# Praise for *Intelligent Databases: Object-Oriented, Deductive Hypermedia Technolgies*

"Parsaye's theoretical approach to what he calls *'intelligent databases'* just may be the key to the troublesome issue of full integration of the database world to the knowledge-base systems world. This solution might indeed be the solution for which users have been waiting."

### Software Magazine

"This book is not only about databases but about the information explosion as well. [This] is an excellent investment for any professional."

### Data Resource Management

"The book presents an interesting method to seamlessly integrate deduction, object orientation, and databases. The book's presentation is succinct, with simple and understandable sentences. The book should be of interest to research scientists as well as practitioners in various disciplines."

### IEEE Computer

"This is not just another book on databases; it might very well become *the* book on databases. I thoroughly enjoyed this book. It is very well written and held my attention from the preface throughout the summary."

### PC/AI

"These essays are excellent, stand-alone explanatory representations of the progressive development of the technologies and offer superb insights into their intricacies without getting bogged down in superfluous details. Perhaps the major strength of the volume will be to stimulate the creative efforts required within the computing community."

### Choice

"This book is a highly useful guide for database and hypertext users and expert systems designers."

### Information Today

"Managers trying to understand how their new, fresh-from-the-university employees think about software systems will find this book to be a valuable tool. The book is a valuable contribution."

### Computing Reviews

"The book is well illustrated and full of charming nuggets of information. You'll be a lot smarter about databases when you're done."

### Software Maintenance News

# INTELLIGENT DATABASE TOOLS & APPLICATIONS

## Hyperinformation Access, Data Quality, Visualization, Automatic Discovery

**Kamran Parsaye**
**Mark Chignell**

**John Wiley & Sons, Inc.**

New York • Chichester • Brisbane • Toronto • Singapore

| Associate Publisher: | Katherine Schowalter |
| Senior Acquisitions Editor: | Diane Cerra |
| Associate Editor: | Terri Hudson |
| Managing Editor: | Jacqueline A. Martin |
| Composition: | Michelle Neil, Editorial Services of New England, Inc. |

*This book is printed on acid-free paper.*

**Library of Congress Cataloging-in-Publication Data**

Parsaye, Kamran.
Intelligent database tools & applications: hyperinformation access, data quality, visualization, automatic
    discovery / Kamran Parsaye, Mark Chignell.
        p. cm.
    Includes index.
    ISBN 0-471-57065-6 (alk. paper). – ISBN 0-471-57066-4 (pbk.)
        1. Data base management. 2. Expert systems (Computer science) I. Chignell, Mark. II. Title. III.
Title: Intelligent database tools and applications.
QA76.9.D3P3485 1993
006.3'3–dc20
                                                                                    92-33080
                                                                                    CIP

Printed in the United States of America
10 9 8 7 6 5 4 3 2 1

# PREFACE

There have been many visions of the future, but the future has its own way of unfolding.

In modern times, we have often turned to science fiction to foretell what the future will be like. However, our collective vision of what is to come has sometimes been shaped by fear more than foresight. Most science fiction depicts the future as a world of robots and high technology warriors whose capabilities far exceed those of the humans. These scenarios often see the future as a world in which our machines compete with and overtake us.

For instance, consider Arthur C. Clarke's book, *July 20, 2019: Life in the Twenty-First Century* (Clarke 1986). The term "database" does not appear in the index to that book. Instead, there is a great deal of focus on physical systems and robots that work autonomously or take over activites currently done by people. Likewise, most current science fiction ignores the fact that we could learn a great deal by automatically analyzing our existing stores of information.

However, current indications are that the future impact of enhanced information processing on society will be orders of magnitude greater than the corresponding impact of electromechanical devices. In addition, these information processing impacts will complement our intellectual abilities, rather than compete with us. In our view, intelligent information systems will have as much impact on human cultural evolution as any other field of endeavor.

Since the book *Intelligent Databases* appeared in 1989, the basic concept of an intelligent database has achieved widespread acceptance. The idea of combining various technologies to extend large data stores with flexible abilities that complement our intellects has struck a resonant chord within a variety of fields. That earlier book (Parsaye et al. 1989) introduced the fundamental concepts of intelligent databases. In this book, we focus on the application of intelligent databases to various scientific and industrial fields. This book has three main goals:

**a.** To introduce a completely new set of ideas pertaining to intelligent databases

**b.** To provide perspective and background information on a number of topics related to intelligent databases

   **c.** To initiate a dialog between computer professionals and domain specialists for the joint use of these intelligent database techniques

We present a number of new ideas in this book, relating to both computer science and other application areas. For instance, we provide new methods of system design and user interfaces and suggest the use of hypertext and icons as query tools, as well as suggest new graph types for quality control and project management. We also provide the background information that sets the new ideas within suitable contexts, (e.g., we discuss the history and evolution of fields ranging from user interfaces to data analysis, to market analysis).

The technology is usually not a solution in itself. Thus a dialog between computer professionals and domain specialists is essential for the implementation of intelligent database applications. This dialog needs a common ground of knowledge of the computer domain as it relates to application domains. This book provides the common ground by introducing computer professionals to some domains of application for intelligent databases and by familiarizing domain specialists in those fields with the technology of intelligent databases.

Our quest for promoting intelligent databases has not been merely philosphical and theoretical. We have developed commercial tools that conclusively prove the fact that the technologies discussed in this book are viable for industrial application. For instance, with *Iconic Query*$^{TM}$, we initiated the use of icons and hypertext as an interface to database systems, rather than operating systems and text processing. In the case of rule discovery from large databases, as some of the examples in this book suggest, it is now a foregone conclusion that we can automatically analyze large databases in a variety of fields and uncover knowledge that no one previously possessed. In fact, our commercial programs (such as *IXL*$^{TM}$ and *IDIS*$^{TM}$) have found more rules in more databases in more applications than any other in history. Other commercial products will continue this effort.

We have been assisted in the preparation of this book by a number people, with both long-term help and immediate assistance. We would like to thank David Barnhart, Bob Blum, Jim Brown, Jim CaJacob, Diane Cerra, Max Chern, Jim Chelton, Amy Chen, Sandra Chignell, Ron Cook, Son Dao, David Garabrand, Bernice Glenn, Bob Glushko, Joel Hadary, Justin Holland, Reiner Keiser, Bob Leong, Alan Lemons, Ray Lee, Rosa Leonuro, David Liati, Diana Lin, Kirsten Lottman, Jakob Nielsen, Chehri Parsaye, Jenny Parsaye, Gary Poduska, Bill Sands, Arthur Scribner, Christel Silva, Clay Sprowls, Felix Valdez, Wilson Yang, Yuh Lin Yau, Tak Wakimoto, John Waterworth, Ray Weiss, Gio Wiederhold, Harry Wong, and Patricia Wright, among others.

It is our hope that this book will stimulate the field of intelligent database applications both by introducing new ideas and by providing the necessary common ground for a widespread dialog between computer analysts and domain professionals. This interaction will usher in the true information age.

*Los Angeles, California*
*January 1993*

# CONTENTS

## 1

## INTELLIGENT DATABASES 1

## 2

## ARCHITECTURES AND METHODOLOGIES 24

# 3

# GRAPHICAL USER INTERFACES 81

# 4

# INFORMATION DISCOVERY 132

# 5
# DATA VISUALIZATION                                   202

# 6

# HYPERINFORMATION AND HYPERDATA                    233

# 7

# INFORMATION PRESENTATION 295

# 8

# EXECUTIVE INFORMATION SYSTEMS 320

# 9

# PROJECT MANAGEMENT AND VISUALIZATION      367

# 10

# MARKETING         407

# 11

# INTELLIGENT QUALITY CONTROL 459

# 12

## CONCLUSIONS 511

## REFERENCES 513

## INDEX 525

# 1

# INTELLIGENT DATABASES

*"Human civilization and the conditions of life are changing so rapidly around the world that phylogenetic evolution, the development of species, is becoming practically irrelevant. It is as though the evolution of phyla stood still."*

— Konrad Lorenz*

*Corollary*: Evolution is now focused on the improvement of concepts, ideas, and information.

## ■ 1.1 INTRODUCTION

The history of human evolution is one of challenge, struggle, and achievement. The vicissitudes of harsh climates, limited resources, and natural disasters require us to develop methods to deal with these challenges. From the time of hunting and gathering to the days of modern business, we have always looked for the competitive edge in survival by refining and innovating our tools and methods. From adding a handle to a flint adze to purchasing a cluster of RISC-based workstations, change through competition has always been the driving force.

Information presentation and transmission have always played a major part in this process, whether it be in the codification of laws by Hammurabi, the use of oracles and various forms of "supernatural" tools to foretell the future and see events at a distance, or the use of fire beacons across southern England to announce the arrival of the Spanish Armada.

While the amount of information has grown, innate human capability has remained roughly constant. Unaided, we still read and speak at almost the same rate as 2,000 years ago. If they could somehow be transported to the present, Aristotle and Archimedes would still be exceptional people. Yet one of the lessons of modern research in cognitive science and artificial intelligence is just how impressive the human mind

---

* *On Life and Living*, St. Martin's Press, 1990. Konrad Lorenz was born in Vienna in 1903. After receiving a medical degree, he traveled worldwide, becoming a leading naturalist. He received the Nobel Prize in 1973.

really is. Capabilities that we take for granted, such as vision and language understanding have proved very difficult to implement on a computer. People and computers both have vast but, for the foreseeable future at least, somewhat different potentials.

The flexibility of the human mind is well-documented. However this flexibility comes at a price. Most people find it hard to remember more than 100 phone numbers, say, over a period of time, and we are relatively poor (compared to computers and software) at carrying out more than fairly trivial numerical calculations. Thus in terms of the ability to store sizable amounts of raw data and to perform numeric operations on it, our minds pale in comparison with modern computers. This discrepancy between human and machine computation will only increase as computers continue to evolve. There is no evidence that human ability to compete with computers in this regard is increasing in any significant way (Figure 1.1).

However, human minds are superior to current databases and computers in many ways. Mostly, in their power to deal with data flexibly. We automatically notice unusual patterns and derive general rules of thumb without conscious effort. For instance, if we see a London cab in New York, we notice it, but if we see the same black cab in London we may not even be aware of it, for we have concluded that it fits our expectation (i.e., the existing pattern). We remember partial names and vague descriptions far better than large databases do. We can deal with many types of data in an integrated form. We deal with pictures, text, and sound simultaneously. A comparison of human and computer abilities with respect to various tasks is shown in Figure 1.2.

The goal of intelligent database applications is to bring the flexible power of the human mind to large data stores. Thus, we need computing systems in general, and databases in particular, that are as flexible as the human mind. Like scratchpads and notepads that help us with our weakness in remembering precise details, and the calculators that have become so pervasive, intelligent databases will also become indispensable assistive partners of the late twentieth century.

Banks, supermarkets, and many other organizations can no longer operate for any length of time without computers. This trend is due to competition. As more segments

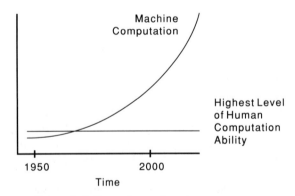

**Figure 1.1** The evolution of machine computation.

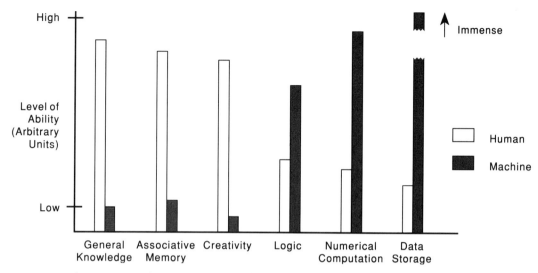

**Figure 1.2** A schematic comparison of human and computer abilities (relative heights of bars are intended to represent schematic, not exact, relations).

of industry and society utilize intelligent databases, their competitors will be compelled to follow suit. Soon everyone will find intelligent databases indispensable.

The strategy behind intelligent databases involves cooperation, rather than competition, with humans. In fact, the kinds of tasks that intelligent databases handle, unaided humans could not possibly compete in. This is in contrast to traditional artificial intelligence applications whose aim is to replicate and replace human ability, as discussed in the Preface (Figure 1.3).

Design of information systems for intelligent database applications thus capitalizes on having people as partners in information interpretation and analysis by allowing them to do what they do best. So information should be presented to them in such a way that it can be chunked and integrated with what they already know.

As human activity has become more complex, information is being produced in ever greater quantity and variety. While the form of information has undergone enormous changes over the past few thousand years, its content seems to have changed relatively little, still relying on annotations of one type or another that can eventually be mapped back into sounds and pictures.

Every day of the year, around the world, the number of databases increases at an astonishing rate — outpaced only by the daily growth in the size of each database. These databases contain vast amounts of information invaluable in making decisions. But as they grow in size, the meaning of the data in these enormous databases becomes harder and harder to understand. This well-known problem is called "info glut." We often tend to accept info glut and our inability to deal with it with the same type of fatalistic approach as people in the Middle Ages accepted early death due to lack of medical care or crop failures due to poor agricultural management. This book argues that rather than accepting info glut, we have to develop and use new technologies that can help us benefit from it.

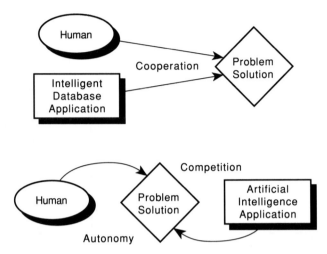

**Figure 1.3** The contrast between the approaches of artificial intelligence and intelligent databases.

If we are to master information and survive in today's world of information glut and systemic complexity, we need to access and use information, and *develop intelligent database applications that will provide more people with better access to the information they need.* More information is being created and stored than can possibly be analyzed or utilized effectively using traditional databases and information systems. Intelligent database applications are designed to overcome the problem of information glut. We need to be more intelligent in our approach to information, emphasizing the essential trends, much as a skilled reader will skim to get the main points rather than stumbling over grammatical structures and other extraneous details.

Development of intelligent databases is motivated by the need to present large amounts of information in a format that is easy to query and understand. Intelligent databases can be loosely defined as *databases that manage information in a natural way, making information easy to store, access, and use.* It is said that you get out of life what you put into it, but with intelligent database applications you can get a lot more out than you put in by recognizing previously undiscovered relationships in the data.

Parsaye et al. (1989) introduced the concept of intelligent databases as a merger of several key technologies (Figure 1.4) and provided a three-level architecture, as shown in Figure 1.5 on page 6. This book describes new types of intelligent database applications that follow these prescriptions, making access to large amounts of information easy and natural. This is achieved by integrating a variety of technologies including discovery, data visualization, and hyperinformation. These methods add value to existing approaches to data querying and provide the flexibility that is needed.

The goal in developing any intelligent database application is to first understand the processes that generate the information and then use this information to control or exploit these processes. This book will develop a model for applying intelligent

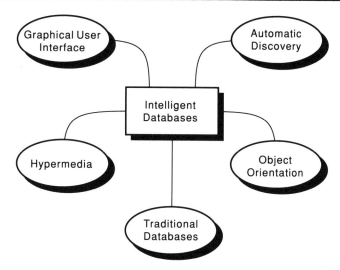

**Figure 1.4** Intelligent databases represent the evolution and merger of five distinct technologies.

databases with particular emphasis on heterogeneous (e.g., numbers, text, sounds, etc.) data. This model will be based on the key technologies of information discovery, data visualization, and hypermedia. This book will then show how intelligent database applications can be developed using these technologies for a number of important application domains.

Also emphasized are the methods and technologies that make intelligent databases useful in application environments. The general focus is on practice rather than theory much as an electrician focuses on wiring rather than subatomic physics. Electricity is a fundamental resource that powers much of our society, but electricity by itself is just a technology. We need devices such as the telephone to put technologies like electricity to work for us.

The difference between intelligent databases and intelligent database applications is like the difference between electricity and telephones. Electricity is used to transmit phone signals down a wire, but the phone as a device collects and organizes the signals in the first place. In similar fashion, an intelligent database organizes and transmits information, but it is the intelligent database application that interprets the information within the context of a meaningful task. Thus this book will focus on the practical issues of developing intelligent database applications in realistic and useful tasks. In order to achieve this goal, the following chapters will discuss tools, application areas, and methodologies.

As our ability to accumulate information has increased exponentially over time, information has become a problem as well as a resource. How can we make effective use of the vast amounts of information available to us? The world's storehouse of information in all its forms is a challenge to us, a resource that is waiting to be exploited effectively. Organizations and nations destined to succeed in the global economy are those who can meet this challenge and profitably and wisely use the wealth of information resources that are available.

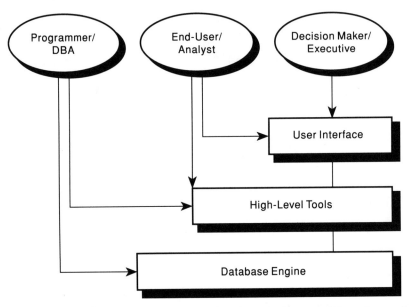

**Figure 1.5** End-users, analysts, and programmers may independently access different layers of an intelligent database.

Oil was a gift left to humanity by a combination of geology and prehistoric life forms. Since the invention of the car it has been one of the world's most valuable resources. Information is potentially a far more valuable resource that has accumulated over thousands of years of human activity. Resources like oil are depleted more rapidly than they can be replaced, but the paradox of information is that it is one of the few resources that multiplies without any effort needed in encouraging exploration or production. We are profligate in our production of information. Much of the world's information was never formally written down or packaged, but it informs us nevertheless. For instance, glass beads in the ground tell us about the trading practices of Indian tribes and the growth of trade between the new world and the old world in the seventeenth century. Old Roman coins tell us about the spread of the Roman Empire. This unintentional or epiphenomenal information can be just as informative as packaged and published information. Every radio broadcast is an unintentional message into space that tells whoever or whatever might be out there about the nature of current human civilization and our priorities in terms of the information that we think is worth transmitting.

The electronic computer provides flexible storage of and access to information (text and data). In a world where there has been a consistent trend towards ever more information over thousands of years, the development of computers and information systems has been equivalent to pouring gasoline on a fire. In fact, the value of information increases exponentially with the size of the database (Figure 1.6). This is because the value of information increases according to the number of connections and relationships between objects that can be identified.

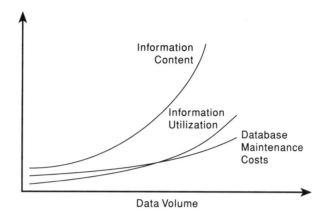

**Figure 1.6** The relative utilization of data assets as database grows.

Computers and related technologies (such as fax machines) have "globalized" corporations and changed the international power balance. People are now performing tasks that would be inconceivable without computers, and those who don't have access to up-to-date tools and technologies cannot survive the competition. People who can't master information are becoming victims of it, drowning in the glut of information.

Consider a book like *War and Peace* or the Bible. How long would it take you to read either? Now imagine the millions of books that have been published. How many of them contain useful ideas or information that you will never read? It is one thing to be selective, but quite another to be ignorant. We never get the chance to see how much of this excess information might actually be useful to us. Imagine that you go on a holiday. You book a flight, accommodation, and rental car at the best rates you can find, but these are still higher than the best rates you could have had if you had had the right information. Alternatively, imagine the predicament of an auditor trying to monitor a complex web of business activities. Hardly a month goes by without news of some huge fraud that was obvious, providing that someone had the right information and was prepared to blow the whistle.

At present we are overwhelmed by the quantity of information and we make decisions that are wrong or suboptimal as a result. Just keeping track of all the telemetry data from a single satellite or all the data from a few supercollider experiments is overwhelming. There are billions of electronic documents and newspaper articles to choose from, along with an unimaginable stream of numerical data from a wide variety of sources, and everyday millions of people have to make decisions without being able to analyze and interpret all the appropriate information.

In most situations people want information quality rather than quantity, because it is information quality that determines decision quality. People need focused and interpreted information, not raw data, about which resources are available for a task, or why products are faulty. This book is based on the fundamental realization that information quality can be attained by making specific types of intelligent database system for different kinds of application.

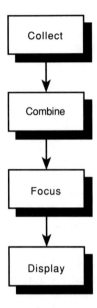

**Figure 1.7** Preparing an information display in an intelligent database application.

There are many ways in which to make databases "intelligent." For instance, they can be built as "all-knowing" databases that have complex representations of knowledge and can interpret information in terms of various models of common sense knowledge and different domains. However, this is a practical book dealing in the kind of intelligence that can provide focused and relevant summaries of information for particular application areas. Based on the authors' experience, a practical model of intelligent database application will be described in the following chapters. The main elements of this model involve collecting information from a variety of sources, combining and focusing it, and projecting it to the user in terms of interpretable views as shown in Figure 1.7.

## ■ 1.2 THE INFORMATION CHALLENGE

In prehistoric times communication was through speech or signs. The invention of the written alphabet allowed information to be stored indefinitely and to be accumulated in libraries. Thanks to the dialogues of Plato one didn't have to know Socrates personally in order to get acquainted with some of his ideas and beliefs. Other inventions in the "form" of information, such as books and movable type have had a great influence on the cost and ease of access to information, but they have not fundamentally changed the content of information.

Changes in the form of information (i.e., how it is stored and transmitted) have largely been driven by the need to handle efficiently ever larger amounts of information. For instance, invention of the book was necessitated by the demands of large-scale classifying, storing, and retrieving of information. Previously, manuscript rolls had been of varying lengths. Sometimes a roll would hold one short work only;

sometimes the writings of several authors in sequence. Books were constructed out of manuscript rolls cut into standardized lengths and bound together thereby making the information much more manipulable and browsable.

Books became mass products when Gutenberg invented the printing press after seeing a wine press during a wine festival in Germany. As books multiplied after the invention of movable type, up-to-date and useful information about various topics became dispersed amongst books from different sources and authorities. As the quantity of information increased, the quality began to suffer and it became more difficult to "find the right book." Society was also becoming ever more complex, particularly after the industrial revolution. The organization of labor, the purchase of parts and supplies, the maintenance of inventories and customer records; all required large amounts of record keeping. The growth of competition among different industrial concerns also placed a high premium on efficiency, quality, cost effectiveness, and technological innovation. Thus the demand for quality information was increasing while the availability of focused quality information was decreasing.

The problems that arose with the cheap printing of books seem to be inevitable by-products of improved information technology. There is something insidious about new technologies for creating, publishing, and handling information because while they facilitate the process of creating or storing information, they also allow us to build bigger information haystacks in which to hide relevant needles of information. The modern computer is, of course, the biggest information haystack builder of them all. Like most havoc-wreaking technologies, the computer started off like a cloud the size of a man's hand, computing missile trajectories and other calculations, and giving no warning of the deluge of possibilities and transformations it was destined to bring.

Information systems on early computers were nonexistent because they had pathetically small input bandwidths and mass storage capability. However, each component of the computer has undergone rapid technological change. The earliest input device was the toggle switch, which was replaced by paper tape and card readers. Today these seem clumsy and unusable, and there are a wide variety of input devices available, including touchscreens, digitizing tablets, keyboards, lightpens, trackballs, joysticks, and mice. Similar advances have occurred in all phases of computer hardware, and we will briefly note some of the important recent developments that are having a large impact on information technology:

> *Mass Storage* — In recent years there has been an exponential increase in the amount of information storage available. Evolution in disk technology has replaced the few memory registers of early computers with gigabytes of information available at high speed on optical media. This has led to the development of massive databases. Since storage media have a tendency to absorb data, information is being stored far more quickly than it can be analyzed or interpreted, hence the problem of information glut.

> *Electronic Publishing* — Much of what is being published today is electronically published, using word processors, so the electronic versions of documents typically precede the corresponding print versions. Thus, huge text databases are developing on every field of human endeavor.

Furthermore, the use of Standard Generalized Markup Language (SGML) and document representation systems is increasing the inherent value of electronic information. For instance, markup tags can be used to create hypertext links.

*Networking* — One of the most significant developments in databases and information retrieval in general has been the connection of computing systems through local and wide area networks. Connectivity and data sharing amongst computing systems have evolved from electronic mail and file servers in local networks, to heterogeneous databases spanning multiple platforms and data models. Many thousands of researchers are already linked by networks that span the globe. Very high bandwidth networks are now being contemplated that will serve as an interstate highway system for information.

*On-line Databases* — As the capabilities for building text databases have evolved along with relatively cheap mass storage, large on-line databases have been developed that collectively contain many millions of documents of various types. These on-line databases represent a vast storehouse of information and they will grow even faster as they become more integrated with electronic publishing.

*Computer Graphics* — Recent advances in computer graphics and animation have been astounding. So much so that there are ongoing attempts to create "virtual realities" where computer graphics generate an artificial world which the user can navigate around (as if it were real). The state of computer graphics can be measured in terms of such units as the number of polygons that can be displayed per second, or the number of pixels and levels of color on the screen, but the bottom line now is that information can be presented on the computer screen as graphics and animations in very compelling and useful ways.

*Multimedia* — Early computers were character-oriented, but multimedia is becoming a powerful force within computing. Multimedia presentations can include text, data visualization, graphics, animation, full motion video, and high fidelity sound. Rapid compression and decompression tools, coupled with huge mass-storage capabilities are making multimedia workstations a reality, so that information from various media can be integrated and presented to the user in a compelling and highly visual environment.

*Automatic Discovery* — Extraction of patterns and trends in data can be carried out through rule induction and automatic discovery. The practical benefits of machine learning research are particularly important in discovering the patterns in large databases that would otherwise remain hidden.

*End User Querying* — One of the most important trends in computing is empowerment of users. With new querying interfaces, anyone can access a database. Now that programming is no longer a hurdle, everyone can interact with data and interpret information for themselves.

*Collaborative Work* — Improved communication and networking have made it possible to link the work environments of different people. This integration of collaborative infrastructure is being followed closely by software applications that integrate applications and desktop activity with video communications so that teamwork can be carried out in collaborative environments where software has evolved into groupware.

The de facto removal of memory limitations in mass storage allows one to store a great deal of information in ways that make it easy to use. Thus, it is possible to have multiple representations of information at different points in information networks or hierarchies. Similarly, with recent improvements in the quality and resolution of visual displays, along with mass storage and compression, it becomes possible to store and use images and live video within information systems. Advances in visual storage and transmission will enhance the importance of video conferencing in project management, pictorial archives of defects in quality control, and so on. Similarly, groupware puts software where it belongs, in the hands of collaborative teams. Thus the component technologies for intelligent databases are in place. Now they need to be integrated and put to use so we can effectively meet the information challenge.

## ▪ 1.3 PEOPLE AND INFORMATION

In discussing intelligent databases, we need to discuss how they impact the people who use them. The interaction between people and information is one where human preferences and constraints have a huge impact on the effectiveness of information system designs. Thus there are a number of general precepts that have motivated the approach to intelligent databases described in this book.

People want to deal with information, not data, and they are notoriously bad at detecting changes in streams of numbers. In contrast, people are extremely good at detecting changes when those changes are represented visually. As an example of this, consider Figure 1.8. Panel *a* on the following page shows a stream of 98 numbers. The numbers represent the populations of 49 U.S. cities in 1920, and 1930 respectively. Although it is hard to detect from just viewing the numbers, there is a shift so that the second group of 49 numbers is greater on average than the first group of 49. Panel *b* on page 13 of the figure shows two histograms representing the frequency distributions for the each of the two groups of numbers. From visual inspection, the change in the magnitude of the input stream is immediately obvious. Wherever possible, intelligent databases should not just provide the data, they should show what is happening in as intuitive and direct a fashion as possible.

The human mind is designed to deal with relatively small amounts of data, but to do so with a great deal of flexibility. When we compare the information requirements of the human mind they seem relatively modest compared to the huge amount of information that is available on-line. For instance, the vocabulary of words for a skilled user of a language, or the vocabulary of positions for a skilled chess player, appear to be in the order of about 50,000. These numbers are just a drop in the bucket compared to the huge amount of information that can be stored electronically. This should tell us that simply dumping huge amounts of information on people is not going to be very helpful to them.

We can add value to the various information technologies that are available by merging them into integrated systems. We need to give people more credit for their ability to handle multimodal information in parallel, interpret patterns, and make associations between different pieces of information.

Intelligent databases need to have a multilayered architecture. Humans don't want to worry about the details, but database systems certainly need to. At the lowest level there should be database engines that handle the basic data, and at the highest level there should be the user interface that displays information in the most natural and useful way. An intelligent database:

- Provides high-level tools for data analysis, discovery, and integrity control, allowing users to both extract knowledge from, and apply knowledge to, data.
- Allows users to interact directly with information as naturally as if they were flipping through the pages of a standard text on the topic, or talking with a helpful expert.

This functionality is provided by tools such as the following:

- Information discovery tools
- Data visualization tools
- Hypermedia presentation tools
- Information filtering and interpretation tools

Each of these tools assists in the essential task of interpreting the information that lies waiting to be discovered and understood within large sets of data.

## Sampling Techniques

### Sizes of 49 Large United States Cities (in 1,000's)

| 1920 |
|---|
| 76, 138, 67, 29, 381, 23, 37, 120, 61, 387, 93, 172, 78, 66, 60, 46, 2, 507, 179, 121, 50, 44, 77, 64, 64, 56, 40, 40, 38, 136, 116, 46, 243, 87, 30, 71, 256, 43, 25, 94, 43, 298, 36, 161, 74, 45, 36, 50, 48 |

| 1930 |
|---|
| 80, 143, 67, 50, 464, 48, 63, 115, 69, 459, 104, 183, 106, 86, 57, 65, 50, 634, 260, 113, 64, 58, 89, 63, 77, 142, 60, 64, 52, 139, 130, 53, 291, 105, 111, 79, 288, 61, 57, 85, 50, 317, 46, 232, 93, 53, 54, 58, 75 |

(a)

**Figure 1.8** Sampling techniques. Part *a* reprinted, by permission, from W. G. Cox, *Sampling Techniques* (New York, J. Wiley, 1977) p. 152.

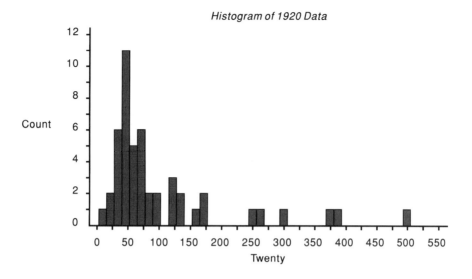

*Histogram of 1920 Data*

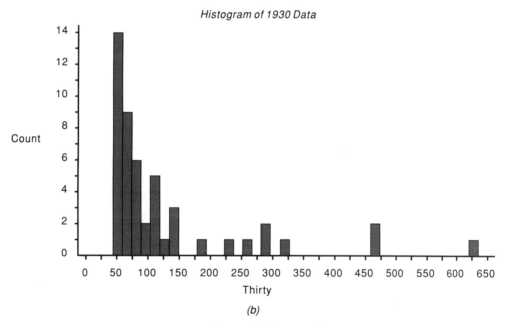

*Histogram of 1930 Data*

*(b)*

**Figure 1.8** *(continued)*

# ■ 1.4  AN INTEGRATED ARCHITECTURE FOR INTELLIGENT DATABASES

Databases typically include a data model, an indexing system, and a querying language among other components. Intelligent databases represent the latest step in the evolution of database technology. Intelligent databases handle a variety of functions ranging from data modeling and management to information discovery, summarization, and presentation. Not surprisingly then, they utilize a variety of tools and technologies and represent the merging of a number of different technologies (Figure 1.4) into an integrated environment. This environment consists of a three-level architecture as shown in Figure 1.5.

The basic architecture of an intelligent database consists of three layers (as discussed in Parsaye et al. 1989), the intelligent database engine, the object model, and a set of high-level tools that tend to vary somewhat according to the application. The intelligent database handles the storage, retrieval, and management of information. It also handles extraction of data from heterogeneous databases and the various communication and transaction protocols required by this activity.

The user interface tends to vary somewhat between applications, but includes querying tools, visual templates for displaying information, and hypermedia tools for navigation and browsing through information. The user interface of an intelligent database will reflect the state of the art in user interface design. Chapter 3 discusses the use of graphical user interfaces. User interfaces to intelligent databases can also use virtual reality, pen-based navigation, speech interfaces, and other methods for enhancing the effectiveness and bandwidth of communication at the user interface.

As we move up the three layers in the intelligent database architecture there is a trend for the components to become more application specific. Thus similar intelligent database engines arose through different applications, while the high-level tools tend to reflect the special needs of each application. The user interface represents a mixture of general and domain dependent features. For instance, specific types of visual containers (templates) or metaphors can be used within the user interface for particular applications.

The high-level tools and user interface serve to customize the intelligent database for a particular application. In marketing, for instance, these high-level tools include geographic information systems (GISs) and associated tools for projecting data on relevant maps. In project management these tools include various tools for network analysis, resource allocation, and scheduling. Some high-level tools are appropriate across a range of applications (e.g., statistics), however, most tools would have at least some application specific components (e.g., graphics are charting tools would include general pie and bar charts as well as Gantt charts for project management, control charts for quality control, etc.).

Parsaye et al. (1989, Chapter 7) formalized the requirements for an intelligent database by presenting the formal object representation model (FORM). This included a model and system that they defined by the equation

$$\text{End-User System} = \text{Hypermedia} + \text{QBE} + \text{Inference} + \text{Object Orientation}$$

This book focuses more on data applications (rather than text). For these applications the equation above has been modified to read

$$\text{End-User System} = \text{Hypermedia} + \text{Data Visualization} + \text{Information Discovery} + \text{Inference} + \text{Iconic Data Access} + \text{Specialized Tools}$$

Using the earlier analogy, the three-layer intelligent interface depicted in Figure 1.5 is like electricity without an appliance. To use it effectively we must now incorporate it with an application and a suitable user interface that integrates the application and the intelligent database. We can then use this strategy to generate a wide range of intelligent database applications from the intelligent database technology. Figure 1.9 shows how the application specific tools and user interface components are merged with the more general intelligent database components to create intelligent database applications.

As shown in Figure 1.9, we distinguish seven types of high-level tools.

1. End-user query tools
2. Knowledge discovery tools including discovery, visualization, and data quality control tools
3. Hyperinformation management tools
4. Information presentation and display tools
5. Executive information system (EIS) tools and decision support system (DSS) tools
6. Data fusion and format management tools (reformat data, etc.)
7. Intelligent system design tools

The following paragraphs sketch the features of each category of tool.

*End-user query tools* allow users to carry out their own detailed querying of data using simple methods (often visual) for expressing their queries. They also provide facilities for selecting and filtering information. Although they are easy to use, the query tools allow unrestricted and full-functioned access to information. In particular, querying with icons lets users have detailed access to information without any need of programming.

*Knowledge discovery tools* include tools for data analysis, machine learning, and statistical analysis. These tools allow us to extract knowledge from data by automat-

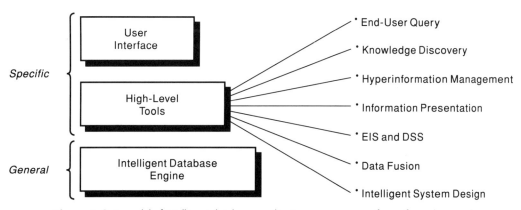

**Figure 1.9** A model of intelligent database applications as a merger of specific and general components.

ically discovering hidden (and often totally unexpected) relationships that exist in a large database. For instance, by using information discovery on a database of car trouble reports, a car manufacturer discovered the reasons for wiring problems, while a computer manufacturer discovered that a large number of disk drive problems were due to one specific error repeatedly performed by one operator in one process. Thus, these tools discover relationships that users would not have even expected. Since today's oceans of data abound with such relationships, these tools will dramatically increase our ability to distill knowledge from databases.

Additional discovery tools are needed due to the unwanted side effects of the increasing number and size of databases. In particular, two conflicting side effects are (a) we are becoming extremely dependent on data stored in databases, and (b) there is an increasing number of errors appearing in databases. Thus it is imperative to have tools that automatically detect or signal errors in databases. These range from tools which use the encoded knowledge of an expert to detect errors in data to tools which signal statistically deviant records.

*Hyperinformation management tools* allow developers and users to build hypermedia information systems that combine free-form linked text, data, images, sounds, and so on. This category reflects the fact that information may be expressed in many different forms or media and that methods are needed for organizing and accessing these different forms of information.

Given a large database, most users wish to see and display some of the data (or summaries thereof). Thus, *information presentation and display tools* provide graphics, forms, and other types of data presentation. Although this category is logically separate from the previous one, in practice the display tools will often be an extension of the hyperinformation management tools.

*Executive information and decision support tools* allow for a uniform merger between spreadsheets, databases, financial modeling systems, and so on. This stems from a view of executive information systems as requiring a special kind of information management, retrieval, and utilization, where the information is tailored towards particular decision-making activities.

Data never seems to be in the format that it is needed in. *Data format management tools* allow users to transform data between formats, for example, to merge an ASCII file with data in dBASE format and data obtained from IBM's DB2 with an automatically generated Structured Query Language (SQL) query. These tools are indispensable for applications that rely on the analysis of real data.

*Intelligent system design tools* provide facilities for designing intelligent databases. Although the fields of database design, information system design, and expert system design have maintained a separate existence in the past, their integration in an intelligent database is essential. These tools allow system developers and administrators to better design and maintain intelligent databases.

In order to be usable, these tools need to be integrated into a uniform and seamless environment. Obviously, there are different classes of users, as discussed in Chapter 2. However, the look and feel should be the same for user and analyst so that the analyst also finds it easy to move between the different tools, as discussed in Chapter 3.

## ■ 1.5  AREAS OF APPLICATION

Intelligent databases can be applied to any problem or domain that deals with large amounts of data. For instance, large projects require scheduling of tasks and the allocation of resources, and keeping track of all the details generates a great deal of data. In this case an extended set of project visualization tools would be invaluable. This includes tracking of a wider variety of information that is relevant to the project, the creation of new types of graphs and charts for summarizing the progress of the project, and the use of a hypermedia interface to allow the manager to visualize all the facets of the project quickly.

Quality control is another activity that may deal with large amounts of data. Intelligent database applications for quality control can create new types of data summarization as well as integrating these with existing methods such as control charts to give quality assurance personnel a bird's eye view of the entire production process. Design, too, is an information intensive activity. The designer has to make numerous decisions in the course of designing a product that is more than a slight modification of an existing one. These decisions may be based on previous test data, specifications and tolerances of supplier parts, availability of parts in inventory, and so on. In complex design projects, design is a collaboration between people with different types of expertise, and this collaboration emphasizes the role of an intelligent database application as a shared workspace and presentation tool.

Design leads to manufacturing. Manufacturing requires effective factory information systems which can be implemented as intelligent database applications. An intelligent database application for manufacturing can then support a diverse range of activities including inventory management, process planning, scheduling, and equipment maintenance. Specialized manufacturing applications can be developed for focused tasks such as quality control, but there is also a need for intelligent database applications that can serve as more general factory information systems.

In marketing, the emphasis is on matching the product to the consumer and on persuading (through product design, quality assurance, service, pricing, and advertising) the consumer to buy the product. In a large market there is a wealth of data that may be relevant to decision making and the formation of marketing strategies. This information includes demographic information (e.g., census data), market research data (e.g., questionnaires and focus groups) and point of sale information (e.g., data collected based on bar code scanning of products at the point of sale). Information discovery will be particularly useful in a marketing intelligent database application in order to determine what the main market segments are and what segments tend to buy which product in a product family.

Financial analysis and investment is another area where there is a continuous stream of potentially relevant data. This ranges from hard data like interest rates, unemployment figures, cost of living increases, and the index of leading economic indicators, to soft data such as new reports about political upheavals in the Middle East, the impact of new technologies, or changes announced in the annual report of a large company. For instance, in the analysis of common stocks, various charts of data are often used to extract trends and predict future price movements. Such charts can be integrated into an intelligent database application for financial analysis of stocks. They can also be supplemented with information discovery to predict future prices of stocks based on past performance.

Almost every intelligent database application will involve decision making of one type or another. For instance, decisions about where to locate a new store, or where to put a new sports franchise should be based on a wide range of representative data that is summarized and interpreted in a suitable way. Relevant information for locating a new sports franchise might include the demographics of the town, the amount of corporate support available, the interest of the townspeople in the sport and so on. Since intelligent database applications emphasize high quality visual presentations of information in an easily assimilable form, they also serve as decision support tools, although they will generally need to be customized to handle particular decision-making applications.

Having high-quality access to data is particularly important for complex decisions where there is a lack of hard data and people are acting on the basis of their own assumptions. For instance, the effectiveness of social welfare or anti-drug education is extremely hard to measure. Effective access to information can only help the process of creating social policy, and in many (but of course not all) cases, ideological differences may be less of a factor if the appropriate information is available and well summarized. Thus intelligent database applications hold the promise of throwing light on some of the dark corners of social policy.

Intelligent databases also help in medicine by extracting critical information from the huge morass of available data. Health costs are one of the largest components of the budget in most industrialized nations. Large medical organizations process a huge amount of information ranging from the results of laboratory tests to billing information and the results of epidemiological studies. Medical intelligent databases help find relationships between diverse variables and factors. At present, relationships such as the effects of dietary fibre and fat intake on cancer incidence, and the effect of aspirin intake on heart disease risk must be studied in focused research studies where much of the effort is concerned with extracting and summarizing the relevant data. Intelligent databases can automate these activities and avoid duplication of effort, which currently occurs as each research group starts from scratch in picking through the available information and records. Researchers and physicians should be able to browse focused summaries of up-to-date medical information so that public health crises can be recognized more quickly.

As another example of how information discovery can help, consider an auto manufacturer, Global Motors, which maintains many databases consisting of various kinds of customer, dealer, shipper, plant, and product information. There are so many of these databases and they are so large that no single person at Global Motor Corporation knows what they all contain. These databases actually contain a wealth of knowledge that utilized correctly can help increase productivity, decrease customer complaints, and improve the company's business. Automatic discovery can be used to detect trends in the data and these trends may then assist policy planning, quality control, and other activities within the corporation.

The topics listed above represent just a few of the many application areas that are suitable for intelligent database development. However, these topics indicate how useful effective analysis and interpretation of large amounts of information may be for decision makers in business, industry, and government.

∎ **1.6 ROADMAP OF THE BOOK**

The first two chapters of this book introduce the essential concepts of intelligent databases and the architecture and functionality of intelligent database applications. The next four chapters introduce the tools and technical information needed to build intelligent database applications and to understand how they work. These tools include graphical user interfaces (Chapter 3), information discovery (Chapter 4), data visualization (Chapter 5), hyperinformation (Chapter 6), and presentation (Chapter 7). There is an explanation of a detailed model of intelligent database applications beginning with the user interface in Chapter 3. This is followed by an explanation of how the display objects in the user interface are created using tools such as information discovery (Chapter 4) and data visualization (Chapter 5), and how hyperinformation (Chapter 6) is used to provide a navigation environment where users may select and manipulate display objects within a point-and-click style of interface. This leads to a discussion of presentation in Chapter 7. Chapter 8 then discusses how these intelligent database tools and technologies may be merged with other technologies such as groupware and video-conferencing to create an executive information system. More specific tools may then be added to the resulting executive information system platform to create different intelligent database applications. Thus Chapter 8 is a key chapter that serves as a bridge between intelligent database tools (Chapters 3–7) and intelligent database applications (Chapters 9–11). The reader will find that designing for the requirements of an executive information system provides an environment that can then serve as a platform for developing intelligent database applications in a wide range of areas.

Chapters 9 through 11 introduce three applications that demonstrate the effectiveness of the intelligent database approach. They also show how intelligent databases may be constructed. The applications described in this section show how the executive information environment can be customized to create intelligent database applications for project management (Chapter 9), marketing (Chapter 10), and quality control (Chapter 11).

As part of a discussion of intelligent database application, there will be a review of fields such as marketing and project management in the later chapters of this book to provide a minimum level of knowledge about the field of application. A major problems in applying intelligent databases is that most computer scientists don't know very much about topics such as marketing and quality control, while specialists in those domains typically don't know much about intelligent databases. Thus one of the goals in this book will be to bridge this gap between database and content specialists, in addition to providing a model of intelligent database application.

## ■ 1.7 WHAT IS NEW?

The answer to the question "What is new here?" is as follows:

- Chapter 2 presents an architecture for intelligent database applications and introduces the concept of concentric design, which is diametrically opposed to some traditional approaches such as the waterfall model.
- Chapter 2 also introduces new application guidelines for applying intelligent databases based on a set of behavioral constraints. A set of concrete steps is provided here.
- A new taxonomy of database user interfaces is presented in Chapter 3 that includes methods of iconic and hypertext data access. This chapter provides the first discussion of how icons and hypertext may be jointly used for data access.
- Chapters 4 and 5 provide a unified discussion of automatic discovery in terms of statistics and induction and merge data quality, discovery, and visualization. Various approaches are compared and contrasted.
- In Chapter 6 the terms hyperdata and hyperinformation are coined as an extension of hypertext and hypermedia. The relationship of these technologies to discovery, visualization, and automated presentations is discussed.
- Chapter 8 provides a new discussion of executive information systems and relates it explicitly to group information management within a hyperinformation environment.
- Chapter 9 discusses a hyperinformation model for project visualization, and provides several new diagramming techniques for project management, including the first 3D hyperdiagrams for this purpose.
- A new model of project risk management in terms of Critical Risk is also introduced in Chapter 9. This ties in well with the discussion in the same chapter on interactive requirement explanation within a group-oriented project environment.
- Chapter 10 suggests how rule discovery is used to find dynamic clusters for market segmentation as an alternative to traditional clustering methods. These techniques identify market segments that are dynamically determined by product type and which change with time.
- The 8th, 9th, and 10th tools of quality control are introduced in Chapter 11, extending the traditional seven tools. Also shown are discovery technologies which go beyond statistics and which improve upon the traditional methods of statistical quality control.

These new ideas are not presented in isolation, but are interweaved with three components: historical perspectives on the various fields discussed; basic concepts in the application domain; methodologies for the use of the ideas and technologies. Thus each chapter begins with a historical overview, then outlines the traditional subject matter before discussing the impact of intelligent databases on the topic under discussion. Following this, methodologies for application are discussed. In the earlier chapters appendices are provided with supplementary material.

## ■ 1.8 APPENDIX: TRENDS IN DATABASE TECHNOLOGIES

The basis of database technology consists of methods for structuring and organizing data. Data needs to be organized if it is to be useful, and data models specify how separate pieces of information are related in a database. Information is generally broken down into data structures such as records and fields. At the file level, records are the basic units of data storage. However, the physical level of description is only one of three different ways of describing databases.

The conceptual view of a database is a somewhat abstract representation of the physical data and the way that it is stored. The same conceptual model of the database can apply to a variety of different physical implementations. In contrast, the logical level of database description consists of the definition of the logical structure of a database, written as logical schemas within a data definition language.

The functionality of database management and information systems rests on a well-established technology. The basis of this technology consists of methods for structuring and organizing data. Data needs to be organized if it is to be useful. Data models specify how separate pieces of information are related in a database. Information is broken down into data structures. The most basic of these structures are records and fields. Fields, such as Social Security number and birthdate, are the elementary data items. Syntactically, the information that a field contains conforms to a certain type, such as a real, an integer, a character or a string. Semantically, the meaning of information within a field corresponds to the concept or attribute represented by the field.

The hierarchical model of data was one of the first steps away from flat file structures. A hierarchy (or tree) is a network in which nodes are connected by links such that all links point in the direction from child to parent. Another way of saying this is that nodes in a hierarchy are strictly nested, that is, every node has a parent node except for the single root (top) node of the hierarchy.

The basic operation in a hierarchy is the tree search. Given a query to a hierarchical database, the hierarchy will be searched and nodes that meet the conditions of the query will be returned. In a hierarchical database, the nodes of the hierarchy consist of records which are connected to each other via links. In a tree, data has to be strictly nested (i.e., each node has only one parent), but real-world data does not always conform to this requirement. One piece of data may need to be repeated in several different locations of the database. This repetition may occur in the same database tree or in several different trees. Virtual records are used to achieve a situation where data appears to be repeated within the hierarchies without having to waste storage or increase the difficulty of updating the database. Instead of data, a virtual record contains a logical pointer to a physical record.

Maintenance of a hierarchical database requires flexible methods for changing and updating records. Each change is equivalent to deleting the old version of a record and inserting the new version. The type of insertion and deletion that is possible depends on the way that pointers are used to create virtual records. In general, a pointer to a hierarchical database record consists of (a) the address of the first block of the database record, and (b) the value of the key field or fields for the record in question.

Hierarchical databases often exhibit poor flexibility, but because of the "hard-wired" access paths, they often provide very good performance for preconceived applications. Many "classical" programs and applications (accounting, payroll, etc.) have been written in hierarchical Database Management Systems (DBMSs) such as IBM's DL/1. It is somewhat ironic that in the age of relational databases we are now looking beyond to object-oriented databases that will return to some of the hierarchical structuring principles that were tried and rejected in earlier database systems.

The network model of data uses additional pointers to add flexibility to the hierarchical model. In its most general form, a network is a collection of nodes with links possible between any of the nodes. These links can be assigned meanings and the creation of links between nodes can be constrained in various ways. The hierarchical model, for instance, is a special case of the network model (a directed acyclic graph) where each node is linked to a parent node. In a pure hierarchy, each node may have only one parent although it may itself be the parent of more than one lower-level node (i.e., have multiple children). Networks may be implemented in different ways, depending on the way in which records and pointers are organized. One method utilizes a multilist structure. In a multilist organization, each record has a pointer for each link that it is involved with.

The relational database model followed on from hierarchical and network databases and is presently the most widely used data model for databases. Prior to 1970, mainframe database applications were dominated by the network and hierarchical models. Then Codd (1970) proposed the relational data model. IBM at San Jose implemented the first working version of the relational model in their System/R (Astrahan et al. 1976).

Each row in a relation represents a relationship between a set of values. One reason for the widespread acceptance of the relational model may be that it is based on this straightforward and easily understood conceptual model. The relational model can be summarized in terms of tables and operations on tables using the relational algebra (Parsaye et al. 1989, Chapter 2). A relational database consists of tables. Each table bears the name of a relation and contains rows and columns. We can define a relation scheme as the set of attribute names for a relation. New tables can be constructed from these tables by cutting and pasting rows and columns from the existing tables. The process of constructing new tables in the relational model is governed by the operations of the relational algebra.

Once we attach attribute names to the columns of a relational table, the order of the columns (attributes) becomes unimportant. Conceptually, operations on this relational database consist of cutting and pasting portions of the existing tables to create new relational tables that satisfy certain criteria. The relational database model offers the simple notion of tables as the only data structure for user interaction. Its close relationship to set theory and first-order logic allows the relational model to inherit many elegant properties and operators since it is based on a well-defined logical structure, namely, the relational algebra.

Data retrieval within the relational model is handled by using the relational algebra to manipulate relations. The five fundamental operations in the relational algebra are Selection, Projection, Product, Union, Set difference. In addition, the join is another operation that may be defined in terms of the Cartesian product and selection operations.

A number of languages were developed to provide efficient querying within the framework of the relational algebra. Two major approaches are based on the languages SQL (Chamberlin et al. 1976) and QUEL (Stonebraker et al. 1977). Another innovative query language was known as Query-By-Example (QBE; Zloof 1977).

SQL has become the standard database language for all platforms and has been adopted as an ANSI standard. SQL is, in fact, more than merely a database query language. It includes features for defining the structure of the data, modifying the data, and specifying security constraints within the database. SQL includes the basic relational algebra operators. Selection is represented in SQLs where clause, while projection is performed in SQLs select clause. Product is represented by the from clause of SQL. SQL also handles set operations including the union, intersection, and set difference, and the logical connectives AND, OR, and NOT. Other features of SQL include the use of aggregate operators such as avg (average), provision of statistical and related information, and sorting procedures that can be used to order records according to their attributes. The flexibility of SQL can be further enhanced by linking it with general-purpose languages such as Pascal and C. This allows the development of customized routines to manipulate the database and makes the SQL language extensible.

Object-oriented databases represent a new philosophy and implementation for storing information and data. Fundamental concepts of object orientation include abstract data typing (encapsulation), inheritance, and object identity (Parsaye et al. 1989, Chapter 3). The object-oriented model is far broader than the relational model and can be applied to a wide range of contexts outside database management. For instance, Parsaye et al. (1989, Chapter 3), discuss the use of object-orientation in discrete-event simulation, design engineering, and software engineering. The field of databases includes both relational and object-oriented systems. In our view, there is no need to make a forced choice between these different styles of database implementation. Our preference is to use a relational database model at the lower layer and overlay this with an object model which then provides object-oriented functionality from the user's perspective, while still implementing low-level queries within the relational model.

# 2

# ARCHITECTURES AND METHODOLOGIES

*"An extremely important factor in voluntary activity is feedback. It is a phenomenon which we understand very thoroughly from a quantitative point of view."*

— Norbert Weiner*

*Corollary*: Feedback is an integral part of Concentric Design.

## ■ 2.1 INTRODUCTION

One of the main lessons of the industrial revolution was that while craftsman cannot satisfy the needs of the mass market, mass produced items can. In medieval times certain goods or services (e.g., orchestral music and opera) could only be owned or experienced by the privileged few. However, with modern methods of automation and mass production, serviceable (if not collectable) goods and services (e.g., recorded music) can be owned by most people. Like handcrafted products, handcrafted intelligent databases are costly and limited in their availability. We need architectures and methodologies for intelligent database applications that can produce usable and effective applications on the scale that is required.

Thus we are concerned with methods that support the rapid development of database applications and large-scale generation of interactive summaries and presentations of data. We want to automate processes of information discovery and presentation so that we can mass produce intelligent databases without sacrificing information quality.

This chapter provides architectures and methodologies for constructing intelligent database applications. It is concerned with a number of issues including the hardware, software, and data architecture of intelligent databases, along with their construction

---

* *Cybernetics*, MIT Press, 1948. Norbert Weiner was born in Cambridge, MA, in 1894. He was a gifted mathematician who recieved his doctorate from Harvard at 18. He taught mathematics at MIT and was the originator of the concept of cybernetics.

process and life cycle. The discussion here gives domain specialists sufficient information to understand some of the basic technical issues in constructing intelligent database applications. These issues will be pursued in more depth in the following five chapters. Since intelligent databases are an integrating technology computer scientists will also be informed about some application domains to which intelligent databases can be applied. This is done in later chapters on project management, marketing, and quality control. These chapters also demonstrate how the unique features of each application domain tend to affect the issues that an intelligent database addresses, and which components of the intelligent database receive more emphasis.

The chapter begins by discussing who the users of intelligent databases are and how and why intelligent database applications are used. This is followed by a description of the architecture of intelligent databases, and the life cycle of an intelligent database application is then considered. The issue of how intelligent database applications are designed is addressed, focusing on a concentric model of design that emphasizes design as an iterative process that reduces the uncertainty of specifications and requirements over time. This is followed by a view of the behavioral model of intelligent database applications as cooperative partnerships between human users and software systems. This model shows how information should be presented in order to enhance its analysis and interpretation, and it also includes a number of principles that guide the presentation of information.

## ■ 2.2 USAGE OF INTELLIGENT DATABASES

Intelligent databases are large and flexible information systems that are typically used by people representing a heterogeneous mix of user types. These different user types may be characterized by a number of attributes, including: level of computer literacy, organizational position, work-group structure, reasons for use, and type of application.

When grouping by computer literacy, as shown in Figure 2.1, the different groups of users include:

- Non-computer-oriented people (such people do not even use a word processor)
- End-users (i.e., people who use word processors and spreadsheets at a simple level or who may write very simple spreadsheet macros)
- Analysts (i.e., people who can write more complex spreadsheet macros and who can also implement dBASE, Toolbook, or HyperCard systems
- Programmers (i.e., people such as database analysts who use C Compilers and similar programming environments)

Intelligent database users can also be classified according to their position in the organization structure. Executives need instant answers to questions from a graphic user interface. They are sometimes assisted by end-users and analysts. End-users know how to use a spreadsheet, but they do not program. Examples of end-users are

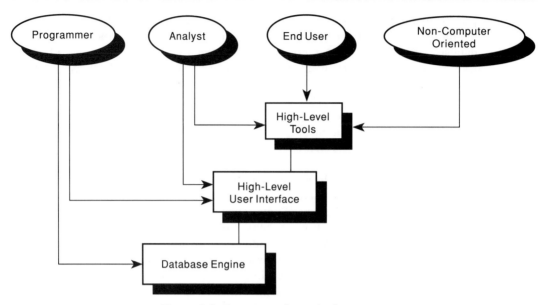

**Figure 2.1** Grouping intelligent database users.

sales people, market researchers, scientists, engineers, physicians, and administrators. Managers at times assume the role of both executives and end-users. Analysts know how to interpret data and do occasional computing but are not programmers. They may be financial analysts, statisticians, consultants, or database designers.

Intelligent database usage also varies with the type of work group structure. We can distinguish three main classes of usage based on this attribute: individual users, working alone; group users, working asynchronously; and group users, working synchronously.

Individual users tend to focus on information exploration and question answering, without any concern with collaborating with other users or members of the workgroup until after the transactions with the intelligent database application are completed. In contrast, group users use the intelligent database application as a tool for communicating with other members of the group. Groups may work either synchronously or asynchronously. Electronic mail is an example of an asynchronous group activity. Asynchronous interactions are characterized by messages and replies. An example of a synchronous activity is group decision making and various forms of meetings or conferences. In such cases the intelligent database application can be used as a form of shared presentation and as a tool for making assertions, testing ideas, and supporting argument and discussion in general. Intelligent database applications are likely to be particularly valuable in synchronous group work because they allow people to focus on the data and on what's really happening, thereby lessening the chances that particularly aggressive or dominant individuals will sidetrack the discussions and ram through questionable decisions on the basis of emotion and force of personality.

Presentation is the essence of group communication. A huge number of work tasks today are presentations of one form or another. Reports are presentations (in synchronous group work), as are design reviews, lectures, and demonstrations. Almost any time people meet to discuss task related issues there is a presentation of one sort or another, whether it be reviewing a data printout, sketching a plan, or presenting an argument verbally. Similarly the interaction between individuals and software applications may be thought of as a set of software generated presentations that are based on the inputs of the user. Thus making presentations more effective and easier to generate will have a huge impact on productivity. The following section considers the issue of presentation further, as it relates to the types of intelligent database applications that are used and the reasons why people use them.

Intelligent database applications can be used for many different types of reason and types of task. These include:

- Querying and reporting
- Presentations
- Visual understanding
- Information discovery
- Data quality management
- Hypertext management
- Data fusion

Some of the main reasons for using intelligent databases are considered in the remainder of this section.

## 2.2.1 Querying and Reporting

Querying is the process of asking questions about data. It generally requires the use of a formal query language with a specialized syntax. The requirements of learning and using this formal query language tend to lock out a lot of potential users. An example of such a formal query language is SQL, which is based on the relational algebra used with relational databases.

Visual querying allows people to query information in a more natural way, without having to learn the formal language. Visual querying still involves a language, but it is a largely visually-based language and as such it is generally easier for most people to use.

Visual querying begins with the selection of a scenario which is then "filled in" according to the requirements of the query. This process is further explained in the discussion of querying with icons in Chapter 3.

Reporting is the process of displaying the results of a query to the user. Reports are typically shown as tabular summaries of the records that match a query in a database. However, people benefit greatly when query results are presented in a more compelling and visual way, using various forms of presentation.

## 2.2.2 Presentation

No amount of words can convey the same impression as a photo or video of a startling or moving event. In fact, the impact of pictures on the general population is so well known that military censors, campaign staff, and public relations personnel will go to great lengths to ensure that the images associated with an organization or campaign are as positive as possible.

Intelligent database applications harness this undeniable power of pictures and visually presented information through the use of interactive graphics. In addition to pictures, photos, full-motion video, and animations, interactive graphics provide pictorial views of data. Interactive graphics bring numbers to life. The model of intelligent database usage in this book includes two types of interaction with graphics; visual querying and point-and-click navigation.

Intelligent database applications provide effective and efficient information presentation. They support a variety of different types of information exchange, including:

- Synchronous presentation (lectures, speeches, reviews, broadcasts, etc.)
- Asynchronous presentations (e.g., memos, letters, and messages)
- Reports

When people analyze and interpret information it usually ends up as a report of one kind or another. Reports are presentations of information that are designed to convey the main points of the information to the reader. Reports are longer and more structured than memos. They may be presented electronically (e.g., as multimedia, or electronic text) or they may be presented in printed form. In the latter case they will benefit from data summaries and data visualizations (charts and graphs) provided by intelligent database applications.

In an intelligent database application, a report can be created as a sequence of charts, graphs, and textual annotations. It can then be read by the user on-line, or printed off to hardcopy and published. It would be a mistake to assume that linear reports are no longer needed when multimedia information on-line is available. In fact, the available research evidence suggests that linear presentations of information are just as useful on-line as they are in hardcopy both in terms of legibility (Jorna and Snyder 1991) and in terms of facilitating comprehension of the information (e.g., Wright 1991).

Another form of presentation usage considered here is the information overview. Since the number of data visualizations that can conceivably be generated from a large database is huge, the intelligent database developer may choose to focus and filter at least some of this information into an interactive briefing. An interactive briefing is a subgraph of the entire point-and-click network that is judged to be most useful to users (Figure 2.2).

An interactive briefing may be thought of as a special type of nonlinear presentation that is designed to be read fairly exhaustively, but which needs to be sufficiently flexible so that people can read through the briefing in different orders. This flexibility may also be useful in presentations where the presenter can use the interactive briefing to change the presentation of the briefing by visiting the nodes in the subgraph in different orders based on the questions asked and the topics that appear to interest the audience.

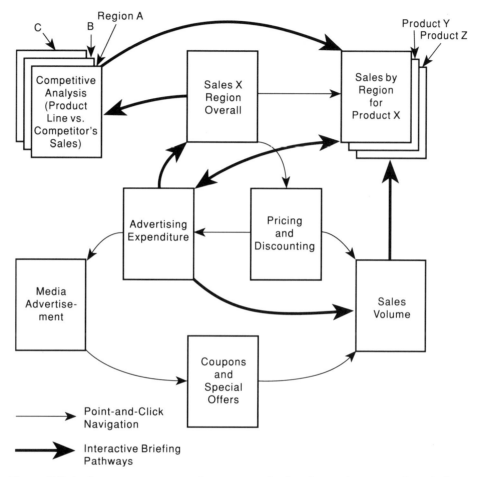

**Figure 2.2** A schematic representation of an interactive briefing showing how it is a subgraph of a point-and-click network.

### 2.2.3 Visual Understanding

Point-and-click navigation is used in hypermedia systems. It is like viewing a slide show where you can click on things that interest you and have new slides appear. For instance, if you are viewing a budget breakdown showing different departments in your company you might then click on a particular department to get a detailed breakdown of its budget. The real feature of point-and-click navigation is that it is very flexible and one can explore trails of information or paths of ideas in interaction with visualizations of information.

Lessons learned with hypertext (summarized in Chapter 6) show, however, that point-and-click navigation only works well when it is embedded within an appropriate structure and in the context of other navigational tools, so that the user doesn't end up feeling lost or disoriented in a labyrinth of slides and charts.

The usage model demonstrated in this book avoids the problems of point-and-click navigation by providing alternative styles of navigation, including visual querying and menu-based access. In addition, intelligent database applications tend to be strongly task-oriented, and this also reduces the danger of disorientation. For instance, an executive who is trying to track down the source of a bad number will tend to have a model of the company and its operations that serves as a strong orienting structure and guide while using point and click navigation. Executive information systems are applications that seek to promote visual understanding, as discussed in Chapter 8.

### 2.2.4 Information Discovery

Perhaps the most valuable function of an intelligent database application is to surprise people with unexpected information that lay buried in the data. Consider, for instance, a manufacturer who discovers that one particular product has a disproportionate number of breakages to its lid. Armed with this information, the manufacturer is then able to trace the problem back to the packaging, which is inappropriate, leading to breakages during shipment and storage. Discovering rules such as "the lid of product X is more likely to break in shipment or storage than the lid for any other type of product" is thus extremely valuable. In many cases, these rules or patterns are there in the data waiting to be discovered, but no one has the time or people on hand to chase after all the possible rules that may lie buried in a large mass of data.

This book will be concerned with two types of unexpected information. The first type consists of new rules that summarize patterns in the data (as in the example about broken lids given above). The second type of unexpected information consists of anomalies. Anomalies can be thought of as the flip side of rules, instances or cases that don't fit a rule or pattern that otherwise explains the data very well. Anomalies are exceptions to existing rules and in some cases they may be accounted for if new rules are added to the database.

Discovery of rules is best done with a machine learning tool. The basic idea is to generate goals or rule conclusions that are of interest, and then see what combinations of other attributes tend to lead to particular values or ranges of the goal attribute of interest. For instance, a disk drive manufacturer may want to know what conditions tend to produce particular defects in a drive. If data is available about when defects of various types occurred, along with various attributes that describe the conditions under which the disk was manufactured and assembled, then rule generation can be used with the particular defect as the goal. Rule generation in this case is equivalent to asking the question, what conditions tend to produce a defect of type X?

The user may ask a few such questions and then wait for the answer to be discovered in the form of rules. In a large database, this process might be fairly lengthy, depending on the hardware available, and it will often make sense to submit a batch of information discovery questions to be processed overnight.

Alternatively, fairly complete information discovery may already have been run on the database in developing the application. In this case, the rules have already been stored in a knowledge base within the application, and information discovery then becomes a process of matching the appropriate discovered rules to each new user's queries about interesting patterns in the data.

Exceptions to rules can be just as important as rules themselves. Imagine that there was a database of information about mechanical breakdowns in cars. We might carry out information discovery on this database and find there is a rule that frozen fuel lines or gas tanks tend to occur when the temperature drops below a certain temperature and there is less than a certain amount of gas in the tank. In the days before fuel additives to prevent freezing this might have been accepted as a normal part of life in a cold climate and the recommendation would be to keep the gas tank full during cold weather. However, an anomaly in this case would be a case that matched the premises of the rule (i.e., cold weather, relatively empty gas tank) but where the conclusion (i.e., frozen gas line) didn't occur. Since this anomaly was an exception to the rule it would be of interest. Say, for instance, that the car belonged to a chemical company that was testing a new fuel additive. Here the anomaly was actually a sign of a case where the rule didn't apply because the freezing point of the mixture of gas and water in the fuel tank had been chemically altered. Thus anomalies can be signals of cases where old rules don't apply and the reasons why they don't apply may lead to new insights or rules being discovered.

In an intelligent database application, a user can ask the system to look for anomalous cases that don't fit a rule. For instance, there may be a rule in a retailing system that small stores will generally have a lower operating margin than large stores because fixed costs and other overheads consume a larger proportion of their budget. Looking for anomalous small stores that seem to buck this trend may provide useful insights into how smaller stores can be run so that they are more profitable.

### 2.2.5   Data Quality Management

Intelligent database applications can be used to enhance data quality and the interpretation of the information inherent in high-quality data. Thus intelligent databases may be used as an important part of a program for managing data quality.

One of the most important aspects of a data quality program is that it should enforce data quality throughout the organization. Thus data collectors, data analysts, and data interpreters should all be concerned with data quality. Furthermore, there should be incentives and controls to ensure data quality enhancement. This will include data quality audits that can identify instances of faulty data collection or input, along with relevant feedback to those responsible.

There should also be a central archive for data schemas throughout the organization. Each new or modified data schema should be checked for compatibility with this archive. Any incompatibilities found during data merging (fusion) or information discovery should be reported back to the managers of the data schema archive.

Errors in data will often be found through information discovery, and through visualization. Intelligent database applications enhance data quality by making the analyst more familiar with the properties of the data, and thus more aware of any errors that exist in the data.

### 2.2.6   Text Management

Text databases represent a critical component of intelligent database technology. Much of human knowledge is stored in the form of text and we face the issue of linking this text-based knowledge to knowledge-based representations that can be used in reasoning. Since the development of intelligent database applications is a large topic, this book will focus on analysis and handling of data (numbers) rather than text. However, even in some of the applications discussed here, text management will still be useful. For instance, report generation, memo generation, and mail filtering systems are extremely useful parts of executive information systems (Chapter 8).

Data visualizations produced by using an intelligent database application also add value to text and assist in organizing and managing it. This is particularly important in report generation where various forms of textual annotation need to be merged with quantitative data. Thus intelligent databases assist in the management of text both by providing a variety of tools for organizing, browsing, and retrieving text, and by providing visualizations that can be used to annotate text and assist in its interpretation.

### 2.2.7  Data Fusion

Although tools are important, they are of little use without data. Therefore, we need to ensure that a good base of data is available before the tools can be used. In practice, most organizations have problems knowing where their data is and what format it is in. This occurs even before they can assess what level of quality the data conforms to.

In many cases, databases grow on their own without a central plan. Different departments continue to gather data and use different pieces of hardware and software that fit the needs of the moment. However, as data assets are accumulated, it becomes clear that a large amount of power is gained by bringing all the data together and merging it into one consistent form. Often data is in different formats and locations and has to be merged between multiple sources and formats. The process of merging data in this way is referred to as "data fusion."

Examples of inconsistencies are different schema structures for similar tables, different field names being used for the same items, different abbreviations being used for the same item, and different scales being used for the same quantities.

Data fusion is thus an important factor in making data available for use by the database tools. Thus the data is the fuel that makes the database run, while data fusion is the process of making that fuel available. At times, data conversion and transformation or fusion is viewed as a very pedestrian activity and this is sometimes true. However, it is a very important activity.

Although data transfer seems easy there are a number of engineering problems that have to be tackled carefully. For instance, date and integer formats typically differ amongst different databases. In addition character strings at times have single quotes, double quotes, or no quotes in different systems. Similarly keywords in different databases may be used in textual segments. These are all examples of inconsistencies that a data fusion system has to cope with.

Data Transfer Utility™ (DTU) is a product that transforms and fuses various data formats together. It brings together data from various database forms ranging from relational tables in products such as Oracle™, Sybase™, Paradox™, and DB2™ to hypertext.

Experience has shown that after data fusion, the level of power in data querying and analysis is greatly enhanced.

## ■ 2.3 ARCHITECTURES FOR INTELLIGENT DATABASE APPLICATIONS

The architecture of an intelligent database has three layers:

1. The user interface
2. The analysis module
3. The search engine

The user interacts with the user interface. The user interface accepts information about the criteria to search for, the topics of interest, etc., and displays results to the user.

The analysis module constitutes the "thinking part" of the system. It makes decisions as to what patterns should be looked for and submits queries and statistical tests to the search engine. The interaction between the discovery module and the search engine is *on-going* (i.e., based on the results obtained from one query, the analysis module generates new queries and submits them to the search engine). However, the level of interaction can be substantially reduced by pre-analysis.

The search engine is responsible for executing queries and statistical questions within the database. The queries may take the form of SQL statements to be executed by conventional database architectures or may be expressed in other proprietary forms suitable for induction.

Since the architecture is fully scalable, at one end of the spectrum all three components may reside on one workstation, while at another end the components may be fully partitioned and may rely on special purpose hardware. The remainder of this section will consider the hardware architecture of intelligent database applications, the special requirements of distributed databases, and the software architecture.

An intelligent database environment consists of hardware, software, and data.

In terms of hardware, we can distinguish between the frontend and backend hardware that is required. Database access, for instance, can be handled using a client server architecture, where queries are sent to a database server and results are processed and displayed on the local (client) machine. The database engine runs on the server, which is also responsible for collecting and fusing data from external databases.

The client machine may be a PC or a powerful graphics workstation, typically situated on a desktop. The point-and-click navigation style in intelligent databases is well suited to input devices such as mice and pens. It can also be adapted to work well with speech input. While intelligent databases can work well with existing hardware, the potential for fast and powerful intelligent database applications will only increase as the state of the art in computing technology advances.

All of the components of intelligent databases are currently available although some of them were originally designed as standalone applications. Reliable relational database engines have been around since the late 1980s, as has the IXL information discovery tool (IntelligenceWare 1987). There are also a wide number of data visualization tools available. Viable intelligent database applications can be constructed in a variety of operating system environments including UNIX, and PC operating systems.

The two stumbling blocks in the application of intelligent databases are the know-how needed, and the availability of good data. This chapter provides methodologies and architectures for applications and discusses how data quality and fusion of data from several sources can overcome these stumbling blocks.

Data transfer is another key enabling technology for intelligent databases. Much of the value of intelligent databases comes from the active data concept, where visualizations can be constructed on the fly with the latest data. This presupposes that the relevant data can be transferred into the intelligent database environment quickly and efficiently. In some cases, external databases may be queried on-line, and this mode of information acquisition will become more viable as the reliability and bandwidth of high-speed data networks increases. In other cases critical data may be downloaded from external databases hourly, daily, or weekly. However, ultimately intelligent databases will act as extremely large virtual databases with almost instantaneous and transparent access to widely distributed and heterogeneous external databases.

Another aspect of intelligent database usage is the work structure. Different intelligent database applications tend to have different styles of usage depending on the task, the users, and the organization where the application resides. For instance, inspection within a quality control application might require a highly portable workstation that can be used to access relevant information from within different inspection environments. Design, on the other hand, is a collaborative activity and typically involves teams of people working together. Thus users of an intelligent database application to support design might be more collaborative and may require networked versions which provide a shared view of data visualizations as they are called up.

An executive information system may work in a number of modes or environments. For instance, if the staff of the executive office are preparing a briefing, they will tend to navigate through the various data visualizations that are available and choose a selection that highlights the most relevant trends and relationships. Alternatively, a briefing to or by the executive may involve use of the application within a meeting environment, with the data visualizations being projected on to a large screen.

While issues of hardware, software, connectivity, and work structure are certainly important, they do not change the basic mechanics of the model of intelligent database application introduced in this chapter. Provided that a minimum level of hardware and software support and connectivity is available, database querying, information discovery, data visualization, hyperdata, and executive information presentation methods can be used across a variety of environments and work structures.

### 2.3.1 Hardware Architecture

There are four basic scenarios for partitioning the hardware architecture (Figure 2.3) for an intelligent database application:

> *Architecture 1* — All three components reside on one PC/workstation. This approach was used for the first implementation of IXL and worked well for data on personal computers. However, as soon as users realized

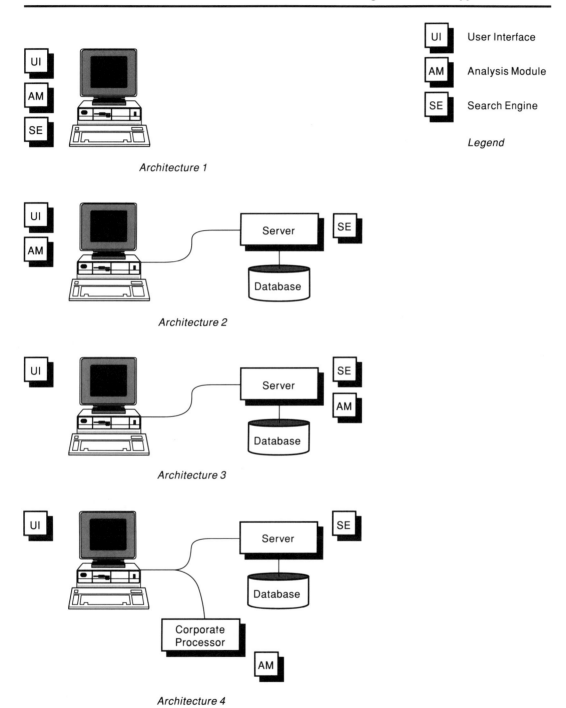

**Figure 2.3** Four scenarios for positioning the intelligent database architecture.

the benefits of the program, many of them began to push for its use on mainframes with gigabytes of data.

*Architecture 2* — The user interface and analysis module reside on a PC/workstation, while the search engine runs on a backend server. The advantage here is that workstations with good graphics may be used in conjunction with existing database management systems.

*Architecture 3* — The user interface runs on a PC/workstation, the analysis module and the search engine both run on a backend server. The advantage here is that a fast backend server may be fully devoted to the tasks of discovery and database search.

*Architecture 4* — There is a separate hardware component for each module. Thus the analysis module runs on a dedicated computer, and submits queries to the search engine residing on a backend server. The user interface runs on a PC/workstation. The advantage here is that a single analysis module computer on a local area network may serve several client PCs running the appropriate user interfaces.

The hardware architecture of an intelligent database should be fully scalable in the sense that although in the early stages it may be implemented on simple general purpose computers, it may later be partitioned to use fast, dedicated hardware within each of its modules.

For extremely large intelligent database applications, involving many gigabytes or terabytes of data, the database engine ideally should satisfy the following properties:

1. *Virtually Unlimited Database Size* — The ability to deal with databases of arbitrary size is very important. The architecture should be expandable so that it can deal with data storage clusters holding many terabytes of data.

2. *Parallel Processing* — Intelligent data analysis is an ideal application for parallel computation. Most of the database accesses performed by the search engine are read-only and the analysis module may pursue several hypotheses at once.

3. *Combined Induction and Deduction* — The analysis module should merge induction and inference to process inductive and deductive database queries. This requires an intelligent database engine as discussed in Parsaye et al. (1989).

The key issue about hardware architecture is that it should be easily expandable as the size of the database grows. Thus the user can start with a small database set and let it grow without having to change the hardware or software architecture.

## 2.3.2  Software Architecture

At the top level the software architecture of an intelligent database application has three components (Figure 2.4): user interface, application logic, and database interface. Each of these components has further subcomponents. For instance, the user

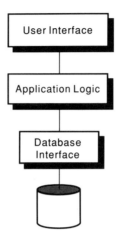

**Figure 2.4** The software architecture of an intelligent database application.

interface consists of generic capabilities as well as application specific terminologies and dictionaries. Similarly the application logic consists of generic components such as graphic routines and discovery engines as well as domain dependent components which relate to quality control, marketing, etc.

However, we may also view the architecture from a different perspective, based on the application specific and generic components. The three main components of the software architecture (as in Figure 2.5) from this perspective are:

- Application dependent terminology
- Generic modules
- Domain specific logic

A combined view of these two perspectives is provided in Figure 2.6.

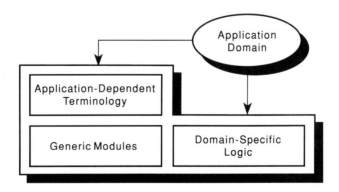

**Figure 2.5** Application specific and generic components of an intelligent database.

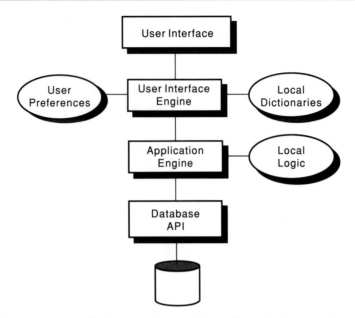

**Figure 2.6** Overall software architecture of an intelligent database application.

Good setup environments are crucial for good applications. Each intelligent database application must have an interface customization tool such as the Corporate Vision™ (see Chapter 8 for a detailed description of this system) setup environment. The user or on-site developer may then setup the kinds of graphs, text, menus, etc. that are needed.

In many applications this setup can take place without programming. In this way, two advantages are achieved:

**1.** More applications can be built because analysts can set them up very quickly.

**2.** The quality of many applications goes up since the feedback loop between the user and the developer is shortened and more modifications can be made easily, raising the satisfaction level of the user.

As discussed later in Chapter 3, a customization tool creates interfaces based on the "base tokens" or basic functions available to it. If no base token for a function like dynamic hypermedia is available, then no such feature can be added. Thus, it is crucial to have rich functionality of features in the customization tool.

Setup and customization help to satisfy the specific needs and requirements of the user interface in a particular application domain. Relevant customization tools include a hypermedia customization tool, a variety of interface building tools (e.g., Interface Builder on the Next), and a dictionary tool for jargon. This latter tool allows key terms in the interface to be changed to fit the needs of the application (i.e., to become aliases). For instance, the word "field" can be changed to refer to "product" in a marketing context.

The intelligent database frontend varies from application to application. Its most salient feature is a hypermedia interface for point-and-click navigation among a set of charts and graphs that are constructed interactively. Other application specific tools may be linked in as buttons within the hypermedia interface. In a quality control application, the standard set of charts would be extended to include control charts, Pareto diagrams (see Chapter 10), etc. These modifications would occur in the visualization procedures.

Other extensions for the quality control application would appear as buttons in the hypermedia interface. For instance, some quality control charts are constructed not from the data themselves, but from the analyst's interpretation of the data. Thus the quality control specialist may first view the various visualizations of the data within the hypermedia interface and then click on the "interactive diagramming" button and select the cause-and-effect diagram option. This allows the specialist to build a model of defect causation in, for instance, a production or assembly process that could then be viewed by other users.

Specialized diagramming and other application specific tools are accessible from the user interface (the intelligent database frontend) but they are actually part of the domain dependent component of an intelligent database application. Other parts of this domain dependent component include specialized visualization tools (e.g., PERT networks and Gantt charts in project management), and other specialized tools (e.g., financial analysis tools in an executive information system, a geographic information system, or GIS, in a marketing application).

The domain dependent part (shared kernel) of an intelligent database application includes the database engine and information discovery tools. The database engine is particularly important. We should not think of an intelligent database application as a monolithic vertically integrated application, but as a set of modules that work together. The intelligent database engine is itself a module and will change as database technology evolves. At present, we envision the database engine as a high performance relational database, and SQL querying forms a natural interface to this module. The discussion in the remainder of this book will assume a relational database engine with an SQL interface. However, it should be understood that the relational engine can be replaced with a different database engine, provided that an appropriate querying interface is available and that the engine affords sufficient performance to support intelligent database operations.

Information discovery is the process of extracting large amounts of knowledge from data. Information discovery is useful in making explicit the hidden properties and patterns within a database. The rules thus generated can then be used directly to create data presentations, or they can be filtered by a human expert and used to update an object model of the application domain. However, while the rules discovered will vary widely across different applications, the induction processes used to discover rules are domain dependent, as are related statistical tools that may be used to discover patterns, trends, or groupings in data.

Data visualization involves both domain dependent and domain independent aspects. The domain independent aspect includes a wide range of chart types and charting conventions. Thus pie charts, bar charts, and scattergrams can be constructed in almost any domain, while charting conventions such as plotting the cause on the horizontal axis and the effect on the vertical access are also widely accepted across different domains. In practice, data visualization will often rely on a standard set of chart or plot types that are used to create visual representations of combinations of variables.

Data visualization can also be used to corroborate the results of rule generation. For instance, the effect of a rule generated through information discovery can be conveyed visually by constructing charts or graphs based on various combinations of the variables that appear in the rule. By convention, the conclusion of the rule (i.e., the size of the long-distance phone bill in this case) would be shown on the y-axis as it is an effect (dependent variable). As will will discussed in Chapter 5, effective interactive data visualization systems can be constructed using a combination of heuristics such as the above.

Throughout the development of the intelligent database application, most of the software is developed in such a manner that the underlying database can be changed or upgraded without major effort. This is achieved through the use of a relational database management system (RDBMS) with an independent Application Programming Interface (API), as in Figure 2.7. The API provides a standard set of input and output functions with which external functions and applications may communicate with the RDBMS. Thus the API allows the RDBMS to be used as a plug compatible module that can be wired to work with a variety of different external functions or modules.

### 2.3.3 Data Architecture

The architecture of the data for an intelligent database application involves two components: local structure and global structure. The local structure consists of the data schemas and normalization issues within a single node or database. The global structure consists of the distribution, partitioning and arrangement of the data amongst

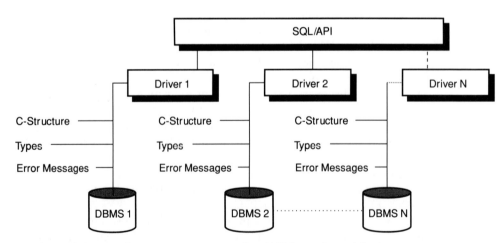

**Figure 2.7** An application programming interface (API) for a relational database management system (RDBMS).

geographically distinct nodes or databases.

In regard to local structure, there are guidelines in relational database design that govern the "well-formedness" of relation schema. These in principle consist of the normalization guidelines. Several "normal forms" for relational database design have been proposed. These normal forms are designed to prevent data duplication, inconsistency, and update anomalies.

Normalization is a step-by-step process for converting data structures into a standard form (relational tables). This standard form then satisfies the following constraints:

1. Each entry in a table represents one data item (no repeating groups).
2. All items within each column are of the same kind.
3. Each column has a unique name.
4. All rows are unique (no duplicates).
5. The order of viewing the rows and columns does not affect the semantics of any function using the table.

There are several types of normalization that differ in the extent to which the resulting standard table is constrained. Fifth normal form is the most restrictive, whereas first normal form is the least constrained normal form. Normal forms actually go beyond standard relational mathematics by referring to "facts," for example, an appeal by the relational model for more semantics!

First normal form restricts the values in each record to atomic. In other words, a table is in first normal form if there is no variable-length or repeating group in any of the fields of the table. Second normal form ensures that no field that is not part of a key is a fact of a subset of a key. Third normal form is violated when a non-key field is a fact about another non-key field. For more examples on normal forms, see Parsaye et al. (1989, Chapter 2).

In local data design for intelligent database application, traditional normalization issues need to be taken into account. Moreover, issues regarding on-line query, discovery, and visualization on large datasets come into play. These issues are often very application dependent. For instance, the ratio of reads to updates for both on-line and historical databases and this in turn affects how one designs the schemas, etc.

Intelligent database applications often link together a variety of diverse data sets stored separately within distributed databases. A distributed database system is a collection of data distributed across many computers (often at different sites), which are connected by a communication network. The system must support local applications at each computer as well as global applications in which more than one computer is involved.

At the top level there are two types of partitioning, either horizontal (where different rows of the same table are stored at different sites) or vertical (where the columns are separated). Some hybrid of these two types may also be used. However, the goal of a distributed database is to achieve transparency of partitioning.

Distributed databases have their own form of distributed database management system (DDBMS) that lets users specify high-level queries stating what they want rather than how they want to get it. In an intelligent database application the users are shielded from the effects of distribution so that they may operate under the impression that they are using a single centralized database. While data may be stored in a fragmented way, the user need not be aware that the fragmentation occurs when using the system.

The users should also be protected from side effects of interference between their own activities and other queries or actions currently in the system. In addition, site or communication-link failures should affect only applications that currently use these resources and should be transparent to all other applications in the system.

Transparency involves hiding details from the user. The view of a function and of a set of data should not be obscured by various wiring and communication details. Two forms of transparency in databases are location transparency and fragmentation transparency. With location transparency the details about the geographical location of the data are hidden so that the user appears to interact with a single virtual database. With fragmentation transparency the splitting of data between different tables and databases is hidden from the user.

As an example of distributed data usage and the associated problems in maintaining transparency, consider the case of three sites in a network. As shown in Figure 2.8. the table SUPPLIER is fragmented into three relations SUPP1, SUPP2, and SUPP3, and they are stored in Site 1, Site 2, and Site 3 respectively. Suppose that we want to retrieve the name of a supplier whose supplier number is 1234. If we have to use the following interaction

*Select Name NAME*
*From SUPP1*
*Where SNUM=1234;*

*if not #found*

*Select NAME*
*From SUPP2*
*Where SNUM=1234*

*if not #found*

*Select NAME*
*From SUPP2*
*Where SNUM=1234;*

then fragmentation transparency is not achieved, but location transparency is present because the user does not have to specify the location of the tables.

In order to achieve a high degree of transparency, the system must automatically record and maintain information about the location of the data in the database, status of transactions, failure of different sites and communication links in the network optimization algorithms. The system also needs to maintain protocols for ensuring transaction atomicity property, commit and recovery mechanisms, and so on.

There are two major additional features that add to the complexity of query processing in a distributed database system as compared to a centralized one. The first

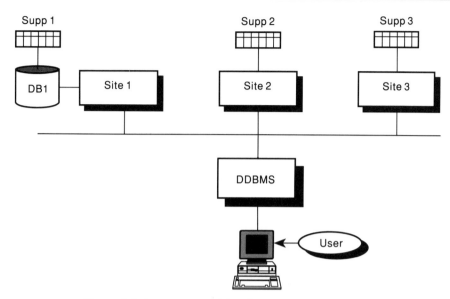

**Figure 2.8** Representation of data from three sites in a network.

is that cost of communication between different sites must be taken into account in developing a query execution plan. The second is that the opportunity for parallelism of execution in multiple sites must be taken into account in developing an overall strategy. The objective of a query optimizer is to minimize response time to the query, which consists of transmission time between sites and local processing.

Query optimization generally decomposes the query into a sequence of serial and parallel operations that yield the correct result. This is followed by grouping together operations which can be performed on the same site and constructing a query processing graph in which each node represents the execution of a group of operations at a single site and arcs represent transmission of information from one site to the other.

Another source of complexity in the design of efficient query-processing strategies arises because of the dynamic nature of a distributed system. Each local processor has its own workload to deal with in addition to processing multisite queries. This workload, which varies with time, may affect the time for local processing of a subquery.

For an example that demonstrates the dramatic performance difference a query optimizer can make to the same query in a distributed database, see Parsaye et al. (1989, Chapter 2).

## ▪ 2.4 INTELLIGENT DATABASE DEVELOPMENT

Intelligent database applications add value to data. They may be built from the ground up as new standalone applications. Alternatively, they may be additions to existing systems. In many cases the data has already been partially collected and the intelligent database is added to what already exists.

This section discusses the process and life cycle of intelligent database development, comparing and contrasting it with traditional database development. A new method of design is presented, based on concentric refinement of ideas. Examples of how this new style of design and development is carried out in different contexts are also provided.

One generally begins building an intelligent database with a set of questions in mind. These questions include:

- Why are we developing this intelligent database?
- Will the effort in building the system be justified?
- What will the return on investment be?
- How are we going to build it?
- Who is going to help us?
- What development tools do we have?
- What are the skills, needs, and requirements of the users?
- What can go wrong?
- When do we stop development?
- How do we maintain the system after it has been built?

These questions may be viewed as being concerned with some general issues in the development of intelligent database applications (as shown in Figure 2.9):

- Building components
- Integrating components
- Evaluation
- Refinement

Feedback is essential between these three issues. As the system is progressing, all of these issues must be continuously reevaluated.

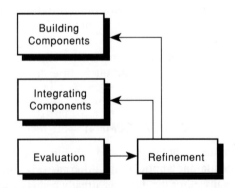

**Figure 2.9** Development of intelligent database applications.

The components include items such as query processors, graphics packages, and discovery systems. In addition, a method of navigation is needed to move smoothly between these different components. This is done using hyperdata, a hypermedia interface applied to various data forms to move between the different parts of an application.

Hyperdata is discussed in detail in Chapter 6. For now, we will introduce briefly the basic idea of hyperdata in terms of a functional model where actions within the user interface are referred to an event handler. This event handler then calls up different components (modules) as appropriate. The functional model of this event handler is shown in Figure 2.10. This figure also serves as a roadmap of the following chapters, showing how the different topics addressed by each chapter are interrelated.

Construction of intelligent database applications is not an open loop process (to use a term from control engineering). An open loop process is one where an instruction is carried out without need of feedback. In contrast, closed loop processes evaluate the results of prior actions in deciding which new actions to initiate. One cannot simply build the components, link them together and then expect users to find the resulting system ideal. Each application and user population will have its own specific features. These features are clarified through a prototyping process where a series of prototypes and evaluations indicate the special needs of the application domain.

The user should be involved early in the prototyping process so that the functionality, and the user interface, can be molded to personal needs. This is particularly

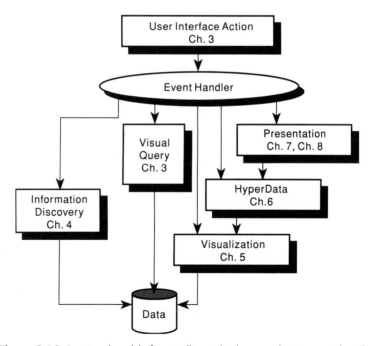

**Figure 2.10** Functional model of an intelligent database application event handler.

important for intelligent database applications that need to be customized for use by executives.

The developer should think through the stages of building the intelligent databases at the beginning of the project and anticipate any flaws or pitfalls that may be encountered. One of the most frequent problems encountered is poor data quality. Without good data quality the presentations of the intelligent database application will be at best misleading. Threats to data quality can arise from a range of sources such as harried data entry operators (e.g., one study found that almost a third of all patient records entered in by emergency room staff at a hospital had errors), or errors in optical character recognition when scanning data printouts into an electronic format. Thus it is frequently necessary to develop special measures for ensuring data quality at the outset of the project.

The process of intelligent databases development can be compared with the traditional software life cycle. Traditionally, the software life cycle has not included much feedback. An overview of the development process from the point of view of a generic software life cycle is shown in Figure 2.11a. (An alternative view of design is shown in Figure 2.11b.)

Development begins with a feasibility analysis. If the project is feasible, the next step is to define the conceptual structure of the system, along with a specification that describes the way in which the application will work for the tasks of interest. The specification is then followed by domain modeling, including development of a standard set of visualizations for the application, and design of appropriate user interfaces that capture the relevant features and requirements of the task domain. Domain modeling may also include analysis to determine which causal relationships and dependencies occur between different attributes.

Domain modeling is then followed by visualization knowledge. This knowledge consists of mapping between constraints and the charts that are produced. For instance, certain types of budget data might be represented by pie charts while other types of data are represented by bar charts. Visualization knowledge is required to know these preferred mappings (although these mappings can always be overridden by user preferences).

In intelligent databases, hyperdata knowledge consists of the rules that determine transitions from one visualization to another based on user inputs. Thus a hyperdata system is really a knowledge base of transition rules referring to available visualizations and the currently active constraints.

Once the application is close to completion, it needs to be validated. Validation can be either internal or external. Internal validation tests the internal consistency of the application. For instance, are visualization and hyperdata rules consistent? Are there any charts and interaction contexts for which appropriate transitions are not defined by the available hyperdata knowledge?

External validation assesses the effectiveness of a working prototype of the application. The development and testing of prototypes will be discussed in a later section of this chapter.

During the implementation phase, the intelligent database is moved into an operational environment, and its structure and use are gradually modified through maintenance.

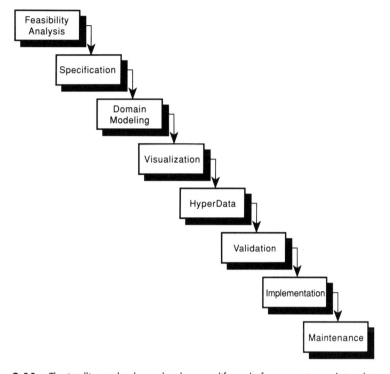

**Figure 2.11a** The intelligent database development life cycle from a static, traditional viewpoint.

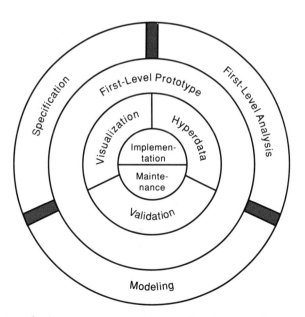

**Figure 2.11b** The concentric viewpoint on intelligent database implementation.

Even at a late stage of development the application and its interface should remain somewhat customizable. Developers within the operational environment should be able to customize the interface without too much difficulty. In addition, analysts may also modify the hyperdata knowledge base to provide better presentation sequencing, based on comments from the users within the organization.

The phases outlined above for intelligent database development are not always distinct and sometimes involve some overlap. For instance, in doing validation one may uncover new knowledge about the task that requires modification of the user interface or that calls into question the assumptions that were made in the initial feasibility analysis.

Section 2.4.2 will discuss concentric design as an alternative to the traditional approach to design. Intelligent database design requires a new form of design that differs quite widely from traditional database design. The next section reviews traditional methods of database design before outlining the novel characteristics of design for intelligent database applications.

## 2.4.1  Traditional Database Design

Traditional database design  has been a fairly linear, open-loop process where it is possible to plan ahead used data modeling and then flow through a well ordered process of conceptual, logical, and physical design. This three-level architecture dates back to the early database structure defined by DBTG (see Parsaye et al. 1989, Chapter 2).

The initial stages of database design traditionally require a process of conceptual design. The conceptual view of a database is a somewhat abstract representation of the physical data and the way that it is stored. The conceptual view is defined through conceptual schema, written in a conceptual data definition language (DDL), or is often expressed in terms of an entity-relationship diagram. In general, these conceptual schema only describe the information content and structure of the database, avoiding issues concerned with specific storage structures and retrieval strategies. This allows the same conceptual model of the database to apply to a variety of different physical implementations.

The development of a conceptual database generally precedes the definition and implementation of logical and physical databases. A conceptual database models the elements of information from the user's point of view.

The representation of the conceptual schema  can be expressed in many forms. For example, it may be expressed as an object-oriented or semantic data model where the key object types, events, and constraints are identified and modeled. The realization of conceptual schema can also be achieved by mapping the constraints in the semantic data model into definitions, procedures, and constraints in a particular data model, such as the relational model. An informal method of sketching out a conceptual schema is to use a combination of narrative descriptions and formal data structures to capture the important entities and their activities.

The logical level of database description consists of the definition of the structure of a database, written as logical schemas within a DDL. The schema includes a description of the various record types and of the ways in which these record types are related. It does not, however, include information about the actual values or records.

Once they are identified, relations and attributes are cataloged in the data dictionary. The data dictionary is itself a database consisting of the information that the user should know about when working with the database management system.

The physical design of the database includes breaking the data up into tables and defining the physical structure of the database. For further information on this topic see Parsaye et al. (1989, Chapter 2).

Next, the object-oriented, semantic, and entity relationship techniques typically used in database design are discussed.

**2.4.1.1  *Data Modeling***    There are several approaches to conceptual and logical data modeling. These include the use of object-oriented designs, semantic models, and entity-relationship diagrams.

Interestingly, all these techniques have a great deal of common structure expressed in terms of items and connections, as shown in Figure 2.12. For instance, objects correspond to entities or concepts, while relationships correspond to associations or messages.

The object-oriented approach views the world in terms of objects which are conceptually identifiable items. Each object has a set of attributes that can have values. Objects have associated methods which describe a behavior with respect to other objects. Objects interact with each other through messages. Objects have inheritance in a class structure (i.e., children or instances of an object share the properties of their parents). For more on object orientation, see Parsaye et al. (1989, Chapter 3).

Semantic data models are designed to overcome the problem of the limited understanding that traditional databases have by incorporating more meaning into the database (e.g., Hull and King 1988). One approach to semantic data models breaks the problem of adding meaning to a database into four stages.

1. Identify a set of semantic concepts that describe relevant information and meaning. This set of concepts might, for instance, include entities, properties, and associations. These concepts may then be linked in a descriptive formalism where the world is described in terms of entities, which are described by properties and linked together by associations.

2. Represent the semantic concepts identified in stage one in terms of a set of corresponding symbolic objects, such as those provided in the entity-relationship model.

| E/R | Logic | Relational | Object-Oriented | Semantic |
|------|-------|-----------|-----------------|----------|
| Entity | Argument | Record-Table | Object | Concept |
| Attribute | Predicate | Field | Attribute | Property |
| Relationship | Predicate | Table | Message | Association |

**Figure 2.12** Equivalence of data modeling approaches.

**3.** Devise a set of integrity rules that govern the description of the semantic concepts in terms of the symbolic objects.

**4.** Develop a set of operators for manipulating the symbolic objects.

Some approaches to semantic data models attempt to bridge the worldviews of Artificial Intelligence (AI), object orientation, and data modeling (Mylopoulos et al. 1980). For example, the concepts of semantic networks, procedural attachments, and frames from AI are finding their way into semantic data models.

The entity-relationship (ER) approach is a widely accepted technique for representing data models (Chen 1976). In the ER model, an entity is an object or thing that exists and can be distinguished from other entities. An entity might be a person, an institution, a flight, and so on. Entities are described in terms of attributes or properties. In terms of the regular database constructs, entities generally conform to records while their attributes are represented as the fields of those records.

A relationship is defined as an ordered list of entity sets. In a family database, for instance, *sister-of* represents a relationship between one set of entities and their sisters. In terms of the relational data model, the relationship corresponds to the name of the table, while the different entity sets correspond to columns in the table.

Entities and relationships can also be used as a diagramming technique in conceptual design of databases. The standard notation for such diagrams is as follows:

- Rectangles represent entities.
- Circles represent attributes.
- Diamonds represent relationships.

Relationships are generally described by verbs, such as supplier *supplies* customer or customer *is-supplied-by* supplier.

Figure 2.13 shows an entity-relationship diagram for a manufacturing process. This process has to deal with the following data:

Numerical-controlled machine data

Work-in-progress

Assembly structure

Vendor

Master parts

Customer

Finished-goods inventory

Raw-materials inventory

Orders

Accounts receivable

Departments that use this information would include:

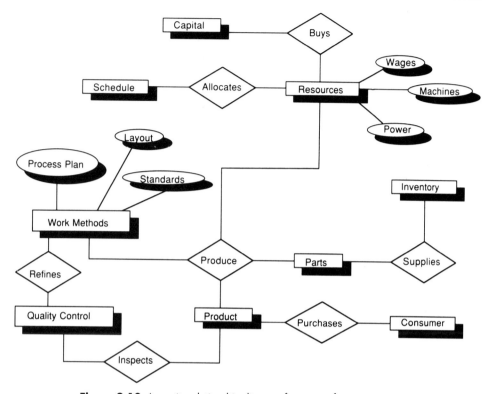

**Figure 2.13** An entity-relationship diagram for a manufacturing process.

*Purchasing* — to determine parts needs and vendor data

*Marketing* — to determine the availability of product in the finished goods inventory

*Production control* — to update work-in-progress

*Inventory control*

*Facilities planning*

*Engineering*

Although there is a close analogy between the relational data model and the entity-relationship model, there are also important differences. The entity-relationship model is a conceptual description of the data that does not determine which relations are necessary and which relations can or should be omitted. In spite of these differences, the entity-relationship conceptualization can be a useful starting point for building a relational database. The graphic representation shows the relations that exist within the data. This must then be supplemented with constraints and relationships that are added to the data dictionary.

One frequently used model of software development has been the waterfall model (Figure 2.14). The waterfall model assumes that software design and development is

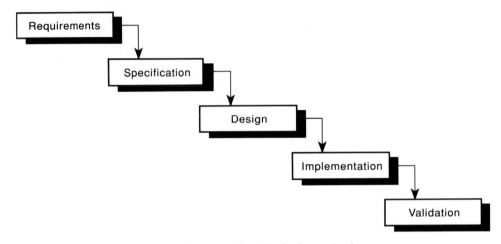

**Figure 2.14** The waterfall model of software development.

a fairly orderly succession of (possibly overlapping) stages.

The waterfall is really a linear model of development. It assumes that there is a sequencing of stages through which development must pass. In intelligent database design, however, development is largely driven by the requirements and needs of the user, combined with the properties of the application domain and the requirements of the task. Often there are considerable uncertainties over what these requirements are, and they only become clearer to the developer after considerable analysis, discussions with users, and experimentation with prototypes.

The waterfall model may be too idealized for many software engineering problems, but it is particularly poorly suited to the requirements of intelligent database design. The real shortcomings of traditional linear development lie in (a) the lack of feedback throughout the design process, and (b) early commitment to ideas which must later be abandoned.

The following section considers an alternative concentric design process that is more appropriate to the demands and uncertainties of intelligent database development.

### 2.4.2 Concentric Design

Traditional database design is not well suited to the needs of intelligent databases. Concentric design is an alternative approach that was developed specifically for intelligent databases, although it applies to other domains. The basic idea behind concentric design is not to commit too fast to a decision. Concentric design uses the principles of:

- Nonlinear progress
- Least commitment
- Design with feedback

One of the key features of concentric design is its *nonlinear progress*. The various steps in concentric design are carried out in parallel rather than in sequence. This allows the other two components to interact. Feedback can be used to finalize decisions that have been delayed.

The principle of *least commitment* means that noncritical decisions are not cast in stone early on in development. Because of this, costly mistakes may be avoided if an early specification for one step is found to conflict with a later specification for another step.

Finally, the principle of *design with feedback* is that design is iterative, and specifications and decisions will need to be evaluated and sometimes changed, based on the performance of design prototypes and interactions and tradeoffs between various specifications.

In concentric design the overall components of the system are gradually identified until the picture becomes clear. Following the principle of least commitment, constraints are delayed until necessary. Therefore, one does not implement a constraint that rules out some key options too early. In this way, one reduces the risks of committing to any direction until the interaction between the components are better understood.

Concentric design assumes that a large and complex design has problems similar to those faced by early mapmakers. In the beginning, the mapmaker understands only a few key landmarks in the geography, in the same way that the designer only has a few key specifications or requirements to go by. Early maps only showed a few well-known features like the "Pillars of Hercules" (the modern Straits of Gibraltar) or the island of Sicily. Once the map was outlined in terms of its major features, succeeding generations of mapmakers filled in the details, and the coastlines, mountains, and river systems slowly became more precisely delineated. Similarly, the concentric designer begins by sketching out the main features, based on the key constraints, and then successively elaborates these until the details are crystallized.

The basic ideas of concentric design can also be compared to the way we see an elaborate picture or a scene. From a distance, the key features of the picture are vaguely seen "all at once," but without full clarity. As we get closer, the real identity of the components becomes clear.

It is a mistake to focus on one piece of the picture too early and prematurely decide exactly what each part of the picture is. If one makes premature assumptions then as one gets closer, the assumptions need to be revised. In practice, revising the assumption will be very expensive in a large-scale project and will cause significant delays and cost overruns. The different pieces of the picture should become clearer in parallel, and these different pieces all influence each other in how they fit together.

In concentric design, we keep the overall picture in mind and proceed along several fronts carefully so that the right decisions are made at the right time. Moreover, we use feedback throughout to reconfirm that what we see is what is actually there.

The feedback provided through prototyping is essential to concentric design. Prototyping allows one to test aspects of a system before it is completely built. Mistakes or faulty assumptions are then corrected. Often, in concentric design, a first level prototype is constructed to illustrate the *look and feel* of the system. The prototype is constructed on a personal computer with the same fields as the eventual database but with fewer records.

The structure of the prototype is constructed by using a prototyping system which interactively builds up the display with the user's participation. The prototype allows the user to see graphs and reports and to selectively "zoom into" pertinent pieces of information using a point-and-click approach.

Prototypes may be categorized into horizontal and vertical prototypes. Horizontal prototypes show the overall functionality of the system. (i.e., the overall look and feel) without delving into too much detail at any level.

Vertical prototypes focus on just one specific detail (e.g., the performance on a specific type of query). The distinction between horizontal and vertical prototypes is similar to the difference between breadth-first and depth-first search in a tree structure. Horizontal prototypes test the general structure of the overall design, while vertical prototypes test the details of specific functions. The use of horizontal and vertical prototypes needs to be balanced within a prototyping plan.

Prototypes can be useful since they help demonstrate some basic features of a system. After a prototype has been constructed, it can often be extended to a fully functional system while its basic structure is preserved. It is generally considered that a prototype has succeeded if its structure is preserved in the final system.

There are two ways of using prototypes in design (Parsaye and Chignell 1988): One can either discard the prototype or evolve it. For intelligent databases, the decision as to which style of prototyping to use depends on the characteristics of the application domain and the quality of the prototype. In some instances, not discarding the prototype and insisting that its structure be preserved increases the likelihood of project failure. Once the decision to extend rather than discard a prototype is made it really becomes an early version of the eventual application.

From an organizational point of view, a linear representation of the basic steps in concentric design is as follows:

- Identify the overall boundaries of the design space and separate it into two or three key components. Identify the top-level classification of user groups.
- Establish the most predominant *landmarks* or constraints for each component, listing the noncritical options or issues without committing to them.
- Elaborate the top-level list of absolute constraints and landmarks. Rank these in a numerical order.
- Determine the local structure by getting immediate user feedback about the above categories of information and make the necessary corrections.
- Explore the global structure and build a first-level prototype. Weigh the extent of horizontal and vertical prototyping.
- Get further user feedback and reevaluate the situation. Begin to identify a complete list of constraints for the design problem.
- Integrate the views of different users into a "wish list" that is subject to trade-off analysis and compromise among the users, and from which further requirements are derived.
- Begin to commit to the next level of design details. Further refine the goals and requirements by talking to the users, ensuring that a clever gadget or application that has few users isn't constructed.

- Look for opportunities for improvement based on user suggestions and availability of new technology.
- Finalize the design. Allow for the customization of user views and fill in the details. Allow for expandability of the system as usage load increases.

Due to the nonlinear nature of concentric design, these steps may be carried out in a variety of iterative loops. For instance, one may begin by building an outright prototype to test user reactions to a new set of ideas. Then this prototype may be discarded and the process begins as before.

Since the ideas presented above are somewhat abstract, the following section illustrates the application of concentric design with the example of building an information clearinghouse, a task that many organizations face.

### 2.4.3 Building an Information Clearinghouse

Suppose you are building an information clearinghouse to provide various user groups within an organization with on-line, multilevel access to historical data. The system provides the organization with better information and better turn-around time for getting the information. When people in the organization can get the right answers more easily, they inevitably ask more questions, becoming far more informed.

One of the key goals of the information clearinghouse is to reduce the reliance on intermediaries for information access. The system allows end-users to walk up to a terminal, click on a few icons to perform queries, and obtain graphs and reports without talking to a programmer, as shown in Figure 2.15.

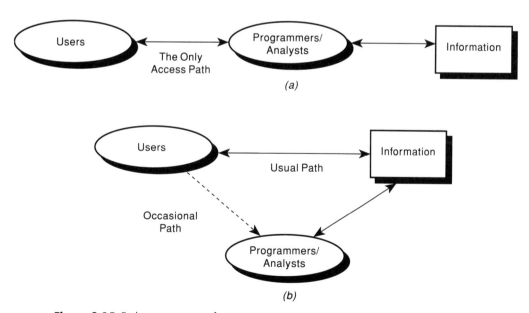

**Figure 2.15** End-user access to information. (a) programmer as intermediary; (b) programmer as occasional assistant.

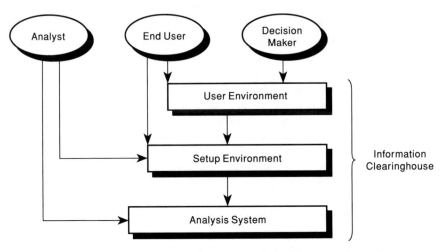

**Figure 2.16** Interaction of different user groups with the information clearinghouse.

To begin with, based on the methodology of concentric design, we identify the *key components and landmarks* for the system. These include the user groups and the system components.

The system has three distinct groups of users, supported by programmers and database administrators, as in Figure 2.16. One class of user is the executive or manager who performs no development and will only use a point-and-click interface. A second class of users is an end-user who is not a programmer but who is familiar with word processors or spreadsheets. Such end-users can customize the interface for the executives or for themselves. Another class of user is the analyst who is somewhat technically oriented and who is prepared to spend time thinking about problems and trends in large databases. Each of these groups is supported by the information clearinghouse.

At the top level, the information clearinghouse has three distinct components, as shown in Figure 2.17:

1. *The data store,* which is a relational database management system (RDBMS) housing records, several gigabytes or perhaps terabytes of data
2. *Access and analysis tools,* which access the data clearinghouse and provide information, either based on user queries or data analysis
3. *Historical data,* which includes a wealth of hidden information and knowledge that is going untapped without the other two components

The data store provides access to the *data,* while the access and analysis tools provide *information.*

One question encountered at the outset of developing an information clearinghouse is what to do first:

- Select a computer platform and a DBMS engine.
- Decide on the tools used for access and analysis.
- Decide on what data to gather, merge, and store.

None of these decisions should be made too quickly or before considering the constraints imposed by the rest of the system. We should first clear the fog of issues, then decide on specific cases. Next, we analyze the choices for each of these components and identify the key constraints.

**2.4.3.1** ***The Data Store***    There are several options for selecting a hardware architecture and a DBMS engine for the data store. These choices include:

- A large mainframe system with a central database housing all of the data
- A small set of departmental super minicomputers, each housing portions of the data
- A set of fast workstations fully distributing the data throughout the organization
- A backend parallel database machine, storing all of the data and supporting either the mainframe or the fast workstations as clients

Of course, each of these options has a different cost structure, performance characteristics, and maintenance costs. Which is "best" greatly depends on the nature of the application, the characteristics of the organization, and the environment in which the system is to be used.

The traditional approach may be to order the hardware first and then think about the software and the data to populate it with. Concentric design approaches the problem differently, allowing for experimentation and user feedback before purchasing expensive hardware.

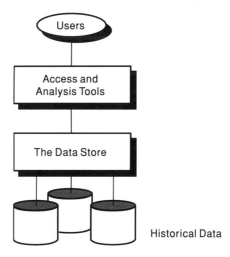

**Figure 2.17** The information clearinghouse.

A good approach to implementing the data store is to evolve it in two or three stages. In the first stage of development, the schemas and fields of the data store are prototyped on a sample database with fewer records. In this way modifications to the schema are more easily managed. The first stage thus uses a fast workstation to prototype the system horizontally and to obtain user feedback. Also, in parallel, a number of vertical prototypes are built to determine the system bottlenecks and response times.

Moreover, the types of data required and desired by the users are confirmed. This may require the search for and acquisition of further data, or the modification of the current schemas. Furthermore, a first glance at the quality of the data is obtained.

The second stage focuses on performance tuning based on the access trends of users, as well as information tool refinements. This stage determines whether the performance bottlenecks identified in stage one can be easily remedied with the introduction of additional hardware components or if the problems are inherent in the design. Moreover, based on user feedback, additional access and analysis tools are provided and the design is modified. A substantial amount of data is used in this stage.

The third stage introduces hardware upgrades (if needed) and additional user interface tools (if desired), and commits to the final software and hardware configurations. In this stage the database is fully populated.

This gradual approach is based on the following rationale:

- Major hardware expenses are not incurred without justification.
- System performance and usability is measured as user needs are tested.
- Unnecessary risk is avoided until the benefits of the system are determined.

Thus with the first and second stages of the data store we measure user response and satisfaction level towards historical data analysis and determine if the data available is of any use. This also allows us to fine-tune the set of tools the users need for information access.

In the process of evolving the data store, planned expansion may be used. Suppose that to begin with, in the third stage we use a large mainframe system. In later stages, fast processing machines should be considered for performance enhancement of data analysis and routine reporting tasks. Some available architectures are shown in the panels of Figure 2.18.

The reason we can evolve the hardware and the DBMS used in the data store is that throughout the development process, most of the data access and analysis software is developed in a manner so that the underlying database can be changed or upgraded without major effort. This is achieved through the use of a RDBMS independent Application Programming Interface (API).

The use of this layer allows the application-level software to be mostly unaware of what DBMS is being accessed. For instance, if the decision support system is found to be useful and many users begin to use it, causing an overload on the mainframe, migration to a new parallel DBMS engine can be achieved transparently without major modification to the application-level systems.

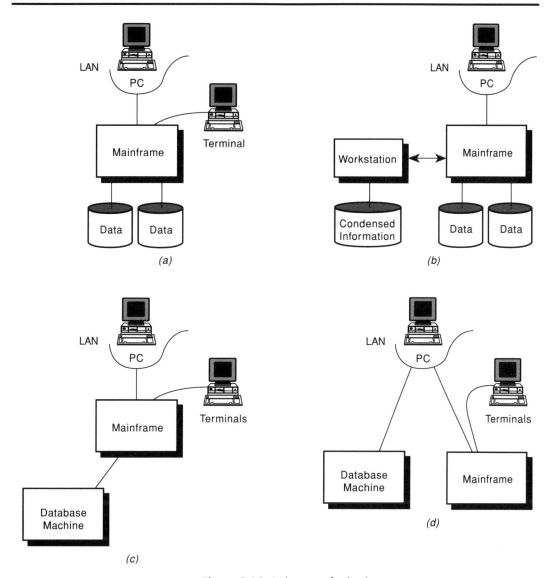

**Figure 2.18** Architectures for the data store.

Since development of an intelligent database application may take some time, depending on the state of the organization's databases, the availability of development resources, and the technological solutions chosen may also change during the development process. For instance, a project might begin with one piece of hardware being assumed for the database engine only to find that these assumptions have to change drastically due to a down sizing process that has occurred in the organization. New architectures or approaches such as client server may also have a large impact. While there are no canned solutions to deal with such problems, decisions should be based on available hardware and made in the context of concentric design. The concentric design strategy allows us to carefully determine the usability and access patterns of the users and provide them with the best system in the long run.

**2.4.3.2  *Analysis and Access Tools***    The analysis and access tools are what the users see and use. They greatly impact the user's perception, satisfaction, and level of success with the system.

Since the goals of users and their levels of computer background vary greatly, the tools provided are separated into several different categories.

The tools have three components:

**a.** Query and reporting system

**b.** Data visualization system

**c.** Data analysis system

The zoom-in capability is very important in all systems. As a trend or a graph is displayed, the user has to be able to zoom in and get further information on demand. The query and reporting system allows end users without prior training to pose two types of queries to the system: traditional, fixed format queries, providing reports and graphs, and ad hoc queries formed by clicking on representative icons.

The data visualization system allows for interactive graphing of trends and patterns. The user can click on any segment of a graph to zoom in and get a further graph. The interface may be customized for the decision maker by end users and analysts.

The data analysis system is used by the analysts to find significant trends and rules in the data. The system complements statistical analysis by finding specific rules that categorize clusters of information.

**2.4.3.3  *The Data***    The need for an information clearinghouse becomes clear when an organization discovers that it is not using its data assets properly. However, at the outset of development the typical organization is often unaware of three facts:

**a.** What data is available in-house and what can be purchased

**b.** The quality and reliability of the data

**c.** The usefulness of the data to the users

In most cases, organizations have large amounts of data in storage, often in sequential access form only (e.g., old magnetic tapes). However, it is not clear exactly what the data contains or what quality it is. In addition, a good deal of power is provided by combining one's own data with data purchased or obtained elsewhere. Therefore, data mapping is a key issue in the first stage.

It will not be clear what data the users really want and what data will be useful before the first prototype has been tested. It is only then that one can begin to determine the actual data that needs to be focused on. Of course, the data required may be in different formats and so needs to be transferred and reformatted before use.

Before relying on the data, it is essential to use data quality management methods as discussed in Chapter 4. Moreover, an ongoing data quality program must become an integral part of the information clearinghouse. Once the issues of data quality and data usability have been addressed in the first and the second stages, the data store can be populated in the third stage. Thus concentric design differs from traditional design by progressing along several paths in parallel until the eventual solution emerges.

## ▪ 2.5 METHODOLOGIES FOR THE USE OF INTELLIGENT DATABASES

Intelligent database applications should be explicitly designed for use by humans. Thus in building such applications we should be guided by the requirements of ergonomic (human-oriented) information presentation. The study of information ergonomics is still a relatively new field (e.g., Shackel 1991) so that most of our knowledge about information and display comes from accumulated experience in fields such as psychology, linguistics, graphic art, and user-interface design. However, at the very least we need to have a model of information transmission that can guide and inform development of intelligent database applications. There are many ways of modeling the transmission of information, a few of which are considered in the following section.

### 2.5.1 Models of Information Transmission

All models of information transmission necessarily deal with a source, a target, and some communication channel or transmission process. The electrical engineer, for instance, models information in terms of the flow of elementary units of information (bits) down a communication channel (e.g., Shannon and Weaver 1949). The psychologist models information transmission as a cognitive coding and decoding process (e.g., Anderson 1982). The linguist models information transmission in terms of transmission of meaning that simultaneously occurs at phonemic, syntactic, semantic, and pragmatic levels. Finally, the advertiser or propagandist looks at information in terms of the effectiveness of the message in influencing the recipient's behavior. Each of these models of information transmission is valid in its own way.

We have chosen to focus on the psychologist's model (which in turn has been strongly influenced by the electrical engineer's model, as is evident in the work of Attneave, 1957, and others) and the advertiser's model of information transmission. Figure 2.19 shows our version of the psychologist's model. In this model the information display is a coded message in the form of a schema or template that has

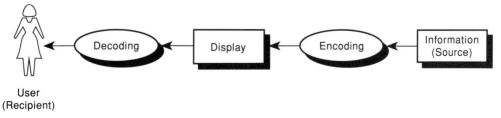

**Figure 2.19** The psychologist's model of information transmission.

been filled in according to the value of relevant attributes in the data. The coding process consists of analyzing the relevant data and converting it into the form required by the template/display. The resulting information display is presented to the users (recipients), who then interpret (decode) the information display according to their task goals or interests.

This model of information presentation is a useful beginning, but it lacks an evaluative component (feedback loop) that can diagnose the effectiveness of the information presentation and the errors or difficulties in coding the display that should be corrected. The advertiser's model shown in Figure 2.20 includes an evaluative component which is useful in developing information displays and in selecting appropriate visual templates. It also focuses more on the medium and the message. Evaluation is carried out in the context of the communication goals and the extent to which the stated objectives are matched by the interpretations of those who see the display.

### 2.5.2 The Hyperdata Model of Information Access

A criticism of all the information transmission models considered in the previous section is that they are fundamentally reactive. That is, these models assume that the user is responding to information displays. This may be true for a medium like noninteractive television, where the viewer has no direct control over which program or advertisement will be shown next on the currently selected channel, but in a medium like a newspaper, the reader actively navigates through the various sections and articles, choosing what is of interest. It turns out that there is relatively little literature concerning this type of active navigation process. However, one of the transformations that intelligent databases should bring about is a transition from

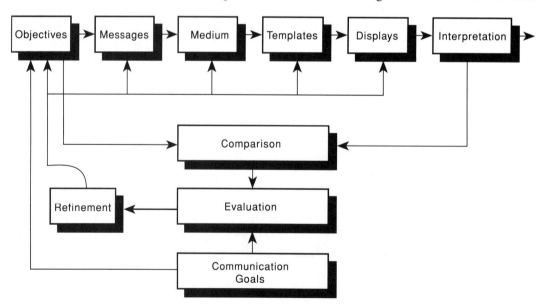

**Figure 2.20** The advertiser's model of information transmission.

electronic information transmission systems to information access systems that are more than menu overviews or keyword search systems.

Hyperdata is a fundamental technology in permitting information access. A hyperdata system is a linked network of visualizations of data where the user may navigate from one visualization to another by modifying parameters or clicking on different regions (buttons) of the current visualization. A hyperdata system will typically overlay a data visualization system. The data visualization system will have a standard set of visual templates (information containers) and a set of transformation rules that convert data from database tables into the format of the visual template. For instance, a field in a table may contain a category attribute with seven different levels or values. A transformation rule (procedure) for creating a pie chart from this field might consist of counting the frequency of each category value of the attribute (within the table) and then constructing a corresponding pie chart, where the sectors of the pie are proportioned according to the frequency of each category value in the table.

The hyperdata system links together the data visualizations according to a prescribed set of navigation rules (or procedures) that are typically customized for each application. We might, for instance, have one visualization that is a pie chart showing sales of mineral water across different regions in a country. A navigation rule then defines what happens when the user clicks on one of the segments of the pie. In one application, such an action might be interpreted as a request for more detailed information about sales in that sector. The navigation rule might then initiate a request to the visualization system for the corresponding pie chart, which in turn may send a request to the data querying system to extract the appropriate sub-table for the selected region and then return the frequencies of category values for the appropriate field (e.g., states, provinces, or cities) within that sub-table.

This discussion assumes an active or dynamic hyperdata system where user inputs are interpreted as navigation actions and transformed into requests to the data visualization system (Figure 2.21a). An alternative form of hyperdata is static (Figure 2.21b), where "canned" visualizations and manually authored navigation links are used. In practice, the creation of static hyperdata will be too costly in most applications. Fortunately, hyperdata is viable because of the well-structured nature of data within relational tables in particular, and databases in general. This stands in contrast to the less structured nature of textual material in hypertext, where it is much more difficult to develop unambiguous rules or procedures for converting user inputs to navigation actions. For instance, imagine that we have an extract from *Hamlet* as part of a large hypertext document and the user clicks on the word "Yorick" in the subtext "Alas, poor Yorick! I knew him." How is the system to interpret such an action? Should the system scroll to the next mention of Yorick, or to a glossary that explains who Yorick is, or perhaps show a video clip of an actor holding a skull? The problem of hypertext, and navigation in text generally, is that the semantics of text is very complex. In contrast the semantics of data summarization and visualization is much more stylized, and a concentration on numerical data allows us to focus on general questions such as: Which number is bigger? Has this number changed? Is there a relationship? These questions apply generally to numbers, no matter what objects or processes they represent.

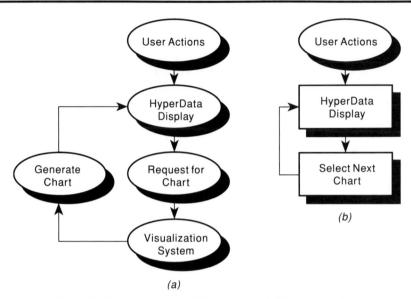

**Figure 2.21** A comparison of (a) dynamic and (b) static hyperdata.

### 2.5.3 Construction of Navigable Information

Navigable information must be developed within the larger context of a complete information system. After all, a display can only be viewed in the first place if the user is able to navigate to it, and once viewed, the interpretation of that display may well depend to some extent on the context of previous displays and the goals of the current task.

Dynamic hyperdata requires a process of automatically creating information displays from data. Figure 2.22 shows a simplified representation of the construction model used in this book. The data passes through several transforming processes that add value to it and make it "presentable." First the data is summarized and filtered, then it is visualized, linked, and finally presented. Further, this process occurs in response to the navigation and selection actions of the user, so that there are a series of arrows leading back toward the data that allow user-driven creation of information presentations.

In developing intelligent database applications it is necessary to consider several models of information display and presentation. The communication model analyzes the codings and decodings that occur between data and interpretation. The evaluation model compares the interpretations with originally intended messages, or with some normative description of the data (if the user perceives clustering effects or differences in data as represented in the display, is it statistically valid?). The construction model builds the displays that may then be interpreted and evaluated.

Thus the creation and use of intelligent database applications involves interrelated activities of construction, communication, and evaluation. It is important to note that, unlike the graphic artist, we are not creating one graphic or display at a time, neither can we envision a system with a small and fixed number of display alternatives.

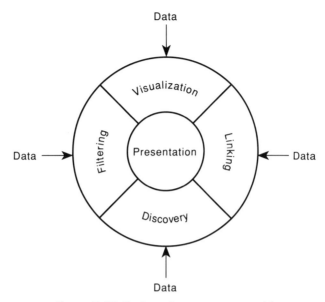

**Figure 2.22** The hyperdata construction model.

Instead, the intelligent database application is a tool for exploring, where a vast number of (virtual) displays are available depending on the interests and selections of the user. These displays are not stored in a chart database, but are created interactively (on the fly) as they are needed. Furthermore, these virtual displays will contain active data, so that their appearance will change as the corresponding data changes. For instance, a display that plots the recent closing prices of shares in common stock will change from week to week as the corresponding stock prices change.

### 2.5.4 Principles of Information Usage

This book describes a method for building intelligent database applications. This method is based on the best technologies (information, visual discovery, hyperdata, Executive Information Systems) that are currently available for converting raw data into meaningful presentations. This section will look at the problem from a different angle and consider how humans prefer to work with information. The following pages will also show that the model of intelligent database development used here fits in well with behavioral principles of information usage.

The goals of an intelligent database application are to improve the quality of information by focusing and interpreting information that is meaningful to people and to take account of the relevant psychological principles of how people handle information. Part of the task of developing better information quality involves adding value to the information. Relevant technical issues include how to combine information from different sources, focus it for the problem or context at hand, and then project views of this focused information through the user interface.

How should information be focused or projected? The answer to this question depends on the needs of the human user. Since intelligent database usage is an interaction between people and machines, the guiding principles of intelligent database usage are behavioral. While technology is changing and advancing, human capabilities are relatively stable. Thus it makes sense to use behavioral issues to drive at least part of the intelligent database development task. This behavioral approach has the useful property of generating fairly clear intelligent database design guidelines.

We can get considerable insight into how people will use intelligent databases from how they use information in general. Figure 2.23 shows how people generally filter, view, and interpret information. In this behavioral model, what goes on inside the person's head is just as important as what goes on in the software prior to the presentation of information views at the user interface. The software will work better

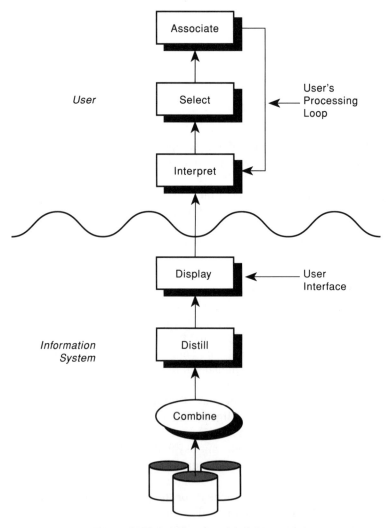

**Figure 2.23** Behavioral model of IDB usage.

if it anticipates to some extent the needs and characteristics of the cognitive interpretation and handling of information. The perceived quality of an intelligent database will be measured in terms of how information is filtered and projected to the user at the user interface.

The behavioral model (Figure 2.23) of intelligent database usage (Chignell and Parsaye 1991) consists of five basic information processing operations (Distill, Display, Interpret, Select, Associate), two of which are handled by the computer software, and three of which are handled by the user's cognitive processing. In the first step of the model the information is *distilled*, based on the users' inputs. This distillation or filtration step extracts trends and patterns in the data and creates summary descriptions of the data and comparisons. Induction or information discovery may also be used at this point to detect rules or trends in the data.

In the second step of the model the distilled information is then projected as *views* in the user interface. Users then *interpret* these views, *select* the information from these views that is judged to be relevant or useful, and then *associate* this selected information with their prior knowledge.

One of the features of this behavioral model is that it locates the center of activity within the user. This reflects the belief that measures of information quality are ultimately subjective and depend on how the user responds to the information. This user-oriented approach should lead to better design of intelligent database tools.

The behavioral model suggests five important processing steps in intelligent database usage, two of the steps being handled by software, while the other three steps are handled by user cognition. What can these five steps tell us about intelligent database application development? General principles are proposed in the following pages that should guide the development of intelligent database applications (Chignell and Parsaye 1991) based on each of the steps in the behavioral model. Each of these principles facilitates in some way the general goal of controlling and exploiting information.

### 2.5.4.1　The Distill Step

**Principle 1.** *Ensure that information is representative*　　One of the problems in summarizing information is that the summary should represent the underlying information. This principle is in fact a lot trickier to handle than one might imagine. For instance, people are not always very good at choosing which information is representative. Consider the following question: In a typical year in North America, are more people killed by tornadoes or by lightning? Most people who are asked this question assign a significantly higher probability to death by tornado, although the correct answer is exactly the reverse. However, we can explain this result in terms of information representativeness. Newspapers and television report tornadoes far more extensively than lightning strikes (except when they happen at the U.S. Open) so people base their judgments on the unrepresentative way in which the information has been summarized for them. In this example the relevant medical records and death certificates would be more representative than the newspaper reports.

As another example, consider the problem of summarizing the performance of a stock-based mutual fund. Say that the information is summarized in terms of the appreciation in value of the fund between 1975 and 1990. The answer varies greatly depending on which month one starts calculating from, due to the joint effects of a stock rally in 1975 and compounding since that time. So, in many cases information is not neutral. The way that information is treated critically affects the way it is perceived.

In the model of intelligent database application used in this book, the information is distilled in a number of ways. The act of data collection is part of the distillation process in that an active choice is made about which data to keep and which to exclude. Other aspects of distillation are very important but tend to lie outside the scope of the definition of intelligent database application development used here. For instance, the definition of what constitutes advertising dollars may not be clear-cut. When a firm gives money to support a team for the summer Olympics, is that advertising? In part it may be, although the dollars spent in supporting the team should probably be handled differently from dollars that are put directly into advertising. In some places, such donations may also be tax deductible, so that the line between corporate generosity and advertising becomes further blurred. In general, distillation of variables, such as deciding how to get an accurate number for advertising expenditure, will require considerable knowledge and expertise in the application domain, and lies outside the scope of the intelligent database application model defined here.

**Principle 2.** ***Provide information that is statistically meaningful*** It has been said that there are lies, damned lies, and then statistics. Descriptive statistics are certainly misused a great deal, especially around election times. One person may point to the fact that unemployment is increasing, based on seasonally adjusted data, while another person may show that it is decreasing using unadjusted data. Similarly, one person may show that there has been a huge drop in the foreign trade deficit, while another will show that there has been no decrease in the deficit once the effect of lower oil prices has been discounted.

Arguments such as these are often rooted in our goals and assumptions about information and how it should be used. However, there is no excuse for making comparisons that are statistically unreliable. For instance, while the truck sales for Global Motor Corporation increased last month, the apparent increase might be accounted for entirely by normal month to month variation. If so, we would be wary of attributing a chance variation to the effectiveness of a promotion that was carried out last month. Of course, it is difficult to root out long-standing habits of misusing numbers in the general population, but attempting to ensure the quality of numbers and comparisons is certainly an important issue in providing high information quality.

This principle applies very strongly in the case of information discovery. We must be wary of discovering useless rules. One way to do this is to ensure that rules apply to a high proportion of a large number of cases. Another application of this principle is to make the statistical measure of correlation and significance level available when showing scattergram relationships of data. This will provide the user with a statistical measure that gives an indication of whether or not there is a systematic linear relationship in the data. This principle could also be used in the creation of hyperdata by giving higher priority to charts where there appears to be a statistically significant relationship between the attributes being plotted.

### 2.5.4.2    *The Display Step*

***Principle 3.*    *Present meaningful views of information***    Even after treatment and filtering it is rare that relevant information can be boiled down into a single number or screenful of text. More likely there are a number of views of the information that are shown to the user.

Since humans have preferred styles of viewing and navigating around information, it is important that meaningful views be provided that can be readily assimilated. For instance, graphic artists are well aware that the form of a book or figure can promote or interfere with the communication of its content. In fact, there is considerable knowledge about how to make effective visual presentations of information (e.g., Tufte 1983). This knowledge should be exploited in developing effective displays of information for intelligent databases.

This need for meaningful views is handled in several ways in the intelligent database application model. The basing of the hyperdata links on attribute and object pivots ensures that there is a tendency to show meaningful views in the domain, since the objects and attributes were defined by the developer so as to be meaningful. The use of drill-down facilities allows users to explore information at different levels of detail, and to do this with respect to a meaningful context variable that they have selected.

***Principle 4.*    *Structure information using familiar templates or metaphors***    Familiarity may breed contempt in some circumstances, but it is also very helpful when people are dealing with new information. Maps are examples of familiar templates. Views of sale information, for instance, can often be effectively overlaid on a map of the sales area. In this case the map serves to structure the information according to geography, but does this structuring in an intuitive and natural way. In the intelligent database application model, maps can be added as part of the process of customizing the user interface during the final application development step.

The principle of familiarity is generally applicable when building interpretable presentations of information. For instance, people are used to seeing time as increasing to the right, having larger numbers represented higher on the page, and so on. Violating these types of expectation can lead to misinterpretation of data. For example, early altimeters in aircraft worked like clocks so that a small hand rotated according to thousands of feet and a big hand rotated according to hundreds of feet. This led to a number of accidents (controlled descent into terrain) where the altimeter was misread by the pilot. The big hand, small hand mapping used in early altimeters makes sense with clocks because people want to know how time is moving (i.e., they focus on the local information). For altimeters though, the big question is how high one is from the ground, and the global trend (thousands of feet) is more important than the local trend (hundreds of feet). Thus it is important to use familiar cues in appropriate contexts.

Further scope for building familiar metaphors is given to the developer in the application stage where customized user interfaces and bit-mapped graphics may be added. For instance, icons may be defined for various products so that whenever a chart refers to a particular product the corresponding icon may be shown.

***2.5.4.3   The Interpret Step***   We now shift to the first step of cognitive processing. The user is trying to figure out the meaning of the views being displayed. At this stage, users don't want to be overwhelmed with complexity, they just want to see information that tells them what they need to know. The following two principles capture these needs.

***Principle 5.   Hide complexity until it is needed***   "Information hiding" is a useful technique in software engineering that can also be applied to intelligent database design. Extraneous information is noise that distracts the users from what they need to know. As a general strategy, it is best to show people the big picture first. Once they have formed a basic mental model or structure for what is going on, they can begin to incorporate the details within this structure. Thus one should not throw away the complexity, but delay showing it until the user expresses an interest in it.

Drilling down is in accordance with this principle in that the details are hidden, but they can be called up by navigating through the menu hierarchy. Thus the hierarchical organization of the data serves to hide the details at the lower levels until they are needed.

***Principle 6.   Provide diagnostic information***   Diagnostic information tells people what they need to know. When people go to a doctor they don't want a diagnosis of a stuffy head and a runny nose. They want to be told what is causing the symptoms and what to do about it. Similarly, spotting a defect in an inspection process is less useful than fixing the problem that is causing the defect in the first place. So information presentation should be oriented towards causes rather than symptoms where possible. This type of task-oriented information selection and presentation will work best with a highly specific intelligent database application where domain knowledge can be used to define relevance and diagnosticity.

The preparation of reports within the executive information system development step is an example of selecting a set of highly diagnostic information from the mass of available data.

***2.5.4.4   The Select Step***   Processing information from an intelligent database can be likened to the well-known process of studying a book. The interpret step is like reading and understanding the text. The select step is like selecting material and taking notes or highlighting while one is reading. Finally the associate step is the learning that occurs as a result of reading. The following two principles address the issue of selection.

***Principle 7.   Focus the information***   This is a general principle that probably applies to all the steps in the behavioral model. However, having focused information simplifies the select step a great deal. Focusing requires a good understanding of the goals of the user. In practice this will generally mean that users should be given powerful tools for zooming in on different pieces of information. Even if the intelligent database software cannot focus the information automatically, it should interactively work with the user to define a focus.

Focusing is the flip side of complexity hiding. The same hierarchy that is used to hide the more detailed levels of information can also be used for focusing as the user drills down to more detailed information.

**Principle 8.** *Organize information according to its value*    In any situation some information is more valuable or useful than other information. A businessman may attach more value to information in the *Wall Street Journal* than information in *National Geographic*, while for a high school teacher it may be the reverse. For a long-term mortgage, information about the interest rate may be much more critical (an ongoing expense) than information about the loan appraisal fee (a one-time expense). Thus, where possible, information should be ranked according to its value to the user and shown in the order of its value. This ranking of information by value might utilize a relevance feedback strategy (as in information retrieval systems) where the user indicates which views of the information are more useful, and the system generalizes this information and uses it to determine the value of other information views that may be shown later. Ranking of information value may also be based on a profile of user interests or on measures of uniqueness or novelty of information.

The issue of information value ranking is not directly addressed in the model used in this book. However, it is implicit in the way that the developer constructs the object model, and in the way in which reports are constructed during the executive information system step. Information retrieval systems sometimes use relevance feedback (Parsaye et al. 1989, Chapter 6) to predict the value of information based on users' judgments of whether or not previously retrieved information was relevant. It is possible that one could also construct a form of relevance feedback for hyperdata, where users mark a "relevant" button if they find a chart particularly useful or interesting. However, this issue will not be considered any further in this book.

### 2.5.4.5 The Associate Step    Viewed from outside the human head, the associate step is particularly mysterious. However, we do not need to model or describe the associate step. The task of the intelligent database is simpler (i.e., to encourage and assist association). In part this can be done with flexible tools for manipulating and viewing the data. In addition, we propose the following two principles.

**Principle 9.** *Combine and interrelate information*    One of the weaknesses of the human mind is in handling lots of details. One of its strengths is detecting patterns and seeing correspondences and links between things that are objectively very different. Tools that allow people to combine and interrelate information are very important. For instance, for numerical data it is useful for people to view plots of how one variable varies relative to other variables. Thus the wealth of visualizations that are provided with the hyperdata of an intelligent database application are an excellent way of allowing people to combine and interrelate information.

**Principle 10.** *Present information in a variety of ways*    One of the fundamental axioms of behavior is that everyone is different (the other fundamental axiom is that everyone is pretty much the same apart from the differences). To capitalize on the differences between people, the intelligent database application should provide a range of choices for viewing and navigating around information. While this may seem to promote redundancy, people often extract different information from different views of the same data. In the present model of intelligent database applications, users are able to explore the data using SQL queries, point and click navigation within hypermedia, hierarchical menu access in an executive information system, and can also view the same data relationships with different charts (e.g., bar charts versus pie charts). Thus the system provides considerable opportunity for presenting information in a variety of ways.

### 2.5.5    Intelligent Databases and Organizational Change

Intelligent databases require new organizational methods for their successful implementation. Like many new technologies, intelligent databases are far more likely to fail due to problems in the management of the technology than to problems inherent in the technology itself. Thus intelligent database design needs to consider the relevant portions of the software-user-organization system. Methods of building intelligent databases should not be grafted on to the existing practice within an organization in order to meet the needs of the moment.

The situation is further complicated by the asynchrony in the development of companion technologies for intelligent databases. While the key conceptual problems for an intelligent database application are concerned with the user interface, Hyperdata, and data visualization, the key enabling technologies are the database engines and distributed databases that support the other functions. In addition, the failure of many organizations to implement sufficiently high data quality standards threatens to undermine the potential and effectiveness of intelligent databases.

However, problems in data quality are likely to recede as automated tools are used to input and filter data. Some of these tools will be discussed in Chapter 10. Data quality is as much a symptom of a faulty attitude towards information as it is a problem in its own right. It may be much easier to fix the technical problem than it is to fix the attitudes that produce the problem. The attitude problem is that people don't give data enough respect. Too many decisions are made "by the seat of the pants" and many organizations are too busy fighting today's fires to use the available data effectively to prevent fires in the future. Any firefighter can tell you that it is much easier to stub out a cigarette than it is to put out a forest fire, but this lesson is often lost in a complex world where "management by crisis" seems the only option.

Unless harried managers find the time to draw a deep breath and plan for a future with intelligent databases, they will not receive the benefits described in this book. Intelligent database development is more than a technological fix, it requires a new way of thinking that makes data, and the information within the data, central to planning and decision making.

## ■  2.6    CONCLUSIONS

This chapter has reviewed the main components of intelligent database applications and their development. The success of intelligent database applications is determined by the quality of information interpretation provided within the context of the task being performed.

The problem of data quality management, which is a critical issue in intelligent databases, was also discussed, as was the architecture of intelligent databases from the perspectives of hardware, software, and data.

The chapter also outlined methods for developing and using intelligent database applications that generate the required characteristics of ease of use, with effective handling of large amounts of information relevant to real tasks. The model of intelligent database usage that was discussed included three main classes of information exploration (i.e., discovery of unexpected information, interactive graphics, and information overviews).

Concentric design was introduced as the best approach to intelligent database application development. This is a very flexible approach to design which should be appropriate for a wide range of application domains. A description followed of a behavioral model of intelligent database usage that included five basic information processing operations (Distill, Display, Interpret, Select, Associate). Also outlined, ten principles of intelligent database usage, and how the model of intelligent database application development related to these principles.

## ■ 2.7 APPENDIX: CLASSES OF INTELLIGENT DATABASE APPLICATIONS

This appendix illustrates briefly how intelligent database applications will work for a number of different problem domains. The purpose here is to show the general applicability of the approach. Later chapters will provide more detailed presentations for some of these application domains.

### 2.7.1 Project Management

People generally find it difficult to evaluate a large number of competing options simultaneously. Thus software tools often act like prosthetics (assistive technologies) that make it easier for us to think without having to "sweat the details." For instance, spreadsheets are tools that allow people to look for patterns in data without having to worry about making the detailed calculations themselves. Computer support of project management extends the envelope of manageable project complexity by assisting human managers to see overall trends in the project and to anticipate problems that may arise because of slippage in the project schedule.

Project management tools have generally been seen as ways of assigning resources to tasks so as to complete projects in reasonable time while utilizing resources effectively. However, the real goal of project management is not to optimize criteria such as cost or quality on the basis of a static world, but rather to guide decision making in the face of an uncertain and dynamically changing environment.

Consider a typical project management application of constructing a building. After the architectural drawings have been approved, a schedule of tasks is set up. This will be visualized in terms of a Gantt chart that shows resource allocation to tasks over time, and a PERT/CPM analysis which is helpful in scheduling activities so that the project can finish on time.

An intelligent database application can take these traditional methods of visualizing projects and link them to the database through an object model so that when the charts need to be viewed they can be updated with the latest data. In addition, these can then be linked to other visualizations of project information, including pie charts showing the budgets consumed by different tasks, bar charts showing resource usage, and so on.

The executive information system in this case provides report generation capabilities that summarize the current status of the project, highlighting tasks that are on the critical path and resource shortages that are likely to impact those critical tasks. These reports also provide up-to-date estimates of budget expenditures on the project and variances from expected expenditures. One of the most important of the drill down menus is be based on the hierarchy of tasks and subtasks. For instance, if a budget problem is detected, the manager can drill down and find out which subtasks were causing the problem. Another drill-down hierarchy can be built, based on the organization chart for the project. This allows the user to see which departments or resources within the organization appear to be responsible for delays or cost overruns.

## 2.7.2 Marketing

Marketing is a difficult but crucial part of consumer society. Marketing is a response by businesses to the environment they find themselves in. For any business the environment is both a threat (challenge) and an opportunity. Marketing information supports a variety of decisions relating to such issues as product design, advertising strategy, and production policy (how much stock to produce or store in inventory).

Marketing may be thought of as a chain of derived demand that begins with the consumer and works back through retailers and wholesalers, to manufacturers and parts suppliers. An intelligent database application for marketing could support the task of reviewing marketing information in order to make strategic decisions about product design, advertising strategy, and production policy.

The role of an intelligent database application for marketing is to integrate the various sources of data available and to present visualizations that reflect the patterns in the data. Consider the task of a market researcher for a soft drinks producer who has been given the task of attempting to expand the market share of the company. The researcher may initially consider a number of strategies to handle this problem. One strategy is to identify which segments of the market are currently more likely to purchase a competitor's product and then investigate why those segments are acting in this way.

The first task of the intelligent database application in this case would be to provide the information that the market researcher needs in determining the "relative performance" of the various marketing segments. Say the average person consumes $x$ gallons of carbonated soft drinks in a year. Then an under-performing segment would be an identifiable group of people (e.g., pensioners) that consume less than $x$ gallons per year on average. Now there may be very good reasons why one segment of the population should buy more soft drinks than another segment. For instance, one segment may be more inclined to the sweet taste or fizziness of carbonated soft drinks, while another segment might think that soft drinks tend to rot their teeth or give them wind.

Information discovery can be used to generate a set of rules that predict the level of soft drink consumption based on different attributes of people. Rules can also be generated on the basis of more complex attributes that are significant within the market researcher's model of the world. For instance, what may be of interest is not the overall consumption of soft drinks, or even the overall consumption of a particular brand, but rather the market share. Thus we can define market share as the proportion (market share) of our own brand that is drunk, versus the overall amount of all soft drinks consumed by a particular type of person or market region. This analysis is very important because there are significant differences in preferences for soft drinks across people of different ages, in different locations, and so on.

Using market share as the goal or conclusion, information discovery would then generate rules of the form:

> Market share is between X and Y%
> if
> the consumer has the following attributes . . .

These rules would then indicate the important attributes that determine market segmentation based on market share of the brand in question. Visualizations can then be constructed and linked into a hyperdata model. Viewing this hyperdata, the researcher might notice that market share for his brand is particularly weak in the important 13–18-year-old group. Analysis of advertising dollars spent on this age group versus an aggressive campaign aimed at the youth market by the competitor might then explain the source of this weakness. The research could then use the executive information system to put together a report showing the key presentations and suggesting a new advertising campaign to recapture market share among teenagers.

### 2.7.3 Quality Control

The basic idea of quality control is to measure some critical parameters that are related to the quality of a product over time, determine the level and variation for each of these parameters, and then feed back this information so as to adjust the production process in line with greater quality.

By the time that data is analyzed in the corporate headquarters and the printouts sent to the shop floor, the production process may have changed several times due to various disturbances. The solution to the problem of lag in the system has been to make quality control part of the production process. Operators themselves monitor the production process and detect when the process deviates from desirable limits, using specially designed and easy-to-use tools.

The problem of quality control is closely related to the problem of observing a statistical process and detecting when changes occur. Any production process will have "natural" variations that are outside the scope of the production process and "production-related" variations that are due to factors such as the skill of the operator or the mechanical status of the machine. The task of quality control is to monitor the production related variations and make sure that they remain steady and that the output of the production process remains at a consistently high quality.

Quality control tools track the production process and tell operators when a control input is required. Examples of such tools are *flow charts, cause and effect diagrams* (also called fish-bone or Ishikawa diagrams), *check-sheets, histograms, scatter diagrams, Pareto charts,* and *control charts*. These tools have had widespread success because they enable a quality control engineer to "see through" the data and understand the reasons for quality problems and come up with solutions for eliminating them.

Thus a quality control system consists of a set of visualizations or summaries of the data along with rules about how to interpret and handle unusual patterns of data that are observed in the visualizations. For instance, Figure 2.24 shows a quality control chart. In this case the points that are outside the control limits are circled. This indicates that the process has changed in some way and that steps need to be taken to get the production process back under control.

Consider the task of manufacturing an automobile. From a total quality management (TQM) perspective there are almost limitless possibilities for improving quality, ranging from designing better bumpers and fuel injection systems, and developing better methods for painting and welding, to weeding out faulty or defective parts provided by suppliers. Each day, a huge amount of data will flow in that is potentially relevant to the quality of the product (i.e., the finished automobile). If we focus on some critical welds on the body frame, for instance, there may be a number of physical attributes that are measured and available to us concerning the size and strength of welds. We may even have a model that allows us to predict whether a weld is satisfactory, based on the combination of attribute values observed. In this case, we have a number of relevant visualizations of the data. The first visualization reports the number of defective welds as indicated by our model, against different values of worker, assembly line, day of the week, and so on. We can also construct a control chart to see whether the rate of defectives is increasing. We may also be interested in tracking the individual attributes themselves, since changes in them over time may lead to defects if not attended to quickly enough. For instance, the temperature at which the welds are being made may decrease, or impurities in the materials may gradually change the properties of welds. Thus we will be interested in various visualizations of the data with time on the x-axis.

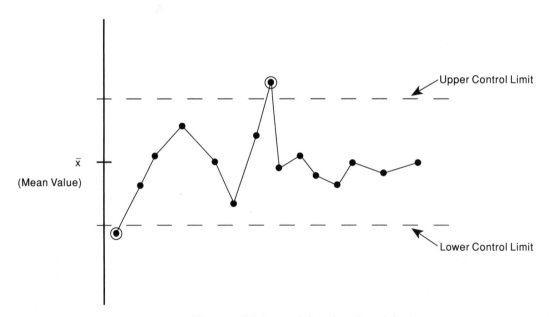

**Figure 2.24** A control chart (hypothetical data).

The quality assurance manager may then use the intelligent database application to forestall problems before they happen or to diagnose problems after they have been detected. For instance, defective welds might start to appear. By tracking the pattern of physical data over time, the manager may be able to determine which part of the production process is causing the problem. This will include looking at the rules generated by information discovery to determine which physical attributes are associated with defects, looking at plots of these physical attributes, and possibly reviewing video data showing the creation of welds that were later judged to be defective. In this example it seems natural to build this type of video record into the application interface.

### 2.7.4 Financial Analysis

Financial analysis is a complex area that combines the basic laws of supply and demand with other factors such as market psychology. Consider the use of an intelligent database application for financial analysis of common stocks to support investment decisions. Shares of common stock are the basic units of equity ownership in a corporation. They can be bought and sold (e.g., on the stock exchange) and their market values are based primarily on investor expectations of future earnings and dividends.

Stocks have a particularly rich set of data associated with them corresponding to information about the companies that issue the stocks. From a stock investors point of view the most important information concerns the health of the company and other factors that predict the future value of its stock.

We can divide information that predicts stock prices into three kinds; fundamental information about the company; technical information about price movements, and external factors. External factors include general political and economic considerations such as changing interest rates, availability of commodities due to war or shortages, and even general market psychology. Technical issues revolve around the history of stock prices and trading volumes for the stock or security under consideration.

Consider how an intelligent database application for supporting technical analysis of the stock market might look. An analyst begins by examining a particular stock and looking at various charts associated with it. For instance, a chart showing daily highs, lows, and sales volumes over the past three months (quarter) might be shown. Clicking on the volume attribute label may brings up a menu of choices such as: on balance volume chart for the past quarter, ten highest volume stocks for the past week, comparison of volume with peer stocks. In this case peer stocks may be defined according to some market model. For instance, banks might form one peer group while utilities form another peer group.

The analyst might also want to test out some ideas on past data. For instance, she is considering buying the stock based on an apparent rising trend from a previous low that is supported by good buying volume. The application interface might be customized so that she can look at previous charts that reflect a similar situation in the past. This will help provide a context for the current situation and provide some indication of the degree of risk involved.

In addition, a more comprehensive tool may actually provide predictions about future stock prices based on information discovery. Such a system could then be integrated into the intelligent database application so that the analyst could later plot past performance versus earlier predictions for different stocks to see which models tended to fit the predictive model better or worse than others.

### 2.7.5 Manufacturing

The nature of manufacturing has changed considerably with technological innovations such as robots, machine vision, computer aided design, and computer control of equipment generally. An essential component of all these technologies is electronic information. This information provides a wealth of data that can be used by an intelligent database for manufacturing.

While it is possible to instrument everything that can be instrumented and collect streams of transient data, selection of manufacturing information to record should be done carefully. After all, collecting noise simply makes it that much more difficult to hear the signal. The goal of the intelligent database approach to manufacturing is not to set up a parallel "data factory" for its own sake (although it could easily be done), but rather to collect and interpret precisely the information that is relevant to productivity, quality, and profitability.

Process planning is one manufacturing activity that may benefit from the intelligent database approach because it requires detailed information from all the other manufacturing activities. Process planning deals with the difficult problem of planning the detailed fabrication and assembly operations required in the manufacture of a product. Process planning requires detailed information about design (including specifications and tolerances), fabrication, assembly procedures, and the status and capabilities of the various machines and cells that are available as resources.

Consider how an intelligent database application may assist a process planner in manual process planning. The process planner begins by studying the engineering drawing to identify the basic structure and potential difficulties. The planner then identifies the outer envelope of the part. This includes geometric shape and surface finish. The planner then chooses the best stock. This choice is usually made from a set of standard stock shapes.

The next step is to recognize part features. Features are the geometric shapes that are cut into the stock to form the part. These features should correspond to the features that can be made with available tools and the paths that they can follow. The planner then considers alternative methods for producing each feature. There are often a number of ways in which the same part feature can be made. Some are less expensive, or produce better quality. At this stage judgment has to be exercised in ranking the alternatives, and often trade-offs have to be considered (e.g., cost versus accuracy). At this point too it may be useful to use the intelligent database to examine plots of cost versus accuracy for different parts and features. The planner may also be interested in knowing about the availability of machines on the shop floor (e.g., charts or graphs may show the current or expected loading of the different machines). Another plot might show the availability of different parts in the inventory. Thus the ability to navigate through a hyperdata representation of factory information may be of considerable benefit to the process planner.

## 2.7.6 Design

Design is an information intensive process. It is also a synthetic activity where there is no obvious right answer. Early automobiles, for instance, were designed as well as they could be at the time, but as technology developed, and designers became more experienced and more aware of what is possible, the automobile improved greatly. The steering wheel now seems the obvious way to steer a car, yet early cars often had levers as the main form of steering. Some design changes are based on conceptual insight, while others require technology change. Early airplanes were made of wood and cloth. The use of metal skins and cabin pressurization in later aircraft required improvements in materials fabrication and engine technology.

Consider the task of a reliability engineer who has been assigned to a team designing avionics for a supersonic commercial airplane (Malcolm, Poltrock, and Schuler 1991). The engineer begins by browsing through the project notebook to learn about the project. A preliminary design review is scheduled in a few weeks. The schedule for analyzing each avionic component shows that the reliability analyses are ahead of schedule except for one component which was scheduled for analysis a month ago. The schedule slippage in this case was caused by an unexpected problem in fitting all the required logic on a single board.

In this case, the alternatives were to pack more integrated circuits on the board with potential risk of thermal problems, or to design an application specific integrated circuit (ASIC). A thermal analysis conducted by a predecessor is linked to the first alternative. Since the high temperatures generated by this alternative would lead to reliability problems the team decided to build a customized integrated circuit for the application. The new reliability engineer now uses an intelligent database to view the thermal characteristics of alternative integrated circuits that are available. The engineer may also use it to look at performance data or specifications for related components of the design. Pointing and clicking through the hyperdata representation of this information speeds up the task of getting acquainted with the project. Furthermore, by linking the intelligent database application with an electronic mail system that can transmit graphics, the new engineer can send messages to other members of the team, showing them plots of the data and asking questions or resolving uncertainties.

The scenario above presents the view of an intelligent database application from the perspective of one member of a team. While this example does not explicitly illustrate collaborative work within the team beyond simple querying, it does show how an intelligent database application can serve a valuable role as a project memory, so that new members to a project team can get up to speed quickly.

## 2.7.7 Understanding, Prediction, and Control

We can divide the motivations for purposeful information exploration and analysis into three broad categories (see Chapter 4 for more discussion of this topic, with particular emphasis on discovery tools): understanding, prediction, and control.

Most applications will have a mixture of these motivations, in varying degree. For instance, while the main goal of management is control of the project schedule, understanding the current status of the project will be a necessary part of achieving the main goal of control. Similarly, quality control also shares aspects of understanding.

| | Understanding | Control | Prediction |
|---|:---:|:---:|:---:|
| Project Management | ✓ | ✓ | |
| Marketing | ✓ | | |
| Quality Control | ✓ | ✓ | |
| Financial Analysis | ✓ | | ✓ |
| Manufacturing | ✓ | ✓ | |
| Design | ✓ | | |

**Figure 2.25** Different types of IDB applications classified according to the activity (understanding, control, or prediction) that they emphasize.

Figure 2.25 shows a categorization of six general application areas in terms of their main categories of motivation. This figure represents a somewhat idealized view and it might be more realistic to fill percentages in for each cell (e.g., project management might be 30% understanding, 60% control, and 10% prediction) except that it would be difficult to justify particular values, and the balance between the three categories of motivation would probably vary from project to project.

Intelligent database applications generally work best in enhancing understanding, and in providing insight which can then be used in control or prediction. Thus an intelligent database should help a manager in tracking down delays in a project and in identifying resources that can be reallocated, but the managerial actions required to reward or reprimand workers, or otherwise enforce compliance to the schedule, lie outside the scope of an intelligent database application as it is conceived in this book.

# 3

# GRAPHICAL USER INTERFACES

*There is a difference between a sign and a symbol. The sign is always less than the concept it represents, while a symbol always stands for something more than its obvious and immediate meaning.*

— Carl Jung*

*Corollary*: Iconic interfaces have an inherent advantage since they rely on symbols rather than signs.

## ■ 3.1 INTRODUCTION

The user interface is the visible aspect of software. Users most often tend to judge the quality of a software application by the quality of its interface. The user interface should be one of the starting points in developing an intelligent database application. The functionality that the user sees in the user interface specifies the behavior of the system. Thus a description of intelligent database applications should start with the user interface, the window of opportunity for the intelligent developer, and the pit of despair for the careless and unwary.

According to various estimates, roughly half of the code in many applications, and about half the overall development effort is concerned with the interface. A survey by Myers and Rosson (1992) found that, out of a sample of 71 systems, an average of 48% of the code was devoted to the user interface portion of the application. They also found that the average time spent on the user interface portion of the application was about 45% during the design phase, 50% during the implementation phase, and 37% during the maintenance phase. This effort required to build the interface was in

---

* *Man and his Symbols*, Anchor Press, New York, 1964. Carl Jung was born in Switzerland in 1875, and obtained his medical degree in Zurich, where he spent most of his life. He worked with Sigmund Freud before developing his own school of psychoanalysis, being regarded as a founding figure of the field.

spite of the fact that 74% of the systems were built with the assistance of a toolkit, user interface management system (UIMS), or interface builder.

This confirms the general impression that user interfaces are costly and difficult to construct even with the much improved user interface development tools that have become available. While survey data should always be treated cautiously it seems reasonable to state that roughly half the overall effort and half of the final code is devoted to the user interface in a software engineering project.

At the broad level, there are in fact two kinds of interfaces: one for input and one for output. For instance, data entry is a task for input only, while the displays used for power plant operators might be for output only. Many traditional and existing interfaces combine both input and output aspects. In the context of intelligent databases, these two issues should be carefully separated. However, intelligent database applications are often more concerned with output (e.g., end-user query, data visualization, discovery, etc.). In fact, as databases are getting larger by the nanosecond, methods of data collection and input are being streamlined into electromechanical processes such as collecting point-of-sale data in supermarkets and records of electronic fund transfers.

Accessing to large amounts of data is a challenge. The only thing keeping us from using large amounts of data is the tools for accessing them. Often the user interface is a key bottleneck. It is essential to reduce the mental effort of the user while the system is being used so that the user can concentrate on better planning and decision making. There *is no end* to how good a user interface should get. The more you provide, the more the user will ask for, because the user benefits more.

One of the great achievements of our species has been the ability to deal with ever more abstract concepts. The leap of imagination that enabled a bone to be seen as a tool or a weapon conveyed power and led people on the path of technology development that has been accelerating ever since. As our world has become more complex, the methods for dealing with various technologies, artifacts, and the systems they are embedded in have become correspondingly more abstract.

The user interface is a defense against unwanted abstraction. It serves as a bridge between people and representations of tasks in software. Good user interfaces contain familiar visual objects that allow users to express their intentions in an intuitive way. These visual objects or icons can be both signs and symbols. The distinction between signs and symbols has been described by Jung (1964). As Jung points out, we use the spoken or written word to express meaning. Our language is full of symbols, but we also employ signs or images that are not strictly descriptive. The signs Track, Swim, etc., somehow signify less than the symbols representing these activities (shown in Figure 3.1). Words and signs acquire a recognizable meaning through usage. In contrast, a symbol is a term, name, or picture that possesses specific connotations in addition to its conventional and obvious meaning. A word or an image is symbolic when it implies something more than its obvious and immediate meaning. It has a wider "unconscious" aspect that is never precisely defined or fully explained.

Jung's notion that "a symbol always stands for something more than its obvious and immediate meaning" may explain the satisfaction that one gets in dragging a file into the trashcan in a graphical user interface. Yet we must also be concerned with

**Figure 3.1** Icons representing Olympic sports.

the broader context of the application and the way in which it manifests itself to the user. Fortunately, the task of visualizing an intelligent database application is somewhat simpler when it is focused on a particular domain.

Iconic and graphic interfaces have now become commonplace in operating systems. This chapter shows how such interfaces can also dramatically facilitate access to databases. These days, end-users do not expect to type in commands to the operating system — they should have a similar interface to databases, expressed as icons. In addition, the associative style of hypertext also extends the use of icons in database interfaces.

This chapter begins with a review of the history and evolution of user interfaces with an emphasis on the emergence of graphical user interfaces. The problem of building user interfaces for databases is then discussed. Various methods for displaying objects and building queries, including the widely used SQL language, and new methods for querying with icons and hypertext are reviewed.

In the section on querying with icons the preferred user interface paradigm for intelligent database applications is described. Some of the technical aspects of querying with icons, including the handling of joins and the creation of iconic schemas are also discussed in that section. This approach is then supplemented with parameterized querying, which provides a powerful means of revising and editing queries.

The discussion on user interfaces for intelligent databases is followed by a discussion of user interface methodologies. This review includes a discussion of evaluation and usability analysis and the role of evaluation in user interface design. A discussion of different methods of navigation is also included. The chapter concludes with a discussion of future interfaces. An appendix provides a tour of existing graphical user interfaces using screenshots from a variety of systems.

## ■ 3.2 HISTORY AND EVOLUTION OF USER INTERFACES

User interfaces existed long before there were computers. The handle of a primitive adze, for instance, is a user interface that serves functions such as increasing the range of action (the handle is like an extension of the arm and allows the adze to be applied at a greater distance from the body) and increasing safety for the user (the hand is removed further from the cutting edge and receives reduced mechanical energy and tissue damage from the blows that are made). All of these "affordances" (Gibson 1979) of the device of application are communicated to the user in one way or another through its physical appearance and the user interface.

The earliest computer interfaces were by today's standards prehistoric — just as some of today's interfaces will seem antiquated in the not-too-distant future. The computer user began by being an electrical engineer, intimately involved with the various wires and switches that made the machine run. The slow development of user interfaces in the early years of computing is demonstrated by the fact that the punched card was perhaps the third generation of computer interface (after toggle switches and paper tape), even though punched cards had first been used in the late eighteenth century by Jacquard to program the activity of automated looms. It is ironic that the interface to the Jacquard Loom (which has probably been seen in museums for a century or so) was punched cards, and that similar punched cards were still being used as the preferred user interface for computers until the early 1980s in some installations, including major universities!

### 3.2.1 History

The interface to the early computers such as the ENIAC were basic toggle switches and flashing lights. Even the idea of the console, where all the user interface functions were concentrated in a small location, was relatively slow to arrive. Until relatively recently, the user interface was something of an afterthought, a sideline to the central activity of computation and data management. Figure 3.2 shows the evolution of user interfaces.

The toggle switches of early computers soon evolved to paper tape. However, toggle switches still remained in evidence. For instance, users of the PDP 11/20 and similar machines in the 1970s may still remember using toggle switches to reboot the machine or carry out other low-level operations. Paper tape was a messy medium, and it was all too easy to wrinkle the tapes or break them. Following the paper tape came punched cards (which were often bent, mutilated, or spindled). The user interface had now reached the level of automated looms of the eighteenth century! The advantage of punched cards over paper tape was that, like book pages versus papyrus rolls, the information was easier to edit and update. Punched cards may also have improved the general fitness of computer users, as people could be seen gamely lugging large boxes of cards between the computer center and their offices.

Punched cards served as the input medium while the printout served as the output medium. For many users this was a frustrating state of affairs. In some cases there would be a day or more turnaround between input (through the punched card reader) and output (with the return of the printout). Along with punched cards, teletype terminals came into being. The frustration with the batch-oriented card reading

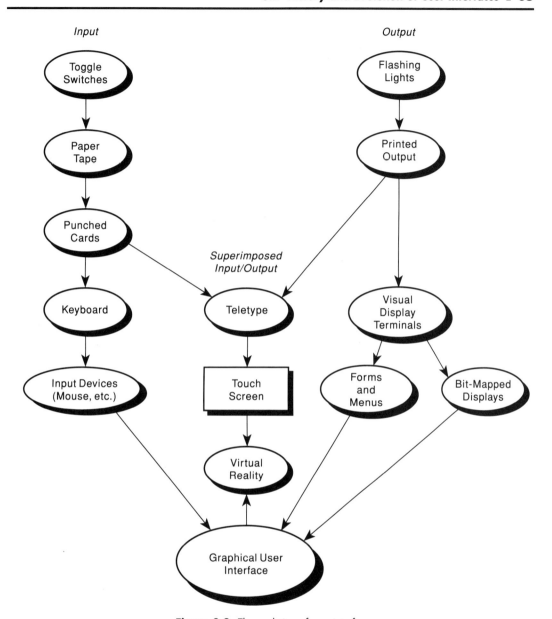

**Figure 3.2** The evolution of user interfaces.

interface was relieved to some extent by the teletype input device, which was generally used in smaller, or even single-user, systems.

The teletype was really a cross between the card reader and the printed output. In this case, the user typed directly onto the teletype keyboard rather than punching the cards and sending them through the reader. The teletype was also supplemented with more convenient storage devices such as magnetic tape, and later, cassette tape, so that transporting large programs and sets of data became less of a problem.

One of the weaknesses of the teletype as an input medium was that it was not really an editing environment. Unlike a screen, one could not erase or edit something and see the result easily. For instance, in entering a sequence of commands, one would retype the line. Thus the teletype, card reader, printer, toggle switch, and paper tape interfaces all failed to give the user a sense of communication, except in the weakest form. In a sense, users had to run their programs in spite of, instead of with the assistance of, the user interface.

In many ways the visual display terminal (VDT) was a huge advance over the earlier interfaces. The VDT was typically part of an interactive system, so that users could carry out tasks and get the results back fairly quickly. Yet, in spite of the inherent flexibility of the screen, early VDTs tended to be used as if they were punched card readers, with each row of the screen representing the equivalent of an 80-column punched card. Any editing had to be done line by line, and most terminals were character based and had no graphics capability. Figure 3.3 shows the asynchrony between technology and its uses (e.g., VDTs used as punched card models). The same applies to many applications today.

With hindsight, it seems amazing how long the character-based 80-column row-by-row model of user interfaces lasted. Until the early 1990s, many PCs were shipped with editors that worked like teletypes, (e.g., edlin, included with DOS).

Yet, while many users were struggling with character-based VDTs well into the 1980s, researchers at Xerox Palo Alto Research Center (PARC) were developing a new paradigm for computing in the 1970s. They replaced character-based terminals with integrated personal computers that supported full screen applications. In this radically different user interface, the screen became a model of the task that the user could interact with directly. The Xerox PARC researchers developed the model of a desktop as a metaphor for the operating system. In this metaphor, files could be saved or stored in folders, and later deleted by placing them in the trashcan.

Software developers also began creating new forms of interface on the newly emerging microcomputers. Thus Visicalc was developed for the Apple II and was enthusiastically accepted because of its use of an onscreen model of a spreadsheet. In fact, the feedback and the synergy between the Visicalc and the Apple II were essential to the success of both products and laid the groundwork for business computing as we now know it.

By the late 1970s, the pieces of the modern user interface were falling into place. Now that the screen was becoming a model, rather than simply a collection of characters, users needed a way to point to different objects within these onscreen models. They soon found that the cursor keys (the up, down, right, and left arrows) on the keyboard provided a rather tedious way of moving the cursor around the screen. Thus a pointing device was needed to supplement the typewriter keyboard that had been the mainstay input device for so long. One of the early pointing devices was the joystick. The joystick became prominent because the early microcomputer was largely a hobby and game playing machine. This rapidly evolved into games such as Pong,

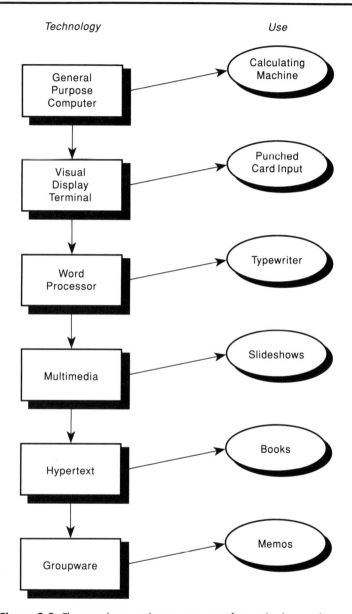

**Figure 3.3** The asynchronomy between user interface technology and its use.

Space Invaders, Galaxians, and a host of other video arcade games that needed a good pointing device if users were to invest their coins and save the universe.

These early interfaces and hardware started to impact the games industry more than the computer industry. Nolan Bushnell, the inventor of Pong, went on to make Atari successful in games. But competitors were catching on and Atari did not exploit the computer interface market — Apple did. If Atari, or Commodore, had exploited new user interfaces early on, instead of just focusing on games, the history of computing may have been very different.

## 3.2.2 The Emergence of GUIs

The joystick was a very successful game-playing input device, but it was the mouse that entered mainstream computing. The mouse was invented by Doug Engelbart in the 1960s and like much of his other work, was far in advance of its time. It wasn't until the 1970s that user interface technology (with full screen editable displays with high quality bit-mapped graphics) caught on to the potential of the mouse and similar devices (e.g., the trackball). It turned out that most people had no trouble moving the mouse along the desktop and seeing the cursor move as a result on the screen (in a completely different plane of motion).

As screen and display technologies advanced, more and more sophisticated and detailed graphics could be displayed on the screen. The Apple Macintosh led the way for PCs in the 1980s with a resolution of up to 80 pixels per inch. This made it possible to display very convincing pictures (icons) on the screen of objects such as trashcans, file folders, and even people. In the new bit-mapped display, more and more complex images could be displayed, first in black and white, and then in color. Whole models could be created on the screen, and the mouse could then be used to point to and manipulate the objects within these models, thereby carrying out various tasks.

The graphical user interface (GUI) had arrived. Although early GUIs are now synonymous with the Macintosh, graphical user interfaces were developed at Xerox PARC, and were first implemented in a commercial product in the Xerox Star computer (Johnson, Roberts, Verplank, Smith, Irby, Beard, and Mackey 1989). In their book, *Fumbling the Future,* published in 1988, Smith and Alexander describe how Xerox abandoned its early opportunity because it saw itself as a copier company and chose to market a simple word processing system instead of its revolutionary computer interface. The Xerox PARC researchers also developed the language Small-talk, as an integral part of user interfaces. Smalltalk (Goldberg and Robson 1983) was one of the first languages to combine object orientation and graphics with a program-ming system.

One of the main elements of early GUIs was the menu that allowed selections to be made. The rather staid bullet list type of menus that had begun on the character-based terminal were transformed into visual entities such as menu bars, tool palettes, and pop-up menus. By the late 1980s menus were embedded as highlight words within text (hypertext) or different visual objects on the screen that could be clicked on to select the corresponding option.

At first, the GUI revolution had its main effect on the operating system, being assimilated into the computing mainstream via the Macintosh desktop finder, Micro-soft Windows for the PC, and X Windows for Unix systems. Once they saw the GUI operating system, users got to like the look and feel of GUI, and developers began building GUI applications using the general principle of "what you see is what you get" (or WYSIWIG). For instance, a GUI application for aircraft reservation shows a representation of the aircraft and the seats that had been filled so that the ticket agent has a much better sense of the current loading. See Section 3.3.4 for an example of how WYSIWIG can be extended to WYSIWYA ("what you see is what you ask™") in *Iconic Query*.

There were, and still are, many shifting crosscurrents that have influenced the evolution of user interfaces. One of the most interesting currents of influence is the relationship between the computer screen and the laser printer. Xerox PARC originally developed the graphical user interface as part of an ambitious program for building a new paradigm of office automation. Xerox wanted to become *the* document company, and thus the computer was seen as a way of generating better documents. It is interesting to speculate on how a different company such as Polaroid might have influenced the modern computer if it had built its own research facility and motivated the new computer paradigm with the camera rather than the copier. The invention of the laser printer (also at Xerox PARC) made it necessary to show the user what printed documents would look like while they were still on the screen. This led to the simultaneous development of sophisticated printer and onscreen fonts. The computer was now integrated into a desktop publishing system, and it was desktop publishing that kept GUIs alive in the mid-1980s, when business users still thought of them as toys.

Desktop publishing turned everyone into a potential publisher. Better interfaces to tasks undermined the role of the expert intermediary. In many cases the skills of the typesetter were no longer required. Similarly, with word processing, people who could type their own documents could now format them without a great deal of skill or effort. Removing the need for the intermediary has empowered the user in a number of tasks. This trend is continuing in querying and data analysis. More and more users are going to carry these tasks out for themselves, particularly if they have intelligent database applications to support them.

This discussion of the evolution of user interfaces will be amplified by a consideration of how that evolution has affected some representative fields of computing, beginning with operating systems.

If you want to experience an early operating system interface (not recommended for the impatient) try using a mainframe interface like MVS. Operating systems like MVS have many esoteric and idiosyncratic features that serve as barriers to potential users. Another operating system interface was job control language (JCL). In card input, the JCL cards would "wrap around" the program and data, setting things like the memory allocation and the priority in the queue. Some people who used JCL more than a decade ago still hate it. The revulsion with which people regard some early user interfaces shows how important the user interface is to overall acceptance of a system and how intolerant of systems people become once they know that better alternatives are available.

Unix was one of the first widely distributed operating systems designed for interactive use. Technological development is generally influenced by the prevailing culture that surrounds the innovators. Unix was built by and for computer hackers and power users who had their own world. The ability to master obscure Unix commands served as a form of membership to the inner circle of users. Unix was originally developed at Bell Labs because a researcher (Ken Thompson) needed an operating system for his DEC PDP mini-computer.

As Thompson said, one reason for the success of Unix was that its design had no specific design goals. It was developed to be used by its creators. The kernel of Unix was written by two people in short time and is very elegant. Today it remains the standard operating system on workstations and is the preeminent multi-tasking operating system.

While many people find Unix difficult to use (Norman 1981), no one has come up with anything better in 20 years from an operating system point of view. However, from a user interface point of view, Unix was developed for the power user, but its designers deliberately traded off fewer keystrokes for less interpretability. For instance, the command "rm" is used to delete a file, while the command "cat" is used to display a file. Further, typing "<" instead of ">" can be a critical error with disastrous results. Thus attempts at "sugarcoating" Unix are underway, e.g. within the neXTStep operating system for the neXT computer.

On the micro front, CPM was the preferred operating system for microcomputers in the late 1970s, developed by Gary Kildall at Digital Research in Monterey, California. The fact that DOS quickly replaced CPM as the operating system of choice for small computers in the early 1980s is an historical accident, one of many that have created today's computing environment.

In 1980, IBM was looking for an operating system for its new line of personal computers. At that time, IBM was threatened by an antitrust suit, and the PC was developed as a form of diversification and to stave off a potentially devastating loss of business in the mainframe market. The development of the PC proceeded in secrecy. Under the impression that Microsoft owned CPM, IBM approached them to license an operating system. The confusion was, however, quickly cleared up.

When IBM approached CPM's actual owners, Digital Research, they probably had little knowledge of how important the PC would become. As it turned out, IBM didn't get together with Digital Research. Instead they turned again to Microsoft who had a version of BASIC for microcomputers. The result was Microsoft DOS, and the success of the PC in the marketplace created a mass market for personal computing and a mature software industry.

DOS didn't have the power of Unix, but it was easier to use. Like UNIX, the user typed in commands in response to a command line prompt. Of course the users were still left to fend for themselves in many ways. For instance, "format a:" was a frequently used command used to format floppy disks. In contrast, "format c:" was a dangerous and infrequently used command that erased all the data on the hard disk. The problem was that users would type a and c somewhat interchangeably, as in the command for copying a file from the a (floppy) drive to the c (hard) drive (using a command such as "copy a:myfile c:myfile"). It was all too easy for the user to type format c: instead of format a: with devastating consequences. Many people found themselves losing megabytes of information from their hard drive when they had only wanted to format a floppy disk. Every cloud has a silver lining, though, and in this case a minor industry developed for recovering data from formatted hard drives. (One of the best known data recovery tools is part of the Norton Utilities software package.)

In spite of its deficiencies DOS was installed on over 20 million computers and was the dominant operating system throughout the 1980s. Yet the replacement for

DOS was evolving before DOS was even off the drawing board. One of the products of the innovative work at Xerox PARC in the 1970s was a radically different operating system based on the direct manipulation of objects. For instance, instead of writing a command to move a file into a directory (in basic DOS this generally involved two commands, a copy and a delete) the user could simply drag an icon that represented the file over an icon that represented the directory (folder). The visual effect of this was that users felt as if they were dropping the file directly into the folder. People who used this new form of operating system soon got to like it.

One of the people who liked it was Steve Jobs. He saw the new operating system at Xerox PARC and came back to Apple later that day convinced that the direct manipulation, windowing operating system was the way of the future. It was a hard sell, but if anyone could do the selling it was Jobs. At that time, Apple relied entirely on the Apple II which had a stranglehold on the educational market. Apple formed a group to go after the vision that Jobs had seen at Xerox PARC. The first result was the Lisa, a remarkable machine in many ways, but one that was too expensive to achieve much market penetration. The Lisa was followed by the Macintosh, which was released in 1984. The first 128K Macintoshes were underpowered for work of any scale (early Mac users will remember the lengthy disk swapping episodes with little nostalgia), but they had the graphical user interface, and they attracted an almost fanatical group of users.

By the mid-1980s the personal computing world had split into IBM and the clones versus the rest (which included machines from Atari and Commodore). DOS-based machines were significantly cheaper than the Macintosh, largely because IBM had kept the PC architecture open, and the IBM name still carried a lot of weight in the business world, resulting in a high volume of business usage. When John Sculley took over as CEO of Apple, there was a conscious redirection of marketing towards business users. With the introduction of the Mac SE and Mac II in 1987, the performance of the Macintosh line increased greatly, and the Macintosh became a viable machine for business. Business users began to take notice, and while business didn't embrace the Mac wholeheartedly (for a variety of reasons, including price and the large installed base of PCs) people started clamoring for the graphical user interface. Microsoft responded by releasing Windows, its graphical user interface, and the unofficial battle between DOS and the graphical user interface was over.

Even the workstation world was not immune to the GUI revolution. The GUI for the workstation was developed as the X Windows system (an environment for constructing GUIs). X Windows then formed the basis for MOTIF, promoted by the Open Systems Foundation (OSF).

In the new multimedia world we take GUI functionalities for granted and wonder how people could have tolerated the highly constrained environment of the earlier generations. Operating systems are moving towards a virtual world presentation where high quality computer graphics and animation are used to present the user with a set of tools that are easy to visualize and manipulate.

The Information Visualizer (Card, Robertson, and Mackinlay 1991) project at Xerox PARC is an early attempt to move beyond the graphical user interface of the Xerox Star and the Apple Macintosh. The Information Visualizer is based on the premise that the task of managing and accessing large information spaces is a problem in large-scale cognition, and that emerging technologies for 3D visualization and interactive animation offer potential solutions to this problem, especially when the structure of the information can be visualized. The Information Visualizer uses a number of techniques including 3D rooms and information visualization for interacting with information structure.

The ROOMS interface (Henderson and Card 1986), was originally designed to reduce space contention in windowing interfaces. A typical room might contain a mail-reader window, a prompt window for messages, icons for performing actions, and a command window for entering in commands. The room would also have "doors" linking it to other rooms, including a "back door" that returns the user to the room from which he or she came.

The basic rooms idea was extended (Robertson et al. 1989) to include 3D rooms. An example of a 3D room is an exploration room which has a whiteboard and a table with an object placed on it. The user may then "move around the room, interacting with the objects encountered in order to discover their content and function." The 3D rooms system (Mackinlay, Card, and Robertson 1990) allows the user to "walk" around room-like objects represented within the computer interface and interact with artifacts which represent information. The information workspace is a simulation of a physical space. The goal of the information workspace project is to evolve the rooms multiple desktop metaphor into a workspace for information access. In addition to the 3D rooms, information visualization is assisted through the use of what Card, Robertson, and Mackinlay call cone trees and perspective walls.

Cone trees are three-dimensional visualizations of hierarchies within a "room" (Robertson, Mackinlay, and Card 1991). The top of a hierarchy is placed near the ceiling of the room, and is the apex of a cone with its children evenly spaced along its base. The next layer of nodes is drawn below the first, with their children in cones. The aspect ratio of the tree is fixed to fit the room. Each layer has cones of the same height (the room height divided by the tree depth). Cone base diameters for each level are reduced in a progression which insures that the bottom layer fits in the width of the room. One of the interesting features of cone trees is that they can be animated, thereby using the sensitivity of the visual system to movement and displacement to help in picking out information. The rotation of the cone tree can also help the user better understand the structure of the hierarchy.

The cone tree is a way of viewing hierarchical structures. In contrast, the perspective wall is designed to handle large amounts of information that is linearly structured. The perspective wall is a method for visualizing linear information by smoothly integrating detailed and contextual views (Mackinlay, Robertson, and Card 1991). The method uses 3D visualizations that have a center panel for detail and two perspective panels for context. A physical metaphor of folding is used to distort an arbitrary 2D layout into a 3D visualization (the wall). The wall has a panel in the center for viewing details and two perspective panels (partially folded back so that they appear to recede into the distance) on either side for viewing context. Like a fish-eye view (Parsaye et al. 1989, Chapter 5) the perspective view has the advantage of making the neighborhood of the detailed view larger than the more distant parts of the contextual view.

3D rooms, cone and cam trees, and perspective walls are ingenious ways of visualizing information. One of the most interesting aspects of projects like this is that they point the way towards the merging of operating systems and databases in the future.

The management of data is one of the most important functions of the computer. From the intelligent database perspective, the development of user interfaces for databases is particularly interesting. Early database systems like IMS used COBOL programming as the interface. Systems such as IMS and IDMS used character-based terminals with little flair.

The advent of the relational model and microcomputers in the 1970s changed the user interface for databases in several ways. dBASE brought databases to the wider PC community, and the PC monitor provided new possibilities for display over the earlier dumb terminals. The dBASE programming language allowed developers to set up customized user interfaces for databases.

The use of menus started with dBASE. Control and Alt keys were used to move between menus and the interface became familiar to many users. Rbase had a similar interface. These interfaces remained unchanged until the early 1990s.

Meanwhile, the relational model led to languages like Structured Query Language (SQL) that provided formal querying capability. Early attempts at "dressing up" SQL were mostly based on Query by Example (QBE). The database system Paradox began using QBE as its method of end-user access. The field of database interfaces was in flux in the late 1980s and early 1990s.

The real reason why database interfaces did not evolve with the operating system interfaces was the lack of a database tradition within PARC. Without PARC's lead, few people worked on creating more attractive and usable database interfaces. One exception to this pattern was the QBE system developed by Moshe Zloof at IBM. QBE provided a form-like template for entering queries (Zloof 1975).

In the early 1980s, the company Metaphor proposed their own interface to databases, based on ideas from Xerox PARC. However, the two-handed, multi-buttoned, cordless mice originally developed by Metaphor did not penetrate the mainframe market. Thus Metaphor chose to become a software vendor. However, the Metaphor style influenced other database interfaces (c.g., Trimble and Chappell 1990).

In the late 1980s the influence of HyperCard led to HyperSQL, a graphical form of SQL. However, querying systems did not yet have a completely visual model of the database and the queries that could be carried out on the data.

Performing queries with full-fledged icons and GUIs was pioneered by the system *Iconic Query* developed by IntelligenceWare in 1992. The system provides visual querying by representing tables and attributes as icons, and by allowing various logical querying operations to be carried out by manipulating hypertext in conjunction with the icons. The system will be described in detail in a later section of this chapter. The key analogy here is that *Iconic Query* extended the "what you see is what you get" metaphor of GUI's to the "what you see is what you ask™" metaphor for database systems.

### 3.2.3 The GUI Model of Access

The functionality that is provided by intelligent database applications has to be communicated back to the user in an effective way. Flexible access to data is only useful to people if they can make use of it. This then is the task of the user interface, to take the application functionality and make it visible to and manipulable by the user.

This section will review the nature of graphical user interfaces (GUIs) which have become the standard paradigm for connecting users with software applications. We will then adapt the GUI (pronounced "gooey") paradigm to cope with the task of displaying visual objects as representations of data within an information system.

Since its development in the 1970s, the window-based graphical interface has become the predominant style of physical user interface. It was first popularized in the Apple Macintosh after its development at Xerox PARC and since then has moved into both the PC (e.g., Microsoft Windows) and workstation environments (e.g., X Windows, Motif). In contrast, the technology for representing and building the conceptual aspect of user interfaces is much less well developed.

Graphical user interfaces have generally been used as operating system interfaces. This is because the operating system represents the most stable aspect of a computing environment, one that is shared across all applications. Thus it is relatively easy to standardize the look and feel of this shared environment.

While graphical user interfaces have proved their worth as operating system interfaces, there is also a need for GUIs to be interfaces to database systems and other applications (e.g., project management). Most importantly, any GUI that is designed should cover as much as possible the shared aspects and properties of a family of types of application. In the case of intelligent database applications, the authors of this book have developed a GUI that consists of interconnected visual templates (charts and graphs) that can be browsed through point-and-click navigation and queried through a style of querying with icons. This GUI strategy was deliberately designed to be as application independent as possible within the broad context of information presentation based on large amounts of numerical data.

The following sections consider some issues associated with the development of GUIs, beginning with a look at the structure of user interfaces and the metaphors that motivate their development.

**3.2.3.1 *Layers within the User Interface*** Good user interfaces express information abstractions in human terms without undermining the power or functionality of the application. This is achieved by carefully designing the various layers of the user interface so that the necessary transformation between information abstractions and manipulable objects is feasible.

Beyond the basic look and feel, the user interface is a complex communication process consisting of several layered protocols (Taylor 1988) where each layer has its own coders and decoders (Figure 3.4). In conversation, for instance, there is one layer for coding and decoding acoustic waveforms, another layer for coding and decoding words, and a third level for coding and decoding concepts (within which the other two protocol layers are nested). Each of these protocol layers communicates at a different level of human information processing. From a linguistic perspective, we

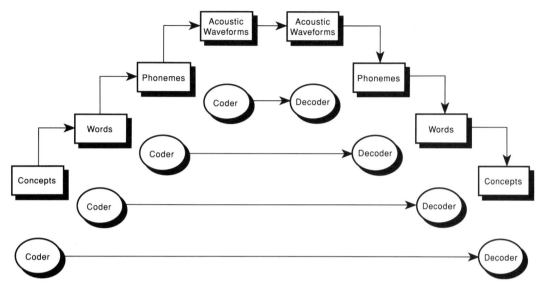

**Figure 3.4** Speech represented as communication through layout protocols.

may distinguish physical, lexical, syntactic, semantic, and pragmatic levels of the interface as we transition from the physical to conceptual aspects of communication (Figure 3.5). Perhaps the most basic distinction, however, is between the physical (physical, lexical) and conceptual (semantic, pragmatic) aspects of the interface. The physical interface is the "obvious" part of an interface, and it is probably for this reason that it tends to receive more attention.

The conceptual interface is non-obvious and is also more task dependent. Thus a chess-playing program and a spreadsheet may both use a similar graphical user interface while having very different conceptual interfaces. But what is the conceptual interface? Like minds, conceptual interfaces exist even though it seems impossible to

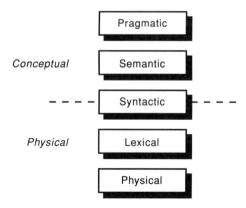

**Figure 3.5** Different levels of a communication interface.

show what they look like or how they work. The conceptual interface may be thought of as the meeting place of the human mind and the software machine. In many instances it is difficult to maintain a clear distinction between the physical and conceptual interfaces. Icons, which are a major part of physical interfaces are simultaneously major components of the conceptual interface, often representing conceptual entities and relations. For instance, in an entity-relationship model on the screen, the icons are simultaneously physical objects that can be manipulated or viewed and conceptual objects that form part of the conceptual model of a database or of an application domain.

**3.2.3.2**    *User Interface Metaphors*      User interface development for advanced information systems is challenging because the rules of communication have to be written anew. In the "invented" setting of the intelligent database application the user interface is in fact a formalism that creates the communication channel between user and computer (e.g., Jacob 1983). There are few naturalistic rules that guide the design of this communication channel and symbolic elements such as icons.

Recently there has been a trend towards interfaces to technology that allow us to feel that we are directly manipulating objects, even when they are quite abstract. Direct manipulation has been especially strong in computer software and has led to the graphical user interfaces discussed in this chapter.

Direct manipulation interfaces are a way of making abstraction more palatable for people. In spite of its importance to information technology, abstraction does not come easily to people. Working with visible and tangible objects is generally more appealing than dealing with abstractions. Thus one of the challenges in designing user interfaces to information systems in general and intelligent database applications in particular is to display information abstractions in terms of recognizable and manipulable visual objects.

The key to making abstractions obvious and manipulable is to use natural or obvious signs and symbols in the user interface that behave in accordance with the rules that govern the underlying abstractions. These signs and symbols must then be embedded within an appropriate visual language that allows the user to manipulate the interface objects in a meaningful way and provides appropriate feedback to the user about how the device, software, or system is reacting.

Metaphors provide a useful framework for embedding effective signs and symbols within computer interfaces. Direct manipulation (Shneiderman 1989) is a metaphor consisting of a world of physical objects that are represented on the computer screen. Tasks can be performed by manipulating these objects using a pointing device such as a mouse or trackball. An alternative metaphor is the agent metaphor. In this model the computer and the user are seen as two agents that communicate with each other through the language of the user interface. In terms of the model world of the application, the agent metaphor replaces direct manipulation of the model world by the user with indirect manipulation of the model world via the agent.

The simplest form of a software agent is a command language interface where the user issues commands to the software which then manipulates the model world accordingly. Command language interfaces have often been used in more abstract tasks such as statistical analysis and database management.

Form filling interfaces fall somewhere between the agent and direct manipulation metaphors. Here the model world is restricted to forms or documents that can be filled in various ways (e.g., the QBE method of database querying, Zloof 1977). Many early expert system interfaces (particularly those involved with diagnosis and classification) can be characterized as types of form-filling interface, with adaptable forms. Here the user is asked a series of questions (later questions will be chosen based on the answers to earlier questions) and reasoning is carried out as the implicit form is being filled in.

Direct manipulation and indirect manipulation via a software agent are the two predominant computer interface communication paradigms. The direct manipulation style of interface has been particularly effective in tasks such as drafting, drawing, and designing where the emphasis is on creating and manipulating graphical objects (e.g., Myers 1990). Much of this book's approach to user interfaces for intelligent database applications is based on the direct manipulation metaphor. However, user interfaces for intelligent database applications, as for other collaborative work environments, may ultimately profit by having a judicious mixture of direct manipulation and conversational dialogue.

Within the direct manipulation approach to interfaces, more specific metaphors can be constructed. For instance, the "desktop" metaphor motivated the development of the GUIs seen in the Macintosh operating system and Microsoft Windows. Elements of this metaphor include file folders, documents, and the trashcan.

There are a large number of metaphors that can be constructed, and few guidelines on which metaphors will work best. One intriguing metaphor is the "pile" metaphor for casual organization of information (Mander, Salomon, and Wong 1992). This metaphor is based on the way people often tend to loosely organize documents and papers into piles rather than file them away. The pile metaphor includes direct manipulation actions (and associated visual feedback) for adding documents to a pile, spreading out a pile, and selecting documents from a pile and reading them. In spite of its apparent informality, the pile metaphor can be used to retrieve information based on different scripts, and to collect items into piles based on scripts (rules).

Desktops, rooms, and piles are strong metaphors that reflect common and familiar objects and structures in our everyday environment. These metaphors tend to be highly evocative and memorable. However, these very strengths can also lead to problems particularly if the metaphor as implemented contradicts in some way the behavior of the underlying objects and environments that motivated it. The "desktop" metaphor was compromised to some extent by the fact that windows opened and closed on the desktop (which is not something that tends to happen on desktops in the real world. However, in this case the GUI based on the desktop metaphor now seems to have transcended it, and few users seem to think they are actually working with a desktop when they use a system like Microsoft Windows.

It is unclear to what extent a strong metaphor should be used in the user interfaces for intelligent database applications. Rather than slavishly adhere to some real world situation that is modeled in a metaphor it is probably best to strive for the advantages that metaphors provide: consistency, familiarity, and predictability.

Following is an example of a "weak" metaphor based on an interactive business slide presentation. The metaphor for intelligent database applications is as follows:

Imagine that you are at a presentation on your topic of interest (e.g., the management of a project or marketing information about your company). At any point you can stop, point to something, and ask for more information about it. You can either ask specifically for some detailed information (querying) or you can vaguely point to something and ask to see more about it (point-and-click navigation). As soon as you make this request, an extremely agile and quick-witted assistant searches almost instantaneously through a huge pile of slides and then shows the one that matches your interests. The end result is a personal guided tour through a large amount of information that allows you to make the most useful interpretations with a minimum of effort.

Future metaphors of data access are likely to merge current approaches such as "rooms" and "piles" with virtual reality technology to create attractive and compelling user interfaces to information. In one such approach, the user is situated in a virtual room which contains maps, filing cabinets, organizational charts, and so on. Each of the objects in the room is actually a tool that the user can interact with. For instance, one of the maps on the wall might be a geographic information system, with embedded data at various locations on the map. The user might touch one of the points on the map and zoom in to a corresponding city. The user might then point to another large chart showing industries and companies and touch a node corresponding to a company. This could then result in the head office and retail stores for that company being displayed and highlighted on the map of the city. Pointing to the head office of the company would then give access to financial data, while pointing to a specific store would then provide access to the sales data for that store. Another tool might be a timeline. This might also be mounted on the wall, or could even be part of a "virtual watch" that the users saw themselves as wearing in the virtual reality. The user could then "wind back" the timeline to see sales data for the preceding year.

A printer might be standing in a corner of the room. Users could grab an icon representing last year's sales data for the store of interest. They could then drop the icon on to the printer, resulting in a report of last year's sales data being printed. They could also drop the icon onto a fax machine located in another corner of the room and point to a picture of one of their colleagues on the wall, thereby sending an electronic copy of the data to that colleague.

Scenarios such as this demonstrate the power of virtual reality for providing natural, intuitive (and fun) access to information and functionality. Virtual reality is the ultimate antidote to the problems of interface abstraction and information abstraction alluded to earlier.

**3.2.3.3 *Windowing Environments*** The majority of existing visual interfaces are characterized by windows, icons, menus, and pointing (or in some formulations, windows, icons, mice, and pull-down menus). The desktop metaphor (i.e., a metaphor where files are stored in folders and deleted by throwing them into a trashcan) and today's graphical interfaces can both be traced to the Xerox Star computer (Smith et al. 1982) developed at Xerox PARC, after which they were perfected and widely distributed in Apple's Macintosh microcomputer from 1984 onwards.

Window-based graphical interfaces have the advantage of implementing basic look and feel functionality in a consistent way (but see Grudin 1989 for arguments against user interface consistency). However, graphical interfaces do not address the funda-mental issues of communication in the computer interface. Like a chess game, the user and the system alternate moves, but the physical interface is like a description of the positions of the pieces, rather than an analysis of the goals and resources of each player.

Graphical interfaces provide a set of tools for constructing the user interface. Windows, icons, and menus are entities within the visual display that the user can interact with, while the pointing device is the physical mechanism through which interaction is achieved. One of the fundamental features of such interaction is a point-and-shoot style of selection of objects and commands, and a direct manipulation style of interaction where objects may be moved around on the screen to carry out certain operations (Singh and Chignell 1990).

Windows are portions (usually rectangular) of the screen that can overlap and be resized. Use of windows allows different applications or data to be visually separated on the screen. Thus windows provide physical separation or compartmentalization of screen objects that corresponds to different activity contexts, modes, and tasks. For instance, in a word processor, two files may be viewed at the same time, where each file is positioned in a separate window. Windows also allow efficient use of screen real estate by allowing these different activity contexts to be readily available even when there is not enough room for all of them to be on the screen at the same time. This is achieved by allowing screen real estate to be effectively shared between activity contexts through techniques such as overlapping, stacking, and resizing.

Menus allow users to select what they want from a set of choices rather than having to remember what the available choices are and their explicit names. Of course, menus were in use in restaurants well before the development of graphical user interfaces. The usefulness of menus stems from the fact that they don't require people to remember what the available actions or choices are. In return for this reduction in "cognitive load" users must be able to select from appropriate menus and be able to "navigate" to the submenus that hold their choices (since menus are frequently nested). Menus may also be presented in a number of different visual formats such as a menu bar, and pull-down, pop-up, and pie menus.

Another element of the graphical user interface is the pointing device (often a mouse or tablet). The pointing device allows the user to move to a region in the workspace and then select it. The pointing device is extremely important in the point-and-click style of navigation. In addition to selecting an object so that it is highlighted, the pointing device can also activate the object (if it is an icon represent-ing an application, it may then be highlighted) or move it (often called "dragging"). These devices have been shown to work extremely well (Card, English, and Burr 1978; MacKenzie, Sellen, and Buxton 1991).

*3.2.3.4* *Icons*    Icons are an extremely important part of user interfaces that serve as bridges between the physical interface and the conceptual interface. They are used to represent manipulable objects within the interface as well as functions such as cutting and pasting. Icons also serve as visual landmarks within the user interface (Glenn and Chignell 1992). Early user interfaces tended to use labels to distinguish generic objects, but since the Xerox Star, icons have been an essential part of graphical user interfaces. In spite of our considerable use of icons, icon design remains more of an art than a science.

Icons are abstract and stylized representations of objects or functions. For instance, the "cut" function in a word processor might be represented by a pair of scissors. A good example of an iconic system are the pieces used in a chess game. The pawn represents a foot soldier, yet the stylized representation of the pawn in most chess sets gives little hint of this. The king is distinguished by a cross, while the queen is generally indicated by the appearance of a crown (without a cross). These iconic features tend to help beginners when they start playing chess, e.g., they refer to the rook as a castle because it has what appear to be castle battlements. Skilled chess players, however, simply see the pieces in terms of the functions they perform on the chess board. Thus they think of rook in terms of the straight line moves that it makes, the bishop in terms of the diagonal moves that it makes, and so on.

The issue of what makes a good icon or visual symbol with appropriate visual semantics (Saint-Martin 1990) is still unresolved in spite of the ability of graphic designers to produce usable icons. Jung's view on symbols suggests that unlike iconic signs, iconic symbols cannot be designed but have to stem from our collective unconscious. At first glance, this role of the collective unconscious as a progenitor for iconic symbols may seem incongruous in the high technology world of user interface design, yet the whole point of icons is that they be intuitive and that they denote something more than a sign-like representation of the underlying object or function.

The requirements that icons be obvious and intuitive across a range of cultures and experiences are met by few icons, but when icons do work they can be very compelling. Some people get an almost visceral satisfaction when they manipulate icons in a graphical user interface, such as the trashcan (and its closely related cousin, the black hole in the NEXT interface) used to delete files or remove disks in the Macintosh operating system and Microsoft Windows. While the particular nature of the symbology in question could be debated (does the symbol represent a return to the womb or the banishment of an enemy?), there seems no doubt that the effectiveness of the trashcan stems in large part from its symbolic properties as well as from people's general familiarity with trashcans.

In applications like international road signs where some users rely completely on the pictorial content of the icon in order to determine the meaning, the symbolic aspects of the icon become paramount. While one might not be able to design a good symbol from scratch (if we are to believe Jung), it should still be possible to recognize an effective icon in terms of its usability, (i.e., the ability of people to recognize the object or function that it represents). The sign-like properties of an icon can be measured by how well it represents what it purports to represent, while the symbol-like properties will be reflected both in the universality of that recognition and in the satisfaction that people experience in using the icon.

Most of the icons that are available as of now seem to fall far short of the goal of universal recognizability. Empirical studies of icons indicate that they do not guarantee instant understanding across or between cultures (Barnard and Marcel 1984). Thus design of effective icons is an iterative process that should be directed according to the measured usability of icon prototypes. Some issues to consider in designing icons (Huang 1990) are:

1. *Application and cultural dependence.* The icon is designed to represent a class of objects, not a specific one. The icon should use the natural symbol or sign to reflect the semantic meaning of the application and its cultural background. For example, the octagonal stop sign and stylized pictures of men and women can be used to distinguish between male and female restrooms.

2. *Easy recognition.* An icon designed with precise meaning will help the user to remember and identify the icon. Scissors provide a good representation of "cut" because that is the main function of scissors. An icon that showed a film director would not work as well because although film directors sometimes yell "cut," they also represent other things, leading to ambiguity in the meaning of the icon.

3. *Distinction from other icons within the system.* The icons within a system should be consistent and each icon should be easily distinguished from other icons in the user interface.

4. *Consistency.* Icons should be used consistently across different environments. International road signs are a good example of the consistent use of icons. Stop signs tend to look the same in different countries as do signs indicating a bend or curve in the road up ahead.

Icons are abstract and stylized representations of objects or functions. A concept related to icons is that of the "bit-map," which is essentially a pictorial representation obtained by giving values to a set of pixels on a screen. In most systems bit-maps are distinguished from icons. However, by defining mouse-sensitive areas on a bit-map or graphic, the same effect as an icon can be achieved.

Icons and overlapping windows play an important role in making the desktop metaphor work. This metaphor has been widely used as an interface to operating systems. A later section of this chapter will discuss the use of icons to develop an improved user interface for database querying.

### 3.2.4  User Interface Development Tools

While half of the software engineering effort being devoted to user interfaces may seem like a lot, there is little doubt that current graphical user interfaces are a great deal better than their character-based counterparts of 20 years ago. It is extremely difficult to compare the amount of effort that has been spent on constructing user interfaces over time, but most likely the amount of effort devoted to the user interface has remained roughly constant over the past few decades. For instance, one early IBM study (Sutton and Sprague 1978) found that the user interface portion of code at that time varied from 29% to 88%.

Thus the amount of effort devoted to the user interface has grown over the past two decades, while the overall quality of user interfaces has improved as more user interface development tools and methods have become available (Figure 3.6).

A central question for human-computer interaction has become, "What methods of

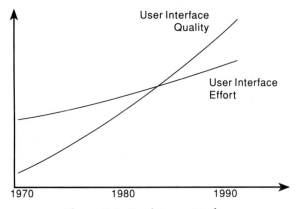

**Figure 3.6** Trends in user interface.

user interface design will produce products with good user interfaces in a cost-effective and timely fashion?" Gould and Lewis (1985) proposed three principles for good user interface design: early focus on users and tasks, empirical measurement, and iterative design.

While the iterative approach seems eminently reasonable, industry has been slow to adopt it, most likely because of the costs (actual or perceived) associated with it . However, convincing arguments have been made for the cost effectiveness of good user interface design (Mantei and Teorey 1988; Nielsen 1990). The challenge of designing usable artifacts in the face of an inherently nondeterministic design process has led to the development of an iterative design method that relies heavily on rapid prototyping and usability testing. This iterative design method is represented schematically in Figure 3.7. In iterative design there is a cycle of three phases that are carried out repeatedly. These phases are prototype, test, and evaluation. In this iterative model of design, evaluation provides feedback to the designer, who then develops a new prototype based on the lessons learned about the performance of the previous prototype.

Application of the iterative model of design has been limited by the cost of developing prototypes. As the ability to rapidly prototype designs develops, the iterative method of design is becoming more feasible.

There are a number of commercially available software tools for designing and developing graphical user interfaces (de Baar, Foley, and Mullet 1992). These include Devguide (Sun Microsystems, Inc. 1990), Interface Builder (neXT Computer, Inc. 1990), and Interface Architect (Hewlett-Packard Company 1990).

These tools, along with other user interface development systems, can be used to lay out the various widgets and tools in a graphical user interface and then generate source code, typically in the C programming language. However, it must be remembered that whatever these tools do, the same could have been done in C or assembly language — or in hardware! The key advantage here is that the interface building tool makes it unnecessary to drop down and use the programming language, significantly reducing the effort in the development of the user interface. People still expend effort, but now build much better interfaces.

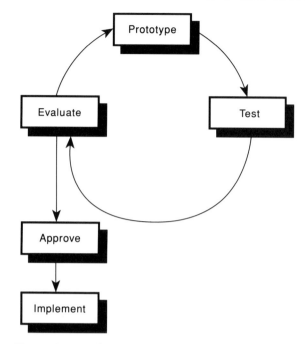

**Figure 3.7** A schematic representation of interactive design.

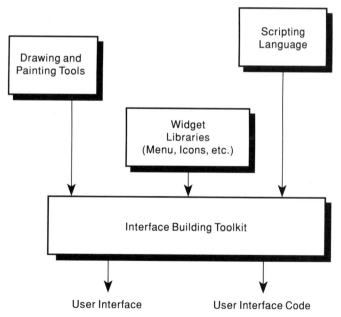

**Figure 3.8** Components of interface building tools.

Moreover, interface building tools allow people who cannot write programs to develop interfaces. Thus it is important to separate the point-and-click components of the interface building tool from the programmatic components, as in Figure 3.8. For instance, HyperCard has two distinct components, the interface builder and HyperTalk, its scripting language (Parsaye et al. 1989, Chapter 5). One can do a great deal in the language, but the main attraction of HyperCard is not the scripting capability but the point-and-click interface and the tools for building the user interface.

Another key issue in the use of interface building tools is the separation of the user interface from the application logic. This allows the user interface to be modified independently of the application. This principle was exploited by the User Interface Management Systems (UIMSs) used by developers in the 1980s. This has now evolved to the user level in terms of "soft interfaces" that can be customized by users to their needs and requirements. For instance, a user may not only change the terminology and the look within the interface by changing aliases and icons, but different users can switch between different styles of interfaces with the same application logic, based on their preferences.

Every user interface has a specific conceptual model. For instance, the conceptual model for many interface builders is a stack of cards, a notebook containing pages, or some similar model. The interface works by moving between different cards in the stack. However, apart from the conceptual model each user interface building tool also has a specific set of tokens and building blocks which are used to construct user interfaces. It is by plugging these components together that a specific interface is developed. For an example of a user interface building tool, see the description of the corporate vision interface setup environment in Chapter 7.

These building blocks effectively define a specific class of user interfaces which may be built with the tool. These operations form the *algebra of interface* for the tool. Buttons, graphics, scrolling fields, and menus, etc., form the building blocks of traditional interface builders. Interface building tools always lag behind the best interfaces by one generation. As new techniques are identified, tools based on that algebra appear just as the better techniques are being found. However, there is no doubt that interface building tools are essential in the development of almost all intelligent database applications. Without them the turnaround time and the feedback needed to deliver a good application will never be provided.

## ■ 3.3 INTELLIGENT DATABASE INTERFACES

Like other classes of software application, much of the functionality of intelligent databases depends on the usability of their user interfaces. The issue of usability is particularly important for intelligent databases where the user is dealing with a considerable amount of complexity. The user interface needs to be good in order to allow the user to handle these massive amounts of data and convert them into information. In some senses, the user interface of the intelligent database application can never be good enough, since there will always be more information available than the user can practically access or digest.

The task of user interface design is complicated somewhat by changing conceptions of what computers are and how they may be used, and by the changing role of the user in design. The computer, as an artifact has changed over the years from an electronic calculating machine to a kind of Swiss army knife of tools, each of which is supported by a particular software application. As computers and the understanding of computers has evolved they have come to be seen as workbenches (workspaces) containing tools such as databases, schedulers, spreadsheets, or word processors, with different tools being provided by different software programs.

As the role of the computer has changed, so too has the role of the user. Programming expertise or special computing knowledge is no longer assumed for most applications. The resulting shift to end-user computing has meant that computer applications generally need to be usable with relatively little training. Users expect to walk to a terminal and be able to use the interface instantly.

As a minimum, intelligent database interface should include the following functions and characteristics:

**1.** Immediate dynamic hyperdata access everywhere.
**2.** Soft interfaces which allow users to customize for themselves.
**3.** Walk up and use query and access.
**4.** Different interfaces to the same data for different types of user.

Section 3.1 distinguished between input and output processes related to user interfaces. It is possible to subdivide user interfaces for end-users and executives into various (at times overlapping) classes: querying, hyperinformation browsing, graphic visualization, analysis and discovery, and briefing and presentations.

There are, of course, other activities such as data modeling and schema design that are performed by database administers and analysts, but the focus here will be on the activities listed above. Of these activities, the most frequently performed activities are often querying and presentations, although querying may in turn lead to production of graphs or materials for presentations. In an integrated intelligent database, on-line querying takes place during an interactive presentation. This section will focus on querying. Discovery and data visualization are discussed in Chapters 4 and 5 respectively. Presentations and browsing are discussed in chapters 6 and 7.

Conceptually, the process of querying may be separated into (a) selecting subsets of information from the database, and (b) deriving new columns (descriptors) from the existing information. An example of (a) above would be to select customers living in a particular city. An example of (b) would be to add up the sales to each customer in a year to obtain a new descriptor representing the yearly sales to each customer.

Another important point to note about querying is that querying can be nested. For instance, in SQL subqueries can be nested within the *where* clause of a query. However, subqueries can also be viewed as separate tables that are then operated on by another query. Nesting is a concept that can cause difficulty for people (like recursion), and it is probably preferable to express nested queries as a succession of simpler queries where the output of one query becomes the input to the next. For query formulation using some type of visual representation this has the useful side effect of

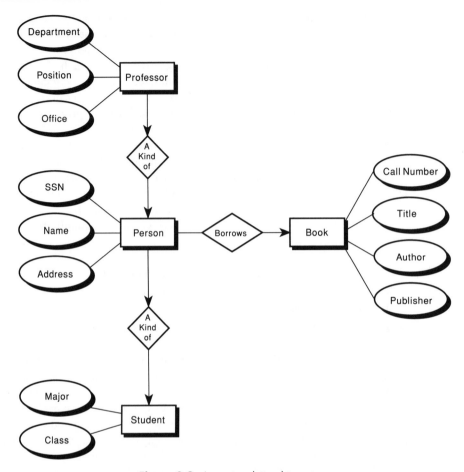

**Figure 3.9** An entity-relationship system.

providing visual feedback on what the query is really doing as it is implemented (thus providing useful information for debugging).

In view of the preceding discussion, the visual querying system should:

- Be interactive
- Be progressive instead of nested
- Clearly distinguish between selection of information and manipulation of information
- Represent a query as an analog of a record rather than a table.

A simple example will help to better compare and contrast these styles of query. The following is a database of five tables, representing books borrowed from a library by students and professors. As in Figure 3.9, tables and attributes are represented in an extended entity-relationship system as follows:

Table PERSON
 type: ENTITY
 attributes:
  ssn: char(9)
  name: char(50)
  address: char(80)
  phone: char(10)
 Table STUDENT
 type: ENTITY
 supertype: PERSON
  (PERSON.ssn = STUDENT.ssn)
 attributes:
  ssn: char(9)
  major: char(4)
  class: char(2)
Table PROFESSOR
 type: ENTITY
 supertype: PERSON
  (PERSON.ssn = PROFESSOR.ssn)
 attributes:
  ssn: char(9)
  dept: char(4)
  position: char(20)
  office: char(12)
Table BOOK
 type: ENTITY
 attributes:
  call#: char(20)
  title: char(80)
  author: char(50)
  category: integer
  publisher: char(50)
Table BORROWS
 type: RELATIONSHIP connecting PERSON and BOOK
  (ssn = PERSON.ssn, call# = BOOK.call#)
 attributes:
  ssn: char(9)
  call#: char(20)

Query interfaces can currently be categorized into the following basic classes:

- Command oriented (e.g., dBASE or SQL)
- Table/Form based (e.g., QBE and Paradox)
- Graph oriented (e.g., Metaphor or Quest)
- Icon based (e.g., *Iconic Query*)
- Hypertext oriented (e.g., *Iconic Query*)

The following five sections discuss these different styles of interfaces.

### 3.3.1 Command Driven Interfaces and SQL

In the 1970s database querying was a highly skilled activity. Initially it utilized programming ability in a database management language which required similar programming skills to general purpose programming languages. As the relational model started to dominate database management, specialized querying languages were developed. Of these languages, SQL has become preeminent. However, although SQL is certainly much easier to use than early languages for database querying it still requires quite a bit of skill and is beyond the capability of many end-users who wish to develop their own applications and queries.

In a command driven querying system, programming systems such as the dBASE language are used, or structured query methods like SQL are employed, where a user types in a SQL command. SQL is the most widely used relational query language today.

To retrieve data the SQL "select statement" is used. SQL select statements are made up of three clauses: *select*, *from*, and *where*. A query in SQL has the form:

> *Select Attribute 1, Attribute2, . . . , AttributeS*
> *From Relation 1, Relation2, . . . , RelationS*
> *Where Predicate*

In this notation, the list of attributes may be replaced with a star (*) to select all attributes of all relations appearing in the *from* clause.

The result of an SQL query is a relation. The *select* clause is used to list the attributes desired in the table produced by a query. The *from* clause specifies a list of relations to be used in executing the query. Finally, the *where* clause corresponds to the selection predicate. If the *where* clause is present it consists of a predicate involving attributes of the relations that appear in the *from* clause.

Some features of SQL are not available in the relational algebra. For instance, aggregate operators such as avg (average) operate on aggregates of records, providing statistical and related information, while sorting procedures can be used to order records according to their attributes.

In order to perform a query in SQL, the user has to understand the table structure and know the commands. Performing selections from a single table is at times manageable. However, SQL's problems appear when a user has to join several tables to perform a query. For instance, suppose that we want to find the titles of all books borrowed by those students whose major is math. The user has to do the following:

1. Select the fields of interest to be displayed, (i.e., Book.Title and Person.Name).
2. Perform a selection based on the value of the field Major being equal to Math.
3. Perform a join between the tables Person and Student to find the names of students who have borrowed books.
4. Perform a three-way join between the tables Books, Borrows, and Person to find the titles of the borrowed books.

There are, of course, optimization issues involved here with respect to the order in which these operations are performed, (e.g., value selections are better performed before joins, etc.) For further discussion of query optimization see Parsaye et al. 1989, Chapter 2. In SQL this query is represented as:

```
Select BOOKS.Title, PERSON.Name
From BOOKS, BORROWS, PERSON, STUDENT
Where    STUDENT.Major = Math and
         STUDENT.ssn = PERSON.ssn and
         PERSON.ssn = BORROWS.ssn and
         BORROWS.Call # = BOOK.Call #
```

This is obviously more than most business people want to do. Some of the problems with using SQL directly are:

1. The user forgets the table names and field names, mistyping them and getting errors after wasting computation time.
2. The commands to be entered are too long.
3. The user has to think of join paths which are irrelevant from the user's perspective.

To overcome these problems, and since many business users are unable or unwilling to learn SQL, several attempts have been made at making SQL more friendly to users. One of these early attempts was the Query by Example system of Zloof (1977), discussed in the next section. A more recent attempt is the Visual SQL approach of Trimble and Chappell (1990), which is the basis of some commercial systems, and is described in Section 3.3.3. The use of icons and hypertext for query is discussed in Sections 3.3.4 and 3.3.5.

## 3.3.2  Tables and Forms

In a form filling approach such as Querying by Example (QBE), the user sees either a form or a table schema and enters values. QBE is designed to build queries interactively and contains a number of features not found in early relational query languages.

The idea of QBE is that instead of describing the procedure to be followed in obtaining the desired information, the user gives an example of what is required. The advantage of such systems is that many users are comfortable with forms and tables. However, one of the problems cited above is still not solved, (i.e., the user has to see the join paths). Although QBE incorporates a number of the features of the relational model and is expressed in a table format, it does not conform as closely to the relational model as does SQL.

One advantage, however, of most QBE implementations is that the schemas of the tables are visible on the screen, so the user does not have to remember field names. For example, to display the column Title in the table BOOKS, first ask the system to display the skeleton of the table BOOKS (Figure 3.10 shows a section of the skeleton), then enter the command "T." under the column of Title (Figure 3.11). This is equivalent to the following SQL query:

*Select BOOKS.Title*
    *From BOOKS*

Here, placing a period after the letter T makes T a variable.

To select specific rows, conditions are specified on the columns. For example, Figure 3.12 contains a QBE query to find all the Titles in BOOKS where category is *Physics.*

Multiple conditions using all the predicates and operators as in SQL can be specified on the Table skeleton. For example, Figure 3.13 specifies a QBE query that finds all books written by *A. Smith* whose category is *Physics* or *Chemistry.*

| ISBN | Title | Author | Year | Publisher | Cost | Category |
|------|-------|--------|------|-----------|------|----------|
| — |  |  |  |  |  |  |

**Figure 3.10**  A section of the skeleton for the table BOOKS.

| ISBN | Title | Author | Year | Publisher | Cost | Category |
|------|-------|--------|------|-----------|------|----------|
|  | T. — |  |  |  |  |  |

**Figure 3.11**  Select the Title from a table in QBE.

| ISBN | Title | Author | Year | Publisher | Cost | Category |
|------|-------|--------|------|-----------|------|----------|
|  | T. |  |  |  |  | 'Physics' |

**Figure 3.12**  A QBE query to find all books where category is Physics.

| ISBN | Title | Author | Year | Publisher | Cost | Category |
|------|-------|--------|------|-----------|------|----------|
|      | T.    | 'A. Smith' |   |           |      | 'Physics' 'Chemistry' |

**Figure 3.13** A QBE query to find all books written by A. Smith where category is Physics or Chemistry.

Commands are also available in QBE for specifying the output order. Expressions involving built-in operators such as arithmetic operators, data functions, and aggregate functions can be specified in QBE, as well as in SQL. For more on QBE see Parsaye et al. 1989, Chapter 2.

However, one key observation about QBE is that while tables are a very good way of visualizing databases, they are not the most natural way of visualizing queries. This is because queries are descriptions of the conditions that relevant data must match, rather than a visualization of all the records that meet that description.

A related visual interface for a database frontend is the form such as that used in a product like ObjectVision™. A form looks like a paper version, with boxes representing the different fields of interest. Forms are generally used to input data or show output, but as QBE shows, form-like representations can be used to express queries. Forms or similar visual representations may also be used to show the results of a query record by record. The collection of records in the result may then be conceptualized as a stack of filled-in forms, where the details on each of the forms match the values of the fields in the corresponding record.

A *form* is an information-holding object consisting of two parts: (1) a form heading that describes form name, form structure, and component names; and (2) one or more form instances (or form occurrences). The form heading assumes a role that is commonly known as data-structure definition or schema definition.

As an example, Figure 3.14 shows the heading of a PRODUCT form. The top line contains the form name. Components of the form are represented by their names. The form structure is represented as follows: field names are represented in the columns, groups names are placed on top of their components, parentheses are used to denote repeating components. A corresponding hierarchy graph is also included in Figure 3.15. Forms are a natural way to represent hierarchies.

The collection of all form instances belonging to a particular form is known as a file of that name (e.g., collection of all instances of STUDENT form is referred to as the STUDENT file).

Most common data processing applications (including the manual ones) can be viewed as manipulations of forms. An application may consist of one or more

| (PRODUCT) | | | | | | |
|-----------|-------|------|-----------|-----------|-----|-------|
| PROD_NO | PNAME | TYPE | (SUPPLIER) | (STORAGE) | | PRICE |
|         |       |      | VNAME | BIN_NO | LOC | |

**Figure 3.14** The heading of a PRODUCT form.

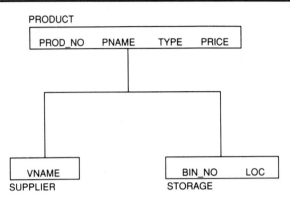

**Figure 3.15** The information in Figure 3.14 represented as a hierarchy graph.

processes. Each process produces or modifies one form. Thus, specification of an application involves capturing information about the forms that are being manipulated. Very often the information on form processing is embedded in the manual office procedure and/or partially implemented computer systems. The actions (processes) on these forms can themselves be described using forms by specifying the effect (output) they have on forms. Therefore, to describe a process involves three parts.

1. A form heading that defines the form name, form structure, and its components.
2. A description of the data that constitutes the form, including statistical information (such as data types, data volume, and value distribution) as well as integrity constraints on the data (such as value constraints, etc.).
3. A description of the operation that produces or modifies the form, including the type of operation (such as insert, delete, update, print, or query), the mode (on-line or batch), and frequency of the operation, as well as the cost-bearing characteristics of the operation such as the necessity of accessing more than one file to produce an output, testing for conditions, aggregation that requires accessing of many records, (e.g., sum, max, etc.), the need of sorting to meet the ordering or grouping requirements, and so on.

The basic operations of setting up a form, including the definition of fields, buttons, and the pasting in of graphics are provided in products like HyperCard on the Mac on ToolBook on the PC. Forms may be used to interactively implement standardized procedures when entering in new records. Forms also provide a useful way to display database records. For many applications they can also be printed directly as invoices, shipping receipts, and so on.

Decision trees may be used to define dependencies between different fields in a database and to set up the logic for calculating field values. The decision trees are actually rules or sets of rules that calculate field values and provide considerable flexibility.

For most people decision trees are likely to be much easier to design and debug than standard spreadsheet formulas. The use of a simple decision tree can be illustrated with an example. Consider the following set of rules that define the amount of discount that different types of customer get depending on the quantity of items that are ordered:

1. Discount is 40% if the customer is a wholesale distributor.
2. Discount is 30% if the customer is a retailer who orders 100 items or more.
3. Discount is 20% if the customer is a retailer who orders less than 100 items.
4. Discount is 20% if the customer is a corner store who orders 100 items or more.
5. Discount is 5% if the customer is a corner store who orders less than 100 items.
6. Discount is 50% if the customer is an educator who orders 100 items or more.
7. Discount is 30% if the customer is an educator who orders less than 100 items.

These rules can be represented as a decision tree as shown in Figure 3.16. Now, using this decision tree, if for instance, we know that the customer type is a corner store who is ordering more than 100 items, then we can deduce that the discount is

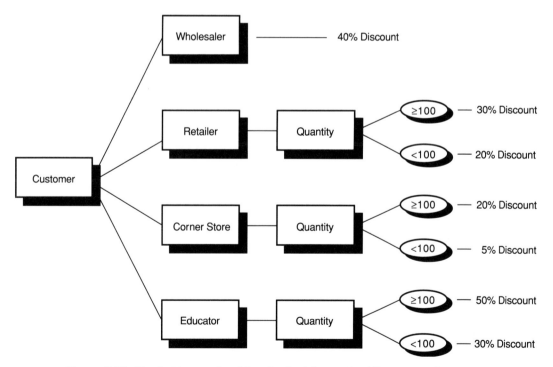

**Figure 3.16** The decision tree that defines levels of discount for different types of customers.

| Jackson's Clearinghouse | |
|---|---|
| Name:  Jim Bennett | Order Date:<br>3/15/93 |
| Company:  Acme Electronics | Customer Type:<br>Retailer |
| Address:  2502 Hansen | Discount:  20% |
| City:  Shreveport, LA | Unit Price:  $10 |
| Sale Item:  Printer Ribbon | Quantity:  40 |
| Amount:  $400* | Discounted Price*<br>$320 |
| Sales Tax | Shipping Cost |
| Comments | Final Price |

**Figure 3.17**  An example of a form. Fields marked with asterisks have been calculated from other data.

20%. Using this logic, the system can then make such calculations while the form is being filled in so that the number of manually entered fields is kept to a minimum and the user is spared repetitive calculations.

Decision trees can also be used as a form of querying where the end result (e.g., the amount of discount) is queried and the decision tree is used to calculate the response, with unknown variables being calculated by sending appropriate queries to the database. Thus forms can be linked directly to external databases. Figure 3.17 shows an example of a form. In this form the amount field is calculated from the values of the quantity and unit price fields (a simple multiplication), the discount is calculated from the customer type and quantity fields (using the logic of the decision tree shown in Figure 3.16), and the less discount, total price, sales tax, shipping cost, and final price fields are also calculated by the database application based on prior data and the other fields of the record that are input manually or retrieved from a database.

### 3.3.3  Graph-Based Query

In a mouse driven diagrammatic query system, such as that described by Trimble and Chappell (1990), the user still sees either tables or entity-relationship diagrams. However, the user can now click on tables to form queries by having the SQL commands represented as menu items. Thus this approach provides a full user point-and-click interface system for making SQL queries. The key difference in this approach is that the user can now click on table and views, as they appear in the database. The same approach can be applied to entity-relationship (E-R) type systems, where the E-R diagram is used as a clicking anchor for forming queries.

Thus the entity-relationship (E-R) model and similar schemes are useful in the visual specification of queries. The basis of such visual querying environments is first the creation of a graphical model or view such as symbols overlaid on a map or other bit-mapped graphic. The next section will consider a point and click style of navigation that takes the graphical approach of E-R modeling one step further.

Point-and-click querying provides a general form of querying that can be used across a variety of applications. With an increased amount of development effort it is also possible to develop highly customized visual querying interfaces that simplify the querying process still further. We can illustrate the functionality of using highly customized visual querying interfaces with the example of an airline reservation system (Huang 1990).

A visual representation of aircraft seat availability allows a passenger to see all the seats and their relationships to exits, no-smoking areas, aisle, windows, and so on. Each seat is then a selectable object in the interface and clicking on a particular seat will call up information about its location, class, and seating section, and if occupied, the passenger's name and any special information associated with the passenger. The use of the visual interface also allows other information to be conveyed very easily. For instance, first-class seats can be distinguished from economy-class seats on the basis of their relative sizes in the display, or empty and occupied seats can be displayed in different colors.

Seat selection can be handled visually because occupied seats look obviously different from unoccupied seats, and dialog boxes can be used to explain if a requested seat is already taken, or to enter information about a new passenger currently making a reservation.

**3.3.3.1  Visual SQL**    For many people it is much easier to express a query visually than to write a set of statements in a language such as SQL. This is the motivation for the development of a visual analog of SQL (e.g., Trimble and Chappell 1990). A relational table can be represented as a box. For instance, Figure 3.18 shows a table and Figure 3.19 shows an equivalent visual representation as a box. Consider the following query as expressed in SQL:

*Select Title, Call#*
*From BOOKS*
*Where Category = Math*

| ISBN | Title | Author | Year | Publisher | Cost | Category |
|------|-------|--------|------|-----------|------|----------|
|      |       |        |      |           |      |          |

**Figure 3.18**  The BOOKS table.

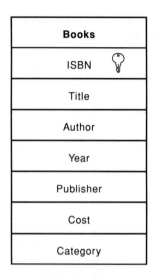

**Figure 3.19** The BOOKS table represented as a box.

Figure 3.20 shows the same query represented in the box notation. The checkmarks beside Title and Call# in the box show that these are the fields that will be returned while the condition Category = Math attached to the row in the box shows that only those records that meet this condition will be selected.

A *where* clause may contain multiple conditions as shown in Figure 3.21. Here the query has been modified so that we are looking for the math books by Johnson.

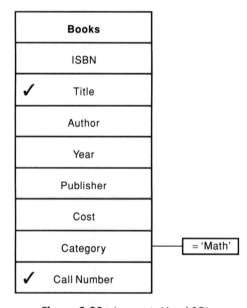

**Figure 3.20** A query in Visual SQL.

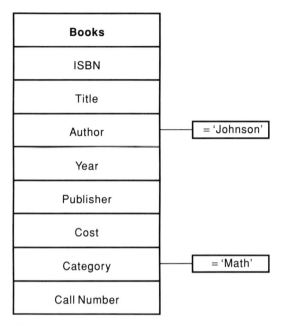

**Figure 3.21** A query in Visual SQL with two conditions.

Attaching two conditions in the query diagram is equivalent to having an AND in the *where* section of the SQL statement. Thus Figure 3.21 represents the following SQL query:

Select Title, Call#
    From BOOKS
    Where Category = 'Math' and Author = 'Johnson';

One method for distinguishing between AND and OR is by explicitly writing "OR" or "AND" on the query diagram as appropriate. An example of the use of AND and OR in the same query diagram is shown in Figure 3.22. This diagram corresponds to the SQL statement:

Select Title, Call#
    From BOOKS
    Where (Category = 'Math' or Category = 'Physics') and Author = 'Johnson';

In principle, it might be possible to develop an inclusive visual metaphor or representation system that provided a visual diagramming technique for each and every keyword in SQL. However, in practice it seems reasonable to develop a basic visual structure and then add more specific operations as textual annotations to the basic structure.

One of the problems in the approach outlined above is that the user has to explicitly setup the join conditions between various tables. Most end-users do not wish to do

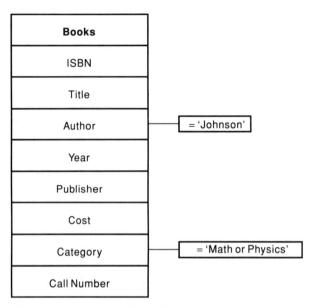

**Figure 3.22** Using AND and OR in the same query diagram.

this. Moreover, the interface described above still works at the logical database level, rather than at the conceptual level.

**3.3.4   *Querying with Icons***   The entity-relationship model is a good way of displaying objects and their structure and interrelations. However, it is difficult to develop a visual language that is fully expressive in terms of specifying rules and procedures that can be carried out using the display objects.

Interactive construction of queries using pointing and clicking can be combined with a naturalized version of SQL to create a style of interaction that can be called querying with icons.

Querying with icons, and other forms of point and click querying rely on a visual representation of the data model. This visual representation may be used to create display objects that are then manipulated by the developer in building the system or else manipulated by the user in querying or navigating around the information.

This section will describe a style of querying with icons that supplements the direct manipulation of display objects with dialog boxes that allow the user to set constraints and conditions on various components of the display object model. This querying with icons will be used in intelligent database applications to express relational queries in an intuitive way at the user interface.

Querying in a language like SQL is not intuitive for most people. Thus it is useful to consider how querying can be made with respect to a visual representation of the object model of data. The basis of such visual querying environments is first the creation of a graphical model or view such as symbols overlaid on a map or other bit-mapped graphic. The second step in the development of a visual querying environment is specification of how the object model will handle user interactions and

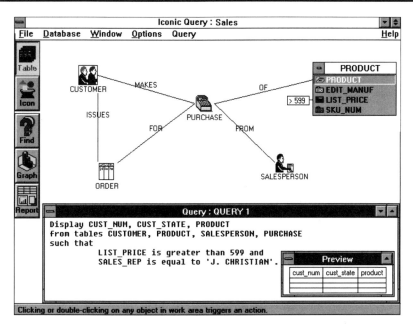

**Figure 3.23** A screen shot from the Iconic Query System.

show feedback about the effects. These effects will include highlighting of active objects and the popping up of dialog boxes or menus when parameterized actions are selected. The third step will be linkage of actions in the graphical interface to the underlying application functionality. For the present purposes this underlying functionality will be transactions in the object model and the SQL queries that are executed as a result of these transactions.

*Iconic Query* is a commercial system developed by IntelligenceWare to provide visual querying for relational databases. Using *Iconic Query*, SQL queries may be simply and natural expressed within a visual querying environment. One of the features of *Iconic Query* is the use of an iconic graphic user interface (see Figure 3.23). In the *Iconic Query* model, scenarios are set up within a development environment and these scenarios are then employed by users to carry out querying. A scenario is an entity-relationship graph that is represented as a graphical user interface where the user can express queries by directly manipulating the various entities and relations.

**3.3.4.1** ***Overview of Iconic Query*** Iconic Query provides a method for accessing databases with an iconic interface, composing queries by using a point-and-click method, clicking in and dragging icons to form queries. Querying with icons uses a set of representative icons, pictorial representations, and hypertext with a point-and-click user interface, relying on automatic query path calculations, rather than commands or systems for pointing at tables. In order to use *Iconic Query*, the database application developers first create an iconic representation for the underlying database. End-users issue queries by clicking at the proper place on the screen. These queries are translated into SQL statements to the underlying relational database.

*Iconic Query* uses representative pictures instead of dealing with database tables. Instead of learning a query language, the user clicks on icons to get answers by creating English-like queries. Behind the graphic art is the linkage between several databases and multi-table joins.

*Iconic Query* introduced the concept of "what you see is what you ask™". This concept:

- Uses pictures instead of tables in a query system. The user no longer sees the shape of a table, but sees a background picture or an icon.
- Inserts background scenes as bit-maps on which active (mouse sensitive) areas are defined.
- Uses another layer on top of the physical and logical structures to represent the conceptual structure of the database.
- Allows dragging of text to form queries with hypertext.
- Provides facilities for defining alternative text labels for tables or fields, so that the end-user does not see the coded or shortened table names. It also provides facilities for defining alternative text labels for field values, so that the end-user does not see the coded values in the database.
- Provides facilities for defining alternative keywords for SQL commands and table join paths and for translating these into readable English text as queries are formed.
- Provides facilities for the automatic calculation of paths during query, based on the keywords used when an application is setup.

Thus querying with icons involves the application of the iconic data model to existing SQL, object oriented, hierarchical, and network databases. Entities and relationships are represented by bit-maps, drawings, and icons, providing an easy to understand interface.

**3.3.4.2 Scenarios**     In the *Iconic Query* model "scenarios" are set up within a development environment and these scenarios are then used by users to carry out querying. A scenario is essentially equivalent to an application. A scenario may be an entity-relationship graph that serves as a graphical database interface, or an iconic representation of a database. The user can express queries by directly manipulating the various objects within a scenario.

Thus a scenario consists of a set of visible icons, representing tables, objects, or items. Each icon has a set of "fields" which correspond to table columns, entity attributes, object attributes or variable slots. Each field can have a set of "values."

The process of building a scenario is carried out as follows:

1. The developer chooses a bit-map as the background or opens and modifies an existing scenario.
2. The developer then adds tables, objects, or entities as required by the application.

3. The developer then creates links between entities by selecting pairs of tables and joining them with a link icon that represents a relationship. In this process, the developer also has to specify the descriptive attributes for each of the tables in the relation. In addition to general relations, entities can also be structured using "is-a" links.

4. After selecting all the tables or objects needed, each table or link can then be replaced with an icon. The icons or labels that represent each new table are then located in the bit-map.

In addition, the developer may set up new table and field names within the iconic model, in place of the existing table and field names. One key issue in querying with icons is that the end-user does not need to see the underlying table structure. In *Iconic Query*, the developer rebuilds the conceptual model, adds iconic images to make it more easily understandable and then allows users to query it directly. The end-user can then carry out querying using a previously constructed scenario in the following fashion:

1. The user chooses a scenario.

2. The user selects attributes from the icons/tables in the scenario and sets up the conditions for the query, (e.g., name, age, etc.).

3. The user may also create new attributes for this query, where the new attribute is a combination of attributes, functions, and operators, (e.g. average age).

4. The user may also browse a table directly to see the raw data.

5. When the user is satisfied with the query, it is executed, and the result is shown in a separate window.

**3.3.4.3** ***Handling Joins*** *Iconic Query* provides methods for creating joins between tables in an intuitive way, two of which are described below.

> Method 1. To connect *all* common fields between two tables, begin by dragging a line from one table icon to another. Holding the right button down on one icon, draw a line to another icon in which you want to make a relation. If there are no common fields between the two icons a join cannot be made.

> Method 2. To connect *specific* fields of two tables, double click on the table icons in the background that you want to join. Holding the right button down on one field of the first icon, draw a line to the corresponding field in the second field.

**3.3.4.4** ***Creation of the Iconic Schema*** Iconic Schema Definition helps database developers create an *Iconic Query* interface. To begin with, the developer merges the definition of each table (represented by icons) and its attributes into a background bit-map, as well as defining the position of each icon and attribute. A bit-map background is any graphic drawing that acts as the background for a scenario. It may be a picture or graphic that is scanned in, or it may be created directly using a paint tool or bit-map editor.

The developer can define active areas that are sensitive to mouse clicks. This is simply done by defining the absolute or relative coordinates of a rectangle on the bit-map and associating it with a table name or icon. The following steps provide a simple mouse driven method of specifying the icon locations.

1. Select a specific icon, object, or table by clicking on it.
2. Place the cursor where *the left upper corner* of the active area should be.
3. Press the left mouse button down and drag to open a box. When the mouse button is released, the new active area is now defined for the item.

Defining new areas is very simple. The areas may be changed and renamed by using the delete menu item, or by dragging and placing another icon over an area.

**3.3.4.5** *Computation with* **Iconic Query**     The process of performing a query is very simple for the end-user. It takes place as follows:

1. The user clicks to open the fields window for some icons.
2. The user selects a set of fields to be included in the result table. This is done, for instance, by double clicking on a field to highlight it or mark it with a check mark.
3. The user may define a set of new fields by using the pop-up operations or the menu. These create fields such as Average Age, Count of Books, etc.
4. The user defines a set of conditions on the fields, by selecting a condition operator from the pop-up menu or the top level menu. For instance, Age = 18 can be selected as a condition.
5. The user selects the find or report option from the menu and the SQL query is generated. After generation, the SQL query is submitted to the database manager for execution and the results are displayed.

The key issue is the construction of the path for adding the *from* and the *where* clauses. Actually, it is easier to generate the *from* after generating the *where*. For instance,

> *Show-all*
> > *Name of Person, Title of Book*
> *Such that*
> > *Major of Student = Math and*
> > *Category of Book = Physics*

may be selected by the user by double clicking on Name, and Title in PERSON and BOOK and adding conditions to STUDENT and BOOK. Here *Iconic Query* has to find a path for connecting the various tables together. This query will be translated into the following SQL statements:

```
Select PERSON.name
    From   PERSON, STUDENT
    Where PERSON.ssn = STUDENT.ssn
    And    PERSON.ssn = BORROWS.ssn
    And    BORROWS.Call# = BOOKS.Call#
    And    STUDENT.Major = Math
           BOOK.Category = Physics
```

The *select* clause is generated from the "selected" columns table just by writing out the names of the fields and tables.

The fields in the Connection Table actually represent a graph of connections. The nodes of the graph are fields, the edges are links. The SQL must have a fully connected graph or a tree of conditions.

For connecting the *where* clause *Iconic Query* finds a "minimum spanning tree" from the Connection Table, based on the tables and fields included in the selections and connections. In this way, a set of fields which connect all selected fields and conditions are computed.

The *where* clause generator then uses the minimum spanning tree to build a set of join conditions automatically, e.g.,

```
PERSON.ssn = STUDENT.ssn and
BOOK.Call# = BORROWS.Call#
```

is now automatically added, to make sure that a correct SQL statement is issued. Depending on table sizes, the generated SQL statement may not be optimal in terms of execution time. Improving this, however, is the task of a query optimizer. The database query optimizer may re-order the SQL query, or indeed generate another path, depending on table sizes, etc.

**3.3.4.6  *How Iconic Query Works***    The following example shows how querying with icons works. Suppose we have a database with five tables:

```
PERSON(ssn, name, address, phone)
STUDENT(ssn, major, class)
PROFESSOR(ssn, dept, position, office)
BOOK(call#, title, author, category, publisher)
BORROWS(ssn, call#)
```

In the setup environment, the developer clicks on the scenario icon to build a scenario. He selects a bit-map or background for the scenario.

The developer then clicks on the table-pool icon to display the tables, then drags the icons to place them on the background. The icon pool is reminiscent of a clip-art repository, and may have an icon archiving system that simplifies the task of finding the right icon in a large icon pool.

By clicking on the icon pool table, the icons are displayed and the developer can drag an icon anywhere and place it on a table. The icon is then assigned to that table and serves as a surrogate for it. Once the icon-table assignment has been made, clicking on the icon shows the fields of the table. A direct manipulation action may then be used to create links between tables. By clicking the right mouse button, holding it down and dragging to another table, the developer can build a link between two fields. For instance, a link between the fields Call# in the tables BORROWS and BOOK. The *Iconic Query* system automatically matches the names of the fields which are the same, or the developer may select or deselect a link.

The developer may also define a few predefined queries, and assign them icons so that end-users can just invoke them. These predefined queries may be completely "hard-wired" or they may be query templates with one or more parameters or arguments to be filled in.

At any time, the user can browse a table by double clicking on the icon that represents the table. The records in the table are displayed in a window. The user can then browse the table by scrolling through this window.

Suppose a user wants to find the name of all the students who majored in math and borrowed books whose category is physics. This query is the following SQL statement:

```
Select Name
    From PERSON, STUDENT
    Where PERSON.ssn = STUDENT.ssn
    And STUDENT.Major = Math
    And PERSON.ssn = BORROWS.ssn
    And BORROWS.Call# = BOOK.Call#
    And BOOK.Category = Physics
```

Most end-users would have to think for a while before they could type in this SQL statement. Actually, in *Iconic Query*, the statement above is automatically generated, but appears as:

```
Find-all Names of People
Such-that
    Major of Student is Math and
    Category of Book is Physics
```

The text is made plural here not by natural language understanding, but by simple alias definitions at the time table names are defined (i.e., the plural of Person is People). This may be turned on or off with a simple menu selection (i.e., we could also get Name of Person or Person.Name), if desired.

In *Iconic Query*, the user first clicks on the icon STUDENT on the screen. All the attributes (fields) of STUDENT including those inherited from Person (e.g., name) are shown on the screen. Since the attribute Name should be included in the output, the user selects this attribute by double clicking on it. This attribute will then be marked with a check mark.

Now, the user can specify conditions on the attribute Major by holding down the mouse button and selecting the equals function from the pop-up menu. A dialog window will pop-up for the user to key in the condition: Major = "Math".

Similarly, the user selects Category = Physics from the book icon. Then, the user clicks on the *find* button to find the name of all the students majored in Math. The *Iconic Query* system automatically calculates the join path, generating the SQL query and providing the result in a report.

### 3.3.5 Hypertext Querying

Iconic Query actually has two styles of query: with icons and with hypertext. Either method may be used to construct queries. Different users prefer different methods of using the system. Some users prefer icons, other like hypertext, yet others mix the two modes.

Hypertext querying also uses a point-and-click style of interaction that minimizes the need to type in various commands and names of tables, fields, and values. Instead, queries are constructed through a series of hypertext selections. Hypertext querying works best when it is combined with querying with icons.

In *Iconic Query*, pop-up text is used both to provide field and condition definitions, and to drag text fragments and icons to perform querying. The user clicks in the query edit window and a pop-up menu shows the list of tables and fields (Figure 3.24). After the user selects a table and a field, pop-up conditions are defined as in the upper right portion of Figure 3.24. The user is essentially entering the query text without typing.

Moreover, the user does not see the full join path or see the SQL keywords. Instead the user sees English phrases substituted for the field names, table names, commands, and operators. These aliases may be easily changed, as discussed later.

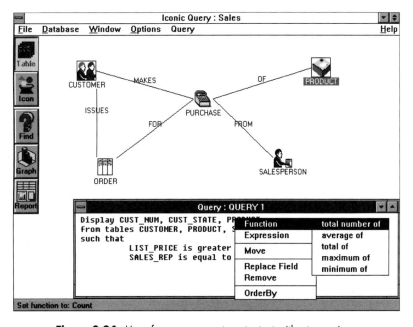

**Figure 3.24**  Use of pop-up menus to enter text without querying.

Previously defined queries can also be revised and edited. For instance, we might already have constructed the query:

*Find-all*
      *Name of Person*
*Such-that*
      *Age of Person > 18 and . . .*

but we now wanted to find people whose age is more than 21. Parameterized querying allows us to avoid extra effort in this type of situation by modifying an existing query. In this case the previous line: Age of Person > 18 and . . . is modified to become: Age of Person > 21 and . . .

In parameterized querying, modifiable parameters are shown as editable hotspots, as if they were hypertext anchors (see Chapter 6 for a discussion of hypertext anchors). For instance, our parameterized query might be:

*Find-all*
      *Name of Person*
*Such-that*
      *Age of Person > <u>18</u>*

Here we have underlined the term 18 to distinguish it. On a color screen, the modifiable term is shown in a different color (or otherwise highlighted). The user can now edit the query by clicking on the term "18" to pop-up an edit screen: Age of Person > . . .

In this way, *Iconic Query* can combine textual command-based query with parameterized querying where terms may be modified using pop-up edit windows.

A great deal of readability can be added in hypertext querying (and other forms of querying) if the developer replaces table, field, and command names with more readable terms, and allows for field values to be replaced with more understandable terms.

There are several reasons why many database terms are difficult to understand. Database designers often use short table and field names because they do not want to keep typing these terms again and again, (e.g., they typically use SSN instead of "social security number," and CUST instead of "customer," etc).

Another reason is that the database may be very large and values have to be coded. For instance, the public domain United States imports database for 1987-88 has 10 million records. The field COUNTRY in this database has less than 200 values. However, there are 10 million records with values for country. The database designers therefore "code" the country names to shorter integers to save disk space, (e.g., they use 17 for Italy and 21 for France, etc.). However, the end-user who queries the database may not remember these values.

Therefore, there is a need to have an encoding table which translates and retranslates these values, (i.e., it reads 17 from the database, but prints Italy for the end-user). This facility may be provided using a "value alias table" for each field. Once the appropriate encoding has been made, if a user clicks on a value, appropriate textual descriptions appear, (e.g., a paragraph about trade practices and trading treaties with Italy).

Specific phrase templates can be used to relate fields and values in queries. For instance, the developer may wish to use:

*Field* of all *Table*

as a generic way of referring to the construct Table.Field in a SQL statement. The developer may even allow for different singular and plural structures, e.g. Table and Tables, Person and People. Other terms such as "Average of," "Maximum of," etc. may also be defined. The developer may thus create very readable sentences such as:

Show the Name of all People such that Age of Person is equal to 18.

In addition, the terms "18" and "is equal to" may be highlighted, so that the user may click on it to open a hypertext edit window and change the query to:

Show the Name of all People such that Age of Person is less than 21.

In this way, new end-users begin to feel at home with the query system and then add their own queries.

Querying with icons and hypertext querying can also be adapted to construct textual queries. Here the user drags fields and icons to within predefined query templates to form new queries. The main steps in the process are as follows:

1. A set of text fragments corresponding to query operations are shown in the "command pool," (e.g., Find-all, Such-that, Equal-to, Less-than).
2. The field names are shown within the icons, (i.e. by clicking on the icon PERSON, the fields Name, SSN, Age, etc., are shown).
3. The query window is populated by dragging commands and field names together. In this way, readable queries are formed by the easy "drag and drop" style of operation, common to many GUIs.

For instance, suppose that the developer has set up the correspondence for *Attribute* of *Field* within the application, then a user builds a query as follows:

1. The user drags the word Find-all to the query window.
2. The user drags the field Name from the icon PERSON to the query window. When the user places Name within the query window, the term "Name of Person" appears. Now the query window reads:

*Find-all*
   *Name of Person*

**3.** The user now drags the word Such-that from the command menu:

*Find-all*
> *Name of Person*
*Such-that*

**4.** The user can now add conditions by dragging other fields and conditions:

*Find-all*
> *Name of Person*
*Such-that*
> *Age of Person > 18 and . . .*

In this way, queries are built up very easily. Such queries may be saved for future use by other users.

In addition, *Iconic Query* provides hypertext and hyperdata as discussed in Chapter 6. The user can click within a table display to obtain hypertext dynamically. Thus *Iconic Query* introduces several innovations at once.

## ■ 3.4 THE FUTURE OF USER INTERFACES

Today, user interface design is at times more of an art than a science. There are many reasons for this. Each new application and software interface is an experiment. We may be able to spot obvious problems in an interface using general principles such as compatibility or obviousness, but aside from that it is difficult to predict exactly how people will respond to a complex interface ahead of time.

It might be possible to systematically examine various interfaces to extract general principles of human computer interaction, except that the nature of the technology and associated artifacts is continuously changing. As the software interfaces (artifacts) change, so too does the nature of the human-artifact interaction.

Scientific research requires a minimally stable environment, and we have yet to achieve this in the field of user interfaces to computer applications. This is a good thing in many ways, since it is symptomatic of rapid innovation and development in the field of user interfaces. Thus while it may be possible to develop a science of the stable or non-technology-dependent aspect of user interfaces, the other aspects change too quickly to build stable scientific theories and models. If user interfaces were described by scientific theories, there would be a Kuhnian revolution (cf. Kuhn 1971) every few days.

The development of graphical user interfaces to operating systems and other computer functions was a surprisingly lengthy process. It was certainly not clear to most people in the early 1980s that graphical user interfaces would become dominant. The evolution of graphical interfaces was to a large extent a hit and miss affair, exemplifying the general principle that fit and compatibility of technology interfaces tends to improve over time, but often relatively slowly and painfully. Early cars were operated by levers (the analog movement of the modern steering wheel is however much more compatible with the steering task), and early computers were operated by toggle switches, paper tape, and punched cards. It seems incredible now, but punched cards and printed output remained a common form of user interface well into the 1980s.

Video display terminals and interactive processing were a godsend to all those poor souls who had dropped their boxes of cards in the snow or had been victimized by huge decks of dog-eared cards that would no longer run through the card reader. However, the early terminal interfaces still retained the 80-column character based structure of the punched card and the teletype.

Diffusion of technology can be surprisingly slow. The mouse had been invented in the 1960s, and the graphical user interface was invented by scientists at the Xerox Palo Alto Research Center in the 1970s. Yet graphical user interfaces did not come into widespread use until the late 1980s. The work at Xerox PARC on high quality bit-mapped graphics paved the way for a new user interface paradigm based on direct manipulation of screen objects as the preferred form of interaction.

It is something of an irony that the graphical user interface is now synonymous with the Apple Macintosh, a machine that was not introduced until 1984 (although Apple introduced its graphical user interface a couple of years earlier in the ill-fated Apple Lisa). A recent informal survey of 39 undergraduate students of engineering at the University of Toronto found that almost all of them thought graphical user interfaces had been invented by Apple. Perhaps it is only a matter of time before it is popularly believed that the graphical user interface was invented by Microsoft.

Even after the graphical user interface became widely available on the Apple Macintosh, the predominant style of computing continued to be character-based terminal interactions. It was not until the late 1980s that business finally embraced the graphical user interface with the success of the Microsoft Windows operating system.

Meanwhile the technology of user interfaces continues to evolve. While today's intelligent databases use graphical user interfaces, we can expect that future interfaces may include three-dimensional models and stereoscopic views, virtual reality, and other technologies that are yet to be conceived. Scientists at Xerox PARC are continuing the tradition of the 1970s with the information visualization project, a vision of a new form of user interface.

There appear to be multiple future directions for user interfaces. These can be broken down into three main classes. First there are speech and language based interfaces. These are inherently natural in the sense that speech and writing are the most common forms of communication between people. Yet software recognition of natural language has proved to be a surprisingly difficult problem. It is still not clear when Hal 9000 (the vastly intelligent computer envisioned by Arthur C. Clarke) will be available, certainly not until well after 2001. Anyone who has tried to carry out a conversation in an unfamiliar language knows how difficult it is to express ideas in a language other than one's own. Typically, one knows what to say, but not how to say it. It is the act of translation that is difficult.

Database querying should not be like speaking in a foreign language. Users should be able to express their intentions without being overtly aware of extraneous linguistic knowledge needed to translate their ideas and intentions into the querying language of the database management system.

Natural language is the way we express ourselves in everyday life, and thus the idea of using natural language to query databases is also appealing. Considerable effort has been expended on the development of natural language understanding systems (e.g., Schank 1975) over a number of years, but in spite of various hopes and claims the goal of natural language understanding is a long way off. Even if natural language understanding were available today, there is no guarantee that it would provide a satisfactory querying interface. This is because natural language is imprecise and full of nuances, while database queries need to be well-defined and unambiguous.

It is possible that a restricted form of natural language may be appropriate for database querying. This restricted, but comparatively natural language would lie on the continuum currently defined by SQL at one end and natural language at the other. One can approximate this language to some extent by adding "syntactic sugar" to SQL, so that more palatable aliases are used to describe database operations.

Meanwhile, there are still some exciting applications for voice-based user interfaces. Speech interfaces actually require two separate technologies, voice recognition for input, and voice synthesis for output. Of these two technologies, voice synthesis is much easier and has already been solved to a great extent. Programs are available for making computers talk fairly well, provided they are given a script.

The process of generating text automatically (i.e., self-scripting for the computer) is also difficult and may not be much easier than the problem of language understanding except in situations where the dialog between computer and user is highly predictable due to the constraints of the task.

Speech recognition is the problem of converting the sounds of a voice into recognizable words. The problem is 95% solved (i.e., speech recognizers can perform at about 95% accuracy) but getting from 95% to 100% accuracy is likely to be much more difficult than getting from 0% to 95% was. Thus voice interfaces remain an attractive possibility that will almost certainly arrive at some point in the future.

The second main class of interface can be referred to as experiential interfaces. The idea with these interfaces is to move around inside the problem. The current model of the experiential interface is the virtual reality. Here the user is ushered into a model world that faithfully represents the characteristics of a situation or task. For instance, in the ultimate form of virtual reality, a pilot might become a virtual aircraft, and guide the aircraft by moving his or her own body through a computer generated version of space. The movements of the pilot through space would then be mimicked by the aircraft. Another form of experiential interface involves the use of physical metaphor to represent task situations. For instance, the information visualizer project at Xerox PARC allows the user to move through different three dimensional rooms to perform different tasks.

The third type of future interface is gestural. Here the basic gestures of point and click are expanded to become a full vocabulary or language of expression. The current implementation of gestural interfaces is in pen-based computing. For instance, a markup editor might allow the user to edit text by crossing out words with a light pen, or by using various proofreader's marks and annotations to modify the text. The repertoire of gestures could then be expanded to meet the needs of a variety of different applications. Already we are seeing how people can adapt to gestures in the various operations (such as dragging and double clicking) that are required in graphical user interfaces.

Considerable research and development is currently being expended on these three avenues of future user interfaces. As these new user interface paradigms mature, they will merge into a qualitatively different style of user interface that will make current user interfaces look as incongruous and misplaced as the unwieldy levers that were used to steer very early models of car.

■ **3.5 CONCLUSION**

Communication issues are subtle, while the physical interface (e.g., screen and keyboard) is obvious. Thus legal arguments about the ownership of user interfaces have focused on the issue of look and feel (Samuelson and Glushko 1990) rather than on communication style and language.

This chapter has discussed graphical user interfaces in general and their relevance to the information presentation task in particular. A number of different methods for querying and navigation were reviewed, and a method of querying with icons that is designed especially for end-users was described. The advantage of querying with icons is that it allows queries to be expressed directly in terms of a visual model of the data. Queries can then be expressed through a combination of point-and-click navigation and dialog completion.

The task of information visualization needs to be considered within the context of user interface design in general. While GUIs dominate the design of physical interfaces, they say little about how the conceptual interface for an application should be designed. In our model of intelligent database application we sidestepped the issue of how to construct a conceptual interface for information visualization by creating a direct mapping between display objects at the user interface and information objects within the data model. Interactions at the user interface then map directly onto transactions on the database level.

Thus it is the visual representation of the data model that the user appears to be manipulating as he or she explores the data and its various summarizations and visualizations. This approach was illustrated with the *Iconic Query* method of executing queries to a relational database based on direct manipulation of an entity-relationship model of the data, but the same style of point-and-click navigation can also be used more generally in the model of hyperdata presented in Chapter 6. While this style of navigation is simple and obvious once one begins to work with it, it requires a considerable amount of machinery to support it. In particular, effective methods of information discovery and data visualization are needed, and these topics will be addressed in the next two chapters.

# 4

# INFORMATION DISCOVERY

*Unless exploratory data analysis uncovers indications, usually quantitative ones, there is likely to be nothing for confirmatory data analysis to consider.*

— John Tukey*

*Corollary*: Automatic discovery is the way.

## ■ 4.1 INTRODUCTION

How much is a crystal ball really worth and what are the limits to the "value" of knowledge? With the increasing complexity of today's society, we need an electronic crystal ball to understand the present and predict the future. Understanding, prediction, and improvement require information. In the right hands, information can be exponentially more valuable than any other asset. Information is usually obtained by performing experiments, by stumbling upon discoveries, or by getting the information from someone who already has it. In today's information society, information is more valuable than ever before, and its value continues to increase, as shown in Figure 4.1.

We need to accelerate the discovery of information and the generation of knowledge. Simply working harder is not the answer. There will never be enough statisticians and scientists to meet the demand. We must automate the discovery of information and generate knowledge automatically. Fortunately, the underlying technology for performing these tasks is not only available, but has been in use for some time (e.g., Blum 1986; Parsaye 1987; Mahnke 1988). What we need to do is to accelerate its use and thereby learn from the past in order to guess the future.

The history of human civilization consists of continuing efforts to distill the lessons of the past into knowledge which can be used for making the right choices in the future. To learn from the past, we need data and examples. Fortunately, minute by

---

* *Exploratory Data Analysis,* McMillan Publishing Co., 1978. John Tukey was born in Massachussets in 1936 and received a PhD from Princeton, where he later taught. He has been one of the major proponents of data analysis, inventing numerous techniques for the visualization and understanding of data.

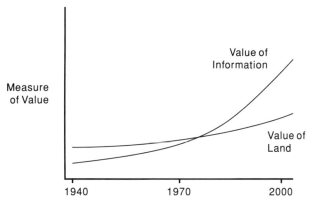

**Figure 4.1** The increasing value of information as part of the assets of society versus value of land.

minute and hour by hour the amount of data in the world's databases increases inexorably. With the widespread use of databases, there is no real shortage of data or examples. If anything, many organizations have more data than they can deal with. This data represents an almost endless well from which knowledge can be extracted.

All data is a challenge to our models of the world. While other luminaries of the age watched objects fall without comment, Isaac Newton sought to incorporate this data within his world model, thereby defining and explaining the concept of gravitational force. Models of the world seek to provide causal explanations for patterns and relations observed in data. Sometimes new data can be so surprising that we are forced to abandon our existing models and scramble to find new explanations of phenomena. An example of this process was Johannes Kepler's rejection of the Ptolemaic model of the solar system in favor of a new model where the motions of the planets are elliptical, with the sun being at a focus of the ellipse for each planet. Analysis of the data collected by Tycho Brahe forced Kepler to abandon previous assumptions about the circular motion of planets. Similarly, evidence of the "red-shift" in light emanating from distant galaxies and related data forced astronomers to revise their models of the universe and cosmology in favor of a universe that is still expanding since the "big bang" billions of years ago.

Data is a prod to our thinking, a reality test for our abstractions. However, the data must first exist before it can be examined and analyzed in terms of its patterns and implications. In the scientific method, data is collected through experimental observation. By manipulating or changing one variable at a time, while holding others constant (or by assuming them to be constant in their effects due to the use of randomized sampling), the scientist charts the effect of each variable setting (e.g., Box, Hunter, and Hunter 1978). There is a great deal of data collected in the world every day, and only a small fraction of that data results from scientific experiment.

Satellites are transmitting huge streams of data about the condition of the earth, its oceans and atmosphere. Supermarkets and retail outlets using bar codes and scanners are constantly recording information about what is bought, where, and when. Factories record detailed information about product defects, labor productivity, inventory levels, and the list of information generating sources goes on and on. We need methods for adding value to all this information collected as a side effect of human activity, and for discovering knowledge and meaning that is buried deep within our burgeoning databases.

We stand awash in a sea of data. Who knows what monsters or opportunities lurk in these deeps? In most cases, we can learn very little from simply "eyeballing" the vast streams of data. Instead, we need sophisticated tools for information discovery that can highlight the important patterns and rules in data and distill the lessons of the past into knowledge which can be used for making the right choices in the future. To learn from the past, we need *data* and *examples*. The current information/data glut may be a blessing in disguise, providing organizations with many opportunities to learn, using cooperative software intelligence for discovery.

Discovery methods can generally be classified as either exploratory or confirmatory. Exploratory methods look for patterns or differences in data, while confirmatory methods confirm whether or not expected patterns actually exist. For instance, confirmatory statistics include analysis of variance and t-tests. In contrast, factor analysis is generally used as an exploratory technique.

Humans are good at exploratory types of analysis, but the assistance of software intelligence is needed in order to deal with the vast amounts of data that can potentially be analyzed. Software intelligence has often been seen as emulating or competing with human intelligence rather than supporting or cooperating with human intelligence. But information discovery can be used as the basis for automated acquisition of knowledge from a database that may then be pooled with human knowledge and expertise in information interpretation and decision making.

Information discovery is a way of adding value to data (particularly large amounts of data) by summarizing it in terms of key trends and patterns. In the special case of rule generation, the output of information discovery is a set of rules that summarize the data. In many situations there is little alternative to the use of automatic information discovery as a means of extracting patterns and trends from data. Some of the factors that encourage the use of information discovery include:

- Huge amounts (oceans) of data to be explored
- Unused machine capacity
- Expensive human resources
- Unexpected associations between widely dispersed pieces of data

Automated information discovery allows us to distill knowledge from large databases. For instance, it can be used by medical researchers who gather reams of data each day from hospitals across the country. This data is often collected with the intent of analyzing it to assist in diagnosing future patients and preventing disease. One example of a relationship that is implicit in data is the striking correlation that can be found between average fat intake and the cancer rate in various countries. A tool for discovering these correlations or diagnostic rules in the midst of huge databases can be of tremendous assistance to medical research, both in speeding up the testing of hypotheses and in automating the generation of hypotheses.

Statistical methods of exploratory analysis are a useful supplement to information discovery. Methods such as cluster analysis have proved to be useful in a number of applications, such as marketing. However, the two methods of information discovery that are particularly useful in large data-bases are rule generation and anomaly detection.

Discovery methods include neural nets and machine learning as well as statistics, rule generation, and anomaly detection. Statistical methods were originally developed to analyze the results of designed experiments and were based on work done on probability in the eighteenth and nineteenth centuries. Neural nets are of more recent origin, although they have many similarities with certain types of statistics, including the use of numerical calculations as opposed to symbolic reasoning and a fundamental similarity to linear regression models. Machine learning includes a broad range of discovery tools that have been developed to handle discovery problems in artificial intelligence.

This chapter will describe some tools for information discovery and discuss their application. These tools are particularly useful in adding value to data and are essential to most intelligent database applications. The focus will be on information discovery through statistical methods and machine learning of patterns and rules in data. All the available discovery methods will be reviewed, with an emphasis on rule generation. When combined with anomaly detection and visualization it provides a powerful way for discovering patterns and relationships that lie hidden within information systems.

Why is rule generation special? Rule generation relies on discovery by value. This means that we can discover rules of the form: If attribute A has value A1 and attribute B is within the range B1, then attribute C will be within the range C1. This reference to values is fundamentally different from statistics, where relationships are expressed as trends such as: Variable Y will tend to increase as variable X increases, or an object will be in category A if attribute X is large while attribute Y is small.

This chapter begins with a review of information discovery concepts and presents a brief, and selective, history of information discovery and related techniques. A model of information discovery is then developed based on the goals of understanding, prediction, and improvement. The discussion of discovery tools includes a review of general data processing techniques, emphasizing the importance of data quality and the relevance of statistical methods of discovery.

The section on discovery methods discusses methods of rule generation and anomaly detection, along with neural nets. This is followed by a comparative analysis of the different tools and methods introduced in this chapter. Chapter 5 will then consider another form of adding value to data where visualizations of data are presented to the user.

## ■  4.2  HISTORY AND EVOLUTION OF DATA ANALYSIS

There are several disciplines concerned with information analysis and discovery. Until the early 1980s data analysis was almost synonymous with statistics. The only tools and theories available for understanding data were couched in terms of the numerical science of statistics. The early prominence of statistics was due to the fact that it was the first information discovery discipline to mature. More recent disciplines include induction and neural networks. These both extend the field of statistics and complement it, as discussed later in this chapter. The field of discovery has been influenced by many researchers working independently of each other. These researchers have often used very similar terminology in different ways.

Information discovery is the process of extracting patterns and trends from data. It requires the ability to relate different pieces of data together in order to establish a pattern or causal relationship. For instance, in 1854 a vicious cholera epidemic swept part of the city of London. The cause of the epidemic was eventually found to be a polluted well. Information discovery in this case consisted of plotting the cases of cholera on a map and then comparing the location of these cases with the location of water sources. This map showed very clearly the high concentration of deaths in the vicinity of the Broad Street pump. After more than 500 deaths, the epidemic was ended by removing the handle of the tainted pump.

Until the middle of the twentieth century information discovery techniques were rather rudimentary, relying mainly on human wit and various plots and charts that summarized the data. One of the reasons for this was that information discovery methods generally required extensive computation, and this was impractical for most large problems until computers and appropriate software became more readily available from the late 1960s on. Thus we will find little hint of modern methods of discovery in the history of data analysis reviewed in the following section.

### 4.2.1  History

Uncertainty is one of the most important concepts in data analysis. When we compare differences between sets of numbers we have to do so in the context of the background variation (arising from uncertainties for individual numbers) that will tend to make two sets of numbers look different even when they are the same.

Economic necessity produced a numerical allowance for uncertainty as early as 1100. Shortly after the Norman conquest of England, inspection was used to maintain the integrity of coins produced by the mint. The contract between the king and the mint allowed for a tolerance in the weight of a single coin.

Developments in mathematical probability began with correspondence between Pierre de Fermat and Blaise Pascal in the 1650s. The early motivation for the theory of probability came from gambling and the need to compute the odds for winning. Right from the start data analysis was about beating the game by knowing more. This trend still continues in major corporations.

The mathematics of many games of chance was well understood by the end of the seventeenth century. The early work looked at how to predict the chance of a red ball being drawn if an urn was known to have particular numbers of red and black balls. However, the different problem of figuring out the proportion of red and black balls in the urn given the colors of the balls drawn from it had not been addressed. This problem was solved by Jacob Bernoulli and appeared in a book published after his death in 1705.

However, Bernoulli left plenty of work for those following him. He set severe standards for determining the uncertainty with which a proportion was estimated (1 in 1000). He found that a coin tossing experiment would require over 25,000 tosses in order to estimate the proportion with such accuracy. However, modern statisticians have found it more convenient to work with a 1 in 20 chance that their conclusions are wrong (i.e., an alpha level of 5%).

The work on mathematical probability proceeded apace in the eighteenth century. Two landmarks that occurred in the early 19th century were the central limit theorem (first read to the French Academy by Pierre Simon de Laplace in 1810) and the method of least squares described by Adrien Marie Legendre in 1805 (in his book, *Nouvelles Méthodes pour La Détermination des Orbites Comètes*). The method of least squares has formed the basis of modern statistical computation, and the central limit theorem enshrined the normal distribution as the preeminent probability distribution used in statistics (statistics based on the normal distribution are generally referred to as parametric statistics).

While early work on probability was inspired by games of chance, early work in statistics (applied probability) was inspired by the problems of astronomy (as can be seen in the title of Legendre's book). In the nineteenth century, the focus of statisticians shifted to the problem of dividing social data into homogeneous classes or categories. For instance, how should information about crimes be grouped over different locations and times?

Statistics, as a form of applied probability, developed in the nineteenth and twentieth centuries. Although it was not motivated by gambling, it too sprang from its own set of interesting motivations. Francis Galton, a cousin of Charles Darwin, used methods of correlation and regression in the nineteenth century in his own studies of heredity and hereditary genius (a tradition that continues today in the correlational studies of identical and fraternal twins, investigating the hereditary components of conditions such as schizophrenia and alcoholism). This was the first example of a close relationship between psychometrics (the measurement of human intelligence and personality) and statistics that still continues.

The discipline of experimental psychology began in the mid-nineteenth century, and due to the variability of human behavior it has been involved with statistics throughout its existence. Experimental psychology has long been concerned with the reasons for differences in reaction time that frequently occur between different people and within the same person, when performing slightly different experimental tasks. The study of human variability in reaction time provided one of the motivations for the use of statistics in psychology in the nineteenth century. The problem of reaction time originally arose in astronomy, where it was observed that time estimates for meridian crossings by stars tended to vary between different astronomers. In 1796, the British astronomer Maskelyne fired his assistant Kinnebrook for having reaction times (i.e., estimates of meridian crossings) that were consistently different from his own. However, by the 1820s Friedrich Bessel found that differences in reaction times between astronomers were the rule rather than the exception. Towards the end of the nineteenth century differences within the same individual's reaction times were recognized (one astronomer noticed that his times were faster when he was hungry).

Gustan Fechner conducted numerous experiments in psychophysics, (i.e., the study of sensation). This tradition continued in the work of Wilhelm Wundt and in other branches of psychology. These studies showed that variability is the rule rather than the exception in human performance, and that the variability in making astronomical readings was duplicated in most other human activities.

By the end of the nineteenth century the core of statistics had been transferred from astronomy to psychology. Statistics thrived in psychology because of experimental design and the control of experimental conditions. In contrast, astronomical "experiments" were more observational, since the movements of stars and other heavenly bodies could not be manipulated.

Galton was an intuitive statistician who first proposed the concepts of regression and correlation, which were later formalized by others, including Karl Pearson, for whom Pearson's r (the standard correlation coefficient) is named. Pearson studied correlation, and Charles Spearman continued this study as part of his quest to prove that there was a single factor of general intelligence. This led to the statistical method now known as factor analysis, which rapidly became a weapon in spirited debates over the nature of human intelligence (Spearman 1927; Cattell 1943; Guilford 1954).

In the early twentieth century statistics was further enriched by input from a new field, agriculture. Sir Ronald Fisher joined an agricultural station in England after working for a few months on a farm in Canada. In doing so he turned down a university position in London with Karl Pearson, one of the best-known statisticians of the time. It is perhaps fortunate for modern statistics that Fisher made this seemingly strange career choice.

Fisher had to develop a method for assessing whether the differences between plants in different plots of land were statistically significant. This led to what are sometimes called "split-plot" experimental designs, and the analysis of variance to determine whether the means of two or more samples could really be considered different (i.e., whether or not the samples were really drawn from the same underlying population) when background random variation was taken into account.

While correlational statistics was being developed as a psychometric tool, the fundamentals of inferential statistics were being laid by Fisher and by another researcher in an unlikely setting. Antonin Gossett (who wrote under the pseudonym "student" and hence the well known student's t-test) worked for a brewing company and developed statistics as part of experimental analyses of the brewing process. The Gaussian distribution (named after Karl Friedrich Gauss) had been known to have interesting statistical properties for some time, and came to be referred to as the normal distribution because it fitted a wide variety of statistical attributes such as height and weight. Gossett developed the t-distribution as the difference of two normal (Gaussian) distributions. He then showed how the t-distribution could be used to test whether two samples (assuming normally distributed data) belonged to the same parent population or not.

Fisher extended Gossett's work, generalizing the t-test, which worked with comparisons of two samples at a time, to the analysis of variance, where n samples could be tested simultaneously to see if they belonged to the same population. He also developed what is now known as factorial analysis of variance. Fisher has been referred to as the greatest intuitive statistician ever, and his legacy lives on, not only in analysis of variance, but in a classic text on experimental design (Fisher 1951) and a well known test case (Fisher's Iris data, described in SAS 1988) that will be used later in this chapter to compare induction and statistics.

Since Gossett and Fisher, modern statistics have developed to the point where there are now an impressive array of techniques for evaluating and testing data. Today there are a huge number of books on statistics and there are also powerful statistical packages available for carrying out a wide range of statistical analyses on computers. Some of the well-known statistical packages include SAS™, SYSTAT™, and SPSS™. Aside from the computer revolution, three of the most important developments in modern statistics have been the development of multivariate, Bayesian, and distribution free methods.

Multivariate statistics consider more than one dependent variable or outcome variable at a time. Multivariate methods include factor analysis, canonical correlation analysis (where a linear model is constructed that relates a set of predictor variables to a set of outcome variables), and multiple discriminant analysis (where entities or records are classified into different levels of a category variable based on a linear combination of a set of predictor variables). Bayesian statistics explicitly take into account the prior probability of an event or measured difference before calculating its posterior probability in light of new data. Distribution free statistics use combinatoric methods of analysis and avoid the need to assume a particular parent distribution such as the normal or Gaussian distribution. Further discussion of these topics and other issues such as nonlinear model fitting lies outside the scope of this book.

### 4.2.2  The Evolution of Data Analysis

This discussion of the history of data analysis has so far concentrated on statistics and on methods of confirmatory analysis. A standard approach in confirmatory statistics is to somehow invent a hypothesis (e.g., that the mean of one set of numbers is significantly greater than the mean of another set of numbers) and then see whether or not this hypothesis is true. Statistical methods for this type of analysis are sometimes referred to as inferential statistics.

Where do the hypotheses come from that are used in confirmatory data analysis? This is one of the great mysteries of statistics. The general view is that they are formed in the mind of the researcher based on careful analysis of prior theories and data. In essence then, there has to be some kind of exploration that precedes the formation of hypotheses and confirmatory analysis. This is the point made in the quotation by John Tukey that began this chapter. Exploratory analysis is the discovery process of finding interesting patterns and relationships in data. Confirmatory analysis is the validation process of showing that these discovered relationships really do hold true.

Recently, under the influence of John Tukey and others, there has been an evolution in data analysis towards more emphasis on exploratory methods. Exploratory data analysis methods look for unanticipated patterns in data. In statistics, they include cluster analysis, which developed out of work in biological taxonomy (Sokal and Sneath 1963) and multidimensional scaling (Torgerson 1958; Kruskal 1964a; Kruskal 1964b), which developed out of work in mathematical psychology. Cluster analysis is a method for finding groupings in data, while multidimensional scaling is a method for estimating an unknown set of attributes or dimensions based on data about the similarities or differences between a set of objects. Factor analysis is another exploratory method that tests a set of attribute descriptions of objects and finds a reduced set of underlying factors that explain the variation in those attributes.

Other forms of statistics have been developed to handle the special problems posed by time series and other forms of specialized data. For instance, econometrics is concerned with the statistical analysis of economic data, while biometrics is concerned with the analysis of biological data. However, each of the subdisciplines of statistics employs a common set of statistical tools (found in the widely used statistical software packages) even though their relative importance and use may vary between disciplines.

While the statistical methods of exploratory analysis (information discovery) are quite good at describing and organizing data, they are not designed to discover explicit rules. Thus they are ill-equipped to handle one of the most important components of knowledge. Methods for discovering rules developed out of a completely different paradigm. Statisticians were concerned with describing the strength of numerical relationships, fitting linear models, and assessing significant differences. Meanwhile, researchers in artificial intelligence were attempting to represent knowledge in a machine-readable form and develop methods for automated discovery of knowledge (i.e., machine learning).

The quest for machine learning developed out of the general quest for intelligence in machines. In the early 1960s, John McCarthy (who coined the term "artificial intelligence") said that the key ability of an intelligent machine was to learn. In their quest for automated discovery and artificially intelligent learning systems, early researchers began developing techniques that could be used by game playing programs.

The literature on machine learning covers a wide spectrum of topics, many of which go beyond the basic style of rule generation that is needed for intelligent databases (e.g., Goldberg 1989; Porter and Mooney 1990; Davis 1991; Michalski et al. 1983; Holland et al. 1986; Quinlan 1983; Langley et al. 1986; Gaines and Shaw 1986). This chapter will focus on algorithms which discover rules and patterns by analyzing a set of examples available as records in databases. This style of learning is called rule generation, or more generally, information discovery.

A variety of programs that aim to "learn" were developed in the early days of artificial intelligence, with one of the successes being a program that learned how to play checkers (Samuel 1963). These programs were mostly what are called "parameter adjustment" programs. They would begin with a predetermined structure for performing a task, (e.g., playing backgammon), and perform repeated experiments on different games until the "best" set of parameters were arrived at, just as neural nets do. As an example of parameter adjustment, consider the equation:

$$\text{Move-Value} = A * (\text{Number of empty neighbors}) + B * (\text{Number of opposing pieces in neighboring squares})$$

which measures the value of a cell in a game in the checker family. The goal of parameter adjustment here is to find the best values for A and B to produce a winning game program. However, the developer must invent the equation first, then perform tests to train the program to set the best values. As we will see, this approach is very similar to the methods used in neural nets.

These early learning programs were characterized by two features: First, they worked on an existing large database, but constructed their samples for learning on the fly. Second, they did not produce explicit rules of knowledge, instead they adjusted the parameters in an equation.

Although Samuel's checkers program succeeded, it was not on an evolutionary path towards learning machines. Another approach to discovery was independently started by Earl Hunt, a psychologist who was thinking about the problem of discrimination and classification. Hunt, who moved to the University of Washington from UCLA, developed the CLS algorithm there in 1966 to generate a decision tree by repeatedly separating a set of examples into smaller subsets, characterized by the values of attributes for each example. Ross Quinlan, who was also at the University of Washington, extended the divide and conquer strategy used in CLS, which eventually evolved into the ID3 (Iterative Dichotomizing 3rd) algorithm (Quinlan 1979). Quinlan's work then influenced Donald Michie's work at Edinburgh University and led to the development of a number of early ID3-based programs (Michie 1984).

The ID3 group of algorithms were the first set of programs to begin to analyze large data sets to find explicit patterns expressed as decision trees. One of the early successes of the ID3 approach was the generation of a decision tree for a specific chess end game, involving tactics previously unknown to any chess master (Quinlan 1983). So, although ID3 would easily go astray and generate monstrous decision trees that made little sense (Michie 1984), it proved the point that a program can by itself extend current human knowledge. This was just the beginning of many discoveries to come in the field.

Another early start was made by Michalski's group at the University of Illinois. His work focused on conceptual clustering, but generated explicit rules. Michalski's family of programs were called AQ, with AQ/11 being the best known (Michalski 1986). These algorithms were used in a number of systems, including one for soybean pathology. These programs generated more general rules than ID3, but they went astray more easily as the database size increased. On small sets AQ family programs generate many rules. As the database grows, the programs become overwhelmed very quickly due to exponential growth problems.

Thus although the AQ algorithms appear to be much more powerful than ID3 in generalization power, the main problem with using the unguided AQ algorithm on large databases is that far too many generalizations are produced. More recent versions of the AQ algorithms include some basic methods of limiting generalizations, but given a large database the heuristics may go astray since the induction method has no "knowledge" of the induction domain.

Another independent effort under way in the late 1970s and early 1980s involved the RX and Radix projects at Stanford University (Blum 1982, 1986). These were good examples of pioneering work in distilling information from large databases (Parsaye et al. 1989, p. 410). RX relied on statistical techniques for determining correlations between time-oriented events recorded in the American Rheumatism

Association database. RX's Discovery Module used lagged correlations to generate a set of tentative relationships. The Study Module then used a knowledge of medicine and statistics to create a study design which was then executed by a conventional statistical package. The RX approach is distinguished by the fact that it deals with a large database and combines statistical observations with model analysis. This approach has shown its viability in dealing with the effects of the steroid drug prednisone (Blum 1986).

The work of Brian Gaines and Mildred Shaw was carried out independently of other induction efforts and was influenced by psychological issues relating to inexactness. The ENTAIL system (Gaines and Shaw 1986) produces inexact measure based either on fuzzy minimum/maximum measures (Zadeh 1965) or distance measures. This approach was not designed for application to large databases, but is suitable for inducing relationships between sets of items represented with inexact values.

Automatic Interaction Detection (Sonquist and Morgan 1969) is a technique that resembles ID3 in some respects. It builds a tree by splitting off branches according to the values or range on predictor variables that best differentiate values on a criterion (goal) variable. Chi-squared automatic interaction detector (CHAID) is a variant of Automatic Interaction Detection that overcame some of its shortcomings and inflexibility. Classification And Regression Tree (CART) can be combined with CHAID to provide increased flexibility. CART procedures search for ranges in which the dependent variable does not vary significantly on the predictor variable. These calculations can become quite complex because of the matching of continuous predictor and criterion variables. Thus CHAID and CART tend to get too slow as the size of the database increases. This has generally restricted their use to the domain of discovery in marketing.

Yet another group working on induction and learning was influenced by biological factors. Genetic algorithms were first invented by John Holland in the 1970s (Holland 1975) to mimic some features of natural evolution (Davis 1991). These algorithms rely on the assumption that generalization from poor examples to better knowledge can be performed by modifying values within example records, just as mutation may modify genetic code in natural evolution. Thus genetic algorithms use mutation and crossover to create children that differ from their parents. Genetic algorithms manipulate fragments of information (schemata) that serve as the building blocks of good solutions. These schemata are combined through crossover (the equivalent of biological mating and reproduction) and they then spread in the population according to the relative fitness of the "chromosomes" that they contain.

There are many different genetic algorithms that can be constructed using these basic principles. For instance, different algorithms may use a different method of selecting parents for creating the next generation of chromosomes in the population. One method of selecting parents is referred to as the roulette method. The roulette method is equivalent to allocating pie-shaped slices on a roulette wheel to chromosomes (members of the population) with the size of the slice allocated to each chromosome being proportional to the fitness of that chromosome. Once this roulette wheel is spun, the probability that a chromosome will be chosen as a parent will then be proportional to its fitness (in somewhat similar fashion to the fact that the probability that a mature salmon will successfully return to its spawning ground will depend on its fitness).

Neural networks are another discovery technique of relatively recent origin. Neural nets had earlier precursors in the neural modeling of Hebb (1949) and McCullough and Pitts (1943). Computer simulation of neural networks of one type or another began in the 1950s. Neural nets received a major setback in 1969 when Minsky and Papert published their book on perceptrons, demonstrating problems with early approaches to neural nets. However, a hardy group of researchers continued to develop new types of neural nets in the 1970s, and their efforts led to a comeback for neural nets in the late 1980s.

There have been numerous examples of learning systems based on the neural modeling approach including Perceptron (Rosenblatt 1959), Pandemonium (Selfridge 1959), and connection machines (Hinton, Sejnowski, and Ackley 1984). Neural modeling tends to use manipulation of numerical parameters to achieve learning.

While most neural nets up to 1990 were research systems, there were a few applications that demonstrated the promise of the neural net approach (Nelson and Illingworth 1991, Chapter 1). These applications included adaptive noise canceling in telephones, a filtering technique that was developed in the 1950s and that is still used in today's telephones.

Once we go beyond the main building blocks that are shared by all neural net paradigms we become immersed in details of particular paradigms such as Perceptron, ADALINE/MADALINE, Brain-State-in-a-Box, Hopfield Networks, Back Propagation, and Self-Organizing Maps. There are in fact many neural modeling paradigms available. Given the state of neural net research it is still too early to say which paradigm or paradigms will eventually dominate. In time, the neural network field will stabilize and become part of the computer industry.

Induction on eXtremely Large databases (IXL), the first commercial induction tool for large databases, was released in 1987 by IntelligenceWare. Its development was influenced by mathematical considerations, as well as statistical issues. With the introduction of IXL, which has since evolved into the Information Discovery System (IDIS) system, discovery became a serious tool for industry. Rule generation and induction can be carried out routinely on large databases. IDIS is an industrial reality, rather than a research project. What distinguishes IDIS is that:

- It works effectively on very large databases (say 100,000,000 records).
- It routinely finds more powerful rules more efficiently than systems based on other methods.
- It uniformly combines discovery with anomaly detection and visualization within a hyperdata user interface.

IXL and IDIS have found more rules in more databases for more people in more application areas than any discovery program in history. They are now routinely used in major organizations as a means of gaining competitive advantage. They can complement and extend statistical approaches rather than competing with them. As an example of this, see Section 4.6.1, where the difference between IDIS's value-based analysis and the trend-based approaches of statistics become apparent. The discussion in Section 4.6.2 also shows why IDIS does better than neural nets that have to rely on sampling of data sets. Section 4.3.3 provides various case studies of IDIS, ranging from U.S. imports and chemical analysis to finance.

The technology of exploratory data analysis and discovery has now matured to industrial use. The next sections discuss this technology in more detail.

### 4.2.3  The Modern Age of Discovery

In the fifteenth century, Prince Henry of Portugal became known as Prince Henry the Navigator because of the exploits of his sailors in charting the oceans. During a period of about 100 years, the major landmasses of the world (with the exception of Australia and Antarctica) were charted and an age of conquest and colonization followed (led by Portugal and Spain, with England and France following in the seventeenth century), which has shaped the political and economic structure of the world ever since.

The age of discovery in the fifteenth and sixteenth centuries had some very powerful motivating goals. To understand, improve, and conquer are goals shared to different degrees by all discovery processes.

Each expedition represented a mixture of goals. The scientists, naturalists, and geographers accompanying the expeditions sought to understand the unknown lands that were visited. The priests and educators sought to improve the indigenous people (often against their will and better interests). The soldiers and adventurers sought to conquer and exploit, with such enthusiasm for gold in particular, that the Incas believed the Europeans ate it.

We tend to forget how ignorant people were about geography prior to the age of discovery. Many thought that Columbus would sail off the edge of the world. Columbus himself had no idea how big the world was. The West Indies are so named because Columbus underestimated the circumference of the earth and thought he had arrived in India. Today's database explorers are often similarly ignorant about the information contained in a large database.

Information interpretation is both a family of techniques and a process for assisting in the transformation of data into interpretations, satisfying the goals of discovery and exploration. Figure 4.2 summarizes this process. The data must first be collected and checked (these early processes are discussed further in Section 4.4 on data quality). Once the data is in good shape one or more of three techniques may be used to assist in its interpretation. These techniques are information discovery, visualization, and data analysis.

The model in Figure 4.2 also has cycles leading from interpretation, information discovery, and so on back to the data collection and checking stages. This is because the interpretation process may indicate flaws in the data that need to be corrected.

Like the explorers in the original age of discovery, explorers in this second age of discovery are motivated by a number of reasons. Information may be interpreted in order to understand, predict, or improve. We shall discuss each of these uses in the following sections.

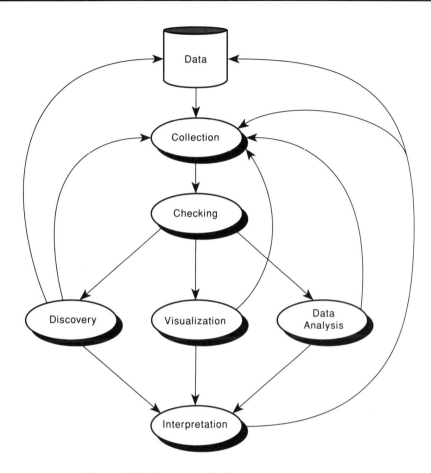

**Figure 4.2** The process of information interpretation.

## 4.2.4 The Three Stages of Discovery

The three stages of information discovery are understanding, improvement, and prediction. Each of these stages is important, although different applications will tend to emphasize different stages of information discovery.

It is extremely difficult to manage or control a process that one doesn't understand. This may be why economists generally find it so difficult to predict or control the performance of a complex economy. Thus understanding is frequently the goal of information discovery and interpretation. Understanding allows us to reduce the knowledge gap between the system as it is and the person's perception or knowledge about the system (Figure 4.3).

There are many forms of understanding. Three types of understanding that are particularly important are differences, trends, and relations.

Market researchers want to know which groups of consumers are "different" from each other (form different segments). Quality analysts want to know if a process has

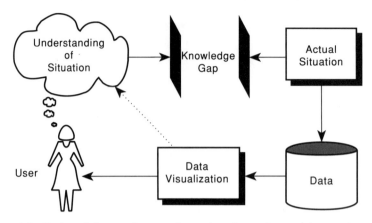

**Figure 4.3** The knowledge gap between the user's understanding and the actual situation.

changed (is different) from its specifications or from the way it was working the previous day. Brokers want to know which stocks have an increasing trend, and which are on the way down. Manufacturers want to know why equipment breaks down and where the bottlenecks in production are. They also want to know the relationship between tool wear and defects in the parts or products they produce.

Understanding is followed by improvement. In the fifteenth century improvement meant correction of behavior in terms of some ideal norm. For the database explorer, improvement means having the power to do things better. It is one of the fundamental assumptions of civilization that things should get better, and recent emphasis on total quality management (Chapter 10) reflects this quest for systematic improvement.

Knowing what causes a defect in a production process, one can modify and improve the process. Knowing more precisely what consumers want can help design better products. This chapter will describe information discovery methods that can be used for improvement. The general approach will be to identify a set of problems or error conditions and then use rule generation (with the error conditions set as goals) to discover when and how errors or problems occur. Anomaly detection may also be used to identify errors or problems that frequently show up as anomalies.

The third goal of the explorers of the sixteenth century was conquest and exploitation. Modern database explorers may not see themselves as conquistadors, but they still want to exploit the knowledge that lies hidden in their data, like a vein of gold buried in rock. They want to know which product will be successful, which stock will rise, or what future glitches are likely to occur in a project.

It is difficult to quantify understanding. Typically, one understands some things but not others. One doesn't know what one doesn't understand until an error is made that shows the extent of the misunderstanding. Prediction is different from understanding because there is a more direct measure of success or failure (i.e., how well the prediction matched reality).

One form of prediction is extrapolation. This involves identifying a trend and then judging from the trend what will happen in the future. Say, for instance, the rate of inflation had increased by 5% for each of the past three years. Judging from this trend we might extrapolate and predict a further 5% increase in inflation in the following year. Linear regression is a statistical technique that fits straight lines to data, using the related idea of interpolation. One can then predict new data points by seeing where they would lie on the fitted (regression) line (Figure 4.4). Obviously this type of prediction can be dangerous if the process is inherently unpredictable or too complex to be fit by a simple model.

Rules can also be used for prediction. A company might find that each time the outside temperature exceeds a certain value some of their computers break down. They might then encapsulate this experience as a rule and predict their next break-down (or take preventive steps to avoid it, such as getting a more powerful air conditioning system).

There will usually be some uncertainty associated with a prediction. A statistical prediction is generally accompanied by a confidence interval (i.e., a range of values in which the predicted value is likely to fall). For instance, pollsters tend to talk about a margin of error when predicting support for a candidate (e.g., 49% support for candidate A with a 3% margin of error). A rule generated during information discovery will also have a margin of error associated with it. Dealing with predictions is complicated by the uncertainty associated with them. Thus it is usually necessary to exercise judgment in deciding what to do in response to a prediction.

## ■ 4.3 AUTOMATIC RULE DISCOVERY

Information discovery is the generation of rules and detection of anomalies based on large amounts of data. Any database, large or small, contains knowledge in the form of relationships and patterns among the records and fields therein. These patterns may or may not be explicitly known to the database user. *Rule discovery* is the process of extracting this knowledge from a database. It is an important component of intelligent databases (Parsaye et al. 1989).

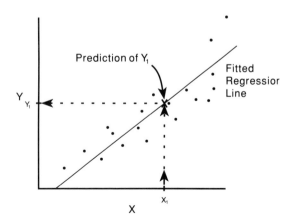

**Figure 4.4** Prediction based on regression. $Y_1$ is the predicted value of Y when $X = X_1$.

Rule discovery involves looking into a large database and discovering rules and knowledge in the form of significant patterns and relationships. For instance, consider a database table with four fields A, B, C, D, and a set of records:

| A | B | C | D |
|---|---|---|---|
| a1 | b1 | c1 | d1 |
| a2 | b3 | c2 | d2 |
| a1 | b1 | c3 | d3 |
| a1 | b1 | c3 | d1 |
| a1 | b1 | c3 | d1 |

In the data shown above, there are four records that have the values a1 and b1 and three of these records also have the value d1. Thus we can capture this relationship in the following rule:

```
Confidence = 75%
If
        A = a1 and
        B = b1
Then
        D = d1
```

This means that 75% of the time, the values a1 and b1 for A and B produce the value d1 for D. Rule discovery analyzes large databases and automatically generates such rules. The information discovered is often unexpected.

Rule generation or discovery begins with the selection of an attribute that serves as the goal (i.e., the conclusion of the rules to be discovered). Rules are then generated that predict different ranges or values of the goal attribute (conclusion) based on combinations of values or ranges on other variables (the premise). Further focusing can be made by selecting a subset of attributes for possible consideration for inclusion in the premise with all other attributes being eliminated from consideration. Alternatively, the method can be completely unfocused by letting rule generation consider all possible attributes as possible conclusions. In practice, this style of unfocused rule generation is not very productive since most applications have relatively few attributes that make useful goal attributes. In addition, this type of exhaustive search through all possible rules in a large database can be extremely expensive computationally.

Rule generation is a relatively autonomous process, once the data is available and goal attributes have been specified. The user may then let rules be generated on the basis of default parameter settings, or may guide rule generation by setting criteria such as how many cases needed to be accounted for by a rule or what proportion of cases that match the premise of a rule should also match the conclusion predicted by the rule for the goal attribute.

Rules provide a detailed summary of the information in a database. They show how different combinations of attribute values and ranges are interrelated. This is different from the general summaries of data that are often made. Summaries tend to be statistical in nature, such as "this attribute has an increasing trend" or "these two attributes are positively related." Summaries often blind people to the important details. A general summary may only scratch the surface of the information available in the database. Using simple summaries of data is like using a bucket to collect oil oozing from the surface of the ground, while rule generation is like drilling a well and extracting a steady stream of oil.

Anomaly detection is the natural follow up to rule generation, as discussed in a later section of this chapter. Anomalies are generally examined as possible outliers that may indicate faulty data or unusual situations. However, a sufficient number of "anomalies" may indicate the need to develop a new rule that will handle special cases.

The combination of rule generation and anomaly detection provides a powerful method of summarizing patterns in data in an interpretable form. However, since rule generation is carried out automatically and without the guidance of "common sense" it will tend to generate useful rules as well as other rules that are best discarded. An important part of rule generation is the selection of the rules by a human analyst who is familiar with the domain of the application.

### 4.3.1 Understanding the Character of a Database

Each database has its own character, reflecting the type of data it contains. The first step in understanding a database is understanding what the tables and fields are and what types of data they contain. In large databases, it is often unclear as to what the fields signify and what type and range of values they contain. For instance, if one has a field such as "Age," one may hazard a reasonable guess about the range of values it contains. However, for a field such as "Complaint," one does not know the number of complaints or the most frequent complaint, etc.

A first-level understanding of the database is essential before proceeding to perform further discovery. Without it, one is proceeding in the dark. An initial understanding of the character of a database is best achieved using interactive graphics. In the information discovery system IDIS (IntelligenceWare 1992) the data characteristics module provides this facility.

In general, the best graphical form(s) to study during data characterization will vary with the database and the intentions of the user. Data characterization is typically an interactive process and it may take several attempts to produce a set of graphics that provide a sufficient characterization. Therefore, one should be familiar with a variety of graphical techniques, including pie charts, bar charts, boxes, surface diagrams, etc., so as to quickly arrive at the best possible representation of your data. (Methods of visualizing data will be further discussed in Chapter 5. A useful set of graph types for data characterization is listed in Table 4.1.)

Each type of graph tends to reveal different characteristics in the data. For instance, a bar chart reveals the actual (and relative) frequencies of each of the values (or ranges) of the field displayed on the x-axis. Characteristics of particular importance are the values that have the largest frequencies (the modal values), the values that have negligible frequencies, and the overall shape of the frequency distribution.

A pie chart is a useful way of showing which values or ranges predominate in a particular field. For instance, a large slice denoting missing values may indicate a problem with data quality.

**Table 4.1 Useful graph types for data characterization**

| Field Types | Fields | Available Graph Types |
|---|---|---|
| Nominal/Ordinal (Non-scalar) | 1 | Pie Chart, Bar Chart |
| Integer, Real, or Date | 1 | Plot, Sorted Plot, Pie Chart, Bar Chart |
| Nominal/Ordinal (Non-scalar) | 2 | Box Plot, 3D Bar Chart |
| Any* except 2 Non-scalars | 2 | Histogram, Box Plot, 3D Bar Chart |
| Nominal/Ordinal (Non-scalar) | 3 | 3D Box Diagram |
| Any* except all Non-scalars | 3 | 3D Bar Diagram, 3D Box Diagram, or Surface Diagram |

*Any* refers to any data type, including String, Integer, Real, and Date.

Plots may be used to display the values of a field across the records in the database. In general, these values should be distributed randomly, so that no pattern is discernible in the plot. If different blocks of records tend to have low or high values, this often says something about the field, and about the way in which the records were collected or entered.

The distribution of values for a field can be seen in histograms (discussed in Chapter 5) or in a sorted (cumulative) plot where the records are ordered by their

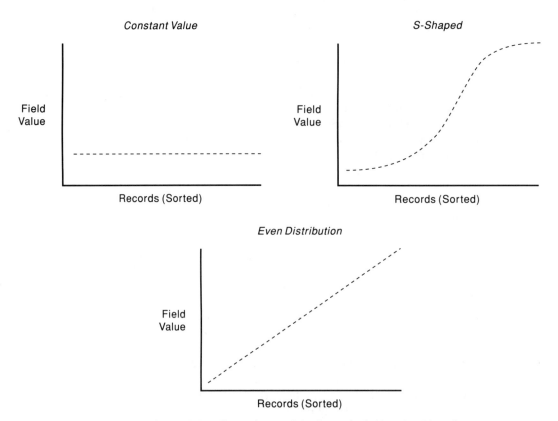

**Figure 4.5** Different shapes of distribution for fields ordered by values.

value. Since such a plot is sorted by the ordinate — that is, the field displayed on the y-axis — it will generally trend upward from left to right. The shape of the plot will help to clarify the nature of the distribution (Figure 4.5). For example, a flat plot indicates that the field values are constant throughout the database. An S-shaped plot indicates that observations tend to cluster at both low and high levels of the field. A plot which creates a 45 degree angle with respect to the x- and y-axes indicates a similar frequency of records at both low and high field values (i.e., uniform distribution).

After getting a general feel for the nature of the data in a database, onc can begin visualization and discovery. However, as Figure 4.6 shows, it is important to have raw (rather than summarized) data, since summarizing data inevitably loses information.

### 4.3.2 Rule Generation from Databases

Throughout the development of database systems, the paradigm for database management generally consists of the following steps:

1. Collect data (e.g., maintain records on clients, products, sales, etc.).
2. Query data (e.g., ask "which products had increasing sales last month?").
3. Try to understand data (e.g., "what makes a product successful?").

When using a query language such as SQL it is necessary to know what to ask about. Ask a relevant question, get an interesting answer. However, often there is so

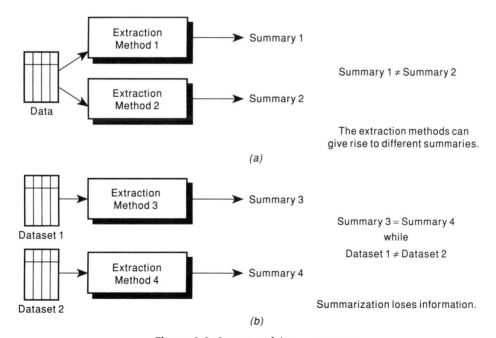

**Figure 4.6** Properties of data summarization.

much data it is not possible to know what the relevant questions are. Information discovery finds the relevant questions by performing an intelligent analysis of the data. Often this points out totally unexpected relationships which may be further pursued with queries.

Rule discovery may be viewed as a layer on top of the database query system. A query language such as SQL can deal with questions like "Which products had increasing sales last month?", but it cannot automatically answer questions like "What makes a product successful?", since we do not know what to ask for in this latter case. All we may have are hypotheses which may be tested with repeated queries. But we need to form the hypothesis, since a querying language like SQL will not form it for us. The answers to questions posed in this more exploratory analysis are often unexpected, and we may not be creative enough to come up with the appropriate hypotheses, or patient enough to work through the many different possibilities.

Using querying alone to explore a database is tedious, as is shown in the steps that a "human analyst" who is well versed in statistics and query languages might take:

- Form a hypothesis.
- Make some queries and run a statistics program.
- View the results and perhaps modify the hypothesis.
- Continue this cycle until a pattern emerges.

These are exactly the steps taken by information discovery algorithms automatically. The human analyst would have to perform these tasks himself, again and again. But, as we know, there will never be enough statisticians to analyze all of the world's databases.

In essence, rule discovery has a closed loop architecture with respect to hypothesis formation and analysis. It continues to query the database and performs statistics and induction until knowledge is discovered. Statistics programs, on the other hand, have an open loop architecture for their operation—that is, a human analyst has to close the thinking loop.

Information discovery can be guided by setting hypotheses. Say we are interested in knowing the situations in which car transmission failures tend to occur. We do this by describing the hypothesis as the conclusion that is to be fired by relevant rules. For instance, in the example shown below, we are really asking the question "What conditions produce or are associated with faulty transmissions?"

*PROBLEM = Transmission*
*If*

‾‾‾‾‾‾‾‾

*and*

‾‾‾‾‾‾‾‾

*and*

. . .

This hypothesis (goal) is indicated by entering "PROBLEM = Transmission" to the information discovery system. In this case the user is asking the rule generation system to predict which cars will have faulty transmissions. This type of rule generation from a hypothesis is very different from a query, since the information discovery process will find the relevant *fields* and *attributes* for the user, not just records. In a query, on the other hand, the user needs to know which fields to ask about.

Rule discovery also allows the user to specify which attributes are of more interest (i.e., how the user would prefer to have the blanks in the above rule filled in) by specifying levels of interest for each of the fields—for example, the user might be most interested in the relationship between faulty parts and the plants in which the parts were made.

Experience has shown that rule discovery can often turn up unanticipated, useful rules (patterns within the data). In an automobile example, the rule discovery system might be told to operate on the combined database of dealer locations and dealership account information, and to search for rules that predict which dealers generally have a large number of complaints. It might then discover that 90% of the "new" dealers in some state had a large number of complaints.

Thus rule discovery is generally far more practical than querying for discovering information. However, the model of intelligent database application described in this book also allows users to execute their own queries directly on the data should they wish to do this (e.g., by using the iconic querying method described in Chapter 3).

The general process of rule discovery will now be described, followed by some of the steps that need to be taken in rule generation (defining goals, setting interest levels, setting discovery parameters), and how the results of rule discovery are interpreted.

### 4.3.2.1 *Rule Discovery*    Rule generation from databases can be carried out with a program such as IDIS. The way IDIS works is shown schematically in Figure 4.7. A goal attribute (variable) is defined and then relationships between different values or ranges of the goal attribute and corresponding ranges and values of other attributes are found. The process by which rules are generated involves the use of search in a space defined by the various combinations of attribute values and ranges that exist across the different records in the database. This search is guided by principles for assessing the significance of different splits in the data.

The process of rule discovery from a database consists of choosing one variable as a conclusion and then seeing which combinations of other variables in the database can predict particular values or ranges in the conclusion variable.

Consider a simple example: Global Motors Corporation makes and sells about one million automobiles yearly through a network of several thousand dealers. Parts for these automobiles are manufactured at a number of company plants and by outside suppliers. They are then assembled at various locations, and the finished products are shipped to thousands of dealers by a number of trucking firms. In addition, imagine that Global Motors is plagued by a major problem: Customers are returning a high number of faulty cars. Unfortunately, Global Motors' far-reaching operations make it impossible for any one human analyst to understand all of this data. By using rule discovery, however, the company can discover valuable knowledge hidden in their databases. For example, rule discovery may reveal that:

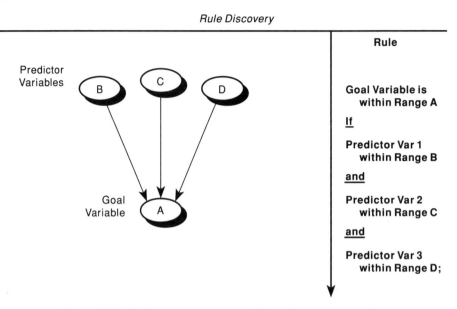

*Rule Discovery*

**Figure 4.7** A schematic representation of how rule generation works.

- Cars sold by dealers in California during January are very often returned with battery problems.
- Large cars shipped to New Jersey by truckers A, B, and C are often returned with scratches.
- Cars with transmissions made at the Cincinnati plant during the spring of 1991 are being returned.
- Cars with transmissions made at the Cincinnati plant and drive shafts made at the Decatur plant are having many problems.

These rules help the quality of Global Motors' overall operation. To maintain quality, the process of rule discovery should be ongoing, as discussed in Chapter 11.

As mentioned earlier, rule generation may be conceptually viewed as a search process, as shown in Figure 4.8. The user may be interested in rules that apply to a large number of cases, or may be interested in some rules that apply to only a few cases. The basic issue may be conceptually represented by the following equation:

$$\text{Rule Discovery} = \text{Generation} + \text{Filtering}$$

The goal controls the generation component, while the parameters control the filtering. Next, the setting of goals is discussed.

**4.3.2.2** *Defining Goals and Interest Levels*    In most situations it will be appropriate to specify a set of goal attributes before carrying out rule generation. For instance, a user may only wish to analyze the Global Motors data with respect to faulty transmissions, and may

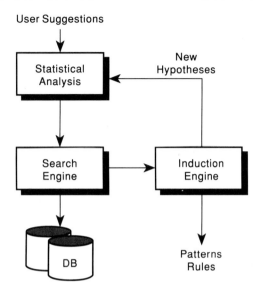

**Figure 4.8** The process of rule generation.

not be interested in other data such as faulty tires, etc. In that case the following goal might be specified: "PROBLEM = Transmission". The user might also want to see rules which predict what models of cars get returned and why. This could be done by specifying as an additional goal: "MODEL = any". In general, there is a trade-off between setting goals that focus the discovery system to find particularly relevant knowledge and minimizing the number of goals (constraints) so that the discovery system can find totally unexpected information.

Exhaustive search can be a computationally expensive process. It can also be time consuming, and many realistic situations require discovery to be carried out under time pressure. In addition, the user might want to focus or limit the number of rules generated to prevent having to wade through uninteresting rules in order to find those that are of genuine interest.

In addition to specifying goals to be analyzed, the user can further focus discovery by setting interest levels on the various attributes. For instance, suppose the discovery system is asked to analyze the goal "PROBLEM = Transmission". There may be many criteria available in the database (e.g., the telephone numbers of the dealers), but the effects produced on the goal by the fields MANUFACTURER and MANUFAC_DATE are of particular interest. Interest levels may be set high on these fields to bias the rule generation process to focus on what the user is interested in.

For instance, suppose that for the goal PROBLEM = Transmission, the following levels of interest are set:

| | |
|---|---|
| *MANUFACTURER* | *80* |
| *PART_NO* | *10* |
| *MANUFAC_DATE* | *50* |
| *DEALER* | *0* |

These values mean that we are very interested in the effect that the field MANU-FACTURER has on the goal, but not very interested in the effect of PART_NO. Conversely, while we are moderately interested in the date the part was manufactured, we have no interest in the dealer.

For example, when analyzing faulty brakes, Global Motors might want to specify that the dealer's location is almost irrelevant to any other data in the database, and therefore give that an interest rating of 10. On the other hand, the experience level of the dealers and the failure rate of parts are both very interesting and relevant fields which should receive a level of interest of 100.

Simply stated, the higher the interest rating of a field, the more the discovery system will prefer to have that field involved in the premise of a rule. However, interest levels, like goal settings, act to constrain the discovery process. So there is also a trade-off between finding unexpected information and focusing on particular fields in discovering rules.

**4.3.2.3 *Setting Discovery Parameters*** The rule discovery process can be tailored by using a number of parameters. For instance, the IDIS information discovery system has parameters which tailor its performance to user needs. Users might not want to see rules that exceed a certain length (their reasoning might be that overly long rules describe only special cases anyway). Similarly, they may want to concentrate only on those rules that have at least 90% confidence.

The margin of error for a rule may be influenced by the number of records involved in a rule. For instance, if only 10 records were involved in forming the rule, then the margin of error might be close to 50%, due to the fact that not enough data had been available for judgment.

The maximum number of clauses in rules parameter limits the number of clauses that may appear in the premise of a discovered rule. The lower this number, the fewer the rules generated and the quicker the discovery process is. One justification for limiting the number of clauses is that rules with large numbers of clauses will tend to represent relatively small numbers of cases.

A record is said to match a rule if it satisfies all the clauses in the premise of the rule. The confidence in the rule is then the number of matching records that actually have the same value or range for the goal attribute as appears in the conclusion of the rule. So, if there are 100 matching records, and 80 of those records have the same value of the goal attribute as appears in the rule conclusion, then the confidence is 80%.

This confidence level really means: If everything stays the same as it was when the data in the discovery sample was collected, then this rule should work 80% of the time in predicting the value of the goal attribute in future cases. In many cases, this estimate might be either pessimistic or optimistic, because of chance variation in the sample.

The maximum margin of error concerns the range over which the true value of the confidence level actually lies. From the viewpoint of statistics, the margin of error corresponds to what is known as a confidence interval. Thus if the confidence level of a rule is 85%, then we may still want to know whether it is possible that the rule might really only be about 70% accurate once we discount effects of chance variation.

In this case, if the margin of error was 15%, then it is possible that the real confidence level is only 70% or so, whereas if the margin of error was 5%, this would be much less likely.

### 4.3.3 Rule Discovery Works

Rule discovery is the process of looking into a large database and discovering knowledge in the form of significant patterns and relationships. With discovery, the user may influence what the discovery system searches for, or may let it roam through a large database at will. The user need not know statistics or a query language. The system discovers the important queries to ask, executes them itself, and shows the key factors which shape the data.

Rules constitute the language by which knowledge in a database is expressed. Rules use the language of *logic* which involves *if . . . then* statements as opposed to the language of statistics which uses polynomial equations. Discovery works well because:

1. It finds unexpected information.
2. It does more than statistics.
3. It is usable by nonexperts.

Discovery helps people make better decisions faster and more economically. For instance, The US Army and Air Force Exchange, a large retailer, uses discovery with IXL/IDIS to determine sales patterns based on the demographics of their customers. Knowing how much their customers spend annually on different items helped the exchange target its advertising and sales toward the appropriate customer base. Before using discovery, the retailer paid a consultant $30,000 to do all the demographic analyses manually with statistics. This usually took two to three weeks to accomplish. Now, with rule discovery, Mr. David Barnhard of the exchange performs the same analyses in a matter of days.

This section describes some other rule discovery case studies. The results reported are based on actual experience with the programs *IXL* (Induction on eXtremely Large databases) and its successor, *IDIS* (The Information Discovery System). The programs have made significant discoveries in a number of fields, ranging across sales forecasting, crystal catalyst design, forest fire prevention, financial analysis, and medical research, among others. To illustrate the wide range of applicability of rule discovery, following are six case studies, on various topics ranging from imports analysis, to oil exploration, to finance, science, and medicine. These applications were chosen to include both hard data areas such as the number of electrons in various orbits in elements or oil well acidity levels to soft data areas such as the mental state and the heart rate of U.S. gymnasts during training. These examples show that in practice rule discovery works in a really wide range of areas, wider, in fact, than most of us imagine.

#### 4.3.3.1 *Information Discovery on U.S. Import Data*    Analysis of the balance of trade and the size and composition of imports and exports is important in showing shifting trends in trade, productivity, and aggregate consumer preference. Customs data may also be

used to show where imports arrive and how they are handled. This type of import data is voluminous. This case study shows how information discovery may be applied to a large data set.

The U.S. imports database consisted of approximately 10 million records, and the overall size of the database was about five gigabytes. Table 4.2 shows the database field definitions. Information discovery in this case was carried out by IXL on an IBM PC connected to a Teradata database engine storing the five gigabyte database. Some of the discovered rules are shown below:

*Rule 3*
*CF = 100*
        *"IMPORT_TYPE" = "1"*
*If*
        *"IMPORT_YEAR" = "89"*
*% Applicable percentage of sample: 30 %*


*Rule 11*
*CF = 97.89*
        *"DE" = "23"*
*If*
        *"DU" = "23"*
*% Applicable percentage of sample: 1 %*


*Rule 41*
*CF = 70.99*
        *"IMPORT_YEAR" = "90"*
*If*
        *"DE" = "05"*
*And*
        *"DU" = "31"*
*% Applicable percentage of sample: 0.0036%*


Rule 3 states that most imports during 1989 were of import type "1." This was not true of the other years, indicating the variation in import types. Rule 11 shows that for district 23, the district of entry and unloading tended to be the same. However, the counter examples for the rule (i.e., the almost 2% excluded) were very interesting. Similar rules were generated for other districts, suggesting a generally high correlation between the district of entry and the district of unloading, and the counter examples.

However, rule 41 shows a change in the relationship between DU and DE for one of the districts in 1990. This rule says that in 1990 a pattern was observed in which the district of entry was "05" and the district of unloading was "31." This pattern was new in 1990, and the analyst wanted to investigate why this new relationship between the two districts had suddenly occurred. Analysis of a large database points out facts that would otherwise go totally unnoticed.

**4.3.3.2** *Information Discovery in the Oil Industry*    This case study demonstrates the use of rule generation using data obtained from standard geological and geophysical information

**Table 4.2  Database field definitions for the USA imports database**

| # | Field Name | Field Type |
|---|---|---|
| 1 | IMPORT_YEAR | CHAR (2) |
| 2 | TSUSA | CHAR (10) |
| 3 | SIC | INTEGER |
| 4 | SITC | INTEGER |
| 5 | SIC_3 | INTEGER |
| 6 | COUNTRY | SMALLINT |
| 7 | CSC | CHAR(1) |
| 8 | DE | CHAR(2) |
| 9 | DU | CHAR(2) |
| 10 | IMPORT_TYPE | CHAR(1) |
| 11 | MONTH | CHAR(2) |
| 12 | CONSUMPTION_QUANTITY_0 | DECIMAL(13,0) |
| 13 | CONSUMPTION_CUSTOMS_VALUE | DECIMAL(13,0) |
| 14 | VESSEL_CUSTOMS_VALUE | DECIMAL(13,0) |
| 15 | VESSEL_SHIPPING_WEIGHT | DECIMAL(13,0) |
| 16 | AIR_CUSTOMS_VALUE | DECIMAL(13,0) |
| 17 | AIR_SHIPPING_WEIGHT | DECIMAL(13,0) |
| 18 | CONSUMPTION_CIF_VALUE | DECIMAL(13,0) |
| 19 | CONSUMPTION_QUANTITY_2 | DECIMAL(13,0) |
| 20 | DUTIABLE_VALUE | DECIMAL(13,0) |
| 21 | CALCULATED_DUTY | DECIMAL(13,0) |
| 22 | RECORD_COUNT | DECIMAL(13,0) |

about a sample of Texas oil wells. The source of this data was a survey publication from the Texas Railroad Commission. The objective in exploring this database was to determine the geophysical characteristics associated with oil field productivity levels.

Table 4.3 shows a set of sample records from the database. The definitions of each of the fields in the table are as follows:

1. Discovery year (e.g., 42 = 1942)
2. End of primary production (e.g., 53 = 1953)
3. Depth, in feet
4. Area, in acres
5. Pay thickness, in feet
6. Porosity, in percentages
7. Permeability, in millidarcies
8. Gravity, in API units
9. Pressure, in pounds per square inch
10. Primary oil production, in barrels
11. Secondary oil production, in barrels

**Table 4.3 Sample records from the Texas oil field database**

| Field | Record 1 | Record 2 | Record 3 | Record 4... | Record 353 |
|---|---|---|---|---|---|
| Year | 40 | 53 | 49 | 60 | 30 |
| End | 66 | 61 | 74 | 69 | 66 |
| Depth | 5200 | 5100 | 5502 | 2250 | 4400 |
| Area | 1100 | 360 | 467 | 960 | 20408 |
| Thickness | 22 | 165 | 10 | 13 | 92 |
| Porosity | 15.5 | 23 | 14.9 | 12.9 | 9.1 |
| Permeability | 700 | 4 | 195 | 10 | 5 |
| Gravity | 43 | 0 | 43 | 39 | 34 |
| Pressure | 2421 | 2550 | 2385 | 1200 | 1800 |
| Primary Production | 4204 | 3144 | 4485 | 497 | 106490 |
| Secondary Production | 1058 | 3076 | 17 | 260 | 77889 |
| Total Production | 5262 | 6220 | 4502 | 757 | 184379 |
| BAY | 147.0 | 1091.7 | 384.2 | 57.5 | 144.9 |
| BAFY | 6.68 | 6.62 | 38.42 | 4.42 | 1.58 |
| Productivity | AVERAGE | AVERAGE | LOW | VERY LOW | VERY HIGH |

**12.** Total oil production, in barrels

**13.** Barrels per acre per year (BAY)

**14.** Barrels per acre-foot per year (BAFY), or production

**15.** Productivity, a concept variable consisting of five ranges of production (Very Low, Low, Medium, High, and Very High)

The sample used for knowledge discovery consisted of all 353 records in the database. The goals used for rule generation were:

- Productivity = Very Low
- Productivity = High
- Productivity = Very High

No rules were found for Productivity = Very High, but some meaningful results were obtained for the other two goals, as revealed below:

```
Rule 2
CF = 100
     "Productivity" = "High"
If
     "10" <= "Pay Thickness" <= "14" and
     "64.38" <= "Barrels/Acre/Year" <= "89.3"
% Margin of Error 10.0 %
% Applicable percentage of sample 1.4 %
```

*Rule 10*
*CF = 100*
  *"Productivity" = "Very Low"*
*If*

  *"34" <= "Discovery Year" <= "35" and*
  *"36" <= "Gravity" <= "37" and*
  *"0" <= "Production" <= "0.14"*
*% Margin of Error 10.0 %*
*% Applicable percentage of sample 1.4 %*


*Rule 19*
*CF = 100*
  *"Productivity" = "Very Low"*
*If*

  *"0" <= "Prime Product" <= "12" and*
  *"0" <= "Barrels/Acre/Year" <= "1.74"*
*% Margin of Error 8.3 %*
*% Applicable percentage of sample 1.7 %*

According to rule 2 above, if pay thickness is between 10 and 14, and barrels per acre per year are between 64.38 and 89.3, then a high productivity level can be expected. In this example, the yield or productivity of an oil field in barrels per acre-foot per year served as the goal attribute in the rule generation. The information provided by the induced rules could then be used to predict and improve annual yields and oil well productivity.

The second case study used data provided by James Brown, an oil industry consultant in Houston, Texas. The original raw data was obtained from the U.S. Department of Energy. The DOE database was predominantly quantitative—that is, it was composed of real and integer values. That data (sample records are shown in Table 4.4) was transformed into descriptive labels such as Sweet, Sour, Deep, and Hi Grav, so that the rules produced during knowledge discovery could be more easily interpreted.

The goal in analyzing this data was to develop a set of objective criteria for predicting whether a prospective site is likely to produce oil, and the quality of oil that can be expected. The database attribute definitions for the data shown in Table 4.4 are as follows:

1. State (LA = Louisiana, MS = Mississippi, OK = Oklahoma, TX = Texas)
2. Age of production (Miocene, Cretaceous, Ordovician, Pennsylvanian, etc.)
3. Depth of oil production (Shallow, Mid, or Deep)
4. Gravity of oil (Lo Grav, Mid, or Hi Grav)
5. Color of oil (Dgreen = dark green, Brngreen = Brownish Green, Grnshbrn = Greenish Brown, etc.)
6. Sulfur content of oil (Sweet = low, Int = intermediate, Sour = high)
7. Viscosity of oil (Lo Visc, Mid, or Hi Visc)
8. Gasoline concentration (Gas Lo, Mid, or Gas Hi)

**Table 4.4 Sample records from a second Texas oil example**

| State | Age | Depth | Gray | Color | Sulfur | Visc | Gas | Resid | Arom/ Paraf |
|-------|-----|-------|------|-------|--------|------|-----|-------|-------------|
| LA | MIO | MID | HI | DGREEN | SWEET | LO | LO | LO | MIX |
| LA | MIO | DEEP | MID | BRNGREEN | SWEET | LO | LO | MID | MIX |
| … | … | … | … | … … … … | … | … | … | … | … |
| MS | CRE | DEEP | HI | GRNSHBRN | INT | LO | LO | MID | PARA |
| OK | ORD | DEEP | HI | DGREEN | SWEET | LO | MID | MID | MIX |
| OK | PEN | DEEP | HI | GREEN | SWEET | LO | LO | MID | MIX |

9. Residuum, or residue (Loresid, Mid, or Hiresid)
10. Aromatic/Paraffinic, or ratio of aromatic to paraffinic content (Para, Mix, or Arom)

A sample of 100 records from the database were run using high gasoline concentration (Gas Lo and Mid) as the goals. Some of the rules that were generated are shown below:

*Rule 102*
*CF = 100*
   *"Gasoline" = "Gas Lo"*
*If*
   *"Depth" = "Shallow" and*
   *"Gravity" = "Lo Grav" and*
   *"Color" = "Brnshblck" and*
   *"Sulfur" = "Sour" and*
   *"Viscosity" = "Mid"*
*% Margin of Error 8.3 %*
*% Applicable percentage of sample 6.0 %*

*Rule 168*
*CF = 82*
   *"Gasoline" = "Gas Lo"*
*If*
   *"Gravity" = "Mid"*
*% Margin of Error 14.7 %*
*% Applicable percentage of sample 33.0 %*

*Rule 239*
*CF = 90*
   *"Gasoline" = "Mid"*
*If*
   *"State" = "TX " and*
   *"Sulfur" = "Sweet" and*
   *"Viscosity" = "Lo Visc" and*
   *"Residuum" = "Mid" and*
   *"Aromat/Paraffin" = "Mix"*
*% Margin of Error 23.6 %*
*% Applicable percentage of sample 10.0 %*

Rule 239 reveals that if an oil well is located in the state of Texas, the sulfurosity is sweet, the viscosity is low, the amount of residuum is moderate, and there is a balanced mix of aromatic hydrocarbons and paraffin, then we can expect with 90% certainty (plus or minus 23.6%) that the its oil will have a moderate concentration of gasoline. Within the database, there were 10 wells which conformed to all of the premises of the rule (i.e., "State" = "TX", "Sulfur" = "Sweet", etc.), nine of which also fulfilled the conclusion or goal (i.e., a moderate concentration of gasoline, or "Gasoline" = "Mid").

**4.3.3.3** *Information Discovery in Chemistry*    When a database contains a large number of attributes, it is often difficult to discern all of the significant relationships among the attributes. In such circumstances, rule generation can be particularly useful, since it is able to detect subtle interrelationships among any number of fields. This case study demonstrates the value of rule generation in uncovering significant interactions among a set of attributes.

Eltron Research, a biochemical research organization, provided the database used in this case study. This database contains the chemical and physical characteristics of metallic elements, such as gold, molybdenum, platinum, and vanadium. The objective of rule discovery by Dr. Ronald Cook was to discover patterns of relationships among the various physical and chemical qualities of the elements, especially with respect to catalytic properties and crystal structures. Table 4.5 shows a sample of the records used in this analysis, while Table 4.6 shows the corresponding database field definitions.

**Table 4.5 Sample data records for the chemistry discovery example**

| Field | | | | |
|---|---|---|---|---|
| METAL | aluminum | chromium | titanium | palladium |
| RADII | 125 | 0 | 132 | 128 |
| ENC | 4.07 | 5.13 | 4.82 | 7.84 |
| MP | 933 | 2130 | 1933 | 1825 |
| H_FUSION | 10.67 | 15.30 | 20.90 | 17.20 |
| HEAT_CAP | 24.35 | 23.35 | 25.00 | 26.00 |
| DENSITY | 2698 | 7190 | 4540 | 12020 |
| THRML_CON | 237 | 93 | 22 | 72 |
| RESISTVY | 2.65 | 12.70 | 42.00 | 10.80 |
| MAG_SUSCP | 0.770 | 44.500 | 40.100 | 6.700 |
| MOL_VOL | 10.00 | 7.23 | 10.55 | 8.85 |
| LATTICE | fcc | bcc | 0 | fcc |
| LAT_CONST | 405 | 288 | 0 | 389 |
| ATM_NUMBR | 13 | 24 | 22 | 46 |
| S_LEVEL | 3 | 4 | 4 | 0 |
| NUM_S_ELEC | 2 | 1 | 2 | 0 |
| P_LEVEL | 3 | 0 | 0 | 0 |
| NUM_P_ELEC | 1 | 0 | 0 | 0 |
| D_LEVEL | 0 | 3 | 3 | 4 |
| NUM_D_ELEC | 0 | 5 | 2 | 10 |
| EA | 44 | 94 | -2 | 98 |

**Table 4.5 *(Continued)***

| Field | | | | |
|---|---|---|---|---|
| IP1 | 577 | 653 | 658 | 805 |
| IP2 | 1816 | 1592 | 1310 | 1875 |
| IP3 | 2745 | 2987 | 2652 | 3177 |
| EXCG_CURR | 0.0 | -6.4 | -6.9 | -2.4 |
| W_FUNC | 4.20 | 4.40 | 4.10 | 5.00 |
| D_PERCENT | 0 | 39 | 27 | 46 |
| RECOMB | 0.4 | 64.0 | 40.0 | 80.0 |
| CH4_FE | 0.01200 | 0.74000 | 0.00001 | 0.08300 |
| CH4VJ | L | M | LL | L |
| CO_FE | 0.00001 | 0.49000 | 13.50000 | 11.60000 |
| COVJ | LL | L | HM | HM |
| C2H4_FE | 0.00022 | 0.05000 | 0.00001 | 0.01100 |
| C2H4VJ | LL | M | LL | M |
| C2H6_FE | 0.0040 | 0.18000 | 0.00000 | 0.01400 |
| C2H6VJ | LL | M | 0 | HL |
| HCOOH_FE | 0.78000 | 0.15000 | 5.20000 | 16.10000 |
| HCOOHVJ | LL | LL | L | M |
| H2_FE | 95.70000 | 92.20000 | 69.40000 | 73.30000 |
| H2VJ | H | HM | HL | HL |

**Table 4.6 Data field descriptions for the chemistry example**

| **METAL** | **Name of the element** |
|---|---|
| RADII | Distance between adjacent atoms |
| ENC | Energy of crystal lattice |
| MP | Melting point |
| H_FUSION | Heat of fusion |
| HEAT_CAP | Heat of catalytic reaction |
| DENSITY | Relative to water (density = 1.0) |
| THRML_CON | Thermalconductivity |
| RESISTVY | Resistivity |
| MAG_SUSCP | Magnetic susceptibility |
| MOL_VOL | Molecular volume |
| LATTICE | Lattice structure type |
| LAT_CONST | Lattice constant |
| ATM_NUMBR | Atomic number |
| S_LEVEL | Level of outer S electrons |
| NUM_S_ELEC | Number of outer S electrons |
| P_LEVEL | Level of outer P electrons |
| NUM_P_ELEC | Number of outer P electrons |
| D_LEVEL | Level of outer D electrons |
| NUM_D_ELEC | Number of outer D electrons |
| EA | Activation energy |

**Table 4.6 (Continued)**

| METAL | Name of the element |
|---|---|
| IP1 | Ionic potential energy, outermost eletron |
| IP2 | Ionic potential energy, penultimate electron |
| IP3 | Ionic potential energy, antepenultimate electron |
| EXCG_CURR | Amperage of exchanged current |
| W_FUNC | Work function |
| D_Percent | Diamagnetic shielding factor |
| RECOMB | Propensity toward crystalline recombination |
| CH4_FE | Catalytic reactivity with methane, relative to iron |
| CH4VJ | Catalytic value in methane |
| CO_FE | Catalytic reactivity with carbon dioxide, relative to iron |
| COVJ | Catalytic value in carbon dioxide |
| C2H4_FE | Catalytic reactivity with propylene, relative to iron |
| C2H4VJ | Catalytic value in propylene |
| C2H6_FE | Catalytic reactivity with ethane, relative to iron |
| C2H6VJ | Catalytic value in ethane |
| HCOOH_FE | Solubility in formic acid, relative to iron |
| HCOOHVJ | Catalytic value in formic acid |
| H2_FE | Catalytic reactivity with hydrogen, relative to iron |
| H2VJ | Catalytic value in hydrogen |

The database used for knowledge discovery consisted of 31 elements, each with 40 measurements of various physical and chemical properties. No goal was specified, since the desire was to thoroughly explore the database. Following are some of the parameter settings of an IXL run using this database, and three of the rules which were discovered.

*Rule 46*
*CF = 100*
*　　　"1E-005" <= "CH4_FE" <= "0.39"*
*If*
*　　　"125" <= "RADII" <= "154" and*
*　　　"-1.08" <= "MAG_SUSCPT" <= "27.6" and*
*　　　"7.38" <= "MOL_VOL" <= "13"*
*% Margin of Error 4.5 %*
*% Applicable percentage of sample 35.5 %*

*Rule 53*
*CF = 100*
*　　　"1E-005" <= "CH4_FE" <= "0.39"*
*If*
*　　　"5.2" <= "RESISTVY" <= "24.8" and*
*　　　"5" <= "S_LEVEL" <= "6"*
*% Margin of Error 4.2 %*
*% Applicable percentage of sample 38.7 %*

*Rule 119*
*CF = 86*
> *"0.01" <= "CH4_FE" <= "0.39"*

*If*

> *"8.53" <= "HEAT_CAP" <= "25.1" and*
> *"43" <= "EA" <= "190"*

*% Margin of Error 21.9 %*
*% Applicable percentage of sample 45.2 %*


*Rule 222*
*CF = 91*
> *"0.044" <= "CH4_FE" <= "24.7"*

*If*

> *"330" <= "LAT_CONST" <= "891" and*
> *"4" <= "NUM_D_ELEC" <= "10" and*
> *"1260" <= "IP2" <= "2352"*

*% Margin of Error 21.5 %*
*% Applicable percentage of sample 35.5 %*

Rule 222 indicates that if the lattice constant of an element is between 330 and 891, the number of "D" electrons is between 4 and 10, and the ionic potential energy of the penultimate electron is between 1260 and 2352 electron volts, then we can say with 91% confidence (plus or minus the margin of error of 21.5%) that it will be only 0.044% to 24.7% as effective as iron as a catalytic agent in the presence of methane. Although not everyone is anxious to memorize this fact, to those in the field this is valuable information. The discovery findings in this case illustrate the relationships between various physical and chemical properties of metals and their value as catalytic agents.

**4.3.3.4** *Information Discovery in Medical Research*    The following study exemplifies two information discovery capabilities: (1) the potential for discovering unexpected factors, or relationships between factors, which can lead to new research hypotheses and major scientific advances, and (2) the use of discovery in an orthogonal direction to statistical research.

Prior to analysis with IXL, the data in this case study had been fully analyzed with two popular statistical tools. This was something of a challenge: Could IXL find something that statistics couldn't? As it turned out, IXL revealed that the data was askew anyway and there was no point to the analysis!

The data was provided by the University of Southern California Cancer Registry in Los Angeles, which collects work-related lead poisoning data as part of its occupational health studies. The database under discussion was developed by Dr. David Garabrand and included the measured levels of lead in the blood of research subjects exposed to lead as part of their occupation, as well as other physiological measurements. Table 4.7 shows a sample of the records used in this analysis, while Table 4.8 shows the corresponding database field definitions.

The database consisted of individuals who received a variety of blood and other biomedical tests at one-year intervals. Consequently, there were three measurements of blood lead level and zinc protoporphyrin level for each research subject. Upon analysis with IXL, rules such as the following were discovered:

**Table 4.7 Sample records for the medical discovery case study**

| Field | | | | | |
|---|---|---|---|---|---|
| Hired | 19720110 | 19720619 | 19780430 | 19840610 | 19860203 |
| DOB | 19300608 | 19331210 | 19550416 | 19600528 | 19460810 |
| Sex | FEMALE | FEMALE | MALE | MALE | FEMALE |
| PBB1 | 26 | 12 | 29 | 22 | 26 |
| ZPP1 | 38 | 58 | 16 | 15 | 50 |
| PBB2 | 8 | 10 | 16 | 12 | 22 |
| ZPP2 | 35 | 58 | 20 | 23 | 24 |
| PBB3 | 16 | 4 | 18 | 10 | 14 |
| ZPP3 | 23 | 51 | 19 | 19 | 28 |
| NAG | 2.300 | 0.890 | 1.560 | 0.260 | 0.240 |
| UCREAT | 5.69 | 6.10 | 1.22 | 2.12 | 2.30 |

**Table 4.8 Data field descriptions for the medical discovery case study**

| 1. | Date Hired: first day on the job (Year/Month/Day) |
|---|---|
| 2. | Birthdate (Year/Month/Day) |
| 3. | Sex (male, female) |
| 4. | PBB1 = Blood lead level at first testing, June 1986 |
| | PBB2 = Blood lead level at the second testing, June 1987 |
| | PBB3 = Blood lead level at the third testing, June 1988 |
| 5. | ZPP1, ZPP2, ZPP3 (Zinc protoporphyrin levels at each testing) |
| 6. | NAC (N-Acetyl-Glucosaminidase level at test 1) |
| 7. | UCREAT (Urine creatinin level at test1) |

*Rule 3*
*CF = 100*
        *"NAG Level" = "High"*
*If*
        *"12-6-1960" <= "Date Hired" <= "10-11-1965"*
*And*
        *"Sex" = " Male"*
*And*
        *"Lead 4/87" = "Medium"*
*% Margin of Error: 25.0 %*
*% Applicable percentage of sample: 2.1 %*


*Rule 4*
*CF = 100*
        *"Nag Level" = "High"*
*If*
        *"12-6-1960" <= "Date Hired" <= "10-11-1965"*
*And*
        *"Lead 4/86" = "Medium"*
*And*
        *"Lead 4/87" = "Medium"*
*% Margin of Error: 25.0 %*
*% Applicable percentage of sample: 2.1 %*

*Rule 7*
*CF = 75*
    *"NAG" = "High"*
*If*
    *"Sex" = "Female"*
*And*
    *"10-25-30" <= "Birthdate" <= "8-10-41"*
*And*
    *"Medium" <= "PBB1" <= "High"*
*% Margin of Error: 15.5 %*
*% Applicable percentage of sample: 18.6 %*

After these rules were studied, rules 3 and 7 were found to be very surprising, because there should have been no apparent reason why sex should have any bearing on lead levels in the blood. In fact, prior to these results, there was no medical literature concerning gender differences with respect to lead poisoning.

However, after a few minutes of thinking, Dr. Garabrand had the "Aha" experience often associated with running a rule discovery program. The key issue was not the level of lead, but the level of "iron," an item which had not even been part of the study!

In the study, the enzyme N-Acetyl-Glucosaminidase (NAG) was used to measure the level of lead. However, NAG itself may be affected by the level of iron in the blood. The relatively high levels of NAG may have been a physiological compensatory mechanism, because of the weakened catalytic strength of NAG in the presence of high levels of lead (which inhibits NAG), and the relatively low levels of iron (a facilitator of NAG) in middle-aged women. After discovery elicited this connection, it was obvious that NAG should have been used more carefully. Subsequent studies of job-related lead poisoning now compensate for blood iron level measurements.

As discussed in Section 4.6.1, IXL did what statistics couldn't do, because rule discovery is value-based, rather than trend-based. One wonders how many other statistically analyzed medical studies could have benefited from rule discovery.

**4.3.3.5** *Information Discovery in Finance and Econometrics*    Most mathematical or econometric strategies for investment are processed by computers. However, recently a few market analysts have begun to use the rule-based approach to decision making with good results. As a tool for financial analysis, one of information discovery's advantages is that it presents its results in the form of decision rules. These rules can be immediately applied to investment decisions such as which companies to trade, when to buy, when to hold, and when to sell.

This study focuses on monthly financial data from Japan for the period of January 1980 through the beginning of 1990, provided by Mitsubishi Corporation. The information included yen valuation, money supply, price index, interest rate, stock market, and balance of trade figures. The goal of discovery was to produce decision rules for assessing market movements. Table 4.9 shows a sample of the records used in this analysis, while Table 4.10 shows the corresponding database field definitions. Here are some of the rules:

**Table 4.9 Sample of records for the finance example**

| Field | Records | | | | |
|---|---|---|---|---|---|
| Date | 831101 | 840101 | 850401 | 861001 | 900401 |
| EURO YEN 3M | 6.55113 | 6.41369 | 6.39687 | 5.01358 | 1.43125 |
| EURO YEN %RCB | −0.03220 | −0.25506 | −0.07932 | 0.04768 | −0.12556 |
| EURO YEN %RCL | −0.61932 | −0.14881 | 0.10411 | −1.90403 | 2.71415 |
| YENDOL %RCB | −1.25259 | 0.13266 | −0.32752 | −0.56788 | 3.01631 |
| YENDOL %RCL | 11.0225 | −4.98710 | 12.6453 | −32.5493 | 17.1394 |
| MONEY | 7.0667 | 7.33330 | 8.0667 | 8.7667 | 12.2000 |
| CPI | 1.43351 | 1.82708 | 1.91412 | 0.10072 | 3.22967 |
| WPI | −3.5962 | −2.41000 | 1.2564 | −10.5491 | 3.3587 |
| IP | 6.5218 | 7.92770 | 5.3249 | −0.4947 | 2.3108 |
| INTDEFMA | 3.15842 | 3.44922 | 2.68631 | 1.10635 | 1.07011 |
| DEF %RCB | −0.10087 | 0.12897 | 0.09077 | −0.30978 | −0.05833 |
| DEF %RCL | −0.35728 | 0.91522 | −1.41390 | −0.49448 | −4.29046 |
| SHOHIN %RCB | 0.42139 | −0.16485 | −0.24222 | 0.12668 | 1.25835 |
| SHOHIN %RCL | −0.2463 | 2.23200 | −2.9098 | −20.9283 | 2.7867 |
| NKDOW %B | −0.3906 | 3.05520 | −1.3019 | −5.2778 | −1.3197 |
| NKDOW %L | 18.0432 | 25.82390 | 12.7993 | 30.7206 | −12.2460 |
| WAGE% | 2.35504 | 2.23906 | 2.32722 | 1.70774 | 3.81330 |
| BASIC BALANCE | 4.7709 | 6.88310 | 14.0862 | 12.9312 | |
| BASICMAY | 6.0489 | 5.90940 | 12.1151 | 15.0841 | |
| BASICMAYB | −0.91874 | 0.31892 | 0.23828 | −0.51248 | |
| BASICMAYL | 4.95562 | 3.97130 | 2.82168 | 2.30248 | |

**Table 4.10 Data field descriptions for the finance example**

1.  Date (Year/Month/Day)
2.  EURO YEN 3M (3-month interest rate for the YEN on the London market)
3.  EURO YEN %RCB (% change in EURO YEN 3M with respect to previous month)
4.  EURO YEN %RCL (% change in EURO YEN 3M from same month last year)
5.  YENDOL %RCB (% change in the exchange rate from the previous month)
6.  YENDOL %RCL (% change in the exchange rate from same month last year)
7.  MONEY (M-2 money supply)
8.  CPI (Consumer Price Index)
9.  WPI (Wholesale Price Index)
10. IP (Industrial Price)
11. INTDEFMA (Interest rate difference between Japan and the United States)
12. DEF %RCB (% change in the interest rate difference from the previous month)
13. DEF %RCL (% change in the interest rate difference from the same month last year)
14. SHOHIN %RCB (% change in SHOHIN from the previous month)
15. SHOHIN %RCL (% change in SHOHIN from the same month last year)
16. NKDOW %B (% change in the NIKKEI stock average from the previous month)
17. NKDOW %L (% change in the NIKKEI stock average from the same month last year)
18. WAGE% (% change in the wage index from the same month last year)
19. BASIC BALANCE (Trade balance + direct investment balance/GNP)
20. BASICMAY (Trade balance/Nominal GNP)
21. BASICMAYB (% change in BASICMAY from the previous month)
22. BASICMAYL (% change in BASICMAY from the same month last year)

*Rule 1*
*CF = 90*
        *"Euro Yen 1Month" = "Precipitous Decline"*
*If*
        *"155.772" <= "Yen I Dollar" <= "224.683"*
*And*
        *"187.644" <= "Producer PI" <= "208.574"*
*And*
        *"-9.9242" <= "Trade Balance" <= "-0.1777"*
*% Margin of Error: 23.6 %*
*% Applicable percentage of sample: 8.0 %*


*Rule 83*
*CF = 90*
        *"Euro Yen 1Year" = "Extremely Negative"*
*If*
        *"9" <= "Money Supply" <= "10.6"*
*And*
        *"-0.1646" <= "Wholesale PI" <= "3.824"*
*And*
        *"4.03369" <= "R Diff JAP I US" <= "8.70747"*
*And*
        *"-1.7211" <= "Trade Bal I GNP" <= "0.995"*
*% Margin of Error: 23.6 %*
*% Applicable percentage of sample: 8.0 %*


*Rule 111*
*CF = 91*
        *"Euro Yen 3M" = "Very Low"*
*If*
        *"187.881" <= "Yen I Dollar" <= "231.693"*
*And*
        *"187.644" <= "Producer PI" <= "208.574"*
*And*
        *"-9.5567" <= "Trade Bal I GNP" <= "0.3422"*
*And*
        *"-9.9242" <= "Trade Balance" <= "0.7887"*
*% Margin of Error: 21.5 %*
*% Applicable percentage of sample: 8.8 %*


Approximately 30 monthly records, or 22.4% of the database, were characterized by a "precipitous decline" in the three-month yen interest rate during the period of January 1980 through May 1990. Rule 1 shows that there is a 90% likelihood that there will be a precipitous decline in the three-month interest rate for the yen on the London market *if* the exchange rate is in the range of about 156 through 225 yen to the dollar, the producer price index is in the range of about 188 to 209, and the trade balance is at least slightly negative. Ten of the 125 records fulfill the premises of the rule, or 8% of the entire sample. The margin of errors in this case tend to be relatively high because of the small size of the database.

Many other rules were generated, relating currency fluctations with the trade balance, etc. Such rules provide the professional market analysts with the added edge they need to make better decisions.

**4.3.3.6** *Information Discovery in Sports Medicine*    The following case study summarizes the analysis of a dataset provided by Dr. William Sands of the U.S. Gymnastics Federation National Team. The data was obtained through the tracking forms filled out by the women athletes prior to their daily training routines and included information about health, sleep duration, sleepiness, injuries, and the exercise elements/routines. There were 81 fields and 830 records. Most of the data related to the individual's psychological feelings and the relationship between mood state disturbance and overtraining during busy training sessions.

The data was analyzed by IXL. Some of these results are summarized below.

1. Some obvious personal characteristics were found, (e.g., a rule that states: If the athlete is "quite a bit" to "extremely" cheerful, she is "moderately" to "not" fatigued). The automatic generation of these "obvious" rules confirms that the supplied data was correct.

2. The psychological feelings were found to be closely related to the number of elements/routines performed during regular training hours (athletes "quite a bit" to "not" cheerful performed more of the exercise elements/routines and in longer hours.

3. Psychological feelings were found to be related to the individual athlete's personal habits, etc. (e.g., an athlete is "quite a bit" to "not" cheerful if she goes to bed early and wakes up early in the morning).

This type of "soft" data is very important in international gymnastics competitions, where the athlete's mood may have a direct bearing on performance and whether a medal is won or lost. An example of an obvious result was:

```
% Rule A1
CF=99
      "0" <="Fatigue" <="4"
If
      "3" <="Cheerful" <="4";
%Margin of Error: 1.5%
% Applicable percentage of sample: 20.4%
```

This rule suggests that athletes with "moderate" to "no" fatigue usually have "quite a bit" to "extremely" cheerful feelings. Such obvious information is important since it is not possible to be sure if the data was correct to start with (e.g., errors in data entry, incorrect data formats). However, this type of result provides reasonable assurance that the data is valid.

The amount of time spent and the number of exercise routines performed each day by the athletes were related to their psychological feelings. Here are some rules that were discovered:

```
%Rule B2
CF=97
        "0" <="Fatigue" <= "2"
If
        "136" <= "BBELE" <= "254"
% Margin of Error: 4.5%
% Applicable percentage of sample: 8.7%
```

This rule suggests that athletes experiencing "moderate" to "no" fatigue would perform 136 to 254 balance beam elements.

Other rules were concerned with the relationship of the resting heart rate of the gymnast to certain factors:

```
%Rule B3
CF=97
        "0" <= "Fatigue" <= "2"
If
        "16"<= "RestHR" <= "18"
And
        "5" <= "Hours" <= "15"
% Margin of Error: 3.4%
% Applicable percentage of sample: 13.5%
```

This rule demonstrates that athletes with "moderate" to "no" fatigue and with resting heart rate between 16 and 18 beats per 15 seconds had 5 to 15 hours of training.

```
%Rule B4
CF=97
        "0" <= "Fatigue" <= "18"
And
        "5" <= "BBRout" <= "7"
% Margin of Error: 4.2%
```

This rule indicates that athletes with "moderate" to "no" fatigue and with resting heart rate between 16 and 18 beats per 15 seconds had performed five to seven balance beam routines.

```
%Rule B5
CF=91
        "Nervous"="0"
If
        "16" <= "RestHR" <= "17"
And
        "3" <= "Cheerful" <= "4"
% Margin of Error: 7.3%
% Applicable percentage of sample: 8.4%
```

This rule suggests that athletes are "not" nervous if they have a resting heart rate between 16 and 17 beats per 15 seconds and are "quite a bit" to "extremely" cheerful.

```
%Rule B6
CF=91
        "Nervous" = "0"
If
        "16" <="RestHR" <= "17"
And
        "175" <= "ConDele" <= "530"
% Margin of Error: 7.2%
% Applicable percentage of sample: 9.2%
```

This rule indicates that athletes are "not" nervous if they have a resting heart rate between 16 and 17 beats per 15 seconds and could perform 175 to 530 conditioning elements.

```
%Rule B7
CF=96
        "Nervous" = "0"
If
        "16" <= "RestHR" <= "17"
If
        "5" <= "Hours" <= "15"
% Margin of Error: 4.8%
% Applicable percentage of sample: 9.6%
```

This rule demonstrates that athletes are "not" nervous if their resting heart rate is between 16 and 17 beats per 15 seconds and they had performed for 5 to 15 hours.

```
%Rule B8
CF=92
        "Nervous" ="0"
If
        "16" <= "RestHR" <= "17"
And
        "21" <= "VTELE" <= "150"
% Margin of Error: 6.6%
% Applicable percentage of sample: 10.0%
```

This rule indicates that athletes are "not" nervous if they have a resting heart rate of 16 to 17 beats per 15 seconds and performed 21 to 150 vault elements.

According to the above rules, the athletes' daily performance is affected by how they feel, in other words, by their psychological feelings. They are more cheerful when they are not fatigued or not nervous. This directly increases the number of exercise routines they perform, as well as the amount of time they put into the training.

Several rules relate the athletes' habits of sleeping with their psychological feelings during the day.

```
%Rule C1
CF=99
        "0" <= "Fatigue" <= "2"
```

*If*
      *"8" <= "Bedtime" =< "10"*
*And*
      *"3" <= "Cheerful" <="4" ;*
*% Margin of Error: 3.2%*
*% Applicable percentage of sample: 9.3%*

This rule suggests that athletes are "moderately" to "not" fatigued when they go to bed between 10:30 and 11:30 PM, and they are "quite a bit" to "extremely" cheerful as a result.

*%Rule C2*
*CF=99*
      *"0" <= "Fatigue" <="2"*
*If*
      *"5" <= "TimeAwake" = "7"*
*And*
      *"3" <= "Cheerful" <= "4"*
*% Margin of Error: 2.2%*
*% Appliable percentage of sample: 13.3%*

This rule represents athletes who are "moderately" to "not" fatigued when they wake up between 6:30 and 7:30 AM, and are "quite a bit" to "extremely" cheerful.

*%Rule C3*
*CF=93*
      *"Nervous" = "0"*
*If*
      *"16" <= "RestHR" <= "17"*
*And*
      *"0" <= "BEDTIME" <= "8"*
*% Margin of Error: 6.5%*
*% Applicable percentage of sample: 8.8%*

This rule demonstrates that athletes are "not" nervous when they have a resting heart rate of 16 to 17 beats per 15 seconds and go to bed between 7:00 and 10:30 PM.

These rules tell us that athletes' psychological feelings are directly influenced by how they slept during the night prior to their training. They tended to be more cheerful and less fatigued or nervous when they had had more sleep.

Relationships were found between the characteristics of the athletes and their psychological feelings, the amount of sleep they had had, and the amount of exercise routines performed. The analysis of this dataset illustrates how IXL finds patterns and relationships that help human performance.

The examples in the last six sections show that rule discovery works well in practice in a number of areas. However, rules are sometimes only as good as the database in which they are discovered. The next section discusses the important issue of data quality.

## ■ 4.4 DATA QUALITY

Almost all decisions rely on data in some way. For instance, a company decides to start a marketing campaign. The decision about which segment of the population to market a product to is based on data about who the members of that segment are and what their preferences are. The decision on how to market to that segment and what advertising media to use is based on data about the attitudes and values of that segment and how they receive information or entertainment through the media. If the data are misleading, then any decision based on the data is likely to be faulty. As the saying goes: "Garbage in, garbage out."

The quality of information interpretation and discovery depends on the quality of data. Many large databases are riddled with errors and inconsistencies. There is often a cavalier disregard for data quality, with people assuming that if large amounts of data have been collected they must be good. All too often this is wishful thinking, but poor quality data has a way of staying undiscovered because insufficient efforts are made to identify it and root it out. High quality data is essential because:

- In a complex environment decisions need to be made based on the data available.
- If the data is incorrect or inconsistent, decisions will be unreliable and will include mistakes.
- The cost of recovering from errors increases the longer it takes to discover them.

It is difficult to make decisions when one is unsure about how good the data is. The following are real and apocryphal examples of bad decisions made with poor data:

- The Trojans would not have let the wooden horse into their city if they had known there were Greek soldiers inside it.
- Pollsters probably wouldn't have predicted the election of Dewey in 1948 based on a telephone survey if they had known that most owners of telephones at that time were Republicans.
- Western leaders might have acted very differently if they had known the true state of the economy of the Soviet Union in the 1980s.

Data quality can be compromised because of the collection process, or because of the transcription (interpretation) process. In most data gathering situations there will be multiple sources of error that tend to compromise or diminish data quality. These sources of error can be grouped according to which aspect of data quality they affect. Some relevant aspects of data quality include:

- Using the right form
- Using accurate measurement
- Labeling and spelling correctly
- Using unique identifiers

- Making correct assignments
- Aggregating data correctly

We can illustrate these different aspects of data quality with an example using the filling in of a form. If you misread the form and put your home phone number where you should have put your business phone number that would be an example of an assignment problem (i.e., assigning a legitimate value, but to the wrong attribute).

If you are asked to provide your current weight and base it on a faulty set of scales (or memory), this creates a measurement problem (i.e., the wrong value is assigned to the right attribute). If you fill out the form for yourself, and then discover that it was meant for your spouse, that is an example of a labeling problem (i.e., the data was collected for the wrong object or entity).

The final aspect of data quality considered here is aggregation. Say that we have to sum the entries in two fields and then put the result in a third field (attribute). If our calculation was wrong this would be an example of an aggregation error. Thus aggregation is the process of combining the values of two or more attributes in some way to determine the value of a new attribute.

### 4.4.1 Quality Improvement

Chapter 11 will discuss quality at length. However, for the moment, it is important to remember the following key concept:

*Quality must be based on "Process Improvement" not on "Problem Solving."*

Although this sounds simple, its full meaning is not often grasped at first sight. Therefore, careful attention must be paid to the concept of "process."

Many organizations operate without a fully defined process structure. Such organizations are prone to low quality standards because whenever a problem arises, "Problem Solving" is employed to remedy the situation. The real cause of the problem is often hard to remedy and the same cause will give rise to other symptoms later.

To illustrate the difference between "process-oriented" and "problem-oriented" approaches let us consider the following simple example. What should happen when an employee makes a mistake because he/she is unaware of some facts? One approach is to explain the situation and then provide the necessary information so the mistake is avoided in the future. This solves the "problem." Another approach is to review the overall training procedures for all employees to see why the individual in question was not properly trained and to find out how many other employees also have missed crucial facts. This improves the "process" and can prevent more serious mistakes later.

The same concept applies to data quality. Suppose errors are detected in a database. One approach is to correct the errors by replacing the erroneous data items with correct values. This solves the "problem." Another approach is to review the data quality procedures and modify the on-line error checking system. This detects and prevents the errors in the first place, improving the "process" and providing better long-term quality.

It sounds simple, but in practice the process has to be well identified and stream-lined in order to lend itself to improvement. There are several interacting issues that need to be considered when improving a process. Among them are simplification, parallel improvement, and cyclic reviews. If process improvement does not follow specific guidelines, as gradual "patchwork" improvements are made, the process itself becomes complex and incoherent, lending itself to other quality problems. Therefore, cyclic reviews of the process itself are often needed in order to improve the "improvement process."

To achieve quality one needs:

- Commitment of top-level managemeent
- Quality improvement tools
- Quality improvement methodologies

Without these three components a quality improvement system will not succeed.

### 4.4.2 Data Quality Enforcement

There are many types of data error that can occur. Errors are like weeds — they will spring up spontaneously if we do not guard against them in some way. Fortunately, there are several steps that can be taken to enforce data quality in databases. These include:

- Maintain schema quality.
- Verify data entry in fields.
- Check data dependencies.
- Enforce constraints.
- Check data schema compatibility in multi-table merges.
- Maintain version consistency.

Measures for ensuring that data schemas are not changed need to be enforced. Data schemas also need to be consistent when different tables are merged. Non-unique attribute labels or inconsistent labeling will play havoc with attempts to merge data, effectively creating data islands that prevent people from carrying out information discovery and seeing the big picture.

Some measure of quality may be enforced while data entry is taking place. Type and range checking may be performed. For instance, ages cannot be negative and telephones have to have a certain number of digits (depending on the location). There may also be a variety of relevant constraints on the data, such as a location in a particular zip code needing a compatible telephone area code. Some constraints may be known ahead of time, while others may exist as dependencies in the data. Dependencies, which show up as significant correlations between attribute values in different fields, need to be checked out. Thus the relationship between zip code and area code shows up as a dependency.

Other dependencies may indicate poor or missing data. For instance, in a medical database, the name "John Doe" may be relatively infrequent overall, but very frequent in certain emergency room records. This dependency would serve as a clue to the fact that the name was being used as a missing value descriptor in the patient name field.

The best type of quality enforcement prevents the data error before it happens. For instance there are a number of ways of detecting and preventing errors during data entry. Deterministic checks find obvious mistakes (e.g., inputting an invalid value for an attribute). Probabilistic checks look for unlikely values and then warn the data entry operator. For instance, a numerical value that is far greater than any previous value (i.e., a statistical outlier) might be suspect.

Simple rule-based constraints may be easily enforced during data entry. For instance, a social security number is constrained to have nine digits or the birth year of all active employees is in the twentieth century. Other methods that can improve data quality include:

- The use of special values for "unknown" (not 0) to avoid confusion
- The identification of functional dependencies to check that values are unique
- The use of version numbers to ensure validity across systems

**4.4.2.1** **Data Quality Audits**     Data quality audits are used to detect data errors. One of the first steps in developing a data quality program is to find out how bad current data quality actually is by carrying out a data quality audit. This is done by listing the different types of errors that can occur and devising procedures to check these errors and ascertain their frequency of occurrence in the relevant databases. For some errors it may be possible to develop a deterministic checking procedure that will be applied exhaustively to all the data. For other types of errors it may be possible to apply probabilistic error checking and anomaly detection to identify outliers and anomalous exceptions. These anomalies can then be separately verified and validated.

However, there will be some errors that are intrinsically difficult to detect. It may be too costly or time consuming to track down every one of these errors in a large data set. In such cases one would typically use a sampling strategy. A random sample of manageable size would be extracted from the data set and the frequency of each error calculated. The overall frequency of the errors would then be estimated by generalizing from the sample. For instance, if an error occurs approximately 1% of the time in a randomly selected sample, than we would expect it to also occur about 1% of the time in the parent population (the entire data set) with some margin of statistical error that can be calculated based on the size of the sample. Some of the techniques for error checking in a data quality audit include:

- Range checking for integers and reals
- Value set checking for small number of known values—strings, reals, etc.
- Pattern checking for strings, regular expressions
- Checking for functional and other dependencies
- Logical constraint checking (within records, fields, and tables)
- Inexact constraint checking

- Statistical constraints checking
- Treatment of unknown and inapplicable values

**4.4.2.2** *Data Quality Programs*     One of the first things that one learns in science is to respect data. The greatest sin in science (worse than plagiarism) is to forge or otherwise misrepresent data. The whole fabric of science would disintegrate if critical data could not be trusted. This is one of the reasons why replication of data across different laboratories is very important, even though it is sometimes neglected in the pressure to publish "new" results.

Science has a program for maintaining quality through the system of submitting results for academic peer review before they are published in a refereed journal. Furthermore, it is expected that scientists will provide sufficient details about their experimental methods so that other scientists can duplicate their results. Data quality is maintained in science by ensuring that data is replicable.

Data is the foundation of knowledge, and it must be mined and distilled very carefully. Figure 4.9 shows a simple three-step model of data processing. The first step is to ensure data quality. The second step is to analyze the data appropriately. The third step is to interpret the data. Without data quality, the whole structure and logic of data analysis collapses. Thus data quality needs to be managed as part of an effective data quality program. The requirements for managing data quality closely map the requirements for quality management in general (see Chapter 11).

A data quality program requires:

- Ongoing data quality audits with appropriate tools
- Cleanup and restructuring of current data schemas
- Standards and software for maintaining the quality of the data in the future (a data quality control program)

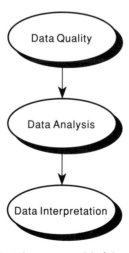

**Figure 4.9** A three-step model of data processing.

The need for a data quality program should be self-evident, but in the rush to better methods of quality assurance data has been left behind. The argument for data quality programs can be summed up as follows: Knowledge is power, knowledge grows out of information interpretation, and information interpretation is founded on data. Bad data leads to erroneous knowledge. An organization that tolerates poor quality data is flying blind.

Almost any large database will have some data problems. Some of the problems that should be paid attention to include:

- *Inconsistent File Naming* — The file names are sometimes used to indicate the file content, but may sometimes be named arbitrarily.
- *Inconsistent Field Lengths* — Field lengths in different files may be different.
- *Inconsistent Field Orders* — Different files may have different orderings for the fields, making the system non-relational.
- *Inconsistent Descriptions* — The documentation that describes various fields and files may be inconsistent or misleading.
- *Incomplete Entries* — The database may contain a large number of missing entries.
- *Inconsistent Identities*—Usage of levels assigned to a category attribute may be inconsistent (e.g., the same product may sometimes be referred to as a cordless phone but be referred to as a portable phone at other times).
- *Inconsistent Value Assignment*—Assignment of values to numerical attributes may be inconsistent (e.g., a zip code may be represented as either five or nine digits, phone numbers may or may not include the area code).

Errors are routinely found in large databases. Think how many times your name has been misspelled on junk mail envelopes. You may have noticed that certain misspellings occur quite frequently. This is most likely because your name has been spelled wrong in a database the junk mailers are using. Often, there are no procedures in place for checking errors in databases or correcting them.

### 4.4.3 Anomaly Detection in Databases

Errors often manifest themselves as anomalies (i.e., exceptions to expected patterns). For instance, Wichita might occasionally be misspelled as Wichitah. The result would be an infrequently mentioned city called Wichitah in the database. The anomaly in this case would be that relatively few records refer to "Wichitah" as a city.

There are many reasons why anomalies occur. However, in most large databases, a fair proportion of the anomalies are due to errors in the data. For instance, data entry errors occur and there are many reasons why we fail to detect them. But one of the major reasons for not finding errors is that we simply do not have the time to examine all the information in the database manually.

As databases continue to grow in size and number there is an ever greater need for error detection to be carried out with the help of automated systems that can detect anomalies. These anomalies can then be screened by humans to determine which of them represent actual errors.

Anomalies are the exceptions to rules. Say, for instance, that a rule is correct 99 times out of 100, then a case that doesn't obey the rule is surprising and possibly anomalous. Using this principle, anomaly detection is an intelligent database tool that automatically analyzes databases and finds anomalous data items and errors. For instance, there is a general rule that every living person is under 150 years old. Using anomaly detection, a 170-year-old man could be checked up on (the first two digits of his birth year may have been entered as 18 instead of 19). Thus anomaly detection is a useful tool in improving data quality and enforcing data integrity.

Consider for instance the problems at a large corporation like Global Motors Corporation. The company maintains many databases consisting of various kinds of customer, dealer, shipper, plant, and product information. There are so many of these databases and they are so large that no single person at Global Motor Corporation knows what they all contain. At times these databases contain errors and anomalies that no one can detect. These errors have a high cost for the corporation.

**4.4.3.1** *Anomalies*   Anomalies are the flip side of rules. Anomalous data contradicts expectations. In general, we can distinguish between different types. An anomaly can indicate an error in the data, or indicate a rule is faulty, indicate an interesting data point.

For one reason or other, anomalies are almost always of interest. Thus anomaly detection is a useful form of information discovery that supplements rule discovery. In practice, anomaly detection follows on from rule discovery. Once a set of rules have been extracted from a large database, the rules can then be applied to the same data (or to new data) to see which data are anomalous (cannot be explained by rules that are otherwise work well within the database). For instance, if we have a rule that says that NBA basketball players are young, tall, and fit, then a 5 foot 7 inch NBA player would be an anomaly. In this case the anomaly would be an interesting data point. It wouldn't invalidate the rule (which still applies fairly well overall), but it would show that in some circumstances fitness, quick hands, and spirit may enable a short person to compete at the highest levels of professional basketball.

Figure 4.10 shows a visual example of an anomaly. Here we have plotted height versus age for a group of professional basketball players (hypothetical data). It can be seen that the data points generally cluster in the tall and fairly young portion of the plot. However, there are a couple of circled points which indicate outliers (exceptionally short or old players). Rules are useful in summarizing data, but the combination of rules and anomalies can provide quite a rich summary of data which can then form the basis of useful interpretation.

**4.4.3.2** *Detecting Errors and Anomalies*   As we noted earlier, Global Motors Corporation makes and sells about one million automobiles yearly through a network of several thousand dealers. Parts for these automobiles are manufactured at a number of company plants and by outside suppliers, are assembled at various locations, and the finished products are shipped to thousands of dealers by a number of trucking firms. All of this data is kept in various databases.

In an earlier section, we showed how rule generation could be carried out on Global Motors' databases. The information discovered in rule generation can then be supple-

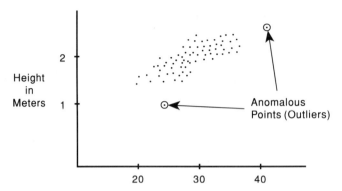

**Figure 4.10** An example of anomalies in (hypothetical) data. A scattergram of height versus age for basketball players.

mented using anomaly detection. Not surprisingly, Global's large databases contain errors, typos, and incorrect entries which cause problems with shipping, receiving, and data analysis. By using anomaly detection, however, the company can discover errors hidden in these databases.

For example, anomaly detection may point out anomalies or unusual cases such as (1) one specific dealer has a very high percentage of cars returned with battery problems, and (2) there is one dealer about whom no complaint has ever been received (perhaps because the dealer is a fictitious database entry).

Anomaly detection may also find the following errors in the database: (1) a trucking company is transporting luxury cars, which it is not authorized to do, and (2) the trucker picking up some cars is not the same as the trucker delivering them.

Anomaly detection has two components:

- It finds anomalous data items and unusual patterns by itself.
- It enforces integrity constraints which are maintained *separately from* databases and application programs by using easy-to-read rules.

In an anomaly detection tool such as Database/Supervisor (IntelligenceWare 1989) one may set thresholds for what level of error is tolerated by anomaly detection, or use a built-in tolerance. For instance, one may specify the tolerance level of 90, which means the system will find *less* anomalies, or a tolerance level of 10, which means that *more* anomalies will be found. One may also enter a constraint such as the following:

*If*
    *Date_Of_Sale > 1984*
*And*
    *Trucker = Transway*
*Then*
    *Plant = Cincinnati*

This constraint would then be checked against the data, and any instances where the date of sale was after 1984 and the trucker was Transway, but the plant was not Cincinnati, would then be flagged as anomalies.

Using constraints, anomaly detection may be based on rules that are input by the user. If the rule in a constraint is completely specified, then for each record that satisfies the IF condition, anomaly detection can check whether the THEN part is also satisfied. Anomaly detection will then report all the records that satisfy the IF condition but fail the THEN part. For example, the following constraint

```
If
        Department = "Sales"
Then
        Salary > 30,000
```

states that the minimum salary in the Sales department is $30,000. If the database contains a record that the person works for the Sales department but only has a salary of $25,000, this record will be caught and reported by anomaly detection. This type of checking is useful when you know the relationships between database fields, and these relationships can be represented as rules. Anomaly detection can then use these rules to check the database and report all the records that violate these rules.

A second type of constraint has only a THEN part but no IF part. This type of constraint is useful for checking value ranges. For example, one can specify the range of allowable employee ages as:

```
If
        (nothing)
Then
        Age > 18
And
        Age < 65
```

This constraint states that an employee can only be older than 18 and younger than 65. With this constraint, anomaly detection will catch and report the records which have the employee age greater than 65 or younger than 18.

A third type of constraint consists of a rule having only an IF part but no THEN part. This type of constraint is useful when specified records need to be caught. For example, one can specify a constraint to catch all the employees that are too young to work:

```
If
        Age < 18
Then
        (nothing)
```

This constraint tells anomaly detection to catch and report employee records that show age younger than 18.

***4.4.3.3*** ***Setting Tolerance Levels***   Just as discovery parameters can be set in rule generation, anomaly detection allows one to specify the tolerance level of errors to be discovered. The higher the tolerance level is, the fewer the anomalies will be found.

Tolerance level can be represented as values in the range of 0 to 100. Tolerance level 100 means all data values are tolerable and, therefore, no anomaly will be reported by anomaly detection. Tolerance level 0 means you do not tolerate any discrepancies in the data values. In most cases if you specify tolerance level 0, you will get all the data values reported. A reasonable default tolerance level is 80.

For scalar analysis, anomaly detection calculates the average value for scalar fields, separating the data values into different value ranges according to the statistical analysis, and screening out those values that fall beyond the tolerance level. For example, in Figure 4.11, the average height is 5 feet 10 inches. If the tolerance level is 100, no record from this table will be reported. However, if tolerance level is 0, then all the records will be reported as anomalies. If the tolerance level is set to 90, then the following entry will be reported:

| 321 | Bob | M | 7.9 | 120 | serious |
|-----|-----|---|-----|-----|---------|

This is because Bob's height is unusually high, which is considered an anomaly and so is reported. If the tolerance level is set to 80, then Andy's record will also be reported, for his height is unusually low.

For non-scalar analysis (e.g., using category variables such as type of occupation or job), anomaly detection uses the occurrence frequencies of values to determine the anomalies. If a value occurs unusually often or unusually seldom, then it is possibly an error. Unlike scalar analysis, where anomaly detection uses values of scalar fields to perform statistical analysis, anomaly detection performs statistical analysis on the occurrence frequencies of the values for each field. The field can be either scalar or non-scalar. For each field, anomaly detection calculates the average frequency, separates data values according to different frequency ranges and screens out those values whose occurrence frequencies fall beyond the tolerance level.

Patient

| P# | Name | Sex | Height | Weight | Condition |
|-----|------|-----|--------|--------|-----------|
| 001 | Mike | M | 5.6 | 150 | fair |
| 003 | John | M | 5.7 | 160 | serious |
| 011 | Andy | M | 5.0 | 100 | fair |
| 025 | Mary | F | 5.2 | 98 | seriuos |
| 128 | Pat | M | 6.0 | 182 | fair |
| 321 | Bob | M | 7.9 | 120 | serious |

**Figure 4.11**  Data for an anomaly detection example.

For example, in the data shown in Figure 4.11, suppose the patient's condition is either "fair" or "serious." Consider the following record saying that Mary's condition is "seriuos," which is a typo of "serious."

| 025 | Mary | F | 5.2 | 98 | seriuos |
|-----|------|---|-----|----|---------|

Normally, typos can only happen every so often. Errors like typos or invalid values can often be caught on the basis of their exceptionally low frequency of occurrence.

**4.4.3.4** *Anomaly Detection and Data Quality*     Traditionally, in database applications integrity has been encoded in terms of procedural programs when the application is developed. Often, integrity constraints are "spread over" a program, with each constraint being coded as a specific set of instructions. As the constraints (inevitably) change, the program needs to be "reopened" for further surgery.

Although most constraints take the form of "should not be allowed" rules, their implementation is often not obvious, since the rules have to be "coded" into procedures. Sometimes, the constraints are not those that you want, since their meaning is lost in the translation to procedures.

Anomaly detection allows comprehensive integrity constraints to be expressed much more easily in terms of rules. This allows the user to change the integrity constraints without changing the application program. Moreover, the system automatically checks for anomalies and deviations in values, based on a set of criteria provided by the user.

With anomaly detection, constraints are expressed in terms of a set of rules which are "separate" from the program. Then as the constraints change, the rules are changed without reopening the program. This has two advantages:

- The chance that the constraints are accurate increases.
- The ability to change the constraints improves.

Anomaly detection also provides a set of statistical features for measuring data quality. For instance, deviations from the standard and from typical correlations are detected. The system thus relies on both statistical and deductive methods for testing hypotheses provided by the user and for enforcing integrity constraints.

## ■ 4.5 PREDICTION

Imagine that you had a time machine and you could move out in time to a year from now and read the business section of the newspaper. That would be helpful in making investments, would it not? Or you might want to go to the stores and see what products are on the shelves two years from now in order to know which products to develop. Knowledge is powerful because it gives us the best alternative to the crystal ball and the time machine for making predictions. This section considers the different methods for prediction that are currently available. However, it is important to note the distinction between chance and systematic variation that bedevils all predictive tools.

All data samples will include relationships that represent fundamental properties of the processes that generated the data, and idiosyncratic relationships that arose by chance or that correspond to rare processes not normally observed or applicable. Statisticians refer to this as the distinction between error variation and systematic variation.

Predictions based on chance variation will most likely be wrong. Say, for instance, that we tossed a coin 10,000 times and then submitted the results to a discovery procedure. We might find all kinds of interesting rules (although most would have a low level of confidence). For instance, a sequence of four heads may always be followed by at least six tails in the next ten tosses. However, almost all such rules would be spurious, because the value of the coin attribute (heads or tails) on each throw is being generated by an essentially random process. Thus prediction needs to be based on predictive tools (whether rule-based, statistical, or neural net-based) that have been applied to representative data samples generated by systematic and reasonably stable processes. Even the best predictive tool will fail if there is no systematic variation in the sample.

### 4.5.1 Prediction with Rules

In some senses every rule is a prediction. A rule says: If the premises are true, then the conclusion will be true. Thus one can use a rule for prediction by predicting the conclusions of all the rules that match the current situation. For instance, if there is a rule that says that the fire alarm is tested at 6:00 PM on every third Tuesday of the month, than at 5:59 PM on a particular third Tuesday it can be predicted that the fire alarm is about to go off.

Prediction with rules is straightforward, providing that an appropriate set of rules can be found. However, what happens if several rules can make predictions at the same time? For instance, one rule might predict that the fire alarm is about to go off, while another rule might predict Chicken Kiev as the blue plate special in the cafeteria tomorrow. This is not a problem because the predictions are orthogonal. The two rules are predicting quite different classes of event.

Problems occur when different rules match the current situation but they make conflicting predictions. For instance, one rule might predict that Coca Cola will have the largest market share for cola drinks in the following year, while another rule might predict the same for Pepsi. In this case the rule set is inconsistent, because two conflicting conclusions can be generated from the same set of data. Yet, such inconsistency can arise in rule discovery, since each rule does not represent a causal relation directly, but rather a pattern of relationship that has been observed in the data. In such cases the user should examine the level of confidence with each rule to determine which one is more likely to be true and hence will make the better prediction.

Another problem in rule-based prediction occurs when the situation under which predictions are to be made changes. It may be qualitatively different from the situation that existed when the data on which the rules are based was collected. For instance, certain rules collected in the relatively controlled environment of the research laboratory may no longer apply for data observed or collected in the messier conditions of the outside world.

An example of applied rule-based prediction is the prediction of demand for stock items on the basis of historical data. In this case the premise of a predictive rule is a set of conditions such as promotional and advertising campaigns undertaken, and the conclusion is the number of orders for a given item within a time period.

The conditions may be expressed either as actual current sales of the item or similar and related items, such as:

$$3000 < \text{Item 433 Sales} < 4000$$

or as an indication of promotional activities, such as:

$$300,000 < \text{TV Reach} < 600,000$$

meaning that a certain audience was reached by television. Here is an example of a rule:

```
Rule No: 18
If
    10 < Cash Rebate < 15
And
    3,000 <= Current Item 433 Sales <= 6,000
And
    300,000 <= TV Reach <= 600,000
Then
    6,500 <= Rebate Claims <= 8,000
    % Confidence: 100.00%
    % Applicable months:
        1991/01
        1991/02
        1991/03
        1991/04
        1991/07
        1992/04
        1992/06
        1992/08
```

The interpretation of this rule is that:

```
If
    an active rebate between 10 and 15 dollars is in place,
And
    sales are currently between 3,000 and 6,000
And
    between 300,000 to 600,000 TV viewers are reached
Then
    Further sales between 6,500 to 8,000 taking advantage of the rebate can be expected.
```

The above rule can be discovered from historical sales data for products. The same pattern appears again and again whenever rebates are offered.

By using Rule 18 one can perform better material resource planning, anticipate demand, and know when to run rebate programs.

There are two groups of issues which can affect a predictive rule:

Group A, Rule specific:

**1.** The fields and factors involved in the premise and conclusion

**2.** The confidence factor for the rule

**3.** The number applicable items to the rule

Group B, Data File specific:

**1.** The fields listed in the data files analyzed

**2.** The historical time period from which the rule is discovered

Suppose that we have four fields, A, B, C, and D, and that the value of items in A is totally dependent on D, but only partially dependent on B and C. If the database selected did not include field D, analysis would probably find a rule relating A, B, and C, but one would never know about D if it was not included in the analysis. Thus this type of rule discovery requires that the right combinations of fields be included in the file when carrying out discovery.

Prediction of the product sales is based upon the rules generated. For instance, a prediction such as

$$6,500 <= \text{Rebates Claimed} <= 8,000$$

means that one can anticipate a specific number of rebates, thus predicting profit and loss for a specific rebate campaign.

When rules are used for prediction they should be generated on the basis of representative data (i.e., the processes that generate the data should be the same as the processes that will generate the situations that are to be predicted). The idea of representativeness is good in principle, but in most situations it is difficult to quantify. When do processes change? Will rules that were generated last week still apply this week, or has the situation changed? We can refer to this problem as predictive stability. Is the environment sufficiently stable for our method of prediction to remain stable?

Predictive stability is not just a problem for rule-based prediction. It affects all forms of prediction. One strategy for dealing with this problem is to continuously test and update rules. Rules should be scored according to how well they predict new data. Rules that fall below a certain level of performance should be discarded and replaced by new rules that provide a better level of prediction. One way of selecting new rules in this situation is to deliberately discard the data that supported the faulty rule and carry out rule discovery on the same conclusion in order to identify the replacement rule. Thus rule-based prediction requires continuous testing, validation, and refinement in order to be maximally effective.

### 4.5.1.1 *Interpreting the Results of Rule Discovery*

When dealing with large databases, users need to be very careful about phantom results. The real world often has many "hidden" variables which may not be represented in the database being analyzed. Two examples are discussed here.

#### 4.5.1.1.1 Too Few Sample Points

Consider the fact that knowledge being looked for may not be available from the data at hand. However, if one looks for something hard enough one will probably find it, even if it is not there! For instance, suppose you have a great deal of data about the weather in New York City, Chicago, Los Angeles, and Washington, DC, and you try to use it to find criteria to determine a stock market crash. Since a crash has happened only so often (three times as of this writing), you can probably find that a certain number of days before any of the crashes, the temperature in all these cities has been exactly equal.

But does this factor determine the stock market crash? In an absolute sense, you may have a rule for some value of X that states:

*Whenever*
   *Temperature in Washington, DC = Temperature in New York =*
   *Temperature in Chicago = Temperature in Los Angeles*
*Then*
   *The market crashes in X days*

It is likely that for some value of X, this relationship may actually be true. When presented with such relationships (which actually may exist), you should use your common sense and avoid them.

#### 4.5.1.1.2 Hidden Variable Effects

Suppose you are trying to determine the cause of certain forms of cancer by analyzing data about daily fat consumption in various countries. It may be that (1) in every country where there is high daily fat intake, there is also high coffee consumption, (2) in every country where there is low daily fat intake, there is low coffee consumption, and (3) you only have data about daily fat intake, and have not even considered databases of coffee consumption.

Your analysis of data reveals a striking relationships between certain cancers and daily fat intake. But, does this mean that by avoiding fatty foods, one lowers the risk of cancer? You do not know. It may be that (a) fat is the main cause, (b) coffee is the main cause, or (c) the combination of fat and coffee is the cause.

Unless data which distinguishes these results is carefully analyzed, it is possible to jump to conclusions too quickly. But how can one ever know if enough variables have been analyzed? Crushed ice in soft drinks may be yet another factor to be considered. In fact, the "real" answer may not be known until the results on many example sets have been experimentally tested. The only solution to hidden variable problems is to be as thorough as possible, include all the relevant attributes in the discovery process, and be conservative in accepting the validity of rules.

Be particularly cautious in ascribing causality to rules that are discovered in data. Rule induction is essentially a correlational analysis of data. It finds relationships in the data, but correlation does not necessarily imply causality. To prove a rule, one generally needs to carry out some type of confirmatory analysis (e.g., a controlled experiment).

### 4.5.2 Prediction with Statistics

Statistical predictions tend to be different in kind from rule based predictions. However, one form of statistical analysis that yields rule like prediction is discriminant analysis (e.g., Tatsuoka 1971). Discriminant analysis uses a mathematical function (a weighted sum of a set of attributes) to predict which among a set of categories a new observation should belong to. If we imagine each data observation as representing a point in a multidimensional space, then discriminant analysis can be explained as partitioning that space into regions separated by planes (which are defined by the discriminant function). However, discriminant analysis will not work well if the categories are irregularly shaped within the multidimensional space.

Cluster analysis also provides information about groupings of objects or individuals which can then be interpreted in terms of the properties or behavior of those objects or individuals. The main difference between cluster analysis and discriminant analysis is that discriminant analysis starts with a sample set of data where the correct categorizations are known, whereas cluster analysis constructs the categories from scratch, a distinction that is sometimes referred to as "supervised versus unsupervised learning" (e.g., Duda and Hart 1974). Multidimensional scaling and factor analysis provide information about the underlying attributes or dimensions that describe a collection of objects.

In terms of the components of knowledge described by Parsaye and Chignell (1988, Chapter 5), data analysis methods generally assist in describing and organizing objects. However, the most useful information often concerns the relationships that exist between objects. These relationships are best expressed in the form of rules. Automatic interaction detection is a style of clustering where the results can be interpreted as rules that allow one to predict the value of one attribute based on values of other attributes. Information discovery based on rule generation is a more powerful and flexible version of this approach. However, rules that are generated through automatic interaction detection can then be used for rule-based prediction just like any other rule.

Other forms of statistical methods predict numerical values rather than categories. Regression uses a linear model to predict the value of one attribute (the dependent or criterion variable) based on values of other attributes (the independent, or predictor variables). The ability of the regression model to capture the variation in the data is expressed as the value R-squared, i.e., the square of the correlation (or multiple correlation if there is more than one predictor variable) coefficient. Prediction stability is also a well known problem with regression. Typically the value of R-squared is much lower (this phenomenon is referred to as the shrinkage of R-squared) when the regression is applied to a new sample of data than for the data upon which the regression equation was originally calculated. This is because the regression equation and all prediction tools capitalize to some extent on the error or chance variation that exists in the original sample.

### 4.5.3 Neural Net Predictions

The neural modeling approach to discovery focuses on general purpose learning using neural nets or self-organizing systems. Such systems consist of a network of interconnected elements which learns by modifying the connection strengths between elements to match the input-output behavior of the net to the process or system being modeled. Consider, for instance, a neural net that was learning to recognize uppercase handwritten letters. As each handwritten letter was presented to the system it would output a decision about what the letter was. Connection weights would then be modified in accordance with whether the answer was right or wrong. A well-designed net would learn over time so that fewer mistakes were made as the connection strengths within the net became better calibrated.

The basic element of a neural net is an artificial neuron, or processing element (Figure 4.12). The basic functions of each element are:

- Evaluate input signals and determine their strength
- Calculate a total for the combined input signals
- Compare the total with a threshold value
- Determine what its own output will be

A neural net will normally contain many such processing elements. Each processing element will have a set of weights that determines how it evaluates the combined strength of the input signals. Mathematically, the calculation of input strength is the dot (inner) product of two vectors, one vector being the input signals and the other being the weights that are assigned to each signal.

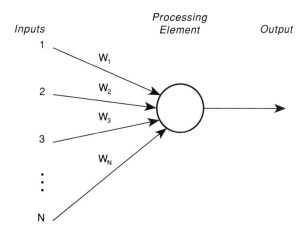

**Figure 4.12** A processing element: The basic element of a neural net. The value of the output is the dot product of the input and weight vectors.

Signals coming into an artificial neuron can be either positive (excitatory) or negative (inhibitory). Learning can take place by changing the weights used by the artificial neuron in accordance with classification errors that were made by the net as a whole. Thus if the net were being trained to recognize the letter A, then connection weights that led to correct detection of an "A" would be strengthened, while connection weights that led to a different letter being predicted when an A was really present would be weakened.

While the operation of each processing element is fairly simple, more complex behavior can be created by connecting a number of artificial neurons together. For instance, a number of neurons could be connected together to form a layer, as shown in Figure 4.13. Further neurons could then be combined to form a new layer and these could be linked so that the neural net then consisted of a number of layers of processing elements (Figure 4.14). In such a situation, the layer that receives inputs is referred to as the input layer, while the layer that generates outputs is the output layer. The layers between the input and output layers are referred to as hidden layers because they have no direct contact with the external environment.

Once we have a multilayered network there is considerable scope for adding further complexity to the system. For instance, the nodes can be highly interconnected. In addition, feedback can be introduced where outputs are directed back to nodes at the same layer or even nodes at previous layers.

Neural nets can be used to predict in a classificatory manner in some application areas. As with other predictive tools, it is important that they be trained on data with sufficient systematic variation. However, one of the advantages for neural nets is that at times they can handle more noise or unsystematic variation than other predictive tools. In return for this advantage, though, neural nets do not explain their behavior so that one cannot look at the knowledge that a neural net uses directly as one might study a set of rules. This is because neural nets are sub-symbolic (i.e., they do not contain any explicit representation of knowledge in symbolic form).

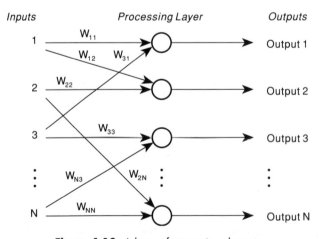

**Figure 4.13** A layer of processing elements.

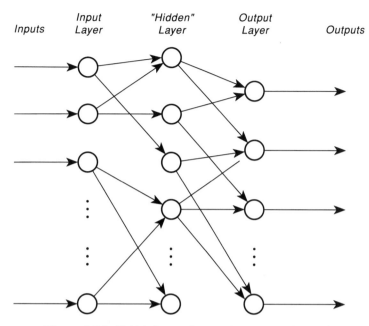

Inputs　　Input Layer　　"Hidden" Layer　　Output Layer　　Outputs

**Figure 4.14** Multiple layers of processing in a neural network.

However, in large database application neural nets generally run into three types of barriers: the inability to handle large amounts of data records (and as a result rely on sampling), the inability to deal with a large number of data fields (due to net suffocation), and the inability to perform value-based analysis with explanations. This is discussed further in Section 4.6.2.

## ■ 4.6 A COMPARATIVE VIEW

Preceding sections have presented a number of different data analysis and discovery methods. However, in the model of intelligent database application development and usage proposed in this book, information discovery based on rule generation, anomaly detection, and feature generation is the preferred method of discovery. This style of information discovery is a relatively novel approach to data analysis and information interpretation. This section explains the rationale for this decision in terms of the advantages that information discovery has over the other discovery methods in dealing with large databases.

### 4.6.1 Information Discovery and Statistics

Rule discovery is useful for large databases, but what does it have that gives it an advantage over conventional statistics in this kind of application? The relationship between statistical analysis and rule discovery is complex and could easily be the subject of extensive theoretical debate. For intelligent database applications, rule discovery is a very important capability that is not handled by existing statistical methods. In contrast to most inferential statistics which seek to confirm statistical differences in parameters such as the mean and standard deviation of an attribute (or set of attributes) between samples or populations, the goal of rule discovery is to find patterns of attribute ranges that predict the value of a goal attribute. This is a fundamentally different process, and one that traditional statistics weren't designed for. One of the reasons for this is that rule discovery can be an extremely computationally intensive process, while the foundations of statistics were developed prior to the widespread use of computers. To put it simply, the goal of statistics is generally to find relationships or differences between distributions of numbers, whereas the goal of rule discovery is to find particular combinations of attribute values or ranges that can predict the value of a goal attribute.

Automatic discovery programs may be used to search large databases and find previously unknown information, rules, and relationships. They generate knowledge in terms of easy to read rules. From a practical standpoint, rules are much more readable than mathematical equations. Many people with databases do not understand statistics well enough to interpret statistical findings, but anyone can easily read through a set of rules. A discovery program with a built-in "expert" statistician can interpret statistical findings, then summarize them as rules.

The basic strategy of most statistical techniques is to look at differences in data sets and use equations to characterize these differences. Statistics packages do not look into a database in order to find the specific values which lead to the formation of logical rules. An information discovery system such as IXL can automatically produce rules such as the one following, where variable names such as Value-1 correspond to actual values in a database.

```
Rule 11
CF = 80
        Field-1 = Value-1
If
        Field-2 = Value-2 and
        Value-3 < Field-3 < Value-4
% Margin of Error 6 %
% Applicable percentage of sample 30 %
```

This rule automatically establishes a concrete relationship between field values. When a database is very large, analyzing each of the values with a separate statistics command is practically impossible, and the value of automated rule generation becomes obvious.

A rule discovery system can form the necessary hypotheses and models itself. In purely statistical approaches, a statistical analyst would have to first form a model, then test various hypotheses. With a large database this can be a lengthy process. In contrast, rule discovery describes the patterns within the database in a format that is easily read by non-statisticians.

While rule discovery does use some statistical methods and principles, it is also based on the mathematics of induction. Explanation plays an important role in assessing the believability of a prediction, and the type of in-built explanation that

**Table 4.11 Sample data from Fisher's Iris Study**

| Sepal-L | Sepal-W | Petal-L | Petal-W | Species |
|---------|---------|---------|---------|---------|
| 5.1 | 3.5 | 1.4 | 0.2 | SETOSA |
| 5.6 | 2.9 | 3.6 | 1.3 | VERSICOLOR |
| 5.9 | 3.0 | 5.1 | 1.8 | VIRGINICA |
| 4.9 | 3.0 | 1.4 | 0.2 | SETOSA |
| 6.7 | 3.1 | 4.4 | 1.4 | VERSICOLOR |
| 6.2 | 3.4 | 5.4 | 2.3 | VIRGINICA |
| 4.7 | 3.2 | 1.3 | 0.2 | SETOSA |
| 5.8 | 2.7 | 4.1 | 1.0 | VERSICOLOR |
| 6.5 | 3.0 | 5.2 | 2.0 | VIRGINICA |
| 5.6 | 3.0 | 4.5 | 1.5 | VERSICOLOR |

rules provide is also an advantage. Thus if someone tells you that the world is going to end soon you might ask them how, or why.

Rules provide a type of built-in explanation. A predictive rule can be read as: I predict conclusion C because the value of attribute A is A1 and the value of attribute B is B1. In contrast, statistics tend to model linear relationships and have no obvious explanation component. For instance, if one obtained a prediction based on linear regression, about the only explanation implied would be "I predict value C because there is a linear relationship between variables A and B and when I compute the model I get the value C for that data point."

**4.6.1.1  *The Fisher Iris Study***    The following is a case study that illustrates the differences between statistical methods and rule discovery. The Fisher Iris Study, a classic in statistics, was published in 1936 by Sir Ronald Fisher. It is frequently employed as a standard test case and is listed in many statistics text books and user manuals. For example, it appears in the SAS manual (SAS 1988) and in the demonstration literature for other statistical packages.

Table 4.11 shows the sample data for the Fisher Iris Study. In Table 4.11 Petal-L means Petal Length and Petal-W means Petal Width, etc. The iris study database contains only 150 records, 50 for each of three species of iris. Using this information, the objective is to identify the species of an iris based upon its physical characteristics—that is, petal and sepal length and width measurements.

Here are some of the base rules discovered from this database using rule discovery:

```
Rule 1
CF = 98
     "Species" = "Virginica"
If
     "4.8" <= "Petal Length" <= "6.7" and
     "1.8" <= "Petal Width" <= "2.5"
% Margin of Error 5.4 %
% Applicable percentage of sample 30.0 %


Rule 7
CF = 98
```

> "Species" = "Versicolor"
>
> If
>
> "1.7" <= "Petal Length" <= "4.9" and
> "0.6" <= "Petal Width" <= "1.7" ;
> % Margin of Error 5.1 %
> % Applicable percentage of sample 32.0 %

> Rule 15
> CF = 100
> "Species" = "Setosa"
>
> If
>
> "1" <= "Petal Length" <= "1.9" ;
> % Margin of Error 1.0 %
> % Applicable percentage of sample 33.3 %

> Rule 16
> CF = 100
> "Species" = "Setosa"
>
> If
>
> "1" <= "Petal Length" <= "3.5" And
> "0.1" <= "Petal Width" <= "0.4"
> % Margin of Error 1.0 %
> % Applicable percentage of sample 32.0 %

Once the rule discovery method is instructed to include concepts such as long, short, etc., more readable rules are produced.

> Rule 7
> CF = 100
> "Species" = "Setosa"
>
> If
>
> "Petal Length" = "Short"
> % Margin of Error 1.0 %
> % Applicable percentage of sample 33.3 %

> Rule 8
> CF = 100
> "Species" = "Setosa"
>
> If
>
> "Petal Width" = "Thin"
> % Margin of Error 1.0 %
> % Applicable percentage of sample 33.3 %

These rules do a good job of summarizing important patterns within the data and of categorizing the different species of iris. With rules such as these, a user should be able to distinguish different species of iris.

Table 4.12 shows an example of what a statistical package might produce after analyzing this database. Based on the comparison of these results with the rules listed above, it is clear that for most people rules are much better than equations in distinguishing the species of irises. Furthermore the information is summarized much

**Table 4.12  Output of analysis using a statistical package on the Fisher Iris data**

*SUM OF PRODUCT MATRIX M = B'A' (A(X'X)-1 A')-1 AB (Hypothesis)*

|  | S-LENGTH | S-WIDTH | P-LENGTH | P-WIDTH |
|---|---|---|---|---|
| S-LENGTH | 61.332 | | | |
| S-WIDTH | -15.583 | 14.193 | | |
| P-LENGTH | 163.141 | -52.047 | 417330 | |
| P-WIDTH | 73.197 | -23.239 | 175.126 | 84.230 |

*MULTIVARIATERESULTS*

*HOTELLING-LAWLEY = 35.727*
*F-STAT = 584.923 DF = 8286 PROB = .000*

*WILKS' LAMBDA = .033*
*F-STAT = 196.491 DF = 8288 PROB = .000*

*PILLAI TRACE = 1.219*
*F-STAT = 56.636 DF = 8300 PROB = .000*

*THETA = .708 S = 3 M = .6 N = 70.1 PROB = .000*

$$
\text{RHO} = 1.0 - \left( \frac{(SUM1-1)}{N(J)-1} \cdot \frac{2P2+3P-1}{N-G} \right) \frac{6(P+1)(G-1)}{}
$$

more conveniently in the rules. The rules indicate that all irises with short or thin petals are iris setosa. In this case information discovery produces clean, easy-to-read rules which are readily understood.

Rules tend to work better than statistics in discovery because they are value-based rather than trend-based. Rules summarize information in the form: When these attributes have these values you can expect the flower to be species X (e.g., when the petals are long and narrow). Many subtle differences in these value combinations can then be captured by different rules. This is generally a much more powerful type of description than just saying: Variable A will tend to increase as variable B increases, or if you multiply the petal length by three and add it to the petal width and the resulting number is between 12 and 15, then the flower is most likely species X.

## 4.6.2  Information Discovery and Neural Nets

In some sense neural nets cannot be fairly compared to automatic discovery since neural nets do not focus on finding unexpected results, while discovery does. Neural nets do not blend rule discovery with graphic visualization either. Instead, they mostly focus on classifying cases based on a training sample. However, for prediction, one can make some comparison between neural nets and rule-based systems. With this comparison it becomes clear that neural nets are oriented towards pattern recognition based on a small number of attributes rather than discovery from large data sets.

One of the interesting features of neural nets is that they are "sub-symbolic." Unlike rules and other forms of knowledge representation, the network carries out "reasoning" without having any explicit representation of symbols. This is certainly not a handicap in reasoning, but if our goal in information discovery is to summarize patterns and present them to people as an interpretation of the data, then the absence of symbolic representation will make it very difficult for people to interpret the structure of the net as an interpretation of the data. Whatever knowledge contained in the network is in the form of connections and connection weights, which works fine computationally, but will be difficult for people to interpret as a data summary.

This weakness of neural nets in explaining their results is well pointed out in a text on neural nets by Nelson and Illingworth (1991). Neural net analysis of data requires considerable expertise and is very different from running a rule generation procedure in terms of the effort required in selecting parameters and setting up the procedure. For instance, one must first select a neural net paradigm (of which there are many). One must then construct the neural net itself since a neural net model for a large database cannot be constructed automatically unless one is willing to tolerate poor performance. In setting up the neural model one has to decide on the number of input nodes and the architecture of the layers.

Another factor that argues against the broad use of neural nets as an information discovery technique for databases is that they generally perform best when they are trained for a particular application. One of the requirements of the training set is that the attributes should be as orthogonal (i.e., independent, with no correlation) as possible. In a very large database finding a training set that has these properties might be a tedious and time consuming task.

Neural nets generally work best on pattern recognition problems. In the case of information discovery from a large database, there is no single set of patterns that the system is trained on before classifying new cases of the pattern. There may in fact be a huge number of patterns waiting in the database, and each pattern only needs to be discovered once. Thus the discovery of knowledge in a large database does not fit the types of problems that neural nets so far have been developed to address. It is possible that a new neural net approach may be developed to handle information discovery in large databases, but even then there will need to be additional mechanisms to present the results in a symbolic form that people can recognize and interpret.

In addition, information discovery in a large database cannot assume that the relevant goal variables have already been classified into discrete values. An attribute such as disposable income might be scaled in dollars (i.e., it is continuous) whereas we want to predict different levels of disposable income based on other lifestyle and demographic attributes. In this case we need a discovery technique that can split off and separately predict different ranges of the attribute of disposable income.

In addition, there are three types of technical barriers that today's neural nets face: (a) the inability to handle large amounts of data records (and as a result rely on sampling), (b) the inability to deal with a large number of data fields (due to net suffocation), and (c) the inability to perform value-based analysis with explanations, as is the case with statistics.

Problem (a) is serious for large databases since it provides too rough an edge for decision making. The pitfalls of sampling can be illustrated by the well-known "loan approval rating" example used for neural nets. Consider a database of one million records. In this type of example, several attributes such as Own Versus Rent are used for training the net. A sample of 30,000 records is taken and some predictions are made.

However, what the neural net cannot induce from the sample relates to the field Occupation, since there are too many values for this field. In fact, there are over 35,000 specific occupations listed by the U.S. government (including interesting and at times hilarious phraseology for describing job categories such as "mobster").

Thus the sample ignores key fields and key pieces of knowledge. Consider the rule for loan approval:

If
      Job Category = Yacht Sales and
      Length of Employment < 2 and
      Inflation = High and
      GNP growth = Low
Then
      Default rate = High

This is a common sense rule that many loan officers know. A neural net with a sampling system cannot find this rule because there are far too many values for the field Job Category. Instead the neural net will focus on the field Rent/Own using a much coarser and less accurate measure for prediction.

More serious problems are encountered when a large number of fields are involved. In addition, neural nets (like statistics, as discussed in Section 4.6.1) do not produce value-based knowledge.

Thus there is no general purpose neural net that will work with a broad class of problems, carry out information discovery across large databases representing data for a wide variety of different domains, and provide the ease of development and use that we require for information discovery in large databases.

The emphasis in using a neural net is on obtaining good classification performance rather than on interpreting what the patterns in the data actually mean. Since inter-pretability is a key issue of intelligent databases and one of the goals of information discovery, the sub-symbolic nature of existing neural nets argues against their usage as a discovery method in development of intelligent database applications. While it may be possible that neural modeling approaches are applicable in some circum-stances, the wide variety of data and databases that may be encountered will often make it difficult to identify a coherent sequence of training examples that can be used to train a neural net or similar classifier.

Another way to look at the issue is this: The neural model for computing was developed because it resembled the workings of the human mind—it aimed to achieve intelligence — whatever it may be. In this sense, neural nets try to "compete" with the abilities of the human mind. However, today's neural nets are not yet reaching the level of average human ability. Now, as indicated in Figures 1.2 and 1.3 in

Chapter 1, it is clear where the problem is: Neural nets compete with the human mind, automatic discovery complements the human mind.

So, it should not be surprising if automatic discovery works better than neural nets on large databases—the neural structure of the human mind is not well suited to very large database analysis, and today's neural nets have yet to achieve this level of competence. Of course, this may all change in a few years with a new generation of neural hardware, but for the moment large databases are mostly a non-neural domain. Thus the focus in this book is on symbolic concept acquisition, and on forms of rule discovery that can be practically applied to large databases.

## ■ 4.7 CONCLUSIONS

For many years, statistical techniques have been the basic tools for viewing and understanding large amounts of data. Statistical techniques emerged as methods of analyzing numeric data and—in the right hands—can be very useful in providing insight into the overall structure of data. There is no doubt that statistics should play an important role in any program which tries to learn from data. However, considerable value can also be added using information discovery, and the use of this tool does not require statistical expertise (which is generally in short supply in any case).

This chapter reviewed the history and evolution of data analysis, along with methods of discovery. Information discovery (rule generation and anomaly detection) was contrasted with neural modeling and machine learning. A comparative analysis of discovery methods was carried out that indicated information discovery based on rule generation and anomaly detection is generally most appropriate for large database applications.

Information discovery can be supplemented with statistical tools for exploratory data analysis. Cluster analysis uses similarities between objects to organize them into groups. Automatic interaction detection also develops clusters but here each cluster corresponds to a value or range on some goal attribute, so that automatic interaction detection can also be used as a rule generation method. Multidimensional scaling uses information about differences between objects to develop a perceptual map of the objects where the dimensions in the map or space represent attributes that are implied in the distance judgments (through inverse geometry). Factor analysis uses proximity data (typically correlations between objects) to reduce a set of descriptive attributes to a smaller core set of factors. Ideally these factors give a concise description of the most important features of objects.

Statistical methods tend to do well at detecting differences and trends, while information discovery does well at identifying relationships. For instance, anomaly detection may be used to identify data that does not fit expected patterns or existing rules. Finding out why anomalies occur will further understanding of the underlying system that produced the anomalous data. Data visualization tends to help all three types of understanding because of the way that good visualizations concisely summarize large amounts of data and because of the way that visual presentations tend to stimulate thinking about data.

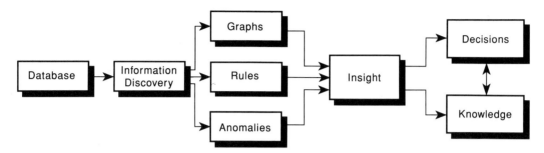

**Figure 4.15** Automatic information discovery turns data into valuable information.

Information discovery is the only practical way to discover patterns in very large data sets. With such large databases, "eyeballing" of the data is out of the question. Similarly, exploration of the data using manual querying is far too time- and labor-intensive. This chapter illustrated the usefulness of information discovery with a number of different case studies.

Statistical analysis, too, requires extensive human involvement, in contrast to information discovery which can be carried out using the many machine cycles that are typically available between dusk and dawn. Rules also have the advantage that they can pick up nonlinear patterns that tend to be overlooked by most statistical methods (which are based on a linear model of data) and they express their findings in a format which is intuitively obvious and easy to remember (i.e., in the form of a premise and conclusion).

One of the main reasons for relying on automatic information discovery is that the amount of data available in many situations overwhelms the ability of human analysts to deal with it. However, by the judicious use of heuristics and statistical principles, automatic techniques can look for trends, rules, and anomalies. This chapter shows how rule discovery is an important part of adding value to databases. This added value is in the form of rules that can be readily interpreted and used. In addition, information discovery also includes anomaly detection which is useful in maintaining the quality and integrity of data. This chapter also showed how anomaly detection can be used to supplement the information provided through rule discovery.

Rule discovery can help a nonexpert understand what the implications of the information in an enormous database are, by discovering relationships and correlations among the data, as well as rules for predicting facts about new data. Information discovery turns databases into active repositories of information, automatically posing queries to the database and uncovering useful and unexpected information. Thus information discovery generates insight, adds to knowledge, and supports decision making (Figure 4.15). However, the validity of information discovery critically depends on the quality of data that is used. Like all forms of analysis, information discovery obeys the dictum: "Garbage in, garbage out." Data visualization as another form of data discovery will be discussed in the following chapter.

# 5

# DATA VISUALIZATION

*Graphic elegance is often found in simplicity of design and complexity of data.*

— Edward Tufte*

*Corollary*: Visualization should be coupled with exploratory analysis to discover key patterns.

## ■ 5.1 INTRODUCTION

A picture is worth a thousand words. However, for understanding large data sets, a good picture is worth many more than a thousand data points.

Data visualization is all about understanding ratios and relationships among numbers. Not about understanding individual numbers, but about understanding the patterns, trends, and relationships that exist in groups of numbers. These patterns, trends, and relationships have to be related to some model of the domain of interest. They are then used to close the knowledge gap between the user's understanding of the current situation and the situation as it actually is (Figure 4.3).

Data visualization tools are an important step in the evolution of databases that parallel the trend towards visual information presentation in the mass media. Visual presentation of information takes advantage of the vast, and often underutilized, capacity of the human eye to detect information from pictures and illustrations. Recognizing the potential of data visualization, many decision makers today would rather have information presented to them in graphical form, as opposed to a written or textual form.

---

* *The Visual Display of Quantitative Information,* Graphics Press, 1983. Edward Tufte was born in Kansas City in 1942 and received a PhD from Yale, where he later taught. His impressive volume of work has had considerable influence on making graphic visualization a science.

As a rough approximation, the world of information can be divided into text, numbers (referred to here as numerical data, or simply data), graphics, and other types of media presentation. While much has been made of the problem of illiteracy, innumeracy (the inability to dealt with mathematical concepts, and numbers in general) may be the larger problem. The majority of people do learn to read and continue reading throughout their lives. In contrast, many people drop out of math classes relatively early in high school and have little involvement with numbers and math thereafter. Most people have difficulty balancing their checkbooks and are not comfortable with concepts such as compounding of interest and probabilities.

Data visualization shifts the load from numerical reasoning (which a lot of people are poor at in any case) to visual reasoning (which most people are very good at). While data visualization helps those with poor math skills, it is also essential for statisticians and other analysts who are dealing with complex data. In a world that is ever more complex, data visualization is a way of reducing the perceived complexity of information while retaining the essential elements of that information and promoting better understanding of data.

The interpretation of information and data is a cooperative effort between the human user/analyst and the machine. Scientific visualization uses animation, simulation, and sophisticated computer graphics to create visual models of structures and processes that cannot otherwise be seen, or seen in sufficient detail. Scientific visualizations are computer generated images and pictures that facilitate a variety of tasks such as understanding the mechanisms and predictions of a complex scientific model. For instance, the shape of a molecule can best be grasped as a visualization where it may be rotated and viewed from many different angles, and scientific visualizations may be constructed to better understand the workings of a black hole in space or the dynamics of a tornado.

Data visualization is generally much simpler than scientific visualization. It is an essential component in intelligent database applications that can present and display information in a way that encourages appropriate interpretation, selection, and association. It utilizes human skills for pattern recognition and trend analysis, and exploits the ability of people to extract a great deal of information in a short period of time from visuals presented in a standardized format. Thus, standard charts and graph types are useful in developing intelligent databases. Visualization using charts and graphs plays a particularly important role in applications such as project management and quality control.

This chapter will discuss data visualization, emphasizing the use of standard charts rather than more exotic tools such as animation and complex visual simulations. Methods for making graphs and charts more truthful and easy to use will be described. A central premise of this chapter is that there are fundamental principles of data visualization that can be used to develop charts, graphs, and displays for particular data and tasks.

This chapter begins by reviewing the history and evolution of data visualization. The use of data visualization for intelligent database applications is then considered. Also introduced and reviewed are a variety of charts and methods for representing and summarizing data, and the subject of how visualization may be automated is considered. Finally, some methodological issues in data visualization, including the role of data transformation, are discussed.

The approach to visual presentation developed in this chapter then forms the basis for the method of HyperData discussed in Chapter 6.

## ▪ 5.2 HISTORY AND EVOLUTION OF DATA VISUALIZATION

As Sherlock Holmes said, "*You* see, but *I* observe." Humans have seen things for millennia, but being able to observe the world in the summarized form of graphics is rather new. The saying "You don't miss what you don't know about" is wrong when it comes to important information. Throughout history, progress was generally made when people questioned their ignorance. With the right knowledge, we observe more and more, although we see the same things.

### 5.2.1 Early Data Visualization

We don't know how prehistoric man viewed the world, but until comparatively recently people were unable to construct pictures and drawings with three-dimensional perspective. Even otherwise advanced civilizations like those of the Greeks, Romans, and Egyptians created essentially flat two-dimensional pictures, although they were able to make exquisite three-dimensional sculptures. To the modern eye, the difference between their life-like sculptures and their flat pictures is quite stunning.

The use of linear perspective to create 3D images was one of the achievements of the Renaissance. One can see just how revolutionary the use of perspective was by comparing pre- and post-perspective paintings of the same churches in Italy. It is like comparing pictures drawn by children and by adult artists. In retrospect, one wonders how people could have accepted two-dimensional representations of people and objects. However, it is easy to criticize something when we know how to do it better, and there are no doubt many things that we accept now that will appear primitive and laughable in a few years time. After having seen color television, most people find it difficult to watch black and white television, and it will probably not be long before the flat screens of today's computer displays also seem limiting and annoying even though millions of people currently accept them without question.

Visualization is the process of transforming objects, concepts, and numbers into a form that is visible to the human eye. Furthermore, photographs are useful because they preserve the appearance of an object at a particular point in time. Maps represent the form of large areas that can generally not be viewed all at once. It is generally easier to read a map than to climb a high hill or charter an aircraft to see the lay of the land. In addition, the clarity of a map does not change depending on the weather. The technologies of maps, graphs, and photographs are merging into a new and integrated method of visualization.

Today's paintings, maps, and photographs are the latest developments in the evolution of the technology of visualization as object representation. The representation of objects as pictures goes back thousands of years to the earliest drawings on caves. Maps, too, have a long history. The first maps were drawn on clay tablets over

5000 years ago. By the eleventh century, Chinese maps showed rivers and coastlines with great accuracy, several hundred years in advance of European geographers (Tufte 1983).

By the sixteenth century, cities were being located within scatterplot-like diagrams where the axes were lines of latitude and longitude respectively. In the late seventeenth century, Edmond Halley created a chart showing trade winds and monsoons on a world map. In the nineteenth century the data map became relatively commonplace, with maps being annotated in various ways with data.

Maps were undoubtedly one inspiration for modern charts and graphs. Another inspiration came from mathematics, and in particular the Cartesian revolution in geometry. It was Descartes's major achievement to relate geometry to algebra by inventing the Cartesian coordinate system. In the coordinate system, the values of points within the coordinate space are related directly to the values of the corresponding locations on the coordinates (reading vertically and horizontally).

The history of visualization was shaped to some extent by available technology and by the pressing needs of the time. For instance, tables of numbers developed relatively early because of the importance of counting in age old activities such as banking. Various accounts and collections of numbers could be represented as tables of numbers. These tables included the concepts of rows and columns. Tables of numbers were particularly important in science and navigation. These interests merged in the fifteenth and sixteenth centuries when tables of astronomical data were used in navigation. It was essential in long voyages to know fairly precisely where one's position was, particularly when there might be dangerous reefs or shoals to contend with, or where a missed landfall could have deadly consequences.

The clock, the compass, and the sextant were critical inventions that allowed a ship to be a traveling observatory, providing that it had the tables of data necessary to make its calculations. In this case, there was a natural data visualization, a map, with the position of the ship being tracked on it. From our perspective, the relatively early emergence of a sophisticated technology of navigation may have arisen not only because of competitive pressure and the prospects for enrichment that came through trading and conquest, but also because the numerical calculations and reasoning, while complex, were nevertheless intimately tied to a natural and familiar visualization (maps).

As technology and civilization developed, people needed better ways of handling large amounts of numerical data so that they could store, summarize, and interpret it. The growth of capitalism, particularly in Britain in the eighteenth century, meant that people urgently needed to understand phenomena such as debt, inflation, interest, and the relative value of different currencies.

In 1786 John Playfair published the first charts showing economic time series, thereby revolutionizing data visualization. These charts were similar in many ways to the charts that are still in use, and they joined the map and table as methods for viewing numerical data. Most importantly, the new charts evolved into standard ways of representing information. These charts are not particularly intuitive when first encountered, as one finds when watching children learn about them for the first time, but once learned they provided people with familiar templates in which to summarize and view numbers. Abstract concepts such as number and time could now be envisioned in terms of more concrete attributes such as position, length, and size.

The slow evolution in data visualization may be partially explained by the difficulty that many people had with the concept of number. Numbers are inherently abstract once we get away from counting objects. It is only after many years of schooling that most people become happy with the concept of number.

Paradoxically, those people who show exceptional gifts in manipulating numbers often do not rely on the formal concept of number. They are usually of two types, visual or auditory (Smith 1983). Visual calculators see number mentally, while auditory calculators associate numbers with sounds and perform calculations accordingly.

Some great mental calculators lose their ability for numerical computation after they have received formal training in disciplines such as math. Jedediah Buxton who was born in England in 1702 had no formal education and could not read or write, but could nevertheless perform calculations involving 40-digit numbers!

Two examples of the loss of calculating ability are Mangiamele and Zarah Colburn who lost such abilities after being questioned by the French Academy. Another example is Richard Whately, who later became the Archbishop of Dublin. Whately was confused by written numbers after attending school and lost his calculating powers. In Whately's words: "In this point, I believe I surpassed the American Boy [Zarah Colburn], and I never remember committing the smallest errors. And when I went to school, at which time the passion was worn off, I was a perfect dunce at ciphering, and so have continued ever since."

Some human tribes have been reported to have only three categories of number, "one," "two," and "many," which suggests that the use of numbers may reflect the complex environment that we live in rather than some innate human trait. This is why educators often stress counting and the mapping of number to physical attributes, such as size, in order to develop an internal concept of number in children.

Not surprisingly, perhaps, some of the earliest recorded uses of numbers were for purposes of accounting and taxation. Numbers were needed to summarize and regulate various transactions. In the early pictographic languages (e.g., the hieroglyphics of ancient Egypt) numbers were represented by visual markers. Thus five cows were represented by a picture of five cows. Later, numbers were represented independently of objects in the form of markings. Remnants of the earlier systems of markings for numbers can be seen in the Roman system of numbers. The numbers one to eight were represented as: I, II, III, IV, V, VI, VII, VIII. However, in the Arabic system of numbering that superseded the Roman system we see little if any hint of counting: 1, 2, 3, 4, 5, 6, 7, 8, 9.

Development of the abstract concept of number was a critical step in the growth of technology. Number theory allowed statements to be made about numbers in general, no matter which objects they represented. For instance, the square root of nine is three, no matter whether the number nine represents cows or bushels of wheat.

The ability to manipulate numbers as abstract quantities is then mirrored in the ability to see representations of relations between numbers as patterns in graphs and charts. For instance, being able to see an increasing trend in a line chart where the line moves up and to the right.

## 5.2.2 Modern Data Visualization

The late nineteenth century (and most of the twentieth century) was dominated by the print medium. This was the age when the newspaper empires of Hearst and Beaverbrook were built, and political and economic information was disseminated to a wide cross section of the population. Charts, graphs, and tables were used for this purpose, and they were also used in the new scientific journals that sprang up at that time.

Graphs were used in various scientific charting applications. A scattergram or bar chart might be used to represent the input-output behavior of an electrical circuit or consumer preferences. Graphs and charts also became popular in the business world as people such as actuaries and insurers began using charts of populations for commercial advantage.

While graphic design and printing methods improved, the basic approach to data visualization changed little. It is only comparatively recently, with the development of highly visual computing environments in the 1980s that a qualitative improvement in data visualization has been possible. The computer medium allowed charts to be created much more quickly, and in a more standardized way. Sophisticated computer graphics also allowed the use of three dimensional charts, which were difficult to draw by hand. Charts could also be treated as data containers that were filled up with new data weekly or daily. As charts became more timely, and could be produced in greater numbers, it was natural for them to be used more frequently in support of information interpretation and decision making.

The personal computer made graphic data visualization possible on a large scale. Before the personal computer, graphing had to be done using special workstations which were expensive. With the advent of the microcomputer, and then software applications such as spreadsheets (beginning with Visicalc), graphing was available to anyone. The early spreadsheets included simple graphing options, and brought with them the vision of graphics.

The ability to provide high-quality graphics on the computer was limited by screen technology and by computer graphics technology. Screen technology evolved rapidly in the 1980s to meet the increased demands of graphical user interfaces. Early screen technology was dominated by cathode ray tubes (CRTs), light source displays that selectively light the pixels in the display. In the late 1980s, liquid crystal displays (LCDs) became prominent, particularly in portable computers. LCDs are light valve displays where the pixels in the display selectively transmit or block the lighting to form the image.

Early computer displays were bulky, being both heavy and deep (rather than flat). Flat panel displays were developed in response to the increasing popularity of portable computers in the late 1980s. Thus by the early 1990s display technologies were evolving in two directions (small and light displays for portable and hand-held computing; very large displays for group work applications). A good example of a project concerned with the use of very large displays in group work was the electronic whiteboard project at Xerox PARC (Elrod et al. 1992). The electronic whiteboard is a computerized display that can be viewed from anywhere in a meeting room. Computerized whiteboards can then be linked by telecommunications to create a work surface that is shared by several remote sites. Marks made on one board then appear on the other connected boards. Documents can also be sent to the board by fax or across an electronic network.

Today, presentation graphics are a core part of the software industry. They are used as an essential part of communication between people in many organizations. At the same time, a different branch of data visualization has evolved as computer aided design (CAD), which represents physical objects. In contrast to object representation technologies such as CAD, data visualization is the representation of ratios and relationships between large numbers of elements as described in a data set. This chapter discusses data visualization, not CAD. Other forms of visualization not discussed at any length in this chapter are the scientific visualization of physical processes such a plasma flow and aerodynamics.

## ■ 5.3 VISUALIZATION FOR INTELLIGENT DATABASES

Data visualization is used routinely to summarize large amounts of data. Many intelligent database applications inherently involve data visualization. For instance, project management, quality control, and other applications are principally fields of data visualization of one form or another. When someone looks at a Gantt chart, they are visualizing the state of a project. When someone looks at a quality control chart they are visualizing an important aspect of the production process.

There are many forms of charts and graphs that are used to visualize data. While certain forms of visualization can be highly artistic, attempts at touching up charts often lead to chartjunk (Tufte 1983). In contrast, a considerable amount of information can be presented succinctly using charts that are constructed automatically. These charts are standard visual templates used to represent numerical data and include bar charts, pie charts, and the like.

Many different forms of chart have been developed. These charts (Figure 5.1) can be categorized as follows:

- Maps
- Coordinate based
- Ratio based
- Hybrid
- Iconic

In addition, there are specialized charts in each domain (e.g., candle stick charts specifically designed for visualizing stock market data). The nature and properties of these charts are reviewed in the following sections.

### 5.3.1 Maps

Maps represent the layout of physical objects. Geographic maps represent portions of the surface of the earth. Other maps represent objects such as the layout of a building or the wiring diagram for the electrical system in a car.

Maps are particularly important tools for data visualization. They are intuitively easier to interpret than abstract charts. Perhaps this is because the human user already

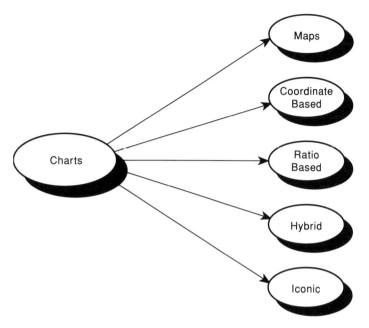

**Figure 5.1** A classification of charts.

has a good mental model of physical space gained from everyday experience with the environment. Thus it is not surprising that cartographic mapping preceded the use of abstract charts by many centuries. For instance, the Yu Chi Thu map (probably dating from the eleventh century) shows a highly detailed and scaled map of south China, yet it was not until 1786 that the first economic time series was plotted.

Maps are a natural way to display information about the environment. They are used in diverse applications ranging from marketing to geology. People find it very useful to see data presented in the context of a map. For instance, one can show separate bar charts of sales figures where the bar charts for each city are located at the position of the city on the map.

## 5.3.2 Coordinate-Based Charts

Maps represent numerical data in the context of a familiar object or physical layout. Coordinate-based charts trace their roots to Descartes, the inventor of the coordinate system. Lines (axes) are used to define a coordinate system where each axis represents different attributes. The values of each attribute are represented along the lines of the axis.

Simultaneous information about the relative values of ratio variables can be provided by projecting each data point onto a set of orthogonal axes. Due to physical and psychological constraints, only three orthogonal axes can be shown at once. Three-dimensional (3D) charts represent information about three variables simultaneously as points within a three dimensional coordinate system. The dimensions (axes) of the coordinate system are mutually orthogonal and are labeled as the X, Y, and Z axes respectively, as shown in Figure 5.2.

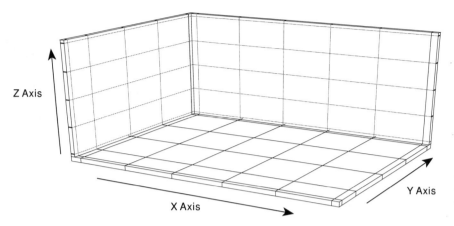

**Figure 5.2** The coordinate system of a three-dimensional chart.

Different versions of 3D charts are appropriate depending on whether the variables being charted are interval or ratio scaled, or ordinal or nominal scaled. If all the axes (variables) are ratio scaled, then a scattergram is generally used to present the information. However, if one of the axes is nominal scaled, then a bar chart may be more appropriate. Finally, if one of the axes is nominally scaled and it is the proportion or split of another of the variables between the nominal categories that is of interest, then a pie chart is appropriate.

Animation can be used to show a fourth dimension of time. Other variables can be added to the basic information in a 3D display by using perceptual attributes such as size, brightness, color, shading, labels, and shape. The choice of which variables to represent directly by position in the coordinate system of the scattergram and which variables to represent by the appearance of the data points may be based on issues such as the importance of variables, how many distinct attribute values they each have, and so on.

Consider for instance a graph that showed height, weight, age, and blood pressure. Height, weight, and age could be shown on the basic three dimensions, and blood pressure could be shown in color range from blue (low blood pressure) to red (high blood pressure). This would create an effective display, but it should be noted that blood pressure is not distributed along a meaningful axis (i.e., some interpretability is lost). Thus it is possible that red (high blood pressure) boxes or data points may be distributed throughout the box defined by the three dimensions.

Theoretically, it might be possible to display an almost infinite number of attributes in a coordinate-based chart. However, in practice, the number of attributes that can be reasonably displayed is limited by human ability to discriminate between different physical information. For instance, one might want to display color and brightness as fourth and fifth dimensions of information in a scattergram. However, the perception of brightness is affected by the type of color, so that these two physical characteristics interact. Furthermore, people cannot reliably discriminate more than a few levels of color or brightness at a time.

**5.3.2.1**  *Scattergrams*    Scattergrams are coordinate-based charts for plotting three ratio, interval, or ordinal scaled variables. However, the appearance of the cloud of data can be changed markedly depending on how the axes are scaled (or stretched or shrunk). One way to add more information to a scattergram is to show the importance or accuracy of each data point. For instance, statistical error bars are sometimes used to show uncertainty about where the point should be located in the scattergram (where the data value is actually the mean of a sample which may contain error).

Scattergrams can also be used to show relationships (correlation). However, since scattergrams show all the data points they provide a good idea about the uncertainty or error in the relationship, but are not so good at showing the trend in more detail. Best fit regression lines are sometimes superimposed on scattergrams so that the trend is more readily seen. If this is done than the square of the correlation ($R^2$), along with the statistical significance of the correlation (i.e., whether or not the slope of the line significantly differs from zero) should also be shown so that the readers can judge whether the visual impressions that they receive are valid.

Hand drawn charts are generally two-dimensional. Computer graphics now make it relatively easy to construct 3D charts. A 3D bar chart represents values on three attributes or variables in a visual representation chart. The chart relates the values of a ratio variable on the z-axis to levels of a category variable or ranges of an ordinal, interval or ratio variable (e.g., time) on the remaining axes. Thus a 3D bar chart is a bit like a stylized city where buildings are placed on a grid of rows and columns. Each building stands in a cell on that grid (e.g., the cell at row three and column four). The height of that building then represents the value of the ratio variable on the z-axis. Cumulative versions of 3D bar charts may also be constructed, where the value of the z-axis variable is accumulated across levels on the x-axis, the y-axis, or across both the x- and y-axes simultaneously.

A 3D pie chart represents values on three attributes or variables in a visual representation (chart) where the values of the category variable are each assigned different slices of the pie. The size of each slice in the pie corresponds to the value of a second (ratio) variable. The height of each slice then corresponds to (is proportional to) the value of the third (ratio) variable. For instance, if we are plotting foods in the average diet as a pie chart, then the height of each slice in the pie can indicate the calorie value of each type of food. The height of the "fat" slice will be 2.25 times greater than the height for the "carbohydrate" slice.

A 3D scattergram represents values on three attributes or variables (each of which may be ratio, interval, or ordinal) in a chart where the values of each variable are converted to positions on the x-, y-, and z-axes respectively. The data are represented as points in the 3D coordinate system. In a confidence scattergram, the 3D scattergram is modified so that instead of being represented as points in the 3D coordinate system, the data are represented by icons (graphical objects) located at the corresponding points in the 3D coordinate system. Information about accuracy of, or confidence in, the location of that data point is then represented by the size (radius) of the corresponding icon (a sphere).

3D charts are a big improvement on 2D charts for many types of data, but sometimes one needs to simultaneously represent more than three variables. Since it is not possible to represent four variables as mutually orthogonal axes, a new approach to displaying additional variables beyond the original three is needed. The trick (which was used above with confidence scattergrams) is to display the data points as graphical objects and then change the appearance of those objects according to the values of the higher dimensions. Using this approach it is possible to define higher dimensional analogs of the 3D graph types previously introduced.

An N-dimensional version of the bar chart can be constructed where the 3D bar chart is modified by using the appearance of the bars (which are the graphical objects in this case) to represent levels on the additional dimensions. These dimensions may be represented using attributes such as color, shading, and box size/thickness. For instance, cost information may be shown on a blue-red continuum with low cost in blue, moderate cost in light blue or purple, and high cost in red.

Similarly, an N-dimensional version of the scattergram can be defined. An N-dimensional scattergram is a modified 3D scattergram where each data point is represented as an object positioned according to the value of the three "location" variables that establish its position in the 3D scattergram. Additional dimensions are then represented by the visual appearance of these objects (e.g., a box) which are modified according to ranges, levels, or values of the data point on the higher dimensional variables. Examples of object features that may be used to represent higher dimensions include color, brightness, texture, size (along any or all of the dimensions of the box or object used to represent each data point), and shading. Different versions of the N-dimensional scattergram can be created depending on how many dimensions are used. If one higher dimension is used, along with the basic three, this results in a 4D scattergram, while a 5D scattergram results from having two higher dimensions, and so on.

### 5.3.2.2 Line Charts

Line charts are coordinate-based charts that are best for detecting trend and showing differences in trend. They work particularly well with time series, although they can be used with other quantitative variables on the x-axis. Line charts are also good at showing correlated data. Typically, the points on the line chart will be averaged for each level of the x-axis, thereby showing the trend more clearly without actually fitting the smooth regression line. Line charts are also good at showing how the relationship between two variables is affected by a third variable. In this case levels on the third variable will be indicated by different symbols. Figure 5.3 shows some of the alternative relationships that can be found in this type of line chart. The parallel lines in panel *a* show that the relationship between the variables on the x- and y-axes is unaffected by the value of the third variable. If the ordering of the lines from bottom to top also reflects the order of values on the third attribute then this also indicates that there is a correlation between that attribute and the variable assigned to the y-axis. Figure 5.3*b* shows a situation where the relationship between the variables on the x- and y-axes depends on the value of the third attribute. For low values of the third attribute there is a positive relationship, while for high values there is an inverse relation.

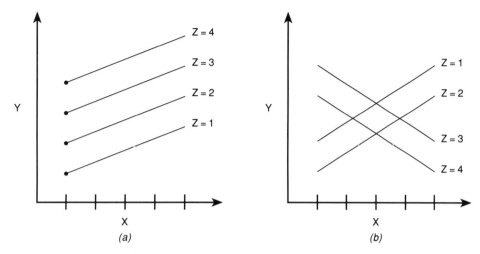

**Figure 5.3** Line charts showing a third attribute coded by symbols. These charts allow us to examine the effect of the third attribute on the relationship between the first two.

### 5.3.3 Ratio-Based Charts

Ratio-based charts emphasize data ratios and proportions. They are quite different from coordinate-based charts which emphasize magnitude, size, and location. The difference between coordinate- and ratio-based charts is clear when we compare a scattergram and a pie chart (discussed below).

**5.3.3.1 Pie Charts** A scattergram has two or three axes that bound the figure, whereas the pie chart has no external axes. Instead the quantities are mapped onto segments of a circle (pie). The size (including angle) of each segment than corresponds to the value of the quantity that has been assigned to it, as a proportion of the total value of all the quantities displayed in the pie chart.

Pie charts are useful in displaying proportions. The segments in pie charts can also be labeled with the corresponding percentages so that precise estimates of the size of each segment do not have to be made visually.

Pie charts are a convenient graphical device for highlighting the proportions of one variable that are assigned to each of the categories of another nominal variable. For

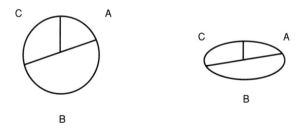

**Figure 5.4** The visual effect of tilting a pie chart.

instance, a pie chart can be constructed to show the proportions of proteins, fats, and carbohydrate in the average diet.

Newspapers and magazines sometimes distort the appearance of pie charts by tilting them on their side or otherwise involving them in a three-dimensional context. Figure 5.4 shows an example of a pie chart where the segments in panel *a* have been distorted by tilting the pie as in panel *b*.

Judgment of relative proportion using pie charts is difficult. This is because the starting point of the segment for a particular category will generally change across different pie charts (as shown in Figure 5.5). Thus there is a shifting visual baseline or starting point that makes comparison difficult. One solution to this problem is to add numerical labels that show the size of each segment in each of the pies being compared. Another solution is to allow each pie segment to be clicked on. Then if a compare proportion option has been selected, the pies will all rotate so that the beginning of that segment is lined up in the twelve o'clock position.

**5.3.3.2 Multivariate Profiles**    Scattergrams are a useful way of presenting information, but they are not always very good at highlighting particular effects in the data. Bar charts and pie charts are good for showing how the data changes for different categories of a variable. One of the most important reasons for looking at data is to make comparisons, such as, "How does this year's budget compare to last years?" or "What's the difference between the way the software engineering folks use their budget and the way the marketing people handle theirs?" Multivariate profiles are sets of pie charts or bar charts placed side by side or in a matrix, for easy visual comparison.

A multivariate pie chart profile is used to provide visualization of multivariate data by using multiple pie charts, where each pie chart represents the data for a different variate (attribute) within the multivariate data set. Profiles can also be created using bar charts. A multivariate bar chart profile, is a combination of 2D and 3D bar charts used to provide visualization of multivariate data, where each bar chart represents the data for a different variate (attribute) within the multivariate data set.

In general, charts may be compared by showing a number of charts, one for each location or logical grouping of the data. Once viewers understand the design of one

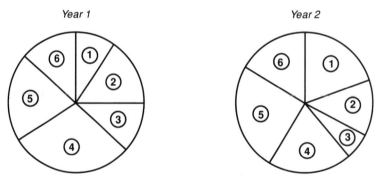

**Figure 5.5** A comparison of pie charts (note that it is much easier to judge the relative change in proportion for segment 1 than it is for segment 2).

panel of the chart they understand all the panels and they can scan across the panels making comparisons and focusing on changes.

## 5.3.4 Hybrid Charts

Other forms of chart mix the properties of coordinate-based and ratio-based charts. We shall refer to these types of chart as hybrid charts. The first forms of hybrid chart that we consider in this section are bar charts and histograms.

### 5.3.4.1 Bar Charts and Histograms

Bar charts, along with pie charts, are perhaps the most familiar and frequently used form of chart. Each bar represents a category, level, or range of a variable, and the height of the bar represents the corresponding value on a second (ratio) variable.

Bar charts are hybrid charts because one variable is represented by a numerical axis, while the second attribute is represented by levels of a category. Thus the relative heights of bars correspond to the relative sizes of segments or slices in a pie chart. As a form of hybrid chart, bars display both size and ratio or proportion information. The height of a single bar shows the size or magnitude information, while the relative heights of different bars shows the ratio information. Since bars generally form irregular patterns that confuse the eye, pie charts typically provide more accurate information about proportions. However, arranging bars in ascending or descending order of height makes relative comparisons between the bars easier. The problem with this strategy is that the user may now be confused by the reordering of the levels of the category attribute that are represented by each of the bars.

The bar chart represents the value of one variable for several different categories of another variable. The bars in the chart may be oriented horizontally or vertically. The size or length of each bar corresponds to the value of the variable represented by the bar. Figure 5.6 shows a number of different versions of bar charts. In tiered bar charts (Figure 5.6*b*) each bar plots several different variables, one stacked on top of the others. It is generally difficult to judge changes in the value of variables in tiered bar charts because the vertical position of the bar segment for a particular variable tends to change from category to category depending on the size of the sub-bars beneath it.

In divided bar charts (e.g., Figure 5.6*c*) multiple bars are plotted side by side in groups. Each group of bars represents a value or level on a category variable. Each bar within the group represents a value or level on a second category variable. Bars can also be used to represent ranges on an ordinal or ratio variable. For instance, age is frequently broken down into ranges, and each age range can then be plotted as a bar.

Sometimes one is not interested in the variable of interest directly, but in a meaningful transformation of that variable. With costs for instance, one might be less interested in how much is being spent in each month than in how much has been spent altogether and how much of the original budget still remains. Thus rather than plotting the total spent in each month one might want to plot the cumulative totals from the beginning of the project up till the end of each month. Figure 5.7 on page 217 shows how a cumulative bar chart can be used for this purpose.

Bar charts can also be used to represent the distribution of a variable. In this special

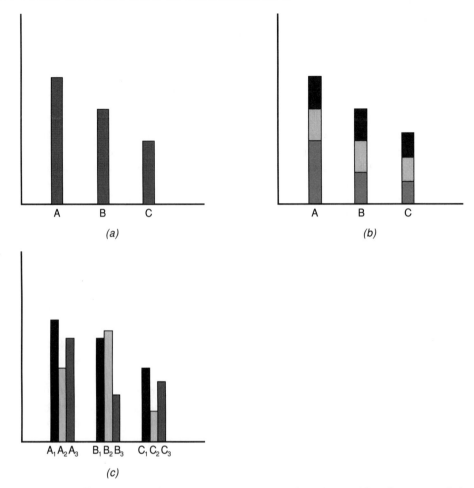

**Figure 5.6** Different versions of bar charts. (a) Standard bar chart; (b) Tiered bar chart; (c) Divided bar chart.

case the bars tend to be quite thin and numerous, and plotted close together. The resulting chart is referred to as a histogram. Figure 5.8 shows a histogram of a grading distribution. Here the height of the bars represents the number of students who were assigned each numerical grade. As is often found, this distribution has a peak around the average value.

**5.3.4.2   Box Plots**   Box plots are another type of hybrid chart that show the range of values on one variable associated with a specific range of values on one (a 2D box plot) or two (3D box plot) variables. The size of each box in the plot is proportional to the number of observations which fall into the specified ranges of the two variables. The box plot is useful for two-dimensional, bivariate (i.e., two-coordinate) map values, and allows a quick assessment of which combinations of values are most prevalent in

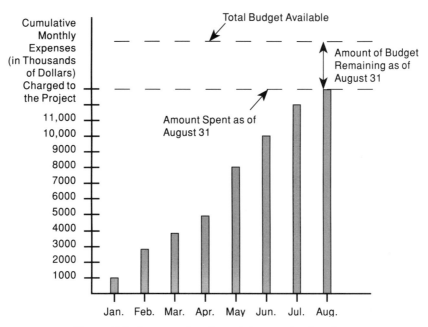

**Figure 5.7** Representation of cumulative costs in a bar chart.

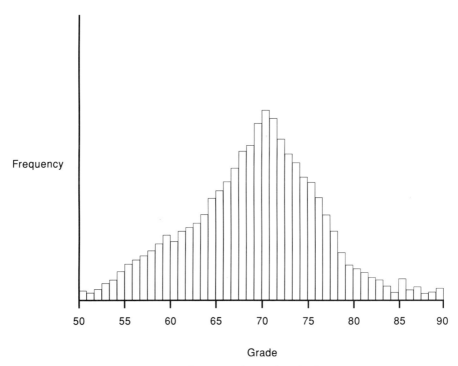

**Figure 5.8** A histogram of a grading distribution.

terms of the relative sizes of the mapped boxes. Box plots are particularly useful as a type of Pareto chart for quality control applications (see Chapter 11).

The 3D box diagram is similar in concept to the two-dimensional box plot. Each box is centered at a point which represents its mean value within a combination of ranges along the x, y, and z axes. Whereas the area of each box in a box plot indicates the relative frequency of its combination of field values, it is the volume of each box in a 3D box diagram which expresses the relative frequency of its combination of field values.

**5.3.4.3  *Hybrid Maps***     Another form of hybrid chart is the map that contains superimposed representations of data. Some of the most compelling examples of graphic representation utilize the projection of numerical information on a visual model or map. The famous graphic showing the fate of Napoleon's army in Russia is an example of this (Tufte 1983). That graphic succeeds in plotting the values of a number of variables: the size of the army, it's location on a two-dimensional surface (two variables), the direction of the army's movement, and temperature on various dates during the retreat from Moscow (the two variables of time and temperature).

Maps are particularly useful in applications like marketing where the data are collected from different geographical locations. Maps generally consist of physical units or locations, a layout or organization of these units, symbols (often with labels) that assign objects (such as cities) to different locations in the map, and data codings that assign attribute values to different locations or units in the map by using different values of attributes such as color, texture, or brightness. For instance, height is frequently represented by colors. In one system, different shades of brown are used to indicate higher regions of the map while greens are used to indicate regions closer to sea level.

### 5.3.5   Iconic Charts

Other forms of chart are iconic in nature. Glyphs are compound marks that can describe the values of multiple attributes. A Chernoff face is a special type of glyph that capitalizes on human sensitivity to faces and facial features. Figure 5.9 (after Tufte 1983) shows an example of a set of faces that represent data. In this case there is one face that stands out from the other faces in its immediate vicinity. As this example shows, "data" faces can be useful in detecting outliers (strangers) and in grouping data visually.

Many different glyph systems have been used to create iconic charts. In one system, data is represented by the length of radiating lines (like spokes from a wheel). Large data values are represented by long lines and small data values are represented by short lines. The resulting glyphs look a bit like "twinkling stars." Another variant of this type of glyph connects the endpoints of each line together to form a polygon figure.

Glyphs tend to be seen as a whole, forming what is known as a gestalt. Thus it is difficult for people to extract the basic number information from a glyph. Instead, they can be used for visually detecting clusters in information or for detecting anomalous points or outliers.

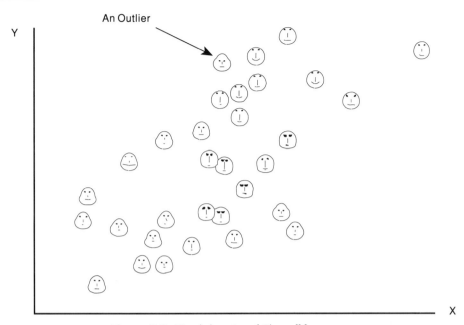

**Figure 5.9** Visual clustering of Chernoff faces.

### 5.3.6 Virtual Visualization

Virtual visualization combines in some way a model of a world with data. The ultimate form of virtual visualization is the visualization of data embedded within a virtual reality (Chapter 3). Some of the benefits can be achieved without using a full-scale virtual reality. For instance, visualization of stock market can be carried out on a map representing different industries and/or different exchanges. Data can then be positioned as cities on a map.

The basic idea of virtual visualization is to create a virtual reality or model world in which the information is located. There are then certain operations for exploring the information by operating on the model world. Different data sets can be selected by pointing to them or by moving to them and grasping them. Different display templates within the world can be selected in similar fashion and the data of interest can then be dropped onto the display template to create a view. The analyst or user can walk around the display in various ways, viewing the data from different perspectives.

### 5.3.7 Domain Specific Charts

The types of charts so far discussed have been generic or domain independent. Charts may be constructed to meet the special needs of specific domains. There are too many of these domain specific charts to describe here, although some of them will be discussed in later chapters (e.g., Gantt charts in Chapter 9; quality control charts in Chapter 11). This chapter will illustrate the domain specific approach to charting with charts that are used specifically for the task of analyzing and interpreting financial data.

Visualization has played a major role in technical analysis of financial data. This section will briefly describe some visualization tools that have been developed for the analysis of stock market data.

Historical data on stocks can be used to estimate the risk of different issues and to assess earnings potential. Charting is a way of adding value to price and volume information in securities prices. In general there is a wealth of information that is relevant to investment decisions. In fact, there is so much information and so many ways of looking at it that it is impossible to identify all the patterns and trends that may be relevant through manual analysis or visual inspection.

A number of charting methods are used for visualizing market data. Using a diverse set of visualizations is important because there may be a number of influences on a stock, and some of the trends in stock prices may be apparent to the human eye when charted appropriately. Graph types that are particularly useful for representing market data are:

*Candle Stick Charts* — A candle stick chart shows the high, low, and close of a stock in daily "candles." Unshaded "candles" indicate days where the stock price rose, while the shaded bars indicate days where the stock market fell.

*Line Charts* — A line chart is one of the simplest ways to see the movement of a stock. It plots the price or percentage of change against time. Figure 5.10 shows monthly stock yields between 1947 and 1970 (after Auerbach 1976, p. 9). Several stocks can be plotted together, even with time lags, allowing visual comparisons to be made. Line charts are generally the best way of conveying basic trend.

*Comparing Stocks* — Comparison charts allow you to see the relative frequency of stocks going up or down together, or the distribution relation in stock price and trade volume of two different stocks. In general two or more stocks may be compared by overlaying them on the same chart, as long as the same vertical scale is used. However, if the volume of one stock is compared against the price of another stock (i.e., different vertical scales), then the comparison should be made in terms of separate panels (one on top of the other).

*Correlation Analysis* — Correlation analysis is useful in showing the correlation between the movement of two stocks together. Correlation may either be carried out with zero lag or with non-zero lags where there is assumed to be some causal relationship so that movements in one stock later affect the other stock. In general, a high zero (unlagged) correlation will occur when both stocks are being influenced by similar factors, while a predictive (lagged) correlation will occur when one stock is a leading indicator for another stock. A stock may act as a leading indicator (e.g., the fall in a price of a major bank stock may affect later prices for other bank stocks) if it is judged to be a trendsetter by the investor community, or if it tends to respond more quickly to fundamental economic variables than the stock whose price it predicts.

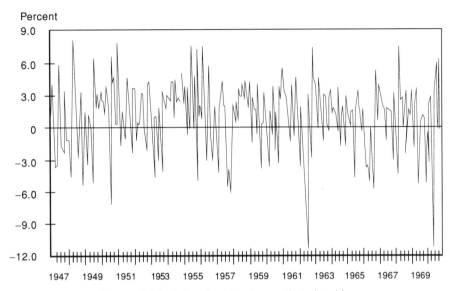

**Figure 5.10** A line chart showing month stock yields.

## ■ 5.4 METHODOLOGIES FOR DATA VISUALIZATION

This section defines the role of data visualization as a tool for presenting the trends and relationships that are implicit in numerical data. A number of technical aspects need to be considered in defining this role, including the use of data transformation to support more meaningful visualizations of data and the use of statistical analyses to assist in the interpretation of charts and graphs, and these are discussed here. The requirements of a good visualization system will also be discussed, and this section will conclude with a summary of how data visualizations can be designed for use within hyperdata systems.

Data visualization is important in all applications where large amounts of data have to be sifted and interpreted. For instance, medical researchers (epidemiologists) gather reams of data daily from hospitals across the country. This data is collected for analytical purposes. The goal of an analysis might be to improve diagnostic capabilities or to prevent disease. A striking relationship can be found between average fat intake and the cancer rate in various countries. A visualization tool can illustrate such relationships by graphically demonstrating the correlation among variables. Thus data visualization can be a great aid to medical research, by speeding up the process of analyzing data, suggesting new research hypotheses, and revealing significant relationships among variables within huge databases.

Data visualization reduces the turnaround time for answering questions. Data visualization systems can be general or they may be customized to deal with particular application areas (e.g., project management or quality control). For instance, in project management, data visualization provides decision makers with a high level view of project status using 3D color pictures and network diagrams. The visual representation of the project network makes it easy to understand the schedule of the project as well as the complexity, cost, and risk involved in each project. The beneficial effects of data visualization can be further enhanced by embedding the various charts and graphs within HyperData (Chapter 6) and by using visualization as a form of information discovery that supplements and corroborates rule generation and anomaly detection.

### 5.4.1 ■ Data Transformation

Visualization is a kind of transformation of numerical data. Numbers are abstract concepts, and to represent them as points and lines requires a transformation. For instance, the size of a number may be represented by the length of a line or bar, and the relationship between two numbers may be represented by the relative sizes of two slices of a pie. We are so used to visual summaries of numbers that we tend to take this type of transformation for granted. However, there are other transformations which can modify the underlying numbers before they are transformed into a visual presentation.

Figure 5.11 shows a schematic representation of the two transformations that generally occur in converting numerical data into a visualization. First there is a

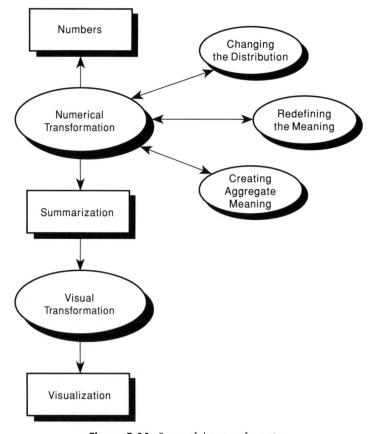

**Figure 5.11** Forms of data transformation.

process of summarization which may include specific data transforms. Examples of data transformations that are frequently used include:

- Linear transformation
- Logarithmic transformation
- Normalizing transformation
- Arcsin transformation
- Square root transformation
- Inverse transformation

The function and use of these transformations is covered in a number of texts on statistics and data analysis. A detailed discussion of transforms and their use is provided by Box and Cox (1964). The transformations listed above are generally used to modify the distribution of numbers so that they are more suitable for analysis or visual presentation. Logarithmic transformation is frequently used when numbers are spread over too wide a range, or if a distribution is "positively skewed" (i.e., there are a lot of data points bunched together followed by a long tail of data points that represent larger numbers). Normalizing transformations are often used to convert data into the form of a normal distribution prior to carrying out statistical analysis (this is done because many statistical analyses are "parametric," i.e., they assume that the data are normally distributed).

Other forms of transformation adjust numbers so that they are more meaningful, or more representative of the concept that the data analyst is interested in. Raw numbers should not be considered sacred and they can often be misleading. For instance, labor economists generally recommend the seasonal adjustment of employment data. This is because many of the increases and decreases in employment during a year can be attributed to seasonal variation. In North America for instance, more people tend to look for work in the early summer when school and college leavers enter the workforce. Similarly, more people tend to find temporary work in November and December during the peak shopping season.

Monmonier (1991) cites a good example of how data may need to be adjusted or transformed to be more meaningful. He showed a figure where the unadjusted death rate across the 50 U.S. states in 1960 was plotted in one panel and the age-adjusted death rate was plotted in a second panel. In the first panel, New England states had high death rates, while Alaska and some southern states had low death rates. However, when the death rates were adjusted by age, Alaska and the southern states had high death rates, while the New England states had low death rates. The reason for this was that the New England states had a much higher proportion of elderly people in their population. This discrepancy in the average age needed to be taken into account before meaningful comparisons about things such as the health of the population or the effectiveness of health services could be made across the different states.

Consider another example from marketing. Say that Global Motors Corporation has a large database on its car sales for the past three years. A marketing analyst might compare the number of cars that were sold versus those that were unsold or sold at a heavy discount. A parts procurement specialist might look at the volume of cars that were made versus the cost and amount of materials and parts that were expended during the production process. A labor productivity analyst might look at the number of person hours of labor required to produce each car. In making these analyses it may sometimes be appropriate to adjust the volumes of different makes of cars depending on their value or cost, or to weight the number of hours of labor input according to the cost of labor for different workers at different plants.

A stock market analyst might focus on the price of the stock from Global Motors rather than on car sales. Her analysis might include fitting moving averages to the data (a form of transformation where the data is "smoothed" by averaging it with a "window" of surrounding data points) or calculating new compound (aggregated) measures that weight price movements according to the volume of trading that was associated with them. Transformations are used to:

- Change the distribution of numbers and make them better suited for analysis
- Redefine the meaning of numbers
- Create new aggregate measures
- Make numbers easy to visualize

The preceding examples indicate that the way in which data is transformed should depend on what the data is required for. Transformation is really an extension of data quality. There is usually nothing sacred about the numbers that we assign to various attributes. For instance, there are a number of different ways that we can measure quantities such as length and temperature and we can convert from one to another using data transformations (e.g., we can transform measurements in inches into centimeters by multiplying them by 2.54). Thus data transformation is the process of finding the right number scale with which to represent an attribute for a particular application.

### 5.4.2   Data Analysis and Data Visualization

Data transformation modifies numbers so that they are more easily analyzed, visualized, or interpreted. Data analysis is the process of applying various methods to data to assist in interpretation. Some of the exploratory data analysis methods available are cluster analysis, multidimensional scaling, and factor analysis.

Data analysis can be used to transform data or to summarize the data itself or its statistical properties. For instance, the average (mean) of a set of numbers is frequently used in calculating data points in a graph. If we wanted to show the relationship between years of working experience and income in a company we might take all the workers with one year of experience and average their incomes, take all the workers with two years of experience and average their incomes, and so on. If we then plotted the graph of the summary data for up to 20 years of working experience, then each data point might summarize the data from hundreds, or possibly thousands of workers' incomes.

Statistical support of visualizations generally includes various numerical quantities and tests of significance that prevent people from making erroneous conclusions based on visual inspection of possible patterns in graphs and charts. For instance, a scattergram may show an apparent relationship between two variables, but is the apparent shape of the cloud of points meaningful, or does it simply reflect random variation? Many people find it difficult to judge the significance of apparent relationships in scattergrams. However, the statistical correlation provides a good quantitative measure of the relationship. In addition, there is an associated test of significance that tells whether or not there is a significant linear relationship between the two variables plotted in the scattergram.

Other tests of significance can be used to determine whether two samples of numbers tend to be different. For instance, with two different histograms of data representing flight delays for major airlines, one of the histograms may seem to be pushed over more to the right (i.e., representing worse delays overall), but is this difference significant? A t-test or analysis of variance is a way of statistically verifying whether or not there is a difference in this type of case.

Another statistical measure that can prove useful in verifying trends in data is the confidence interval. The confidence interval is like a margin of error (see the discussion on margin of error in rule generation in Chapter 4). A 95% confidence interval, for instance, represents the range of values within which we can be 95% sure that the true (or underlying population) mean will be found (in most situations it can be roughly estimated by calculating it as the range of values within two standard deviations of the mean).

For instance, Figure 5.12 shows some hypothetical data giving the average number of minutes of delayed arrivals per week over a ten week period for a particular airline. When we look at this data there appears to be an overall improving trend. However, add in the 95% confidence interval around each point (Figure 5.13) and the apparent trend is well within the random variation to be expected around a sample mean. Extended lines drawn horizontally across the chart show the confidence interval bounds for the first data point in the chart. It is apparent that while there is some variation in the confidence intervals for each data point, none of the data points is outside the bounds defined by the confidence interval for the first point. Thus it would be dangerous to point to this data as evidence of a significant improving trend in the

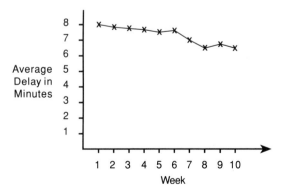

**Figure 5.12** Average number of delayed arrivals per week for a hypothetical airline.

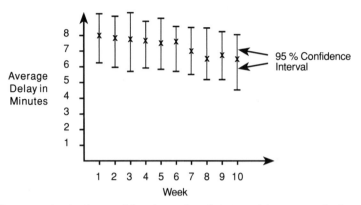

**Figure 5.13** The data on delayed arrivals with 95% confidence intervals plotted.

timeliness of the airline since it is most likely due to chance and things are just as likely to get worse as better in the next ten weeks.

In the ideal case, data analysis and data visualization proceed hand in hand. However, in building intelligent database applications we cannot assume that most people will be comfortable using statistics. In addition, the model of hyperdata described in Chapter 6 requires that the user be able to explore the data entirely with point and click navigation. A good compromise in this case may be to show relevant statistics as annotations to charts where they are appropriate. For instance, the correlation and the significance of the linear relationship could be routinely shown along with each scattergram, while users could also have the option of seeing error bars (confidence intervals) for line charts or bar charts if they request it.

Since the intelligent database application can be envisaged as an exploration and discovery tool, there is nothing to stop statistically knowledgeable users from applying detailed statistical and data analytic techniques to the data after they have got a good overview of the data using point-and-click navigation. If the statistical tools are integrated with the intelligent database environment users can use point-and-click navigation until they get into a particularly interesting display and can then call up some statistical routines to examine the relationship more closely.

### 5.4.3 Graphical Interpretation Tasks

Graphical interpretation is part of a cybernetic (feedback) model of discovery and understanding about processes and systems. Numerical data represents snapshots in time about different aspects of systems. In a marketing application, the system could be products, advertising, customers, and the various demographic and lifestyle attributes that differentiate the response of different market segments to different products. In quality control, the system might be the production process and the various causes of defects, along with the workers who monitor the system, and the customers who react to the quality of the product over time.

Graphical interpretation consists of a few key activities such as judgment of magnitude (and relative magnitude), judgment of proportion (and relative proportion), judgment of trend and slope, and judgment of grouping.

**5.4.3.1** *Magnitude and Change*    There are some basic questions about data. The first of these questions is "How much?" and the related question is "Did it change?"

It is often difficult to separate the concept of magnitude (how much) from the concept of variability. For instance, say that we have five retail outlets and we are told that sales for four of the outlets improved last week. That might actually turn out to be bad news if the fifth outlet had a sharp drop in sales that exceeded the combined improvement in the other four outlets. In this case there is some variability between the outlets, and while the mean (average) change in sales might be useful to know, most managers would also want to know about the store with the unusual or worrisome sales figures.

Examples of similar questions that might be asked include:

- How many defects did we have last week?
- How many nondefective units does a typical new operator turn out on the first day of work?
- How many tons of sulfur dioxide are being emitted by our three largest coal burning plants?

The response to this type of question is generally judged with respect to some threshold or expected value. We might want to know whether the sulfur emissions are meeting an environmental standard. This type of comparison with a standard can be tricky because slight deviations from the standard may be due to chance variation (see the discussion on statistical significance and natural variation in Chapter 4). A 1% increase in sulfur emissions might be due to a slightly higher sulfur content in the coal that was used, or to a potentially troublesome fault in the "scrubber" that scavenges sulfur from the emissions.

Instead of comparing a current value with a standard, one might also compare the current value with a previous value, or with another current value. An airline might want to know if the number of items of baggage it has lost has increased in the past month, or it might want to know how well it is doing in this regard compared to its competitors. While statistics can help in answering such questions, there is often considerable benefit to "eyeballing" the data and examining the relationships visually.

Judgments of magnitude and change in charts generally focus on the absolute or relative length of lines. As shall be seen later, these judgments can be enhanced by allowing the person to judge magnitude by judging position, and by ensuring that the judgment is not distorted by various forms of visual illusion.

**5.4.3.2** *Proportion*    Assessment of proportion is frequently necessary in decision making and resource allocation. A car manufacturer might want to know what proportion of its profits last year was due to trucks versus minivans. A manager may want to know what proportion of the budget ("piece of the pie") was consumed by the capital cost of computing equipment versus software purchases. Not surprisingly, perhaps, information about proportions is well conveyed by pie charts.

Proportions may be compared visually to ascertain relative proportion. Colloquially, relative proportion is concerned with questions like "Is my piece of the pie getting bigger?" Judgments of relative proportion seem to be difficult for people to make using existing methods (pie charts).

### 5.4.3.3 *Trend, Slope, and Correlation*

Trend and slope are particularly important in time series data. Stock market analysts want to know if a stock is moving up or down. Managers want to know if their sales figures are improving. School boards want to know if intakes of children for future classes will increase or decrease. Trend information of this sort can be shown visually in line charts and scattergrams. In contrast, it is very difficult to assess trends by comparing different bar charts.

In time series data with lots of data points, the eye tends to get distracted by short term fluctuations in the data. Consequently, people often need help in seeing data trends, and this can be provided in the form of lines or curves that highlight the trend. In such situations, care has to be taken to balance the need to understand the overall trend with the need to understand the variability and microstructure of the data.

Trend information answers the question "Are things getting better or worse?" If things appear to be getting better (or worse), one can ask the question "How much better (or worse)?" Quantification of trends provides us with slope information. People are not very good at judging precise slope. However, statistical methods such as regression can be used to quantify slope. One can even estimate a confidence interval around the value of the slope.

Visual comparisons work better in comparing relative slope if it is possible to plot the different time series being compared on the same axis. In this case the human eye is very good at discerning the fact that two lines are not parallel due to the readily apparent (and systematic) fluctuation in distances between the two lines.

### 5.4.3.4 *Groups and Outliers*

The human eye is good at grouping based on proximity. It can also group very easily based on similarity of color, size, and shape. Statistical methods of grouping (cluster analysis) are much less well developed than statistical methods for assessing magnitude, proportion, and trend. Thus visual grouping is a particularly important task for the human analyst.

There are a wide range of grouping activities that may occur when viewing data visualizations. For instance, clusters of points might be identified in a scattergram that correspond to market segments, or certain types of car dealer. Other groupings may occur in glyphlike comparison of bar charts. For instance, Figure 5.14 shows a plot of hypothetical data for different sales people in a marketing department. The four panels of the figure show different profiles of sales across different types of product. People are fairly good at scanning across and identifying these different groups in a display of multiple bar charts.

Outliers can also be spotted visually in many instances. Outliers will tend to be spatially separated from other data points in a scattergram. Detection of outliers can be assisted by using confidence intervals and error bars to show what deviations are significant. For instance, error bars drawn around the line of best fit in a scattergram can indicate points that are outliers (assuming that the data conforms to the linear model).

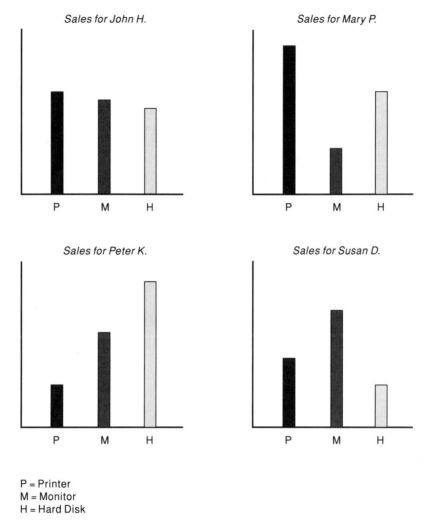

Sales for John H.

Sales for Mary P.

Sales for Peter K.

Sales for Susan D.

P = Printer
M = Monitor
H = Hard Disk

**Figure 5.14** Bar charts showing hypothetical sales data for four different sales people.

### 5.4.4 Data Visualization for Hyperdata

There are many ways in which interactive data visualizations may be defined. For instance, a number of software packages use a model where a data file or table exists and various operations on the data can be selected using menus or tool palettes. These operations include statistical analyses and graphical presentations, where the user chooses which aspects of the data to graph and what types of chart to use. In some cases the user may also choose which symbols to display data points with, what shading to use on bar or pie segments, and so on. These packages provide the user with a great deal of choice in creating visualizations of data, but this choice comes at the cost of some effort in designing the overall visualization.

It is important that point and click navigation be simple and quick to use. It should require little if any expertise in database querying or graphic design. When the user pauses during the navigation process it should be to have a cup of coffee or examine a chart in more detail, not to figure out how to create the next chart to be studied. Thus we need to consider what type of data visualization process can support this style of navigation.

Ideally, charts and graphs should be created automatically, as and when they are needed. How can a visualization system determine what graph should be displayed next? Our answer to this problem is to exploit the natural structure of numerical data. Each data table consists of a number of attributes. Further, these attributes have logical relationships (such as those expressed in an entity-relationship model) and each application will have preferred types of chart (e.g., line charts of closing prices and daily sales volumes for stock market analysis).

The problem of activating interactive visualization during hyperdata navigation will be considered more fully in Chapter 6. For now note that the graphics or charts need to have selectable regions that can be clicked on to indicate users' current interests and to provide some indication of what they want to see next. In this approach, clicking at different points on the visual template is equivalent to asking a well defined question (query) of the data.

Figure 5.15 shows a bar chart with embedded hyperactions. Selectable regions of the figure that a user may click on are marked. At the top of the figure is the label.

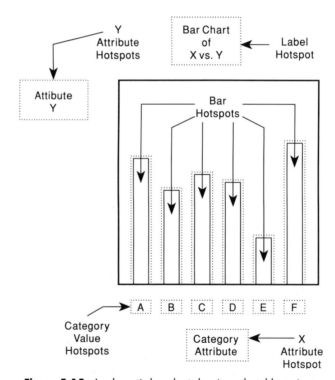

**Figure 5.15** A schematic bar chart showing selectable regions.

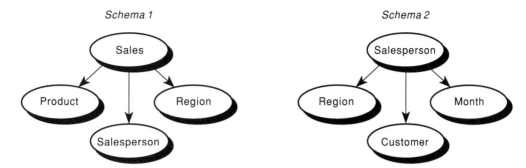

**Figure 5.16** Two attribute schemas for sales data.

When the label is clicked on a description of the chart may pop up. This may either be a "canned" description explaining what a bar chart is and giving the definition of which variables are being plotted, or it may be an annotation that is added by a developer.

On the left is the y-axis. The label at the top left beside the y-axis indicates what attribute the length of the bars is representing. Clicking on the label may be interpreted as interest in that attribute. Figure 5.16 shows a set of transaction schemata for the dollar sales attribute. The regional sales schema shows how dollar sales are linked to regions, salespeople, and products. The customer sales schema shows how the dollar sales for a salesperson are linked to customers, regions, and months. These schemata would normally be set up by the database developer. Clicking on the x-axis or y-axis would then activate the schemata for the corresponding attribute.

The use of well-defined regions of charts (visual templates) as active hotspots allows us to make inferences about which schema should be activated and which objects are of interest. The mechanisms for using these inferred interests to select visualizations in hyperdata will be explained in Chapter 6. For now, note that in order for this to work we need to use visualizations that have well-defined hotspots, where selection of particular hotspots by clicking on them allows the intelligent database application to infer the current interests of the user.

## ■ 5.5 CONCLUSIONS

Most database management systems have tended to emphasize input processes and there are relatively few tools for enhancing the display and interpretation of output. Past emphasis on input processes has been justified, because one can't have good output results without good input in the first place. As the technology of database input processes becomes more mature, the scope for development of new types of output process increases, and the role of output processes in determining the viability and usefulness of databases increases. Data visualization allows people to output database information in a highly summarized form and extract patterns and trends with the aid of the highly developed human perceptual capability. Thus data visualization enhances and amplifies human reasoning.

Computer graphics have long been important for business purposes. There are two main areas of usage, the first being to produce presentation aids such as 35mm slides, overhead transparencies, videotapes, and even multimedia presentations to illustrate points in conferences, meetings, and training sessions. Computer graphics are also used in business to assist the process of decision making. Graphics, when used appropriately, provide a tremendous data summarization capability.

Graphs and charts must be constructed in such a way that they encourage appropriate interpretation of the underlying data. In practice this means that they must conform to principles of good design without triggering inappropriate perceptual cues or other inappropriate perceptual distortions.

Data visualization is a key tool for intelligent database applications because it allows the user to see the patterns in complex data. Data visualization allows users to switch rapidly between different representations of the data depending on their needs.

Information discovery through rule generation and anomaly detection can be supplemented and supported through information discovery by data visualization. For instance, the IDIS discovery system works by combining graphs, rule generation, and anomaly detection within an integrated environment.

In this chapter a model for selecting different chart types in different situations was developed, and a variety of different chart types that may be used in data visualization were described. In Chapter 6 a model of hyperdata will be developed that can combine a set of data visualizations into a hypermedia network that can be browsed and explored using a point-and-click style of user interface.

# 6

# HYPERINFORMATION AND HYPERDATA

*"It is the natural tendency of the human mind to proceed from the simple to the complex."*

— Jean Piaget*

*Corollary*: Hyperinformation allows the user to selectively delay the exposure to complexity.

## ■ 6.1 INTRODUCTION

Mature technologies work well and they don't tend to change. Books are a mature technology, and books work well. Why should we look for an alternative to books? Electronic information systems are faced with this dilemma. How can electronic information provide us with new capabilities without losing the benefit of the navigational tools and strategies that work so well with books?

Hypertext was developed as a type of antithesis to the way books work, a form of nonlinear exploration of electronic text. However, books allow both linear and nonlinear navigation, and thus hypertext and other forms of hyperinformation need to provide flexible access as well. While the basic motivation for early hypertext focused on its nonlinearity, the current focus is towards flexibility. Hypertext structures and documents are versatile because in principle they allow any piece of information (node) to be linked to any other piece of information. This versatility can be extended by adding extra navigation tools such as a table of contents and keyword search.

It is no accident that the word hypertext is spelled hypert-e-x-t. In spite of discussions about multimedia, text is still the dominant medium of communication in many hypertext and hypermedia systems. Making all the hypertext links that are needed in electronic text is costly and time consuming. Hypertext has to represent a considerable improvement over conventional text before people are willing to expend

---

* *Structuralism*, Harper & Row, 1970. Jean Piaget was born in Switzerland in 1896, and received a PhD from the University of Neuchatel. His experiments on the development of perceptual abilities in children have made him well known throughout the world.

a great deal of energy in creating it. Good hypertext linking requires sophisticated text analysis, and often such analysis requires human input.

The emphasis on linking text is largely historical. It stems from the fact that early computer systems handled text a lot better than they handled graphical presentations of data. Intelligent databases require h-y-p-e-r-DATA, (i.e., the nonlinear structuring of data representations within a browsable and navigable information system). Hyperdata systems still include plenty of text in the form of annotations and attached text files, but the emphasis on data visualization within a hyperdata system leads to a somewhat different model of nonlinear and responsive information.

Hypertext, hyperdata, and hypermedia are all forms of hyperinformation (Figure 6.1). Hyperinformation is the linear and nonlinear arrangement of various forms of information into electronic documents. Electronic documents are very different from the printed documents that most people are familiar with. Electronic documents may include video clips, simulations, and animations. Furthermore, the information to be displayed may be calculated or generated as it is being selected or requested. Thus electronic documents are *intrinsically dynamic*.

Printed documents are typically organized as books that contain chapters which in turn contain sections and so on. Thus a book is actually a compound document that contains a tree of subdocuments, although we don't normally think of a section in a chapter as being a document in its own right. Electronic documents can also be constructed as compound documents. Hyperinformation documents often have fuzzy boundaries, since there may be natural links to other electronic documents in any hyperinformation document and it is fairly simple to build that link, effectively incorporating the other document referenced within the hyperinformation (Figure 6.2). Thus hyperinformation documents can expand very rapidly by connecting to large electronic documents already in existence. A large hyperinformation document typically contains a number of nested documents as well as references outside its structure to other electronic documents (which are thus implicitly included within its structure).

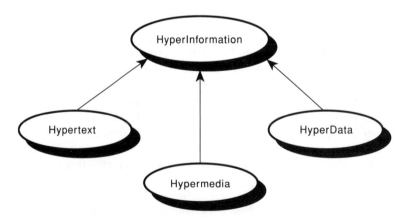

**Figure 6.1** Forms of hyperinformation.

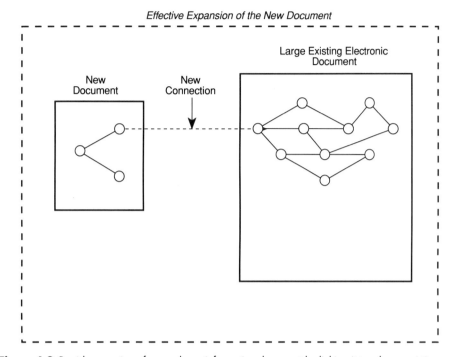

**Figure 6.2** Rapid expansion of a new hyperinformation document by linking it to a large existing document.

Hypertext and hypermedia (the inclusion of other media such as sound, graphics, and video in information networks) are central components of intelligent database technology (Parsaye et al. 1989). In this chapter the third type of hyperinformation is introduced — hyperdata (see also Parsaye and Chignell 1992). While hypertext and hypermedia have traditionally focused on text presentation and accompanying graphics and sound for applications such as documentation and training, the hypermedia model needs to be adapted to the special needs of data presentation within an intelligent database application. The term hyperdata is used here to distinguish this approach from more textual styles of information presentation.

Working with hypertext, hypermedia, and hyperdata requires both vision and pragmatism. Hypertext and related technologies must be handled carefully if they are to be used effectively. At a conference in San Francisco once, Ted Nelson (the person who coined the term "hypertext")was about to begin a typically lively presentation when his assistant dropped the slide carousel, spilling the slides all over the floor. Some wag in the audience called out gleefully, *"Now that's hypertext!"* That incident was an appropriate metaphor for the promise and pitfalls of hypertext and other forms of hypermedia. How can we create nonlinear representations of information without making a disorganized mess?

We coined the terms *hyperdata* and *hyperinformation* to extend the hypertext metaphor to applications which go beyond text. As this chapter will show, the basic concept of "hyperaccess" is useful for many types of information.

There are two components of hyperinformation: nodes and links. There are also a number of different types of nodes and links. Some of the main types of node are text, graphs, sounds, video clips, and charts and diagrams. There are a variety of different types of link that can be used in hyperinformation systems.

This chapter will review the nature of hyperinformation and critique current hypertext research and systems. Hyperdata will then be introduced as a tractable version of nonlinear information well suited for the special requirements of interpreting numerical data. The fundamental principles of navigation will be discussed, and a model of hyperdata use and the hyperdata life cycle will be described. The chapter concludes with a discussion of how the usability of hyperdata and other types of hyperinformation can be assessed.

## ■ 6.2 THE HISTORY AND EVOLUTION OF HYPERINFORMATION

Hypertext is a great idea. Everyone wants unrestricted access to electronic information using an intuitive form of exploration and browsing. Like many great ideas though, hypertext has a few bugs that need to be worked out. For a start, hypertext is still a cottage industry. Fully linked hypertext documents with more than two megabytes of information are rare. People haven't learned how to use hypertexts, and it is not surprising. There is not much payoff in learning how to read when there are only a few books available.

### 6.2.1 Definition

The basic idea of hypertext as described in Bush's (1945) Memex system has not changed conceptually, only the implementation details are different. A hypertext system consists of a set of information containers linked together. Each of the containers of text is called a node. Users are shown the nodes, and "go" to other nodes by selecting, in some way that is system dependent, a link. Links can be organized into two general categories: typed links and non-typed links. Typed links are links which are given a name when created. The name usually represents the type of relationship that exists between the nodes being linked (Trigg 1983).

Hypertext systems often have other functions that are shared by non-hypertext systems (i.e., full text search, history of visited pieces of text, etc.). Thus, in practice, the definition of what is a hypertext system can be quite fuzzy. This has made it difficult to exchange findings or information content between different hypertext systems.

People have some intuitive notions of what hypertext is, but the consensus model of hypertext is extremely broad and still under development (NIST 1990). As of 1990 there were over 100 different hypertext systems reported in the literature (Irler and Colazzo 1990), each representing somewhat different conceptions of the basic notion of hypertext.

Hyperinformation is a broad term that refers to electronic documents consisting of nodes of information connected by links. A hyperinformation System is a system that includes hyperinformation documents along with modules for creating new nodes and links and a user interface for browsing and reading the content material contained in the documents.

Hyperinformation systems provide the following functions and capabilities:

- Navigation
- Querying
- Presentation
- Structuring
- Authoring
- Text Manipulation and Generation

### 6.2.2 The Hyperinformation Metaphor

The overall metaphor of hyperinformation is generally spatial. Browsing consists of navigating through an information structure. This contrasts with the collection metaphor typically used with on-line retrieval systems and with query-based database interfaces. In the collection metaphor users describe what they want and then it is collected by some agent or system and presented to the user.

The navigational aspect of hyperinformation is reinforced by the use of maps (typically 2-D box and arrow representations of nodes and their relative position) to assist in browsing. However, the navigation metaphor is not intrinsic to hyperinformation, since book-like metaphors may also be used. When a person clicks on a hyperinformation hotspot, it is up to the interface metaphor to determine what happens next. In the collection (or replacement) metaphor, a new page is brought to the user and replaces or overlaps the previous page. In the navigation metaphor the users themselves "move" to the new piece of information. These two metaphors are differentiated in the user interface by different cues relating to command names, screen visual effects, and the use of related tools such as maps (navigational) or querying (replacement).

The use of interface metaphors enhances hyperinformation usability (Waterworth and Chignell 1989). The book is a useful metaphor that seems to work well in book-like applications (e.g., Benest and Dukic 1990), but in other situations (e.g., visualization of data) it seems less appropriate. In the model of hyperdata discussed later in this chapter, a "slide presentation" metaphor will be used, where users view a sequence of visual presentations (slides) selected from a huge number of slides and where they are free to change the order at any time.

### 6.2.3 Early History

Hypertext, as the forerunner of hyperinformation, is a byproduct of the age of electronic information. Object representations of text have grown out of the special opportunities that electronic text provides. Originally, authors wrote or typed their manuscripts and these were then typeset from scratch again. Later, as more people wrote with word processors, this duplication of work continued, with people inputting and formatting documents and then producing hardcopy which was input and formatted all over again. Furthermore, organizations such as the U.S. Department of Defense might deal with many different typesetters or print shops, each with their own preferred formatting language. Thus it was recognized that there was a great deal of advantage in having a standardized language for describing documents. Originally, this advantage was seen in terms of preserving formatting across different representations of the document on different systems, however, object representations of documents can also be used by hypertext systems for conversion of text into hypertext, and for creation of different formatting styles "on the fly."

Early researchers saw hypertext as an artificial memory that could make huge amounts of external information available to the human user. H.G. Wells in the 1930s envisaged "a nervous network . . . knitting all the intellectual workers of the world through a common interest and a common medium of expression into a more and more conscious co-operating unity." This idea has continued to some extent in the "docuverse" envisioned by Ted Nelson. Thus the first interpretation of hypertext is as a type of shared world memory and information archive.

The second theme in hyperinformation is for personal access to large information archives (e.g., the Memex idea of Vannevar Bush). Thus the two themes in hypertext are shared access to knowledge and personal access to knowledge. Both are important reasons for developing and using hypertext. In the discussion of hyperdata in this chapter the personal access model of information exploration is used. In chapter eight this model will be expanded to include shared access in the discussions on executive information systems and group work.

Although hypertext often has an explicitly nonlinear structure, nonlinearity is more a property of the style of reading than it is of how the written material is structured. Books can be just as nonlinear as hypertext. This is seen, for instance, in skilled analysis of scientific papers; many readers tend to read the abstract and discussion first, skipping around the key points of the text in a nonlinear fashion.

The modern history of hypertext (e.g., Conklin 1987; Parsaye et al. 1989, Chapter 5) began with Vannevar Bush in his writings about Memex (e.g., Bush 1945). The Memex, as Bush called it, was a mechanical system that would help scientists in storing and retrieving vast amounts of information by the use of "links" between documents.

The Memex idea lay fallow for some time because computing technology was not yet ready to implement it. Then in the mid-1960s things began to move. Engelbart built NLS, a hypertext-like system (Engelbart and English 1968), and Ted Nelson coined the term "hypertext." Meanwhile, the idea of vastly powerful information systems was being absorbed into popular mythology, often embodied in the form of a software agent (e.g., HAL9000 in the film *2001: A Space Odyssey,* or the computer in the "Star Trek" television series).

In the 1960s and 1970s hypertext remained largely a research idea that only a privileged few could experiment with. In the 1980s hypertext hit the mass market (comparatively speaking). In 1987 the well-known NoteCards system had perhaps 100 users, and by 1988 Apple's HyperCard environment had many thousands of users.

Hypertext is in fact best understood as a form of hyperinformation. The essential aspect of hyperinformation is that it is a highly usable and natural interface to information. Thus the intellectual core of hyperinformation is access and retrieval, not storage. Once this fact is realized, the role of hyperinformation as a component of information presentation and interpretation systems becomes much clearer. The role of hyperinformation in presentation will be pursued further in Chapter 7.

### 6.2.4 Evolution of Hyperinformation

The term "hypertext" was coined in 1965 and it was the first component of hyperinformation to be recognized. The term hypermedia became prominent in the 1980s as a means of emphasizing the emerging multimedia nature of electronic documents. Hyperdata was first formally noted as a component of hyperinformation in 1992 (Parsaye and Chignell 1992).

The development of hypertext and the evolution of hyperinformation has been based on systems, real or imagined. Recent developments have been greatly influenced by particular software products. Each of these products has its own features and represents its own view on what hyperinformation (and in particular, hypertext) is.

The NoteCards system was developed at Xerox Parc (Halasz et al. 1987). Although it ran on a Xerox Lisp workstation and was thus not readily available to most users, it probably had the largest (or at least most geographically dispersed) group of users of any hypertext environment prior to the introduction of Guide in 1986 and Hyper-Card in 1987.

The Intermedia system was developed as part of the IRIS project at Brown University over a number of years, with its roots going back to the late 1960s. The Intermedia system is widely regarded as one of the best examples of a hypertext/hypermedia development and browsing environment. Intermedia ran on a Unix platform and used a relational database to store and access the links in hypertext. It also pioneered methods of using anchors to represent different types of links in the text.

While Intermedia was used internally in courses (particularly English literature) at Brown University, it did not become widely used outside that university. In part this was because it was a high-end hypertext environment that ran on expensive equipment not in widespread use (first AIX on the IBM PC RT and then A/UX on the Macintosh II).

Guide was the first mass-market hypertext system, developed originally at the University of Kent at Canterbury in England, and then marketed by OWL. Guide was a strongly textual system (Parsaye et al. 1989, Chapter 5), but it had the advantage of being available on both the PC and Macintosh platforms. Another system was KMS which grew out of the ZOG project at Carnegie Mellon University.

HyperCard is perhaps the best known "hypertext" system, which is ironic since it is not really a hypertext system at all, but rather a general programming environment which can be used to develop hypertext as well as many other types of applications. HyperCard is really a collection of tools, including paint tools, user interface development tools (menus, buttons, etc.), and a programming language. While hypertext systems can be implemented in it, HyperCard has no inherent model of hypertext.

One of the few projects to look at how different hypertext systems create documents was ACM's hypertext on hypertext, where the proceedings of a conference were converted into hypertext as an experiment. This project was highly instructive in showing how different the various hypertext platforms really were.

Current methods of hyperinformation have evolved to meet the needs of browsing in large text structures. As different tasks are explored, the conception of what hyperinformation is will evolve and grow. For instance, methods for collating and organization electronic mail messages, and other artifacts created in collaborative work will drive the development of future hyperinformation systems.

## ■ 6.3 COMPONENTS OF HYPERINFORMATION

Hypertext and related systems are typically used with a mouse or other pointing device. When the user clicks on an item (e.g. the word "grain sales") a window with more text or options appears and provides further information (e.g., "grain sales represents the total tonnage of all grains shipped in the calendar year"), and from there further hypertext may be obtained (e.g., the chart showing grain sales for a particular year).

In spite of their many differences, hypertext systems share the common feature of being composed out of nodes and links. Nodes can best be thought of as objects, with their own internal structure that will tend to differ in different applications. In particular, nodes may be either text objects or data objects.

### 6.3.1 Nodes

Hypertext nodes are used for storing the information users are going to browse through. Nodes are the smallest piece of a hypertext document that can be accessed by links. Nodes can contain text, graphics, sound, or even video (Harrison 1991; Alves 1991). Hypertext which has more than text in its nodes is also referred to as hypermedia. Depending on the system, nodes can also be called pages, cards, units, topics, articles, rames, records, documents, files, components, and so on.

Nodes can be aggregated or composed into higher structures (Lai and Chua 1991). Virtual structures permit the user to compose descriptions of the hypertext and call them by name, instead of hardwiring the hypertext. This capability to create virtual structures as hypertext is sometimes referred to as dynamic hypertext. However, we will refer to this capability here as "modifiable" hypertext and reserve the term "dynamic" for links that are created or calculated at run-time.

#### 6.3.1.1 *Text Objects*    Representation of text objects has come a long way since early systems modeled documents as sequences of paragraphs. In those days, each paragraph was a sequence of characters. Formatting was then linked to text representations in terms of different styles or looks being associated with the individual paragraphs or characters to describe their appearance. This style or look would include such things as the character's font and size, along with features such as underlining, bolding, and italicization. A paragraph's look might include the margins associated with the paragraph, the spacings between the lines of the paragraph, and the positioning of the paragraph on the page (e.g., centered versus left with a ragged right margin).

Other properties or styles could be defined for the whole document. For instance, in the Bravo editor (developed at Xerox Parc), the Page Properties Sheet specified certain properties (such as the margins and the appearance of the page numbering) for the entire document. In more advanced document modeling systems, text objects can be defined within a class system. In such object-oriented text representation systems, modification of the component properties associated with an object can be applied to the type (where it affects all objects of that type), or it may be applied to one specific instance only. The entire document can then be modeled as a hierarchy of text (abstract) objects (Furuta 1987).

The standard generalized markup language (SGML) was a breakthrough in document representation in the 1980s because for the first time it provided a commonly accepted standard for representing documents. In fact SGML was more of a framework than a standard since it allowed considerable scope for varying the way in which the details of the representation were implemented. SGML is a declarative language where the formatter is regarded as a document compiler (Joboloff 1987). The source program for this compiler is the document to format, the object code is the printable form. The fundamental advance made by SGML is that the source document is expressed in a rigorous language and the compiler can make use of general compiling techniques to parse the source document and construct a tree reflecting the document structure.

Markup in SGML is based on enclosing elements that require markup between left and right brackets, accompanied by appropriate symbols. The left-hand bracket, or start-tag, begins with the character <, followed by a label, while the corresponding right-hand closing parenthesis or end-tag is identified with the same tag label (preceded by the character /). For instance, a chapter would be marked up as follows:

```
<chapter>
Section 1
. . .
Section N
</chapter>
```

Authors can also define their own text structure in SGML through the definition of new tags (in a process referred to as element declaration). An element declaration defines a new class of entity with its structure and properties. This style of individualized or customized markup definition provides a metalanguage capability. For example, the following construction could be used (Joboloff 1988):

```
<!ENTITY % title "#CDATA"
<!ELEMENT
01 article        (%title, abstract, section+, references?)
version (draft \| final)
02 abstract       p
03 section (%title, (p \| list \| fig )* )
04 list (p+)
type              (simple, enumeration)
05 fig            (graphics, caption)
   xsize, ysize #NUMBERS
06 graphics       #CDATA
07 caption p
```

The use of the symbol ENTITY makes it possible to define an entity (macro) which will be reused later. In the first construction, a title is defined as a character string. The second construction shows that an article is formed of a title (a character string), a summary, and sections (+ indicates that there is at least one), followed optionally by references. An article also has the attribute "version" which takes the value draft or final. The abstract is then followed by a section, which also has a title, followed by a series of objects which are either paragraphs, lists, or figures. The final construction deals with figures, each of which includes a drawing and a caption. The attributes xsize and ysize then indicate the space allocated to the figure.

More information on SGML is given in the SGML handbook (Barron 1989). SGML and other forms of high-level representation of text objects are mostly concerned with providing a more flexible text formatting or conversion capability. In this case, the interest lies with the representation of nodes as objects in order to facilitate querying. The next section is concerned with the handling of data objects.

*6.3.1.2* **Data Objects**    Data is not usually thought of in terms of objects. However, data is often thought of in terms of tables. For instance, data in a relational database is stored in tables, and data in a spreadsheet is also stored as a type of table. The tuples or rows within such tables are typically instances of an object.

Data objects for display purposes can be constructed based on visualizations such as charts and graphs. In this case, the data from a number of underlying objects are summarized as a new data object that represents those underlying objects. This has the effect of creating a many to one compression of underlying objects into a single visual presentation. In hyperdata, such data objects correspond to the text objects that are expressed as nodes in a hypertext system. Like fragments of text, data objects can be hierarchically organized and linked into network structures. Figure 6.3 shows a set of hierarchically organized data objects that display the sales data for an organization.

Data objects also have their own structure. Text objects tend to be organized in documents, chapters, sections, subsections, paragraphs, and sentences. In similar fashion, data objects are organized into presentations or briefings, chart sequences, charts, and individual attribute data, along with specialized components of charts such as captions, legends, scaling factors, and so on.

The definition of a data object includes both a graphical and logical component. The logical component consists of concepts such as charts and chart labels that were mentioned above. In contrast, the graphical component consists of the object representation of the associated graphical layout and is somewhat akin to the graphical objects used in various drawing software (e.g., MacDraw on the Macintosh).

Much of the functionality of the intelligent database derives from the use of abstract data types that allow the equivalence of information to be recognized and transmitted across diverse representations of that information. For instance, an employee of a company might be represented as a record in a relational employee database for that company. A biography of that person may also appear within a hypermedia document, or that employee may be referred to as an instance of the general class of Person elsewhere in the system. However, no matter where the information about the employee is stored, the descriptions, rules, and so on refer to a common object (i.e., the instance of that person) that is being described.

In similar fashion to a text document, a graph may be defined as a combination of the data associated with the graph and stylistic information that specifies how to present the graph. Presentation style includes such things as axis labels and plotting symbols. This stylistic information is then combined with the data to produce a graph. Thus this information serves as a style sheet for the formatting of the chart or graph.

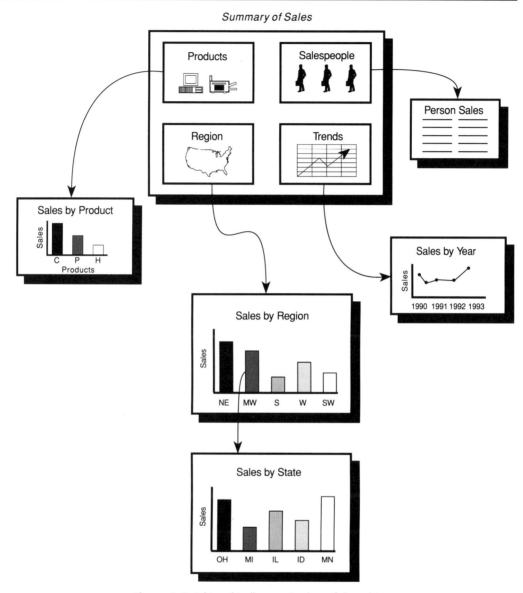

**Figure 6.3** A hierachically organized set of data objects.

## 6.3.2 Links

Links are the elements that let the user navigate from one node to another. Some hypertext systems are designed so that links are untyped, that is, users just see a connection between nodes but there is no explicit meaning for that connection. Other systems have a fixed set of links that authors can use, while still another group of systems lets authors create an unlimited number of types of links.

Parsaye et al. (1989) classified links into three categories: Hierarchical Links, Relational Links, and Execution Links. Trigg (1983) proposed a taxonomy of links for scientific hypertext, while Schuler and Smith (1990) describe a taxonomy of links to be used for the support of argumentation of ideas. Links can produce a variety of different results: transfer to a new topic; show a reference; provide ancillary information, such as a footnote, a definition, or annotation; display an illustration, schematic, photograph, or video; or run another program (Shneiderman 1989).

Links are also classified as static or dynamic. A static link is a link which has been authored or created by a user and will not be modified at use time. Dynamic links are the links that are created, modified, or deleted at run time. These links should be modified by a system of rules (production rule system) which will be activated when certain conditions are present. This will permit the generation of links that will fit the user.

Chaffin and Herrman (1988) report that people are able to perceive and create novel relations. This can lead to an explosion of link types. Trigg (1983) proposed the use of a fixed set of typed links. He argued that giving users the facility for creating their own link types was not the right solution because of the following reasons:

1. Explosion of link types. If users are not restricted in their creation of links, systems are going to become too difficult to manage.
2. Reader confusion: without a standard for naming the links, there will be a chance for users to become confused over the meaning of links created by others. This will affect users when trying to criticize other user's works.
3. System confusion: some of the links proposed by Trigg were only partially understood by the system.

Two types of links that have received attention in the hypertext literature are hierarchical links and relational links.

**6.3.2.1** *Hierarchical Links* These links are used for expressing hierarchical relations and building categorizations of the domain of interest. Frame-based systems like KMS (Akscyn et al. 1988) rely on the idea of categorization. Links low in the hierarchy inherit the properties of the higher level links.

One way of building hierarchies is to have two kinds of link: more general and more specific. The more general link moves to a parent or higher level object in the hierarchy, while a more specific link moves to a lower level object or entity in the hierarchy. Printed documents rely heavily on the use of hierarchical organization of information. Most documents are organized into chapters which in turn are organized into sections containing subsections. Similarly, hierarchical representations of data may also be constructed. Hierarchical links are particularly useful for looking at data at different levels of detail or abstraction. For instance, drilling down in executive information systems is an example of the use of hierarchical links in exploring a data presentation.

**6.3.2.2** *Relational Links* Relational links help to connect objects which are related in a non-hierarchical fashion. Relational links allow the user to make a number of judgments about the relation between concepts or objects, such as Chaffin and Herrman (1988) did. It is possible to:

1. Judge some relations as more similar than others
2. Distinguish one relation from another
3. Identify instances of common relations
4. Express relations using everyday words and expressions
5. Recognize instances of relation ambiguity
6. Perceive and create novel relations

One of the questions addressed in the present description of hyperdata is: What is the set of meaningful relations that link different presentations of data? Fortunately, the set of meaningful relations for data is more restricted than for text.

### 6.3.3    Maps and Search Tools

Nodes and links provide the structure of hyperinformation. However, in large hyperinformation structures one also needs various tools to assist in finding information within the structure and in getting a sense of where one is in the information. A variety of maps and search tools are available for this purpose, and will be discussed in this section.

**6.3.3.1    Book Functions**    The functions we are familiar with from books can be transferred fairly directly into the hyperinformation environment. These include table of contents, index, pages and page sequencing, and bibliography. Most of us are so familiar with these that we take them for granted. However, they are the result of centuries of experimentation, intensified after the invention of movable type in the mid-fifteenth century.

Literacy is largely a modern phenomenon. Various estimates place male adult literacy prior to the year 1500 at below 5% of the population. One of the reasons for low literacy was that books were not part of everyday life. They were expensive and relatively few in number. In Europe, the major advance in literacy occurred between 1500 and 1800 as the number of book titles published per year went from 1,000 to 20,000. Thus books in the fifteenth century were a relatively unfamiliar technology to the general public, just as hyperinformation was a new concept to many people in the 1980s.

When people are given the chance to use book functions in a hyperinformation system they tend to use them quite naturally, often in preference to the hyperinformation links that are also available. This can be explained in part by the fact that people have been trained much more thoroughly in using books than in using hyperinformation. However, it also reflects the fact that book functions are inherently useful, which is not surprising since they have been developed and tested over hundreds of years.

Figure 6.4 shows a screen shot from a hyperinformation system that includes booklike functions. This screen is part of a hypertext fax manual created by Felix Valdez as part of his study of hypertext navigation (Valdez 1992). Several booklike

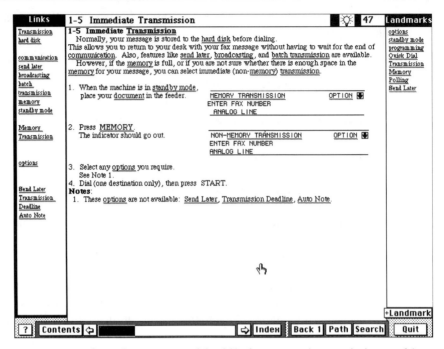

**Figure 6.4** A screen from a hypertext manual (book-like features are shown at the bottom of the screen).

features are shown. One button takes the reader back to the table of contents, while another provides access to the index. The next and previous page buttons are analogous to turning pages in a book. In addition, the slide bar shown at the center bottom of the screen allows the reader to move a portion of the way through the book. The information provided by the position of the slide bar is similar to the information one gets by looking at the profile of the book to see how thick the pile of pages that has been read or how much of the book is prior to the current page. This gives a sense of "how far through the book" one is.

Figure 6.4 shows how booklike functions can be added fairly naturally to a hyperinformation interface. Users then have the choice of using the hyperinformation or booklike functions as they see fit.

**6.3.3.2** *Search Functions*    Search functions are also considered to be outside the essential elements of the hyperinformation paradigm. However, like booklike functions they provide an important additional functionality to the user. Search in text generally corresponds to the use of querying in databases. For text, the most common form of search is Boolean querying.

Boolean queries provide a great deal of power, flexibility, and context independence. A Boolean query consists of a set of keywords connected by the operators AND, OR, and NOT. In addition parentheses may be added to make the meaning of the query clearer. For instance, "Discovery AND Hypertext AND (NOT Statistics)" is an example of a Boolean query which would retrieve documents that mentioned both discovery and hypertext, but not statistics.

Boolean queries are difficult to formulate (e.g., Borgman 1986) for a number of reasons. These reasons range from the ambiguity of AND and OR operators, to difficulties with NOT, problems with nesting and parentheses, and operator precedence.

When expressed textually, Boolean syntax uses the English words AND and OR to represent set union and intersection. By borrowing the words, this syntax implicitly borrows the English meanings of these words (Golovchinsky and Chignell 1992). The problem is that these meanings are sometimes ambiguous without context, and this ambiguity can cause novices to misinterpret the meanings of Boolean expressions. For example, in English the word "and" can correspond either to the Boolean AND operator or to the OR operator. The word "or" in turn, can signify both inclusive and exclusive OR operators, in contrast to the Boolean OR which is strictly inclusive. When a person says that they are interested in football *and* baseball they are usually interested in articles on either topic (i.e., a Boolean OR) rather than in only articles that mention both topics (corresponding to a Boolean AND).

Various methods have been developed to make Boolean queries easier to use. For instance, the Queries-R-Links system (Golovchinsky and Chignell 1992) uses a style of graphical and interactive querying where the user builds a query by clicking on words in the text being read.

Relevance feedback is another method to assist the user in querying. In this method the query is normally expressed as a vector of terms with varying weights. In relevance feedback, the user expresses a query, and then reviews the documents that are retrieved, classifying them as either relevant or irrelevant. The search terms in the query are then modified so that the terms that tend to appear in relevant documents are given higher weightings, while the terms that tend to appear in the irrelevant documents are given lower weightings or removed from the query altogether.

Hyperinformation systems can accommodate a variety of different search functions. However, queries that can be expressed from within the text or information that is currently being viewed will generally be preferable. This avoids the "mode switching" that occurs in some information retrieval systems where the query is viewed in one window while the information is viewed in a different window.

### 6.3.3.3 *Maps and Organizers*

The user of hyperinformation generally needs to be aware of its structure. While aimless browsing is certainly possible, most users will have some goal in mind when they use it. Thus they will want to have at least a rough idea of where various types of information are likely to be found. Maps and organizers provide the type of structural information that people need.

Landmarks (Lynch 1959) are reference points external to the observer. There seems to be a tendency for people in a city to rely increasingly on systems of landmarks for their guides over time.

A key property of landmarks is the ability to stand out from other nodes or objects. Landmarks are easily singled out from other objects in the environment when (1) they have a clear form, (2) they contrast with their background, and (3) there is some prominence of spatial location.

Landmarks add to the organizational characteristics of an environment. Good landmarks provide a strong contrast with their background and have prominent spatial location. Because of their spatial prominence, they are good location cues for users.

Landmarks constitute the first stage of knowledge about navigation. At the same time, expert navigators also use landmarks because they are handy reference points.

Landmarks are useful in moving around hypertext (e.g., Parsaye et al. 1989, Chapter 5) in the same way that they are useful in navigating around physical space. Valdez, Chignell, and Glenn (1988) suggested several methods for identifying landmarks in hypertext and developed a method for empirically assessing the quality of a landmark. The basis of that method is the intuitive notion that landmarks often function as waypoints on the path from one location to another.

Hyperinformation systems generally use physical navigation as a metaphor for the design of their interfaces. The user is assumed to be in one location, or node, where some information is presented (textual, graphical, sound), and is also supposed to have a destination goal in mind (target node). Users are provided with navigational tools as browsers and maps.

Maps provide an overall view or picture about the layout and relationships within the hierarchy. Two questions arise when using maps in information systems: (1) how do users learn about the environment, and (2) how do they learn to use maps in order to navigate through the environment?

Maps can be designed so they have a "fish eye" property, that is, locations closer to the city (or node shown) are given more importance than the rest of the objects. Only "very important" cities located far away are illustrated in these maps.

Furnas (1986) proposed the use of a "fish-eye view" approach to viewing information, where a Degree of Interest function is utilized in order to decide which points of the structure are going to be displayed. This function depends on two factors: (1) the previous interest the subject had on the node to be shown, and (2) the distance from the location of the user in the structure to the point to be displayed. The degree of interest function can be "tuned" in order to display a reasonable amount of information.

The fish-eye view is generally a special kind of map, but expanding and collapsing different sections of an outline can also highlight different information, as shown in Figure 6.5.

Maps provide the knowledge required for navigation. There are three types of navigation knowledge (Wickens 1992): landmark, route and survey. Knowledge is first acquired in terms of highly salient visual landmarks in the environment. Next, route knowledge is acquired, giving the ability to navigate between points by making turns at various landmarks (much as aircraft fly from waypoint to waypoint). With survey knowledge comes the fully developed cognitive map. Survey knowledge allows people to give directions or plan journeys along routes not directly traveled.

Road maps or other types of survey knowledge of information structure are sometimes referred to as advanced organizers. Advanced organizers assist users by letting them know ahead of time the structure of the information or task. Availability of advanced organizers generally leads to improved performance.

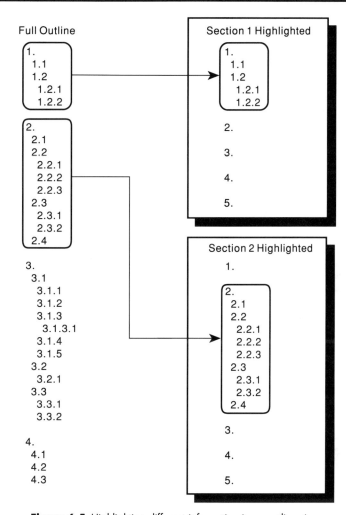

**Figure 6.5** Highlighting different information in an outline view.

## ■ 6.4 HYPERDATA

Hyperdata is a style of hyperinformation for numerical data. It has many of the advantages of hypertext, but few of the disadvantages. Most importantly, there is a specific method for constructing hyperdata, and it is a method that lends itself to automation rather than handcrafting.

One of the motivations for hyperdata is that the task of handcrafting visual presentations of data is just too onerous for very large databases. Thus a method is needed for generating and linking visualizations in an automated fashion. Components of a comprehensive data visualization environment include:

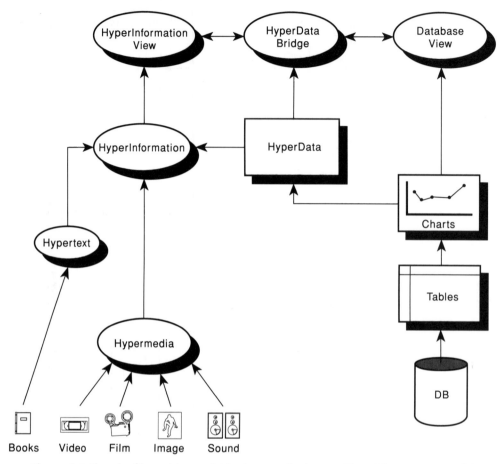

**Figure 6.6** The role of hyperdata as a bridge between database and hyperinformation views of the world.

1. Display of charts and figures
2. Navigation through large amounts of data
3. Visualization of database files
4. Hyperdata linking of charts, data, and annotation
5. Hierarchically organized charts and figures

Nonlinear presentations of data within a browsing environment constitute a special type of hyperinformation. The new term "hyperdata" has been coined to refer to this specialized application of hyperinformation. Hyperdata is an extremely flexible method of organizing presentations of information that is based on predominantly numerical data. Hyperdata is a network representation of information summarized in the form of charts and graphs. The point-and-click style of interaction that a hyperdata

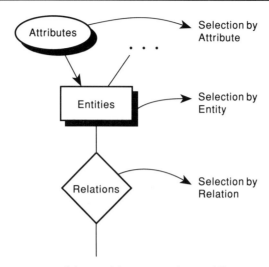

**Figure 6.7** Basic properties of data and their use in selecting different summaries of the data.

interface allows is a natural way to explore visual presentations and summaries of data.

Hyperdata needs its own model, development environments, and design and development methods. Some of the questions considered in designing and developing hyperdata include:

- How can hyperdata help people to manipulate data?
- How can hyperdata help people to navigate around data and information?
- How can hyperdata help people to visualize and interpret information?

Hyperdata is a tool and browsing environment for manipulating, browsing, and visualizing data. Hyperdata is a bridge between the database view of the world and the hyperinformation view of the world (Figure 6.6). The advantage of hyperdata is that it handles the visualization of data in an extremely flexible fashion. However, hyperdata with its extremely dynamic and flexible methods of constructing and linking visual presentations generally works best with manageable subsets of large databases. Thus hyperdata is particularly effective when the user has used some queries or selection criteria to identify an interesting neighborhood of information that limits the scope of possible relevant data to some extent. Judicious use of queries to select the attributes and entities of interest can help in defining a manageable subset of data before navigation is attempted.

Hyperdata takes advantages of the special properties of data. Data refers to entities, attributes and attribute values. Rules express relationships between entities and attribute values, and entities in turn can be selected based on the pattern of attribute values that they have. Figure 6.7 summarizes these basic properties of data.

Hyperdata provides a simple point-and-click style of access to data visualizations, coupled with the use of a control panel and constraint setting to allow the user to customize the behavior of the hyperdata. Other navigation functions may then be integrated with the hyperdata at the level of the intelligent database application user interface, as discussed in Chapter 8.

### 6.4.1 Hyperdata Nodes

Hyperdata nodes differ from hypertext nodes in that they are defined at run-time as customizable visualizations of active data. Unlike text, data is constantly changing. A person's age changes with each birthday, and the prices of various stocks rise and fall from week to week. Thus one of the most important properties of data is that it is active.

Active data is the essential precursor for hyperdata. We must have ready access to the databases that are relevant to our problem domain and this data must be updated regularly. One of the main justifications of hyperdata is that it can use active data to create active information presentations that are automatically updated with the latest data.

Hyperdata nodes are charts and graphs. These charts and graphs are filled with active data. The standard charts and graphs used in hyperdata were described in Chapter 5. They include bar charts, pie charts, scattergrams, and application specific charts like Gantt charts and control charts. Each different type of chart is actually a graphical template, a container for numerical information. These templates benefit the user by allowing display of data in a familiar and consistent context. These templates also benefit the developer by simplifying the task of visualization. Once a template has been chosen it provides a set of constraints that facilitates the development of the corresponding chart for the current data.

Each template has a set of actual or implied axes. These axes correspond to attributes within the data. Thus in bar charts and scattergrams, for instance, there are x, y, and possibly z axes, and an attribute must be assigned to each of the axes. In contrast, axes are not displayed for a pie chart, although the splitting of the pie into segments represents one attribute, and the relative sizes of the segments represents a second attribute.

Once the assignment of attributes to axes has been made, the scale of the axes has to be selected. This will normally be chosen based on the range of values for the attribute. For instance, the prices of houses will tend to be represented on larger and coarser scales than the prices of cars. In addition, for axes that represent ratio variables (e.g., the x and y axes of scattergrams, or the y axis of a 2D bar chart) tick marks need to be selected so that the user can read off more precise numerical values from the chart.

While scaling and tick marks are important issues for assigning ratio variables to axes, category variables need some kind of coding to make them visually distinctive. In a bar chart for instance, spatial separation of the bars, along with labels showing which bar represents which category is a form of category coding. In a more complex divided bar chart, levels of a category within a cluster of bars may be indicated by color, texture or shading. Color and shading may also be used to differentiate segments in a pie. Labels may then be matched to category colors in a key or legend, or if enough space is available, they may be attached near the corresponding segments of the pie.

## 6.4.2 Hyperdata Links

One of the difficulties in developing a model of hypertext is that there are many relations that can exist between fragments of text, including hierarchical relations, argumentation relations, and so on. Fortunately, there is a much smaller set of data relations that are relevant for a hyperdata system.

In a visualization system, data relations are links between hotspots in different charts or graphs. There are a limited set of relations between elements of data that will generally be of interest. Possible data relations include shared attributes, related attributes, entity specialization, and entity generalization.

Figure 6.8 shows a hyperdata node (bar chart) with some links attached to it. Each of these links takes the user to a different screen. Each link is traversed by clicking on the corresponding link anchor. In this case each of the links is dynamic and has a corresponding rule that tells the hyperdata system how to calculate which node is to be displayed next.

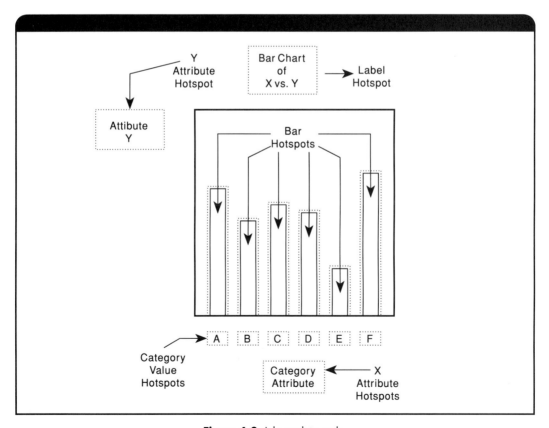

**Figure 6.8** A hyperdata node.

Each of the bars in Figure 6.8 represents an entity. As well as displaying information, these bars are also hotspots. Clicking on one of the bars displays more information about that particular entity. In this case, clicking on the bar is interpreted by the hyperdata system as a question of the form: "Show me more about this entity (or class of entities)." This type of hyperdata link is *entity specialization*. For instance, the bar chart may show sales figures for different marketing personnel. Clicking the bar for a particular salesperson would then show a more detailed breakdown of their sales figures. For instance, their sales figures across a set of product categories could be shown. In this case the choice to show product categories as the variable of interest would be based on the active constraints in the hyperdata interface as explained below in the section on the hyperdata user interface.

The category label below each bar would also be a hot spot. The behavior that occurred when the user clicked on the category label would depend on how the hyperdata was customized. For instance, clicking on the name of a salesperson may show a scanned image of the person along with a selectable audio button providing access to a spoken self-introduction by that person (using a digitized sound resource). Alternatively, the hotspot could be defined for entity specialization, acting in the same way as the bar above it, or it could lead to a dialog box allowing the user to create a customized visualization for that salesperson.

In Figure 6.8 there are two attributes, one representing the x-axis and the other representing the y-axis. The attribute on the x-axis in this case is referred to as the category attribute. Clicking on one of the two attribute labels is interpreted by the hyperdata system as a question of the form: "Show me more about this attribute (or related attributes)." The distinction between a shared and related attribute link can be indicated by whether or not the user holds the mouse button down. If the user simply clicks on the attribute label, a *shared attribute* link is activated and the next presentation corresponds to a similar chart that shares the same attribute (but may differ in terms of the entities or the second attribute plotted). Exactly which chart is constructed for the next presentation will depend on which defaults or constraints are active at that time.

If the user clicks on the category label and holds the mouse button down, a *related attribute* link is activated. The user then sees a list of related attributes. This list can be constructed on the basis of which attributes appear in the same schema as the attribute whose label was clicked on (see the following section for further explanation of this point). The user then selects the related attribute of interest and the corresponding chart is constructed and shown.

When the label or title of the chart is clicked on, a description of the chart may be presented. In a fully developed system this description may actually be a gateway to a hypertext system, and clicking on embedded buttons may take the user to related topics. This is a good way of annotating a hyperdata presentation or of providing a help facility.

Alternatively, plain text or hypermedia information may be shown. This may either be a "canned" description explaining what a bar chart is and giving the definition of which variables are being plotted, or it may be an annotation that is added by a developer.

If the user clicks on the chart title and then holds the mouse down, this is interpreted as a request for entity generalization. In this case a tree diagram might appear showing the superclasses of the current entity or entity set. If no superclass is available, the system might default to an entity selection within the entity space of the control panel, as described in the following section.

### 6.4.3 Hyperdata User Interface

A hyperdata interface can be constructed using a control panel. A control panel interface has the advantage that it encourages a style of mixed initiative interaction, where users can control the extent to which they design or specify the various charts that are produced. The control panel in Figure 6.9 includes an attribute selector, a chart type selector, an entity selector, and a schema selector, in addition to the main

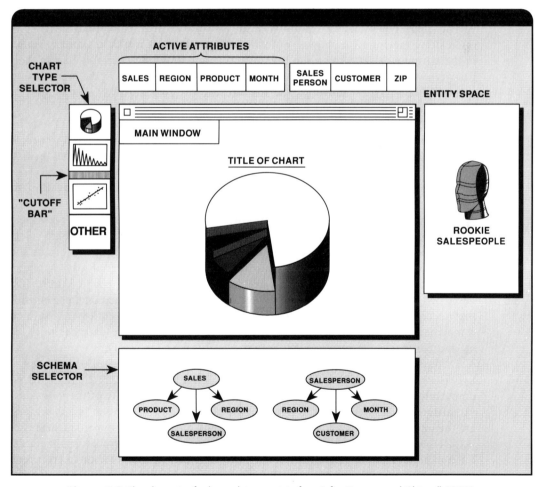

**Figure 6.9** The elements of a hyperdata user interface (after Parsaye and Chignell 1992).

window for displaying charts which can also be used to set constraints via point-and-click navigation. The control panel allows the users to customize the way in which the hyperdata works, and gives them fairly precise control over the visualization process.

Multiple charts can be opened, resized, and tiled within the main window of the control panel so that users are free to design their own composite displays. Figure 6.9 shows the elements of the hyperdata user interface. It is not meant to be a finished graphic design of the hyperdata user interface.

The attribute selector allows users to specify attribute constraints directly. Attributes are ranked in left to right order. Each attribute is represented in the hierarchy (left to right order) by an icon or label. Users may rearrange the attribute constraints by selecting and dragging the icons around the list of attributes. The user may also set a barrier. Attributes to the left of the barrier are considered in constructing visualizations, while attributes to the right of the barrier are ignored (i.e., the weights for the corresponding attribute assignments are set to zero).

The chart type selector (hierarchy) shows the types of chart that the user is interested in seeing (it is shown vertically in Figure 6.9). It works in similar fashion to the attribute selector, with the user selecting and dragging charts to change their priority (weighting) within the list. A barrier may also be placed in the hierarchy so that only chart types above the barrier are active (considered as candidates for visualization or presentation).

The schema window shows the currently active schemas. These schemas may be created directly by the user, be pre-defined by the developer, or be based on rules selected from the rule browser. Selection of a schema makes the attributes in that schema active for use in creating charts. In Figure 6.9 there are four active schemas. The active attributes are defined according to which attributes have been placed to the left of the barrier in the attribute hierarchy.

The entity space is a region where the entities of interest are defined. For instance, the hyperdata user may be interested in examining the performance of rookie salespeople in some detail. This may be done by setting the appropriate conditions on the salesperson and length of experience attributes. There are a number of ways in which this can be done. One method is to define the entity set using iconic queries (as described in Chapter 3). Another way is to define an entity set based on those entities that match one or more rules selected from a rule browser. Once an entity set is defined it may have an icon assigned to it. The user may then select a pre-defined entity set by dragging the corresponding icon into the entity space (selector).

Different applications or different user populations may require different styles of hyperdata interaction. Thus the detailed design of hyperdata systems should be based on usability analysis. The first criterion to be tested is the usability of the individual visualizations. How easy is it to interpret the meaning or information in a chart, and are the interpretations made correctly? The second component of hyperdata usability is the ease with which users can navigate or move around the different visualizations. Ease of navigation is tested by seeing how smoothly a user can move from one visualization to another and how well they understand the different navigation options that are available to them.

Another aspect of usability concerns the frequency with which different hyperdata features are used. For instance: How effective or usable is iconic querying versus point-and-click navigation versus direct setting of constraints through the control panel? This can be tested with experiments or questionnaires, or more simply, by logging the frequency with which each feature is used.

### 6.4.4  Inferential Hyperdata

The use of well-defined regions of charts (visual templates) as active hot spots allows us to make inferences about which schema should be activated and which objects are of interest. Inference can be used to implement a dynamic hyperdata system where user inputs are interpreted as navigation actions and transformed into requests to the data visualization system. The creation of static hyperdata will be too costly in many applications (as is also the case for hyperdata's cousin, hypertext).

Charts and graphs should be created automatically, as and when they are needed. How can a visualization system determine what graph should be displayed next? This problem can be solved by exploiting the natural structure of numerical data. Each data table consists of a number of attributes. Further, these attributes have logical relationships (such as those expressed in an entity-relationship model) and each application will have preferred types of chart (e.g., line charts of closing prices and daily sales volumes for stock market analysis).

Using rules, links between the various charts that describe a set of data can be expressed in a very general way. Instead of saying that the default link for Company X fruit juice sales is to Company X sales by region, one could say that the default link for any fruit juice object when plotted against an attribute is the breakdown for that object by the attribute over region. Using this general form of the default, if we clicked on orange juice while reviewing a chart of advertising dollars spent on each of the fruit juices, we would then move to a chart (e.g., a pie chart) showing the advertising dollars spent on orange juice across each of the sales regions.

Hyperdata navigation at the technical level is a process of selecting constraints that limit the visualizations that can currently be displayed. When sufficient constraints have been identified, either a menu of alternative displays can be shown or one single display can be shown that meets all the active constraints. Two of the important classes of constraint in a hyperdata system are entity constraints and attribute constraints. Attribute constraints are implemented by schemas. The idea of a schema is that certain attributes "hang together" depending on the type of question being asked.

Schemas may be identified based on information discovery and rule browsing. Information discovery systems such as IDIS (IntelligenceWare 1991) generate rules based on patterns that exist within large databases. Rule generation systems select one variable as a conclusion and then see which combinations of other variables in the database can predict particular values or ranges in the conclusion variable. This results in a set of rules which capture different patterns in the database. Once a set of rules have been generated, they may be examined using a rule browser. Users browse through the rules and select those rules that are interesting. They can also choose a subset of the attributes and a separate browser will be chosen for rules that have only those attributes in their premises. In this way the user can segment the rule set to simplify inspection and analysis.

The rules that are selected from rule browsing may then be used to construct schemas. In this case, the premises of the rules define a set of interesting relationships. Figure 6.9 showed two schemas. One schema showed a relationship between salesperson, product, region, and dollar value of sales while the second schema shows a relationship between salesperson, region, customer, and month. Schemas such as these may be identified during rule browsing or set up by the database developer. During navigation, clicking on the x-axis or y-axis activates the schemas for the corresponding attributes.

Discovery is also used to impose constraints on the entities that are extracted from the data. This is done by selecting entities that match the premise or conclusion of a rule. A rule acts as a query that selects all the entities in the database that match the conditions in the premise. For instance, we might have a rule that says:

> If
>> Salesperson is X and
>> "years of experience" of X < 1 and
>> product = computer
> Then
>> "dollar value of sales" < 50,000

Applying this rule as an entity constraint would then select all the data points for computer sales where the salesperson has less than one year of experience. We could then label this constraint as "rookie computer salesperson" and assign an icon to it. Once entity constraints are active they limit which entities will be represented in the chart. In contrast, attribute constraints are used to define which attributes will be plotted, but they do not constrain which entities will be represented by data points in the chart.

## 6.4.5 Hyperdata Navigation

Hyperdata navigation at the technical level is a process of selecting constraints that limit the visualizations that can currently be displayed. When sufficient constraints have been identified, either a menu of alternative displays or one single display that meets all of the active constraints can be shown.

Two of the important classes of constraint in a hyperdata system are entity constraints and attribute constraints. Attribute constraints are implemented by schemas. The idea of a schema is that certain attributes "hang together" depending on what type of question one is asking.

### 6.4.5.1 *Rule Browsing*    Chapter 4 discussed methods of rule generation. This section shows how rule browsing may be used to study the results of rule generation and create a structure for hyperdata knowledge. A visual interface (control panel) for rule generation is described below.

The purpose of this control panel is to allow users to set up rule generation runs in a natural and intuitive way. The style of interaction is through a type of decision table or spreadsheet, as shown in Figure 6.10. The table consists of two rows, one for

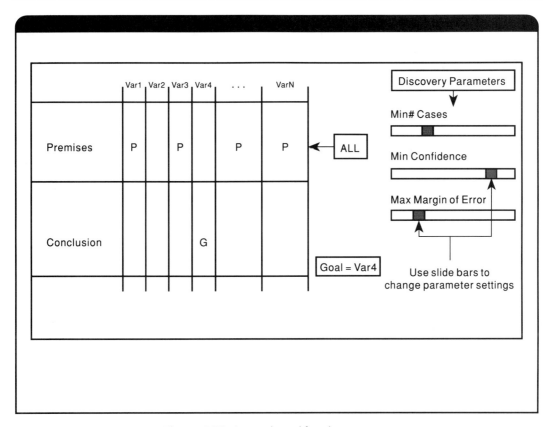

**Figure 6.10** A control panel for rule generation.

premises and one for conclusions. In addition there is one column for each variable. The person begins by selecting the goal (conclusion) by clicking on the cell representing the corresponding variable in the conclusion row of the table. The variable is then removed from the table and the label "Goal" = <selected variable> appears prominently to the side of the table. Beside this is a message saying "No restrictions, click here to customize." If the user now clicks on this message a pop-up is shown with >, = etc. The user can then select a restriction on the conclusion, e.g., Y=Y1, or whatever.

The user may then click a button "All" (to the side of the table) and all the variables are highlight as premises (the premise row of the table is filled with Ps). Alternatively, the user may be selective and click on a subset of the variables to be considered in the premise. The P marker is a toggle so if the variable has been selected as a premise and the user clicks on it again it is removed from the list of premises and the P is no longer seen in the corresponding cell of the table.

To the side of the table (on the right) are a set of discovery panels represented by slide bars. The user then moves the sliders to indicate the settings that are wanted. When the user is comfortable with the settings and variable selections he clicks a discover button.

The rule browser is shown in Figure 6.11. The conclusion of the rule is written on the left followed by the word "If." To the right of this is a scrollable table. Each row in the table represents a discovered rule. The columns of the table represent the variables that were considered in the analysis. The variables are placed in the columns based on how often they appear in the rule premises. The most frequently occurring variable appears in the left most column. If a variable doesn't appear in any rule it is dropped from the table. Initially the cells of the tables are marked with Xs to show which variables appear as premises in each rule. If the user clicks on a row, the corresponding value or range for each of the variables in the rule's premise are shown (within the corresponding cells of that row). The browser has space for about 10 columns. In addition, there are five columns on the right to handle cases where some of the rarer premises appear in the current rule. Thus the table is divided into 10 fixed columns that represent the variables that commonly appear in premises and five variable columns that represent the less frequently appearing variables.

The user may remove a rule from the browser by selecting its row and clicking the delete button. Alternatively the user may hit a "Group" button. This button groups all the rules with similar premises (based on shared variables and variable assignments or ranges within the premises). Ideally, the rules would be grouped by similarity before being entered into the rule browser.

The user browses through the rules and selects those rules that are interesting. Other rules can be deleted. The user also has the choice of deleting a variable (and any

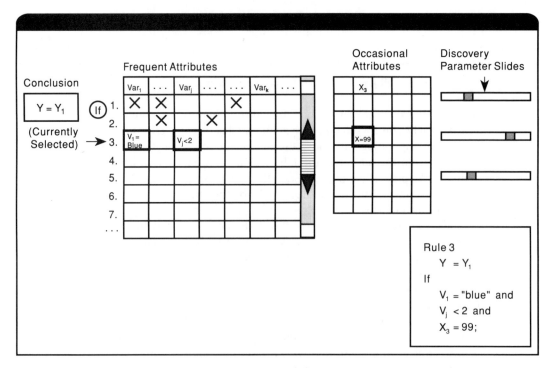

**Figure 6.11** A rule browser.

associated rules) if it is not useful, and can also choose a subset of the variables and a separate browser will be chosen for just those rules that have only those variables in their premises. In this way the user can segment the rule set to simplify inspection and analysis.

To the right of the browser is a set of slide bars showing the values of the discovery parameters such as "Confidence" and "Margin of Error." The user can also ask to see a chart that corresponds to each rule. If this window is selected and open, then as the user scrolls through the rules the corresponding graph for each rule changes.

The user can also annotate interesting rules with a heading or title and a description. The user can save or print the edited rule sets in a standard form, along with the accompanying titles and descriptions. The user may also attach keywords to rules and store them in a database for later access using keyword search. The rules that are selected from rule browsing may then be used to construct schemas. In this case, the premises of the rules define a set of interesting relationships.

Discovery can also be used to impose constraints on the entities that are extracted from the data. This is done by selecting entities that match the premise or conclusion of a rule. A rule may be thought of as a query that selects all the entities in the database that match the conditions in the premise. For instance, we might have a rule that says that: if Salesperson is X and years of experience of X is less than one and product is computer then dollar value of sales is less than 50,000. Applying this rule as an entity constraint would then select all the data points for computer sales where the sales person has less than one year of experience. We could then label this constraint as "rookie computer salesperson" and assign an icon to it. Attributes where the value or range of values of interest is specified serve as entity constraints, effectively limiting which entities will be represented in the chart.

Attributes constraints are attributes that are known to be of interest, but where there are no interesting or required values or levels specified. They are used to define which attributes will be plotted, but they do not constrain which entities will be represented by data points in the chart.

*6.4.5.2* **Model Constraints**    It is often helpful to index pictures so that they are accessible with standard textual retrieval methods. In the case of "chart pictures" there are the constraints that can be used as index terms. Thus a chart that shows the sales in the northeast for Henry across different months of the year and different products might be indexed as:

> Salesperson: Henry
> Region: Northeast
> Months: Any
> Products: Any

In this case the constraints on the entity and attributes form a template consisting of a list of general expressions of the form—Attribute: Value.

Attributes with filled-in values serve as entity constraints, while attributes where values are unspecified serve as attribute constraints. The similarity of one picture to another is defined as the extent to which they share the same entity and attribute constraints.

Relevance feedback in querying is a complex topic that has been studied extensively (e.g., Salton and McGill 1983). A relatively simple approach to the problem will be used in this section. This approach can be employed with hyperdata because of the highly standardized and constrained nature of the visual templates that are used.

Say a person is using a picture menu to select a new chart. First he or she clicks on a 3D bar chart showing dollar sales for salesperson by month for the northeast region. Then the user clicks on a pie chart showing the proportion of dollar sales for each salesperson in the northeast region. Finally he or she clicks on a scattergram showing dollar value of sales for one year of experience by number of sales leads reported in the northeast region.

The information provided by these selections can be summarized as follows:

*Chart: Bar (3D)*
*Region: Northeast*
*DollarSales*
*Salesperson*

*Chart: Pie*
*Region: Northeast*
*DollarSales*
*Salesperson*

*Chart: Scattergram*
*Region: Northeast*
*DollarSales*
*YearsExperience<1*
*SalesLeads*

This may then be interpreted as a query vector where Region=Northeast (assigned a weighting of 1) and YearsExperience<1 (assigned a weighting of 1/3) are the entity constraints, while DollarSales (assigned a weighting of 1) and SalesLeads (assigned a weighting of 1/3) are the attribute constraints. In this case a simple weighting scheme for each entity or attribute constraint has been used by taking the weight to be the proportion of times that the constraint appears in the selected charts.

Picture relevance allows users to express their interest by choosing items from a menu of pictures. A picture menu can be constructed in several ways. The first way is to have a set of pictures already available in an archive. A random selection (or a set of category representatives) is then chosen and the pictures are presented in subsampled (iconized) form. A second form of menu construction is to keep a running list of the visualizations that have been created and viewed. This history of visualizations can then be used to select previous pictures. These pictures can then form launching points for new queries.

In automated chart generation a set of alternative charts that meet the current constraints may be shown in a picture menu. However, this strategy is computationally expensive and requires good graphics hardware.

The final method of menu construction considered here is to define a standard set of charts that are of interest (e.g., pie chart, bar chart, scattergram) and then show how the data fitting the current constraints would appear in each of the chart templates. The user could then choose one of these charts as the starting point for further navigation.

### 6.4.6 Hyperdata Creation

Much of the behavior of hyperdata can be constructed by the user at run-time using the control panel interface. However, a developer may also build in a considerable amount of default behavior and may pre-define a knowledge base of rules that govern the behavior of links, along with hypertext annotations to various charts.

The development of hyperdata knowledge is based on presentation dialogs. Presentation dialogs can be used to create general rules for link generation in an application. An example of a presentation dialog is shown in Figure 6.12. In the left-hand window is some hypertext, a discussion of problems that can occur in cars, along with links to related nodes mentioned in the text (shown with surrounding boxes). The right-hand window has a bar chart showing the frequency with which each of the problems is encountered in the database.

Below this is a set of icons representing alternative ways of graphing the data. Clicking on one of these items changes the view in the right-hand window to the

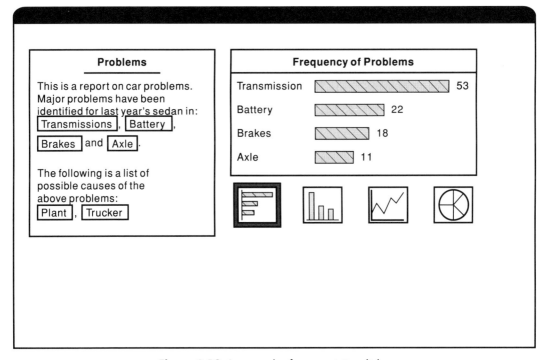

**Figure 6.12** An example of a presentation dialog.

corresponding graph type. For instance, clicking on the right-hand button would change the display from a bar chart to a pie chart.

This presentation establishes a relation between the hypertext window and the graphical (right-hand) window. For instance, if we now selected the "Trucker" link by clicking on it in the left-hand window we would then move to the Trucker hypertext and the graph in the right-hand window would also change. Figure 6.13 shows the result. Now we see a description of the different truckers in the hypertext window and we see a bar chart showing a distribution of the problems across the different trucking companies.

However, at this point we might like to see not only the overall number of problems for each trucker, but also the distribution of problem types within each trucker. For instance, EZBrake Trucking might deliver cars that have a lot of problems, but which types of problem in particular? We can find this out by clicking on the EZBrake bar. A menu then pops up. If we select "Zoom In" from the menu, the screen as in Figure 6.14 is displayed, and the graph window (on the right) shows a bar chart with a breakdown of the problems experienced by the EZBrake Company.

Data modeling can be carried out by the developer or by the user on the fly. One form of data modeling is to select rules through the rule browser and then use those rules to define attribute schemata. Attribute constraints can then be defined by selecting (making active) one or more of those schemata. Another form of data

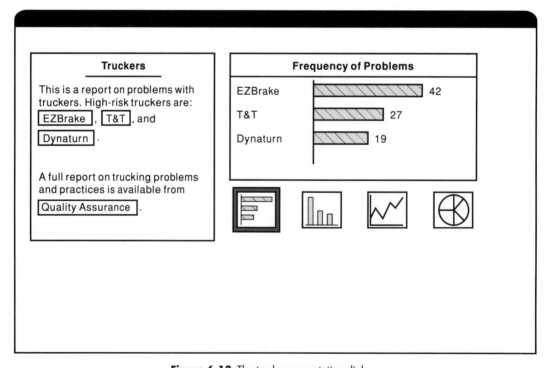

**Figure 6.13** The trucker presentation dialog.

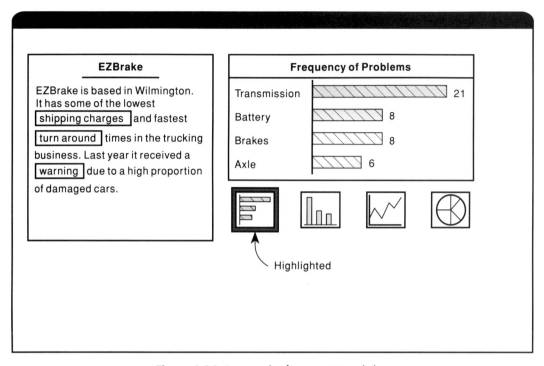

**Figure 6.14** An example of a presentation dialog.

modeling involves the user of a hyperdata modeling diagram. This type of diagram is illustrated in Figure 6.15. Using this diagram, users may construct a data model representation of a chart. The two main elements of the hyperdata model are attributes and entities. In addition, entities may be merged or stratified to create de facto levels of a new feature or attribute.

Data may consist of categories (textual labels or levels) and numbers. Numbers may be ratio (i.e., where zero is meaningful), interval (where equal intervals exist between adjacent numbers) and ordinal (where numbers only provide ordering information). Data also refers to objects that are entities existing in a world or world model. Thus each tuple of data has to be mapped onto an object, location, or other meaningful entity.

One of the advantages of dynamic hyperdata is that the structure of the hyperdata can be customized by the user at run-time. A hyperdata customizing interface can be constructed using a control panel as shown earlier in Figure 6.9. This type of interface encourages a style of mixed initiative interaction where the users can control the extent to which they design or specify the various charts that are produced.

The attribute hierarchy allows users to specify attribute constraints directly. Attributes are ranked in left to right order within the hierarchy. Each attribute is represented in the hierarchy by an icon or label. Users may rearrange the attribute constraints by selecting and dragging the icons around the list of attributes. The user may also set a barrier. Attributes to the left of the barrier are considered in constructing

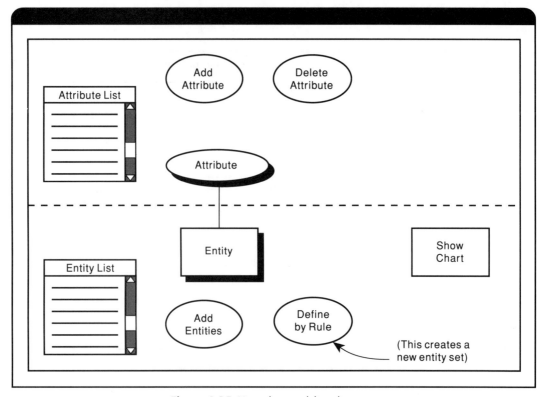

**Figure 6.15** Hyperdata modeling diagram.

visualizations, while attributes to the right of the barrier are ignored (i.e., the weights for the corresponding attribute assignments are set to zero).

The chart type hierarchy shows the types of chart that the user is interested in seeing. It works in similar fashion to the attribute hierarchy, with the user selecting and dragging charts to change their priority (weighting) within the hierarchy. A barrier may also be placed in the hierarchy so that only chart types to the left of the barrier are active (considered as candidates for visualization or presentation).

The user may select which entities are active through a number of mechanisms. One method is to use iconic querying (Chapter 3). Another method is to choose a restricted entity set by selecting a corresponding visual icon. Combinations of entities can be created by dragging them into the entity selection space. For instance, in Figure 6.9 the "Rookie Salespeople" entity set has been placed in the entity space. When multiple entity sets are selected, a graphical style of querying can then be used (Golovchinsky and Chignell 1992) where lines between entity icons (or labels) indicate AND relations while the absence of lines indicates OR relations. A third method of selecting active entities is to use the rule browser to select rules. Entities which match the premise of a rule then define an entity constraint. This constraint may be considered in isolation, or it may be merged with other entity constraints in the entity selection space.

## ■ 6.5 HYPERINFORMATION METHODOLOGIES

This section considers methodologies of hyperinformation concerned with creating a satisfactory environment for navigation. Since much of the work in this area has been concerned with hypertext this review will also emphasize hypertext.

### 6.5.1 Navigation in Hyperinformation

There is much confusion about the nature of hyperinformation. One area of doubt is the way in which it is to be used. Hyperinformation can be used to view data, search for textual information, or just browse for interesting ideas and text. Each of these activities requires a different style of navigation. A well-crafted hyperinformation document should provide mechanisms for moving between nodes that can accommodate different styles of information seeking behavior. Some of the methods for moving to a node are:

- By query (pattern matching of records)
- By gateway or pathway (e.g., via an index)
- By menu selection
- By navigational link
- By map

The process of moving "by query" corresponds to Search in an information retrieval system. Here the query consists of a set of keywords or slot values, and nodes are considered relevant if they match the pattern defined in the query. In the model of intelligent database application used here this move by query is handled by a visual querying system (iconic query).

The process of moving "by gateway or pathway" is frequently seen in hyper-information documents. Here there may be an opening screen and one is required to click on the mouse button after which one is "taken to" a node that the developer assumes is appropriate at this point. Alternatively, in the case of a pathway, one follows a path where the next node is already predefined by the developer. It should be noted that gateways and paths generally constitute "islands of linearity" within a hyperinformation document that are used by the developer to assist the user in finding particularly important information (e.g., a map of the system when it is first used). The construction of gateways may be developed as part of the application that is overlaid on the hyperdata.

Moving by "menu selection" is a common navigation device in software that may also be applied to hyperinformation. The menu may refer to nodes directly, or may refer to another menu of choices. For instance, Figure 6.16 shows a pop-up menu where the user may choose to see an alphabetical listing of the nodes in the system, a list of more general terms (i.e., superordinates of the current node), and so on. Many hyperinformation or hypertext documents use a form of embedded menu (e.g., Shneiderman and Kearsley 1989), where access points to related nodes are indicated by highlighted terms (hot spots) within the current text. This latter case of embedded menus merges the concepts of menu selection and navigation link by providing an

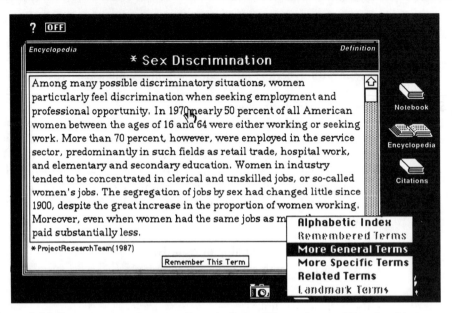

**Figure 6.16** Pop-up menu to other terms. (From the Project Jefferson System, Chignell and Lang 1991.)

embedded menu of navigational links. Thus menu selection is a style of presenting navigational links, or a way of defining the context within which a type of navigation link will be chosen (e.g., more general terms). Moving by menus is handled in the information overview part of the intelligent database application.

"Maps" provide a visual representation of overall hyperinformation structure. Navigable maps allow the user to click on the icon (e.g., a box) representing a node and move to it directly. Hierarchical maps may also be defined where each map represents a different level of detail. Figure 6.17 shows a schematic representation of a hierarchical map. In panel *a* only the general regions of the hyperinformation structure are shown. Then in panel *b* a detailed map of one of the "regions" is shown. This processing of nesting maps to greater levels of detail can in principle be continued indefinitely and the limiting factor is the degree of resolution (natural grain size) in the hyperinformation structure. Hierarchical structuring should be used judiciously as some domains may have inherently fewer levels of abstraction and generalization.

Navigation is a ubiquitous phenomenon that includes moving around the environment as well as operating a computer application. The questions of what to do next and where to go next confront us every day.

Navigation is concerned with where to go and what to do, while search is concerned with finding objects or information. We can summarize the difference between navigation and search in an example. If we go to the library to look for a book, we first have to move (navigate) to the library. We might then go to the front desk and ask for the book (e.g., it might be "on reserve"). We then carry out a search with the

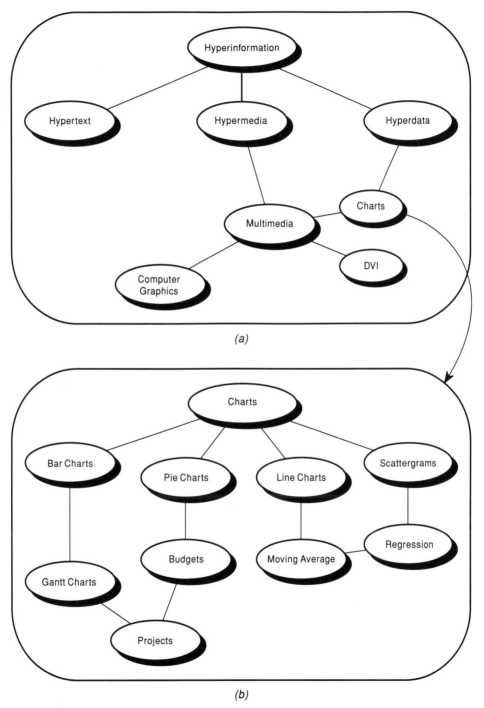

*(a)*

*(b)*

**Figure 6.17** A schematic representation of a hierarchical map.

assistance of the librarian who responds to our query. If, however, we choose to look for the book ourselves we might go to a terminal that has an on-line catalog. We would then carry out a search for the book we are interested in. While we are carrying out this search we might "navigate" through a number of different menus. Then, when we locate the call number of the book we might "navigate" to the shelf where the book is. In this example, search is restricted to obtaining information that we need, while navigation is concerned with the problem of deciding where to go or what to do next based on some goal.

Argument structure may also be used for navigation. Argument structures have received quite a bit of attention in collaborative authoring and design environments. For instance, graphical Issue-Based Information System (gIBIS) characterizes the design process as one of "argumentation" leading to the resolution of design issues. Using the gIBIS framework, designers present arguments for and against various positions relating to each issue. The SEPIA system for collaborative writing (Streitz et al. 1989) is another system that explicitly uses argument structures. The following link types represent a minimalist set of argument types for hyperinformation: supports; contradicts; leads to.

This book can illustrate the use of argument structure. The goal here is to develop intelligent database tools for useful applications. Understanding the role of each chapter in the evolving presentation of material helps relate the chapter to our larger context and purpose. There is a causal flow to the argument that motivates this chapter and the relations of this chapter to the rest of the book. Figure 6.18 shows the argument structure for this book. It could be used as a form of map for a hyperinformation version of this book. Thus if one clicked on the box labeled Quality Control one would then go to the corresponding chapter and so on. Maps and argument structures are not explicitly handled by the model in this book, although like entry points they may be added to the user interface by the intelligent database application developer.

## 6.5.2   Disorientation

Excessive reliance on nonlinear styles of navigation may lead to disorientation. This is hardly surprising given that many hypertexts provide few linear cues, but it has also been confirmed in experience with hypertext systems. Several authors have reported disorientation problems by users of large hypertext systems. (Furnas 1986; Conklin 1987; Campagnoni and Ehrlich 1989; Nielsen 1990). Users of large hypertext systems have to deal with a huge structure of interconnected nodes, but the interface typically lets them display only a restricted view of this structure. This leads to two types of disorientation: (1) not knowing where one is and (2) not knowing where to go next (or what else is available).

Some hypertext systems reduce disorientation by providing users with navigational tools as browsers and maps. Maps are common navigational aid tools used in the physical world.

While maps are perhaps the most obvious navigational tool in a hypertext system, other forms of assistance have also been developed (Gray and Shasha 1990; Walker 1987; Egan, Remde, Landauer 1989). In Gray (1990) the user describes the target location in terms of properties that can be assigned to objects in a frame system. In

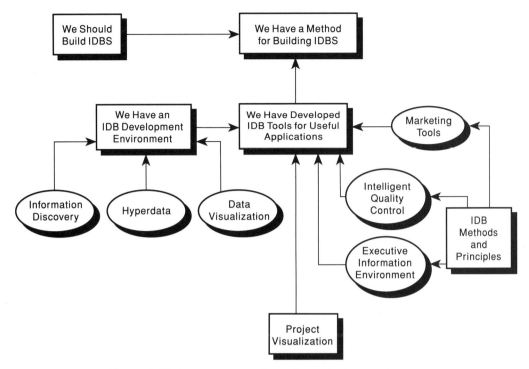

**Figure 6.18** Argument structure for intelligent database applications.

the Guided Tours used by the American History Stack (Oren et al. 1990), the user is guided by "agents," which each have a different perspective on the historical events. For example, a "businessman" agent could guide the user through the most important topics from his point of view, talking about such topics as the influence of gold in the economy, etc. The reader could be shown a different picture by a "missionary" guide, or by a "settler" guide.

In principle, hyperinformation may consist of node and link structures of unlimited complexity. In practice, the ability of users to navigate through hyperinformation structures successfully is a serious constraint. When dealing with large amounts of information people get disoriented unless there is sufficient structure.

### 6.5.3 A Model of Exploration

The classical model of search assumes that the user has a clear idea of the information they are looking for. However, in many cases this is not so. The user often wants to explore information, starting off with a rough idea of what might be wanted, and then exploring the information using a combination of navigation and search.

Hypertext is clearly different from books and printed text both in terms of its electronic format and in terms of its nonlinearity. Similarly, hypertext is different from on-line information systems (e.g., databases accessible through the DIALOG system) because it does not emphasize querying through means such as Boolean search expressions. Thus we need to understand the role of hypertext as an information exploration tool. One model of how hypertext fits into the general scheme of information exploration systems has been developed by Waterworth and Chignell (1991).

The first element (dimension) of their three-dimensional model (Figure 6.19) concerns the concept of navigation. Navigation is unstructured from the system perspective but structured from the user perspective. The assignment of responsibility for handling information structure occurs as a direct result of which agent (i.e., the user or the system) is responsible for carrying out information seeking. In the case of navigation, users are responsible for controlling the search process and as a result it is they, rather than the system, who must be aware of the structure of the information. This role is reversed in the case of mediated information retrieval, where it is the system that is responsible for searching and which must consequently be concerned with structure. This issue of who is concerned with structure represents a primary dimension of information seeking behavior that Waterworth and Chignell (1991) refer to as "Structural Responsibility."

Waterworth and Chignell also proposed a second dimension of information seeking behavior that contrasts the activities of browsing and querying. Browsing is distinguished from querying by the absence of a definite target in the mind of the user. Waterworth and Chignell referred to this second dimension of information-seeking behavior as "Target Orientation." In their model the distinction between browsing and querying is not determined by the actions of the user, or by the configuration of the

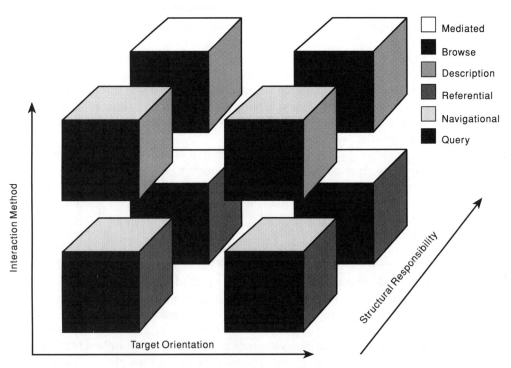

**Figure 6.19** 3D model of information exploration.

system, but by the cognitive state of the user. Presumably, there is a continuum of user behaviors varying between querying and browsing that is differentiated according to the specificity of the information-seeking goals of the user. Given the existence of this continuum, it may be inappropriate to arbitrarily classify user behavior as either browsing or querying and build systems that reflect this strict dichotomy. Thus this view of browsing implies a need for merging conventional information retrieval with browsing.

Structural responsibility and target orientation define two dimensions of information seeking systems. The definition of browsing focuses on the distinction between targeted information seeking and discovery-based information seeking. In contrast, the definition of navigation emphasizes the responsibility of the user, as opposed to the system, for dealing with structure. These two dimensions are clearly orthogonal, since both browsing and querying can occur as part of navigation or information retrieval processes.

Waterworth and Chignell also discussed a third dimension of information-seeking behavior that arises from the method of interaction used in the interface to the information system. They drew a distinction between descriptive interfaces, where the user describes what is wanted, and referential forms of interaction, where the user selects or refers to what is wanted (generally using some variant of a menu). They pointed out that, while descriptive interfaces have generally been associated with querying behavior, and referential interfaces have generally been associated with navigation, there is no intrinsic correlation between the interaction method and target orientation. Similarly, the concept of interaction method is orthogonal to the dimension of structural responsibility introduced above.

Querying and deductive retrieval are useful adjuncts to the basic point-and-click navigation in hypermedia. Browsing and querying are complementary components of information-seeking activity (Waterworth and Chignell 1991). The SuperBook system (Remde, Gomez, and Landauer 1987; Egan, Remde, Gomez, Landauer, Eberhardt, and Lochbaum 1989) shows how information retrieval functionality may be embedded within a hypermedia environment.

## ■ 6.6 HYPERINFORMATION RESEARCH ISSUES

The status of hyperinformation is reviewed in this section. Since the bulk of work has been done on hypertext, most comments here will refer to hypertext systems. However, hypertext is one of the most difficult form of hyperinformation to implement, and thus some of the problems identified with hypertext stem are less of an issue for hyperdata.

This section begins with a critique of current approaches to hyperinformation, followed by a discussion of hyperinformation usability and a review of current trends in the field.

### 6.6.1 A Critique of Hyperinformation

In this section some of the criticisms that may be leveled at current approaches to hypertext and hyperinformation are discussed. While a number of criticisms are relevant, hyperinformation remains a central part of intelligent databases and new methods of handling information. The critique of hyperinformation below largely reflects early approaches to hypertext. The model of hyperdata used here was developed to overcome or avoid some of the problems encountered in early hypertext.

**6.6.1.1 A Solution in Search of a Task**     Hypertext is a great idea. Most people who read Bush's original article on the Memex still find it inspiring. How many other articles written in the 1940s contain ideas and methods that are still at the cutting edge of technology? Perhaps the fact that we are still inspired by many of the Memex ideas shows how much further we still need to go.

One of the enduring problems of hypertext is that there is no single task that motivates the development of the technology. Concepts such as "docuverse" and "world brain" are simply too broad and remote to provide a direct impetus to research and development. People tend to get lost in the details and lose sight of the overall goal.

The field of hypertext is becoming fragmented as different researchers find different tasks to motivate them. We need a better definition of what tasks are appropriate for hypertext, and how hypertext should be developed and used in those task contexts.

**6.6.1.2 A Network in Search of a Browser**     People get lost in hypertext. This comment has been made a number of times, although there is little firm evidence concerning the issue of disorientation in hypertext. Successful browsing generally requires at least a minimal awareness of structure. Hypertext systems as currently implemented generally give the user little assistance in figuring out the structure of the information. This is in contrast to books, where the structure is typically laid out right at the beginning, in the Table of Contents. Where tables of contents have been used in hypertext systems they have generally proved very helpful to the user (e.g., Egan et al. 1989; Valdez 1992).

As well as booklike tools, hypertext developers have also used maps or browsers to show users the structure of a hypertext. One of the best known early examples of this concept was the NoteCards browser. This was a hierarchical (tree structure) representation of the nodes that provided a kind of table of contents overview.

The problem with early browsers in large hypertexts, however, was that it was difficult to show all the information on a single screen. The browsers get so large that they have to be split up into a number of screens and this can lead to navigation problems within the browser, which is ironic, since the whole idea of browsers was to alleviate navigation problems in the first place. However, the use of three-dimensional hierarchical browsers (e.g., Robertson et al. 1991), fish-eye views, and outlining tools with high-quality computer graphics is largely resolving this problem.

**6.6.1.3 Scaling Up**     Rolls Royce cars are handcrafted. So are most current hypertext systems. Rolls Royces are status symbols, but you don't see that many, except perhaps in some small countries where there is a lot of oil, or outside the garages of pop stars and leaders of religious cults. The low volume of Rolls Royce production is part of the car's allure, like a rare painting or a limited edition stamp. However, hypertext documents shouldn't be collector's items, so they need to be easy to produce and distribute.

Early hypertext systems were about as common as Rolls Royces, but we need a family sedan type of hypertext. Switching models to enable mass production of hypertext will probably be traumatic, but it is necessary. We need to develop more realistic and heuristic methods of engineering to develop hypertexts on a large scale (see Glushko 1989). Hyperdata solves the problem of hyperinformation for the special case of data, but better methods are still needed for more efficient construction of hypertext (see the Appendix to this chapter for some approaches to this problem).

The creation of hypertext documents is sometimes called "authoring." The process of authoring involves the selection of a text for the domain of interest. This text then needs to be partitioned into self-contained chunks, or nodes. Finally, those nodes are linked. Manual authoring of a relatively small size hypertext can be time consuming and prone to errors. Manual authoring in Project Jefferson (Chignell and Lacy 1991), for instance, was found to lead to errors in the linking process due to fatigue and forgetting.

Manual linking is probably acceptable for what Rada calls "microtexts," that is, self-contained hypertext documents consisting of up to a few hundred nodes (Rada 1991). For large-volume hypertexts, the common approach today is to rely on indexing documents in order to then use Boolean operators and information retrieval techniques based on word frequency techniques. (Salton and McGill 1983). However, Boolean searches with simple queries yield too many entries to be useful, including many that are irrelevant.

One of the current problems in manually authoring hypertext is that there are few good tools available to support the task, so that it is even more labor intensive than it needs to be. To support authoring of hypertexts Perez (1991) recommends use of tools for:

1. listing links and nodes,
2. providing information about nodes,
3. tools for outlining,
4. indexing,
5. word frequency and analysis report,
6. keyword extraction utilities, based on word frequency

Glushko (1990) challenged hypermedia application developers to create tools for automatic conversion of text into hypertext since in many cases it is not possible to discard vast amounts of information already existing in printed form. He also coined the phrase "hypertext engineering," to point out that there is a need to use systematic methods for the creation of hypertexts. In the appendix to this chapter how this challenge is being met will be considered.

Size and complexity are difficult for any database or information system to handle. The problem is particularly severe with hypermedia because the number of possible binary (leave alone n-ary) links in a graph (hypertext structure) increases with the square of the number of the nodes in the structure. In the large data sets considered in intelligent database applications, size and complexity are also major issues since there could potentially be millions of visualizations that relate to a large set of data.

Shared databases as particularly problematic, because much of the information will not be relevant to a particular user. Thus one of the major issues in reducing the problems of size and complexity is to find ways for quickly and effectively filtering the large database to find the relevant information for a particular user. Such filtering requires better models of information. The main tool to use in handling large and complex data sets is to summarize it using information discovery and present easily interpretable data visualizations. At this point, the process of summarization reduces the data to a manageable size and it can then be incorporated effectively within a hypermedia interface. Note that the original data is still available and the user can refer to it directly as needed.

Browsing works much better on data that is summarized in this way. In a large data set, each record might be involved in tens, hundreds, or even thousands of links. However, in summarized data there are fewer links and the summarization process naturally focuses the data so that links become more relevant as well as being less numerous. One of the best forms of summarization is a visual summary of data; such visual summaries are routinely used in the charts and graphs of science and business presentations.

**6.6.1.4 *Going Nonlinear*** Linearity may not be as bad as some early hypertext researchers felt, and nonlinearity may not be as good. Going nonlinear in hypertext systems cuts people off from a lot of the linear cues that they have learnt to rely upon. As mentioned earlier in this chapter, books have a lot going for them, including hundreds of years of accumulated experience with what is now a successful technology. Linear systems have a beginning, middle, and end, and a clearly defined sequence. Finding out where one is can be fairly straightforward in a linear system.

Many early proponents of hypermedia celebrated its liberating nonlinearity (e.g., Nelson 1987). However, experience with highly nonlinear hypertexts has shown that they can be disorienting and confusing. Hypermedia systems are now evolving to the point where they contain both linear and nonlinear features, thereby getting the best of both worlds.

The notion of nonlinearity in hypertext is sometimes confused with the general responsiveness of electronic text. People have compared hypertext to hardcopy but this really confounds two issues: linear versus nonlinear, and hardcopy versus electronic. Linear features are functions that can be found in linearly-designed documents (whether in electronic or paper form). Examples of linear functions are: going to the table of contents, going to the index, flipping to the next or previous page, etc. Nonlinear functions have a different use: e.g., the users can "jump" to a different page in the document where more information on some topic of interest is presented.

Recently, Valdez (1992) has developed methods for testing the usage of linear and nonlinear functions in books and hypertexts. His research shows that nonlinear functions (jumping between sections and papers) are sometimes used just as frequently in printed documentation as they are in hypertext documentation. He also found individual differences, with some people tending to rely more on nonlinear functions, while others relied on linear functions. These results suggest that the intuitive idea that hypertexts are nonlinear and books are linear is incorrect. Linearity versus nonlinearity is a function of the strategy a person uses in reading a material as much as it results from the particular structure or presentation of the material in the document. The idea that people impose their navigational structure on a document using whatever tools are available, rather than vice versa, is also supported by the finding that with some linear texts, such as scientific journal articles, people frequently read the articles in a different order from the one in which they are written (Dillon, Richardson, and McKnight 1988).

Since people tend to have different navigational styles and use whatever tools or cognitive prosthetics (Wright 1991) are available, in most applications, a judicious mixture of linear and nonlinear structuring will work best. For instance, a table of contents is extremely useful in a hypertext document, and it seems counterproductive to deliberately exclude useful linear structures and tools from hypertext systems.

**6.6.1.5 Bad Psychology** One of the most influential arguments for why strongly nonlinear (associative) hypertext should be easier for people to use has been based on appeal to psychological principles. The argument goes something like this: The structure of human memory is associative. People are very good at making associations between data that is presented to them. Therefore, the best way of providing information to people is in the form of associative structures.

On the face of it, this type of argument seems very convincing. However, it ignores a number of critical factors. First, while everyone does have a memory that is associatively structured, the structures themselves differ widely between people. A young child may be quite happy to say that a whale is a fish or to group Santa Claus in the category of real people. Even adults, who have a more normative model of knowledge will show considerable difference in their associations. Thus the argument above begs the question, *If associative information structures are so intuitive, who's associative structure should we use when we create an external representation of the information?* It hardly helps to say that we will use the associative structure of an expert, because now we have lost the close mapping between external and internal structure which presumably produced the intuitive understanding and use of the hypertext.

This first criticism is certainly troubling, but it is a second criticism outlined below which is most damaging to the commonsense view that the external representation of information should mimic the internal representation in the brain. The basis of the second criticism is simply that while information in the brain is structured associatively, the process of acquiring new information from the environment is linear. This has been shown in countless psychological experiments going back at least as far as the 1950s. This linearity in processing new information is in fact a central component in the dominant model of human information processing and cognition (e.g., Neisser 1967; Lindsay and Norman 1977; Anderson 1987). Processing of new information encounters a bottleneck (Broadbent 1958; Kahneman 1973) which requires that attention be directed to information in a serial or linear fashion. While the amount that people can attend to at one time may be increased by using different modalities or styles of representation (Wickens 1984) as in multimedia, the idea that people can process novel associative information without linearizing it is not credible from the standpoint of modern psychology.

**6.6.1.6** *Text is Tough* Hypertext works best when it adds value to text. Books are highly portable and easy to read, so hypertext must add value in some way since it can't compete with books on their own terms. The big selling point of hypertext is that it can make information more accessible. However, in practical terms, hypertext creates smart relationships between different locations in text. Since we don't want to rely on handcrafting hypertext, many of the relations or links in hypertext need to be created automatically.

Methods for automated construction of hypertext are still in their infancy. Some of the most promising early methods rely on similarity of indexing and on matching text strings in different locations of the hypertext. These approaches are simplistic and they will sometimes produce simplistic hypertext.

More sophisticated techniques are needed to allow automated construction of quality hypertext. There seems to be little alternative but to carry out text analysis in some form in order to do this. But text analysis is a tough research issue that is closely related to the general problem of natural language understanding. It's going to take some time to crack that nut.

**6.6.1.7** *Where's the Model and Method?* It might help if we knew what the model of hypertext was. When we are explaining to people what hypertext is, the definition using nodes and links seems obvious and satisfactory. However, when we are trying to convert a hypertext document from one development environment to another we quickly find that there is a great deal of variation in the implicit models of hypertext that are used.

The first attempt at a hypertext model was the Dexter Reference model (Halasz and Schwartz 1990). This was superseded by the HyTime model of hypermedia. However, this model is incomplete and leaves many issues unresolved. For instance, what types of node and link should be used in hypertext. What styles of navigation should be available? How should the logical structure of hypertext be expressed?

Since we have no firm model of what hypertext is, it shouldn't be surprising that there is no recognized method for building hypertext either. Hypertext developers manage as best they can, relying on intuition and good sense. We are still a long way from the practical process of hypertext engineering envisaged by Glushko (1990).

## 6.6.2 Hypermedia and Hyperinformation Usability

There is no standard on what a hypertext (or hyperinformation) system is. Existing hypertext systems differ in both interface design and in the functionality they offer to users. Hypertext systems share with expert systems the fact that there probably exists a markedly different hypertext interface for each hypertext shell developed. This can be contrasted with other more "stable" interfaces as in the case of spreadsheets or word processors. While there is no standard hypermedia interface model, there is quite a bit of research that has studied the usability of hypertext under different conditions.

**6.6.2.1** *Research on Hypertext Usability*    Most evaluations of hypertext have used somewhat contrived tasks with specially chosen text. One study that has used a realistic task on a large scale is the study of the Document Examiner (Walker 1987) described by Walker, Young, and Mannes (1990). The Document Examiner is an interface to on-line documentation for Symbolics computer systems (equivalent to about 6000 pages of paper documentation) divided into 10,000 titles (nodes). In their study, Walker et al. collected two kinds of data, from a usage questionnaire and from usage monitoring. A usage monitor was built into the software to enable unobtrusive monitoring of system use (potential subjects could disable the usage monitoring if they so wished).

Monitoring took place over a period of 12 months, with over 34,000 interactions being selected for data analysis. One finding was that about 60% of the commands were used for viewing and the remaining 40% were used in finding possibilities and deciding what to view. For locating material to view, keyword search (20%) was strongly preferred over using the Table of Contents (1%). As Walker et al. put it, "The importance of this work is that it describes a very large, real-world example in use commercially for day-to-day work. It is not a research system with limited users and usage."

One of the interesting features of the Document Examiner study was the large overhead (40% of browsing time) that was consumed in finding possibilities and deciding where to go next. Studies such as this suggest that it is fruitful to subdivide the browsing task (and consequently hypertext usability) into components such as search, link selection, and node reading. The usability of each of these components may then be analyzed separately.

Other reports on usage of hypertext systems (Shneiderman 1989) have reported higher preference for use of tables of contents, but comparisons are difficult to make because of the use of different interfaces, different texts, and different tasks. Dillon and MacKnight (1990) investigated six researchers' perceptions of texts in terms of their use, content, and structure. This preliminary research showed that subjects classify texts based on three attributes: why read them, what type of information they contain, and how they are read.

Gordon, Gustavel, Moore, and Hankey (1988) found that subjects reading hypertext versions of short (1000-word) general articles did worse than subjects when reading linear versions, whereas the hypertext and linear versions showed equivalent performance for articles with more technically oriented content.

Monk et al. (1988) found that the relative effectiveness of hypertext depends to some extent on the availability of structural diagrams (browsing tools) while Gordon et al. (1988) found that hypertext may work better for certain types of text content. This pattern of mixed results has been obtained across a range of research studies (Egan, Remde, Gomez, Landauer, Eberhardt, and Lochbaum 1989).

In contrast to other studies, which focused on recall and comprehension as measures of hypertext performance, the SuperBook project described by Egan et al. has looked at the use of hypertext for information retrieval. In the research that they cite (Egan et al. 1989, p. 33) "For text databases of roughly book size . . . full content indexing and rich aliasing markedly improved utility compared to the levels of author indexing and keyword assignment commonly found in conventional documents, on-line documents, and typical hypertext systems where there are a limited number of 'hot' keywords." The findings of the SuperBook project generally indicate that the performance or usability of hypertext is not some fixed quantity, but will depend critically on the particular components that are included in the hypertext system.

Review of the literature suggests that hypertext can be useful and usable, but that usability is determined by many different factors acting on the different components of hypertext. Our views on hypertext usability assessment are reflected in the "method of specific advantages" proposed by Perlman (1989). In this approach, a specific must be demonstrated for each feature/capability in a system. Consequently, we don't believe that there can be a single global measure of hypertext usability. Instead, we must examine the usability of each hypertext feature or capability across different types of task, user, and situation. While this may be bad news for those who would like to propose hypertext as a general panacea for ailing information systems, this approach has the advantage of being directly related to design. Armed with knowledge about which design features do or don't work, designers may then go about the business of refining hypertext systems accordingly.

Nielsen (1990) compared 92 benchmark measurements of various usability issues related to hypertext and found that individual differences are the most important factor for hypertext usability. The biggest difference found was *age*, reported in a study by Baird, Mac Morrow, and Hardman, where the proportion of "young" people (20 years or younger) compared to the proportion of older people who went from looking at Glasgow On-line to using it was reported to be 11.5 to 1. The second biggest difference was reported by Conklin (1987), where *user's motivation* had a 10 to 1 effect on the number of new hypertext nodes created by users. These results led Nielsen to point out that "there is little hope for a single, universal hypertext user interface design which will be optimal to everybody."

Valdez (1992) found that when a range of navigation features were used (booklike as well as hypertext features) subjects exploited a wide range of the features, although there were some individual differences in the frequency with which different subjects used the different features. In addition, Valdez found that while the hypertext features were used 40% of the time, people tended to take quite a lot longer to select the hypertext features, suggesting either that selection of hypertext links is a more complex task or that hypertext links are a method of "second choice," used when other methods of navigation don't seem appropriate. However, the findings of Valdez (1991) show that when given the choice people will freely intermix tools such as the table of contents, next and previous page, and hypertext links. Thus our model of the intelligent database application interface will include a variety of tools including hyperdata, information overviews, visual querying, and information discovery.

Valdez also found surprisingly little variation in navigational strategies between printed and electronic text. In general, he found an approximately 60/40 split between booklike and hypertextlike features. Naturally the exact size of this split will depend on which features are classified as booklike versus hypertextlike. The index for instance, may be used either way, depending on the strategy adopted by the user of the system. However, the 60/40 split is a good estimate of the relative usage of booklike and hypertextlike features in a variety of situations and will be reasonably close to the mark in many instances. It seems likely that the range of booklike to hypertextlike feature usage will tend to fall between a 50/50 and a 75/25 split in most cases.

**6.6.2.2** *Data Visualization in Hyperinformation*    One method for increasing the amount of data that users can handle and interpret is the visualization of data in terms of summary presentations. Some methods of data visualization were discussed in Chapter 5. Data visualization within hyperinformation (hyperdata) potentially poses some problems due to the need for the user to navigate within a complex and often unfamiliar structure. However, hyperdata has the advantage that the user is fairly familiar with the task, and each visualization may be thought of as a template that is filled with pictorial material. It seems reasonable to expect that most users will be familiar with the template and will know enough about the application domain to understand how different charts or visualizations are filled with different data. Thus the transition from single visualizations and presentations to a hyperdata network should be straightforward because there is a natural and obvious structure that links adjacent presentations within the network (see Figure 6.20), and each data presentation is closely tied to a task application, and is not some unfamiliar and abstract textual material (often the case in hypertext systems where users get disoriented).

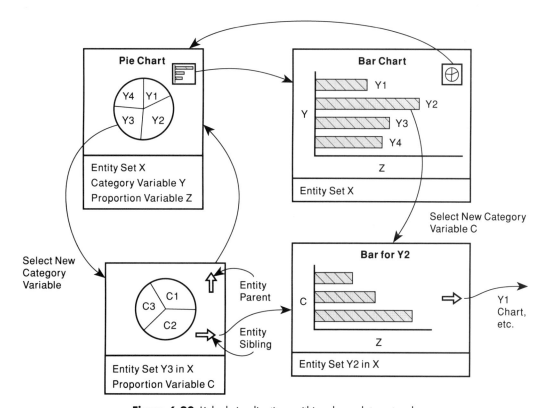

**Figure 6.20** Linked visualizations within a hyperdata network.

At this point it might seem that a further layer of data visualization could be added, where different presentations or visualizations were linked into an overview display or map. The apparent advantage of this approach is that it gives a birds-eye view of the hyperdata structure. However, such overviews of hyperdata should not be needed as much as they are in hypertext. Furthermore, there are many unanswered questions about how such overview visual representations should be constructed.

One of the most appealing methods of visual representation is to represent a hypermedia network as a three-dimensional structure. The user may then move around inside this structure much as they would inside a physical space, but using the mouse to select locations rather than a physical process such as walking or driving.

The use of a three-dimensional network for visualization has been explored, for instance in the SemNet project at MCC (Fairchild, Poltrock, and Furnas 1988). The goal of this project was to allow users to navigate around knowledge bases. Techniques were explored such as using motion parallax to induce a feeling of three-dimensionality from a viewing point, and using scaling, clustering, and annealing methods to create and simplify the three-dimensional configurations. The SemNet method appeared to work quite well for relatively small numbers of nodes (53 in one case) and the well-structured type of information that exists in knowledge bases, but it remains to be seen whether three-dimensional networks will be feasible with messier information structures consisting of larger numbers of nodes. Some of the arguments in favor of the use of three-dimensional networks include the fact that people are very familiar with three-dimensional spaces and with the visual cues associated with them. These arguments at first glance seem so overwhelming and obvious it is not surprising that they have generally been accepted without question. However, the enthusiasm for using three-dimensional networks for visualizing hypermedia should be tempered by the following concerns.

1. People may live in a three-dimensional world, but they tend to navigate on two-dimensional planes parallel to the surface of the earth. The tendency to navigate in two-dimensions was used as a plot device in one of the Star Trek movies when an intelligent but novice pilot still thinking two-dimensionally was out-maneuvered by an experienced star ship pilot who had been trained to think three-dimensionally. Thus, while people are highly skilled at viewing a three-dimensional world, they may require some training in learning to navigate effectively in three dimensions.

2. It is probably unreasonable to expect a large number of information concepts to fit into a three- (or even four-) dimensional structure. Spatial structures generally impose metric constraints (e.g., Shepard 1974) that may be too severe. Associative links can potentially link almost anything to anything else based on criteria that can hardly be predicted from a spatial structure. Spatial structures that represent relatively small (less than 60, say) numbers of nodes or objects may not effectively "scale up" to represent larger numbers of objects.

3. The creation of a three-dimensional structure raises the question of how that structure will be used in browsing. While users may be able to view the structure without difficulty, how will they navigate around the structure? The effective-

ness of browsing may well depend on what techniques are available for viewing the structure from different vantage points. Other navigation features that are likely to have a strong effect on browsing performance include the ways in which the relative salience or importance of different objects, and the different types of links, are represented.

4. Should different subtopics reside in separate spatial representations, or should they be linked within a single monolithic representation? If separate representations are used, how is the user going to switch between them during browsing?

Thus spatial representation in hyperinformation should be used judiciously, and should be supported by appropriate navigation tools. The model of hyperdata described in this book will downplay the role of spatial representation and will instead rely on information overviews and fairly intuitive point-and-click transitions between related charts and graphs as a means of achieving navigation without disorientation.

**6.6.2.3** *Visual Menus and Hot Spots*    Existing hyperinformation systems generally rely on nonspatial solutions such as trees for displaying structure, or use spatial maps relatively sparingly, representing small numbers of nodes, generally in two-dimensional structures.

The use of menu alternatives can provide a limited navigation facility even in the absence of visualization. Menu alternatives may be displayed in a number of different ways. In the HyperTies system (Shneiderman 1987), for instance, menus are embedded in text and menu items are indicated as bold-faced items. Replacement buttons in Guide also serve as embedded menu items. In other approaches, visual menus are used where menu icons are embedded within a visual scene, much as menu items may be embedded as words or phrases within text.

Menu alternatives are good at showing the user local structure, (i.e., what the current node is and what links are immediately available), but they do not allow the user to visualize the larger structure within which the current node is embedded. However, like selectable trees, menus for local navigation have proved to be useful in a number of hypermedia systems and would appear to be good candidates for inclusion in such a battery of visualizing techniques.

The SuperBook project (Remde, Gomez, and Landauer 1987) also shows how navigation can be achieved through nonspatial structures. In this case the book metaphor includes selecting information through index and table of contents. As Remde et al. point out, this approach has the advantage that SuperBook is able to access existing documents while most hypertext systems require authoring of new information structures.

In other systems, trees are often used to convey the overall structure of a portion of hypermedia. Trees are used, for instance, in the NoteCards browser (Halasz, Moran, and Trigg 1987). Trees allow nodes to be organized into categories that are nested at different levels of abstraction. Nodes can then be directly selected from the browser (i.e., the map of the tree structure). Selectable tree systems (browsers) are a good method of visualizing hypermedia. Browse trees are an explicit representation of the hierarchical representation that is otherwise available in a table of contents.

Webs are a refinement of the tree or network visualizing techniques where links may be filtered according to context or interests. Intermedia webs (Yankelovich, Haan, and Meyrowitz 1988) are an implementation of this concept. Webs are an example of a general principle that users should only have to view the subset of links and nodes that are of interest to them. Methods for using inference to dynamically construct or reconfigure hypermedia based on criteria such as the purpose of browsing or user interests are discussed elsewhere (Parsaye, Chignell, Khoshafian, and Wong 1989, Sections 5.6 and 7.2.6).

Menus and hierarchies are powerful and popular tools for improving navigability of hypertext by adding structure. One method for reducing disorientation is to selectively filter or weight information about the surrounding hypermedia structure. The fish-eye lens model (Furnas 1986), for instance, is motivated by the observation that humans often represent their own neighborhood in great detail, yet only indicate major landmarks for more distant regions. This phenomenon can be demonstrated within a city and across larger geographic regions. It also reflects the functioning of the human eye, where closer objects are seen in more detail.

### 6.6.3 Current Trends

The work on the underlying ideas and principles of hyperinformation continues unabated. While the technology and thus model of hyperdata is fairly stable, there are a number of trends that will have a strong influence on other forms of hyperinformation. Some of these trends are described in this section.

#### 6.6.3.1 *The Merger of Electronic Document Technologies*

Hypermedia systems are more flexible than traditional information structuring methods in that they allow information in a variety of forms (media) to be attached to nodes. Nodes in hypertext (hypermedia) will generally include buttons that provide links (send messages) to other nodes. The variety of nodes that can be defined in hypertext make it an extremely flexible knowledge representation tool. This flexibility is further enhanced by providing a variety of link types. Links define the structure of hypermedia and provide the capability for browsing and exploring the nodes.

From the perspective of hyperinformation there has been a somewhat artificial separation between hypertext, hypermedia, and multimedia. As alternative media become available in the form of "clips" these distinctions will disappear. In essence, the various forms of hyperinformation are providing flexible access to heterogeneous electronic information. Each chart or sequence of charts in a data visualization may be thought of as a kind of document. Similarly, the presence of interactive video segments within systems of electronic information also gives video document-like properties. Thus hypertext, hypermedia, hyperdata, and multimedia may all be thought of as complementary aspects of electronic document technology.

#### 6.6.3.2 *Hyperinformation as an Assistive Technology*

Hyperinformation is a partnership between flexible information and the curious user. This approach is reflected in the augmented intellect idea of Engelbart and English (1968). We may view hyperinformation as an external assistant, rather than as a navigation environment that gets internalized or that matches the user's cognitive structures in some fashion.

From this perspective hyperinformation is a tool (cognitive prosthetic) that assists people in carrying out tasks (Wright 1991). The interaction between the user and the hyperinformation is then constrained by the task, simplifying the interaction. In addition, the task provides a strong model of hyperinformation usage and this naturally cuts down on the tendency towards disorientation and uncertainty.

Emphasis on hyperinformation as a cognitive prosthesis or external assistant also counteracts the tendency for hyperinformation to be envisaged as a taskless activity (a kind of liberated and joyous exploration of information for no particular reason). We would argue that the tasklessness of some environments is more disorienting than liberating. Without a task, is it any wonder that people get disoriented?

**6.6.3.3** **Embedded Systems**    The days of stand-alone hyperinformation applications are probably numbered. People want to be able to integrate their activities and cut down on the overhead of switching between applications. Hyperinformation too, should be embedded within other systems, depending on the requirements of the task. While this type of embedded hyperinformation is still relatively rare there are a number of applications that show how it can be done.

One of the first examples of using hyperinformation in an embedded system was the knowledgePro expert system shell (KnowledgeGarden 1988) which used hypertext as an explanation system. One could click on a term in a rule to call up hypertext annotations that explained the meaning of the term. One could then return to the rules, or continue to explore the hypertext and look at the links between different explanations. In this case the hypertext supplemented the traditional how and why method of explanation within hypertext systems (e.g., Parsaye and Chignell 1988).

On-line help is one of the most obvious examples of commercially important problems where embedded hypertext can help. Perhaps the best known example of this is the hypertext environment available for constructing on-line help in Microsoft Windows applications. Hypertext works well in on-line help because when one finds a topic one is often interested in related topics. In this case it is easier to browse through a web of related topics in hypertext than it is to go in and out of an alphabetical index looking for topics.

Customer service is another domain where it is critical that the user have ready access to related information. In this case, the operator/user often has to input data into a database (e.g., a customer service operator may collect information about product defects and this information is then aggregated and passed on to the quality assurance department). An embedded hyperinformation system makes sense in this situation as long as it can be integrated with existing databases and information systems.

Hyperinformation systems are also being developed to help organize electronic mail messages. Anyone who uses electronic mail systems extensively faces the dilemma of what to do with old mail messages. As the list of old messages grows into the hundreds and thousands serial search through them becomes too time consuming. The net result is often wholesale deletion of old messages which is sometimes bitterly regretted at some later date when it is found that some critical information was also deleted.

A number of systems exist that allow the user to tag messages with keywords, or that extract keywords from the subject fields of messages. It is even possible to carry out full text retrieval of terms from stored messages in some systems. Hypertext takes this one step further by allowing one to browse around old e-mail messages. However, it is essential that this hypertext be created automatically or dynamically (for "free") since much effort in creating the hypertext would be self-defeating in this application.

## ■ 6.7 CONCLUSION

Definitions and discussions of hypertext (and by implication, hyperinformation) have generally focused on its nonlinearity, node and link structure, the disorientation problem, and its textual nature. In contrast, hyperinformation and hyperdata are an attempt to sidestep some of the problems with hypertext by developing a workable and usable model for intelligent database applications. In constructing hyperdata as a special type of dynamic hyperinformation, the special properties of numerical data and graphical templates have been exploited.

The field of hyperinformation as broadly defined has been in a state of flux for some time. In spite of a great deal of interest in the technology, a standard model of what hypermedia is has been slow in arriving. Prior models of hypertext and hypermedia were not targeted to handle intelligent database problems. Thus, this chapter reviewed some major trends in hyperinformation and defined a version of hypermedia (hyperdata) that is designed to handle the problem of linking data visualizations within an intelligent database application.

Some of the core issues in hyperinformation discussed in this chapter include the relationship between and use of linear and nonlinear features, and the measurement of the usability of hypermedia system. In this section the frequently discussed problems of disorientation were considered, and it was pointed out that they are less troublesome in hyperdata, because the structure of the numerical data imposes a strong structure on the resulting network of charts and summaries.

The problem faced in hypertext conversion is also less severe in hyperdata because there are fewer nodes to worry about since each chart or diagram will summarize many data instances. The complexity of a hyperdata network will generally be related to the number of major concepts in the object model and the number of main descriptive attributes that are used in constructing visualizations of the data. In addition, the generation of links between presentations exploits natural relationships in numerical data and this also makes the links seem fairly natural to the user who is familiar with the conceptual model of the application domain.

This discussion of hypertext has focused on its relevance to hyperdata and the problem of navigating around data visualizations. For an introduction to hypertext and a broader overview there are a variety of sources available (e.g., Conklin 1987; Parsaye et al. 1989, Chapter 5; Nielsen 1990). There are also numerous hypertext systems, all of which are idiosyncratic in their own way. The best way to get a feel for the types of hypertext system available and current trends in the area is to scan some of the relevant conference proceedings, including hypertext '87, '89, and '91 sponsored by the Association for Computing Machinery and held in the United States, Hypertext 1 and Hypertext 2, held in the United Kingdom, and the European Conference on hypertext held in Paris in 1990.

The hyperdata system described in this chapter forms the foundation for point-and-click interface to an intelligent database application. Hyperdata is an integrated set of tools for viewing data. These tools give rapid and natural access to tables and charts based on interactively specified constraints on data and presentation formats.

In the appendix to this chapter, methods for automatic conversion of material into hypertext are discussed. In Chapter 7 this approach will be supplemented with navigation based on information overviews, using an executive information system approach.

## ▪ 6.8 APPENDIX: AUTOMATED HYPERTEXT CONVERSION

Manual authoring of large hypertexts is very labor intensive. Some of the methods that may be used for conversion of text into hypertext are considered here. The hypertext created using these methods will generally not be as good as hypertext created by a skilled human author. However, for very large hypertexts, automated conversion may be the only feasible way to create all the nodes and links that are required. Thus there is a trade-off in large-scale hypertext creation, with human authoring providing better links, but often at much higher cost.

There are many ways to make a hypertext project fail. One frequent problem encountered in developing hypertext is that it is too expensive. It is like a new cancer drug that is so expensive it can't be tested out in large-enough clinical trials to see if it works and how it should be used. The processes of creating and using hypertext need to be much less expensive. Some of the ideas that people are working on to make hypertext "almost free" include automated conversion of text into hypertext, browsing through interactive querying, and statistical representation of semantic meaning. Some of these issues are discussed below.

### 6.8.1 Hypercompilation by Hyperterm Matching

One of the simplest methods of hypertext conversion is hypercompilation based on keyword matching and indexing. The characteristics of this approach are that it is both simple and effective. Although more elaborate approaches provide more power, in many industrial instances, the trade-offs here are well justified.

The method begins by selecting a set of key terms or phrases which we call *hyperterms*. Terms are selected as hyperterms beforehand, based on various criteria: Are they known as acronyms? Do they tend to be diagnostic (i.e., they appear reasonably frequently, but are unequally distributed, appearing often in some documents but never in others)?

Once the hyperterms are chosen, instances of them are identified in the text using various forms of string matching. Links are then constructed between different instances of the same hyperterm, or they may all point to the node that describes the meaning of the hyperterm in some way. This process of hypertext conversion is represented in Figure 6.21. The typical text entry to the system in an Ascii file looks like this:

*#! Term 1*
*Here is the text for hyperterm Term 1*
*....*

*#! Term2*
*Here is the text for hyperterm Term2*
*....*

*#! Term3*
*Here is the text for hyperterm Term3*
*....*

The symbol #! (or any other symbol) is used to initiate a new hyperterm definition. These Ascii files are then processed by hypercompiler and the appropriate links are built automatically. The hypercompiler has to search through all hyperterm definitions and all text in order to find all instances of all hyperterms and build links for

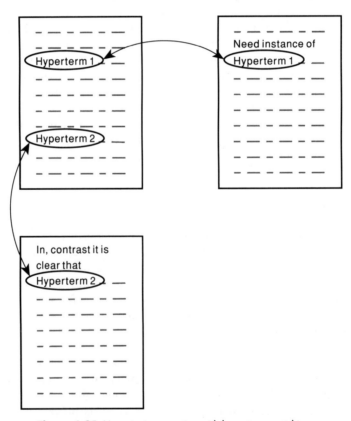

**Figure 6.21** Hypertext conversion with hyperterm matching.

them. Thus this process is at times computationally intensive, but it does not need to be frequently repeated since updates can be processed intelligently.

The system thus has two distinct components: the hypercompiler and the hyperengine.

The hypercompiler builds the links and leaves them in a database for future reference. The hyperengine then accesses the database of links at run-time. This simple architecture provides a great deal of flexibility since the amount of text managed can be very large. When a really large amount of static information needs to be hyperaccessed, a traditional relational database may be used for link management, while optical stores, etc., are used for read-only document and diagram storage.

## 6.8.2  Project HEFTI

This section describes another approach to the automated conversion of text into hypertext, as used in the system HEFTI. This approach differs from the discussion of the previous section in that the system is interactive, providing greater control over link building, while requiring some additional human effort.

The goal of Project HEFTI (Hypertext Extraction From Text Incrementally) at the Institute of Systems Science, University of Singapore, is to extend existing work on the manual creation of hypertext from text by automating parts of the process (Chignell, Nordhausen, Valdez, and Waterworth 1991). The HEFTI model assumes that hypertext conversion is a sequential process starting with some sort of "protomedia" consisting of segmented (and possibly named) text. The current HEFTI model focuses on text nodes and their linkages. Pictures and other media can then be added to nodes manually.

HEFTI systems are able to convert large chunks of textual information into linked hypertext using a semiautomated algorithm. The HEFTI prototype (Chignell, Nordhausen, Valdez, and Waterworth 1991) handled a large book (over 400 pages). The major research issues in HEFTI systems are concerned with techniques for automatic indexing of text nodes, and for identifying hypertext links either through semantic analysis of text (albeit of a limited nature) or else through syntactic and statistical techniques. Other issues concern the refinement of links to enhance hypertext usability, and the organization of links to facilitate the process of navigation during browsing. Commercially important problems where HEFTI-like conversion should prove useful include:

1. Technical documentation for maintenance and repair
2. Software libraries and CASE tools
3. Instructional resources based on text books
4. Electronic encyclopedias on a variety of topics
5. Organization of e-mail messages, notes, and memoranda as part of a project management system
6. Design support tools based on hypertext representation of design specifications, engineering notes, and so on
7. Organization of indexing and thesaurus items for assisting query formulation in information retrieval

The HEFTI model assumes that hypertext conversion can be achieved through the action of seven modular components arranged approximately in sequence. The modules are; text preparation, node preparation, indexing, link creation, organization, link refinement, and hypertext specification. Since each of these seven modules may be implemented in a number of different ways, there are in fact a large number of HEFTI systems that could be implemented within the broad framework of the HEFTI model. Each of the modules can be implemented using a variety of different strategies and computational techniques. However, the inputs and outputs of these modules need to be compatible, and the end result of the process is a text file constructed in a standard format.

The task of node preparation involves segmenting the text into nodes and then labeling (naming) each node. Optionally, an abstract may be added to describe the contents of the node in brief. Node preparation may be simplified in a well structured text. Here the structure of the text (see Furuta 1987) is exploited to provide an a priori node segmentation.

In the next module, the nodes are indexed by a standard set of index terms obtained through manual indexing, automated indexing, or some combination of the two. The output of HEFTI indexing is a set of facts that define which index terms are contained in each node.

Various cues within the text indicate relations between nodes (subsections). These cues may be used to detect similarity between nodes which forms the basis for linking. Several measures of document similarity have been suggested in the literature (e.g., the number of index terms that match divided by the total number of index terms used to describe two documents). Applying one of these measures to our text nodes we can construct a node similarity matrix containing the similarities for all possible pairs of nodes. Similarly, we may define the similarity of a pair of index terms according to the proportion of documents that they co-occur in. Associative links may then be defined using a threshold function on the node similarity matrix.

The task of organizing the hypertext is carried out in the next module of the HEFTI model. The easiest method is simply to take the organization of topics that is represented in the tree structure of the table of contents, if the original material is a book. In other situations, cluster analysis (discussed earlier in Chapter 3) may be used to group nodes based on the similarity matrix created as part of the linking module. This will then build a hierarchical organization of the nodes based on the pattern of indexing or linking.

The final task in the HEFTI model is to specify the resulting hypertext in terms of a standard hypertext model that can then be imported into different hypertext systems such as Guide or KMS. Since such a standard model is not yet fully developed, current versions of the HEFTI system convert the representation into a specific format such as the KMS system.

Other approaches to automated hypermedia creation are less generic and emphasize the role of careful design of the target hypertext document. For instance, Furuta, Plaisant, and Shneiderman (1989) described a methodology for hypertext conversion based on softcopy (electronic) input with machine-readable markup. Their transformation methodology includes the following steps:

1. Design the structure of the target hypertext article.
2. Determine how the source's structure corresponds to the desired target's structure.
3. Specify the conversion process, which must
    a. extract the relevant components of the source's structure,
    b. reorganize the components to form the target's structure,
    c. augment the target's structure with representation of relationship's pinks,
    d. generate the hypertext database files.
4. Automatically convert from source to produce the target hypertext database.
5. Modify the hypertext database, if appropriate, to provide a "wrapper" to incorporate additional articles, and to correct errors.

Nunn et al. (1988) also describe a particular instance of automated construction of a hypertext, and the Chameleon project (Mamrak et al. 1989) has done some related work in converting paper based and electronic documents between different document representations.

### 6.8.3 Interactive Querying

The distinction between information retrieval systems and hypertexts blurs when we consider queries launched while viewing text as an alternative form of browsing (Golovchinsky and Chignell 1992). This hypertext-like behavior of interactive querying from within text is particularly apparent when a powerful text retrieval engine is used that performs searches almost instantaneously.

Queries-R-Links is an interactive querying system developed at the University of Toronto. Queries are expressed by marking text in terms of AND clusters (i.e., using non-negated disjunctive normal form).

The use of AND clusters is appropriate for Boolean querying since any Boolean expression constructed out of keywords and various combinations of AND and OR operators (possibly with parentheses used for disambiguation) can be converted to the AND cluster representation (disjunctive normal form). This conversion can be carried out using De Morgan's law and the distributivity law of logical equivalence in similar fashion to standard methods of converting predicate logic sentences into clausal form (e.g., Clocksin and Mellish 1984).

The avoidance of the negation operator (NOT) reduces the generality of the method somewhat, but may actually be beneficial given the problems that many people have in using NOT effectively during Boolean querying.

Users of the Queries-R-Links system are able to form a query, examine the results, adjust the query to produce a new set of hits, and iterate in this manner (potentially backtracking to previous states) as they collect information. Figure 6.22 is a screenshot from the Query-R-Links system showing how a graphical query is formed. Terms are selected by mouse clicks and then joined into AND clusters by dragging between the terms to form lines. First, the word "white" was clicked on. Next, the word "rabbit" was selected. The two words were then joined with an AND. The graphical query is

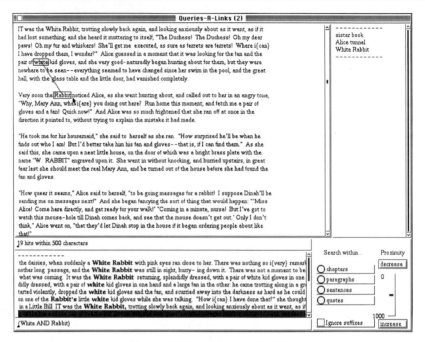

**Figure 6.22** Down the rabbit hole.

thus marked on the text (upper left window) while the sections of text referring to white AND rabbit are shown in the lower left.

Queries-R-Links has also been designed to allow queries to be formed interactively even if one of the words to be used in the query does not appear on the current screen. This is done by allowing the user to click in the right margin of the test to enter a new term which can then be added to the query. Alternatively, the user may click on an existing word on the page and then duplicate it in the margin. This allows a query of the form (A and B and C) or (A and D) to be expressed easily even though the term A may only appear once on the current screen.

The simple paradigm for interactive querying can be extended in a number of ways. For instance, a "slider" within the user interface of Queries-R-Links shown in the lower right of Figure 6.22 allows the user to set the scope of the AND operator. This allows the range or scope of the AND to be defined for any number of characters within a document, where a range of 100 characters, say, will lead to more precision than a scope of 500 characters. Then, as the slider is moved up and down, the number of hits contracts and expands, giving a highly visual representation of the changing precision.

Marking up queries in this way creates a dynamic, interactive, immediate, and reversible interface to an information retrieval system that encourages a style of exploration and navigation that is typically associated with hypertext. In other words, Queries-R-Links makes interactive querying look and feel like hypertext browsing.

However, interactive querying does not constitute hypertext per se. For instance, the user must expend some effort in constructing the queries, in contrast to simply pointing and clicking at preexisting link anchors. In return for the greater expended effort the user is able to express more complex relations between elements of information.

### 6.8.4 Statistical Representation of Meaning

The last method for getting hypertext functionality on the cheap discussed here is based on the work of Tom Landauer and others at Bellcore (Landauer et al. 1990).

The basic idea is to develop a statistical representation of meaning. This is done as follows: First a large amount of text is chosen and segmented into nodes (or documents). Then the text is indexed, either manually or using a process like term weighting (discussed earlier in this appendix). Then a rectangular data matrix is calculated showing the number of times that each index term appears in each node or document (as illustrated in Figure 6.23). This matrix is then subjected to a form of eigenvector analysis (e.g., the Bellcore researchers used a method known as singular value decomposition). Conceptually, and mathematically, this method is similar to the method of factor analysis.

The output of the analysis is a vector space representation of the terms and nodes. This vector space is assumed to represent the meaning of the texts used in some way (the entire process has been referred to as latent semantic indexing). The dimensionality of the vector space is a parameter that can be set during the analysis, but typically about 100 dimensions have been used for analysis of large bodies of text. The "meaning" of the terms and nodes or documents is then represented by their position in the 100-vector space. Nodes that appear in closely related positions in the vector space are assumed to be similar. In addition, if it is possible to interpret some of the dimensions in terms of some construct, then more specific types of hypertext link are possible. For instance, say that one dimension corresponded to size or strength. Then

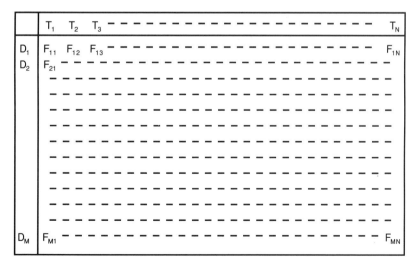

**Figure 6.23** A rectangular data matrix for statistical analysis of meaning. ($f_{ij}$ is the frequency with which term $T_i$ appears in document [node] $D_j$.)

nodes that had the same value for that dimension would be similar in terms of size or strength.

This type of statistical analysis of meaning is still very experimental although some promising results have been obtained. Further, if the vector space representation of a large set of nodes is available, then it provides a natural type of hyperinformation environment, where links are established between nodes that are close in the space. Further, landmarks may be defined in the space and browsers can be constructed automatically by projecting close nodes and moderately distant landmarks into a two- or three-dimensional "subspace."

The ultimate expression of this statistical approach to meaning would be a dictionary where the meaning of words would be defined as vectors. Naturally there would be different vectors for each sense of a word. The dimensional representation of word meaning is in fact quite consistent with some theories of semantics (e.g., Leech 1974).

# 7

# INFORMATION PRESENTATION

*Those who distinguish between education and entertainment, don't know the first thing about either.*

— Marshall McLuhan*

*Corollary:* In effective presentations, the audience interacts with and is engaged by hyperdata, achieving two-way communication between entertaining and informing presentation and interested user.

## ■ 7.1 INTRODUCTION

Presentations are essential to organized group activity. Many of the activities we routinely perform are presentations. For instance, when someone makes a sales presentation, teaches a class, delivers a speech, or addresses a meeting of one type or another the process of presentation is under way. Presentations are an essential part of intelligent database applications. Project management often involves presentation of Gantt charts, etc. Quality management and control often center around group meetings.

Presentations occur in synchronous communication during meetings and differ from television newscasts since they allow for interaction between the presenter and the audience. Presentations are distinguished by the existence of feedback and the use of visual material to make a point.

Mathematics has always distinguished between proof by induction and proof by deduction, but good presentations create proof by persuasion, a much more powerful type of proof in many instances. Proof by persuasion has to be interactive and the presenter has to respond to feedback and objections from the audience. This puts a premium on agile and flexible access to information, as is provided by hyperdata.

It is instructive to contrast presentation with visualization. Visualization is a more analytical exploratory activity which aims at understanding, while presentation is

---

* Marshall McLuhan was born in Edmonton, Canada, in 1911. He taught at the University of Toronto and originated the phrase "The medium is the message." His books on human and electronic communication issues are read worldwide.

inherently a group-oriented activity which aims at persuasion. Thus presentations often provide acts of analysis, discovery, and visualization, nested within the synthetic process of persuasion.

Why are presentations important? Presentations are needed to coordinate the activities and assumptions of people. Education, for instance, is a way of sharing culture and knowledge about technology. Business meetings are often used to negotiate, reach agreement, or persuade. In our complex world, more and more work activity revolves around presentations. People routinely complain about the number of meetings that they have to attend in a day. This is because presentations have become the glue that holds people and organizations together in a complex world. Improving the efficiency of presentations is a key method for enhancing the efficiency and productivity of an organization.

This chapter will examine the nature of presentation and its role in intelligent database applications. The history and evolution of presentation is examined first, followed by a discussion of how presentation may be used in intelligent database applications, and finally, methodologies of information presentation are reviewed.

## ■ 7.2 HISTORY AND EVOLUTION OF INFORMATION PRESENTATION

Humans receive a high proportion of their information about the environment through vision (as discussed in Chapter 5). In contrast to other methods of communication (e.g., books and printing), the technology of visual presentation of information has developed relatively slowly.

The history of formal presentations is rather brief. Although the ancient Greeks and Romans relied on verbal addresses to large groups they did not use visual materials to support their arguments. The emphasis was on oratory and persuasion with words rather than on the analysis of data and trends. Court meetings, councils of war, performances by court jesters, were held for hundreds of years, but none of these activities constituted a presentation in the formal sense. Perhaps the only form of presentation that appeared earlier than the eighteenth century was when councils of war referred to maps. Generals would consult maps in preparing the disposition of forces and plans of attack and defense.

The first systematic use of charts to represent numerical data is commonly attributed to William Playfair in 1786. This was decades after the development of calculus and thousands of years after the invention of Euclidean geometry. Playfair's activity may well be categorized as visualization rather than presentation. However, the appearance of data visualizations as tools to support argument was quickly followed by the incorporation of those tools in presentations. It is not clear when visualization was formally turned into a presentation. Lectures in universities certainly began to use presentations in the 1800s. The Royal Society and the French Academy were also the scenes of formal presentations with the aid of charts and graphs.

Sophisticated mathematical concepts developed much earlier than basic methods of visually summarizing numerical quantities and relationships because people needed math first. Math was needed for astronomy and navigation, and to explain the behavior of mechanical forces. In contrast, visual presentations were not so sorely needed in a simpler world where meetings were relatively fewer and organizations were smaller. In addition, the technology required for doing math was pencil and paper, whereas the tools for visual presentation were less well developed.

The history of sophisticated information presentation is also relatively brief, except for the technology of books (and before them, manuscripts), which has provided the main method of information presentation for many hundreds of years. Systematic visualization of numerical data is only two centuries old, flexible navigation on electronic media is barely two decades old, and graphical interfaces and large-scale information discovery are of even more recent origin.

In spite of its late arrival, data visualization has spread throughout the industrialized world in the past two centuries. Charts and graphs are now considered to be essential for almost any discussion of numerical data. What people want is not raw numerical data, but summaries of ratios and trends, and visual presentations are generally the best way of presenting such information.

In more modern times, graphics and presentation played a key part in the success of the early spreadsheets. For instance, the ability to do graphics in Visicalc enabled managers in corporations to go to meetings better prepared and with persuasive visualizations. This has since spawned a whole industry of presentation graphics software.

One of the most recent inventions of all (i.e., the graphical user interface) has in the space of a few years become so widely accepted that it is hard to imagine computing without it. The graphical user interface is important to the topic of presentation because it provides a consistent and familiar visual environment within which to embed information displays and navigation tools.

The emergence of GUIs (see Chapter 3 for more on this topic) went hand in hand with the emergence of graphic presentation tools on the Macintosh. This in turn brought about first desktop publishing and then multimedia as an advanced form of computer-based presentation. This trend is now leading to the concept of hyper-presentations where navigation (in a Hyperinformation system) can take place throughout the presentation and the presentation can connect to active data so that it is continuously updated as new data arrives. This trend also goes hand in hand with the issue of executive information systems discussed in Chapter 8.

Hyperdata (discussed at length in Chapter 6) is a manageable and focused technology for navigation of data visualizations. Much effort has gone into creating navigation through screens of text, and a comparable degree of effort needs to be spent on navigation through alternative visualizations of data.

The concept of information navigation has developed separately from data visualization. Nonlinear navigation of text seems to have been common at least for the past few hundred years (McKnight, Dillon, and Richardson 1991) and books have a variety of built-in navigational tools such as tables of contents (a hierarchical overview), indices, footnotes, references (i.e., "see also, hypertext links"), and citations (references or bibliographies).

Yet in spite, or perhaps because, of the extensive experience of navigation in books, navigation in electronic media generally took a back seat to numerical computation in the early years of computing. It was only in the 1980s that widespread availability of hypertext systems brought the focus back to navigation in electronic documents. The early emphasis was on the nonlinear nature of hypertext systems and on comparisons between hypertext and books. This tended to obscure the relevance of point-and-click navigation as a means of exploring large networks of information presentations and data visualizations. In other words, a great deal of effort has been expended in looking at hypertext as a replacement for books, rather than looking at how hypertext and other forms of nonlinear access to electronic information might help us to interact with information in new ways.

Today the fields of executive information systems, presentations, and hypermedia have merged in the context of intelligent databases. Now, distributed presentations are emerging as presentation technologies combine with new communication technologies such as broad band ISDNs, video conferencing, and group decision making.

## ■ 7.3 PRESENTATION WITH INTELLIGENT DATABASES

The fundamental tenet of intelligent database presentations is that the process of converting data into presentations can and should be automated. The key benefits are increased organizational productivity and better information flow throughout the organization.

It is impractical to author presentations from huge data sets by hand on a routine basis. Consider, for instance, the information generated by the 1990 U.S. census. Say that there were 10,000 interesting ways that the data could be partitioned on the basis of region, state, county, city, or zipcode. Then each of these data breakdowns might be summarized and displayed differently for different applications such as marketing, city planning, demographic analysis, and so on. There could conceivably be hundreds, if not thousands of different ways of summarizing and viewing each breakdown of the information. The situation gets even more complex if we allow broad artistic license in the way in which the displays or presentations get constructed. There are simply not enough graphic artists to create all the presentations that might conceivably be called for in summarizing or interpreting a large data set.

A second reason for automating data presentation is even more compelling. Human authoring of charts and displays takes time, but increased competition requires instantaneous response. For instance, a busy executive wants to see a particular breakdown of the information as a pie chart now, not tomorrow. In the same way that computing in general was revolutionized when processing moved from being batch-oriented to interactive, so exploration of, and interaction with, data is revolutionized when interactive presentation of the data is possible based on user selections with a set of navigational tools.

A third reason why automated presentation is so important can be summed up in the phrase "data knows about data." Construction of a good presentation of data is more than graphic art. It also requires an understanding of patterns in data. However, detailed understanding of large amounts of data is extremely hard to achieve. People in general are not good at absorbing masses of details. Therefore it is preferable if the data itself can determine what its important patterns and properties are. In practice this means using information discovery and data visualization tools to add value to the data, *to make it fit for human consumption.*

A fourth reason for automating information presentation is that it allows more scientific control over the presentation process. For instance, more consistent graphic formats or visual templates can be used and various unwanted effects such as "chartjunk" (Tufte 1983) can be avoided. In addition, the statistical significance of a relationship can be calculated and conveyed to the user along with the graphic.

In automating information presentation we avoid the dilemma faced by artificial intelligence researchers where domain independent methods were too weak while domain dependent efforts required too much knowledge engineering effort (Parsaye and Chignell 1988). We develop a solution that uses both domain independent (e.g., the intelligent database engine) and domain dependent (specific charts and user interfaces) components. Thus, while customized versions of intelligent databases need to be developed for each application, there is still a considerable kernel of domain independent functionality that is shared by all intelligent database applications.

### 7.3.1 Categories of Presentations

A number of different types of presentation have evolved to handle the different requirements of meetings between people. For instance, presentations can be classified as internal: group meeting and external: involving outside personnel.

Internal presentations generally assume a much greater shared context or "group literacy." In contrast, external presentations will tend to focus more on terminology and terms of reference. External presentations tend to be "funnel shaped" in that they start broad by sketching in the missing context before getting down to shared specifics. Group meetings tend to be more focused from the outset.

Presentations can also be classified into the following two groups, (1) cyclic presentations: fixed format, at given times, etc., and (2) single case presentations: new idea, no fixed format. Examples of cyclic presentations are monthly project reviews, department meetings, and so on. These regular meetings are the glue that hold most organizations together. They provide a chance to update the different members of a group on what has been happening. Regular meetings generally have a fairly fixed format. Single case presentations tend to be arranged to meet a particular challenge or need. As such they tend to be oriented towards a particular goal (e.g., solving a problem) rather than generally updating people.

Presentations can also be distinguished in terms of the flow of control within the meeting. Thus presentations may be oriented towards information delivery or oriented towards group discussion. For instance, there may be a single speaker who delivers most of the material and generally controls the floor, or there may be a group discussion with no clear leader. Group discussions are necessarily more interactive, and they tend to involve spontaneous (e.g., suddenly sketching an idea on the whiteboard) presentations rather than planned slides and the like. In fact the inappropriate use of a particular style of presentation is often viewed with disdain. An example of this is when a person attempts to give a more formal presentation in the midst of a group discussion. The different types of presentation are shown in Figure 7.1.

Presentations may also differ in terms of their amount of technical content. There

| | Internal | | External |
|---|---|---|---|
| Cyclic | Formal | e.g. Dept. Meeting | e.g. Dept. Review |
| | Group | e.g. Project Discussion | e.g. Regular Discussion with Contractors |
| Single Case | Formal | e.g. Announcement of Budget Cuts | e.g. Site Visit for Special Contract |
| | Group | e.g. Special Budget Planning | e.g. Lab Visit |

**Figure 7.1** Different types of presentation.

often seems to be a trade-off between the quality of graphics and the amount of technical content. For instance, business charts have tended to be much better prepared than overheads presented in scientific meetings.

All the types of presentation discussed above can benefit from automation. Automation reduces the effort required in preparing presentations and allows people to focus on the real issues rather than on the mechanics of preparing the presentation. Automated presentations are generally carried out with the following steps: (1) put presentation system in place, (2) build series of presentations, and (3) perform interactive discussion.

The presentation system is a platform for building presentations, while each presentation has to be authored or created within that system. Once the presentation has been constructed it is then delivered. Typically this delivery will involve interactive discussion that may require flexible adjustment of the presentation. Strictly linear presentations tend to falter during interactive discussion since it is difficult for the person making or sharing in the presentation to modify a chart or refer to a previous chart. Anyone who has attended scientific conferences and meetings over the years will be familiar with the sight of presenters shuffling laboriously back through previous overheads trying to find one that addresses an issue raised by a discussant. In addition, those making presentations with linear materials will often hurriedly mark up an overhead to make a new point in response to a question or comment.

The overall process of developing and giving a presentation is as follows:

**1.** Data gathering, fusion, transformation, putting the information assets in place.
**2.** Identifying the goal of presentation. Then two other phases:
   a. Analytical—understand visualization goals, discovery, etc. Build your case. Involves exploratory analysis.
   b. Dress up your point and deliver it. Choose color etc.
**3.** Deliver the presentation.

In many instances the preparation of a presentation is an exploratory activity as information is culled in response to a question or a need to update the status of a work group. In contrast, actually giving the presentation is often a confirmatory form of activity. People may question some of the assertions made or findings reported. Thus presentation tools need to switch easily between exploratory and confirmatory modes of operation.

Presentations are often thought of as slide shows. Typically the slides are presented in linear order, although occasionally speakers may move back, as well as forward, within the slide sequence. Some presenter may rely on words (e.g., bullet charts) to make their point, while other presentations may predominantly involve charts and figures.

Modern presentation systems allow presentation via a network of visualizations, including charts, figures, as well as bullet lists and other forms of visual information. This provides considerable flexibility to the speaker, audience, or members of a group discussion to trace different paths through the presentation based on the topics and issues that are raised.

The last distinction considered here in the categorization of presentations is the distinction between analytic and synthetic presentations. Diagnostic and creative presentations represent the difference between analysis and synthesis. Diagnostic presentations are often made to analyze or diagnose a problem. In contrast, creative presentations focus on solutions. They are often made to pitch a proposal of one sort or another.

There are two key phases in the life cycle of a presentation system: (1) developing an intelligent presentation environment, and (2) constructing presentations within the environment. Phase 1 allows for facilities for creating and storing presentations. Phase 2 allows for presentation building, storage, and retrieval. The following section considers the various steps in building an intelligent presentation system.

## 7.3.2 Developing an Intelligent Presentation System

The starting point for any presentation system is the process of collecting the data and fusion of this data into a standard form. At this point, the system is not concerned with getting specific records but rather in getting access to relevant databases so that future presentations can be constructed by querying them. In many situations data fusion is a difficult step because of the variety of formats in which data is stored. The processes involved in this data fusion include getting the data dictionary, designing the schema, verifying the format, and setting up views.

Development of the presentation system also requires data modeling where the developer defines relevant objects (e.g., consumers, products, advertising media, etc. in a marketing application). The set of attributes is listed for each object, and methods are created for calculating other attributes not directly available in the database. For instance, if age is not listed for a person, but date of birth is, then age may be calculated by subtracting the year of birth from the current year (and subtracting one if the birthday in the current year has not yet been reached).

The collection of information for a presentation may then be guided by information discovery. For instance, one discovered rule might say that people who buy video camcorders will tend to be between 18 and 45 years of age, with one or more children and a relatively high disposable income. These people may also be more likely to buy large screen televisions and other consumer electrical products. This could then be used in a presentation to argue that marketing should be targeted to people who match this profile. Thus information discovery is used to construct a knowledge base of rules that summarizes the data. These rules can then be used later to construct particular presentations.

At this stage in the development process it is now possible to use the presentation system to display a set of data visualizations. This can be done by querying the databases that are included in the system and using standard charting tools to construct the visualizations. The challenge now is to link the data visualizations into hyperdata, thus forming a platform for presentation.

The hyperdata component of the intelligent presentation system consists of rules that link together different presentations. These rules are expressed fairly generally so that each rule typically applies to a number of different visualizations. The rules then act as dynamic links between visualizations.

In one style of dynamic link, the user selects an object and then links to other presentations or visualizations that also refer to that object. Say that one were viewing a plot of sales for different fruit juices in the past month. The system would then take the user to the most "interesting" alternative presentation that involved that object, relying on the currently active constraints (as described in Chapter 6).

As with hyperdata in general, links in a presentation can be expressed in a very general way. Instead of saying that the link for Company X fruit juice sales is to Company X sales by region one could say that the link for any product in the presentation when plotted against an attribute is the breakdown for that object by the attribute over region. Using this general form of the link, if one clicked on mineral juice while reviewing a chart of advertising dollars spent on each of the fruit juices, one would then move to a chart (e.g., a pie chart) showing the advertising dollars spent on mineral juice across each of the sales regions.

In another form of dynamic link one moves to a different chart or graph that shares the attribute that was clicked on. For instance, say that one was viewing the advertising dollars spent on mineral water across each of the sales regions. If one clicked on Region (i.e., the attribute on the x-axis as shown in Figure 7.2) one might move to a default presentation showing the total number of advertising dollars spent in each region (aggregated across all products).

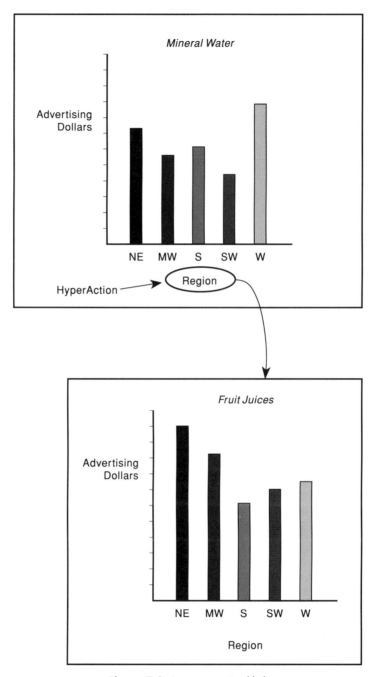

**Figure 7.2** A user-customized link.

Thus the presentation system can be constructed so that navigating via an object tends to lead to a presentation at a finer level of detail, while navigating via an attribute leads to a more summarized or aggregated form of the data. This type of behavior can generally be built into the intelligent presentation system and reflects the type of domain that the presentation system deals with.

The task of constructing presentations using the system then consists of using the dynamic links to create a sequence of charts and graphs that are of interest, and in some cases perhaps constructing additional charts and graphs based on customized queries. Skilled users of the presentation system may also develop their own customized rules for specifying how dynamic links are to be calculated under different circumstances. In this way, the presenter can respond in an agile fashion as questions or comments occur during the presentation. Instead of giving an answer in words, the presenter can click on a button and make the relevant point by showing a different graphic of the data. Thus hyperdata provides a platform for flexibility, leading to a very agile type of presentation.

The intelligent presentation system includes a data set, which is collected and integrated using data fusion tools. It also includes an end-user querying system for retrieving data, and a data visualization system (as discussed in Chapter 5) for construction graphs and charts based on extracted data. These are generally fixed components of the presentation system. Other components, notably the hyperdata rules, and the discovery-based summary of the database, may be variable.

The variable components of an intelligent presentation system are jointly defined by the system itself and by the customizing actions taken by a user in developing a specific presentation. For instance, the presentation system may have a set of pre-specified hyperdata links, some of which are modified by a user in constructing a particular presentation. In the marketing example, one such user-customized link is a special direct link from regional sales figures of a product to regional sales figures for another product that is of particular interest to the group that will be viewing the presentations (as in Figure 7.2).

Another customizable component of the presentation system is the organizing control panel for the user interface. This control panel is an extension of the hyperdata control panel discussed in Chapter 6. It allows the presentation developer to select and edit visualizations, add bullet charts and other notes, and then clip these into a presentation folder. The presentation system is thus a special kind of multimedia authoring and editing suite of tools.

Using the presentation system, the presentation developer may add textual summaries and provide hierarchical menus for access to the different visualizations. Thus the outline or table of contents is an important part of most presentations. Other forms of access to the visualizations within a presentation include an index, search by keyword, and picture retrieval menus (as discussed in Chapter 3). These different forms of access provide an executive overview capability.

The executive overview component of the presentation system includes access to presentations in terms of a hierarchy of menus, along with a drill-down facility (explained further in Chapter 8). Drilling down consists of moving down the hierarchy for one or more of the context variables. For instance, the hierarchy for region could be

region - state - county - city - zipcode.

In the drill-down mode, if the context were defined as a particular state, the presentations then viewed would be restricted to data collected from that state.

Attribute hierarchies to be used for drill down can be built into the presentation system. Other attribute hierarchies may be added for specific presentations. The presentation system also includes an interactive briefing facility. In its simplest form this will consist of a slide show with a sequence of the most important visualizations or presentations being shown. Alternatively, it may be a small hyperdata network containing the most important charts and a few paths of links within this network. The developers of specific presentations may then add value to this focused hyperdata by preparing accompanying report text or briefing notes and by adding various browsers and organizers such as a table of contents or index.

### 7.3.3 Constructing Presentations

The preceding sections outlined a fairly orderly and straightforward method for developing a presentation. Using this process for a marketing domain is the subject of this section.

Data collection and fusion consists of bringing together several different databases containing point of sale information, demographic data, and advertising expenditures for different products. These databases are then integrated in some way into a single "virtual" database although they may still physically exist on separate machines in separate locations.

Assuming that a fairly general presentation system is used, then much of the capability will need to be customized for the marketing domain. For instance, further information discovery will be needed. This discovery looks for relations between types of product and types of consumer, between advertising dollars and sales volume and between other things such as discounting policies and sales. The results of information discovery will then be rules that describe useful patterns in the data. The developer then filters and selects rules that may be used in constructing the presentation. Rules may either be reported directly (e.g., paraphrased as text or in bullet charts) or they may be used to construct visualizations (e.g., the relationship captured in a rule may be shown visually using a scattergram).

The presentation developer than forms additional visualizations using focused queries. Different visualizations will be constructed for different questions relating to products. Thus "who buys the product?" leads to charts relating to the number of sales of a product versus a variety of demographic and psychographic attributes that describe the people who bought the product.

The visualizations are then linked into the hyperdata. Some links are already predefined in the presentation system as described above. The developer can then build in additional links by hand, or by defining rules that govern the transitions (links) between different charts and graphs. An example of a rule (expressed informally) that might be authored at this stage is the following: If someone has been looking at a breakdown of a certain set of data by region then they may also be interested in a similar breakdown by sales manager (if the division of the data by sales manager does not correspond exactly to the division by sales region).

The use of rules in this fashion allows domain knowledge about the application to be entered in a very general form so that a single rule that relates different types of presentation may lead to the generation of hundreds of hyperdata links in the intelligent database application.

Once the hyperdata for the presentation is specified, the developer customizes the user interface. The work that is carried out at this stage will depend on which category of presentation is being targeted (e.g., cyclic or analytic versus synthetic).

In cyclic presentations one is reviewing the state of affairs and the changes in a number of specific parameters. For instance, how has quality been this month? How many returned products? How many new salespeople have been hired and what are the financial results? Cyclic presentations usually have a common format from one meeting to the next. Although, obviously, the format varies for different departments, etc.

During the design of the cyclic presentation we have to decide what charts and graphs will be appropriate in the current application. These will then supplement a library of default visualizations that generally apply across different intelligent database applications. The specification of visualizations will include:

- Which attributes in the relational tables are of interest?
- Which derived attributes in the object model are of interest?
- Which specialized charts (e.g., Gantt charts in project management) should be constructed?
- Which combinations of attributes represent meaningful relationships?

For instance, a derived attribute might be age or likely interest in purchasing consumer electronic products. Specification of meaningful combinations of attributes will be based on the results of information discovery (i.e., attributes that appear together in meaningful rules will be regarded as forming meaningful combinations), object modeling (i.e., attributes that describe meaningful classes of object will tend to be meaningful), and application knowledge (combinations of attributes that are traditionally shown for that application domain will be presumed to be meaningful).

The goal of synthetic presentations is to show how to create something new from existing pieces to shed light on previously unknown facts or to convince others of the existence of an opportunity. In synthetic presentations to executives, a presenter may need to be ready to answer probing questions about specific aspects of the data. This can be handled by adding drill-down facilities to the interface. For instance, the relationship between advertising dollars and sales could be plotted for the United States as a whole. This plot could then be viewed in different geographic contexts while holding the definition of the plot constant while moving down the menu hierarchy for the "region" context variable. The developer may also add text summary templates for particular charts. This tool is particularly useful for generating textual reports after using the presentation system since the user could select a set of charts with accompanying text summaries and then send them to a word processor where they could be "massaged" without too much difficulty into a fairly impressive report. This feature alone, by cutting down on the tremendous amount of time and effort spent in writing reports in most organizations, justifies the development costs of the presentation system.

In analytical presentations the goal is to identify a cause or an event, action or problem. Discovery is particularly important in analytical presentations as people try to track down causes and identify patterns. Analytical presentations often have a hierarchical structure corresponding to the goal tree that is generated by the original motivation for the presentation. For instance, the question — "Why have sales in Arizona been low and what can be done to increase them?" — can be divided into two subgoals: finding out why sales in Arizona have been low and finding out how to increase those sales. In this case, finding out why sales are low might include a presentation on the features that distinguish Arizona from other states.

In an analytic presentation, the presenter may need to discuss the details of the analysis and justify some of the assumptions made. In this case, the ability to carry out what-if scenario analysis is very useful (e.g., given the relationship between advertising dollars spent and sales made in the past, what component of last month's sales could be attributed to increasing the amount of money spent on advertising by 10%?). Frequently this extra capability is best implemented by linking the presentation system to external software applications. For instance, the presentation may be linked to a spreadsheet, so that what-if queries can be smoothly integrated with the presentation.

In the final step of developing the presentation as a finished intelligent database for marketing, the developer adds special multimedia capability to the user interface. This might include full motion video clips showing each of the sales managers commenting on their sales figures for the previous month and explaining their views on why the particular figures were obtained. The presentation may also be linked with a video mail system so that users can send reports of the data to their colleagues along with appended video messages describing their interpretation of the data.

### 7.3.4 Automated Presentation

The development of an intelligent database presentation can be thought of as a series of transformations that add value to data (Figure 7.3). With each transformation a new layer is added to the presentation along with corresponding new tools for interacting with the data or summaries of the data. However, the functionality of previous layers in the presentation continue to be available for users even after newer layers have been added. For instance, the presenter may directly query the data if time permits and the situation demands it.

In the first transformation a set of disparate data from a variety of databases is integrated into a relational database environment. In the second transformation a set of summary rules are added to the data. These may be thought of as an alternative

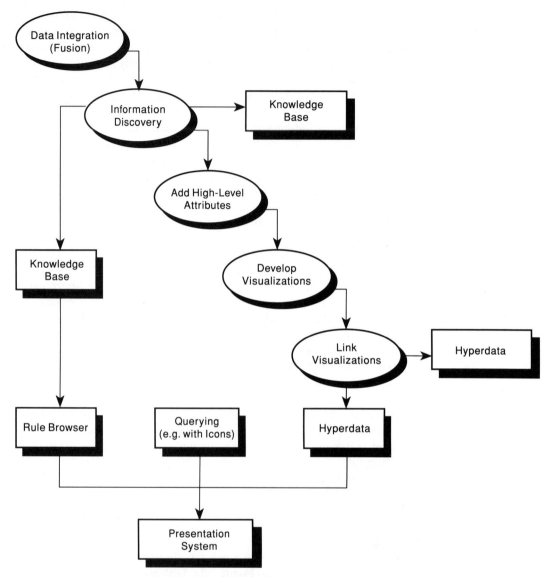

**Figure 7.3** The development of an intelligent database presentation.

representation of the data. They can also be used to answer what-if questions by classifying new cases according to the conclusion predicted by the matching rule.

The summary rules are identified through information discovery. Discovery begins with the identification (by one or more human users or experts) of a set of interesting attributes or conclusions. For instance, in a marketing presentation one of the interesting questions might be "What type of person buys each particular product?" In this situation, information discovery starts with the conclusion being the product variable and then looks for combinations of consumer attributes that predict what sort of person buys each product. Similarly, in a quality control presentation information discovery might begin with the attribute "defect" as the starting point for generating rules since there will be general interest in knowing what circumstances tend to lead to each type of defect.

The output of information discovery will then be a set of rules about which combinations of variable affect or predict the conclusion variable of interest. The presentation developer may then scan these rules to see which ones appear to be meaningful. The developer can also view various plots or charts of the data at this point to check out visual representations of the data that correspond to rules or to look for alternate patterns in the data. The discovered rules will then be stored in a knowledge base so that they may be "rediscovered" by users of the intelligent database application.

Higher level attributes can then be added to the data. This allows new higher level attributes to be added such as socioeconomic type (e.g. young professional, or small town blue-collar) based on combinations of the original attributes such as age, employment, and zipcode. Queries and visualizations may then be constructed in terms of these higher level attributes.

Visualizations may be linked to queries. Thus the user may express an SQL query, and the result will be shown as a visualization. In contrast, the method of interacting with data when hyperdata is available is much simpler. Here links have been constructed between the visual presentations, and the user may navigate around the different presentations using a point-and-click style of interaction. The user no longer has to worry about SQL queries or the object model to interact with the data, although these functionalities are still available of course.

## ▪ 7.4 METHODOLOGIES FOR PRESENTATION

Intelligent presentations incorporate several tools (e.g., information discovery, data visualization, and hyperdata) and are effectively incorporated into working intelligent databases.

Users are largely concerned with the conciseness, relevance, and interpretability of information, and it is these basic concerns that the presentation developer should address. A presenter needs an effective set of navigation tools with which to express his intentions and interests when making a presentation. The presenter should be firmly in control of the presentation. Any hint that some software is guiding and controlling the presentation destroys the credibility of the presenter and makes the whole presentation suspect. It is better to give the presenter the tools to navigate the information in lots of different ways than to have software intelligence figure out which view to show next.

There are certain kinds of questions that people want to ask about large amounts of data. The particular questions asked will vary from application to application. For instance, the quality control analyst might ask questions about whether the proportion of defects changes after a production process is modified or a shift changes, while a project manager may be concerned about deviations from a project schedule or

**Table 7.1. Aircraft Composition of Two Airlines.**

| | (100) World Airlines | (200) Global Airlines |
|---|---|---|
| 727 | 50 | 80 |
| 767 | 10 | 30 |
| DC-10 | 20 | 25 |
| 747 | 20 | 65 |

allocation of scarce resources. Nevertheless, the general nature of these questions is similar across a wide variety of presentations (i.e., people want to know about trends and relationships, and they want summaries of data or information in a readily interpretable visual format). There are questions that people regularly ask of data. The best strategy is to automate what can reasonably be automated (e.g., chart construction and the creation of "obvious" hypertext links) and then provide the user with a rich set of exploratory tools with which to interact with data and interpret the information and relationships that lie hidden within.

## 7.4.1  Information Processing

A chart is just dots on a piece of paper or pixels on a computer screen until someone starts to interpret it. Thus the process of creating a visualization or graphic presentation is followed by the information processing carried out by the person who views and interprets the visualization. The way a person processes the information will depend on the type of question he or she is trying to answer.

Consider for instance, the problem of using percentages and frequencies in presenting and reporting data. Say that we are analyzing the different types of aircraft that comprise the fleets of two airlines. We might carry out such an analysis to predict future purchase decisions of competitor airlines, or to develop a marketing strategy based on the relative safety or capacity of one of the airlines' fleets. We shall call the two hypothetical airlines in our analysis World Airlines and Global Airlines (a subsidiary of Global Corporation, of course) and a summary of the composition of the fleets of the two airlines is shown in Table 7.1.

Notice that there are total of 100 aircraft in the World Airlines fleet and 200 aircraft in the Global Airlines fleet. Thus the numbers for World Airlines can be read directly as percentages, while the corresponding numbers for Global Airlines must be divided by two to get the percentages of each type of aircraft. For instance, 40% of Global Airlines' fleet are 727s and 15% are 767s.

If we want to plot or describe this data we need to consider the problem carefully. Let's say that someone asked, "Which airline has more DC-10s, Global or World?" You could answer this question either way, depending on your assumptions about what was really being asked.

If you think the question being asked is "Which airline has a higher *proportion* of DC-10s in its fleet?" The answer would be World Airlines because 20% of its fleet are DC-10s versus only 12.5% of Global's fleet. However, if you think the question being asked is "Which airline has the higher *number* of DC-10s?" then you would answer Global, because it has five more of those aircraft than World (25 versus 20).

If we assumed that the person was interested in the proportions of aircraft then we would show the pie chart versions of the data (Figure 7.4) while if we though that the actual numbers were of interest we would show the corresponding bar chart (Figure 7.5). In comparing the two pie charts it is obvious that World Airlines has a higher proportion of DC-10s (the corresponding segment of the pie chart is larger). However, when the data are plotted using bar charts (based on frequencies instead of proportions) it can be seen that the bar representing frequency of DC-10s for Global Airlines is higher than the corresponding bar for World Airlines.

Querying data is a bit like asking questions. The answer that you get depends on the question, and the way that you graph or visualize data should also depends on the questions that users are likely to ask or be interested in. Thus data presentation is no more neutral than asking questions in general, and we need to give people tools for exploring data themselves rather than generate reports and summaries that can be easily misinterpreted.

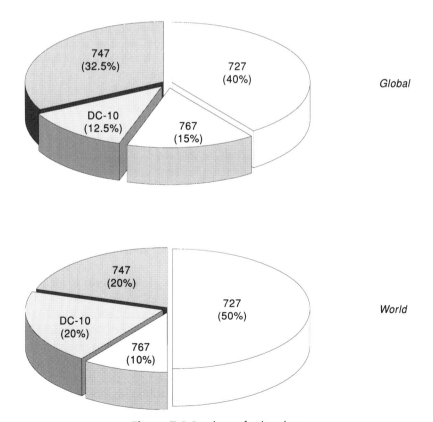

**Figure 7.4** Pie charts of airline data.

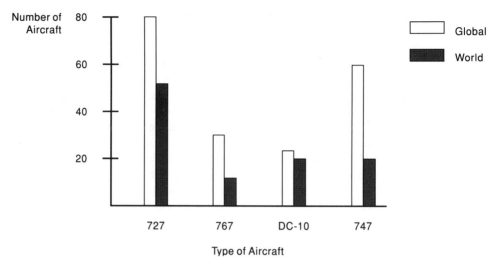

**Figure 7.5** Bar chart of the airline data.

Users should also be discouraged from jumping to conclusions about data. In some cases, it may help to annotate visualizations such as scattergrams with appropriate statistical measures so that users know which apparent patterns are firmly established and which are likely the result of random variation and effects in the data. Consider for instance Figure 7.6 which shows a scattergram of some hypothetical data. In this figure we see a cloud of points representing the relationship between disposable income and the purchase of fast food. It is tempting to see a linear relationship in this data. However, a measure of statistical correlation indicates that there is no strong evidence that such a relationship exists. In fact if we remove the three points that are circled in Figure 7.6, we find that the visual appearance of a linear relationship is also removed. Thus while visual presentations of data can be very useful, people should also be given tools that assist them in making good interpretations.

### 7.4.2  Visualization and Presentation

Presentation is still a field in its infancy. Much of the recommendations for chart development have come from experience in graphic art (e.g., Tufte 1983). The model of data visualization explored in this book seeks not only to identify useful chart types but also to develop a method for creating the presentations. Presentation systems should (1) be extremely easy to use, (2) work effectively with large databases, and (3) present summarizations of data in intuitive and clear pictures. In general, there is a natural model for each type of data. For instance, physiological or medical information can be related to the human body. Marketing or political data often is best superimposed on top of geographical maps. Such maps or representations will be referred to as presentation models in the following discussion.

In addition to the presentation model there is also an abstract representation of the numbers themselves. This abstract representation is independent of the presentation

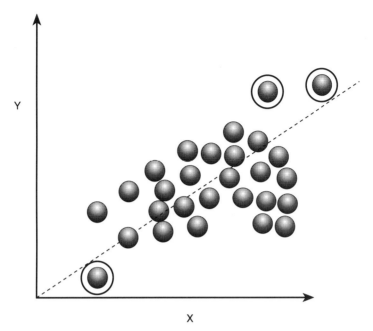

**Figure 7.6** Spurious linear relationships in scattergrams.

model although it can be related to that model by superimposing abstract charts over the relevant location of the model (e.g., having a chart showing housing sales in Chicago and superimposing that chart over Chicago's position on the bit-map of the U.S.).

Data values can also be integrated into the presentation model. Components of the basic presentation model can be systematically distorted to represent corresponding data values. For instance, amount of flow in a pipe can be represented by the width of a pipe, type of material being sent through the pipe can be indicated by color, etc.

### 7.4.3 Graphical Templates

The cornerstone of presentation is the use of graphical templates that serve as containers for numerical information. Objects within a graph or chart may be highlighted in a number of ways (Horton 1991, p. 50). Objects may be enlarged to appear more important or they may be pointed to with arrows or framed in some way. Objects are also more eye-catching if they have a unique shape. Isolated objects may also be more attention-grabbing, particularly if they are near the center of the chart or are noticeably larger than the other objects. It is easier to notice that one object is larger when it is closer to the other objects. Statistical outliers may be flagged by showing them as unusual colors or shapes. Outliers are best shown in scattergrams or line charts.

Grids should be used with caution. They can be helpful in judging the heights of bars in bar charts fairly precisely, but they should not be used with line charts (where the lines of the grid tend to conflict with the line or lines representing the data).

Stratification may be used to show another category in a chart without increasing the number of axes needed. Stratification generally is used with scattergrams and line charts. Typically the levels of the extra category variable are represented by changes in the visual symbols used to represent each data point.

Symbols should be chosen carefully, so that different levels of the category variable are not confused with each other. Color works quite well for category coding in stratification, as long as there are no more than four of five different categories or levels. Regardless of what coding scheme is used, even a good set of visual symbols will be ineffective if the symbols are plotted too small, the points are too numerous, or too many categories are represented (Chambers, Cleveland, Kleiner, and Tukey 1983).

Other aspects of graphical templates are difficult to capture as constraints. One of the aspects of automatically constructed visualizations that should most clearly differentiate them from charts drawn by graphic artists will be in their use of positioning. Different positions in a chart or graph tend to have different meanings (Horton 1991, p. 35). For instance, in diagrams, items on the left tend to refer to causes, problems, or events earlier in time, whereas items on the right tend to refer to effects, solutions, or events later in time. Some regions of a chart may also be natural "hot spots" where things are more likely to be noticed. These include the center of the chart and the top left-hand corner (in left-to-right reading cultures). Thus a good chart designer will tend to modify the scale and tick marks of a chart so as to highlight the important features of the data. This is almost impossible for a data visualization system to do.

However, there are some ways in which presentation systems can be constructed so that they do not violate particular principles of good chart design. For instance, in line charts, rapid short-term fluctuations may distract the eye from perceiving overall trends. In this case variability of the data can be calculated using statistical measures. If the variability is below a certain level, a typical line chart may be plotted, while if variability is above that threshold, a moving average may be fitted to the data to smooth away some of the variability and highlight the trend.

### 7.4.4 Visualization for Presentation

The topic of visualization was discussed at some length in Chapter 5. Visualization always takes place within a context, and often the context is a presentation. The requirements for visualizations within a presentation are particularly stringent. They must be clear and readily interpretable. The audience may sometimes be skeptical or even critical, so it is essential that the visualizations be clear and that they support rather than detract from the arguments being made. The process of creating a visualization for a presentation consists of the following steps: (1) select attributes, (2) select chart, (3) assign attributes to the chart template, and (4) select symbols and labels. Consider the example of a marketing manager who has data on the sales and expenses of salespeople. This data includes the dollar value and volume of sales, along with breakdowns by product, region, type of buyer (e.g., government, education, industry), and sales leads (e.g., advertising sources).

To create a presentation of this data we have to select a set of attributes. For instance, we might be interested in the dollar value of sales for different types of buyer. In this example, there are two attributes of interest, one is a category variable (type of buyer) and the other is a ratio variable (dollar value of sales).

The next step is to select a chart that will serve as the visual template for this data visualization. A pie chart could be used. This chart would have type of buyer as segments in the pie, with the size of each segment depending on the proportion of overall sales that came from buyers in that segment. Alternatively, a bar chart could be used. In this case each bar would represent a different type or category of buyer, and the height of each bar would correspond to the dollar sales for that category.

The pie chart would then be labeled "Proportions of Dollar Segments for Different Categories of Buyer," while the bar chart might be labeled "Dollar Segments for Different Categories of Buyer."

A more complex visualization can be constructed by including who the salesperson was along with the other two attributes. One could then plot a separate pie chart for each of the salespeople. With a large number of segments, overall visual comparison of the different category of buyer breakdowns across salespeople would be difficult using a multivariate profile of pie charts. However, in this case we only have three categories of buyer and pie charts will work fairly well.

We can also extend the bar chart method of constructing the visualization. One approach is to use divided bars where separate clusters of bars are devoted to each salesperson. These bar clusters then function as a type of glyph. After looking at a number of these "glyphs" we can begin to process them as a gestalt and get a general impression of the different distributions of buyers that different salespeople have. The bar chart clusters (glyphs) may then either be distributed along the x-axis of a single bar chart, or else each cluster of bars may be allocated to a separate bar chart, thereby creating a multivariate profile of bar charts. A second approach is to use a 3D bar chart for this data. The x-axis may be used for salesperson and the y-axis for type of buyer. In this case, the natural grouping variable is salesperson rather than type of buyer (in this domain it makes more sense to be interested in the different profiles of buyers that salespeople have than in how the sales for each type of buyer is split across the salespeople). The z-axis will then be the dollar value of sales.

## 7.4.5 Presentation of Data in a Spatial Context

The virtue of pie charts, bar charts, scattergrams, and the like is that they can be applied to almost any data. However, data often has a powerful reference model with which it is associated. For instance marketing or sales data may be referenced to the geographic locations which it refers to. In such cases data presentation is assisted greatly by including the relevant geographic or topological model as part of the data visualization or presentation. For instance, sales figures for major cities may be represented as separate bar charts for each city within a map of the nation. Geographic information systems represent an important area of application for visualization of topologically or geographically referenced data.

In creating topological data presentations the following procedure may be used:

1. Identify a world model that shows the relationships between and locations of the major entities that are relevant to the data.

2. Create a bit-map representation of the world model where each tuple in the database can be referred to a precise location on that bit-map.

3. Select a set of attributes (fields) to be displayed.

4. Select presentation goals for each attribute, such as:
   - Show individual data points
   - Show change in data over time
   - Show accumulated data
   - Show summary statistics (e.g., average, range, max value)
   - Emphasize proportions
   - Highlight outliers or unusual data
   - Emphasize differences
   - Emphasize variation

5. (a) Choose components of the presentation model to represent attributes, and (b) choose abstract charts and graphs to represent the remaining attributes.

### 7.4.6    Rules for Good Graphics

According to UNESCO estimates in 1988, approximately one-third of the world's adults (one billion) can't read (the *Los Angeles Times* 1989, cited in Horton 1991). However, graphics are more than just cartoons or text substitutes for the illiterate. Scientists also use graphics frequently to convey and summarize their results (e.g., Cleveland 1988). In scientific graphics, and in data visualizations for intelligent databases, the most important requirement is to present the meaning in the data without distortion.

In the automated model of data visualization and presentation under discussion some of the virtues of graphic design (and its associated humor) were sacrificed in favor of more standardized templates. In some ways this is a pity. One misses such gems as the graphic in a Chicago newspaper a few years ago that compared the amounts of snow that had fallen in winter, with the minimum amount of snow recorded shown relative to a jockey and the maximum amount of snow recorded shown next to a basketball player.

However, for every example of successful graphic design in charting numerical data there is probably at least one instance where spurious graphics (sometimes referred to as "chartjunk") tend to distort or hide the data (Wainer 1979). One of the worst forms of chartjunk is the inappropriate use of a third dimension in a chart. Thus 2D bar charts are often drawn with 3D bars, even though this tends to hurt rather than help the interpretation of the data. In addition, bars are sometimes shown as receding into the distance, or they may be transformed into barrels or tractors that grow or shrink depending on the value of different data points.

When bars are shown at different distances, it makes their size ambiguous. Should the height of the bar be judged as it actually is, or as it would be if it were really at that distance (i.e., increasing the judged size of the bar to take account of the fact that it is further away so that its image will appear smaller)? Similarly, the base of bars at a distance will tend to rise in the page. Should the size of the bar be judged based on where the top is, or should it be judged based on the shifting baseline? Figure 7.7 shows an example of a bar chart that uses a meaningless third dimension.

The requirement that charts be generated automatically eliminates problems like chartjunk. In addition it forces us to be more systematic in activities like choosing templates and labeling axes. Even so we will need to follow prescriptions such as:

- Use redundancy wisely
- Use familiar templates
- Label axes clearly

In the midst of all these prescriptions, the need to accurately represent the data is paramount. The physical representation of numbers as displayed on the graphic should be proportional to the corresponding numbers themselves (Tufte 1983). For instance, if one number is twice as big as another in the data it should also look twice as big in the graphic. Other prescriptions that apply to visual templates are:

- A line plot should only be used to plot a continuous function.
- Line plots should not be used if data values are irregularly spaced along the horizontal axis (Tukey 1988). This would happen, for instance, if data were available for some years but not others (e.g., 1971, 1971, 1974, 1977, 1979, 1983, 1988).

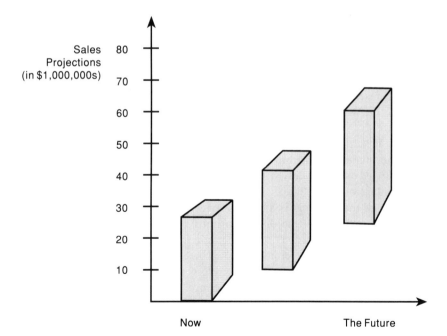

**Figure 7.7** A bar chart with a meaningless third dimension.

- Do not use line plots if wild points are common since connecting up the points will lead the eye and brain to focus on those points to the exclusion of other features in the data (Tukey 1988).

- Varying shades of gray rather than color are better at showing relative size or quantity (Tufte 1983) because they have a natural order (unlike colors which appear to be arranged in a circle where the two ends of the spectrum (red and violet) tend to merge together.

- If the data bunches near the zero point, change the scale or use a log scale (Tukey 1988).

- If points at the upper right in a scattergram are much more widely scattered than those at the lower left, then use logarithms (Chambers, Cleveland, Kleiner, and Tukey 1983).

While it is often good to use redundant coding of data points, one should not code linearly-dependent data as if it is independent. This typically occurs when the probability, portion, or size (out of a fixed total) of two mutually exclusive events is plotted. Suppose one plotted the percentage of people employed in the service sector versus the total employed in all other occupational sectors. At each time point plotted the two data points must sum to 100. This results in a bar chart or line chart where the points are mirror images of each other and tends to confuse more than help.

### 7.4.7  Rotation and Color Coding

In addition to carefully visualizing data in terms of visual templates, tools using rotation and color coding can help the user to interpret these charts.

3D graphs can be rotated for better viewing. For instance, in a project management system, multiple tasks can be displayed on a 3D rotatable graph without overlapping. Overlapping is where the position of a display primitive has the same x- and y-coordinates as another display primitive. The x-,y-, and z- coordinates of a task representing a box will differ for each task. A task has four display primitives that define it: the upper side of the box, the front of the box, and each of the ends of the box.

Rotation of graphical objects can be used to show their position unambiguously to the human eye within a three-dimensional coordinate structure. Rotations may be carried out separately with respect to the x, y, and z axes, in order to get a better overall picture of the graph or chart. Without this type of rotation it would be impossible to see all the data that is hidden or overlapped in a complex chart.

In rotation, all the display primitives are rotated about one of the axes (e.g., the z-axis). A standard set of fixed angle increments can be used for rotation (e.g., in 45 degree steps). Different visual projections or apparent viewpoints in 3D graphs, charts, and plots can also be used to permit viewing of hidden or overlapped objects. Using a Data Visualization Projection System, the user may rotate the x-, y-, or z-axes, or combinations thereof to get a clear picture of how the data is laid out in the graph or chart. The difference between rotation and viewpoint projection is that in rotation the user imagines that the graph is rotating while the user remains still, while in viewpoint projection the user imagines that the graph or chart remains still while the user moves to the rotation viewpoint. This distinction between rotation and viewpoint projection is important to the user, but does not require different software algorithms since a rotation to the left is equivalent to a viewpoint projection to the right.

Color coordination may also be used for easier reading of complex data. The colors of graphical objects such as bars or pie slices may be used to convey information about a dimension. One method of coloring is to disambiguate the position of a graphical object within the 3D coordinate system by using colors to mark off ranges on each of the three coordinates and then color the surfaces of the object in the corresponding colors. In general, coloring of surfaces on a bar or other graphical object may be used to indicate position, level, or coordinate values with respect to a three-axis coordinate system.

## ▪ 7.5 CONCLUSIONS

Data visualization, information discovery, and navigation are essential components of information presentation, and each has developed with some difficulty, or with little emphasis on their relevance to information presentation. Other tools reflect the requirements of specific applications. This chapter reviewed the often neglected topic of information presentation. How visualization and hyperdata can be used to support presentation was shown, and a classification of different types of presentation was developed.

It is easy to forget that the visualization tools used in most domains are fairly recent inventions. However, presentations of one sort or another are now a major human activity, playing a crucial role in training, communication, and decision making.

# 8

# EXECUTIVE INFORMATION SYSTEMS

*We were probably ten years ahead of most other retailers in scouting lo-cations from the air, and we got a lot of great ones that way. From up in the air we could check out traffic flows, see which way cities and towns were growing, and evaluate the location of the competition—if there was any. I loved doing it myself. I'd get down low, turn my plane up on its side, and fly right over a town. Once we had a spot picked out, we'd land, go find out who owned the property, and try to negotiate the deal right then. That's another good reason I don't like jets. You can't get down low enough to really tell what's going on, the way I could in my little planes.*

— Sam Walton*

*Corollary:* An executive needs to have the ability, on demand, to selectively zoom into any detail of his business.

## ■ 8.1 INTRODUCTION

Executives in charge of any large organization are inevitably out of touch with the facts. The question is, "How much out of touch?" The issue of being in touch was well argued by Heineke in regard to societal executives. His point was that centrally organized totalitarian systems were inevitably inferior because the information flow to the decision-making center would always be at a lower rate than in a decentralized economy. However, the same argument applies equally well to large corporations, in which the CEO has very little time to deal with the vast amount of potentially relevant information.

As pointed out in Chapter 1, the rate at which people can read has not increased dramatically since the invention of the computer — thus the form of information delivery has to change if we are to handle the problems of data glut and info glut

---

* In an interview with *Fortune* magazine, 1992. Sam Walton was born in Oklahoma in 1918. He turned a small local store into the largest discount-store chain ever. He was regarded as one of the twentieth century's best businessmen.

effectively. Executive information systems (EISs) handle the problem of data glut for decision makers.

Many of the goals and functions that have been defined for executive information systems also apply to intelligent database applications. This chapter will review the topic of executive information systems and describe a general executive information environment that combines the tools discussed in earlier chapters (information discovery, data visualization, hyperdata) with additional features such as information overviews. The resulting information environment allows all users (not just executives) to interact with large amounts of data in a powerful and natural way.

An intelligent database application provides easy access to large amounts of information in the form of summaries and visualizations, with a point-and-click interface. This functionality is also the goal of executive information systems. Executive information systems are fundamentally different from other types of information system (but similar to intelligent database applications) because of their emphasis on the big picture and highly interpretable visualizations.

In later chapters of this book the executive information environment will be used as a platform for building more specialized intelligent database applications. Thus the executive environment integrates the intelligent database application tools and serves as a platform for intelligent database application development (Figure 8.1).

This chapter begins with an informal review of the history and evolution of executive information systems and a discussion of the motivation for them and their functionality. The architecture of executive information systems is then described, focusing on a system called Corporate Vision™, and some of the tools and components of executive information systems are reviewed. Issues in groupware and computer-supported collaborative work are discussed, before a review of some executive information system methodologies, including the use of drill down. The chapter

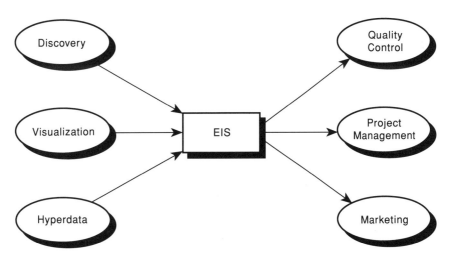

**Figure 8.1** The Executive Information System as a platform for intelligent database application development.

concludes with a discussion of the characteristics and needs of executives as information users.

## ■ 8.2 HISTORY AND EVOLUTION OF EISs

EISs are a recent phenomenon. However, executives throughout history have craved information to support their decisions. The executives of prehistoric times were generally military commanders, since war was the main large-scale organized human activity of those times. These executives inevitably needed information about their own troops, the enemy's movements, the amounts of rations left in a fort, just as today's automobile executives would like to know about the competition's advertising budget next quarter.

In *The Art of War* Sun Tzu describes several methods of information gathering with spies. The *Art of War* remains popular reading among today's executives as they study ways of beating the opposition. It was Attila the Hun's knowledge of the internal workings of the Roman system of defense that ensured his victory. Similarly, reconnaissance missions during the second world war provided the military executives with the information they needed about troop movements, etc.

The nature of business competition has changed over the years as business itself has changed. After the crash of the stock market in 1929 and the ensuing depression in the 1930s, large corporations became better defined and began to go through a personality change. The large corporations of the 1930s had access to large amounts of low cost labor that was desperate for work. The 1920s and 1930s also saw the beginnings of the science of market research and advertising. Once the smaller corporations began to disappear through the effects of the depression, the larger corporation began competition in earnest. This often meant competition for market share and size, a process that still continues.

The best way to beat competition was to grow, and this meant increasing the size of warehouses, the number of stores, the number of employees. This trend toward growth resulted in the emergence of mega corporations in the 1950s and the 1960s. To beat competition the mega corporation looked for any means available. As discussed in Chapter 9, one of these avenues was advertising coupled with market research, forming the now-familiar triad of industry, advertising agency, and the media to sell products from cars to toothpaste.

Another key avenue for competitive advantage was keeping the house in order, keeping costs down and profits high. The mega corporation now had more employees, more inventory, and more consumers than ever before. To keep track of things on paper was becoming increasingly difficult. Thus the mega corporation began to look for the solution in the digital computer.

Computers began to keep track of sales and inventory, customer names, and product shipments, etc. A new partnership was formed between the corporations and hardware vendors. At that time the software industry was still almost nonexistent. Software was delivered by the hardware companies. This gave rise to the management of information systems (MIS) department as part of the company.

Today major corporations can no longer survive without their computers. Thus the age of information-based corporations is upon us. The executives at the top have wanted information about who sells what, where, and when since well before the 1960s. But it was only at about this time that widespread computerized reporting by MIS departments became feasible. These reports included sales figures, statistics, consumer information, etc.

As the quote from Sam Walton reflects, this information was not limited to computer-generated information. As time went on, the demand for more and more reports gave rise to the well-known MIS backlog in the 1970s, where sometimes managers had to wait two months for a programmer to write a suitable report to provide them with the information they needed. The MIS backlog however illustrates two distinct points: (1) the information is useful, or there would not be so much demand for it, and (2) the tools for delivering the information are not up to date, causing part of the backlog.

The arrival of personal computers allowed some managers to get views of smaller subsets of their data without going through the MIS backlog. In addition, now people could interactively think with their spreadsheets. However, the top-level executives of many organizations still wanted the information fast and they could afford to pay what it took to build a system. Hence the first generation of EISs came into being as customized programs written for delivering information to the executive. Companies such as Comshare provided the service of implementing highly customized information delivery systems.

As more and more executives and managers began to ask for information, the "off the shelf" EIS industry emerged in the mid to late 1980s. The early 1990s are now seeing the full-scale push for personally customized EISs.

Executive information systems are the result of an urgent need for executives and senior management to get better and more timely information. In the early days of computing it didn't make sense for senior management to have computers on their desks (they were too big in any case). The best way for executives to get focused information was to get people to filter the information for them. All the early computer could give you were rows of blinking green numbers. However, times have changed and computers are giving us radically new views of information as well as allowing us to build systems of ever increasing complexity. More and more, businesses who don't have good information systems may just as well start writing checks out to their competitors that can handle information. Similarly, governments and organizations who are unable to handle extremely large amounts of information complexity are unable to compete.

The demands of executives for easy and natural access to information, without sacrificing power bring into sharp focus the goals of intelligent databases. If we can develop intelligent database applications that can satisfy executives then similar applications should satisfy most other users as well.

Executives typically are voracious consumers of information as well as extremely busy people. Thus executives have evolved a number of strategies for extracting the most important principles and patterns from vast amounts of information. These strategies include using subordinates to collect and filter the information, and using various summarization, reporting, and newsletter sources in the information industry to provide "predigested" information.

This process of information abstraction results in summaries of one kind or another and is very effective in focusing information for executives. However, it also has the side effect of distancing executives from the original sources of their information. Consequently executives have become reliant on the particular interpretation or "spin" that their subordinates choose to put on the information. In a large corporation, the information may go through a number of preprocessing or abstraction steps before it reaches the executive. Over time, the process of collecting and filtering the information will become more entrenched, so that the executive will have difficulty in implementing changes in information collection and filtering policy all the way down the line. Like the captain of the modern supertanker who is a victim of physical inertia (it takes several miles to turn a supertanker around due to its large weight and inertia, so tanker captains need to plan a long way in advance) modern executives are victims of information inertia, and competitive forces may not give them the time they need to turn the corporate ship around should trouble arise. The problem of information inertia and the "information chain of command" is illustrated in Figure 8.2.

Thus executives and other high-level decision makers are faced with a dilemma. The vast amounts of information that are potentially relevant to any problem have to be filtered and summarized, yet the process of summarization throws away potentially useful information. As the information chain of command becomes more extended the executive has relatively little control over what information is kept and what information is thrown away. Executive information systems offer a solution to this dilemma by allowing the executive to have the best of both worlds. In this approach the executive is also provided with focused summaries of the information, but now these summaries are linked to the underlying data sources, so that the executive can drill down to the detailed data when the need arises. This ability to provide summaries and details within an integrated environment is the main functional requirement of an executive information system. A related requirement that also determines the usability of such a system is that the interface be intuitive and easy to use so that the executive can focus on the interpretation of information rather than on the computational details.

Executive Information Systems are intended to satisfy the rigorous information needs of top management. The first EIS tools were developed in the mid-1980s and provided multimedia slide shows, and later EISs added the data integration and drill down tools that were needed. Executive information systems were not developed prior to the mid-1980's because:

1. There wasn't enough networking between databases or within organizations.
2. There was still not enough computing power on the desk top to provide sophisticated frontend tools without losing efficiency.
3. The client-server model was not implemented and heterogeneous data could not be handled in an integrated way.
4. There weren't enough multimedia and graphics packages to excite people about seriously looking into the possibility of EISs.

Fortunately this situation has changed and interest in EISs and the characteristics of available technology are both advancing rapidly. This chapter will describe the

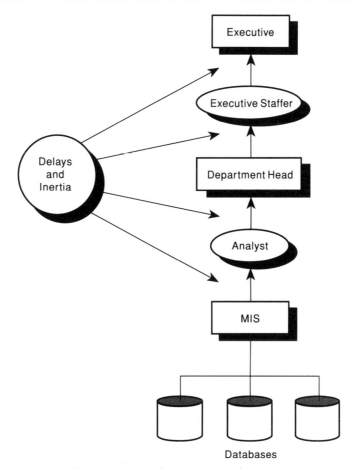

**Figure 8.2** The information chain of command.

properties of executive information systems in general and then describe a particular executive information environment (Corporate Vision) based on the intelligent database tools discussed in the earlier chapters of this book.

### 8.2.1 Early EISs and Information Management Software

An EIS should be designed to enhance the positive traits of an executive, including high-energy level, high-achievement motivation; high effort and capacity for work, and perseverance. A good EIS should also reduce the amount of time that the executive needs to collect and absorb information, and this will lead to less stress, better time management, and higher productivity.

The explicit goal of executive information systems has been to provide up-to-date answers to key questions raised by executives without burying them in vast quantities of unnecessary details. Most EIS applications feature colorful graphic displays that emphasize trends and exceptions. Some also provide project-managementlike tools that show which projects are on schedule and which are in trouble.

The London underground is an interesting example of the use of an EIS. The London underground authorities were concerned with four main performance areas: trains, station services, safety and security, and finance information. Each of these performance areas focuses on different sets of data. For train operation the relevant data includes what percentage of the schedule was operated; how many trains ran in peak service; the average waiting time between trains; failures, delays, and incidents.

Relevant information for station services includes the status of 70 lifts and 275 escalators in the system, information on the 272 station booking offices, and data such as average queuing times, station closures, and passenger congestion.

Some EISs provided spreadsheetlike data manipulation facilities. These information spreadsheets could then be linked to active external data some of which was textual (e.g., external news feeds, market analysis reports, electronic mail, customer satisfaction surveys), while other data was numerical — stock market quotations, interest rates and other financial data, sales figures, and budget estimates.

Color is used in existing EISs to highlight critical data. For instance, bad sales figures can be colored red. The user (executive) may then drill down on these numbers by clicking on them, after which another screen is displayed that breaks the numbers down further, provides textual explanations, or trend graphs, and so on.

An electronic briefing book or some similar functionality (report template) is a particularly important feature for an EIS. With briefing books, each executive can receive a personalized selection of reports and charts, reducing the amount of irrelevant information he or she sees. An electronic briefing book may be personalized with color highlighted exceptions responding to tolerances set by the executive. The electronic briefing book may also be updated at any time, eliminating the frustration of not seeing any information until all of it is ready. In practice, the briefing book is a form of personalized report. Using the electronic format, it becomes possible to electronically publish different versions of the report for different users much more easily and cheaply then can be done if equivalent versions of the report are to be published as printed documents.

Users generally want to see information in context. Another way to add context to reports is by offering predefined paths through the information. Thus the report can act as a hypermedia document that presents the key information in an easily browsed format. In one model, the executive staff and other managers use the EIS to create a personal report which is then read by the executive.

The report might contain hierarchical as well as associative links. Data is often inherently hierarchical in nature. For instance, information about car sales in Dallas can be broken down by dealer, and within dealers it can be further broken down by model and make of car. Thus higher level report values may point to lower levels of detail or alternative perspectives and the user may zoom in and out of information using these links or pointers. Lateral (associative) movements are also possible. For instance, one can go from a budget/variance report format into a trend format, showing months, quarters, or years, or to an explanatory memo from an analyst.

### 8.2.2 Why are Executive Information Systems Needed?

EISs are sorely needed because of the following principle: The cost of an error rises exponentially according to the level of the organization at which the error is made.

Detailed information can be put to good (and timely) use in an EIS (Malone and Rockart 1991). For instance, in 1990, 10,000 route salespeople in one company used handheld computers to record daily sales information about 200 grocery products in 400,000 stores. The stored information was then transmitted nightly to a central computer which in turn returned pricing and product promotions to the hand-held computers. The resulting data was then combined with external data about the sales of competitive brands on a weekly basis and this information was summarized and provided to executives through an executive information system.

Detailed information can be extremely useful in developing marketing strategies in response to competition, using handheld computers, EIS software, and telecommunication. Accurate and timely information is essential for good decision making in a competitive environment. For instance, at one time there was a drop in regional tortilla chip sales for a major supplier. The chief executive officer (CEO) noticed a red number on the EIS, indicating reduced market share for tortilla chips in the central business region. Using the EIS the CEO located the problem in Texas and then tracked the problem to a specific sales division and eventually to a particular chain of stores. It turned out that the problem was due to a regional competitor who was marketing a new white-corn tortilla chip. A few months later the company launched its own white-corn tortilla chip and was able to restore its lost market share. In this case the EIS probably saved two or three months in locating the problem and allowed the company to get the new product to market much faster. This example shows how an EIS can give CEOs intimate knowledge of how the company is working and with this knowledge at their fingertips large organizations can get new products to market and react to the competition as quickly as their smaller competitors.

### 8.2.3 General Functions of an EIS

In our view, an EIS is an intelligent database application that allows executives or their assistants to visualize, interpret, and understand relevant information, while being closely integrated to other executive tools such as project management and electronic mail. The EIS should be designed to add value to the other tools and to information databases, rather than act as a standalone monolithic application or system that subsumes all the other tools and capabilities.

The EIS should also contain a hypermedia interface that is customized to the particular needs of each executive and provides sophisticated information access within a point-and-click environment. While the available literature says relatively little about what an executive does, it is clear that executives perform ill-defined and almost impossible tasks, and that well-focused and easily interpretable information could be extremely useful to them.

Data can be better focused when meaningful patterns and trends are abstracted from the many and separate databases where the raw data is stored. This requires distributed databases with an easy-to-use common frontend. Further, since different trends or patterns may be important to different organizations, it should be possible to customize the interface to highlight different features of data.

In addition to focusing of data, presentation of data is also very important. These principles are true for any intelligent database application, but due to the level of abstraction of the executive's deliberations and the huge amount of potentially relevant information, they are particularly important for an executive information system.

The presentation of the data should be in meaningful formats where the definition of "meaningful" may vary to some extent between individuals and industries. For many people, visual and graphical presentations of data are more meaningful and data visualization tools can provide such presentations (see the earlier discussion of such tools in Chapter 5). Skillful use of color and form can assist in separating out visually different categories of information and reveal underlying patterns (Tufte 1983, 1990). Presentation can also be enhanced by annotating the information and creating links between pictorial, numerical, and textual types of information. Thus hypermedia is a convenient framework for presenting information where the user can navigate easily between different components. Presentation of information should not only highlight important patterns and trends, it should also allow annotation of information by subordinates and navigation between text, numbers, and pictures.

### 8.2.4 Prioritizing Information and Applying Strategic Focus

The collection and interpretation of information within an executive information system should be driven by the goals and objectives of the organization. Those goals and objectives will then generate priorities for different types of information. Information should be distilled and focused so that the high priority aspects of information are emphasized. The measurement of information value during such prioritization is difficult but essential. The following excerpt (Hopper, as cited by Barron 1991, p. 170) illustrates the importance of establishing the value of information:

> I know of an oil refinery that's operated by computer. Information comes in from marketing and goes to the computer, which opens valves and pushes stuff through pipes and tells inventory how much of the finished product has been made. The computer puts out payroll reports and makes out the checks, as well as generating reports on all the activity that occurs. Let's suppose that two pieces of data simultaneously enter that flow. One comes from a valve out in the plant and says, "if you don't open me, the plant is going to blow up. You have 45 seconds to act to save 78 lives and a $120 million plant." At the very same instant, from another part of the system, comes the fact that Joe did 2 hours more overtime. Which is the more valuable piece of information? And what are our criteria?

Thus information value should be based on what the executive needs to know. In most cases this will be a very small proportion of the total information available. In medical triage, a battle or disaster can produce an overwhelming number of injured people that exceeds the capacity of available medical services. The accepted solution in such situations is to divide the injured into three groups: those that are healthy enough to wait for attention or recover by themselves; those that are too badly injured and should be left to die; those that need immediate attention. Similarly, when faced with an overwhelming amount of information, some of it critical, some of it trivial, a form of information triage is needed. We can summarize the activity of information triage in terms of three categories: dump; delay; display (Figure 8.3).

The need for relevant information can be illustrated with an example. Imagine that

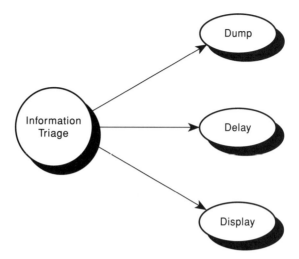

**Figure 8.3**  Categories of information triage.

a manager needs to know how much gas is required for a fleet of corporate vehicles in the next two quarters and how much to budget for that gas consumption. One estimate is to determine how much money was spent on gas in the previous two quarters. This type of estimate is questionable, because the price of gas may fluctuate considerably in the coming months. Another way of looking at the problem is to consider how many gallons of gasoline the fleet is using and how many miles each vehicle travels on average per month. Knowing some of the trends and pressures on the oil market may then allow estimates of the price of gasoline to be derived. Subsequently, estimates could also be made of how many gallons of gasoline the fleet would use based on predicted business demand.

Figure 8.4 shows a special information template (an "iconic display") that can be used to provide an estimate of gas costs and is updated continuously based on the latest information on gas usage and gas pricing. With a combination of such information, including what-if scenarios, the executive could receive a presentation, in terms of figures and charts, of several possibilities of what the firm may have to spend on gasoline for the rest of the fiscal year.

An EIS may be customized with a toolkit to handle particular situations or tasks. In the model discussed here, the functions of collecting, filtering, and displaying information are central activities for any EIS. Other tools may be added to provide additional functionality for different situations or organizations (Figure 8.5 on page 331). One toolkit that would be useful is a financial toolkit, since one of the key jobs of an executive is to understand where the money comes from and goes to within a company. This knowledge is brought into sharp relief when someone tries to value the operations and assets of a large company or conglomerate when putting together a merger or takeover bid. The financial toolkit will include information relating to costs and profitability and will highlight a variety of critical accounting ratios.

Another important toolkit involves communications. The executive needs to promote the company's image in the community, and also needs to know about new products

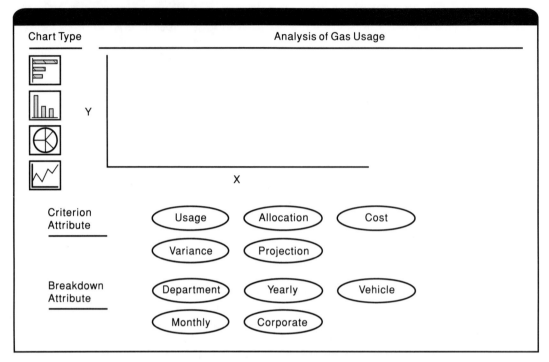

**Figure 8.4** An iconic display for viewing gas usage and pricing, and for estimating gas costs.

being developed so that he can grasp the central issues in choosing when to launch the products, how to advertise them, and so forth.

The executive projects his power and influence through a variety of communication tools. These tools are in a state of flux as technology advances. Face to face meetings and telephones are now supplemented with electronic mail and videoconferencing. Electronic mail has emerged as a particularly important form of communication within and between organizations, and it will be considered in more detail in a later section.

## ■ 8.3 ARCHITECTURE OF EXECUTIVE INFORMATION SYSTEMS

Corporate Vision, developed by IntelligenceWare, is a general executive information environment that can be customized to the needs of different executives and organizations. It lets users filter information and provides a graceful way of moving from generalities to details should the executive want to follow up the sources of summary data. Corporate Vision also incorporates tools that allow assistants to communicate their results and strategies to the executive as quickly and effectively as possible.

### 8.3.1 The Structure of Corporate Vision

Corporate Vision allows the executive to carry out visual information discovery, compare the results with visual presentations of the appropriate attributes, drill down

*Customized Application*

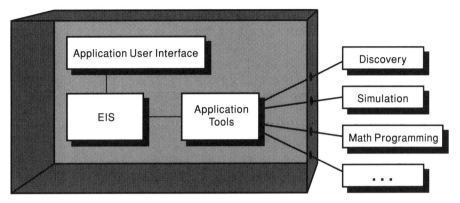

**Figure 8.5** Customizing an EIS with application tools.

into information all the way to the raw data, and point and click through a network of related views (visualizations) of the data.

There are two modules in Corporate Vision: the setup (development) module and the use module. Setup is by an analyst or assistant. The use module is for use by the executive.

Setup has several components:

- Database definition (name your data sources)
- Window and dialog setup (build a user interface, including graph definitions)
- Hypertext management
- Note taking and e-mail
- Group communication

The developer chooses the tables of interest. The user then creates windows. Each window represents a view of the data. The view is defined by selecting a graph type and choosing the variables to be plotted in the graph. Conceptually, the creation of the graph plots a region in the data space defined by the chosen variables. In fact, this is a subspace of the data space defined by all the attributes or variables that are available. The question at this point is how should the variables that are not being plotted be handled? Say, for instance, that we plot a 3D bar chart showing sales for different months and states. What do the heights of the bars represent? Do they represent the sales for one sales person, the average across the salespeople, or the grand total of sales? Thus not only must developers or users define the attributes that are actually plotted, they must also define how records will be handled in creating the plot. In other words, as well as having a data space that defines what is being shown in the graph (e.g., within the coordinates of a 3D scattergram), there is also an entity space which is defined by which entities are to be plotted. Consider the following example. We have a data table with the following fields:

- salesperson
- state
- product
- month
- dollar sales

We choose to plot state, month, and dollar sales in a 3D bar chart where the height of the bars is represented by the dollar sales. Thus all the different values of state, month, and dollar sales will be plotted. Now we have to define the scope of the 3D bar chart (i.e., what it refers to). The scope of the chart is the *entity aggregate* (i.e., the combination of entities as defined by the non-plotted variables that constrain the data values that are actually plotted). For instance we might have the following entity aggregates:

- a single salesperson
- a single product
- a combination of salespeople (e.g., salespeople with more than 3 years experience)
- a combination of products
- a combination of salespeople and products (e.g., experienced salespeople selling computers)

At this point we still haven't defined exactly what will be plotted. The final step required is to specify the aggregation operation across the eligible entities (records). Some possible aggregation operations are:

- the total (sum)
- the average (mean)
- the maximum
- the minimum

Thus the process of specifying a chart consists of:

1. Selecting the graph type
2. Selecting the data attributes (construct the data space)
3. Selecting the entities (by fixing or specifying the combinations on the remaining attributes eligible to be displayed)
4. Defining the aggregation operation for mapping multiple entities to a single data point

Using Corporate Vision charts can be constructed very quickly by following these four steps repeatedly. Once charts have been made the developer can link them into a presentation structure.

The first thing to note is that windows may contain a number of tools in addition to the basic chart. For instance, pull-down menus may be added representing one or more of the attributes that define the entity space, as shown in Figure 8.6. Say that we want to drill down to get information about who among our salespeople are selling modems and where. In this case we activate the product pull-down menu by clicking on it and dragging down to the value "modem." Then, when we release the mouse button, the chart is updated and shows the data just for modem sales. Similarly, a salesperson pull-down menu can be used to drill down to a particular salesperson, while both pull-downs can be used simultaneously to get the detailed data for a particular salesperson and a particular product. This example shows that drill down is really a process of restricting the entity space by fixing the values of those attributes not directly plotted in the chart.

Corporate Vision also allows the developer to define selectable regions on the chart with associated actions. For instance, in the 3D bar chart we may define an action

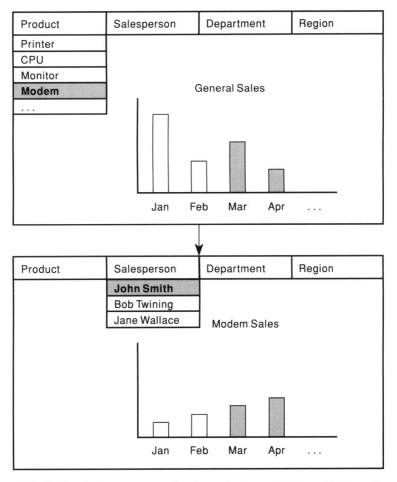

**Figure 8.6** Drilling down as a process of setting attribute constraints to restrict the entity space.

where another chart is linked to the current chart, say a pie chart. In Figure 8.7 the proportion of sales for John Smith is shown across different products. By linking the pie chart to the bar chart we now have a situation where clicking on a cell in the bar chart modifies the data displayed in the pie chart. For instance, clicking on the cell representing New York in April shows the pattern of sales for John Smith in the New York region during the month of April. A backward link can be similarly defined to the bar chart, so that if the modem segment of the pie chart is selected, then the bar chart will display the sales data for modems only.

In addition to linking charts, other actions show a schema indicating where the application is currently in the entity space, a hypertext note (which can then be linked to other hypertext notes attached to different charts), or a pop-up window (showing another chart or graphic).

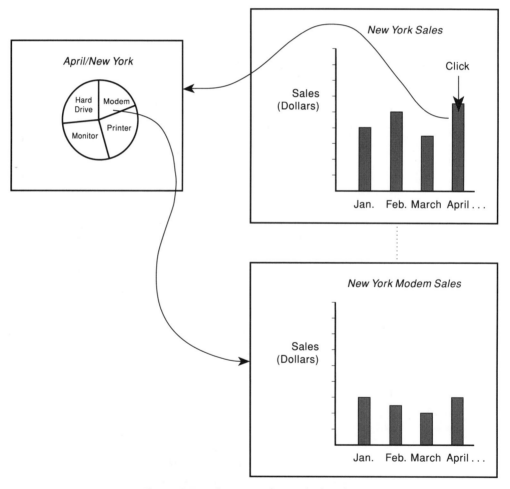

**Figure 8.7** Linking a pie chart and a bar chart.

Links within a window that change the data displayed in one chart based on a mouse click in another chart are referred to as "slaved" or tandem links. Links that go across or between windows are more arbitrary and reflect relations of particular interest. We refer to these as "interest" links. For instance, in the sales example, we might have a line chart showing the trend in overall sales for the past 12 months for the different salespeople. Clicking on the name of the salesperson in the title of the bar chart might then pop up the corresponding line chart.

Another useful feature of Corporate Vision is the chart network diagram. Here the user or developer may view the connections between various charts. The chart network diagram shows the links that exist between the various windows, each of which may contain one or more charts.

Developers who want to specify more complex entity combinations (e.g., salespeople in their twenties who sold more than 10 printers in Texas during the past year) may use iconic query (described in Chapter 3) to define the entity aggregation for a chart.

The setup environment for Corporate Vision can be used by skilled end-users to explore their data, but it can also be used to create presentations. This can be done either by creating a network of linked charts and windows which can then be navigated during the presentation (either by the presenter or by an executive) or by editing the various charts into a presentation. In the latter case, Corporate Vision provides a storyboarding tool for constructing the presentation. This consists of a work area onto which the charts of interest may be clipped, after they have been constructed in the presentation environment. The developer also has the option of shrinking the size of these selected charts (i.e., converting them to icons by subsampling them as described in the section on picture relevance menus in Chapter 3) so that they are easier to manipulate on the storyboard. The user may then create a hyperdata network by creating links between the presentation (using a point-and-click style of interaction). When making a link the developer also specifies the anchor of the link in the source node. This anchor could be a hot spot on the chart or one of its labels or it could be a specially created button or a highlighted word within a text field.

The developer may also construct bullet lists and hypertext annotations. These may then be aggregated with nodes, or set as independent entities that pop up during the presentation. Links may then be created between the hypertext annotations, providing an alternative form of navigation in the presentation to the link structure of the charts. In practice, a smooth presentation can be created by alternating navigation between the chart structure and the hypertext structure. Figure 8.8 illustrates this latter type of mixed navigation. Here the presenter is reporting on the performance of the staff in the sales department. She begins by showing a chart with the overall sales figures for the department across the different product categories (a bar chart). She then clicks on one of the bars, this leads to a chart showing the breakdown for that product across the different sales regions. Attached to this chart is a hypertext note explaining the important trends in that sales region. One portion of the note says: "Sales of printers in New York were hurt by the departure of one of our most experienced salespeople mid-year. However, Bill Johnson joined us in July and has already been picking up the sales in this product category, flying out to New York several times in the fall."

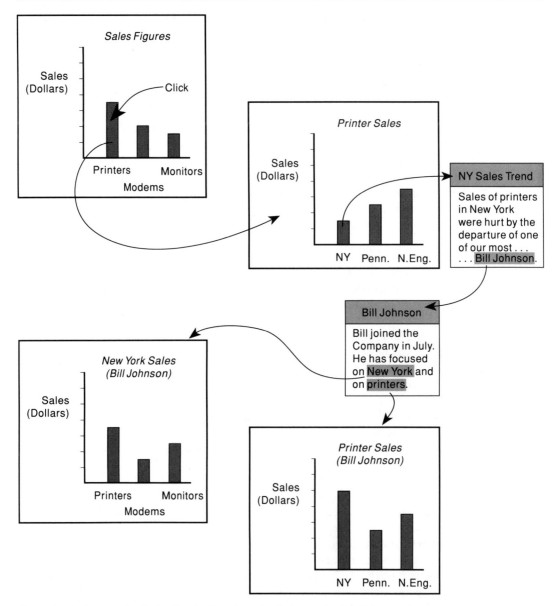

**Figure 8.8** An example of mixed navigation alternating between charts and hypertext.

At this point the presenter could click on Bill Johnson, this would then take her to a hypertext annotation on Bill Johnson's performance, attached to a couple of bar charts, one showing his sales of different products and the other showing his sales in different regions.

An executive information environment like Corporate Vision consists of an intelligent database engine, a user interface, and a set of executive information tools. The end-user will normally interact with the upper and middle layers of the Corporate Vision architecture, while the Corporate Vision developer will interact with the middle and lower layers in building the object model, collecting and integrating the data, and creating an appropriate interface and set of presentations.

Corporate Vision is implemented as a set of modules. The intelligent database engine is an efficient relational database, coupled with an SQL query generation capability. Corporate Vision also contains the tools discussed in earlier chapters: information discovery, data visualization, and hyperdata, along with a set of executive information tools: information overview, visual querying, briefings, and report generation. In addition, the user interface is enhanced with an interactive dialog construction tool and a storyboard facility that gives the executive or a Corporate Vision developer a fine degree of control over the visual presentations that are constructed.

## 8.3.2 Information Discovery

Information discovery is a useful feature that needs to be integrated into Corporate Vision carefully. This is because information discovery will often generate a number of rules, of which only some will be relevant or useful. Thus information discovery is probably an activity that is best done by an analyst, with the results of information discovery after filtering and selection being placed in a type of database that can then be queried by the Corporate Vision user. For instance, the user may ask for rules that predict which stores were profitable in a given year. A relevant rule may then be matched to the query (as shown in Figure 8.9) that shows store profits were related to the size of the store, its location, and the socioeconomic status of its zip code. The user could then use these results as a starting point for further analysis by looking at visualizations that plotted store profitability against attributes, mentioned in the premise of the rule that predicted store profitability. Thus in a focused use of Corporate Vision, information discovery can provide a very good starting point for data exploration.

## 8.3.3 Hyperdata

In Chapter 6, hyperdata was discussed as a data-oriented version of hypermedia that provides access to large amounts of data through a point-and-click interface. Hyperdata fits right into the requirements of an executive information system interface and is an ideal way of organizing data visualizations. It also complements the hierarchical

```
Store Profit > 20%
If
3,000 sq. ft. < Store Size < 10,000 sq. ft.
and
Location of Store = "suburban"
and
Zip Code Status = "middle income";
```

**Figure 8.9** A hypothetical rule that predicts profitable stores.

structuring of information overviews and associated drill-down tools.

Hyperdata is a considerable advance over executive slide shows using multimedia presentation. It gives the flexibility that a presenter needs to respond to feedback and inquiries "on the fly." Furthermore, powerful hyperdata functionality can be achieved without too much development cost, and can be smoothly integrated within an executive information system.

For instance, Corporate Vision provides a variety of powerful features for building and customizing sophisticated presentations. Further value can be added to this system by using rules (scripting) to define general purpose links between charts (as discussed in Chapter 6 concerning the hyperdata knowledge base). Here the developer may define the links using rules of the form:

> *destination chart is of graph type X*
> *with data attributes Y and*
> *entity aggregates Z*
> *If*
> *source chart is of graph type X1*
> *with data attributes Y1 and*
> *entity aggregates Z1 and*
> *action A is taken.*

In this case the particular rules that are created will depend on the application domain and the goals of the presentation. However, it should be noted that this rule template has a very stereotyped form. To create the rule, the developer simply has to fill in the graph types for the conclusion (target node) and premise (source node) along with the attributes defining the data space for source and target, the entity aggregates for source and target (which may have been selected using Iconic Query), and the initiating action in the source node.

### 8.3.4 Information Overviews

Information overviews in Corporate Vision consist of a menu hierarchy, briefings, and linear reports. Menu hierarchies can be constructed on the basis of the object model of the application domain. Menu hierarchies may then be used in a drill-down mode of operation.

Briefings are subgraphs within a larger hyperdata network. They are created by flagging a subset of the conceptual objects and attributes within the domain as being of interest. Typically a briefing will have been 10 and 100 visualizations on the network, depending on the willingness of the user or executive to explore the briefing extensively. Naturally, the greater the willingness to explore, the more information can be included in the briefing.

Linear reports provide the information in a more familiar linear form. They are also useful if there is a natural order to the information or if a particular case or point of view is being argued. A linear report can be created from hyperdata by browsing the network and selecting relevant presentations to be included in the report. The linear order of the resulting "slides" can then be constructed using a slide sorter facility as available in presentation software such as PowerPoint (Microsoft 1990).

In addition to the information overview tools described above, maps and organizers may be constructed at the discretion of the developer. We shall consider these types of overview further in the next section.

### 8.3.5 Interactive Dialog Construction

The use of an EIS involves several processes (Figure 8.10). These uses include:

1. Looking for patterns and problems in the data.
2. Making assertions about the data.
3. Collecting evidence to support assertions about the data.
4. Linking assertions and evidence into a coherent presentation.
5. Creating a report.

When used effectively, an EIS is a vehicle for decision making and has strongly rhetorical and argumentative components. The goal of an EIS is not to make pretty pictures, but to develop the arguments and evidence necessary to make effective decisions and convince others of the need to implement those decisions. The fourth and fifth steps listed above are particularly important in this regard. Interactive dialog

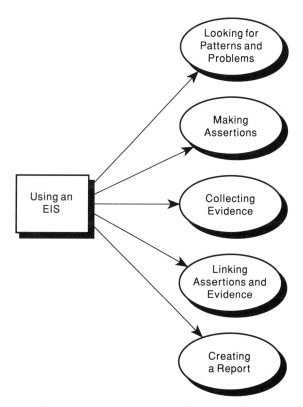

**Figure 8.10** Processes involved in using and EIS.

construction allows the user to link assertions and evidence. In the simplest form of this approach, the user will use a "record" feature to take interesting snapshots of the interaction with the EIS. These snapshots can then be played back later in the form of a slide show, or linked into a hypermedia presentation. An overview of the presentation may then be constructed using thumbnail views of each slide (i.e., iconized or reduced bit-map images).

Another type of presentation is the use of a bit-map to help interpret data. For instance, a map of the United States is often used to convey marketing information as shown in Figure 8.11. Here the location field of data records corresponds to particular positions on the bit-map and it is natural to overlay information about a particular location on the corresponding portion of the bit-map. In this hypothetical example, the number of World Motor Company cars sold in several cities are represented by the height of the bar at the location of the corresponding city on the map. Further detail has been added by subdividing each bar into two pieces representing truck sales and car sales, respectively. From Figure 8.11 it is easy to see that New York, California, and Texas have a large number of cars sold overall, while truck sales are disproportionately high in western states.

A good example of a dialog tool that tends to be taken for granted is the spreadsheet. Spreadsheets are an extremely popular class of software, partly because they are relatively easy to use, but also because they allow people to ask a variety of "what if?" questions concerning a set of (active) data. A spreadsheet can be thought of as a special tool that has a corresponding model represented in the interface (Parsaye et al. 1989, Chapter 7). In the case of the spreadsheet, there is a close mapping between

**Figure 8.11** Hypothetical data on car and truck sales in the United States.

the underlying data manipulations and storage and the physical operations performed by the user on the interface's model of the task. In other cases this mapping may not be so immediate or apparent. A simplified version of the spreadsheet model outlined here is implemented as the hypercalc example distributed as part of the original HyperCard package on the Apple Macintosh microcomputer.

Figure 8.12 shows the basic hypercalc structure consisting of six fields. The entire card may be viewed as an object. This object then has six fields or attributes: miles per year, gallons per year, miles per gallon, cost per mile, price per gallon, and cost per year. The values for three of the attributes are dependent on the values of other attributes. The relevant equations are as follows:

$$\text{gallons per year} = \text{miles per year} / \text{miles per gallon}$$

$$\text{cost per mile} = \text{price per gallon} / \text{miles per gallon}$$

$$\text{cost per year} = \text{gallons per year} * \text{price per gallon}.$$

Each of these equations is then implemented by a method attached to the object. These methods act like "if-needed" attached predicates during object access.

Figure 8.13 shows the extended hypercalc structure. Each spreadsheet is defined as an class. Columns within the spreadsheet are attributes, and rows of the spreadsheet are objects. The functionality of the spreadsheet is then implemented by permitting the user to select a subset of objects within a class and to update attribute values. The

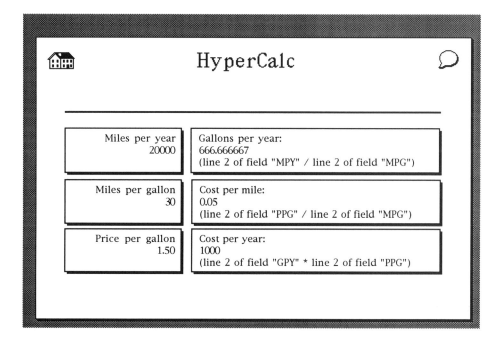

**Figure 8.12** The basic hypercalc structure.

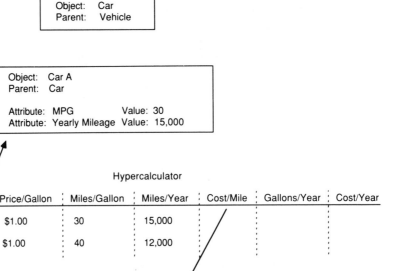

**Figure 8.13** An example using the extended hypercalculator.

modification of an attribute value then triggers updating of all the dependent attribute values via the appropriate methods. In this case the spreadsheet updating is analogous to the operation of an "if-changed" attached procedure in a object system.

Ideally, representation tools present operations at the database modeling level to the user in a natural and obvious way. One of the most "natural" ways of viewing information is in terms of objects that can be manipulated. The spreadsheet is one representation tool that embodies these three features of visuality, familiarity, and manipulability. The extended hypercalc spreadsheet is a tool for representing, at the interface level, what is occurring at the level of the database model in such a way that the user can operate on the representation and thereby have the desired actions occur at the level of the database model.

### 8.3.6 Report Generation

Chapter 6 discussed a variety of hypermedia applications and the differences and similarities that occur in navigation in hardcopy and electronic documents. In the case of EISs, there are two types of report generation to consider: generation of electronic reports and generation of printed reports. Generation of reports as electronic documents is now feasible in situations where the recipients of the report are networked by computer and where the quality of screen presentations and displays is sufficiently high. It is clear that there is no fundamental difference in legibility between paper and screens once physical parameters such as brightness, resolution, and visual contrast are controlled for (Jorna and Snyder 1991), and thus there is no intrinsic disadvantage to presenting documents and reports electronically.

The advantage of electronic report publishing is that the report becomes more flexible (it can be navigated in a variety of different ways, e.g., as hypermedia) and it can incorporate a number of multimedia features. For instance, full-motion video sequences can be inserted as figures in the report and played back using video control buttons beneath the figure. This feature was introduced in 1991 with Apple's Quick-Time tool, and it is likely to revolutionize reports and presentations of data. One use of inserted video sequences would be for the author of the report to provide an interpretation of what a particular chart is indicating or to advocate that a particular decision should be taken. Another video clip might show samples of a product line in the supermarket with a salesperson collecting the basic data that was used in the report. In cases where the report is the major outcome or artifact generated by the EIS, the success and effectiveness of the report generation facilities will be a major determinant of the overall success of the EIS.

### 8.3.7 Using an Executive Information System

The utility of the intelligent database approach can be demonstrated with an example. Consider the situation of a busy executive looking at sales figures for a family of products. The sales figures may be stored in a variety of databases and tables representing different types of product, different sales regions, and so on. Most of the time it may be possible to specify what the executive is interested in, with a standard set of charts (i.e., a profile of presentations). This might include a pie chart showing sales by region, a bar chart showing sales of the different types of product over the past month (in decreasing order), and a scattergram showing the sales of each type of product over the past month versus the number of advertising dollars spent on that product.

There might be some concern on the part of the executive that advertising for one product may be hurting sales for another. Is the advertising budget generating new sales or market share, or is it simply cannibalizing sales away from another product? Questions like this might motivate the executive to look for new relationships in the data that are not part of the regular profile. For instance, one relevant chart might show advertising dollars spent on one product versus sales of a somewhat similar product in the following month (Figure 8.14). With this hypothetical data we can see that there is an apparent relationship as the cloud of points tends to run from upper left to lower right. This suggests an inverse relationship where low advertising in the previous month for the other product tends to result in higher sales, while higher advertising tends to result in lower sales figures for the other product in the next month. With enough data on month to month variations of this type it might be

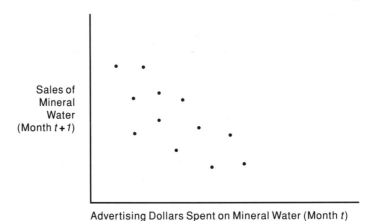

**Figure 8.14** The effect on advertising on one product on next month sales of a different product.

possible to test whether or not this apparent relationship is actually statistically significant. A significant inverse relationship in this case may then indicate that promotion of one product is actually hurting (cannibalizing) sales of another.

In this situation the executive will often have considerable task and domain knowledge. The task knowledge will include the ability to ask the right questions and know about what aspects of the data are critical. The domain knowledge will include general knowledge about marketing as well as specific knowledge about products, advertising budgets, and the like. Intelligent databases allow non-database specialists, who nevertheless have a considerable amount of domain expertise, to explore data and extract what they need from it. This is made possible through a point-and-click style of navigation and the use of supporting tools such as data visualization and hyperdata. Information presentation can be automated in an intelligent database because the construction and selection of charts and graphs is based on the intelligence and wishes of the user, rather than on some covert software reasoning process.

## ■ 8.4  GROUPWARE AND COMPUTER SUPPORTED COLLABORATIVE WORK

People working with early computers tended to work alone. When people worked in a group they typically did not use a computer as an integral part of their activity. The role of the computer as a tool for individuals is changing as groupware develops.

Ellis, Gibbs, and Rein (1991) define groupware as computer-based systems that support groups of people engaged in a common task (or goal) and that provide an interface to a shared environment. Groupware is used for communication, collaboration, and coordination. Figure 8.15 shows a convenient way of classifying groupware systems (after Ellis et al. 1991, Figure 2) according to whether or not the people using the groupware share the same time and space. Synchronous communications occur at the same time, while in asynchronous communications a message is sent by one person in the group and may be read by other members at a different time. Thus phone

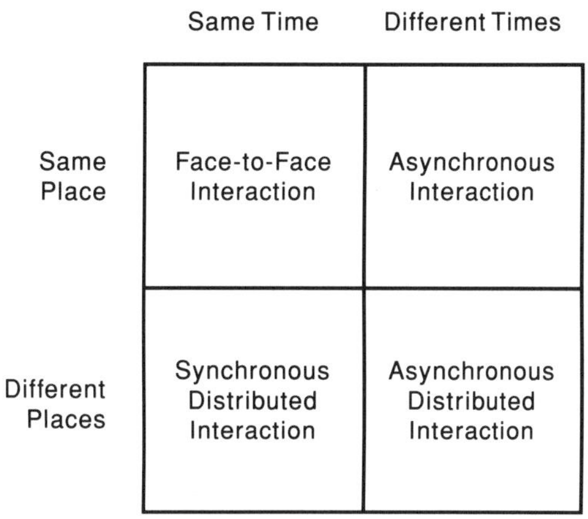

|  | Same Time | Different Times |
|---|---|---|
| Same Place | Face-to-Face Interaction | Asynchronous Interaction |
| Different Places | Synchronous Distributed Interaction | Asynchronous Distributed Interaction |

**Figure 8.15** A classification of groupware systems (after Ellis, Gibbs, and Rein 1991, figure 2).

conversations are examples of synchronous distributed interaction, while electronic mail typically involves asynchronous distributed interaction. An example of asynchronous interaction at the same place is the use of notes attached to the refrigerator as a way of communicating between people sharing an apartment or busy working couples.

The potential for supporting collaboration using computers seems almost unbounded. Collaboration can be supported using a variety of applications. The enthusiasm with which early collaboration tools such as electronic mail and electronic bulletin boards have been adopted in some quarters shows the need for collaborative tools. Collaborative tools generally perform one or both of two functions: coordination and communication. Coordination can be supported by providing a shared information space that different people can work on together or at separate times, but where messages and annotations are left for the other person. Shared information spaces are evolving out of more familiar shared drawing spaces such as chalk boards and whiteboards. Shared information spaces play a role not only in storing information and presenting ideas, but also in developing ideas and mediating interaction amongst members of work groups (e.g., Tang and Minneman 1991).

One of the emerging groupware and collaborative work technologies relevant to the executive is group decision support systems (GDSS). GDSSs are often set up within "electronic meeting rooms" and they use computer-based tools to assist decision structuring and improve the efficiency and quality of decision making within meetings. Some of the functions addressed by existing GDSSs include alternative ranking and voting tools, and tools for idea generation (Applegate, Konsynski, and Nunamaker 1986), and issue analysis (Conklin and Begeman 1988).

Since word processing is one of the most widely used computer applications, it is not surprising that collaborative writing of one form or another has been a focus of groupware research and development. Collaborative word processing, like individual word processing, consists of two somewhat distinct processes: writing and editing. Collaborative writing seems to be a more difficult problem since it requires selection of ideas, creation of narrative arguments and expression of these narratives in terms of words and rhetoric. Collaborative writing systems include the Writer's Assistant from the University of Sussex, England, the Writer's Environment (WE) from the University of North Carolina, and SEPIA, a collaborative authoring system under development at GMD-IPSI in Darmstadt, Germany.

Collaborative editing may not have the same level of creativity as collaborative writing, but it still requires the solution of some difficult technical problems. The process of distributed editing is very different from face to face editing. One of the properties of distributed editing is that it tends to equalize the power roles of the participants much as electronic mail tends to reduce differences in authority between the participants, at least as far as the content of e-mail communication is concerned.

### 8.4.1   Collaboration and Intelligent Databases

Information discovery, object modeling, data visualization, and hyperinformation provide a tremendous platform for intelligent database applications. However, as information technology evolves, we cannot expect users of intelligent database applications to cluster around a single screen at a single work site.

People work and interact in groups by meeting together. Videoconferencing and desktop conferencing enable people to meet over a distance. Groupware such as electronic mail, conferencing and on-line editing is particularly well suited to the way teams of people actually work (Perin 1991).

Electronic mail has proved to be a useful adjunct to face to face communication, the telephone, and mail because it provides easy and quick connection at any hour, and the receiving party does not have to be standing by. It is not really possible to play an electronic mail analog of phone tag unless there is a fault in the computer system or one deliberately throws away messages from a particular person and then claims not to have seen them.

Electronic mail and other new technologies also appear to be encouraging different types of communication and  extending communication possibilities in the same way that intelligent database applications facilitate the process of interpretation of large amounts of information. For instance, one study found that up to 60% of messages sent by e-mail would not have been sent if e-mail had not been available (Feldman 1986). We expect that intelligent database applications will similarly allow people to make important interpretations of information that are currently being missed.

Other forms of communication that can be facilitated by information technology include voice mail and voice annotation (both of which, like electronic mail, allow people to communicate asynchronously). Intelligent database applications should incorporate the new communication technologies and support the collaborative aspect of work, allowing members of a group to view different data presentations and discuss them in a collaborative computing environment.

Some new technologies tend to amplify existing styles of social interaction. For instance, it has been observed that men tend to interrupt women more than vice versa, and we can probably expect this trend to continue in videoconferences as it does in face to face meetings. However, other technologies do seem to break down social hierarchies, acting as a neutralizer. It has been observed that electronic mail is something of an equalizer, smoothing out differences in the organizational hierarchy. Many people are able to be much more direct and assertive with electronic mail than they are in face to face meetings with people higher up in the hierarchy. As a result, some managers feel electronic mail is subversive and have tried to take steps to curtail its use.

It is difficult to know how intelligent database applications will affect group work and organizational power structures. However, it is likely they will be amplifiers like video conferencing, rather than neutralizers like electronic mail.

Coordination can sometimes occur without explicit communication. For instance, planes get filled fairly efficiently even though the task of filling a plane involves many different travel agents and airline employees who never communicate with each other except in special circumstances. Coordination works in cases such as this because the physical constraints of a plane, coupled with an efficient database system that handles simultaneous access effectively, ensures that agents only need to refer to the current status of seating availability in order to advise potential passengers and make reservations. Thus we can expect that some intelligent database applications will need more in the way of explicit support of collaborative activity than will others. Marketing and project management are likely to be more collaborative in nature and need more in the way of groupware than an activity such as financial analysis.

### 8.4.2 Cooperative Document Editing

Publication of documents of one form or another consumes an amazing portion of human resources. While the exact amount of this portion is difficult to quantify, there is no doubting its economic importance. Thus it is not surprising that the most frequently used application in personal computing is word processing or that publication in all its forms is such an important industry. Of course, the importance that is attached to documents is hardly a new thing. From the code of Hammurabi in Sumeria to the Magna Carta and the Declaration of Independence, documents have been used to inspire and regulate human activity. In the case of someone like Thomas Jefferson, writing consumed much of his activity, as is evidenced by the more than 10,000 letters that he wrote during his lifetime (without the aid of a modern word processor!).

### 8.4.3 Electronic Mail

At its most basic, electronic mail allows the user to compose, edit, and send messages to other users or groups of users, along with (optional) attached files. However, in practice e-mail systems are starting to merge with scheduling, project management, and collaborative work tools.

Nowhere is the problem of information glut more graphically illustrated than in the experiences of active and well-connected users of electronic mail. There have been reported cases of people returning from holiday trips to a backlog of literally thousands of messages. Not something to think about while sipping a piña colada on the beach.

Fifteen messages that require attention and response per day is more than enough to provide a significant work load, and it doesn't really help to disguise this work load by taking it home and doing it early in the morning or late in the evening. Sometimes one can only feel glad that a lot more people don't use electronic mail. The telephone, fax, and regular mail service all put natural filters on communication, something that is almost entirely missing with e-mail. This is because e-mail is asynchronous, and with the reliability of today's computers and networks an e-mail message can be sent almost anywhere at any time. The situation is complicated by the fact that there is a great deal of junk e-mail such as circulars, routine reminders, and even automatic replies generated while someone is out of town. Thus sorting out the wheat from the chaff becomes a significant task for all but the most undifferentiating of e-mail users.

Although e-mail has been the realm of the privileged (e.g., academics) in the past, things are changing, and being "on e-mail" is becoming more and more routine. As the possibility for e-mail connections increase, so inevitably will the number of e-mail messages. According to some projections, the number of electronic mailboxes will soar from 17 million in 1990 to 65 million in 1995.

Electronic mail is perhaps the most widely used form of groupware (i.e., software that helps people perform tasks jointly). However, electronic mail is a very primitive form of groupware that has little intrinsic task focus. Even so, many people add value to e-mail in terms of how they use it (e.g., using subject headers to indicate the priority of a message, transferring sections of text files by mail in a form of asynchronous collaborative authoring). The fact that people are willing to do collaborative work in a fairly impoverished environment (basic e-mail) suggests that there is a need for groupware and that it will be a tremendous boost to productivity if appropriately designed and implemented.

Experience with e-mail has indicated a number of problems with the medium that need to be addressed. Some of these are technical, others may reflect basic human behavior in a novel communication environment. One of the things that people comment on most frequently with respect to e-mail is the phenomenon of flaming. Here mild-mannered people sometimes become extremely aggressive while making their opinions known. It is as if the normal social inhibitions have been removed due to the relative anonymity of the medium.

Other problems occur due to "bugs in the technology" and how it is used. For instance, separate functionalities that may have been created for very good reasons may interact badly. An example of this is a list server. Here a group of people define a list where they can post messages and have discussions. In principle list servers are good ideas. However, in some systems, if you get a message from the list server and reply to it, then your reply goes to all the people on the list. One problem with this is that people sometimes forget whom they are replying to. For instance, if friend X sends a message to the list server and friend Y happens to get it, Y may reply in a somewhat personal vein only to find out that the confidential message was broadcast around the entire list.

Holiday messages are another "good" idea. Regular e-mail users often leave messages to let people know that they are out of town and when they'll be back. If someone sends mail while the person is away, the holiday message is automatically sent back as a reply. Holiday messages can get pretty annoying, but they generally function well. However, mixing holiday messages with broadcast list servers can sometimes be a disaster. Say that the list server sends out a message and 10 people are on holiday. Their ten holiday messages get broadcast through the list server and go to everyone including themselves (!). This in turn triggers a new round of holiday messages that get broadcast and the process continues ad nauseam until the network breaks down or the operators take evasive action. This process can lead to some "flaming" messages.

### 8.4.4 Voice Mail

During the early years of their availability, voice mail systems were often given to inappropriate work groups, such as those who could easily communicate by just walking down the hall. Many users were also unclear about how to take advantage of voice mail. Voice mail could reduce telephone tag by allowing people to leave detailed messages, but early users who left only name-and-number messages missed this benefit. It took about ten years, but voice mail has become a standard communication tool for many businesses. Yet problems remain with voice mail, for some users at least. Elderly people and others who want a human touch in their business dealings are turned off by voice mail.

In general, voice mail technology is a mixed blessing. If it is used to replace direct human contact (as it often is), then it can become a method of avoiding unwanted callers as well as an "electronic wall" that can turn valued customers, clients, or colleagues away. Voice mail makes it easier to leave accurate, precise messages but it also makes it more difficult to use the excuse that the message didn't reach you.

Much of the frustration with electronic answering systems, may stem from how infrequently callers actually reach the people they want. According to some estimates only about 20% of calls go where they were intended to go. The other 80% land on answering machines or voice mail systems or are answered by someone other than the person to whom the call was made.

One of the most frustrating forms of voice mail or answering system is the "automatic information line" where the following type of transaction might occur: "Welcome to the generic information service, if you are calling form a touch tone phone press 1 now (user presses one). If you want to continue hearing this message in English press 1 now (user presses one). If you want information about our new line of products press 1 now . . . . If you have a problem with your screen blinking when you start up the software, press 2 now . . . . If you are calling about your warranty press 3 now (user presses 3). If you are calling about the Write-Right word processor press 1 now . . . . If you are calling about the Excellent Spreadsheet press 2 now . . . . If you are calling about Data Cruncher press 3 now . . . . If you would like to talk to a member of our service department press 4 now (user presses four)." At this point the user listens to a minute or two of muzak and then a voice comes on the line: "All of our service personnel are busy at the moment, please stay on the line and your call will be answered by the next available technician. . . ."

Voice mail offers several interesting lessons for implementation of new communication technologies. Most importantly, there needs to be an effective and easy interface. Alternatives should be available so that someone in voice mail, for instance, has the option of talking to a human operator if they want to. In addition, users want a quick response so that they do not have to waste time listening to options or hearing pauses as a standard message is retrieved. One way of improving the response in this case is to cut down the number of alternatives to those that are really needed, and to place the most popular or generally applicable alternatives first.

### 8.4.5  Videoconferencing

The computer-controlled video environment, "Media Space," pioneered the use of video technology for the support of remote collaborations (Ishii and Miyake 1991). Media Space made video available as a work media, and other computer-controlled video environments such as CRUISER (Root 1988) and CAVECAT (Mantei, Baecker, Sellen, Buxton, and Milligan 1991) have been developed. In these video-based approaches to collaboration a group can share information on physical desk tops using cameras to capture desk top surface images. Other video-based systems can be used in conjunction with a shared computer application such as the team workstation (TWS) system (Ishii and Miyake 1991).

Videoconferencing technology has been round since the 1960s and was part of the celebrated NCC demonstration by Doug Engelbart in 1968. However, there was little infrastructure to support it and it was too expensive to achieve widespread use. Early videoconferencing systems required dedicated rooms with special acoustics to house the bulky video and sound systems. They typically cost several hundred thousand dollars to set up, and on top of this, costs for using satellite links might run up to $1500 per hour.

Advances in compression and decompression technology now mean that adequate video signals can be squeezed into much smaller bandwidths. This is making videoconferencing much cheaper and as a result it is being used more frequently. Videoconferencing is also attractive when international tensions restrict business travel. Essential videoconferencing equipment currently includes codecs (compression/decompression systems); remote control cameras; audio systems; video switchers; network interfaces; television monitors. Some systems also allow incoming video signals to be routed to a computer screen, as in the CAVECAT system developed at the University of Toronto (Mantei 1991).

Lincoln National Life is an example of a company that has adopted videoconferencing (Bernstein 1991). It chose equipment that could comfortably service meetings of approximately seven people. The system was designed to be easily understood and operated after a single training period using what is termed the "Ph.D. (Push here, Dummy) approach." In 1990, videoconferencing at Lincoln National was judged to be a success by their director of telecommunications, with an average usage of between six and nine hours per day. At that time Lincoln was planning to add five more videoconferencing rooms to its facilities.

As the costs of videoconferencing continue to fall, some of the advantages of videoconferencing are becoming more apparent. Video conferencing saves time out of the office and traveling, permits more timely solution of problems, and maintains links between employees that are separated geographically. Videoconferencing is likely to become an increasingly important tool in companies, and like politicians, executives may find that video communication skills will become a necessary prerequisite for the job. Videoconferencing within the work place as a routine activity now seems inevitable, and use of picture phones in the home may follow hard on the heels of business video. However, many unanswered questions remain about how videoconferencing differs from face to face communication on the one hand, and the audio-only telephone on the other (Harrison 1991). Videoconferencing technology has been available since the 1960s, and the picture phone was originally launched in 1964. Video communication didn't take off in the 1960s for a number of reasons including cost and the lack of an infrastructure to support it. However, even as these problems are solved, interesting questions remain about how video communication can and should be integrated into work activities.

## ■ 8.5 EXECUTIVE INFORMATION SYSTEM METHODOLOGIES

This section will consider some of the issues that an EIS needs to address and a set of requirements will be formed based on the analysis. One model of an EIS consists of an integrated environment where all the executives tools are gathered together within a common interface. There are a number of problems with this approach, not least of which is the difficulty of finding a system interface that will handle such diverse tasks as brainstorming, project management, and data visualization within a common interface structure. Based on the discussion in Chapter 1 on the behavioral model of intelligent database usage, the argument here is that the key function of an EIS is to filter and display information that is easy to interpret. A model of EIS based on these key functions will be developed in this section.

### 8.5.1 Drilling Down and Highlighting

In its most general form, drilling down is the practice of getting down into the detailed information or data that underlie the general trends or patterns observed at higher levels of information abstraction and presentation. In practice, drilling down often consists of working through a hierarchical model of the data (e.g., the data hierarchy may correspond to the organizational hierarchy) to see what is generating or driving the high-level numbers (Figure 8.16).

One advantage of drill down is that it enables executives and high-level managers to diagnose problems in the data, thereby bypassing the intervening layers of the organization information hierarchy in order to get access to the basic data. This top down access to data contrasts with traditional views of the organization where information is passed in a bottom up fashion, while task delegation is carried out in a top down fashion (Figure 8.17).

Drill down is a useful tool, but there also needs to be a way of signaling interesting places to begin drilling down from. A large part of information interpretation involves separating the wheat from the chaff. Important data values or patterns may be disguised within a surrounding mass of irrelevancy. The irrelevant data acts like the metal fragments that are dropped from aircraft to confuse radar operators, or like any other form of decoy.

The goal of data highlighting is to differentiate the useful information from the decoy information, providing promising start points for drill down and indicating those regions of the database where further analysis is required. Successful data

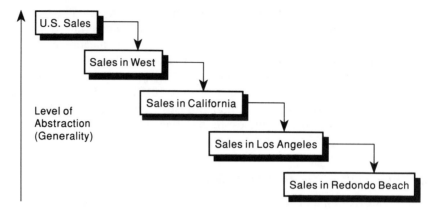

**Figure 8.16** An example of drilling down in a hierarchical model of sales data.

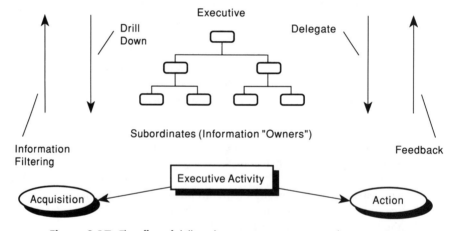

**Figure 8.17** The effect of drilling down on communication in the organization.

highlighting requires tools that differentiate data and presentation tools that highlight data in a way that is immediately obvious to the human visual system. For the majority of the population, color is a particularly effective form of data highlighting. One strategy that has been used in EIS software is to use a traffic light analogy where satisfactory information values are colored green, worrisome values are colored orange, and critical values (e.g., those values falling below some threshold) are colored red. The executive can then focus in on the red colored values and drill down to find the source of the problem.

### 8.5.2 Flexible Query Processing

When searching for information, partial match is often better than no response. In traditional query systems, a database record either matches a query or it does not. For example, a person is either *young,* or not. A flexible query system, on the other hand, gives the executive the ability to deal with inexact queries, and provides best guesses. It provides a degree of confidence for how well a record matches a query—for example, 80% sure.

As an example of flexibility in information processing, suppose you are a detective and you have a description of a suspect: He is tall, in his thirties, and drives a yellow car. As it turns out, the car is listed as orange, and the suspect is 37 and 6 feet 4 inches. Your mind can match these descriptions (e.g., you don't have to know the suspect's exact height), but a database query can not.

A flexible query system can solve queries involving inexact numeric values (e.g., someone is almost 18 years old), inexact words (e.g., Janssen, Jensen, etc.), and other types of inexact data. Using flexible querying one can specify conceptual terms upon which the system will base its queries. For example, ADULT might mean those people who are older than 21, YOUNG might mean those people who are less than 30, and BRIGHT COLOR might mean the colors Red, Yellow, Green, Blue, Orange, and White.

A flexible querying system finds partial matches and inexact answers such as:

- Close string matches—e.g., *Rogers* and *Dodgers.*
- Inexact concepts—e.g., *young, tall,* etc.
- "Educated" or "best" guesses—e.g., "I think the age is about 30."

This helps the user of an executive information system to gather potentially useful information using inexact queries as a starting point. As another example of how inexact queries can be of help, consider a customer-support person. Customer queries are very often partially specified or *imprecise* queries, as information-desk and order-desk personnel well know.

Traditionally, the set of conditions have been two-valued (i.e., given a record R and a set of conditions C, either R satisfies C or not). In a flexible query system, a degree of confidence is used to reflect how well R satisfies C.

How well R matches C depends on three factors:

1. How well each field of R matches the conditions.
2. How well the fields of R match the inter-field criteria.
3. How important each field is to the query.

To use SQL as a notation, an inexact query has the format:

*Select Name, Age, Telephone*
*From PERSONNEL*
*Where*
       *Name = Dovid Smth and*
       *Age is-close-to 18*

In this case, the name *Dovid Smth* is misspelled, but the system matches it to *David Smith.* The condition Age *is-close-to* 18 is similar to "age is around 20," or "age is about 20." (inexact ranges and concepts for fields are defined in the *concept dictionary*). The system can also provide a guess (i.e., a hypothetical answer which is not a record in the database). For instance, if you know someone's zip code, it can try to guess the make of that person's car.

As another example, suppose you have a database about the people in the U.S. To obtain interesting information, you may simply pose a set of queries. For example, to know where old people live, you may ask the following question:

```
Select GUESS(CITY)
From USA-DATA
Where
        Age is-close-to 80
```

In this case, the answer may be Miami, Florida, or perhaps Sun City, Arizona.

A flexible query may also have a degree of importance (or weight) associated with each condition. The weight is a number between 1 and 100 which shows the importance of the condition, e.g.:

```
Select Name, Age, Telephone
From PERSONNEL
Where
        Name = Dovid Smth, weight = 70 and
        Age is-close-to 18, weight = 50
```

Here the Name condition is more important than the Age condition. A query also has a *query output threshold* to filter all the records in the relation that have a *combined query confidence factor* less than the threshold.

Flexible queries can use inexact comparators such as *Near*. To use this comparator, a user must first specify a *closeness* value $C$ which is a percentage on the field. Field values will be compared with the *value* in the subcondition according to $C$.

For example, a user may specify *closeness* on field *Age* of relation *Person* using the following table:

| Age value | Confidence Factors |
|-----------|--------------------|
| 33 | 100% |
| 36 | 90% |
| 39 | 81% |
| 42 | 73% |
| ... | ... |

A similarity matrix can be used to define a user-defined comparator. A set of values can be defined in a similarity matrix by specifying the level of similarity between them. For example, a user-defined operation *similar-color* can be defined on a set of values {yellow, orange, red, green} by the following similarity matrix:

|        | Yellow | Red | Orange | Green |
|--------|--------|-----|--------|-------|
| Yellow | –      | 30  | 70     | 10    |
| Red    | 30     | –   | 60     | 0     |
| Orange | 70     | 60  | –      | 5     |
| Green  | 10     | 0   | 5      | –     |

This matrix suggests that yellow is more similar to red than to green. The matrix need not be symmetrical. Using repertory grids and related methods it is possible to use an automatic knowledge-acquisition system to obtain such matrices (Parsaye and Chignell 1988).

### 8.5.3 Communication and Report Generation

An EIS may be thought of as a vertical integration tool for an organization. It brings executives closer to the information they rely on. It can also be used to assist executives and managers in delegating and monitoring tasks. Often, such communication is facilitated when it takes place in the context of relevant data. For instance, the executive may institute a change in policy based on disappointing sales in the previous quarter. In communicating the policy change it may be useful to provide a summary of the data which motivates and justifies the change. In this way, policies and decision making are not only better informed, but they will seem less capricious to those who must implement them or be affected by them.

Currently there is a merging of EIS applications with related communication technologies such as electronic mail and videoconferencing. This allows a powerful combination of interpersonal communication and data sharing. As information technology advances and systems become more complex, collaborative work is likely to be a major activity in many organizations. People will not only work together at the same location, but they will work together (both synchronously and asynchronously) at different locations using shared information tools. Thus the task of managing and interpreting large amounts of information in an EIS will tend to merge with related communication within a distributed work group (e.g., electronic mail and videoconferencing).

Reports and memos are a traditional way of communicating and getting things done in many organizations. The report is often a summary of previous activity that is used as a basis for decision making, and memos are often the vehicles for various directives and suggestions for implementing decisions. Traditionally, reports and memos have been printed products. However, electronic mail has already usurped much of the function of memo writing and transmission. The challenge now is to develop automated tools that can relieve much of the work of report generation. Ideally, executives or their subordinates should be able to browse through the visual presentations in an

EIS, tag and annotate the interesting graphs and charts, and then output the resulting figures and text in a standardized format that serves as a draft report.

### 8.5.4  Detecting Patterns

The past is often the best predictor of the future. Thus analysis of long-term trends and patterns in data can be very important in predicting problems ahead of time. Tools that help the executive or decision maker to detect important patterns in large amounts of data should be part of the value added that an EIS provides. Some of the patterns that may occur in data include:

- Trend (increasing or decreasing?)
- Acceleration (increase or decrease in the rate of change?)
- Transition through an important threshold (e.g., red ink to black ink)
- Cyclicity
- Correlation between variables
- Lagged correlation between variables (indicative of causality)
- Clustering and grouping
- Singularities and cut-off points
- Interaction

Each of these patterns can be detected with the appropriate tool. There are a variety of methods for detecting trend. For instance, linear regression attempts to fit a straight line to the data and develop a precise estimate of the slope of the resulting line. If the data is not linear (i.e., if it can be fitted better by some form of curved line) then polynomial regression or some other form of nonlinear regression may be used. A simpler form of test which makes fewer assumptions about the data is the sign or run test. Here successive data points are compared to see if the value of the data has increased or decreased. This analysis assumes that each new data value is like tossing a coin, where an increase is like heads and a decrease is like tails. If the proportion of heads in a sequence is higher than can be expected by chance an increasing trend is signaled. Conversely, if the proportion of heads is significantly lower than chance, than this is evidence of a decreasing trend.

Acceleration or deceleration is a change in the slope of the underlying trend. For instance, a company may be studying demographics to decide whether or not they should launch a new line of baby food. A significant question might be, is the birthrate among the targeted market segment increasing or not? Evidence for changing slope can be collected using nonlinear regression, or by carrying out "piecewise" regression where the slope is calculated at different points in the data stream. The various estimates of the slope at different points in time are then analyzed to see if there is an increasing or decreasing trend in slope (i.e., acceleration or deceleration).

Transition through an important threshold can be assessed by direct comparison (e.g., is the number less than zero?). Alternatively, we might adopt a looser criterion, reflecting the fact that some of the variation in numbers will be due to chance. In this case we might set a confidence interval around the actual threshold we are interested in, thereby including some margin for error. For instance, in analyzing monthly sales volume in dollars for an organization over the past 36 months we might find a certain amount of background (random) variation that can't be attributed to systematic factors in the market place. We might have, for instance, a standard deviation of one million dollars among the monthly sales figures. This means that a relatively small loss in any one month may be due to random variation. However, if the organization lost more than two million dollars in a particular month then we could be fairly confident that it was a significant loss rather than a random blip in the data.

Cyclicity tells us something about the underlying causal structure of data. For instance, beer and soft drinks tend to be consumed in greater quantity in the summer, whereas there is less season variation (cyclicity) in the sale of wine. Cycles can be detected as consistent peaks and valleys in data. There are standard methods in econometrics and time series analysis for detecting cycles and systematic seasonal variation. One class of methods (spectral analysis) fits waves (e.g., sine waves) to the data, explaining it as a summation of various waves of different frequencies and amplitudes.

Correlation between variables is used to show a relationship. This relationship may be causal, or the two variables may both be responding to the causal influence of a third variable. For instance, tobacco companies have long claimed that the well-known correlation between cigarette smoking and lung cancer does not indicate a causal relationship. For instance, nervous people might be prone to cancer and may tend to smoke more. This kind of alternative explanation also gets around the problem of the dose-response relationship (i.e., that the risk of lung cancer increases in proportion to the amount of cigarettes smoked). Dose-response relationships are sometimes taken as evidence for causality, but in this case it might be argued that the more naturally nervous a person is the more he will tend to get lung cancer *and* the more cigarettes he will tend to smoke. At this point one might then show that nervousness is not a good predictor of lung cancer risk, but tobacco proponents might then suggest a different third variable as the possible real cause of lung cancer risk. This type of smokescreen can of course be constructed indefinitely.

Dose response relationships are one way of trying to demonstrate causality, lagged correlations are another. We generally assume that the cause should precede the effect. For instance, we know that the discharge of electricity in lightning causes thunder, rather than vice versa, because lightning always precedes thunder. Thus a consistent lagged relationship between variables is often indicative of causality. Lagged correlations are calculated by taking the data from one variable (the cause) and correlating it with data from the other variable (the effect), but collected at some later time (after the lag). This method works best when the lag is consistent. It would be difficult to determine that lightning causes thunder solely on the basis of lagged correlation, for instance, because each instance of lightning will tend to have a different lag before the ensuing thunder, with the length of this lag depending on how far the lightning strike was from the listener. In many situations, though, constant lag relationships do occur at least to an approximate degree. For instance, the relationship between amount of advertising and resulting sales will be lagged, with the length of the lag depending on the "diffusion time" for the advertising medium and the product.

Clustering and grouping are carried out using a variety of techniques including cluster analysis (as described in Chapter 4) and discriminant analysis. Singularities and cut-off points are generally estimated using curve-fitting techniques. For instance, the executive might be interested in points of inflection on a curve (i.e., points where the trend changes). Mathematically, an inflection point occurs when the second differential of a point on the curve equals zero. Or, in terms of data analysis, an inflection point or region has approximately zero slope and is surrounded by regions of non-zero slope (normally the executive will be interested in inflexions that represent peaks or valleys, where the inflection point or region is surrounded by regions of opposite valued slopes (i.e., one has positive slope while the other has negative slope).

Interaction between attributes can be detected using analysis of variance. The presence of a significant interaction means that the value on one variable (the effect or dependent variable) is jointly determined by the levels of two or more other attributes. For instance, success in a training program may depend on both the amount of prior knowledge or experience a person has and on their motivation. Either one of these alone may not be enough. In this case there is an interaction between the variables. In our complex world there are many interactions, and a failure to understand them will lead to faulty decisions.

## ■ 8.6 EXECUTIVES AS INFORMATION USERS

Executives have particular needs as information users. However, they tend to differ from other users of information systems in terms of degree rather than kind. Thus an executive may want faster response, more point and shoot simplicity, and the ability to fire off memos quickly based on patterns in data. Other users would appreciate these features as well, although their needs may not be as sharply focused or their specifications quite as demanding. Consequently, executives can be characterized as prototypical users of intelligent database applications, and their characteristics will be considered in more detail.

### 8.6.1 The Character of an Executive

One of the maxims of software design is that the way the software looks and functions should be adapted to the particular needs and characteristics of those who will use the software. In the case of an EIS, the executive is interacting with the system directly or is viewing the output of the system.

The role of executives is very different from that of middle managers, and consequently executives need different types of information systems and tools. While information is the essential resource for all managers, communication and control are major tasks of the executive. Most importantly, the executive wants to know when things are going wrong (and why) and when there is an opportunity that should be taken advantage of quickly (e.g., an acquisition or new product).

An error made at the top of an organization can cost literally billions of dollars. Not having an EIS can get a manager on the cover of *Fortune* magazine for the wrong reason. Thus it is not surprising that executives constantly search for information that monitors the vital signs of their company and their competitors. By its nature, such information is widely dispersed and often subjective. Many executives spend an hour or more of each day trying to keep up with general and business news so that they can understand trends and predict possible impacts on their own organizations.

In many ways the executive in a large organization is involved in a never-ending and demanding job where each success is likely to be matched with a new crisis. In this stressful situation it takes a particular type of person to adapt successfully. Executives tend to have more drive and more dominating personalities than the norm. Since most executives have a fairly dominant motivation, the user interface to an EIS should reflect this need, allowing the executive to call the shots, and hiding irrelevant details.

The executive uses a number of skills and capabilities that are enhanced by good work habits. The components of executive skill are jointly determined by factors such as education; experience; reasoning ability; and judgment. The effective executive uses these skills to make decisions wisely. Executive behavior is important not just to EIS design, but to the future of the company. Errors made by executives tend to be much more costly than errors made lower down in the corporate hierarchy.

### 8.6.2 What Does an Executive Do?

The development of an executive information system should be based on what executives do and what they need in order to carry out their tasks. However, since executives typically work at a much higher level of abstraction than other managers, their activities are harder to track and define.

For executives there is a fuzzy line between business and social activities. For instance, if the executive of a large corporation is out playing golf with supermarket executives, is that part of his formal job description? Similarly, how concerned should the executive be with the stock price versus the day to day operations of the company? If we define the task of the executive as that of keeping the company board and the shareholders happy, then these goals are abstract enough to include almost any activity. However, we can safely say that a major part of the executive's task involves assimilating and acting upon the information that is relevant to corporate planning, scheduling, and decision making.

The activities of the executive can be divided into 10 distinct roles Mintzberg (1973), organized into the major categories of interpersonal roles, decisional roles, and informational roles (Figure 8.18). The executive acts interpersonally as a figurehead, leader, and liaison, and in decision making as an entrepreneur, disturbance handler, resource allocator, and negotiator. These first seven roles may each require certain information (e.g., knowing the needs and expectations of the other side during negotiation). The final three roles are more explicitly informational—monitoring and disseminating information and acting as spokesman for the company.

However from the intelligent database point of view, there are two general classes of activity for the executive: (1) monitoring of information and (2) control of information. Much of the communication activities of the executive (e.g., coordinating meetings, reviewing documents) may also be vehicles for monitoring and controlling information. An EIS can assist monitoring activity by providing an alternative means

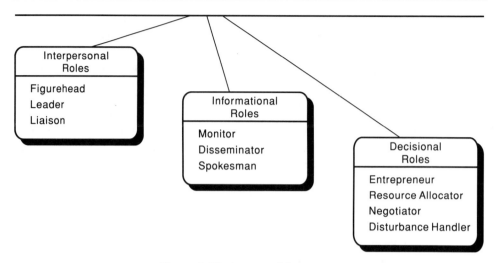

**Figure 8.18** Activities of the executive.

of directly interpreting information (Figure 8.19). Other groupware tools (discussed later in this chapter) provide ways of controlling information and the people and processes that generate it.

Another approach to understanding what executives do is to see them as architects of an exceedingly large and complex system (the organization) as it moves into the future. Insights about system architects and system architecting (Rechtin 1990) will also apply to executives. System architects, and people concerned with conceptual design generally, often need associatively structured information. This makes hypertext and hypermedia a natural way to present and store information for the designers and system architects. For instance, a hypermedia document can show how all the different parts of a spacecraft interact. Hierarchical structuring is an alternative to associative structuring. Hierarchical organization of information, for instance, can be used to provide a zooming capability (where the user moves up or down the network to explore less or more detail). However, such hierarchical structuring should be used judiciously because the hierarchy has to depend on an a priori defined set of questions or structuring principles. The general solution is to use hybrid forms of representation that allow hierarchical overlays on associative systems (Parsaye et al. 1989, Chapter 5). Thus the model of an executive information environment used here will be supplemented with point-and-click hyperdata with hierarchically organized information overviews.

System architecting and management highlights the need for information of the right kind. For instance, in manufacturing, there is a great deal of information that is collected, but how much of that information is useful? Just in time (JIT) manufacturing represents an interesting trade-off between the desirable goal of reducing inventories and the side effects of increasing information load and transportation costs. JIT has reduced inventory costs but creates additional transportation costs and requires the system to track things much more closely (e.g., bar coding of operations). Thus

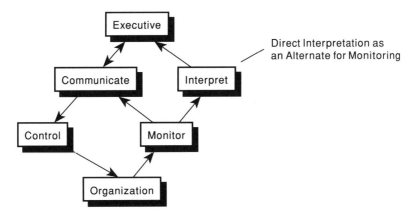

**Figure 8.19** The role of the EIS in assisting monitoring activity.

JIT has increased traffic congestion in Tokyo by requiring smaller, but more frequent, shipments. Excessive need for information may actually be a diagnostic symptom of problems. The lesson from JIT and similar tools is that one needs to have a good model of the task that is driving information collection and interpretation.

Even if data is relevant and important it may not be useful because the key trends and relationships are hidden for one reason or another. Information often needs to be enhanced and highlighted so it can be more easily interpreted. The following are some basic principles for enhancing information, each of which is exploited in intelligent database applications.

- Create effective visual presentations
- Organize the information (e.g., as a hierarchy)
- Look for deviations from norms and exceptions

Ultimately the usefulness of information is determined by its relevance to the tasks of monitoring and control that preoccupy the executive. One of the potential pitfalls in developing EISs is to assume that since executives work at a high level, they only need high-level (general) information. This may be partially true, but it is the importance of the information to the company that should drive the executive's interest, and if a minor detail is about to bring the company grinding to a halt, then that detail suddenly becomes exceedingly important to the executive. Shakespeare put it well in his epitaph on Richard III and the battle that ended the Wars of the Roses "for want of a nail the shoe was lost, for want of a shoe the horse was lost, for want of a horse the crown was lost. . . ."

Executives look at issues in terms of what they mean for the system as a whole. Thus some (but not all) details may be critical to the entire system. Executives are interested in "selected detail." They should be able to dive (or drill down) into detail when necessary. Thus the executive may need to have very detailed knowledge in some areas. For instance, the executive of a corporation that is thinking about acquiring a tobacco company may need to delve quite deeply into the details of tobacco-related litigation and its likely effects on the future of the acquisition candidate.

Some executives put posters with pithy sayings on their walls or captions on a variety of desk ornaments. Like bumper stickers, these are statements of underlying philosophy that can often be very revealing about the attitudes and motivation of the person behind the statement. In the case of executives, one of the most common sayings is, "The buck stops here." The corollary of this approach is the saying, "If you have a problem make it someone else's problem." The point here is that the executive is ultimately responsible for dealing with problems, but that the solution to the problem is carried out through a process of delegation. An executive will generally receive a great deal of information, attached to which will be value judgments that are part of the process of filtering and massaging information that subordinates carry out in order to make it more interpretable and digestible for the executive. Since this information has been filtered and massaged, it is important that the executive be able to judge and scrutinize it so that decisions are made on the basis of trusted and trustworthy data. Executives need to be skeptical, and their information tools need to give them the ability to exercise and test their skepticism.

### 8.6.3 Information Needs of Executives

For the executive, the conduit for the information needed has been other people, with subsidiary sources being news presentations in a variety of media (e.g., books, magazines, and television). Executives have been largely insulated from the computer revolution by layers of support staff. In organizations in the 1980s it was striking that the higher one went up in the hierarchy, the fewer computer workstations there were to be seen. Computers were considered useful mainly for clerical tasks and routine activities. In contrast, the subjective analyses, insights, and interpretations of executives did not seem to benefit from computer support.

Today, more and more executives are finding uses for computers and the main reason for this appears to be the ready access to appropriately packaged information (e.g., Rockart and DeLong 1988). While a few pioneering executives have used computers for electronic mail (establishing better lines of communication and access to subordinates) or even word processing, the major payoff for executive-oriented computing will be in providing targeted information that meets the needs of executives.

Executives need a variety of tools to perform their various tasks. First and foremost is a broad field of view. A typical manager may control up to five or six people, while an executive may need to monitor the activities of many more subordinates. Necessarily then, the executive works at a higher level of abstraction and is concerned with the big picture. By definition, the chief executive of an organization can never perform all the tasks, or monitor all the information, that his job description requires. Thus most executives have a strong sense of time shortage and are motivated to find systems that can give them greater efficiency and more time to think and plan.

Executives don't want to be interrupted by details unless they are details that count. Thus pages of printouts are generally not welcome in the executive suite. Instead, they want critical information that is easy to digest and highly relevant to the "big picture."

They are generally future-oriented, and want to be able to anticipate (and if possible circumvent) crises before they occur. Naturally, there are considerable individual differences between executives ranging from the extremes of the "hands off" style of management to details-oriented micro-management. However, it is often advantageous for the executive to check the facts on which interpretations are based rather than blindly accepting submissions from subordinates. Ideally the executive should be well-informed about the information that pertains to key decisions and issues without second guessing his subordinates.

### 8.6.4 Executive Tools

Chapter 3 reviewed the desk top metaphor of user interfaces. The desk top metaphor can be extended to handle the information tools needed in the executive suite. For instance, an executive needs an effective filing system with files on people, correspondence, finances, and scheduling. In an EIS, these files can be integrated and extensively cross-referenced, so that the executive can move smoothly between the different types of information.

While some of the information that an executive uses may be of a general nature, most of the information will be tied to particular tasks and contexts The presentation of information will generally reflect the task and context. Thus most of the information that an executive sees or uses is packaged within one tool or another. These tools generally fall into one of four major task categories (communication, monitoring, control, planning).

Communication includes a variety of tools such as electronic mail, video conferencing, report and memo generation, and meeting schedulers. Monitoring includes data visualization tools, and such features as data triggered alarms (e.g., when a key financial ratio goes bad) that alert the executives to potential crises as quickly as possible. Control tools include project management, scheduling, decision analysis, and performance evaluation. Planning tools include the ubiquitous spreadsheet, along with a variety of groupware tools that allow executives to plan in a group environment.

There are a variety of information tools needed by the executive. To what extent is it possible to build an overall EIS that handles the most important information in a general way? Part of the solution to this problem will be to handle the task-specific features of executive information needs by allowing customization of the EIS to meet the needs of specific companies or executives. In other words, the goal here is to define a general EIS environment that can be modified and extended in different ways to meet different needs.

Attention is often paid to issues such as time management with its well-known strictures, e.g.:

- Try to handle each piece of paper (or information) only once.
- Make a clear distinction between the in-tray and out-tray.
- Carry out information triage.
- Don't hide things in manila folders, make them visible.

- Delegate where possible.
- Set apart quiet time for big projects or creative work (e.g., 90 minute blocks of time).
- Make up a to do list of target tasks for each day and check them off when done.

However, it is information monitoring and communication that are probably the most critical of executive skills. John D. Rockefeller said (cited by Wareham 1991, p. 74) "I will pay more for the ability to deal with people than for any ability under the sun." Perhaps if J. D. Rockefeller were around today he would also be paying a lot for the ability to monitor information as well.

In many instances, what the executive really needs is information triage. One problem with information triage, like medical triage, is that even the process of triage itself can consume valuable time and energy. Thus one might imagine using an electronic assistant to sort through mail or messages and select out the important ones for immediate attention and throw out or file the rest. These ideas motivated the Information Lens project at MIT (Robinson 1991). The Information Lens uses a computer-based assistant to sort incoming messages into meaningful categories and prioritize the messages based on importance and urgency.

Information Lens was originally implemented as a prototype running on Xerox 1100 Series workstations connected by an Ethernet network. Users sent different types of messages including action requests; notices; commitments; general messages. Each message type had a template. The message template for a meeting announcement is shown in Figure 8.20. The template for each message type contained a number of fields and associated with each field were three properties: a default value, a list of possible alternative values, and an explanation of the field and its relationship to the template. The Information Lens also included a rule editor which allowed users to find, filter, and sort messages. The rule editor used templates that were similar to

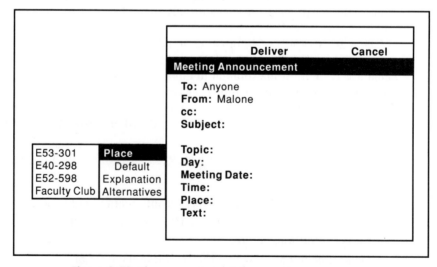

**Figure 8.20** The message template for a meeting announcement.

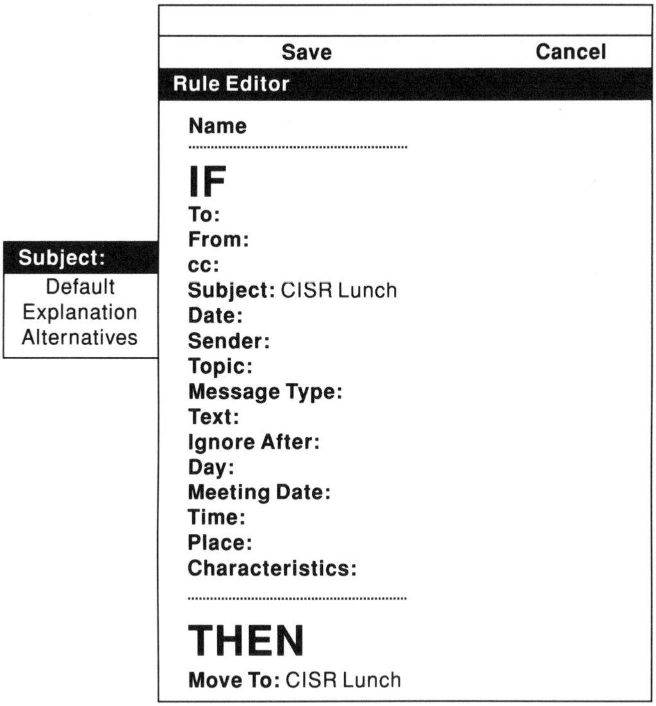

**Figure 8.21** An example of a rule in the Information Lens (after Robinson 1991, figure 4).

message templates except that the rule template contained both a condition and action part as shown in Figure 8.21. An example of a rule for processing messages is

*If Message type action request and*
        *Action deadline Today, Tomorrow*
*Then Move to urgent*

In the Information Lens system rule and message types were organized into frame hierarchies. Rules could be defined by individuals for themselves or be unstructured for groups for automating a variety of communication and coordination procedures.

Information triage also seems like a great idea for executive information systems. The model of the executive information environment discussed here includes a type of information triage capability by providing a briefing capability that presents a restricted hyperdata network focused on the most important data objects and attributes.

## ■ 8.7 CONCLUSIONS

The essential problem of executive information systems (and of all intelligent databases to some extent) is the problem of getting the right information. One of the reasons cited for using EISs is that people like information, and executives are rewarded if they feel they've got ready access to data at their fingertips. This is only partly a technology issue. It is also a user interface problem, a task analysis problem, and a knowledge acquisition problem. Executive information systems highlight the importance of information focusing and interpretation. The principles of making information focused and interpretable are axiomatic for intelligent database applications in general. Further important principles will be discovered as other intelligent database problems are explored.

This chapter addressed the issues of what information executives need and what functionality an EIS should contain. EISs were defined as sophisticated intelligent database applications that generate information, reports, and presentations for executives and other users who need to make decisions on the basis of large amounts of data. Corporate Vision, an executive information system and an effective platform for developing intelligent database applications, was described. Later chapters will show how this platform can be modified for specialized intelligent database applications in areas such as marketing, project management, and quality control.

# 9

# PROJECT MANAGEMENT AND VISUALIZATION

*But there will be no new man to do these staggering tasks. The manager of tomorrow will not be a bigger man than his father was before him. He will be possessed of the same endowments, beset by the same frailties and hedged in by the same limitations.*

— Peter Drucker*

*Corollary*: The only way to succeed in increasingly larger and more complex projects is to have better information systems.

## ■ 9.1 INTRODUCTION

The ability to manage large projects is one of the distinguishing features of civilization. Today there are numerous examples of project management on a grand scale, including the construction of large buildings, the development of new computers or airplanes, and the construction of satellites. While many large projects are spectacular successes (e.g., the Apollo moon missions or Hannibal's crossing of the Alps), some large projects fail completely, finish late, or fail to meet all their objectives. Examples of the latter include Napoleon's invasion of Russia or the Hubble space telescope.

There are many ways for projects to fail outright or to exceed their time or cost budgets. Successful projects require careful planning and management, but they also require responsive management, so that unexpected events, harsh winters, and inaccurate test results do not sidetrack or derail the project.

Projects come in all shapes and sizes. The word "project" generally refers to the process of planning, managing, and carrying out a task. Most useful tasks are actually a sequence of more detailed tasks each requiring its own resources. Even apparently simple tasks such as changing a tire on a car must be handled carefully to ensure, for instance, that the lug nuts are loosened at the right time and in the right way.

---

* *The Practice of Management,* Harper & Row, 1954. Peter Drucker was born in Vienna in 1909 and was educated in England and Germany. He was professor of management at New York University and the Claremont Graduate School and acted as a consultant to many top organizations in the US. His books on management are widely read and respected.

As tasks increase in scope, requiring more resources to carry out more subtasks, the complexity of managing the overall project increases exponentially. Consider, for instance, a task where there are three subtasks, each of which can be carried out by one of three people, on one of three machines. In this case, if we assume that any of the people can perform any of the tasks on any of the machines, there are $3\times3\times3=27$ different combinations of task carried out by human resource on a machine resource. However, if we have four tasks with four people and four machines, then there are 64 different combinations. Thus the complexity of managing the various interfaces between tasks in a project tends to increase exponentially as the number of interacting tasks increases. For multifaceted projects involving hundreds or even thousands of people using different resources the resulting complexity can be enormous. Further complexity may derive from constraints on how the tasks should be performed. For instance, there may be sequential dependencies so that some tasks cannot be performed unless some prerequisite tasks have already been completed. The key point here is that as society becomes more complex, projects become exponentially more complex. The only solution is the systematic use of advanced computer technology for all phases of project management.

This chapter will review the major issues in project management, including monitoring and control and the visualization of project activity. Some of the visualizations (charts) that are useful for project visualization will then be discussed, including some new graph types developed especially for project visualization. How these charts may be integrated within a hyperdata presentation environment for project exploration will also be explored. Other issues discussed in this chapter include the iterative refinement of requirements and expected functionality, the notion of critical risk, the use of data quality control for managing project data, the merging of projects and presentations, and the use of groupware for project management.

## ■ 9.2 HISTORY AND EVOLUTION OF PROJECT MANAGEMENT

There are relatively few visible reminders of past civilizations. Much of what we know about past cultures is based on the analysis of garbage dumps, burial places, and building foundations. Thus most of archeology involves digging of one type or another. Large works of ancient civilizations above the ground are particularly awe inspiring. The pyramids in Egypt, the megaliths of Stonehenge, the Aztec pyramids in the Yucatan, and the Great Wall of China all attest to the ability of earlier civilizations to plan and manage large projects.

Some large projects have left their mark in recorded history, even though they did not produce monuments still visible today. One such feat was the crossing of the Alps by Hannibal and the Carthaginian army, which was a logistical marvel of its time. Other large projects focused around the activity of shipbuilding, which required the transportation, coordination, and processing of many different resources, often under time constraints. The construction of Greek and Roman fleets in times of war must have had many parallels to the more recent frenetic construction of aircraft and the "liberty" ships of the second world war.

Tasks such as early shipbuilding and pyramid construction must have strained methods of project management to the limit. They appear to have been carried out in very authoritarian (hierarchical) societies and they must have involved exceptionally gifted planners and architects.

As projects became ever larger, project managers were less able to deal with all the constraints and communications inside their heads. Things came to a head in the 1950s with the Polaris missile program. In the Cold War atmosphere of the time that incredibly complex project was placed under severe time constraints. The complexity of the Polaris project led to the development of the Program Evaluation and Review Technique (PERT) method as a reporting technique for evaluating and monitoring the phase-by-phase progress of the various subtasks in the overall project (Martino 1964). Also in the 1950s, the critical path method (CPM) was developed as a computer-oriented planning technique designed to control construction, engineering, and plant maintenance projects.

The critical path method (CPM) was developed by DuPont and Rand. An independent and parallel path was followed by the U.S. Navy in the development of PERT for the Polaris project (U.S. Navy 1960). CPM and PERT share a great deal in common, particularly in their use of nodes and links to represent activities and durations. Differences between CPM and PERT are largely based on the calculations made and the emphasis placed on various aspects of the network. However, variations in the way different users tend to use each method are greater than the overall differences between the methods (Martino 1964). Thus PERT and CPM are often seen as a unified technique referred to as PERT/CPM.

While PERT/CPM tends to be the predominant project management tool, other tools and methods have also been developed. In the mid-1960s, Graphical Evaluation and Review Technique (GERT) was developed by Pritsker for use within the Apollo project. It deals with more complex modeling situations than can be handled by PERT/CPM (Meredith and Mantel 1989). GERT differs from CPM and PERT by being a simulation-oriented model which allows for alternative branches and cycles.

As these examples show, large-scale government projects have frequently led to the development of new computer technology for project management. More recently, experience in fielding a hyperinformation project management system for the strategic defense initiative (one of the largest projects in modern history) has led to a new generation of project management technology.

The strategic defense initiative (SDI) is a large and controversial project. In any case, the issues raised by SDI have challenged the field of project management, ushering in a new set of technologies for project control. The Project Visualization System™ encompasses these technologies, as discussed later in this chapter.

Modern computer support of project management has extended the envelope of manageable project complexity (Figure 9.1). Just as spreadsheets allowed people to look for patterns in data without having to make the detailed calculations themselves, computer-based project management tools now assist human managers on even the most complex projects. Project management is necessary in these cases because humans generally find it difficult to evaluate the large number of competing options available in coordinating a variety of tasks occurring in parallel.

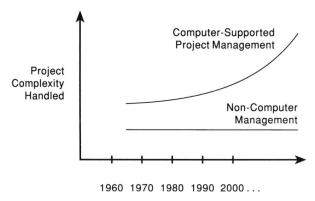

**Figure 9.1** Project complexity and computer support.

## ■ 9.3 BASIC CONCEPTS OF PROJECT MANAGEMENT

The basic terms and ideas in project management will be defined in this section. The next section shows how the technology of intelligent databases impacts and advances the field.

The basic elements in a project are tasks and schedules. A *task* is an activity that needs to be performed. A *project* is a collection of related tasks that share a common deadline. All the tasks must be completed before the project is completed.

For instance, consider a project for building a park. The community wants a park for the children to play in. The park must be built in a specified amount of time. It has to be finished before the next election. The mayor is planning to make his reelection speech in the new park. Here, two tasks might be "Choose the Site" (which should be somewhere near the center of town) and "Level Ground."

The descriptions of the desired nature of the project form the project *requirements*. For instance, it may be a requirement that the park must have a good children's playground. There are different methods of building a good children's playground, and one of these is chosen as a *functionality expected*. For instance, the functionality: "three swings, two slides and a see-saw" is used to implement the requirement for a children's playground. If no swings are to be found, the functionality may be changed to "two slides and three see-saws."

A number of activities need to be coordinated before the park is completed on time and on budget. These are called *tasks*.

Tasks are organized into a tree structure (e.g., the "Shrubs" task may have subtasks including the purchase, transportation, and the planting of shrubs). The shrubs subtasks are "Purchase Shrubs," "Transport Shrubs," and "Plant Shrubs." Subtasks may also have subtasks.

Some tasks *depend* on others. For instance, shrubs need to be purchased before they are transported. Therefore, the "Transport Shrubs" task depends on the "Purchase Shrubs" task. Dependencies thus link tasks such that the start or end of one task must follow or lead the start or end of another task. A dependency defines the relationship between tasks. Dependencies always involve two tasks. One task is always the successor and the other is the predecessor. One task might be "Choose Site" and another may be "Level Ground." The "Level Ground" task depends on the "Choose Site" task. "Level Ground" is the successor. "Choose Site" is the predecessor.

A *critical task* is a task which cannot be delayed without the project's end date being delayed. Therefore, critical paths have no "float time" or flexibility of delay for their completion.

A task consumes *resources,* including time and money. For instance, it may take one hour and cost $50 to plant a shrub. Also, transportation may only be provided by a specific number of trucks which are also needed for the transportation of other material.

Thus a project consists of seven key components:

1. A set of *requirements* for the project
2. A specified type of *functionality* derived from the requirements
3. A set of *tasks* which need to be completed and *dependencies* between the tasks
4. A set of *agents* or *resources* which are needed to perform tasks
5. *Time* and *cost* estimates for task completion by agents or resources
6. Estimates of *risk* for functionality delivery and task completion
7. *Alternative methods* for performing tasks and for functionality

A project supervisory system not only keeps track of what tasks are to be completed, their progress rate, etc. but also provides tools for supporting negotiation between project team members and for facilitating the implementation of various decisions.

### 9.3.1 Gantt Charts

Gantt charts show when different tasks are being carried out in relation to the schedule of the entire project. They are particularly useful for tasks such as resource allocation. A Gantt chart is a two-dimensional graph which usually plots time on the horizontal x-axis and lists project tasks on the vertical y-axis, as in Figure 9.2. A Gantt chart shows the projected start, duration, and end of tasks. Tasks are typically arranged in chronological order, so that a steplike pattern emerges in the chart. Gantt charts can also be modified during the course of a project. For instance, extra information can be added to the chart such as the percent of task achieved or the end date for each task. Already completed portions of the task can be shown as dotted lines while yet to be completed tasks can be shown as continuous lines. Milestones can be shown as rectangular markers and a dotted vertical line can show the current date.

The information in the Gantt chart is very useful in conveying the status of the project. As time goes on, the continuous lines should change to dotted lines and milestones should be marked with checks. In this way the project manager can quickly

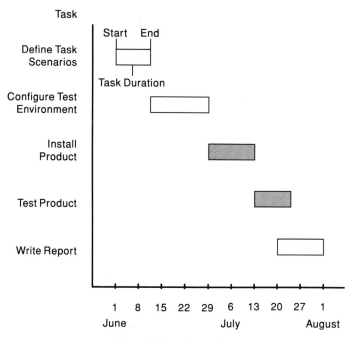

**Figure 9.2** A Gantt chart.

see which parts of the project are on time or delayed based on the visual features of the modified Gantt chart and can sense changes in rate of progress and possible problems based on changes in the visual appearance of the chart.

### 9.3.2 PERT/CPM

PERT/CPM is a method for determining when resource allocation needs to occur but it is not designed to guide decisions about how to implement resource allocation. The PERT chart is also a useful way of showing which tasks depend on other tasks (subtasks). In the production of a newspaper, for instance, articles must be written before they can be edited, and must be edited before they can be laid out, and so on. A large amount of domain knowledge is needed to determine how one resource can be substituted for another, or whether available resources can be extended (e.g., who may be willing to put in some overtime).

PERT and CPM are network analysis tools. Their goal is to produce a schedule defining when each job will start. Some activities are relatively unconstrained and can be started at almost any time, while other activities may be heavily constrained to start on a particular day or at the completion of a particular task. Thus the scheduling information about each job should include not only the earliest possible starting time for each activity, but also the permissible variation in starting time (referred to as the total float). If the total float is zero, then no variation in the starting time for the activity can be tolerated. Where some variation can be tolerated, the total

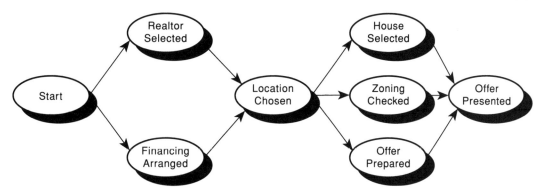

**Figure 9.3** A network diagram for selecting a house (one of several strategies that might be used).

float is the difference between the earliest possible start time and the latest possible start.

### 9.3.3 Diagramming of Projects

Developing a network diagram of a project provides a unified representation of activities, problems, decisions, and operations that relate to the management objectives (Miller and Starr 1969). Figure 9.3 shows an example of a network diagram of a project, selecting a house. In this diagram, each activity is shown as an arrow. The completion of each activity is called an event and is shown as a circle. Thus each arrow (activity) points to a circle (event) that represents the completion of that activity. The sequence of arrows in the diagram indicates the order in which the activities should be performed.

Visual inspection of a network (arrow) diagram is useful because it shows the entire scope of the project and the prerequisite work for each task is always readily apparent. It takes a great deal more time to prepare an arrow diagram than it does to read it. However, this diagramming (project analysis) time is generally well spent because it forces the manager or diagrammer to think carefully about what the project really involves. Many problems can be anticipated and resolved while constructing the diagram.

### 9.3.4 Dealing with Uncertain Durations

PERT is a planning method designed to deal with tasks that have uncertain durations. PERT uses three time estimates to approximate the time for each operation. This reflects the fact that the duration of an activity is not a certain or precise quantity, but is rather a random variable having some probability distribution. The three time estimates used by PERT are a most likely estimate, an optimistic estimate, and a pessimistic estimate. These time estimates define the peak and tails of a hypothetical frequency distribution (the distribution that would be obtained if it were possible to run the task independently many times and measure how long it took). Figure 9.4 gives a schematic representation of this probability distribution showing the location of the three time estimates.

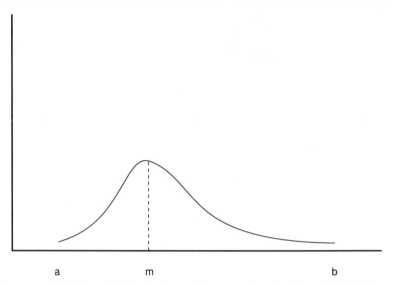

**Figure 9.4** A model of the probability distribution for PERT approach with most likely (m), optimistic (a), and pessimistic (b) estimates.

PERT uses a weighted average of the three time estimates to estimated the expected time for the task. For instance, under one weighting scheme the weighted estimate is given as

$$\text{expected time} = (a + 4m + b) / 6$$

where *a* is the optimistic time, *b* is the pessimistic time, and *m* is the most likely time. Estimates of expected time can then be used to calculate the critical path, slack times, etc. Under certain probability assumptions, the difference between the optimistic and pessimistic time estimates for tasks can then be used to estimate the variability of task duration (e.g., Hillier and Lieberman 1980, p. 252). For instance, one estimate of the standard deviation of the activity duration distribution is that it is one-sixth of the difference between the optimistic and pessimistic times.

Given the estimated expected values and variances for each of the activity times (along with assumptions that the activity times are statistically independent, and that the critical path always requires a longer total elapsed time than any other path), it is then possible to calculate the expected value and variance of the time for the entire project as being the sum of the expected values and variances, respectively, of the times for the activities on the critical path.

Consider the PERT network illustrated in Figure 9.5 where the three time estimates are shown for each activity. Using the method as described above, the expected values and standard deviations of the activity durations have been calculated and are shown in Figure 9.6. The scheduled completion time is 25 days. However, the expected completion time, taken by summing the expected activity durations along the critical path is 24.5 days. This shows that the expected completion time is within the scheduled completion time. However, the variance in the overall completion time is

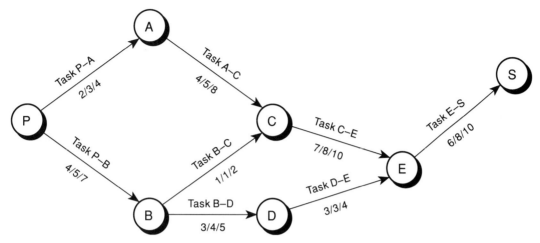

**Figure 9.5** A PERT network with three time estimates for each activity. Each activity is labeled by three time estimates (optimistic, most likely, pessimistic).

| Task | Expected Time | Standard Deviation of Estimated Time |
|------|---------------|--------------------------------------|
| P–A | 3 | .33 |
| P–B | 5.17 | .5 |
| A–C | 5.33 | .67 |
| B–C | 1.17 | .17 |
| B–D | 4 | .33 |
| C–E | 8.17 | .5 |
| D–E | 3.17 | .17 |
| E–S | 8 | .67 |

**Figure 9.6** Expected values and standard deviations of the activity durations for the chart shown in Figure 9.5.

2.17 days (using the calculation method described above as applied to the critical path).

What is the probability that the project will in fact be completed late? We can estimate this probability by noting that the scheduled completion data is .23 standard deviations above the expected completion date. We can then compare this value for z with the table of probabilities of a standard normal distribution (Box, Hunter, and Hunter 1978) to estimate the desired probability. In this case the probability that the actual completion time will be greater than .23 standard deviation units from the expected completion time (i.e., that the project will be late) is .41 (i.e., 41% chance of being late). Given the size of this probability, the project manager can decide whether or not it is necessary to take action to try and reduce the expected completion time and thereby reduce the probability of being late.

### 9.3.5 Finding the Critical Path

The critical path method (CPM) identifies the tasks that control the completion time of a project. Knowing the critical path is very useful in planning and controlling a project. Using the critical path, the manager can distinguish between those tasks that can be delayed without delaying the entire project and those critical tasks that have to be performed on time if the project as a whole is to be completed on time. CPM employs the following steps:

1. Identify the individual tasks for the project.
2. Identify the duration or effort for each task and the resources required.
3. Identify the critical path:
   a. Identify the earliest start times.
   b. Identify the latest start times.
4. Manage the project to obtain the most economical and efficient schedule without delaying any of the critical tasks.

It should be noted that the critical path may change during a project. Even though a task may be off the critical path initially, it may switch to being critical if sufficiently delayed.

Figure 9.7 shows a very simple task network. In this network there are two parallel paths, each consisting of two tasks. The upper path (as drawn in the figure) can be completed in a total of 12 days, while the lower path can be completed in a total of 8 days. Thus the duration of the project as a whole is controlled by the longer path (the upper path in this case).

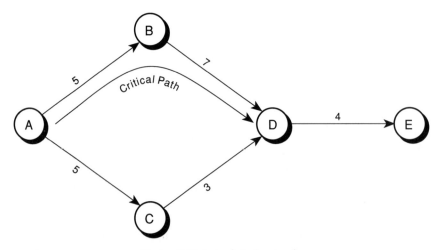

**Figure 9.7** A simple task network.

Any operation not on the critical path has a certain amount of slack time associated with it. In Figure 9.7 the lower path has slack time of 4 days because the two tasks in the path can be delayed up to four days without affecting the overall project time. In this example there are linear dependencies that constrain the sequence in which the task activities are performed. In other tasks there may be much less sequential dependency and as a result considerably more freedom for changing the schedule around. In the extreme cases, the tasks may only be performed in a serial fashion, or they may all be performed in parallel (Figure 9.8). However, in practice most projects have a network that falls somewhere between these two extremes.

Having slack time available can be very useful in load leveling and resource allocation. This is because resources can be temporarily reassigned from a noncritical task to a critical task for the duration of the available slack time. Thus CPM is a method for identifying those tasks that are noncritical so that resources from those tasks can be allocated to the critical tasks in such a way as to minimize the overall completion time of the project.

In addition to finding the critical path in the task network, CPM also finds the slack time (if any) for each task. Tasks that are on the critical path will, of course, have no slack time. Another way of saying this is that there is no permissible variance in the start and finish times for the tasks on the critical path. In contrast, noncritical times can start later, up to the amount of slack time that they have. Thus the start of the first

*A Serial Project*

*A Parallel Project*

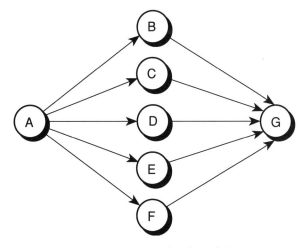

**Figure 9.8** Serial and parallel projects.

job in the lower path can be delayed by up to four days, but the second job would then have to start immediately and should not be delayed. If for some reason the first job in the lower path were delayed by two days, then this would consume two of the days of slack time for the lower path and only two days of slack time would remain for the second job in that path.

Figure 9.9 shows a hypothetical histogram of resource loading for Dan, a software engineer, over a five week period. It can be seen that there are sharp fluctuations in the requirements for Dan's time. Panel *b* of Figure 9.9 shows hypothetical resource requirements for Dan's department as a whole. It can be seen that the resource requirement fluctuations affect the whole software engineering department, thus it is not possible simply to get existing software engineers to help Dan when he is overloaded.

Aside from hiring temporary resources (which can be difficult for a number of reasons) another way of resource leveling is the modify the start and stop times of tasks so that resource requirements are more evenly distributed. This is possible because some of the tasks will not be on the critical path, and consequently their start and stop times can be shifted somewhat without affecting the project as a whole.

Figure 9.10 shows a simple example of poor resource loading using a graphical technique. The critical tasks (with their resource requirements) are shown with shading in the lower part of the figure. The noncritical tasks are free to vary somewhat.

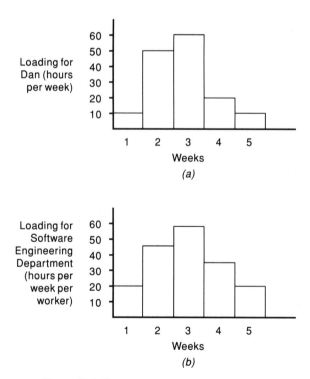

**Figure 9.9** Fluctuations in resource requirements.

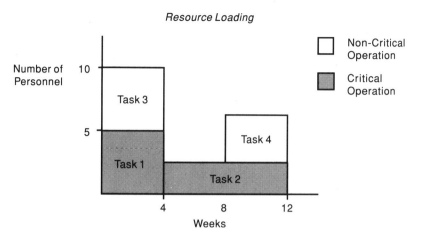

**Figure 9.10** A set of tasks with non-uniform loading on the personnel resource.

Task 3 can be slid to the right (as shown in Figure 9.11) to produce a more uniform resource loading. Note that this type of resource leveling can be used for machine as well as human resources.

## ■ 9.4 INTELLIGENT DATABASES FOR PROJECT MANAGEMENT

Conventional project management tools have proven very useful in managing large projects. However, they were developed in an era prior to powerful graphics workstations, hypertext systems, and multimedia. Thus the methods of visualization used (Gantt charts, PERT diagrams) are necessarily limited. This section will describe a project visualization system that combines the traditional project management tools with hypertext features and visualization of supporting data using a number of different types of view.

The Project Visualization System™ (PVS) is a commercial system from IntelligenceWare that complements Corporate Vision. PVS has been used as part of the largest projects in modern history, i.e., the strategic defense initiative (Schwartz 1992). An analysis of PVS highlights two axioms of intelligent database application: (1) information should be combined and interrelated, and (2) information should be presented in a variety of different formats. Thus PVS allows for hyperdata access to many components of projects, including Gantt charts, cost charts, textual documents, etc. The user can click on a Gantt chart to get text, then click within the text to get another graph, etc.

### 9.4.1 Projects and Group Information

A large project requires a team of people, generally with differing skills and expertise, to carry it out. This team may be melded out of one or more existing working groups, or it may even cut across existing work group boundaries, as different people are selected for the project team.

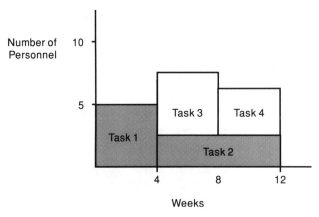

**Figure 9.11** A more uniform resource loading.

Thus the different members of the project team may have vastly different interests and backgrounds and this needs to be taken into account in the project management software. For instance, some users may want to customize the software for their needs, while others may want an off-the-shelf solution. Customization may be provided by allowing the user to modify the user interface to some extent or it may be provided by a programming language.

Technical expertise and managerial level are also important user aspects for project management software. Analysts generally have very different requirements and expectations from executives.

The software may also need to be adapted or selected based on the characteristics of the project. Some of the relevant dimensions of projects include the degree to which it is experimental or routine, its complexity, and whether its duration is long or short term.

Large projects require relevant (group) information that can be shared by the various members of the team as needed. In this case, the requirements for data quality may be even more stringent than usual, because some of the users may not be as familiar with the data as others. Obviously, if one collects one's own data, one is more likely to know about typical misspellings or digit combinations that are used to indicate missing values. However, as data is shared, the "lore" surrounding the data tends to get lost in the transmission. Thus more and more of the "accessory knowledge" about the data needs to be compiled and made explicit.

A more stringent data quality control is needed for managing project data. Ideally, the quality should be designed into the original model or definition of the data and the data collection. Attribute names and value labels should be understood to mean the same thing by all members of the project, and standardized methods of data collection should be enforced. In addition, group discussion of data should be encouraged, so that the most knowledgeable people are available to discuss the subareas of the project. For instance, part of a satellite may be overheating under normal operating conditions. The electrical engineer might find this mysterious until the layout planner explains that the component was moved away from the vent in order to reposition another component.

## 9.4.2 Project Visualization

Information is very important to large scale projects, and it should be as accessible and interpretable as possible. Project visualization enhances interpretability by summarizing the key trends and relationships within the project in terms of charts and graphs.

Project managers need tools that help them keep track of the big picture for the project. What project management software does well is to calculate things such as the critical path time, the current slack time for a task, and so on. However, there is a relatively limited amount of visualization capability in terms of Gantt charts, hierarchical representation of projects, PERT charts, and miscellaneous charts or tables such as spreadsheets showing the allocation of resources to tasks. In addition, it is not easy to switch between alternative views of the project.

Some of the information that is relevant to the management of a large project (Figure 9.12) includes:

1. Description of tasks and subtasks
2. Description of resources
3. Assignments of resources to tasks
4. Estimates of task duration
5. Dependencies between tasks
6. Milestones
7. Holidays, due dates, etc.

A lot of this information is interrelated and can be shown in different ways. For instance, the assignment of resources will be jointly defined by the requirements of tasks and the availability of resources.

Histograms are used to represent resource usage over time. Other basic graphics such as pie charts and bar charts are also used in traditional project management systems.

Each representation emphasizes different features of the data. In designing a project visualization system consideration should be given to which types of graph or chart can supplement Gantt and PERT charts in providing the critical information about a project in a form that can be easily assimilated.

Most Gantt and PERT charts are designed to be displayed on paper. Thus it is necessary to ask how charting methods should be modified or extended to take full advantage of the computer as a display medium. For instance, the computer allows creative use of three-dimensional graphics to better display project information.

A number of different presentation styles to display the project status can be defined. The relevant set of variables of project status include schedule (time), costs, complexity, and risks. Different combinations of these variables may be combined into graph types which assist in answering different questions about the project status.

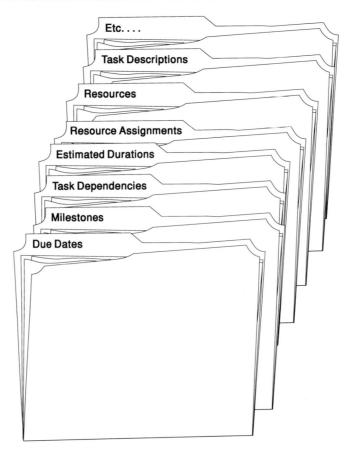

**Figure 9.12** Relevant project information.

Some of these new types of graph and chart for project visualization will be described in a following section.

The Project Visualization System is an example of an advanced project management system. The system presents the executives or decision makers with a network diagram which represents the project interdependencies. The project network display presents the project dependencies from left to right based on chronological order. When you first begin to use the system, you will notice that *ProjectName*, which is the name of the project database you have just created, is the only project in the network display. Usually, the project status has been prepared and maintained in a project database. Therefore, the chronological interdependencies of projects will be displayed using the project network.

The project network diagram, which is displayed during the entire session, shows at a glance the task interdependencies of each project. At any time, the user can invoke the hypertext facility to obtain project descriptions, project cost or complexity, risk assessments, etc. By selecting an individual project or task with the direction keys or a mouse, the next level (detail) project network will appear.

A project may be represented as a bit-map and used as an access or entry point for project information. In this case the user selects one of the project components in the bit-map after which a pop-up menu appears and a Gantt chart is chosen. This bit-map visualization of the project structure provides a useful alternative to the PERT network presentation.

**9.4.2.1   *3D Gantt Charts***      While 2D displays are informative, they do not have the impact a 3D display has. Having the third dimension is particularly useful in Gantt charts where one wants to display cost as well as time and resources. Other 3D versions of the Gantt chart focus on risk and resource usage. The three main types of 3D Gantt chart are as follows:

1. *The 3D Gantt/Cost Chart* shows three (or more) levels of information by using the third dimension to represent cost as in Figure 9.13. The use of color and shading can introduce two other parameters (e.g., high risk is shown in red and shading and hatching represent agents or resources).
2. *The 3D Gantt/Risk Chart* shows three (or more) levels of information by using the third dimension to represent either risk or complexity. The use of color, shading, and box size/thickness can introduce three other parameters (e.g., high cost is shown in red).

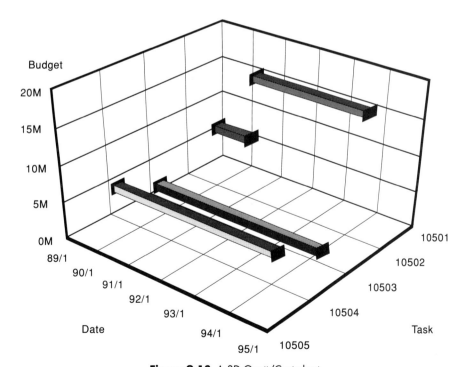

**Figure 9.13** A 3D Gantt/Cost chart.

**3.** *The 3D Gantt/Resource Chart* shows three (or more) levels of information by using the third dimension to represent resource usage. The use of color and box size/thickness and shading can introduce two other parameters (e.g., high risk is shown in red).

3D Gantt charts gives user information in spatial form. Although earlier project management systems give a numerical printout of the data, the project visualization system graphs it in a more comprehensible form. For instance, in a 3D Gantt/cost chart, the three axes are TIME, TASK, and COST. TASK is a discrete unordered (categorical) variable. COST and TIME are linear real variables. The higher the cost of completing a task, the higher it appears on the z-axis. Thus the trend in costs over time and tasks is then readily apparent to the eye (and thus quickly assimilated and interpreted) in terms of the relative height of the different data points.

**9.4.2.2  3D PERT Charts**     PERT charts can also benefit from the use of a third dimensions. The most important 3D PERT charts cover cost, risk, and task duration as alternative ways of using the third dimension.

**1.** *The 3D PERT/Cost Chart* shows three (or more) attributes of information in a PERT chart presentation by using the third dimension to represent cost as in Figure 9.14. The use of other parameters such as color, box size/thickness, and shading introduces additional attributes (e.g., high risk may be shown in red and different shading and hatching may represent different agents or resources).

**2.** *The 3D PERT/Risk Chart* uses the third dimension to represent either risk or complexity. Other coding parameters (e.g., size and color) can be used to represent additional attributes.

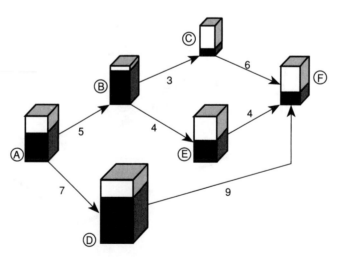

**Figure 9.14** A 3D PERT/cost chart. Note the use of frames to ease the task of judging heights of the bars.

**3.** *The 3D PERT/Duration Chart* works in similar fashion, with the third dimension representing duration for each box as a bar.

The different types of 3D PERT chart (cost, risk, and duration) are then distinguished in the project visualization system by different labels. In addition icons (e.g., dollar signs for cost) can be shown to remind the viewer of the type of 3D PERT chart being used.

**9.4.2.3** *Multi-Subtask Status Charts* Other charts are particularly useful in a computer presentation where charts are linked together within a hyperdata interface. For instance, multi-subtask status charts show each subtask's ratio for a given parameter of interest. The basic multi-subtask status chart can be modified to emphasize progress to date.

1. The *Multi-Aspect Subtask Status Chart* shows four (or any other number of) pie charts reflecting each subtask's ratio for a given parameter of interest. Figure 9.15 shows a multi-aspect subtask status chart with the parameters budget, expenditure, duration, and risk. Similar charts can also be constructed showing different aspects of the subtasks, such as percentage of delay, percentage of time remaining, percentage of budget remaining, etc.

2. The *Progress-to-Date Chart* shows the percentage of each subtask completed and the percentage of the budget remaining with 3D bar charts. Again, the color, shading, and the thickness of the bars may represent other parameters, according to the requirements of the user.

Multi-subtask status charts are extensions of pie charts. They show the proportions of the subtasks relative to the main task for budget, duration, risk/complexity, and cost. They evaluate the subtasks in a variety of ways, characterizing subtasks in terms of familiar categories. One task may be labor intensive. Such a task might require extra supervision. Another task may be time intensive (i.e., waiting for cement to dry). This task may require security since one does not want anyone to interrupt that process. The categorization of tasks into chart segments (and attachment of icons to these segments) helps to invoke themes associated with those tasks.

**9.4.2.4** *Snake Charts* The snake chart is a 2D graph, with time as the x-axis, and cost as the y-axis. For the tasks, or group of tasks, specified, the $/day is displayed. Each task

*Status Charts for the Installation Subtask*

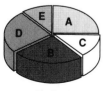
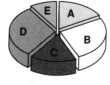
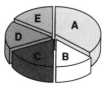
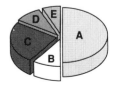

*Budget*    *Expenditure*    *Duration*    *Risk*

**Figure 9.15** A multi-aspect subtask status chart.

has a line of a different color. The total cash expenditure can be graphed. This is helpful in anticipating problems with cash flow. Also promoting solutions to this problem is a graph of the cumulative $ spent on the project. Project reorganization can minimize the cost of completing the project. Usually there is a time-cost trade-off, where the project can be completed sooner if more money is spent on it.

The cost-time graph can also display resources. The amount of money spent on a resource or a type of resource can be displayed over time. This is useful in analyzing the benefits of resource leveling. If a resource is leveled it will never be allocated over 100%. People are resources and allocation over 100% results in overtime and doubletime. The cost-time graph can show the benefits of resource leveling and allow one to ponder the question of how much it will cost to finish the project on schedule.

### 9.4.2.5  Multi-Estimates Charts

Multi-estimates charts show the differing estimates about tasks from different people in 3D bar charts or boxes (e.g., differing estimates of task risk or complexity). These charts allow managers to use their expertise in quantifying certain parameters, such as risk and complexity, relevant to the project. These judgments may then be incorporated within other charts. For instance, Figure 9.16 illustrates the process of collecting judgments about the complexity of various tasks within a project. In this case, the manager estimates how *relatively complex* each task is (with respect to the other tasks in the project). For each task the complexity estimate can be made by different estimators with different confidences. 100% means most complex and 0% means least complex.

### 9.4.2.6  Traditional Charts

The new types of chart described above augment, rather than replace, the charts that have traditionally been used for project management. However, even the traditional charts may be improved with appropriate computer presentation.

One aspect of projects that traditional charts have focused on is the budget. The budget is a large part of any project and is of particular interest to the finance department. How much money will be required must constantly be monitored. If the required amounts of funding are too high, the project may run out of cash. Or it may take more time to finish, as fewer resources are dedicated to it and time is used to get more funding.

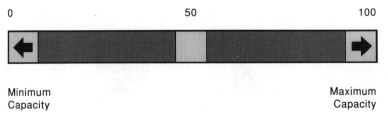

Consider task installation. Use the slide bar below to indicate the complexity of that task relative to other tasks in the project.

0                    50                    100

Minimum                              Maximum
Capacity                             Capacity

**Figure 9.16** Judging task complexity.

Tasks on the critical path may be given a higher funding priority, while other, noncritical, tasks get delayed. This is one way to reduce short term financial requirements without delaying the end date of the project. However, there is still a resource being consumed in this case. Tasks that are off the critical path have slack time. This is the time at the end of the noncritical tasks, over which they can be extended. Slack time is an important resource. However, when the slack time for a task is used up, that task ends up on the critical path. Thus the project manager may need to evaluate both the budgetary issues in a cost-based Gantt chart and the scheduling issues in a PERT chart in order to find a viable strategy for prioritizing tasks and allocating resources.

The budget-task pie chart shows the proportion of budget (relative to the budget of the main task) allocated to each of the subtasks. The graph may be displayed not only in different colors but in different shading patterns. The budget graph has three labels. These labels identify the subtask, state the percentage completion, and give the numerical value from which the proportion was calculated.

A project visualization system can call upon a wide variety of different charts and graphs relating to a variety of important issues such as costs, duration, and risk. However, to be effective, these different views of a project must be integrated within an effective and easy user interface. The following section will show how hyperdata may be used to create such an interface.

### 9.4.3 Exploration and Project Visualization

One of the conclusions drawn in Chapter 6 was that due to the way in which it developed, hyperinformation has become closely associated with text browsing, while there are many promising applications in the areas of data querying, summarization, and visualization that have yet to be developed. This is particularly relevant to project management, where it is imperative that the project manager be able to visualize the progress of the project and anticipate problems.

Hyperdata is a natural interface for project management. It is a commonly accepted truism that the user interface is critical to any application or environment. In the case of project management, a hyperdata interface can link the various views of the project into a coherent and easily visualizable whole.

Multivariate profiles are particularly useful as entry points to project-related data within hyperdata. Charts may also be organized to show the hierarchical structure of tasks and subtasks, resources and resources components, etc., in terms of a hierarchy of pie charts, where the user may "zoom in" to a lower level in the hierarchy by clicking on the corresponding slice of the parent pie chart and may then zoom out to return to the higher level pie chart.

Representations of the project with Gantt and PERT charts are particularly useful when they are linked to hyperdata features. A network may be used to show project interdependencies. Zoom-in and zoom-out capabilities then allow users to move between different project levels.

#### 9.4.3.1 *The Hyperdata Interface*    Hyperdata is the ideal user interface for advanced tools for project visualization because it links the various charts and graphs that are critical for understanding and planning the progress of a project. Project exploration can be

carried out through navigation of the project hyperdata along with other forms of more structured access. This section will consider how project visualizations may be integrated within the hyperdata interface.

A good starting point for visualizing the project is the project network. By double clicking any node in the network, a more detailed view of the project network for the selected node is displayed. The use of colors, shades and size allows the project manager to see very quickly where the problems are. Colors such as green, yellow, and red are used to code dimensions such as risk (e.g., green for low risk and red for high risk).

Hyperdata access provides text displays, graphs, picture images, and diagrams within a multi-window environment. Data visualization provides displays of project schedule, costs, complexity, and risks in terms of 2D and 3D diagrams. Extensive use of graphics and hyperdata makes the project visualization system very easy to use. The following are some brief examples of how the hyperdata interface may be used.

Hypertext may be active for the "Choose Site" task in a Gantt chart layout. The user may then click on the "Choose Site" task and additional text will appear. This text may be the note "Joe Ferrante may be consulted." Alternatively, voice annotation might have been used to attach a message to a node. Another example is the display of resources dedicated to a particular task. A task might be "Level Ground." If this is selected by the user, a dialog will appear displaying the resource list. The resource list might be "Bulldozer, Dump Truck, Earth Mover, . . ."

The budget-task pie chart shows the proportion of budget (relative to the budget of the main task) allocated to each of the subtasks . Hypertext is active during the budget graph. The graph is displayed not only in different colors but in different shading patterns. The budget graph has three labels. These labels identify the subtask, state the percentage completion, and give the numerical value from which the proportion was calculated.

The use of a hyperdata interface does not preclude other forms of interaction in addition to point-and-click navigation. For instance, a query system may inquire, upon user request, what amounts have been paid to, and are budgeted for, contractor X. The user is first given a menu from which to select the contractor to inquire about. Next a set of dates or a period of time may be given from which to select. The amounts paid for a particular month may also be of interest. A query may then be executed based on the selections made. Another type of querying is provided by drill-down access, as explained in the following section.

***9.4.3.2 Hierarchical Charts and Drill Down***     Hierarchically linked charts are particularly useful in project management because they allow the manager to zoom in and out of the information, examining it at different levels of abstraction or detail. Moving from one level of the hierarchical chart to another can be carried out as a hyperdata (zoom in or zoom out) action.

A hierarchical pie chart is a 3D pie chart or a conventional pie chart that is modified so that individual slices within each pie chart are expanded into pie charts of their own. This creates a set of hierarchically linked pie charts that may be used to provide zoom-in, zoom-out views of data at different levels of abstraction or detail.

Similarly, a hierarchical bar chart is a 3D bar chart or a conventional bar chart that is modified so that individual bars within each bar chart are expanded into bar charts of their own (this process is similar to expanding a slice of a pie in a pie chart hierarchy). This creates a set of hierarchically-linked bar charts that may be used to provide zoom-in, zoom-out views of data at different levels of abstraction or detail.

Since Gantt charts are particularly important in displaying project-related information, they may also be expanded into hierarchical structures. A hierarchical Gantt chart, is a 3D Gantt chart or a conventional Gantt chart, that is modified so that individual bars within the Gantt chart are expanded into Gantt charts of their own. This creates a set of hierarchically-linked Gantt charts that may be used to provide zoom-in, zoom-out views of data at different levels of abstraction or detail.

**9.4.3.3** *Converting Project Data to Hyperdata*    The Project Visualization System has to be used effectively if it is to have a positive impact on how well a project is managed. First, the available time resources will have to be budgeted, and this process begins with setting the calendar, which is then used to define the hours that can be worked.

The tasks to be performed in the project should then be defined. Tasks may be organized into related task groups in an outline representation of the project (task hierarchy). Figure 9.17 shows an example of a task hierarchy. The outline view can also be used to schedule multiple projects, where each project is a separate branch at the top level of the hierarchy.

Tasks are special objects that may be defined using forms (cf. Parsaye et al. 1989, Chapter 7). The representation of the task object will include a name and a list of resources that will be involved with the task. The representation of the task object may then be annotated with descriptive comments, and other key parameters such as start and end dates for the task, the task duration or effort required, and whether or not the task has already been started.

The skill in project management comes in defining dependencies (sequencing) between tasks. If all the tasks in a project could be run in any order without damaging the schedule, then the only need would be to schedule the resources so that they are used most efficiently. In practice, however, there are dependencies between tasks, for instance, one can't design a new product without first specifying what the functionality of that product should be.

Dependencies are timing relationships between a predecessor and a successor task. With a complete dependency, the successor task cannot be started until its predecessor is completed. However, partial dependencies can also be defined where the successor task can begin after the predecessor task has been worked on for a while (e.g., Task B might be able to begin after five days of work on Task A).

Once the dependencies have been defined and the resources assigned, a schedule can be constructed and visualized as a Gantt chart. This schedule can then be updated as the project progresses and used to manage and control the project. Other views of the schedule can also be shown (e.g., the hierarchical structure of the schedule).

Thus the first step in converting project information into hyperdata is the specification of the dependencies and the structure of tasks and resources. The project visualization system can then automatically construct the corresponding visualizations. These visualizations are then updated automatically as the underlying data changes.

Develop Specifications
    User Interface
    Functionality
    Data Requirements

Iterative Design
    Build Prototype
        Data Model
        User Interface
        Select Functions
        Coding
    Test Prototype
        Select User Group
        Develop Test Plan
        Run Tests
        Evaluate Usabilitiy
            Statistical Analysis
            Post-Test Interviews
        Write Test Report

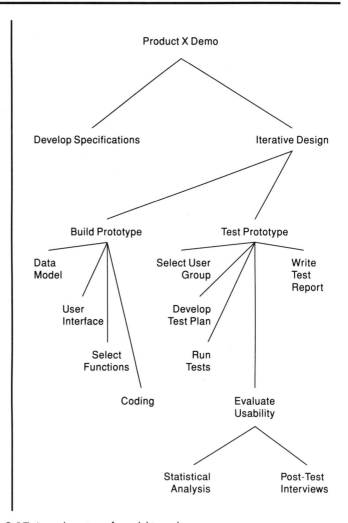

**Figure 9.17** An outline view of a task hierarchy.

The second step in creating the project hyperdata is to create the links between different visualizations, as discussed in the following section.

**9.4.3.4** *Hyperdata and Dynamic Linking*    A major advantage of the project hyperdata system defined here is that links can be defined dynamically as they are needed. Many of these links may be preassigned based on natural correspondences between different charts and graphs. For instance, a Gantt chart showing costs over time may be linked to a PERT representation of the project, and a node within the PERT chart may be linked to a pie chart showing the breakdown of the corresponding task into subtasks.

The task of constructing the hyperdata knowledge base is simpler in project management because of the highly structured nature of project data. Thus when a person clicks on the slice of a pie to get a zoom-in view, the hyperdata link can be calculated, based on a definition of which tasks are the child or subtasks for the task in the selected slice.

The project visualization system automatically creates hyperdata views of database files by plotting the data using hierarchical pie charts, hierarchical bar charts, and hierarchical Gantt charts, along with multivariate pie chart, bar chart, and Gantt chart profiles. Other arrangements of charts and figures may also be used to display visual representations of project resources, costs, and completions. Hyperdata links are then created as needed between corresponding objects, variables, or variable values within data files, charts, figures, and text annotations of the data. The data may then be visualized and browsed using point-and-click navigation.

Project hyperdata can be customized by using dialog boxes to mediate the behavior of links. For instance, when the user clicks on a portion of a pie chart, a set of options are provided for further operation. This allows a deep menu structure to be implemented with less confusion and a clearer indication of submenu relationships. Backtracking is also possible. If a submenu is reached whose choices are unexpected, it is possible that a previous level menu must be corrected. Submenus have a "cancel" option that allow the user to backtrack. After the appropriate number of backtracking steps have been executed, the correct choice can be made. One does not have to "start again from the beginning."

A pie chart may be displayed showing the allocation of time for each of the main tasks. The time taken by a main task is the sum of the time taken by each subtask. While the pie chart is being displayed, the user may select a section of the pie. A new pie chart will be displayed in a window overlaying the previous pie chart. This chart will show the allocation of time for each of the subtasks associated with the pie section chosen previously. The pie section previously chosen will be taken as equal to 100% of the newly displayed pie chart. The sections in the newly displayed pie chart are subtasks.

### 9.4.4 Using Hyperdata in Project Exploration

Hyperdata serves two roles in the project visualization system. First, it is an information-structuring technique that supplements traditional text and record-oriented methods. Second, it is a way of structuring the interface that adds associative links to traditional project manager menu systems.

Links and nodes may be combined with the object-oriented features of the project visualization system for more power. In this way, the charts, graphs, and links of the project visualization may change as the data for the task objects change. For instance, if a task is delayed sufficiently it may become part of the critical path and as it is further delayed, the project will be delayed. This information, which would be part of the object representation of that task would then be propagated to the various views of the project that involve that task and would also affect relevant links between views that involve that project.

The major components of the project visualization user interface contain hyperdata access to two-dimensional and three-dimensional displays of project status. Hyperdata access provides display with texts, graphs, picture images, and diagrams within a multi-window environment with hypertext. Data visualization displays project schedules, costs, complexity, and risks in terms of 2D and 3D diagrams and project networks. Due to its modular design, it is directly connected to multiple underlying databases, which can be easily tailored to specific requirements.

Graph types may be edited within the hyperdata interface. For instance, if the user requests a cost chart showing resource expenditures for all heavy equipment, a graph will be displayed. That graph will show, over time, the $/day for the bulldozer, dump truck, and earth mover. This graph may be labeled "Heavy Equipment." The user may want to add a piece of heavy equipment to the project, such as a steamroller. When the "Heavy Equipment" graph is requested, it will appear as before, but in addition, the steamroller's cost in $/day will be shown, on a new line in a different color.

The project exploration uses hyperdata to switch between the many different components of the project in an easy and natural way. The project manager can move from schedules to budgets to risk analyses through a sequence of point-and-click actions.

### 9.4.5 The Merging of Projects and Presentations

A project is a collection of tasks carried out by a set of resources, under the control of a manager. Coordination is often the most critical part of the project. Coordination in large projects is achieved through communication, principally presentations of one type or another.

The structure of most large projects is defined in and by the various presentations made. Consider the task of constructing a building. The physical tasks will be carried out by construction workers, plumbers, electricians, truck drivers, and so on. However, there is also the planning layer of the project, and this is largely driven by decisions made, or at least elucidated, in presentations. The planning layer exercises supervisory control over the action layer of the project.

The term "supervisory control" refers to tasks where one agent indirectly controls activities through other agents. For instance, modern aircraft are flown by a type of supervisory control. The pilot specifies course, heading, and other general parameters, but no longer directly controls all the flight surfaces of the aircraft, except in special circumstances.

The management of large projects requires a form of multi-agent supervisory control. Consider the task of a wing commander who is trying to coordinate the actions of a squadron of aircraft. First a presentation (briefing) will be made on the ground to ensure that all the pilots are aware of the general plan. Then, further adjustments are made through messages sent when the planes are in the air.

The tasks of squadron leaders are simplified to some extent by the fact that they are clearly in control. In projects, however, there may be a number of specialists who have to negotiate with each other in order to reach agreement on strategies or to extract the relevant information. Even in cases where one person is nominally in charge, they may have to negotiate with others to get access to critical information.

Thus large-scale project management is actually an instance of nonhierarchical multi-agent supervisory control. Negotiation between, and coordination of, the multiple agents (e.g., managers, engineers, information specialists, financial officers, etc.)

is critical. Presentations are the rule rather than the exception.

As projects become ever more complex, and tools for enhancing meetings through groupware improve, presentations and project management are merging to the extent that the overall task of managing a project is becoming equivalent to arranging an appropriate set of presentations and developing a management structure that will enforce the resulting decisions.

### 9.4.6 Presentations in Project Management

The core function of an intelligent database application is the automated generation and sequencing of presentations. This is why project management is a prototypical example of an intelligent database application.

The method of creating presentations for project management is as follows: The data is first subjected to information discovery and descriptive patterns (rules) are generated. These rules are then incorporated within an object model, along with other expert knowledge about the domain. A set of data visualization tools are then defined for the application of interest. In project visualization these include Gantt and PERT/ CPM charts and diagrams. These visualizations are then linked to the object model (defined by the structure of the project data) as necessary. Thus a Gantt chart might refer to time, resources, and tasks.

The object model for the project defines certain objects as resources while others are defined as tasks. The data is then organized in terms of descriptions of the objects at different time intervals. Each task will be cataloged in terms of the resources and time needed for its completion. Using the information in this object model, the visualization system can then automatically construct a Gantt chart representing the actual progress of the project and this can then be compared with the chart showing the original schedule of activities and resources for the project.

Presentations are implicitly linked. A Gantt chart presentation of a project is linked to the budget of that project via the costs associated with the resources required. Thus if the user is viewing an automatically generated Gantt chart of project progress and clicks on a resource, he or she should be able to "pivot" on that resource and move to a budget-oriented representation of that data. This can be done by selecting a resource as the active object and then requesting a new attribute for the presentation.

In this case, a menu of meaningful attributes for the resource object will be shown. One of these attributes will be cost. Once cost has been selected, the active concepts in the object model will be the project, the resources, and the costs associated with the resources. At this point, the user may request that a new presentation be constructed. Given the set of active concepts in the object model, one of the available presentations will be a budget representation, which the user can then choose. The default presentation for this budget information might be a bar chart showing the costs associated with each of the resources used so far in the project.

However, the user may actually be interested in comparing actual costs with scheduled costs. In this case, the scheduled costs need to be active. By clicking on a resource the user returns to the object-attribute menu for resources and chooses scheduled costs. The bar chart representation is now updated so that each resource is represented by two bars, one for schedule costs, the other for actual costs incurred thus far in the project. At this stage the two bars would be distinguished by two different default colors (e.g., blue versus red) or shadings. However, the user can modify these defaults to further customize the presentation. The user can also customize the type of graph used in the presentation, for instance, a pie chart rather than a bar chart.

What this example demonstrates is that interactive presentation of data in the form of user-customized charts and graphs is relatively straightforward as long as the process of presentation and display generation is supported by an adequate model of the project. Furthermore, the point-and-click style of interactively customizing the charts and presentations creates a natural and easily used navigation interface to the project visualization system.

### 9.4.7 Group-Oriented Project Management

Groupware can be used to integrate the project team and support shared work activity. Project status reviews are often used to ensure that the project is on track and to bring the different sources of expertise to bear on the problem simultaneously. However, projects often involve geographically dispersed groups of workers. Thus videoconferencing and other forms of communication technology are needed.

One of the most important classes of groupware for project management involves coordination software. This is particularly important because communications need to be explicit about what is to be done and who is going to do it. In addition, there needs to be some follow-up mechanism to ensure that promised actions really are carried out. Even the best planned project will fail, if the actions specified in the plan are not taken.

Large projects coordinate the efforts of large numbers of different people. The relationships between these people have to be formalized in some way so that things get done on time and to specification. Negotiation is necessary in any project to ensure that people make and keep their commitments. It is the means by which people agree to do certain things at certain times within a project.

Traditionally, negotiation has been a major problem because of the fuzzy and imprecise use of language as a vehicle of communication. The use of language in cross-cultural settings is particularly problematic, because different cultures have different standards and rules about how to act and speak during negotiation. In some cultures, for instance, it is considered to be impolite to say "no" directly to a high status person. Within the culture, this rule is well understood, but an outsider might be in for a rude shock if he or she waits for the actions promised by a polite, but unwilling, "yes."

The solution to the vagaries of language and culture is to formalize the use of language so that the meaning of speech in terms of assertions or commitments made is clearly understood by all parties. In this formal view, speech can be broken down into speech acts of different types, and negotiation and coordination can be based on the assertions and commitments that are indicated in those speech acts. Speech act theory (Searle 1979) provides a convenient framework for describing the way in which negotiation occurs within projects.

Speech acts are important because they provide a standard against which subsequent behavior can be judged. If a promise has been made, has the promised action been carried out and within the time promised? Each speech act has to be judged on the basis of the intention of the utterance. Searle (1979) classified speech acts in terms of five main types.

Assertives commit the speaker to the truth (in varying degrees) of the proposition or assertion that is stated. Directives attempt to make the listener do something. For instance, a question is a directive that directs the listener to make an assertive speech act in response, while commands direct the listener to act in some way. Commissives commit the speaker to a future course of action. Assertives, directives, and commissives are probably the most important type of speech acts for project management. The two other classes are expressives (such as apologizing or praising) and declarations such as pronouncing a couple married (Winograd and Flores 1986, p. 59).

Negotiation of various kinds is necessary to regulate the various requests, promises, and assertions that are made during conversations about collaborative work on a project. The manager then seeks to structure the various requests and promises in carrying out cooperative work.

Coordination software takes the basic ideas of speech act theory and constructs and controls conversation networks in large-scale distributed communications systems (Winograd and Flores 1986, p. 159). Coordination supports such activities as speech act origination, monitoring of task completion, monitoring of temporal aspects of speech acts, display of network status and commitments, and the use of speech act "forms" that serve as templates to handle stereotypical or recurrent types of interaction.

A *request* asks someone to perform an action at some point in the future. Making a request implies a future condition or event that will serve as a satisfactory fulfillment of the request. Requests vary in their strength. An example of a strong request is a driver asking someone to get out of the way, while a weak request is more like a suggestion or invitation. In project management the requesting process needs to be formalized. When a request is made, the time by which the requested action should be completed should also be clearly stated along with the conditions under which the request will be satisfied.

While requests assign actions to other people, *promises* assign actions to the person doing the promising (or to a work group that they represent). Like requests, promises should specify a time of completion and they can vary in their degree of strength. "I'll do the best I can" is a weaker promise than "If I can't finish this job by the end of the month I'll resign." If a promise is a response to a request, then it is obviously important that the conditions of satisfaction are agreed upon by both the requester and the person making the promise.

*Assertions* commit the people that make them to provide evidence in support of the truth of the assertion, should that evidence be asked for. This is obviously far more important in a major project than it is in general conversation. Different standards of evidence may be required in different situations. In general, written documentation will be preferable to reliance on human memory. One of the benefits of collaborative work tools is that they provide an audit trail that serves as evidence of various assertions about commitments or agreements that were made. The presence of this audit trail also serves a motivating function, in that people are held to their word.

In contrast to assertions, *declarations* are judgments rather than factual statements. An example of a declaration might be, "We are spending too much time using electronic mail."

While some conversations plan and discuss actions, other conversations take place within domains of possibility (Winograd and Flores 1986). Various possibilities are discussed about *what* choice or object should be selected, *who* should carry out a task, *how* a task can be performed, and so on. Conversations for possibility generally precede conversations for action. The main difference between the two types of conversation is that those for action produce commitments to action while those for possibilities produce opportunities for commitment to action.

The Coordinator™ is an example of coordination software. Based on speech act theory, it organizes agreements and commitments, for which people are then held accountable in the public record. The software structures conversations for possibilities and conversations for action as part of the coordination process, participants "declare," "promise" and "commit," and articulate the "conditions of satisfaction" of a request.

In The Coordinator's model of the world, there is a process of shifting from possibility to action that roughly approximates the following steps:

1. Declare some possibility for action.
2. Define the conditions of satisfaction for realization of the possibility.
3. Formulate a conversation for action.
4. Commit to action.

In a comparison of work groups using this product in developmental and in action modes (cited in Kling 1991), one study found that the "conversations for possibilities" entailed a "painful" amount of keyboard inputting, created more, not less ambiguity, and were more effectively handled face-to-face. The "action" conversations were direct and more effective. The Coordinator, the study concludes, was helpful for actions but not for developing ideas (Zuboff 1988). Thus the free exchange of unstructured ideas may be inhibited by a built-in "conversational" system, while more structured exchanges (actions) fit comfortably into a regular formula of demand and response.

Studying the way that speech acts and negotiation work makes one realize that project management is not just about setting schedules, it is also about regulating the activity that a schedule requires and about negotiating and monitoring the various commitments to action that are required by the schedule.

Monitored and coordinated speech acts are one way of maintaining the flow of information and commitment in a project. Reports, graphs and charts are also important in sharing vital information about the project. These sources of information often supplement the speech acts that occur with them. For instance, a declaration about the project or some task being late can be backed up by a Gantt chart showing the disparity between the expected completion data and the current date.

### 9.4.8 Requirements and Delivery

Every project is carried out in order to achieve a goal. This goal is often a product, whether it be the construction of a building or the implementation of a large information network.

The general goals of a project have to be made tangible, so that the success of a project can be evaluated. This is done in the initial stages of the project by specifying a set of requirements for the project. Requirements are yardsticks against which the success of the project can be measured.

At the completion of the project the requirements are translated into a set of deliverables (i.e., the things that are actually delivered to the customer). There is usually a gap between the requirements and the deliverables, as shown in Figure 9.18. In general, there will always be some gap, but it should be small enough to be tolerable.

The gap between requirements and deliverables arises because project implementation is not a deterministic process. People get sick, weather gets bad, and resources get scarce for one reason or another. A project might be delayed because vital components are held up in a freight car at the border. Such events are often unpredictable. In the case of project management, Murphy's dictum is: "If anything can go wrong it will, and it will be the thing that you didn't plan for and which will hurt you the most."

From the point of view of specification and evaluation, the sequence of activity in a project is as follows: First the requirements are defined as a set of components or tangible products or milestones that have to be achieved. Then the project as a sequence of actions is formulated in order to create the products and meet the milestones. The project as carried out then creates a set of deliverables and the success of the project is judged by referencing the deliverables back to the requirements. In many cases the success of the project may be mixed. Some requirements may have been exceeded, while others were not met. In general, it is better to meet all the

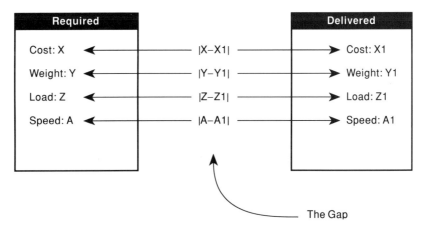

**Figure 9.18** The gap between project requirements and deliverables.

requirements than to greatly exceed some while failing others. However, there is no simple way to evaluate most large-scale projects simply because they involve multiple attributes and goals.

The astute project manager will carry out a process of continuous evaluation. The question uppermost in the project manager's mind should be, which requirements are threatened by the current trend in project activity? Knowing which requirements are under threat allows the manager to take preventive action. The earlier that this knowledge is available, the less costly and painful such preventive actions will be. Project visualization provides the manager with the overall view of the project information that is needed to help identify threatened requirements before they become major glitches. However, other tools may also assist the project manager in evaluating the project and comparing deviations from the original requirements.

Some project requirements typically have to be modified or elaborated over time to make them more specific and to handle changes in the environment and the detailed planning of the project. The remainder of this section will discuss the Requirement Explanation System (RES) that allows project managers and top-level decision makers to gain an understanding of the progress of a project. RES also allows for the development of better requirements by providing a formal requirement specification language.

RES allows base-level requirements to be formally specified using a tree structure. It demonstrates the use of an explanation system for providing interactive information about project status, requirement completion, etc.

RES is implemented as a logic program and uses a number of base tables for retrieving facts. Requirements are specified as a hierarchical system. This means that each requirement may have a number of sub-requirements. In addition to requirements and their hierarchical tree structure, the projects themselves form a tree structure (i.e., each project has a number of sub-projects. There is yet a third tree structure. This corresponds to the physical and CAD representation of the system being built. Generally, here the tree relations are "part-of" relations.

There are three basic graph (or at times tree) structures: requirements, projects, and components. Consider the scenario of building a satellite. There are three structures involved:

1. The requirements for the satellite (e.g., it must be able to send and receive messages at specific frequency ranges, and it must have enough battery life or solar power to last 10 years). These requirements do not specify how things should be done; they specify what is necessary.

2. The project tree specifies "who does what when" in order to achieve the requirements by building specific components. The project tree therefore is an assignment of tasks and timing to various resources: personnel, equipment, etc.

3. The component tree specifies the structure of the satellite and the components that are used within it. For instance, batteries are a component of the electrical system, etc.

There is also a fourth tree, called the functionality tree. This tree represents what is actually being delivered from a project, not what is expected. For instance, the requirement may be that batteries should last 10 years. In reality, the project may only deliver batteries that last six years. Thus, the functionality and the requirements do not match. The question is: "To what extent is this acceptable?"

RES uses several tables to represent the tree structure. The requirement tree is implemented as tables:

1. *Requirement hierarchy table* — shows the list of sub-requirements for each node. Each requirement has some sub-requirements.

2. *Parameter table* — lists the parameters and values associated with each requirement. The parameters and values essentially provide an object representation system. For instance, three parameter requirements for a battery may be:

$$\text{life-time-in-years} \geq 10$$

$$\text{weight-in-pounds} \leq 4$$

$$\text{size-in-cubic-inches} \leq 100$$

The requirement tree gives rise to specific objects which are part of the component tree. Project managers and system designers provide the trees. RES then allows managers and other users to query the requirements and project tables to see how well requirements have been satisfied.

Other facts can be used to link object components to projects. The project component table defines which components are to be delivered by what project. Each project that delivers a component object provides specific values for the attributes of the object. The key function of RES is to detect the gaps between the deliverables and the requirements and explain problems or discrepancies.

RES works as follows. The user begins by specifying a set of requirements, objects and attributes. RES then reads these and begins to compare the requirements with the functionality as being delivered. RES then lists those top-level requirements that are not satisfied and allows the user to interactively zoom in to explanations by selecting sub-requirements and related projects, etc.

The RES interface looks as follows:

*RES > select one of: 1. Requirements satisfaction*
*　　　　　　　　　　 2. ...*
*　　　　　　　　　　 3. ...*

*user > 1.*

*RES > These requirements are not satisfied:　1. batteries*
*　　　　　　　　　　　　　　　　　　　　 2. antennas*
*Please select one.*

*user > 1.*

RES > 1. *battery-weight*
     2. *battery-life*
     *are not satisfied. Please select one.*

*user* > 2.

RES > *The current deliverable from project Plo41 is:*
     *battery-life = 6*

     *while requirement REI says:*
     *battery-life > 10.*

     *Do you wish to see the project manager's explanation notes:*
     *yes*
     *no*
*user* > *yes*

RES > *shows a memo from the project manger*

Thus RES provides an interactive facility for tracking project progress based on functionality.

### 9.4.9  Critical Risk Management

Planning and scheduling is only a part of activity management. Monitoring of project performance is needed to ensure that quality requirements are met and that unexpected occurrences will not delay subtasks and lead to a new critical path and a delayed project. For instance, a manager may be responsible for the production of a report describing what his department has done over the past year. Each member of the department may be assigned a portion of the report to write. Then the copy will be collected and submitted for editing and desktop publishing. The alert manager will monitor activity and ensure that each portion of the report is being written. If he finds that a key project member has been called away, or that two of the staff are involved in a bitter argument over the contents of the report, then he will take steps to overcome these problems before they have an impact on the schedule. Thus the concept of critical risk discussed in this section is often just as important as the concept of critical path in a project.

Every project has some risk associated with it, whether it be the risk of being late, the risk of exceeding budget, or some other risk. Risk can be classified in a number of different ways. For instance, risk may be concerned with internal problems with the project or with adverse impacts that the project has on external environments or systems. For instance, a cost overrun may be bad for the project, or it may have wider consequences, bankrupting a large company, and leading to lost money for investors and lost jobs for employees. The art of critical risk management in a project involves identifying the critical problems and tracking their likelihood, taking steps where necessary to reduce excessive risk.

The functionality of the project as a whole is central to critical risk management (CRM). CRM relies on estimates of how well the system will work if part of the system has reduced functionality. For instance, in building an aircraft, failing to achieve the targeted top speed may have different consequences than failing to achieve the required flying range.

CRM recognizes that the delivered functionality is at least as important as the delivery time. In CRM a project fails not only because it is late, but also if the delivered functionality is not acceptable. In addition, one of the goals of CRM is to detect likely deviations of functionality from requirements early on in the project. Thus CRM is used continuously to monitor the progress and reassess the project risk throughout the life of the project.

CRM is based on the assumption that all projects involve choices and decisions. Therefore in addition to the display of risk, CRM also supports the decision maker with the following information that is available throughout the project: (1) the risk of each component of the project, (2) the existing time and budget for the project, and (3) the new or changed requirements for the system.

One form of visualization that assists in displaying risk-relevant information is the impending risk chart. This chart displays the increasing levels of risk posed by a project with respect to completion time and delay. The impending risk chart can be displayed as a 3D bar graph or a 3D surface graph. The 3D bar graph shows the impending risks of the projects with respect to time (as shown in Figure 9.19). Each bar in the chart may have a color or shading to represent the agency involved. The 3D surface graph shows the variation in risk. With a multi-window project visualization system, both graphs can be viewed at the same time.

Other forms of risk arise from lost opportunities. In leading-edge technology projects, it is often necessary to look for alternative technologies for achieving the goal of the project. Some technologies may work a lot better than others.

Other forms of risk relate to the quality of deliverables, large cost overruns, late delivery, and so on. The combination of risk assessment methods (including expert

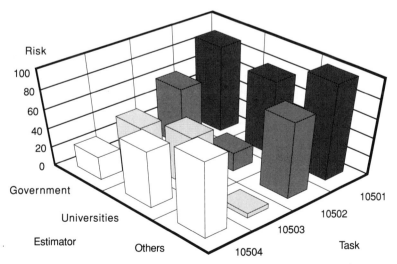

**Figure 9.19** A 3D bar graph showing impending risk. (10501-10504 are codes for project tasks.)

judgment based on usage of the project visualization system) allows the project manager to control risk to the extent possible.

## ■ 9.5 PROJECT MANAGEMENT METHODOLOGIES

The project visualization system provides the tools needed to plan, schedule, and monitor projects. This section will consider the special role that graphs and charts play in project management.

### 9.5.1 Project Monitoring and Control

Project management tools are generally concerned with providing information about project status that can assist in project monitoring and control. Time, cost, and performance form the basis for the operating characteristics of a project. These same factors help determine the basis for project control. The goal of project control is to keep the project on schedule and to minimize the deviation between actual performance and planned performance.

Monitoring is an activity that we humans do naturally and take for granted. However, we are all familiar with projects where no one took responsibility for a particular activity and it was omitted or done poorly. In a large and complex enough project, monitoring can become a problem as it becomes more and more difficult to keep track of every aspect of the numerous subtasks that are involved.

Since projects occur in a dynamic world, complex projects have to deal with changing circumstances and plans and schedules have to be continuously reevaluated. In contrast to basic scheduling, these broader issues of monitoring and evaluation are difficult to quantify and there is still no consensus method for dealing with them. Some of the disturbances that may challenge the manager's control of the project include:

- Change of due dates
- New industry regulations that need time to implement
- Supply delays
- Missed milestones
- Delay of key tasks
- Unreliable time estimates
- Low reliability
- Fragile components
- Cost overruns
- Inadequate resources

The Gantt chart serves as a yardstick for measuring project progress and for providing the information required by project control. Of particular interest is the expected Gantt chart and the actual chart. Examination of the differences between such charts provides an indication of where each activity should be and where it actually is. This information may then be sent to other members of the project team. Schedules generally have milestones and these are used as markers with which to assess slippage. Many activities, such as writing or software development, are hard to monitor because it is difficult to assess the extent of intermediate progress. However, a well-defined milestone is an all or nothing condition that is either satisfied by the time specified, or else the schedule has slipped. Thus plentiful milestones are generally a good way of identifying and controlling problems before they get out of control.

Scheduled variance magnitudes can be plotted on a time scale (e.g., on a daily basis). If the variance continues to get worse, drastic action might be needed. Temporary deviations without a lasting effect on the project might not be a cause for concern.

Cost control is another aspect that can make or break a project. There are well-known examples of buildings that were half finished because the costs had soared and their were no more funds to finish the building. Cost overruns can be particularly damaging to the project's cash flow and they can eventually amount to a point where the project is no longer able to absorb them. Figure 9.20 shows a control chart for cumulative cost. The control limits on the chart are indexed to the project percent complete. At each percent complete point, there is a control limit that the cumulative project cost is not expected to exceed. Figure 9.20 shows an example where the cumulative cost of the project is actually out of control at a couple of points, as marked in the figure. In the first case, the control limit indicated that no more than 28% of the budget should be consumed when the project was 20% completed. However, this control limit was exceeded because the actual amount of the budget used to that point was 30%. In the second out-of-control situation, 55% of the budget had been spent when the project was only 40% completed. (The control limit for that point was 50% of budget.)

The complexity of tracking costs in a large project can be so great that manual cost tracking is almost impossible. Thus computer accounting systems are often used to track project costs. Ten key issues that management must address (Heid 1991) are:

1. Proper planning of the project to justify the basis for cost elements
2. Reliable estimation of time, resources, and cost
3. Clear communication of project requirements, constraints, and available resources
4. Sustained cooperation of project personnel
5. Good coordination of project functions
6. Strict policy of expenditure authorization
7. Timely recording and reporting of project resource usage time, materials, labor, and budget
8. Frequent review of project progress
9. Periodic revision of schedule to account for the current status of the project
10. Critical evaluation of budget depletion versus actual progress

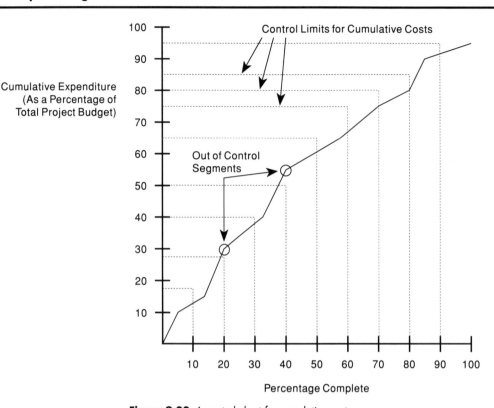

**Figure 9.20** A control chart for cumulative cost.

When variances (deviations) are observed between plan and actual progress, appropriate replanning may be carried out to bring the project back into line with the original objectives. Control limits can be incorporated into charts to indicate when actions should be taken. task duration, quality, or resource utilization. Thus the information obtained from project monitoring can be converted into meaningful charts that indicate when control actions are needed.

### 9.5.2 Product Management

Product management includes not only management of the various subassemblies of versions of the product or system being developed, but also the management of change. Consider for instance, the building of a commuter aircraft. At a certain point in the project a competitor may announce a similar aircraft with a more attractive price and performance for the market segment of interest. Subsequently it may be decided to modify the product design in some way, therefore fundamentally changing the nature of the project. Similarly, a highway development may be modified at a late stage to include sound protection barriers for portions of the highway passing through a residential community. It is rarely the case that the product or system remains unchanged throughout the course of a project.

Even if the specification of the product remains stable, people's perceptions and understanding of the product will change over time. Thus as more details about the product or system are known, trade-offs, conflicts and constraints become apparent, and these will affect the way that various subtasks are defined.

### 9.5.3 Project Planning

A project is an activity with well-defined goals. This activity is complex enough that subtasks require careful coordination and control in order to meet the project goals which are expressed as a set of performance, cost, and time targets (Meredith and Mantel 1989). Once an activity and accompanying goals have been defined, a suitable project plan must be developed for achieving those goals.

Many of the skills that are later required in project management also apply in project planning. The project needs to be represented in terms of a set of tasks and subtasks, resources need to be assigned to these tasks and the tasks need to be scheduled. In addition, decisions have to be made about the best strategy for achieving a goal, often in the face of considerable uncertainty. For instance, in some countries certain construction projects might have to be handled differently in the rainy season, or various tasks may be planned although shipment of some of the required materials may be in question. Thus project planning is a classic case of planning and decision making under uncertain conditions.

A major initial step in project planning is the development of a suitable mission statement and a set of performance goals or criteria of success that are to be achieved. As well as clarifying the goals of the project the mission statement is also an important communication to the rest of the project team. The goals of the project should be understood and shared by the other members of the team. Another feature of project planning is the breaking up of the project into phases such as planning, design, implementation, and testing (i.e., the procedural flow of the task) and the definition of tasks and subtasks within each phase.

A useful heuristic during project planning is to build extra time into the schedule. This is particularly important in the case of uncertainties such as whether a supplier can or will deliver essential parts on time as promised. There should also be contingency plans in case Murphy's Law applies and things start going wrong. Naturally the critical path in the project is the most sensitive to slippage and any problems in the critical path soon start delaying the entire project.

Once a project is planned and initiated a battle ensues to maintain the plan against the forces of entropy. Active management is required to keep the project on track. Bad weather, sickness of critical personnel, and so on can all take their toll on the schedule. Some of these problems will be difficult to circumvent and should be built into the planning fudge factors. However, other problems need to be dealt with speedily and effectively before they start affecting the whole project. The task of project management is to monitor the project and recognize and deal with such problems.

Project management tools have generally been seen as ways of assigning resources to tasks so as to complete projects in reasonable time while utilizing resources effectively. However, the goal of project management is not to optimize criteria such as cost or quality on the basis of a static world, but rather to guide decision making in the face of an uncertain and dynamically changing environment. The task of managing a bakery is very different from managing a domestic kitchen, because the manager is not worried just about basic task sequencing, but also about issues such as conflicts between resources. Presumably a project management tool should not only tell the manager how to plan the overall projects, it should also assist in deciding what to do if the most skilled and productive baker is injured during a particularly important job.

Techniques such as PERT/CPM focus on the problem of scheduling project activities. However, PERT/CPM do not provide managerial tools for actually administering the schedule and ensuring that the various reallocations of resources actually take place. In reality, projects generally involve large numbers of people and various forms of communication. Negotiation must be carried out to resolve conflicts and implement decisions, and in some cases it may even be necessary to renegotiate some of the goals of the project.

## ■ 9.6 CONCLUSIONS

Computer systems greatly assist in the automatic tracking and management of projects. However, today's very large-scale and complex projects defy project management systems that are based on the technologies of the 1970s. This chapter developed extensions to project management (project visualization) that use recent technical advances such as hyperdata, interactive 3D graphics, executive support systems, and risk management to provide the required framework for managing projects successfully. In particular, this chapter showed how traditional charts and graphs for projects could be extended to include the third dimension, and how these visualizations could then be incorporated within a hyperdata system for project visualization. Since Gantt and PERT charts have proved to be so useful in project management, it is not surprising that the most useful new graph types for project management tend to be 3D versions of Gantt and PERT charts.

Making strategic decisions during the course of a project requires the manager to have a good sense of what the project is about, how it is proceeding, and how different combinations of resources can be used to complete the various tasks. A Project Visualization System supports this strategic decision making by providing a kind of "information spreadsheet," which will help to visualize the requirements and progress of the project. A project manager must remember a lot of information. Hyperdata is an interface paradigm that gives the project manager the opportunity to become familiar with the data.

None of the traditional models of project management include the notion of "functionality" or "quality" (i.e., how well a project is completed). This is not something that a project visualization system addresses directly, but good project visualization is an important component of quality management and risk management. Thus intelligent database applications for project management greatly enrich current methods of project management.

# 10

# MARKETING

*If marketing is seminally about anything, it is about achieving customer-getting distinction by differentiating what you do and how you operate. To differentiate an offering effectively requires knowing what drives and attracts customers. It requires knowing how customers differ from one another and how those differences can be clustered into commercially meaningful segments. If you're not thinking segments, you're not thinking.*

— Theodore Levitt*

## ■ 10.1 INTRODUCTION

Within the twentieth century alone there have been massive changes in many technologies and infrastructures of society. One place where this is clearly indicated is in the modern distribution of goods, supported by the growth of advertising, marketing, and the creation of the consumer society.

It is easy to forget how the distribution methods on which society is based have changed in the past two generations. When major societal changes are mentioned, they often refer to mechanical marvels such as cars and airplanes or social phenomena such as fashion and music. Yet great changes have occurred in the way in which goods are produced and consumed. Hardly any households make their own soap any more. The fact that households do not make their own soap may not seem particularly staggering, but it is a key indication of a major change in the flow of goods and services that occurred in the twentieth century.

Soap is just one of many products that is now bought in standardized packages. Industrialized nations have become consumer societies where average people do not produce the vast majority of the items they use. Where once a person may have

---

* *Marketing Imagination,* Macmillan, NewYork, 1986. Theodore Levitt was born in 1925 in Germany and received a PhD in economics from Ohio State University. He taught business at Harvard and was an editor of the *Harvard Business Review.* He originated several new concepts in marketing, including "market myopia."

plucked a feather and fashioned it into a quill, now a large variety of off-the-shelf writing instruments is widely available.

This is not to say that everyone always made their own soap in earlier times. In ancient Egypt, Greece, and Rome, patrician classes devoted themselves to war, arts, politics, and religion, while the production of the goods and artifacts that they used (from soap to swords) was carried out by artisans, laborers, and slaves.

What is unique about modern Western society is that the vast majority of people are predominantly consumers. With mass production and high technology, slavery is no longer needed to support the needs and luxuries of the consumer class. Differences between rich and poor remain, of course, but that distinction is reflected in the quantity of goods consumed, and the quality (brand), rather than in the earlier distinction that the poor produce and the rich consume.

Those who try to produce more than a very small fraction of the items they use are generally considered to be cranks or ideologues. It is difficult for people to justify making the products that they use. The economies of scale and the effectiveness of the mass market make it more expensive for people to make their own household goods than to buy a product from the store.

In many ways consumers are defined by the products they use, and the products they use change them in subtle but important ways. However, some products have a more obvious effect. For instance, an examination of the pictures of soldiers in the American Civil War shows that beards were generally worn. This was probably due to necessity and convenience as much as to fashion. Prior to the development of the safety razor, shaving was carried out with the aptly named cutthroat razor, a dangerous tool in the hands of the unskilled, and one whose use was best left to a skilled barber. Thus shaving was an expensive or dangerous business. The Gillette safety razor changed the rules for shaving. The blades were disposable, so that the user could always shave with a sharp blade, and the level of skill required (and the associated risk to major blood vessels) was much lower.

In this chapter, an intelligent database approach for solving problems of relevance to market segmentation and product positioning is developed. Traditional methods of market research (e.g., using questionnaires and interviews) can be very costly and do not provide up to the minute information. In contrast, this chapter discusses the use of data sources such as point of sale information to provide almost instantaneous feedback on how consumers are responding to products.

This chapter begins with a discussion of the history and evolution of marketing, focusing on issues such as the development of the mass market and the consumer society in the early twentieth century. Basic issues in marketing are then discussed, particularly the issue of market segmentation which is a major focus of this chapter. The various sources of market data are reviewed and classified in terms of product, consumer, and geography. The use of intelligent database tools in marketing is discussed. How information about demographics and life-styles can be utilized in product innovation, product positioning, and in targeted marketing is considered. This chapter also describes the market analysis and segmentation system, an intelligent database tool for market analysis. The chapter concludes with a discussion of marketing methodologies and the use of clustering to identify market segments.

## ■ 10.2 HISTORY AND EVOLUTION OF MARKETING

Sales and marketing are essential traits of most civilizations. While modern forms of marketing and the consumer society have only become prominent within the past century, the careful identification of likely customers and the use of persuasion in selling are age-old practices.

### 10.2.1 History

Since the Stone Age, bartering of goods has been the basis of commerce. The silk route was one of the first attempts at international sales and marketing. Other valued commodities traded over large distances in the ancient world included gold and a variety of easily transported items.

Early forms of payment involved barter. Objects were exchanged according to differences in perceived value. Animal meat might be exchanged for wheat, and so on. In advanced economies bartering was eventually replaced by a currency that was perceived to have relatively fixed value. The use of currency facilitated the exchange of goods and services. This innovation is important because bartered materials often vary wildly in value depending on supply and demand. Thus a bag of wheat might be much more valuable in the dead of winter than at harvest time. As societies advanced, surplus wealth was created, and luxury items were traded. Jewelry and cosmetics were examples of goods whose value was determined to some extent by fashion.

The idea that something could be fashionable meant that it no longer had a fixed or inherent value. Its value could be modified by creating a fashion for it. Evidence for the existence of fashions in clothing, accessories, and even eating utensils can be seen in the earliest civilizations. These fashions were often set by the leaders of the power elite such as royalty and members of the ruling class. The forerunners of today's advertisers may well have pointed out that products they were selling were in use by the king or whomever, in the same way that royal patronage has been a significant factor in British advertising over the past few centuries. The term, "by appointment to her Majesty" appears on some British goods and can translate to millions of dollars of sales. To obtain such a mark the product has to be endorsed by the monarchy. In other countries sports figures, etc., endorse a wide range of products for promotional fees.

Paper currency was a further step in the development of the modern economy. The use of paper currency allowed the supply of money to be set according to the goods and services available, rather than according to the limited amount of gold, shells, beads, or whatever precious or comparatively rare commodity was being used as currency. Since a currency note was no longer intrinsically valuable, the value of the note was created by being a standardized artifact that could only be produced by the treasury. Thus the value of the paper currency came jointly from the production monopoly exercised by the treasury and from the fact that people recognized it as being equal in value to its face value equivalent in bartered goods.

The use of paper currency promoted the growth of capital through the linkage of money to goods and services rather than the inherent worth of the currency as an object. The growth of capital and surplus wealth increased after the industrial revolution with the availability of relatively cheap mass produced goods.

There is little need for sophisticated marketing to sell sausages in a starving city. Marketing became important when people had a choice about what to purchase. Once currency and systems of sale are in place, along with sufficient surplus wealth to motivate sales by persuasion, there are two key questions for a person selling goods: How does one find people likely to buy one's merchandise? How does one convince them to buy?

These two issues gave rise to the science of marketing. As society became more complex, it became essential to be selective in identifying likely candidates. Those who selected their targets appropriately achieved better sales with less effort. One of the techniques used in early marketing was "product enhancement" carried out by those selling the goods. For instance, a farmer might polish his apples or sprinkle water over them in the market to make them look fresher (a practice still continued in modern supermarkets). Similarly shop displays often use special lighting today to make products look more attractive.

Marketing as a more formal discipline practiced by specialists began as a reaction to the needs of the mass market that developed in the nineteenth and twentieth centuries. Early marketing in the nineteenth century proceeded largely on the basis of trial and error. In the late nineteenth century the critical twentieth century concept of a brand was still largely unknown, and most products were identified by the name of the retailer rather than the name of the manufacturer. More modern marketing developed as techniques of mass production created surplus goods and producers scrambled to create a market of consumers willing to purchase these goods through a combination of product design, advertising, and effective distribution.

The ability of a major manufacturer to create a market for a product was shown prior to the first world war by the introduction of Procter and Gamble's Crisco as a replacement for animal lard. Procter and Gamble was then mostly a soap company that wanted to ensure its supply of cottonseed oil (a key ingredient in its soap). Crisco served as a replacement for lard and used a large amount of cottonseed oil. If Crisco was successful then it provided a whole new market for cottonseed oil and put Procter and Gamble in a stronger position when purchasing its raw materials. When Crisco was developed, there was no guarantee that it would be snapped up by a willing public. In fact, a somewhat similar product ("Cottolene") made of cottonseed oil mixed with animal fat had failed a few years earlier.

Widespread acceptance of Crisco by the public followed four years of determined advertising by Proctor and Gamble (Strasser 1989). In 1912 Crisco was advertised in national magazines, and cooperating storekeepers wrote letters to their customers enclosing booklets about Crisco and offering to add it to the delivery order. Demonstrators also toured cities throughout the United States, conducting week-long cooking schools. Some of these demonstrations led to newspaper articles about the product. Procter and Gamble also published booklets of Crisco recipes to further stimulate demand.

The Crisco advertising campaign anticipated the modern concepts of market segmentation and product positioning. For instance, a number of railroads adopted Crisco after a special 10-pound container was created for compact dining-car kitchens, and special packages were marked with the seals of rabbis (who pronounced the contents kosher), advertised in the Yiddish media and sold in Jewish neighborhoods.

The new mass market products of the early twentieth century created new habits and life-styles. Extensive advertising was used to convince people that they needed products such as chewing gum and flashlights that they hadn't even imagined previously. One of the early pioneers of the field of "Scientific Advertising" was Claude Hopkins, whose advertising methods helped Anheuser Bush capture a significant share of the beer market. Hopkins's method of advertising focused not only on the creation of the image, but on test trials and tabulation methods for responses. His methods apply today as well as they did then. Later, advertising became a major industry, claiming a percentage of all media revenues. Thus the triad of advertising agency, medium (e.g., newspaper), and manufacturer was born.

This process of creating demands for new products that change people's life-styles is still continuing. For instance, IBM's "Charlie Chaplin" advertisements for the personal computer that appeared in the early 1980s were aimed at altering the perception of the computer from being a tool for rocket scientists to something that anyone could use in the home or office.

Today's "educational" advertising about new products was preceded by similar educational advertising at the turn of the century. People who had formerly bought cereal in bulk were taught to buy packaged breakfast cereals. People who had never shaved were told how important it was to be clean-shaven, and people who had been shaved by the barber were taught how to shave themselves using safety razors.

Advertising campaigns were used to educate people about a variety of new products, and they were so successful that these products are now taken for granted. The effectiveness of advertising campaigns demonstrated the malleability of consumer markets.

The creation of consumer markets for a wide variety of products that affect every aspect of people's lives has led to the present day consumer society. Improvements in packaging, transportation, and communication allowed products to be shipped over large distances and advertised effectively. As packaging and distribution of products improved, more and more people found it easier to consume and use ready-made products than to go without or make their own. For instance, the safety razor took a commonplace task and made it considerably easier and safer. Once people learned how to use the new tool it became entrenched as a routine part of their life. Industrialization and mass production allowed goods to be produced on the scale required for a consumer society.

The application of marketing has been pursued enthusiastically, and in ever more sophisticated ways, since the end of the nineteenth century. Attempts to explain why marketing works, and how to make it better, also date back to that time. The use of the term "marketing" surfaced sometime after 1900, appearing in the title of a course that was offered at the University of Pennsylvania in 1905 (Bartels 1965). Prior to 1900, the activity of marketing had been subsumed under general activities associated with trade, distribution, and exchange. The process of communicating the customer's needs to the manufacturer was at best haphazard, and as a result the rate at which products and markets developed was relatively slow.

The decade between 1910 and 1920 was a time of increasing urbanization and industrialization. New products were being developed, and they required more sales effort and better quality advertising. Greater awareness of the need for marketing led to description of the major concepts and tools in books, including early books on advertising and the elements of marketing (Cherington 1913, 1920).

One of the key contributions of early marketing was the recognition that the relationship between producer and consumer (seller and buyer) should be a cooperative one rather than a competitive one. While earlier practices of bargaining over price and letting retailers set any price they wanted, emphasized the competitive aspect, educating consumers about new products they could use was part of a new, more cooperative approach. The old competition between producer and consumer was being replaced by more cooperation between producer and consumer, with alternative suppliers competing for the loyalty and custom of the consumer. Producers could only hope to shift allegiances of consumers to the new product if they could convince consumers that it was advantageous for them to do so.

The concept of fixed prices for packaged goods confirms this cooperative relationship between producer and consumer. An interesting historical case in this regard was Hachirobei Mitsui (of the Mitsui group) who in 1673 succeeded exceptionally well because his store was the first shop in Tokyo to sell cloth for a fixed length and price, without bargaining (i.e., he succeeded by cooperating with the customer). When one reduces confusion for consumers, they buy more and more easily. The reverse of this was the VAX configuration problem for DEC equipment in the 1980s, where the bewildering array of peripherals and prices available for VAXes made the purchase a serious undertaking.

However, after packaging has made the concept of the product uniform, competition calls for differentiation. The trend towards differentiation met the needs and interests of different market segments. The most obvious early market segments were based on economic class and on culture. This was particularly true in the multi-ethnic American society of the early twentieth century where about a third of the population were either born overseas or had parents who were. There was generally a strong correlation between shopping districts and economic class, so that "higher quality" products could be sold in the higher quality shopping districts (e.g., Michigan Avenue in Chicago). Similarly, many shopping districts or individual shops were identified with a particular ethnic or religious group, again allowing a very focused kind of product positioning.

Interest in explicit marketing research developed in the 1920s and was reflected in the use of questionnaires in analyzing markets and marketing. The trend towards more rigorous marketing methodology increased in the 1930s as simple opinion surveys were replaced by more complex questionnaire investigations aimed at providing more comprehensive knowledge of markets. However, in spite of the apparent progress and rigor, until the 1950s, there remained doubts about how much progress marketing had really made.

While the theory of marketing may have been problematic, the application of marketing in the form of advertising grew by leaps and bounds as the media of radio and television provided new ways to influence people. The manipulative aspect of advertising was once seen as pernicious (Packard 1957), but today advertising is so pervasive that it is taken for granted in the era of the thirty-second sound bite.

As discussed later in this chapter, the field of psychographics has also had a key impact on modern marketing and marketing research.

The origins of psychographics go back to the 1930s and the competition between large consumer oriented corporations for more market share. At this time, corporate America would try anything that would provide a competitive edge—as it still does. Two distinct groups of experts that corporate executives turned to were psychologists and statisticians. In both cases, the resulting increase in sales was significant, resulting in the emergence of two distinct (and polarized) vectors for marketing research.

To trace the origins of psychographics, we have to go back to Ernest Dichter, a Viennese psychologist who fled Austria just before the second world war, borrowing his way to New York (Piirto 1991). Dichter tried to apply psychology to product marketing research, but at first was laughed at. After several attempts, he was assigned the task of analyzing Ivory Soap at Proctor and Gamble, had a spectacular success, and was featured in Time Magazine in 1939. This was follwed by his successful psycho-analyses of the advertisements for Plymouth at Chrysler. Dichter's approach was non-statistical and relied on interviewing methods used by the psychoanalysts. Later, Dichter formed the Institute for Motivational Research.

One of Dichter's best known successes was Betty Crocker cake mixes at General Mills in the 1950s. The original recipe for the cake mix required only water, but was not a success. Dichter realized that just adding water to the cake mix made housewives feel "unimportant," so they often added milk or eggs to the recipe (despite the instructions) anyway—ruining the taste. When the Betty Crocker recipe was modified to allow the preparer to "participate" more in the baking process by adding milk and eggs, the product became a success.

However, Dichter was not always well accepted. His suggestion to change the color of tea to men's favorite color (namely *blue*) was not followed—needless to say! Nor was his suggestion to American Airlines to install oak beams on the cabin ceiling of aircraft to make passengers feel safer! In fact, Dichter's controversial views gave rise to a heated debate about how marketing research was to be done.

The opposing camp to Dichter's motivational approach was the statistical methods promoted by Alfred Politz. A well-known statistician who consulted for the marketing departments of Time and Life magazines, Politz considered motivational research "pseudo-science"—Dichter in turn called Politz's research "nose counting." Politz was joined in his attacks on Dichter by Elmo Roper, who formed the Roper Organization, and later by George Gallup who went on to become a well-known pollster.

The term "psychographics" itself only appeared much later in the mid-1960s. It is either due to Russel Haley of Grey Advertising or Emanuel Demby, who once worked with Dichter.

In time, Dichter's basic point (Dichter 1947) that "You can not describe a person simply on the basis of age, income, and marital status" became accepted by more market researchers. Eventually, after 40 years of arguing, the two sides started to agree with each other — the motivational people now use statistics and the statisticians use motivational criteria in their studies!

By the late 1960s the field of psychographics was taken seriously by many corporations and better tools became available. Daniel Yankelovitch invented the

Yankelovitch Monitor which measured attitudes and lifestyles (Yankelovitch 1964, 1981). Another key contribution came in 1978 from Arnold Mitchell at SRI International in terms of the VALS system (Mitchell 1983).

Interestingly, Mitchell's road to success was almost the opposite of Dichter's celebrated application of his academic training from Vienna. Mitchell described his training as "poetic" and had no schooling in any related field, except for literature. He was hired at SRI as a technical writer, but soon showed the initiative to lead the VALS project by drawing on the needs hierarchy of Abraham Maslow (Maslow 1970, 1971). In 1987, SRI began the development of VALS 2 system.

By the early 1980s psychographics were widely used by a large number of organizations: MasterCard used them to create the "Master the Possibilities" campaign, while Cezar Chavez and the United Farm Workers Union used them to better focus their direct mail campaign towards Mitchell's Socially Conscious group (Piirto 1991).

Thus after 30 years, the industry fully accepted the title of Yankelovitch's article: "A Marketing Concept should be the Sum of Psychoanalysis and Nose-Counting" (Yankelovitch 1958). In this chapter we suggest that: "A Marketing Concept should be the Sum of Psychoanalysis, Nose-Counting, and Rule Analysis," (i.e., one can use discovery to identify new types of segments).

Thus, modern marketing is now an advanced and complex business. Modern methodologies for market research range from sampling, surveys, and scaling, to information discovery, regression, factor analysis, and multidimensional scaling.

Modern marketing has become heavily dependent on behavioral research and market segmentation as shall be seen in the remainder of this chapter. In addition, marketing strategies have had to adjust to differing rates of innovation for different products. For instance, innovative products like video camcorders and highly portable cassette recorders (e.g., the Walkman) almost sold themselves (once there was sufficient awareness and availability of the product) because they matched the wishes and perceived needs of many potential customers. In contrast, marketing is still key for products with large and stable markets (e.g. beer, soap, glass). For products such as these manufacturing and production methods have stabilized for the moment. These types of product involve mature technologies where there is little competitive advantage to be gained for product innovation. The key to win in selling these products is marketing.

**Figure 10.1** Marketing as a process of communication between producer and consumer.

## ■ 10.3 BASIC CONCEPTS OF MARKETING

One of the issues in marketing is the process of communication between producer and consumer (Figure 10.1). In the consumer society the consumer and the producer are mutually dependent upon one another, and this dependence requires effective communication. The producer communicates to consumers through advertising. Consumers communicate to the producer through their product preferences as expressed in their purchase decisions. Marketing further amplifies and facilitates the communication between consumer and producer through various research methods such as surveys and focus groups, and through scientific analysis of different market segments and their preferences for products.

Marketing may be thought of as a chain of derived demand that begins with the consumer and works back through retailers and wholesalers, to manufacturers and parts suppliers (Figure 10.2). However, the massed responses of consumers within markets are malleable to some extent, and thus the communication between the consumer and manufacturing is modified somewhat by advertising and by the actions of the retailer.

Applying the analogy of a food chain to marketing, manufacturers and retailers feed off the customer, advertisers feed off the manufacturers and retailers, and the media (newspapers, magazines, radio, television) feed off the advertisers (Figure 10.3). This "food chain" has evolved into a complex web of interrelationships where

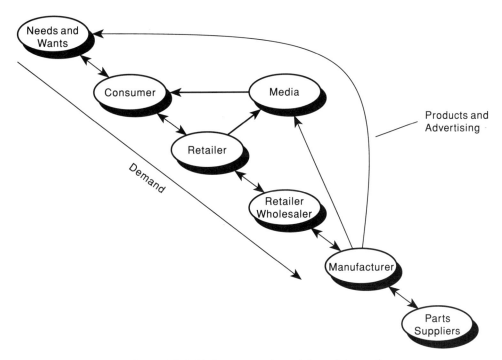

**Figure 10.2** Marketing as a chain of derived demand.

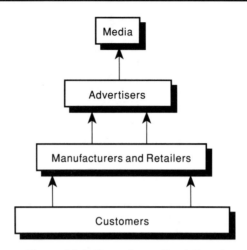

**Figure 10.3** The marketing "Food Chain."

there is a mutual dependency among all the parties (Figure 10.4). For instance, the information that consumers receive in the form of newspapers and television programs is subsidized by advertising, which is in turn subsidized by the purchasing behavior of those same consumers.

Market research is a complex business and there have been numerous attempts to define what exactly market research is. For instance, market research is "a formalized means of obtaining information to be used in making marketing decisions" (Tull and Hawkins 1987, p. 5). Or, more formally, "Marketing research is the function that links an organization to its market through information. This information is used to identify and define marketing opportunities and problems: generate, refine and evaluate marketing actions; monitor marketing performance and improve understanding of marketing as a process. marketing research specifies the information required to address these issues; designs the method for collecting information; manages and implements the data collection process; interprets the results and communicates the findings and their implications" (American Marketing Association).

In fact there are many definitions of marketing. From the perspective of intelligent databases, market research is a process of collecting, analyzing, and interpreting information. Thus two driving elements of marketing are information and decisions. Marketing information supports a variety of decisions relating to such issues as: product design; advertising strategy; production policy (how much stock to produce or store in inventory). This section examines the nature of the marketing problem and the way in which fragmented markets require careful segmentation and appropriate product positioning.

### 10.3.1 The Marketing Problem

Marketing is a difficult but crucial part of the consumer society. For any business the environment is both a threat (challenge) and an opportunity. The challenge of the business environment stems from the way in which resource availability, customer

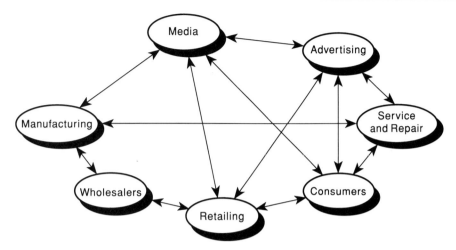

**Figure 10.4** Mutual dependencies in marketing.

needs, and the nature of competition are continually changing. Marketing is a response by businesses to the environment they find themselves in. Some of the activities involved include:

- Forecasting current and future demand
- Market analysis and planning
- Distribution
- Service and quality assurance
- Advertising
- Product planning
- Product testing and pricing

Like design, software engineering, and many other activities, marketing may be thought of as a cycle (Bayliss 1985). The cycle begins with information gathering as shown in Figure 10.5. It then proceeds to analysis and forecasting, strategic analysis and planning, product development and production, advertising, distribution, and market testing and quality assurance. This cycle is then repeated continuously during the life of a product or product line.

In reality, the market cycle is not nearly as smooth as the idealized view shown in Figure 10.5. Products and markets change over time, and sometimes these changes can be very abrupt, particularly in a highly competitive market. One of the biggest challenges for marketing is market fragmentation, where society is becoming more diverse, and people are expecting more and more diversity in the products that are available to them.

Data, or more generally information, is the lifeblood of marketing. Marketing data is used to understand which people are attracted to products and why. There are many

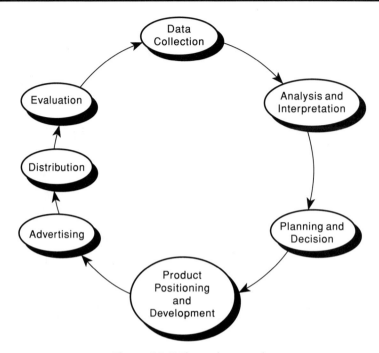

**Figure 10.5** The marketing cycle.

reasons why people might be attracted to a product. For instance, customers tend to be attracted to products that reflect the image they have of themselves (Dolich 1969). Marketing success depends on understanding and meeting consumer needs more quickly than competitors, and this in turn requires the collection of appropriate data.

Perhaps the greatest problem with using surveys and questionnaires is that it is difficult to establish validity. What people say they like may not be what they end up buying, and the samples that are collected by the marketing research team may be biased for any number of reasons. Some people may elect not to participate in the sample while others will tend to volunteer enthusiastically. It is possible that there may be some kind of link between this type of behavior and product usage. These concerns about sample validity should not be put aside easily.

A well-known example of sampling bias in data collection is the "President Dewey" case. In 1948 Truman and Dewey were contesting the U.S. presidential election. A telephone survey predicted that Dewey would win easily, but the reverse happened. The telephone survey had in fact created a biased sample since telephones were much less prevalent at that time than they are now, and there was a much higher proportion of Republican voters among telephone owners than in the general population.

As if sampling bias were not enough, there is also the problem of observation bias. In one famous study a group of workers were observed after their work situation had been modified. Their productivity improved. Then the work situation was changed again and the productivity remained high. After a while however, output returned to prior levels. It turned out that it was not the changes in the workplace that were having the biggest impact on performance, but rather the fact that the workers were being "observed." This "Hawthorne effect" (named after the place where it was first discovered) is well known and makes any intrusive observation of human behavior problematic.

There are a wide variety of data collection tools in market research. However, they will only be mentioned briefly as the emphasis in this chapter is on how to utilize marketing information rather than how to acquire it.

In most instances data is not very useful in its raw form. Thus there are a number of data analysis tools for interpreting and refining data. For segmenting markets and describing the resulting segments, cluster analysis, multidimensional scaling, conjoint analysis, and factor analysis have become prominent in the marketing literature.

For marketing purposes, data analysis tools need to address the following questions:

1. What are the critical features of a product that determines the purchasing decisions of customers?
2. What are the critical features of consumers that predict their response to products?
3. What identifiable segments exist in the market of interest (i.e., what are the identifiable clusters of people who respond to products in similar ways)?
4. What is the rule for assigning people to each market segment based on the profile of feature values that they possess?
5. How can a product be developed, positioned, or repositioned so as to better meet the needs of the market segment of interest?

Question 1 above produces relevant descriptions of products, while question 2 produces corresponding descriptions of consumers. Question 3 identifies market segments, while question 4 addresses the issue of how membership within market segments is determined. Finally, question 5 takes the knowledge represented in the answers to the first four questions and applies it to product design, development, and advertising. The role of data analysis in answering the fundamental marketing questions is illustrated in Figure 10.6.

### 10.3.2 Market Fragmentation

One of the fundamental problems of marketing is positioning products so that they are chosen and bought by consumers. The solution to this problem requires an understanding of the motivations and product preferences of consumers. In a large, homogeneous market, this problem only has to be solved once. However, in the complex and dynamic information society, there are very few such homogeneous markets and market researchers need new types of information to understand the segments of today's fragmented markets.

Each type of product raises its own particular set of marketing problems. In highly

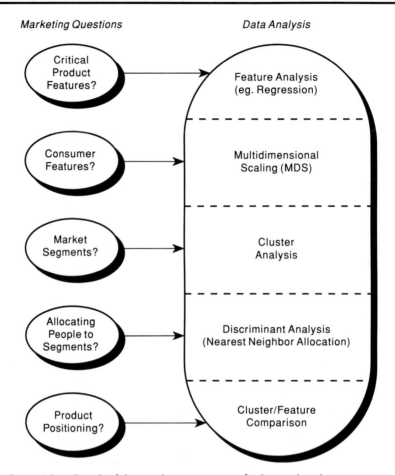

Marketing Questions           Data Analysis

Critical Product Features? → Feature Analysis (eg. Regression)

Consumer Features? → Multidimensional Scaling (MDS)

Market Segments? → Cluster Analysis

Allocating People to Segments? → Discriminant Analysis (Nearest Neighbor Allocation)

Product Positioning? → Cluster/Feature Comparison

**Figure 10.6** The role of data analysis in answering fundamental marketing questions.

profitable market segments the intense competition often forces companies to focus more on individual segments of the market. For instance, an important segment in the food and soft drink market is the weight conscious segment, and the needs of this segment are met by a variety of diet products. The burgeoning youth market is another segment with different body sizes and shapes, views, and preferences. For instance, cereals for children tend to be sweeter and are advertised very differently from cereals containing nuts and bran.

For some products market segments may be in equilibrium. Other products, particularly in new technologies, can have much more volatile segmentation. This has been true for instance in the personal computer market as the hobbyist segment of the mid-seventies was replaced by the education segment of the late seventies, with a business segment becoming predominant in the late eighties. Within the business segment new software (e.g., databases, spreadsheets) opened up the computer to new classes of user, while new hardware and technology (e.g., notebook and laptop computers) continually redefined the nature of the product and how it could be used.

Marketing is an interesting but difficult problem because neither individuals nor groups are predictable in a volatile society where the pace of technological innovation and life-style changes seem to be constantly accelerating. In a society where there are hundreds of hair shampoos and magazines to choose from there is a natural fragmentation of the market as people choose different products for a host of different reasons.

Market fragmentation is exacerbated by fragmentation of the media. The onset of cable television has led to a multiplicity of television channels and similar fragmentation can be seen in the print industry where specialist magazines and suburban newspapers are displacing the big city newspapers to some extent. This fragmentation is obvious in a melting pot like Los Angeles. For instance, in the Pacific Bell yellow pages for Los Angeles there are hundreds of newspapers advertised with names such as *The Beverly Hills Courier, The Buddhist Times and Society, B'Nai B'rith Life, California Japanese Daily News,* and *Chinese Entertainment News* (just a selection of titles from A to C).

Not surprisingly then, the subscribers to the *Los Angeles Times* receive different advertisements and supplements depending on their neighborhoods. As the heterogeneity and mobility of society increases in the future it is likely that there will be much less mass market advertising and more targeting of messages to particular clusters and niches. Watching the same advertisement on two different TV stations (e.g., an English language station and a Spanish language station), shows how the same product may be marketed differently to two different ethnic groups.

### 10.3.3 Market Segmentation

The fragmented market is actually a segmented market. Each fragment of the market is internally consistent to some extent, and its members share similar needs and product preferences. Products and positionings that are effective for one segment may be inappropriate for another. Thus the task of market research is to identify meaningful segments and develop marketing strategies that are targeted towards these segments.

The splintering of markets into smaller segments has been matched by increasing scope and pressure for new products due to:

- International competition
- Rapid changes in product and process technologies
- Deregulation
- Increasing market sophistication
- Changes in consumer life-styles

Thus market researchers and analysts are faced with increased diversity and fragmentation within markets and within products. In addition to understanding segments, the market researcher must also understand product differentiation and the way in which different products or product variants should be matched with different market segments.

This represents a challenge and an opportunity that is tempered by the need to define cost-effective market segments that are neither so broad that they do not effectively differentiate between products and consumers, nor so narrow that they cannot be reached through advertising in a cost-effective fashion. This complex matching between a diverse range of products and the diverse range of markets requires a great deal of information about people and their preferences.

The various advertising media are also becoming more fragmented. Media tend to fragment along the lines of market segments because advertisers tend to choose magazines, newspapers, etc., that have well-identified customer profiles. The readership of a magazine on boxing has an identifiably different profile from that of a magazine about women's fashion. The proliferation of magazines on newsstands is visible evidence of how feedback within the consumer, advertiser, producer triad works. Magazines that appeal to well-defined market segments do better at attracting advertising revenue.

Media fragmentation (and segmentation) is not restricted to newspapers and magazines. Cable television and independent channels have led to more specialized stations that cater for different types of audience. Gone are the days when everyone could be counted on to watch "I Love Lucy" on a particular channel. As a result, advertisers want targeted markets rather than mass markets. Newspapers have responded to the challenge by breaking papers up into different sections that tend to appeal to different segments. Many of these sections are aimed at the critical 25–44 year-old market that in the early 1990s accounted for close to half (44%) of American adults. For instance, "money" or business sections often have a personal finance/career focus that appeals to "baby boomers."

Based on the requirements of complex, segmented markets, two key issues in marketing research are (1) how to get good data and (2) how to analyze and understand it for better decisions. The next section discusses the first issue, while the analysis part is discussed in the intelligent database section of this chapter.

### 10.3.4  Competitive Analysis

This chapter will concentrate on the problem of market segmentation. The fragmentation of the market is partly due to increased competition, as producers find niches where they can insert their products successfully. Thus any analysis of market segments has to be done with respect to the competition. In general, segments that are easier to penetrate and dominate will be more attractive than segments that are already dominated by a competitor.

One of the main tools in dealing with competitors is to use information as a competitive advantage. This is illustrated in Figure 10.7, where knowledge that is known only to some companies provides them with a competitive advantage. Often, companies learn about new information through chance, but discovery places the search for competitively useful information on a sounder footing. Discovery can identify trends and patterns that lie hidden in data, long before they become apparent to the broader community. Thus discovery is a key part of competitive analysis.

Competition is not always unhealthy for a company. Advertising by a competitor may sometimes have a slipstream effect so that it also improves the position of one's own company. For instance, when IBM carried out a large promotional campaign on PCs in the early 1980s it also helped the clone makers, since people got the message

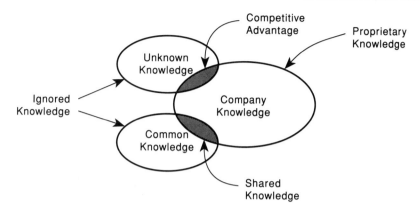

**Figure 10.7** Knowledge and competitive advantage.

about the new product, but could still choose to buy that product from a different company.

However, in other cases the competition can be damaging and this is where competitive analysis is particularly important. For instance, in the automobile market, the mid-size four door sedan is a highly competitive and profitable market segment. Knowing that a competitor is overstocked on a particular model and will lower prices represents a short-term competitive threat. One response would be to lower production and look at expansion in another product category; another response would be to meet the competition head to head, cut prices, and launch an aggressive advertising campaign to make the situation of the competitor even more difficult. A third possibility would be launch a countercampaign that emphasizes quality, in an effort to make the competitor look cheap and to leave the long-term impression with consumer's that one's own cars are of significantly higher quality. Making decisions such as these can be critical for a company, and having the information necessary to make the competitive analysis is a major factor in achieving ultimate success.

Competitive analysis is also important in planning more detailed strategy and tactics. For instance, deciding on the marketing mix (e.g., advertising, personal selling, sales promotion, publicity) to be used in getting the message across to the consumer. The marketing mix should be influenced by the profiles of the consumers being targeted. In competitive analysis, the key questions are "What is the distribution and profiles of current product users? What is the distribution and profiles of competitor product users? What is the profile of customers representing the highest sales potential?"

## ■ 10.4 SOURCES OF MARKET DATA

Smart marketing requires reliable information, which in turn is based on sound and relevant data. Marketing data comes from a vast array of sources. The volume of marketing data can easily submerge a manager or researcher under a deluge of information.

Marketing has a wealth of information to draw on, ranging from census data to sales data. General purpose marketing statistics are provided in volumes such as the *Rand McNally Commercial Atlas and Marketing Guide.* In addition to such encyclopedic collections of data, there are also a number of other major data sources, some of which (like census data) are generally useful, while others (e.g., accounting data) may be useful for a particular company.

A few of the major sources of marketing data will be discussed in the following section. The data is categorized by (1) products and purchases, (2) consumers, and (3) geographic locations, (i.e., who buys what, where, and how). In particular, the focus will be on the type of data that will be useful in identifying market segments.

### 10.4.1 Product and Purchase Data

Perhaps the ideal source of data is the consumer's shopping bags. Naturally, this approach works best when a large number of products are bought at the same time. The one place where almost everyone shops in quantity, and at regular intervals, is the supermarket. Can we cluster people according to the contents of their shopping carts? The answer is almost certainly yes. Standing in a checkout and watching what a person buys in a weekly shopping trip can probably tell you more about that person than a psychologist could discover with the Rorschach ink-blot test.

The type of surveillance involved in looking inside shopper's bags is generally unwelcome and intrusive. However, new technologies allow marketers to find out what is inside the shopping bag without appearing to be collecting this information. This detailed data about what is purchased is collected at the point of sale (the cash register) and is referred to as point-of-sale data.

***10.4.1.1 Point-of-Sale Data*** Point-of-Sale (POS) data is a key source of marketing data. POS data is often collected using POS terminals that automatically record and store data about each purchase, using technologies such as bar code scanning.

As of 1990, there were over 100,000 leased POS terminals in the U.S. and there were close to a million POS terminals in total. While POS systems and payment methods (e.g., debit cards) are evolving, the basic idea of a POS system is that it captures information about individual transactions electronically and then stores them in a database. This information can then be analyzed in a variety of ways (e.g., to assess changing buying trends, product preferences of different market segments, effect of advertising and in-store promotions, etc.).

One of the main aspects of POS terminals is that they collect information unobtrusively. With electronic technology there are many ways of unobtrusively collecting data as part of ongoing activity. For instance, it is becoming more prevalent to collect POS information directly from the customer. Often the provision of this information is used as an inducement or is positioned as a requirement for making a purchase. Consumers are often asked to fill in information when making a purchase. One reason for this is to send catalogs and other information, but it also has POS marketing value. It might, for instance, be extremely useful to know which people buy cordless phones, and whether or not these are the same people that buy fax machines for home use.

POS data collection is widespread and increasing. It is spreading to many types of purchase activity. POS data is no longer restricted to the supermarket or department store checkout. It is also possible to obtain POS information in a variety of interactive formats ranging, in the case of television, from home shopping to interactive game shows.

In the past it has not been possible to tie together information about single households. Information has generally been aggregated in terms of zip codes and portions of zip codes. However, as information technology advances it becomes more reasonable to consider the individual household as the fundamental unit of analysis. It is now conceivable for all the information about product purchases, and precipitating factors such as consumer characteristics, product purchases, and media exposure to be correlated within a single household. The remaining problems in collecting such exhaustive data on households are now social and ethical rather than technical. Many people would prefer not to have the full spectrum of their purchasing behavior available as public knowledge.

The retail point-of-sale system collects valuable market research information as a by-product. It is a timely and relatively inexpensive way of collecting information. It is also relevant, because what the consumer buys today tends to be a good predictor of what he or she will buy tomorrow, and the kinds of things bought reveal a lot about life-style and preferences. For instance, trends toward increased sales of fast food and convenience foods can be correlated with a variety of societal trends, including an increasing number of working mothers and a larger number of relatively affluent elderly.

Most importantly, the marketing research information should be valid. If the information is invalid then it may lead to wrong decisions. In the case of POS, the basic information is demonstrably valid because the customers are indicating their preferences with hard cash (or credit). Of course, whether later aggregations and interpretations of this basic information remain valid is a separate issue. The factual and objective nature of POS data stands in contrast to the subjective nature of many other types of marketing data (e.g., preferences reported in various surveys or consumer panels).

POS has traditionally applied to a cash register terminal environment that converts the task of ringing up the bill into electronic information about the sales transaction. Included in a POS system is the eventual reduction and analysis of this data.

Since point-of-sale information is a by-product of the sale it should not interfere with the checking out or purchasing process. Today's POS systems are unobtrusive. When a product is scanned using a bar code reader, it looks to the customer as if this is being done to get the price (the customer might even rationalize that the store is using this system to prevent customers from substituting price tags from cheaper items). However, in addition to this function the scanned bar code also contains product identification, which can then be correlated with the sales location and time. In principle this information can also be correlated with customer identity if a credit card is used, however, with present technology this would probably require coordination with the credit agency involved. However, even if the identity of the customer is not recorded, there is still considerable information value not just in which individual items were bought, but also in how products are grouped together in the purchases of different shoppers.

POS information has obvious utility for inventory management and this may have distracted people from its market research use. "With the introduction of a cash register terminal which could capture the sales data and make the required information available on a real-time basis, the retailer can now more effectively control his inventory, assure himself that he is reacting to customer needs promptly, and reduce cash losses and receivables." (Auerbach 1974, p.i).

POS marketing is a useful antidote to the problem of market dispersion that is confronting the mass media. Special product displays can be set up on a store by store basis where target segments of consumers are identified both by the type of store that they go to and the location of that store.

**10.4.1.2** *Looking Inside the Shopping Cart*    Traditional point-of-sale tools have been oriented around the cash register. Cash register-based systems can be surprisingly informative when combined with demographic information. However, there are other ways of collecting point-of-sale information.

Supermarkets provide the richest source of POS information at present. They are also a fertile ground for new technologies such as videocarts, which provide a supplementary type of product and purchase data. Videocarts are shopping carts equipped with a multimedia information display. Ostensibly, video carts provide instore information. The video cart is actually a regular shopping cart with a video terminal that can be read while the computer is being pushed. The video terminal is surprisingly unobtrusive after one has gotten some practice in using it, except that with early models one couldn't sit a small child on the shopping cart with the video terminal there.

The video terminal provided basic information about the store including an alphabetical index of products that could be used to find which aisle they were in, and a map of the store. It also provided some entertainment features such as horoscopes. In addition, advertisements would sometimes show on the screen as one passed a product in an aisle.

From a POS perspective, a videocart can provide a wealth of information that cannot be gathered by a cash register system. If the cart is instrumented appropriately, and if the video terminal collects the appropriate data, it is possible to track where the customer goes inside the store, which general shelf positions receive the most attention, and even which times of day different aisles are traveled most (e.g., liquor and snacks may tend to be more heavily traveled in the evening).

The information value of the videocart can also be enhanced by correlating it with the cash register information. Since each product is recorded at check out, and since the position of each product in the store is known, it is relatively simple to determine when each product was picked off the shelf in most cases.

One may then be in a position to answer fairly esoteric questions such as "To what extent are product purchases grouped by category?" Detailed point-of-sales data and data about shopping patterns collected from videocarts may be used to identify market segments and clusters. This knowledge can then be used in a variety of ways, including:

• Stocking goods based on zip location
• Determining advertising strategies and shelf placement
• Using POS info to provide rapid inventory response and to forecast demand

- Labeling products according to who buys them
- Identifying synergistic relations between products (e.g., natural mergers in the food industry, transfer of brand loyalty)
- Determining which products should be located so as to enhance access for customers with low mobility
- Validate and label clusters and cluster profiles using interviews and questionnaires

Clearly, innovations such as videocarts may revolutionize POS marketing research, although the ethics and constitutionality of such information-gathering systems are certainly interesting issues. However, considerable information value can still be found in the basic cash register information, and in the information that stores routinely collect as part of their accounting and inventory management practice.

**10.4.1.3 *Accounting and Control Systems*** Retail store audits provide information about inventory and deliveries over time and thus allow sales to be tracked over time. This data may then be supplemented by an auditor who visits a store and collects observable information about shelf prices, use of display space, and in-store promotion activity.

Retail store audits are becoming progressively easier to carry out as scanning of items at check out becomes more routine. Scanners read the bar code (universal product code or UPC) printed on each package and send the information to the cash register which relates the product code to the current price. All the information in the transaction is then stored in the computer. This information may include, price, product, and coupon use. The information may then be correlated with information about promotions and use of shelf space within the store.

Other point-of-sale data is provided by auditing companies such as the A.C. Nielsen Co. In addition to basic information about sales, distribution, and selling prices, a Nielsen audit might also include analyses of which brands are displayed together (i.e., which brands compete with each other).

Internal records accounting and control systems also provide basic marketing data. The problem with such databases is that they are designed to satisfy many different information needs and their data or reporting formats may be difficult or inappropriate for marketing analysis. Typically the data is designed to be read as summary reports and is therefore highly aggregated. However, marketing will generally require more detailed breakdowns.

Customer feedback in the form of product returns, service records, and customer correspondence provides further data. However, feedback tends to come from a small subgroup of customers who are probably not typical of customers in general. For instance, a customer service center that uses a 1-800 number may get a large number of calls about broken or defective products. Yet the effort of getting extra background information about the customer that is useful for marketing is relatively high. In many instances, such effort may not be justified if point-of-sale data is already available or if it can be shown that service calls represent a biased sample of customers.

Other sources of data include government publications, periodicals, and publicly available reports of various organizations.

### 10.4.2  Consumer Data

There are many ways to classify consumers. Only some of these are relevant for marketing. Some of the most relevant information about consumers includes their demographic profile (where they live, work, how old they are, etc.), and various life-style attributes such as whether or not they like outdoor activities.

*10.4.2.1  Census Data*    Census Data is particularly important in marketing, and U.S. Census data is widely exploited by marketing researchers and planners in North America. Census data has the following structure:

city block -> block group -> census tract

Census tracts have populations of above 4000 and are defined by local communities. In urban areas, census tracts are combined to form metropolitan statistical areas (MSA) which are counties containing a central city with populations of at least 50,000.

TIGER (Topologically Integrated Geographic Encoding and Referencing) is the Census Bureau's computerized mapping system of the United States (Exter 1991). TIGER contains four types of information: census geography (from city blocks on up), postal geography (including street names and zip codes), map coordinates (expressed in latitude and longitude), and reference data that links everything together. When combined with geographic information systems (software for handling geographic databases like TIGER), TIGER becomes a powerful tool for retail marketing. Current systems show where a store's customers live within a trade area and they can also show market penetration by census tract. Once these systems are linked to TIGER they will be able to place customers on the streets where they live. They will also be able to analyze spending patterns by variables such as the customer's driving time to the store, the exact distance from competing stores, and the degree of exposure to promotions.

Data may even be reasonably inferred in cases where it cannot be observed or collected directly. This type of surrogate data is generally based on common sense assumptions about the relations between variables over time. Surrogate data relies on predicting unavailable information based on available data. For instance, the demand for baby food will be highly correlated with the number of births in the preceding two years. In general, predictions about future values of variables represent surrogate data.

*10.4.2.2  Psychographics*    Demographics and similar information provided in census data and the like provide only an incomplete picture of the consumer. In contrast to the basic information of age, location, education, job, and income, psychographics is concerned with the life-style of the consumer. Psychographic variables describe consumers in terms of "how they think and what their activities, interests, and opinions may be." (Bearden, Teel, and Durand 1978, p. 66).

Psychographic influences on purchasing behavior are generally easier to relate to demographics and other observable variables than are other "intrapsychic" variables such as personality. Personality is the internal organization within a person that guides behavior and thinking.

Consumer personality is difficult to track, because personality testing generally requires fairly detailed assessment. However, some well known research sponsored by Anheuser-Busch (Ackoff and Emshoff 1975) shows that personality can be a useful tool in product positioning. Seven fictitious brands of beer were created (all were the same beer, but with different labels). Advertisements were created to make each of the beers appeal to a different personality type. One type of advertisement assumed that the target person drank beer as a reward for self-sacrifice, while another advertisement assumed that the target person drank as a consolation for failure. The experiment was successful in that most people gave the highest rating to the beer whose advertising matched their personality.

In spite of the Anheuser-Busch findings, use of personality data is difficult. In part this is because personality is difficult to measure and there are a number of different theories of personality. Which, if any of the many theories available is best for marketing remains an open question. In addition, personality tests are normally used to assess personality, yet marketers do not have detailed personality profiles for large numbers of consumers. Thus to be used on a large scale, personality variables need to be matched to more readily obtained data such as life-style variables, demographics, and product purchases.

Psychographic descriptions of the customer have proven useful in explaining brand preferences and store loyalty. In contrast to personality theories, which were designed to describe and explain human behavior in general, psychographics is concerned with the goals and motivations that influence consumer purchase behaviors.

Thus a typical psychographic analysis might be concerned with what type of person shops at discount food stores. A survey could be taken of shoppers to determine their shopping behavior and their attitudes towards food preparation. Relevant issues might include the extent to which a shopping list is used, shopping for specials, and looking for the lowest possible prices. The value of the psychographic analysis in this case would be that products could be positioned according to the findings. For instance, more emphasis might be placed on "specials" in the discount store and on price comparisons. The findings of the analysis might then be extended to other forms of discount store. For instance, there might be some overlap between who goes to discount food stores and who buys discount shoes.

Further generality is obtained by creating composite groupings of consumers. Life-style typologies blend various profiles of psychographic measures into composite types. The purpose of creating life-style typologies in marketing is to find clusters or groups of consumers with similar preferences and tastes that can be identified on the basis of readily obtainable demographic and psychographic information.

The PRIZM clusters developed by Claritas Corporation are one way of classifying people. This approach uses 40 clusters of life-styles within the U.S., where these clusters are closely related to geographic locations represented by zip codes, or portions of zip codes.

An alternative approach which is less fine grained is the SRI VALS typology. This groups people according to nine life-styles. The VALS typology is actually a two-level hierarchy (Figure 10.8). At the top level the three major types are need driven, outer directed, and inner directed. The need driven type has two subtypes — survivors and sustainers. The outer directed type has three subtypes (belongers, achievers,

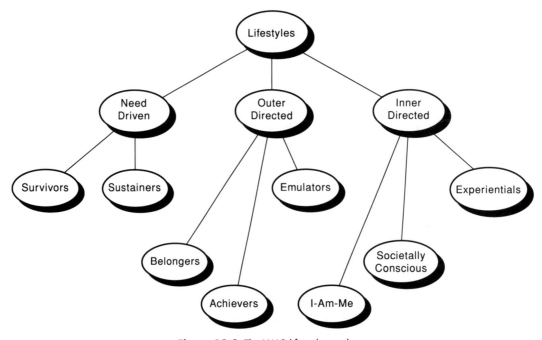

**Figure 10.8** The VALS life-style typology.

emulators). Finally the inner directed type also has three subtypes (I-am-me, societally conscious, experientials). The ninth type is the integrated type.

Survivors comprise 4% of the U.S. population, sustainers comprise 11%, and the corresponding figures (Farquhar 1986) for the other subtypes are: belongers (35%), achievers (22%), emulators (10%), I-am-me (5%), societally conscious (8%), and experientials (7%).

According to the VALS typology, need-driven people have low incomes and are driven by their needs. Survivors tend to be passive and focused on survival, while sustainers have more hope for breaking out of their situation. Outer directed people are by far the most numerous type in the VALS typology, comprising two thirds of the population. Within this type, belongers are middle class with average incomes and consumption (just over a third of the population are classified as "belongers." Achievers are professionals with high incomes who share business values and a power focus. Emulators also have high incomes, but they tend to be more ostentatious and status-oriented.

Within the inner-directed type, I-am-me subtypes tend to be student or artistic types with low incomes, while societally conscious subtypes are also well-educated, but have high incomes and confidence. The societally conscious people tend to be the early adopters of new products and technologies. Finally, the experiential subtype focuses on self-actualization and seeks direct experience.

***10.4.2.3  Consumer Panels***    There are a number of practical and ethical problems with looking inside shopping bags in general, but these can be overcome by "hiring" people to act as prototypical consumers who can be observed in detail (thereby forming consumer panels). Consumer panels are used to learn about the behavior of individuals and the sequence of purchases that they make. Home audits and mail diaries are two ways of capturing detailed information on what individuals or individual households are buying over a period of time. In a home audit, an auditor periodically goes through the kitchen cupboards to see which products are stocked and in what quantities. The household may also save all packaging so that it can be recorded by the auditor. Alternatively, mail diaries contain the detailed purchase records of targeted items. The diary is kept by a representative of the household and obviously the validity of the data in the diary will depend on the diligence with which the diary is kept.

It is also possible to mix the consumer panel and scanning approaches. Exposure to advertising is ascertained by monitoring the home's television sets and surveying household members periodically on what they have read. Each household also uses a special identification card at specific stores each time a purchase is made. Use of this card triggers a detailed record of the purchases made which is then stored. This detailed purchase information can then be related to other details about the household, previous purchases, and previous promotions and advertisements that members of the household were exposed to.

### 10.4.3 Geographic Data

Geographic Information Systems (GISs) are specialized database applications where the data is referenced to some underlying geographical structure or information. Thus GISs deal with spatial data and link this to other types of data. GISs are particularly important to marketing applications because market segments will generally be correlated in some way with geographical locations.

Geographic information systems assemble a range of different data in a cartographic form. The resulting GIS is a potential source of entirely new kinds of information derived from the comparison and combination of the assembled data. As an example, the computer can calculate the distance of a point from any other, producing a tabulation of proximities from towns, services, and physical communications. In the case of marketing, data can be superimposed on the GIS. For instance, demographic information can be added to the GIS along with estimates of memberships of life-style typologies in different regions.

For marketing problems the spatial component of the GIS is a two-dimensional map. Each geographic object in the map is classified as belonging to a particular class (e.g., city, road, park, etc.). Geographical objects may also be grouped into the three generic spatial object classes of point, line, and region (Ooi 1990). Each geographic object will then have a location on a corresponding map or maps. The geographic objects on the map may intersect, be adjacent to other objects, or contain other objects. A fully functioned GIS has the following features:

- A user interface or language that supports queries that select objects of interest satisfying some criteria, queries that may range over any stored information, and the display of selected objects and their attributes in graphical or textual representation.

- A windowing facility that allows users to view a particular area of interest and acts as a top-level filtering device to query only a small section of a global map space
- A query language that is insensitive to the spatial class of the objects (e.g., underlying geometric properties of objects should not affect query semantics)
- Flexible interpretation of errors in spatial information arising from such factors as an inaccuracy in raw data (e.g., coastlines might be smooth in overview maps but shown in detail at a larger scale)

Mapping technology can assist in identifying the marketing potential of different regions for different products. Non-graphic databases can accompany maps depicting the size and distribution of different market segments with known preferences for products. The effectiveness of this information can then be enhanced by linking it to geographic information (i.e., maps and multimedia capability) and other information such as point-of-sale data.

## ■ 10.5 INTELLIGENT DATABASE TOOLS FOR MARKETING

The essence of marketing is matching products and advertising to customers. Marketing is a communication process which in the best cases benefits both customer and producer. Figure 10.9 shows the general structure of market planning and execution from our perspective. An initial set of marketing goals is used to interpret marketing data from a variety of sources that may include census data, life-style clusters, point of sale information, and so on. The outcome of this interpretation is a market segmentation which is then used as a basis for product positioning and further market planning and execution.

Information in general, and databases in particular, are essential to the development and implementation of marketing strategies. However, a recent study of marketing practices among direct mailers (Barney 1991) showed that nearly 70% of respondents did not think that they were effective in using the information in their databases. The actual survey breakdown was not at all effective (1%), not very effective (26%), somewhat effective (43%), effective (25%), very effective (5%). Clearly more could be done with the available information.

Most companies collect more information than they can put to good use. More personnel might be hired to analyze the excess information, but increasing the number of personnel will never keep up with the exponentially increasing volume of information.

Intelligent databases are needed to work smarter, rather than hiring extra personnel to work harder. Managers need to know their customers as the general store owners of the nineteenth century knew theirs. The technology for getting detailed knowledge of customers is now available through the use of intelligent database applications.

If the information obtained in marketing research is to help decision making it should be relevant, cost-effective, timely, and valid. Consider some of the problems that may arise in a typical scenario. A marketing research team sets up a booth in a busy shopping mall. People are given a demonstration or sample of a new product and

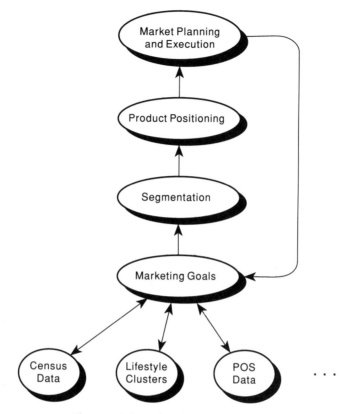

**Figure 10.9** Market planning and execution.

are then asked how it compares to competitor products. This information may be collected either as a questionnaire or through a formal interview. This information is presumably relevant because the shoppers are a fairly typical cross-section of people who buy the product in the mall (the researchers may actually screen people according to criteria, e.g., age, gender, or type of clothing). However, it is a very costly way of collecting information. It is also a fairly slow way of collecting information. By the time responses are entered into a database, tabulated, and a report is generated, several weeks may have elapsed.

Market researchers and managers need marketing decisions support systems (MDSSs) that can provide them with relevant data and summarization in a timely fashion. An MDSS consists of four components:

- Modeling
- Display
- Analysis
- Database

Knowledge about market segments is included in the MDSS, along with models for calculating advertising costs and expected returns for targeted advertising to particular market segments. The MDSS also includes tools that allow the market researchers to explore different scenarios.

One of the main functions of the MDSS is to assist in setting up a marketing strategy that corresponds to the segments identified. This is then followed up by a cost-benefit analysis of whether this strategy is viable. Later in this section, Market Analysis and Segmentation System, is described. It is a new kind of MDSS that brings the power of intelligent database technology to the problem of MDSS development.

Marketing research is an aid to decision making. For instance, a car manufacturer may be concerned about loss of market share. Information that may be important in designing new models of car and in advertising those models might include information about how the market is segmented, information about which features people within each market segment want, and information about what the competitors have been doing that has proven successful.

A number of tools may be used in collecting and analyzing marketing data. Marketing research is an applied type of behavioral research and uses many of the tools that are used by social psychologists and sociologists. Research is needed because the right answer is usually not obvious and cannot be generated from existing theories or models. John Wanamaker (cited by Weiss, 1988, p. 27) once observed that "half of all advertising dollars are wasted; [he] just didn't know which half." Market research is the job of finding which advertising dollars are wasted and how to make sure they won't be wasted in the future by better positioning of the product. It is also about creating the products that people need and getting those products to the right people at the right time.

### 10.5.1  Market Analysis with Corporate Vision and IDIS

The technology of intelligent database discussed earlier in this book has a direct application to market analysis. Corporate Vision and IDIS are two commercial systems from IntelligenceWare that deliver intelligent database applications. Market Analysis and Segmentation System (MASS) is a marketing research and analysis system designed by IntelligenceWare for marketing managers. It is a combination of Corporate Vision and IDIS with some additional features designed especially for the requirements of marketing.

MASS can be used to integrate a company's internal customer information, its sales and promotional information, external demographic data on the market, along with psychographic data and other information on product preferences and attitudes. MASS allows the marketing manager to get closer to the customer and is a tool for supporting strategic planning and increasing market share. The functional architecture of MASS is shown in Figure 10.10. Marketing data is aggregated and analyzed according to marketing goals to produce market segments. These market segments are then used to position products and this in turn leads to planning and execution of various marketing strategies. The description of MASS here will mainly be concerned with the process of market segmentation.

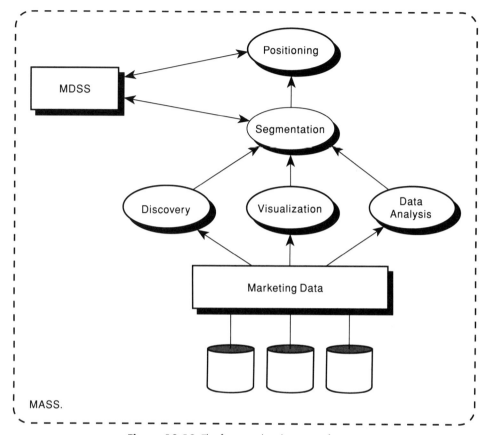

**Figure 10.10** The functional architecture of MASS.

Market Analysis and Segmentation System is a system for visualizing patterns in marketing data and supporting marketing decisions. MASS builds upon the basic functionality of an EIS, with more emphasis on market segmentation through clustering, cluster identification, and linear decision models based on cost of product innovation, positioning, and advertising, versus expected benefits.

In the Market Analysis and Segmentation System, information from a variety of different external sources including customer information, point of sale data, census data and demographics, and geographic information systems is combined into a central marketing database. This information is then categorized and clustered using information discovery and related tools (e.g., with the IDIS system). This data can then be operated on by a data visualization and querying system using an executive information system such as Corporate Vision to determine the nature of the market segments. Segments may then be further refined manually based on this inspection and by using domain dependent tools for competitive analysis. Market segments may also be tailored to correspond better to media and distribution channels that can be readily defined.

## 10.5.2 The Marketing Manager's View

As an example of intelligent database usage a marketing application will be discussed in this section. This example shows the use of information discovery, anomaly detection, and visualization to track down a new market segment for a product.

Consider a MASS user who is looking for relations between types of product and types of consumer and any other information that helps in making decisions about marketing strategy, how to spend advertising dollars, and so on. The user in this case is a marketing manager who begins by looking for unexpected information. We assume that the developer of the system has already generated a set of rules through information discovery and that these rules are now available for review by the user.

In this example the market manager wants to know what life-style factors tend to predict purchases of video camcorders. She queries the information discovery system on this score by setting up purchase of camcorder as the goal of matching rules. The matching rule then indicates that the best predictors of who purchases camcorders are socioeconomic status and the presence of children in the household.

The marketing manager then checks to see what anomalies exist for this rule. She sees that the foregoing rule not withstanding, some purchases of camcorders appear to be relatively poor and with large families. To get a better indication of who these apparently anomalous people are, the market manager describes a new attribute "anomalous camcorder purchases." She then defines this attribute using the condition: An anomalous buyer is a person from a lower socioeconomic class who buys a camcorder. She then submits this new attribute as a goal to information discovery, effectively asking the question "What sort of person will buy a camcorder when they don't appear to have much extra cash?" The result of this query is a rule which says that anomalous buyers tend to have large families and be new immigrants.

At this point the question arises, why are these anomalous people buying camcorders and do they represent a new market segment that we can court with more focused product positioning, pricing, and advertising? The user now switches over to the interactive graphics, armed with the question obtained through an analysis of the information discovery results.

She starts by doing some visual querying. The first query is, "Show me what other purchases tend to be made by new immigrants with large families." This query returns a table and visualization of this table in terms of a bar chart showing that new immigrants with large families tend to purchase a large amount of consumer electronics. This fact seems to conflict with the fact that many of these people are classified as being in a lower socioeconomic class in the database and thus should be expected to have less disposable income.

The marketing manager then uses point-and-click navigation, and begins with the chart showing consumer electronic purchases made by large immigrant families. She then clicks on the immigrant attribute and chooses a new display showing purchases of major items such as houses and cars. This chart seems to indicate that expenditures on houses and cars are much higher than would be expected if there were little disposable income available. She then selects a graph showing the overall expenditures on major items plotted against socioeconomic class, for immigrants and for nonimmigrants. In this hypothetical data, the chart then confirms that immigrants in a lower socioeconomic class have higher than expected expenditures on major items. Finally, the marketing manager switches over to a plot comparing camcorder sales for immigrants and nonimmigrants. This shows that overall, camcorder sales are relatively weak for the immigrant group (Figure 10.11).

At this point the marketing manager reflects on what she has learned. There are a number of reasons why immigrants could have higher than expected disposable income. First, they may have a higher savings rate, and there may be multiple incomes in the family that are pooled in providing the disposable income necessary for major expenditures. Second, the measures of low socioeconomic status may be inappropriate since many of the immigrants may be starting their own businesses, which are not yet recognized by the employment classification scheme used in the database. Whatever the reason is, and there may be several, the information suggests that new immigrants may be a good market segment to focus on in future marketing strategy.

The marketing manager then links some of the screens that she has viewed together into a report and adds textual annotations explaining what she thinks each screen is indicating. She tops it off with a suggestion that an advertising campaign be started in a language other than English to capture this important and under-represented segment of the market.

This example shows the broad scope of intelligent database usage. Users of intelligent database applications do not simply form queries and view the resulting numbers. Instead, they delve into the data, viewing it from a variety of different perspectives and analyzing and interpreting the main trends and relationships from inside the intelligent application itself. Thus an intelligent database application is an integrated environment for exploring, analyzing, and interpreting information.

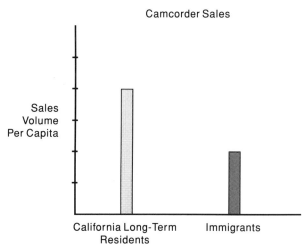

**Figure 10.11** Hypothetical camcorder sales.

### 10.5.3 Segment Discovery

Some problems will benefit from focused analysis using specific tools such as information discovery. For instance, segmentation as a problem is well suited to the characteristics of information discovery where the end result is a mapping between types of consumer and their attributes.

Thus information discovery serves as an alternative to (and at times betters) the traditional clustering methods that are frequently used in market research. Information discovery uncovers the relationships between product selection and customer profiles (demographics, psychographics, etc.).

Rule generation can replicate the results of clustering as well as providing additional information of relevance to marketing researchers and planners. In the Market Analysis and Segmentation System, both clustering and information discovery are carried out on marketing databases to identify market segments. The results of these analyses are also passed to the data visualization system so that the marketing user can compare the different segments identified through rule generation and clustering and can assess the importance of the patterns detected in the data. Further querying can also be carried out within the visualization system using the visual querying tools discussed earlier in Chapter 3.

One of the most important advances of the Market Analysis and Segmentation System over other marketing analysis systems is that it does not rely on "canned clusters" that have been predefined through an analysis of zip codes, product purchases, or whatever. Thus segmentation can be carried out anew for each set of data. However, while this approach is more flexible and leads to clusters or segments that are better at differentiating the consumers for particular products and services, it is also more difficult to use, since no canned clusters means no canned distributing and marketing channels.

The standard visualization tools in marketing are the pie chart and the bar chart. In the Market Analysis and Segmentation System, as with other intelligent database applications, these visualizations are constructed dynamically on the basis of stored data. This dynamic visualization ensures that summaries of the latest data are always available.

Rule discovery may be used to identify different segments in marketing data. In this section we show how information discovery can emulate and extend the findings of the clustering methods that are typically used in market segmentation.

Market segmentation is generally regarded as a difficult problem where useful segments should differ in their response to marketing strategy and tactics and be easily identified in terms of customer characteristics.

Traditionally, cluster analysis has been used to identify market segments. Use of cluster analysis is a highly skilled activity that requires careful tailoring of the clustering method to the particular problem and domain being investigated. This section will review a classical market segmentation study that used clustering and show how an alternative rule discovery approach can be used to advantage.

Blattberg and Sen (1974) carried out an analysis of aluminum foil purchase segments based on purchases made by the *Chicago Tribune's* panel of women in the Greater Chicago area between 1962 and 1966. In their analysis they found eight segments within the market of which five did not appear sensitive to price. Two of the price-sensitive segments shopped around at many stores to obtain low prices, while the remaining segments tended to shop principally at a single store.

Table 10.1 shows the data from a small group of subjects who were each highly representative of a different segment in the Blattberg and Sen study. This data covers seven brands of foil, 10 stores, five different sizes (23.5, 25, 37.5, 75, and 200), and price in cents.

Table 10.2 shows the characterization of the segments that Blattberg and Sen identified. An IDIS analysis was run on the data shown in Table 10.1. "Brand=any" was used as the goal. This led to a number of rules that referred to a customer in the premise, of which we show a selection below.

*Rule 1 (12 cases)*
*Brand = 1*
*If*
*consumer = 11 and store = 7 and size <= 25*

Consumer 11 was classified as representing the dual product segment according to Blattberg and Sen. Referring to Table 10.1 it can be seen that all but two of consumer 11's purchases were split between brands 1 and 2. Rule 1 tells us that consumer 11 generally buys brand 1 in small sizes. A second rule showed that consumer 11 bought brand 2 in a larger size.

*Rule 2 (12 cases)*
*Brand = 2*
*If*
*consumer = 11 and store = 7 and size = 75*

**Table 10.1  Purchase Histories of Individual Consumers, Aluminum Foil Study**

| | Consumer 9 | | | | Consumer 48 | | | | Consumer 4 | | | |
|---|---|---|---|---|---|---|---|---|---|---|---|---|
| Purchase Number | Brand | Store | Size (feet) | Price (¢) | Brand | Store | Size (feet) | Price (¢) | Brand | Store | Size (feet) | Price (¢) |
| 1 | 1 | 3 | 75 | 89 | 1 | 6 | 25 | 31 | 1 | 1 | 75 | 85 |
| 2 | 1 | 3 | 75 | 85 | 1 | 3 | — | — | 1 | 2 | 75 | 85 |
| 3 | 1 | 3 | 75 | 85 | 4 | 1 | 25 | 29 | 1 | 5 | 75 | 79 |
| 4 | 1 | 3 | 75 | 85 | 1 | 3 | 25 | 25 | 1 | 1 | 75 | 75 |
| 5 | 1 | 7 | 75 | 85 | 1 | 1 | 25 | 35 | 1 | 1 | 75 | 85 |
| 6 | 1 | 3 | 75 | 85 | 1 | 6 | 25 | 33 | 1 | 1 | 75 | 85 |
| 7 | 1 | 3 | 75 | 85 | 2 | 3 | 25 | 35 | 1 | 1 | 75 | 85 |
| 8 | 1 | 1 | 75 | 85 | 1 | 3 | 25 | 35 | 1 | 1 | 75 | 85 |
| 9 | 1 | 3 | 75 | 85 | 4 | 1 | 25 | 29 | 1 | 1 | 75 | 85 |
| 10 | 1 | 3 | 75 | 85 | 2 | 6 | 25 | 33 | 4 | 1 | 75 | 75 |
| 11 | 1 | 7 | 75 | 85 | 1 | 3 | 75 | 85 | 4 | 1 | 75 | 75 |
| 12 | 1 | 7 | 75 | 85 | 1 | 1 | 75 | 85 | 4 | 1 | 75 | 75 |
| 13 | 3 | 7 | 75 | 79 | 1 | 1 | 25 | 35 | 4 | 1 | 75 | 65 |
| 14 | 1 | 3 | 75 | 85 | 1 | 3 | 75 | 85 | 1 | 7 | 75 | 75 |
| 15 | 1 | 3 | 37½ | 59 | 1 | 6 | 75 | 79 | 4 | 1 | 75 | 75 |

**Table 10.2  Market Segments for Aluminum Foil Consumers**

| Segment | Label | Description |
|---------|-------|-------------|
| 1 | High Brand Loyal | Same brand almost always |
| 2 | Brand Loyal | Mostly same brand |
| 3 | National Brand Loyal | Prefer national brands |
| 4 | Last Purchase Loyal | Buy same as last purchase |
| 5 | Dual Product | Always buy 1 of 2 products |
| 6 | Deal-Oriented | Buy deals and stockpile |
| 7 | National Brand Deal | Prefer deals on national brands |
| 8 | Low Price Store | Buys cheapest brand at Regular Store |

In this case the IDIS analysis yielded two rules that explain why the consumer was switching between the two brands (depending on the size). Two more rules picked out the fact that consumers 9 and 48 were brand loyal.

*Rule 3 (31 cases)*
*Brand = 1*
*If*
*consumer = 9*

*Rule 4 (30 cases)*
*Brand = 1*
*If*
*consumer = 48*

Consumer 6 was classified by Blattberg and Sen as being in the low-price store segment. In their interpretation, consumers within this segment buy the cheapest brand at the store they usually shop at. This trend was also apparent in the rules generated by information discovery.

*Rule 5 (24 cases)*
*Brand = 4*
*If*
*consumer = 6 and store = 1*

In other words, when consumer 6 is in store 1 he or she will general buy brand 4 (the low-price brand). A second rule for consumer 6 notes the fact that the consumer almost always buys a small size and that most often the brand bought in this condition (77% of the time) is brand 4.

*Rule 6 (30 cases)*
*Brand = 4*
*If*
*consumer = 6 and size <= 25*

A third rule picks up the price sensitivity of consumer 6.

*Rule 7 (26 cases)*
*Brand = 4*
*If*
*consumer = 6 and 26 < price < 31*

Rule discovery also finds the two occasions that consumer 6 bought brand 5 at a low price.

*Rule 8 (2 cases)*
*Brand = 5*
*If*
*consumer = 6 and 7 <= price <= 21*

Consumer 41 was also classified as belonging to the low-price store effect segment, although the data shows a considerable amount of brand switching early on. However, eventually, the consumer settles down into buying a discount brand from a particular store.

*Rule 9 (15 cases)*
*Brand = 6*
*If*
*consumer = 41 and store = 7*

However, an additional rule highlights the fact that consumer 41 is also price sensitive.

*Rule 10 (14 cases)*
*Brand = 6*
*If*
*consumer = 41 and 25 <= size <= 37.5 and 24 <= price <= 29*

Consumer 12 was classified by Blattberg and Sen as "deal-oriented." Thus this customer bought the discount brand (5) when shopping at store 8, as the following rule shows:

*Rule 11 (8 cases)*
*Brand = 5*
*If*
*consumer = 12 and store = 8*

Information discovery using rule generation was able to pick out and characterize five of the eight clusters described by Blattberg and Sen. The other three clusters were described by a number of rules each representing small numbers of cases, and more data was needed to find stable patterns.

Segmentation by customers is of course only one way of looking at the data. One of the advantages of using the information discovery approach is that it has the side effect of discovering other unexpected patterns in the data. For instance, the following rule was also derived by rule generation from the aluminum foil study data.

*Rule 12 (45 cases)*
*Brand = 1*
*If*
*Store = 6*

This rule had a confidence factor of 76%, meaning that 76% of the purchases made in store 6 were for brand 1. This information could then be followed up by finding out why brand 1 was doing so well in store 6 (e.g., because of special promotions, because of a special relationship with the brand 1 sales representative, or because brand 1 was positioned right for the demographic and psychographic characteristics of shoppers at store 6).

A second rule relating to brand 1 was

*Rule 13 (41 cases)*
*Brand = 1*
*If*
*75 <= size <= 200 and 85 <= price <= 198*

This rule suggests that people who are paying more and buying a bigger size tend to purchase brand 1 in this sample. However, much of the effect of this rule in this particular illustrative sample may be derived from the fact that consumer 9 is brand loyal and paying the higher price for the 75 feet size, while consumer 48 also buys brand 1 in the larger size. However, in a larger sample a rule such as this could be particularly interesting.

Consider the use of MASS in examining North American sales figures as shown in Figure 10.12. Through a hypermedia interface, regional comparisons of product performance in various markets can be made. The user may view a screen within the system and then click on any part of the display, thereby triggering a hyperaction (Chapter 3). Once this occurs, a new visualization is constructed and displayed on the screen. The hypermedia provides direct access to database information and employs several graphing functions to reveal particular relationships among system variables. A map with the five primary regions of the United States is used again, only this time it is linked to service history information. If a user clicks on a hypermedia region, area-specific data is retrieved to be used for a variety of functions (see Figure 10.13 on page 444).

### 10.5.4 POS Data Analysis

So far marketing research has been discussed from the perspective of segmentation. However, other problems do concern the market researcher. Insight gained from analysis of POS data can be very useful in dealing with these problems. This section will consider the problem of analyzing coupon using.

Coupons are frequently used to encourage customers to purchase products. In North America alone, over 100 billion coupons are issued a year, although the redemption rate on coupons tends to average only about 4%. More than half the number of coupons

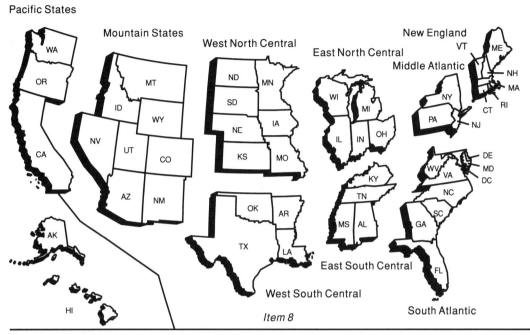

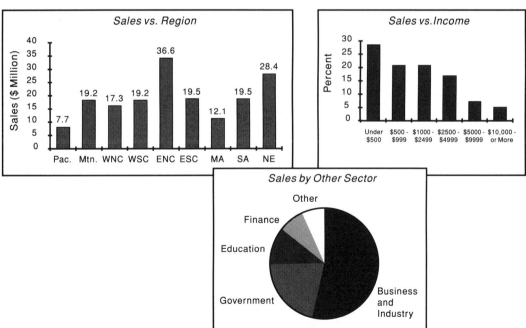

**Figure 10.12** A hypermedia interface to sales data.

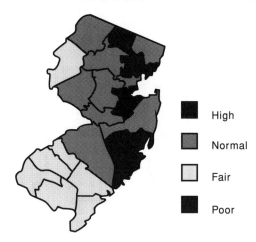

**Figure 10.13** Area-specific data about sales.

are typically distributed with newspapers.

Coupons may either be distributed in a broad spectrum way (e.g., in a citywide way) or they may be targeted to particular market segments using methods such as direct mailing to particular neighborhoods, or inserts in highly specialized magazines or newspapers. Normally, a coupon is turned in at the point of sale, and the retailer deducts the value of the coupon from the cost of the product in billing the customer. The coupon is then returned to the manufacturer who reimburses the retailer.

Coupons are generally used to influence both the customer and the retailer. For the customer, they tend to increase the probability of purchasing an established brand or trying out a new brand. Coupons also encourage retailers to stock and display the brand.

Consider the case of a retailer who would like to know more about how coupons are being used. Some of the questions of interest are:

- Do certain types of coupon tend to get used at certain times of day?
- How effective is advertising in promoting the use of coupons?
- What is the relationship between product category and the value of coupons being redeemed?
- What is the relationship between the price of products, the value of coupons being redeemed, and the product category?

Since coupon redemption rate is fairly low, these questions have to be answered by observing purchasing behavior using POS data, rather than by simply tracking the numbers of coupons being printed.

Discovery was carried out using IDIS on a retailer's sales data. This data included the value of the coupons redeemed, the store, the date, the time, the product price, whether the product was involved in a storewide promotion, and the total value of the customer purchase. A few fields from the database look as follows:

*Store_#*
*Date*
*Time*
*Terminal*
*Transact_#*
*Line_Operator*
*Line_UPC*
*Line_Family*
*Campaign*
*Item*
*Item_Price*
*Key_Campaign*
*Value_Required*
*Oper_Override*
*Coupon_Value*
*Req_Multi-Item*
*OR_Scan*
*Certified_Double*
*Good_for_Free*
*Validation*

Discovery focused on rules that predict the type and value of the coupons being redeemed. Summary examples of discovered rules were (1) coupons for some groups of items tended to be redeemed on weekends, (2) coupons for specific products tended to be associated with a large overall sale, and (3) coupons tend to be redeemed at a faster rate in the early days of specific types of storewide promotions.

Discovery provided a number of insights into how consumers use coupons, in spite of having no knowledge about the different types of coupon and product. With a large data set, discovery usually finds consistent patterns and an analyst can then determine what the rule implies in terms of coupon usage and marketing strategy.

## ■ 10.6  MARKETING METHODOLOGY

This section will consider some of the basic methodology of marketing, focusing on the problem of market segmentation and the use of cluster analysis to identify groups of consumers that tend to have similar life-styles and purchasing behaviors.

### 10.6.1  Identifying the Customer

The information society may be bringing us closer to electronic surveillance of all our activities, but it has not yet reached the point where market researchers have detailed profiles of each customer. Instead, they must rely on descriptions of aggregate or group behavior.

Cash register-based POS systems certainly collect lots of data quickly, but in most cases that information cannot be referred back to particular customers, although there are exceptions (e.g., when a credit card company markets products directly it can correlate customer purchases with a wealth of product information).

However, while POS information is generally not linked to individuals, it can in fact be linked to types of customer using the clues that are available. Thus even if marketing can't predict the behavior of individual consumers, there is still a considerable amount of leverage that can be gained by understanding the behavior and preferences of groups of people and positioning products and promotions accordingly.

The process of classifying people into meaningful groups is referred to as segmentation. Different methods of segmentation are possible depending on what the basis of the classification is. One of the most frequently used forms of segmentation is demographics. People tend to have different life-styles and purchasing behavior depending on how old they are, their family status, and where they live.

Once one understands demographic segments one can fine-tune products so that they are targeted at what people need according to who they are and where they live. Thus demographic reports can be used to identify the critical characteristics of different locations for market planning, and a whole industry has developed around converting census data to marketing relevant information. Some of the demographic parameters important to marketing are:

- Socioeconomics
- Income by age of head of household
- Housing characteristics
- Household composition
- Commuting
- Income and earnings
- Housing loan characteristics

Basic demographic information can be supplemented by more detailed information about where people live, which is one of the best indicators of who they are. Many neighborhoods are fairly homogeneous in terms of life-styles and socioeconomic status. This should not be too surprising since neighborhoods differ widely in their costs and amenities and people with similar needs and budgets will tend to move into the same neighborhoods. For instance, older people may want to live in safe, warm areas, whereas younger married couples may look for neighborhoods with good schools, and singles may look for areas with a good nightlife.

In North America, the suburb is a particularly important location for marketers because suburbs tend to contain a lot of people with high rates of consumption. A suburb is an area within a metro market that lies outside the city. Typically there are a large number of employed people within a suburb who commute to the neighboring city for work and entertainment. In 1950 just over a quarter of the U.S. population lived in the suburbs. By 1970 this proportion had risen to 43%, and current estimates place the suburban population at over 60% of the total population.

At first glance, there seems to be a clear dichotomy between suburban and inner city markets. According to demographic data, more single people live in the cities and more families live in the suburbs. Not surprisingly then, there are a lot more children living in the suburbs. In addition, households in the suburbs tend to be more affluent and have higher discretionary income. Local newspapers offer fairly exclusive coverage in suburban markets. For instance, in the United States, the network of over 1000 small suburban newspapers provides a targeted delivery system based on zip code, age and income demographics, and socioeconomic characteristics (Hemm 1991, p. 40). Each suburban newspaper delivers to an average of just over 2.3 zip codes and 10,000 customers. Thus marketers have turned to strategies such as the following for using suburban newspaper advertisements and inserts as an alternative to direct mail — picking appropriate suburban newspapers by matching against the zip codes of the best customers and picking appropriate suburban newspapers by using demographic and psychographic models that predict good customers based on zip codes or newspapers that match the models.

Picking neighborhoods can be a good way of identifying segments, if those neighborhoods are reasonably homogeneous. The choice of how to segment is also influenced by who has discretionary income. When it comes to making business decisions it tends to be a case of "one dollar—one vote" rather than "one person—one vote."

Discretionary (disposable) income is related to the "buying power" of a household. One estimate of relative buying power (RBP) for different regions is (Aaker and Day 1990, p. 119):

$$RBP = .5Y(i) + .3R(i) + .2P(i)$$

where $Y(i)$ is the percentage of national disposable income in area i, $R(i)$ is the percentage of national retail sales in area i, and $P(i)$ is the percentage of national population in area i.

Traditionally, one of the key indicators of affluence has been home ownership. There is plenty of evidence to show that people who have lived in the same house for more than a few years tend to have good incomes and relatively low mortgage payments. However, the relationship between home ownership and discretionary income is distorted by the fact that home ownership is not always a winning proposition from the financial point of view, and marketers will generally want to target housing winners rather than housing losers.

Separating the housing winners from the housing losers is of crucial importance to any business that sells consumer products and services (Hughes 1991). Neighboring households with identical incomes and similar homes may have vastly different housing costs depending on when they bought their homes and how much of a mortgage they took out.

However, home owners across the U.S. have on average incomes twice as high as those of renters. Most home owners live in married couple households, while renters are most likely to live alone or share with other singles. Home owners also tend to be older, with 35% of them being in the peak earning years (45 to 64 years old) compared with 18% of renters.

## 10.6.2 Using Segments for Marketing Decisions

Segments are frequently referred to as clusters. In practice, clusters are collected from sample data, whereas segments are theoretical groupings of people based on the findings of clustering and discovery.

People within different clusters may be more or less likely to use a particular product. For instance, members of one cluster might use the product at three times the rate of another cluster that tends to contain older people. This information can be used either to focus on reaching those people who are likely to use the product or to reposition the product so that it appeals to the market segment not currently using it.

Clusters interest different industries or organizations in different ways. Politicians might use clusters to determine the profiles of voters versus non-voters and to target their appeal towards "swing voters." On the other hand, a moving company might be interested in which types of people tend to move frequently (i.e., make the best targets for advertising).

One way to answer this question is to take the clusters and collect data on what proportion of people within the cluster have moved recently. Using one clustering approach, for instance (Weiss 1988), one finds that the residents who are most likely to move are predominantly young, single people. This information is then of use to a variety of people in the transportation and moving business including real estate agents, shipping companies, and so on.

From the marketing perspective, interest in life-styles is focused on what people want and need and how they buy products in accordance with those needs. Descriptions such as the VALS typology give us a useful insight into the population, but they need to be linked to some keys that tell us information such as:

- Where do the various types of people live?
- What do they buy?
- How much can they afford to spend?
- Where do they get information (e.g., TV programs)?
- What types of advertising do they respond to?
- What values do they have and how do these affect product decisions?

Life-style types or clusters may sometimes help provide the answers to the questions posed above. Ideally, one would like a single typology or clustering which can be used to describe segmentation for a wide variety of products.

Consider how clustering might assist in decisions about how to target prospective book buyers or how to decide which markets to buy television advertisements in. We might start by looking at which clusters tend to have more or less people who prefer to read more books versus watch more television.

The greatest concentration of book buyers live in suburban areas and have high education and incomes, while the biggest television watchers tend to be the poorest and least educated. Armed with this information, a market planner may decide to advertise in "bookworm" zip codes for advertising a book club, while using television to reach products targeted at low income consumers.

There are many different ways to form clusters. However, the key issue is to use identifiable attributes that can be measured or collected easily, and to relate these to useful differences in purchasing behavior. One simple method of clustering that makes it easy to identify people within clusters is to cluster on the basis of zip codes. Identifying clusters with zip codes has a number of benefits, including making it relatively easy to reach specific clusters by direct mailings in specified zip code areas or through advertising in neighborhood newspapers.

Clustering of neighborhoods in this way is imperfect to the extent that neighborhoods are not homogeneous. However, it works quite well for some products because the differences between neighborhoods (clusters) are greater than the differences between households within the same neighborhood or cluster.

The clustering system described by Weiss (1988) included 40 different clusters representing different life-styles and demographic groups within the United States. Thumbnail sketches of just three of the clusters (using the labels as mentioned by Weiss) are given below to illustrate the type of information they contain. It should be noted that the incomes and home values cited are approximate and refer to the mid-1980s and should be adjusted for inflation to reflect current rates. The three clusters with accompanying demographic information are:

*New Beginnings*

4.3% of U.S. households
Primary age group 18–34
Median household income: $25,000
Median home value: $75,000
Proportion with college degrees: 19%
Demographics: middle-class city neighborhood, single and divorced apartment dwellers, some college educations, white-collar jobs

New Beginnings neighborhoods are characterized by rental housing and residents with high rates of mobility, some college educations and lower echelon white-collar jobs.

*Blue-Collar Nursery*

2.2% of U.S. households
Primary age group 25–44
Median household income: $30,000
Median home value: $67,000
Proportion with college degrees: 10%
Demographics: middle-class child-rearing towns, single-unit housing, predominantly white families, blue-collar jobs.

More traditional families (married couples with children) live in this cluster than any other. Often located on the fringe of midwestern cities, these communities consist of modest homes owned by union men employed as skilled laborers and machine operators, homemakers and working women who serve as nurses and secretaries, and their young children.

*New Homesteaders*

4.2% of U.S. households
Primary age group 18–34
Median household income: $26,000

Median home value: $67,000
Proportion with college degrees: 16%
Demographics: middle-class, single-unit housing, predominantly white families, some college education, blue- and white-collar jobs.

This cluster contains people that tend to live in remote towns in the West, with a high proportion of military jobs. Many residents have moved away from large cities.

On the face of it, the three clusters chosen tend to be fairly similar (mostly young, white, with similar incomes and similarly priced homes). There tends to be some geographical differences between the clusters with New Beginnings tending to be located in the sunbelt, Blue-Collar Nursery tending to be found in the midwest, and New Homesteaders tending to be found in the West. Taken together, these clusters account for almost 11% of the U.S. population.

The ZQ (Zip Quality) defines a scale of social rank. According to the ZQ scale, these clusters rank near the middle of the 40 clusters (New Beginnings = 15, Blue-Collar nursery = 16, and New Homesteaders = 17). Are there reliable differences in life-style and product preference between these otherwise similar clusters? In other words, can zip code-based clustering offer something over and above traditional methods of market segmentation via geography and demographics?

Residents of New Beginnings tend to buy imported cars more frequently (ranging from Hyundais to Acuras), while Blue-Collar Nurseries favor American made cars. New Beginnings residents tend to read *Rolling Stone,* while Blue-Collar Nursery residents seldom read that magazine. New Beginnings residents have a higher than average use of whole-wheat bread, while Blue-Collar Nursery residents have a much lower usage of whole-wheat bread. Blue-Collar Nursery residents show a high rate of hunting relative to other clusters, while New Beginnings residents show a relatively low rate of hunting. Finally, the rate of usage of slide projectors is fifteen times higher amongst New Beginnings residents than amongst Blue-Collar Nursery. This last piece of information would obviously be of particular interest to manufacturers of slide projectors and may also suggest the possibility of a similar split in usage of video cameras.

New Beginnings and New Homesteaders residents both have high rates of consumption of tequila and similar above-average rates of whole-wheat bread consumption. However, New Beginnings residents on average buy almost four times as many jazz records and tapes as do New Homesteaders. New Beginnings residents have a high usage of small cars or sedans, while new homesteaders have high usage of station wagons.

New Homesteaders are almost six times as likely to contribute or belong to environmentalist organizations as Blue-Collar Nursery residents. On the other hand, Blue-Collar Nursery residents are over three times as likely to belong to Christmas or Chanukah clubs.

The foregoing analysis shows that there can be marked differences in product preference, even among groups that seem otherwise fairly similar, at least in terms of net wealth, age, and ethnicity. One can tell a lot about a neighborhood based on clues such as the number of liquor stores or churches.

Our discussion so far has shown the good side of clustering, where identifiable differences can be found between clusters. However, no single clustering scheme can differentiate people on every possible attribute. A clustering scheme that works well in distinguishing amongst the cars that people buy might, for instance, does relatively poorly at predicting the use of toothpaste. The way that the clustering works in practice will depend on how the clusters were formed. For instance, if clustering is based on geography, the clusters will strongly reflect the differences in economic status that tend to differentiate neighborhoods.

In addition, clustering schemes are relatively inert. It is difficult for a clustering scheme to pick up new trends, in contrast to discovery. Thus membership in a cluster should be thought of as just another attribute that describes a person or family. In some situations, the clustering attribute may be particularly useful or predictive. In other cases, the cluster attribute may be no more useful than a demographic attribute like age.

### 10.6.3  Market Performance

The market performance of a particular product within a cluster can be estimated by comparing the use of that product within the cluster with the use of the product in general. Say that on average a particular product is bought by 5% of U.S. households, but that the product is bought by 6% of households within a particular cluster. In this case, the product is being bought at 1.2 times the national average by the cluster. Multiplying this by 100 we have a marketing performance index of 120 for this combination of product and cluster. In general, a cluster with good marketing potential for a product (i.e., a rate of use above the national average) will have a corresponding market performance of greater than 100, while a cluster that uses a product relatively infrequently will have a market performance for that product below 100.

Correlations between variables can also be exploited in analyzing market performance. For instance, do people who have American Express cards tend to buy video cameras, or are people who own personal computers more likely to read science fiction? Market performance can also be ranked for a particular trading area. For instance, we might study Redondo Beach in California and find that there is a high rate of health club membership in that city but a low rate of chewing tobacco usage.

Location based cluster norms can also be used to predict market potential for products in particular locations. The rationale for this is that if members of a cluster tend to subscribe to cable television 20% of the time, but in a particular community with a high proportion of people in that cluster only 10% are hooked up, this suggests there is potential for greater penetration of that market.

Competitive position can also be analyzed by clusters. If the manufacturer already dominates the market at better than the expected rate for that cluster, then chances are it will be less easy to expand sales further than it would be to find a market where the cluster is under-performing. Thus clustering can be used to identify "saturated" versus under-performing markets. This leads to a set of heuristics for using market performance to determine sales and advertising strategies.

If market performance of a cluster is equal to the market performance of a community belonging to that cluster then marketing performance is average for the sector or location. If there is lower market performance for the sector this suggests it is not a good segment to target the product for. More aggressive marketing (or perhaps better positioned marketing) is called for when there is high market performance for the cluster as a whole, but average local performance, since there is a likelihood of a large untapped market.

These high potential segments are of course particularly important in competitive situations where they may be exploited to increase volume and market share over a competitor. In some cases, local performance may be good, but the market performance is even better. In this case, more marketing effort may pay off in reaching the full market potential for that segment and achieving market dominance. Figure 10.14 shows a hypothetical competitive marketing analysis of geographic regions using this type of approach.

### 10.6.4    Targeted Marketing and Market Segmentation

Market segmentation is a tool where the overall market is divided into segments representing different types of consumer. The viability of each market segment will depend on whether it can provide revenues great enough to justify the marketing effort and cost in defining and reaching that segment. Targeted marketing consists of identifying different market segments and then using this knowledge to develop new product concepts, position existing products, develop pricing and advertising and distribution decisions, and to generally gain a better understanding of the market.

This section will consider how segmentation supports targeted marketing. The emphasis will be on using marketing information, applying segmentation methods,

**Figure 10.14** A hypothetical competitive marketing analysis.

adding value to the information, and presenting the resulting information in an intelligent marketing information environment.

Markets may be segmented using a number of criteria including geography, demographics in general, and psychographics, a set of "softer" or less precisely defined attributes that include life-style and values. Some of the information potentially relevant to market segmentation is extremely difficult to quantify and should be used with caution. This is particularly true of psychological variables.

In any market there will be many possible segmentations of consumers. However, only a few of these possible segmentations will be useful from a marketing standpoint. How do we identify useful market segmentations? Segments within a good market segmentation are (Bell and Vincze 1988):

- Clearly identified and measured
- Important
- Economically accessible
- Different from other segments in their response to marketing efforts
- Reasonably stable over time

Even though the preferences of market segments may change fairly rapidly (e.g., fads in the Christmas toy market come and go), well-defined market segments will tend to be more stable. However, new segments may evolve (e.g., the "gray-power" retirement age market grew in recent decades with the increased life expectancy and disposable income of the elderly), so that market researchers need to constantly reassess and refine the segmentation of the market.

Market segmentation is becoming more and more important with increasing population, more variation in life-styles, and rising consumer expectations about how products should be designed for them. However, segmentation can be expensive and time consuming and should be used judiciously.

Segmentation is inappropriate when the market is small, or when one brand dominates the market (appealing to all segments). However, in many situations segmentation provides useful information about how different consumers respond to changes in price, promotion, media, and distribution policies. Thus segmentation is the first step in complex analysis of consumers and their behavior. Segmentation may be based on a variety of criteria, such as demographics, psychographics (life-style variables), and purchasing behavior.

Our model of the segmentation process is shown in Figure 10.15. The four steps in segmentation are:

- Define segments
- Classify consumers in terms of segments
- Describe segments (in terms of customer characteristics)
- Differentiate segments

The first step involves developing a set of segments. This may be carried out using

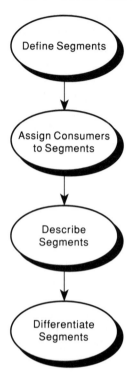

**Figure 10.15** A model of the segmentation process.

techniques such as information discovery or cluster analysis (discussed earlier in Chapter 4). The criteria by which segments are selected, and thus the segments themselves, will vary according to the marketing goals. The next step is to classify consumers in terms of these segments. Once consumers have been so classified the segments themselves can be described in terms of the characteristics of the customers that "inhabit" them. From a marketing point of view however, one must not only describe segments one must also be able to differentiate between them for a variety of reasons. Hence the fourth and final step in the analysis. Segment differentiation will generally be based on issues such as, which advertising media reach which segments, or which types of product or product positioning are most attractive to which segments. Thus segments must ultimately be judged not in terms of their general expressiveness or descriptive power but rather in terms of the leverage they provide us with in making marketing decisions and planning appropriate strategies.

Segmentation looks at the market in terms of smaller units. The more restricted a segment is and the more focused the descriptions of the customers inside it, the more focused one can be in marketing to that segment. However, there is a trade-off, because the more segments there are, the more expense is generated in marketing, product development, and so on. Segmentation is a way of improving the communication between the customer and the product but the economies of scale that are possible with large homogeneous markets tend to be lost. One can trace the history of market segmentation with a product like the automobile. When cars were first mass produced, the claim you could get a Model T Ford in any color you wanted as long as it was black. Now there are a huge range of makes, models, and colors to choose from.

Figure 10.16 illustrates the continuum between mass marketing and micro-marketing. Micro-marketing is an extreme form of segmentation where marketing is carried out with individual households, based on psychographics, product usage, neighborhood characteristics, proximity to stores, and other factors. Micro-marketing requires detailed information that can be obtained by joining census data with the type of information typically held by credit card companies.

There is a clear trend towards more and more collection of information about consumers and the marketing potential of this information naturally leads to attempts to exploit it. For instance, lists are often created as a marketable side effect of other business activity. One publishing company has eight popular book clubs representing 3 million buyers. They created a list of these buyers which can be segmented by age, sex, zip, interests, and a variety of demographic breakdowns. This list is currently being sold, as are many other similar lists.

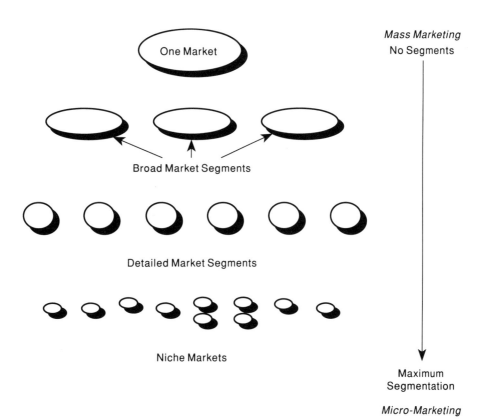

**Figure 10.16** The continuum between mass marketing and micro-marketing.

### 10.6.5 Product Positioning

Product positioning is the natural corollary of market segmentation. Faulty product positioning is a major cause of failure in about 80% of new products introduced (Hisrich and Peters 1991). The term "positioning" has a number of different senses in marketing and advertising, but we will use it to refer to the process of matching products and advertising to the wants and needs of a specified target market segment.

A product's position in the marketplace is determined by such factors as the product itself, its price, its distribution, and its promotion. Some products, for instance, are positioned as being healthy, or inexpensive, while others are position as chic, decadent, and so on. It is fairly easy to see how product positioning shows up in advertising by comparing different types of car advertisement (e.g., pickup trucks versus European luxury sedans).

Product positioning can be critical in segmented markets. Correct positioning can differentiate products from their competitors and make them more attractive to the consumers within the segment. Some of the components of product positioning include:

- Product features
- Product price
- Product applications
- Product user
- Competition
- Product class

Consider the issue of price. Normally, the cheaper a product is the more people will buy it, but this will not necessarily hold for segments where status is an overriding concern. In such segments, expensive products may outsell their cheaper competitors if they are seen to confer higher status. Often, of course, the issue of status becomes confused with quality. In some segments consumers may prefer to buy a Rolex watch over a Seiko, solely on the basis of price, and might actually be less likely to buy a Rolex if the price were lowered significantly.

Positioning by product user can also be very important. People generally identify with the image of the products they buy. In some cases there may be an apparently objective criterion against which to judge the quality of a product. Thus most people would probably like to buy the toothbrushes or toothpaste their dentists buy, or the headache medication their doctors buy, since they assume that such "experts" know best. In other cases there is probably no obvious reason to assume that one brand is better than another, so positioning becomes everything.

Product applications are used to emphasize different ways the product can be used. For instance, the use of baking soda in refrigerators was a breakthrough for that product. For beer (as seen through advertisements) the chief applications seem to be (a) create a party (usually involving attractive people), (b) reward hard work, (c) quench thirst (often in hot, dry, or dusty situations which may explain the high consumption of beer in the Australian outback), or (d) enjoy the taste. Interestingly enough, the one application that isn't stressed is getting intoxicated.

### 10.6.6  Identifying and Reaching Target Markets

Product positioning is ultimately concerned with making the right appeal to the right market. The same product can in fact be positioned differently for different markets. Weiss (1988) for instance, describes two very different market segments for Lincoln Town Cars. One group of consumers consists of the most wealthy of Americans. However, another segment consists of relatively poor blue-collar workers who live in rural communities. For the wealthier segment, the Lincoln Town Car represents sturdy family transportation, while for the less-affluent farming communities it represents a taste of the good life.

Differentiating between two such different market segments for a product requires a detailed picture of market segments constituents and purchasing patterns. Demographic information is useful, but it can be supplemented with psychographics, (i.e., measures of social trends, consumer attitudes, and buying behavior).

Although target markets can be identified, there is still the problem of reaching them. Even if a product is positioned appropriately, relevant consumers may not be aware of its existence or positioning. At this point, the goal is to find a consumer behavior that provides a point of access. Thus one point of access for college students is the college bookstore since most students buy texts from there. Similarly, specialized magazines or newspapers may provide a good way of reaching an approximation of a target group through their subscribers.

The print media understands market segmentation fairly well. Many newspapers and magazines are targeted towards particular market segments or user profiles. For instance, the *Wall Street Journal* targets people who are interested in finance and investment. This market turns out to be a fairly well-defined segment of the overall population.

As of 1989, the *Wall Street Journal* had a circulation of close to 2 million. California had the highest circulation with 240,000, followed by New York with 178,000. Subscribers were 88% male, with a median age of 49 years. 94% of the subscribers had some college education and about half of the subscribers had undertaken some postgraduate study. The median household income for the subscribers was $85,500, and almost 81% of the sample had a household income of $50,000 or more. The median net worth of subscriber households was almost half a million dollars. 80% of the sample owned stock, and over three quarters (76.5%) worked in either business or professions. Of the respondents in business or professions, over half (53.2%) were in top management and 32% were in middle management. 40% of the respondents served on at least one board of directors.

Thus it is clear that readers of the *Wall Street Journal* are a particular segment of the population. Segmentation of readership can also be seen for other journals and magazines. People can be classified to some extent by what they read, and thus particular newspapers or magazines may reach a fairly focused group of people.

Direct marketing is another way of reaching consumers. Direct marketing solicits business directly by mail, and telemarketing does the same thing over the phone. Direct marketing typically uses the mail system to send offers, catalogs, coupons, and general product information to targeted customers. The high levels of complaints about "junk mail" shows that direct mailings are not always selective in reaching target consumers. This has led to a variety of innovative attempts to get better access to targeted groups of consumers. For instance, college students are reached by placing bag inserts at college bookstores. Advertisers are particularly interested in establishing "relationships" with college students because they are young and more likely to be affluent in the future, so that establishing brand loyalty with them can pay long-term dividends.

Direct mailing worked well for the Collins Street Bakery which produced more than 4 million pounds of fruitcake (its only product) in 1990, all of which was sold by mail. Collins Street Bakery sends mailings to 10 million names annually. While the people who buy food through the mail are a relatively small segment of the population, they tend to be affluent, and thus of interest to marketers.

Marketing research information is particularly important for high technology products and services in a highly competitive market. This is because image and technology innovation become very important, and knowing how different types of customer will respond to new product and marketing strategies becomes critical. For instance, when the SPRINT long-distance phone service was initiated in 1986, the direct marketing strategy was based on low price and high quality of fiber optic connections (advertisements showed pins being dropped and heard over a long-distance call). Later, it projected itself as a company that offers enough products and services to meet every customer's needs (offering more than 30 products by 1991).

## ■ 10.7 CONCLUSIONS

Marketing and market research is a huge topic. Marketing research can add value to the huge amount of information that may be relevant, using the intelligent database approach to make it interpretable and usable. This chapter focused on marketing research (i.e., the process of collecting information about customers or potential customers and using that information to design products, position products, or target products at particular demographic or geographical segments of the population). The problems of market segmentation, product development, and product positioning were considered.

The conclusions drawn from this chapter are that marketing research is an extremely information intensive activity with a special need for combining geographic, demographic, and psychographic information. The essence of the marketing problem is the identification of relevant market segments for different products and the matching of product positioning and advertising strategies to these segments. The Market Analysis and Segmentation System can be used in a variety of ways. Product development and testing can be supported through an analysis of market segments.

This chapter also reviewed the literature on marketing and market segmentation and defined the major techniques for identifying market segments. The problem of carrying out an economic comparison of different market segment and advertising strategies was also considered. Finally, this chapter described an intelligent database application for marketing research, the Market Analysis and Segmentation System. The following chapter will examine quality control and improvement as another application domain that will benefit greatly from the use of intelligent databases.

# 11

# INTELLIGENT QUALITY CONTROL

*After the war, we studied quality control and actively incorporated this concept into our operations. The basic idea behind QC of "creating product quality within the process" is essentially identical to Kiichiro's thinking. This was an idea that could have occurred to anyone. What set him apart was his initiative in putting the idea to practice.*

— Eijii Toyoda*

*Corollary*: Quality does not happen by chance. An initiative must be shown for it. The quest for quality within the organization must be unending.

## ■ 11.1 INTRODUCTION

In an increasingly competitive global marketplace customers expect more and more from the products and services that they buy. While the goal of a business is the pursuit of profit, this goal can best be achieved through the creation and maintenance of satisfied customers. If a company or organization can better serve the needs of their customers they will have a significant competitive edge. Thus the goals of an organization are driven to a large extent by the needs of its users or customers and quality is not a luxury but a necessity. Quality should be the first goal of a business.

The idea of quality is directly related to the concept of brand name. The word "quality" is strongly associated with manufactured goods. This has occurred through the growth of the consumer society since the first world war (as discussed in Chapter 10). In the process of building consumer loyalty to brand names, quality became important to manufacturers. When the brand name was associated with quality, quality became a significant business tool.

High-quality products require high-quality information about customer needs and preferences, the reasons why defects occur, and the status of ongoing production processes. With high-quality information, higher quality products can often be

---

* *Toyota, Fifty Years in Motion,* Kodansha, New York, 1987. Eijii Toyoda was born in 1913 in Japan and graduated from Tokyo University with a degree in mechanical engineering. Along with Kiichiro Toyoda he was part of the formation of the Toyota Motor Company, eventually becoming its president.

achieved at little if any additional cost. Thus information, and information technology, is an essential part of quality improvement.

In focusing on internal quality, control has to be preceded by a management structure that can motivate and pursue quality. If the management structure is not suited to pursuit of quality, then effective control of quality is not possible. This expanded view of quality leads to the concept of total quality management which is discussed in later sections of this chapter. This is distinguished from basic quality control in being a single-minded pursuit of quality in all its forms. In contrast, the basic method of quality control (i.e., statistical quality control) is best suited to highly repetitive and fine-grained tasks. These tasks are not necessarily production tasks since one can use measures such as the average call answering times for service operators and so on.

The essence of quality control is setting up quality as a goal to be pursued and modifying practice in order to ensure that the goal of quality is achieved as nearly as possible. As the above quotation from Toyoda points out, assurance of quality is not a revolutionary or controversial idea. It is the conversion of that idea into practice that is challenging.

This chapter reviews the traditional methods of quality control and supplements them with an intelligent database-oriented analysis. Three new tools for quality control extending the traditional seven tools are discussed: the eighth tool—automatic discovery; the ninth tool—3D visualization; and the tenth tool—hyperinformation. These new tools complement the existing array of quality tools (Parsaye and Chignell 1992). Quality Through Discovery, an intelligent quality control system that adds new methods for visualization of quality control data, is described in this chapter. This system links the various methods of quality data visualization with a hypermedia user interface. This chapter also differentiates terms such as quality control and statistical quality control from more holistic methods such as quality assurance and total quality management.

The following section reviews the history of quality control and outlines some basic concepts.

## ■ 11.2 HISTORY AND EVOLUTION OF QUALITY

The history of "nonscientific" quality goes back to ancient times. People have always striven for improvement. At one time, quality was synonymous with craftsmanship. Many early cultures prided themselves on the quality of their craftsmanship, preeminent examples being swords from Damascus, Phoenician ships, and Hittite chariots. Remnants of early craftsmanship live on in museums and private collections. The pyramids in Egypt and Central America are a testimonial to the quality work of the early stonemasons. These ancient structures will likely outlast most, if not all, of today's modern buildings.

While people have generally wanted quality, it has not always been pursued in a persistent and determined fashion. Quality has to be achieved through a quality process, which involves continuous evaluation and refinement.

The scientific approach to quality only dates back to the time immediately preceding the second world war. The origins of scientific quality control began with the work of W. A. Shewhart on statistical quality at Bell Laboratories in the 1930s. These theoretical ideas were put into practice quickly due to the demands of the war. By using the quality standard known as Z-1, the U.S. managed to manufacture military supplies inexpensively and in vast quantities, gaining a significant military edge.

The British Standards 600 were in use in England in 1935, based on the statistical work of Karl Pearson, the inventor of the correlation coefficient. In some sense, the use of quality control helped win the war for the allies.

Following the war, methods of quality control continued to evolve in the West. Many organizations focused on quality and improved products and production processes. However, the lesson to be learned here is that progress alone is not enough. Progress has to be measured against the standards of the competition. While the U.S. was making progress in quality, the Japanese were progressing significantly faster by methodically applying quality control techniques throughout industry.

While Japanese products were known for their low quality in the 1950s, quality and Japan are almost synonymous today. The science of modern quality has been greatly impacted by the systematic use of quality control techniques in Japan.

During the war the British Standards 600 were translated into Japanese. However, they were not fully utilized during the war. In view of the fact that quality has become the key weapon in economic wars, it is something of an irony that the roots of quality control and quality assurance in Japan go back to General Douglas MacArthur who was tired of getting the wrong phone numbers in Tokyo. He arranged for a few quality control people from AT&T to visit Tokyo to teach the Japanese how to fix the phone system, and in May 1946, effectively began the quality movement in Japan.

The Japan Union of Scientists and Engineers (JUSE) was also formed in 1946 and established a quality control research group in 1949. Since then, JUSE has become one of the key forces in introducing the concept of quality to the world. In 1950, JUSE arranged a series of lectures on quality by W. Edwards Deming. Those eight days of lectures were attended by many company presidents as well as engineers, and had a significant impact on the future of quality control. Deming, who was well-versed in statistics, explained the basic ideas of what is today called statistical quality control. He returned to Japan in 1951 and 1952.

In 1954, JUSE invited J.M. Juran to visit Japan for another series of lectures. In his lectures he emphasized the limits of statistical quality control and the need to view quality as a management tool. This contrasted with Deming's approach to quality based on mathematical tools. These two points of view provided a well-balanced recipe for success.

The concept of "total quality management" originated in an earlier idea of total quality control discussed by Armand Feigenbaum, who, in the 1950s, directed quality control programs. He published the first article on total quality control (Feigenbaum 1957), which was followed by a book on that subject (Feigenbaum 1961).

JUSE promoted the seven tools of quality discussed later in this chapter and released the product JUSE/QCASE, which became one the best-selling software products in Japan. The seven tools used 2D diagrams and relatively simple computation, reflecting the conditions of the 1950s. Today we need new tools of quality that exploit the new capabilities created through computer technology. Some of these new tools will be outlined later in this chapter.

Today, quality is a worldwide quest and W. Edwards Deming is the best-known of the quality gurus. Born at the turn of the century, Deming, the son of Wyoming pioneers, later became a statistician and worked with Shewhart. Following his visit to Japan, Deming filled the role of leader for quality engineers in Japan's strongly hierarchical society. Some of his key ideas were:

- Quality is defined by the customer
- In every process, variation must be understood and reduced
- Top management must be continuous and all-encompassing
- There must be ongoing education and training of all employees
- Performance rating schemes are usually destructive

Demingism developed as an approach to quality, and in Japan it was enshrined in the Deming Prize. The Deming Prize is awarded by JUSE as the highest award for quality in Japan. Winning the Deming Prize has been an obsession in Japan since 1951. Winners have to show their ability to master the process of improvement and adapt to new customer demands and market conditions. The rigorous competition for the prize made companies tougher and more resilient in the face of competition in the global marketplace. So great has been the influence of the quality approach in Japan, that by the 1980s statistical theory became part of the basic curriculum in Japanese high schools (Gabor 1990).

Deming did not receive widespread recognition in the United States until the 1980s, when he became a key player in quality improvement efforts in a range of companies including the Ford Motor Company. While there are a number of other prominent quality theorists and practitioners in the United States and abroad, it is hard to imagine what modern quality approaches would have been like without Deming and his contribution.

However, now quality has progressed well beyond the basic concepts laid down in the 1950s. One of the most important components in the successful pursuit of quality has become the recognition that since quality in a competitive environment must be always increasing, a continuous process of improvement is necessary. In Japan this process of "continuous improvement in the system" is called Kaizen. Kaizen (Imai 1986) involves not only abrupt change associated with new technologies and improvements, but also a more gradual and subtle form of continuous change. Some of the groundwork for the Kaizen approach was laid in Deming's early lectures in Japan, when he stressed the importance of constant interaction among research, design, production, and sales, in order to improve quality. One mechanism for improvement was the Deming wheel (reproduced in Figure 11.1).

One of the outcomes of the Kaizen approach has been seven tools of quality that emphasize the information needed for gradual but continuous improvement. Some of these tools are:

*Relationship Diagram* — This diagram resembles an entity-relationship model and is used to show cause and effect relationships between factors.

*Affinity Diagram* — This diagram clusters information into groups. It is frequently used as a brainstorming method.

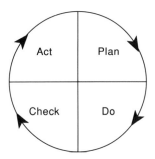

**Figure 11.1** The Deming wheel (also known as the Shewart or PDCA cycle). Adapted from J. Horowitz, *Critical Path Scheduling: Management Control through CPM and PERT* (Ronald Press, 1967).

*Tree Diagram*—This diagram creates a more detailed hierarchical structure showing the interrelations among goals and measures.

*Arrow Diagram*—This diagram uses a network representation to show the steps necessary to implement a plan. It is closely related to the flow process charts used in industrial engineering.

Continuous improvement is more than a matter of using specific tools and techniques. It also requires commitment and a management style that encourages and rewards improvement. One strategy for promoting improvement is to give workers time to think about the processes they use and how they may be bettered. For instance, one Japanese company told its foremen to set aside the half hour before noon as Kaizen time, where they were to think about improvement in the workshop.

With the success of Japanese products the focus on quality is now worldwide. The Baldridge award in quality is the U.S. award for quality improvement. Today quality is no longer a companywide effort but a nationwide effort. For instance, consider the database of human body parts that is being developed at Ibaraki National Labs in Japan. Measurements of finger lengths, arm lengths, etc. from fifty thousand people around the world are being developed to feed into CAD systems for the better design of car seats, etc. This database will then be available to automobile manufacturers for simulation of quality tests. Similar anthropometric databases were developed for the U.S. airforce and are available for various industrial design tasks.

The example above not only shows the impact of databases on quality, but also emphasizes the importance of the M-form cooperative structures discussed by William Ouchi (Ouchi 1984). In the M-form model, several organizations and the government cooperate to establish standards and techniques which have widespread benefits to national industry.

It must be noted that what we know of Japanese QC in the world today is a snapshot of the past. Today many Japanese corporations have developed advanced, proprietary, and closely guarded techniques for corporate management with quality that exceed the familiar methods discussed in the open literature. U.S. and European companies will simply have to follow suit, making quality a key proprietary technology and the key to competitiveness.

Thus, with the renewed interest in quality in the U.S., the quality race is on for the ultimate benefit of the consumer. It is not just quality progress that matters; in today's competitive environment it is the relative amount of progress made by nations and corporations that counts. Information technology is the key factor in winning the quality race since it affects how quickly one can improve quality in an increasingly complex environment. The recent push towards quality in the U.S. has already begun to show positive results, confirming the fact that with the right tools and the commitment of management, quality can be achieved routinely. In Europe, the ISO-9000 standards are also likely to improve quality dramatically.

## ■ 11.3  BASIC CONCEPTS OF QUALITY CONTROL

Quality control is not just a matter of weeding out the defects. In the ideal case it is a process of continually striving for improvement in activities ranging from product design to cost cutting, production processes, and maintenance. Information should be diagnostic, and information should be representative of the process being analyzed. This section will review the concepts of quality control, distinguishing between quality control and quality assurance, beginning with the basic notion of quality itself.

### 11.3.1  What is Quality?

Like motherhood and apple pie, the word "quality" has such positive connotations that its meaning and importance is seldom discussed. What manufacturer would want to admit that it was not selling a quality product, or what organization would not claim that it provided quality service? Since quality is something that everyone claims and aspires to, its meaning is continuously debased. Quality is treated as if it were a standard that can be routinely adjusted to meet current practice.

Even for a single product or system, quality can be difficult to define. What quality is depends on the purpose of the product or system, and the expectations of its users. The first definition of quality, and the one that is probably the most frequently used, is an empty one, where quality is a vaguely defined standard, easy to aspire to but difficult to measure. The new customers in the shop might be encouraged to "feel the quality," knowing full well that many customers certainly wouldn't know quality if they felt it. Similarly, a car might be marketed as a quality product, yet most consumers will not be in a position to assess the validity of that claim.

One of the major problems in assessing the quality of any product is that modern products are generally fairly complex and can be measured along a number of different attributes. Consider a car. It is made up of a number of different subsystems including the engine, drive train, and electrical system. To most people, however, the parts of the car that are readily visible are the exterior and the interior of the passenger compartment, including the dashboard/driver interface. Since each of the subsystems of the car are very distinct, we can separately assess their quality. For instance, a car might have a high-quality exterior, but a poor engine, or vice versa. Thus quality is generally not a unitary concept, but can be separately assessed for different components of each product, service, or process. The quality that matters is the quality that is recognized by customers, which in turn influences purchase decisions. However, experience has shown that, in a competitive environment, customers can be educated about quality. Customer expectations of product quality, and the quality of the competing products, will generally drive each other upwards in a type of positive feedback loop.

Quality is an attribute of systems as well as products. For instance, in a public mass transit system, many of the users may have few alternative means of transport, yet the notion of quality is still relevant. Here quality may be assessed in terms of factors such as safety and cost efficiency, along with the overall satisfaction of the users of the transit system. Thus the notion of what constitutes quality will change depending on the product or system being assessed.

Since quality is relative it cannot be measured on an absolute scale. Yet, we have a concept of quality that is independent of particular products or systems. If people are asked to rank order products such as cars in terms of their "quality," they can generally carry out the task. Similarly, if people are asked to rank order soft drinks or fruit juices in terms of quality they can generally do that too. People treat quality as if it were a yardstick that can be applied to almost anything. The quality yardstick is not like a ruler, however, because it stretches or shrinks depending on what's available. In a famine, overripe fruit will be perceived to have much higher quality than in times of plenty, and in the former East Germany, the Trabant and Lada were perceived to have higher quality than they did after unification, when they were explicitly compared with the Mercedes Benz, BMW, Audi, Volkswagen, and Opel.

Quality is not a fixed standard, because standards are always changing. Nowhere is this fact of shifting standards clearer than in the world of international athletics. A performance that would have won a gold medal at the 1896 Olympic games in Athens would now be laughable in the context of current international competition. When Edwin Flack of Australia ran the 1500 meters in four and a half minutes in Athens in 1896 he received a gold medal for his effort. Today, many high school athletes could easily better that time. Similarly, it took Thomas Hicks of the United States almost three and a half hours to run (and win!) the Olympic marathon in 1904.

Rather than being a fixed standard, quality is a goal and an associated process that ensures that products, services, and processes are as good as they can be within the context of current constraints such as the availability of technology and resources.

Clearly the manufacturer who could sell two boxes instead of one would be better off, so having products that sometime failed wouldn't worry the manufacturer unless it worried the customer. Thus quality goals will not be effective unless there are discriminating customers who show a preference for quality products. Strategies such as planned obsolescence and making profits through service and maintenance, become less viable when competitors are prepared to make a product that works better and lasts longer for the same price. Thus the notion of competition is inextricably linked with quality.

Quality arises in a competitive market where customers choose to buy higher quality products and thereby motivate further improvement in quality. The competition between products in the marketplace and the evolution of products through the economic pressure engendered by consumer preferences and purchases is somewhat analogous to the competition between species in the environment and their evolution under the pressure of natural selection and the survival of the fittest.

When quality becomes a sufficiently important motivating force, manufacturers will seek to "institutionalize" it, using methods and programs such as quality assurance, quality management, and quality control. At this point the organization focuses on quality improvement, that is, the pursuit of products and processes that match customers needs and expectations.

There are two general methods of designing for improvement. The first method corresponds to what is known as "open-loop control" (Wickens 1992) where one attempts to understand or model a process, predict outcomes based on different input alternatives, and then select the input that will provide the most favorable outcome. In this first method of improvement, one utilizes a combination of understanding and prediction.

The second method of improvement is somewhat different in that it uses closed-loop control and negative feedback. It is used frequently when a process or system is poorly understood. The basic idea in this second method of improvement is to recognize problems and then fix them. It is the same idea that drives rapid prototyping and iterative design (as discussed in Chapter 3). This method can be very effective, but it requires much less understanding. However, since it is basically a trial and error method, it will lead to costly failures from time to time, when attempted improvements are made but the cure turns out to be worse than the disease because of a lack of understanding of the process or the ability to predict the effect of design changes.

## 11.3.2 Forms of Quality

Quality is a goal or criterion that can be used to evaluate the success of manufacturing and production systems. However, there are a number of distinct paths to producing quality. This section will briefly distinguish between three methodologies of quality, namely, *quality control, quality assurance,* and *total quality management. Quality control* is a process of making sure that products conform to certain standards or guidelines. In particular, quality control is often associated with statistical quality control (SQC). The idea of SQC is to inspect or sample key attributes of the product or production process and compare variations in these attributes with a statistical model of random variability. When systematic deviations from the standard are detected, the quality analyst then "flags" them and the production process is modified as needed.

One of the problems with this form of quality control is that it is essentially reactive. Errors and problems are detected only after they have occurred. In addition, the production line or assembly process has to be stopped while the necessary alterations and changes are made.

*Quality assurance* attempts to maintain the quality standards in a more proactive way. Thus, in addition to using quality control methods to identify errors, quality assurance may go further by surveying customers to determine their level of satisfaction with the product. Problems can thus be identified early. For instance, a product might tend to develop cracks in its handle after prolonged used. Surveying customers may alert the quality assurance to the problem before customers actually start reporting breakages to the customer service center.

Quality control reacts to identified quality problems, quality assurance attempts to anticipate quality problems. Thus quality assurance conforms more closely to the goal of continuous improvement or Kaizen.

The final step in focusing on quality is to use a *total quality management* (TQM) approach where quality is striven for in every aspect of a business or industry. The total quality approach is concerned with every aspect of an operation, not just the end product. For instance, this approach attempts to reduce scrap and waste as much as possible, so that money is invested in the product, and in profits, rather than in needless waste.

Total quality also involves motivating the workers to perform at a high level and to ceaselessly strive to improve quality within their own sphere of influence. One method for doing this is the quality circle approach. Here, groups of workers (circles) periodically meet to discuss the nature of their work as it relates to quality and to suggest various improvements. The concept of total quality will be discussed further in a later section of this chapter.

Total quality management includes tracking of statistical quantities such as the number of sales leads. However, the essential difference between TQM and SQC is that the former examines all relevant factors in an integrated way rather than focusing on one or a few quantities in particular.

### 11.3.3 Seven Tools of Quality Control

The basic idea of quality control is to measure some critical parameters that are related to the quality of a product over time, determine the level and variation for each of these parameters, and then feed back this information so as to adjust the production process in line with greater quality. This cybernetic (negative feedback) process view of quality control is illustrated in Figure 11.2, which shows the need for a continuous loop of information, decisions, and actions in improving quality.

One of the principles of negative feedback systems is that the shorter the lag between measurement and feedback the more responsive the system is in adapting to change. A simple illustration of this principle is adjusting the temperature of water using hot and cold faucets. A person notices that the water is not at the "right" temperature (i.e., too cold) and turns up the hot water. However, if there is a lag in the system, this change in the control will not yet be reflected in the water temperature. Thus the person may increase the level of the hot water a second time. A short time later the first control input may take effect and the water becomes warm enough, but soon after the water becomes too hot (reflecting the increase caused by the second control input). Not surprisingly, systems with lags in them are notoriously hard to control. Imagine if you had to drive a car where there was a few seconds pause between a control input (turning the steering wheel) and the system response (a change in the direction or heading of the car). This is the problem for the supertanker captain who has to deal with a huge lag in the steering response of the ship due to its large size and inertia.

So, one of the fundamental principles of quality control is that the lag between measurement and control should be as short as possible. By the time data are analyzed in the corporate headquarters and the printouts sent to the shop floor, the production process may have changed several times due to various disturbances. The solution to a lag in the system has been to make quality control part of the production process. Operators themselves monitor the production process and detect when it deviates from

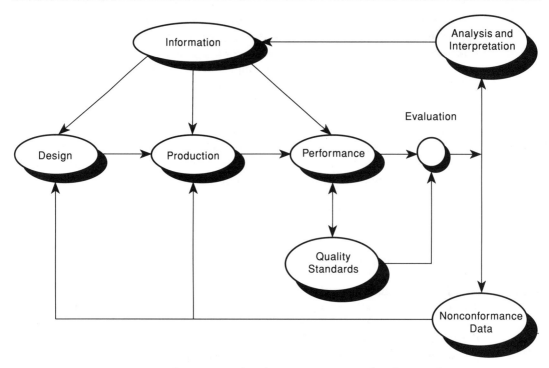

**Figure 11.2** The cybernetic process view of quality control.

desirable limits using specially designed and easy-to-use tools.

The problem of quality control of a production process is closely related to the problem of observing a statistical process and detecting when changes occur. Any production process will have "natural" variations that are outside the scope of the production process and "production-related" variations that are due to factors such as the skill of the operator or the mechanical status of the machine. Natural variations will tend to vary unsystematically. This is not to say that they are not caused by some external phenomenon, but simply that the source of the variation lies outside the system being controlled. For instance, in the water temperature example, there may be momentary fluctuations in the temperature of the hot water due to the on-off cycle of the water heater. These fluctuations will generally be outside the control of the operator and, with a good thermostat, will not lead to significant deviations from the set point. Quality control is a statistical process because a clear distinction has to be made between natural variation and product-related variation.

Attempts to control natural variation will actually increase, rather than decrease that variation. Technically, this is because the control inputs will be uncorrelated with the "natural" causes of variation. For instance, in a well-known demonstration by Deming, a marble is dropped through a funnel onto a target below. When the marble is repeatedly dropped through the funnel, it will sometimes roll to the left of the target and sometimes to the right. To all intents and purposes, the distribution of positions that the marble rolls to can be taken to be the result of a random process. Attempts to control such a random process are doomed to failure. If a "diligent" operator now attempts to move the funnel to correct for the positional error on each trial (e.g., the funnel is moved to the right when the error is to the left and vice versa) the errors will in fact increase! Thus the fundamental problem for quality control is to detect when control inputs are needed.

A quality control tool should track the production process and tell operators when a control input is required. The tool should be easy to understand and use, methodologically sound, and if possible indicative of what the problem is and what needs to be changed. As with intelligent database applications in general, the right tool depends a great deal on how people prefer to visualize information.

Based on years of experience in encapsulating and displaying quality-related information to operators, seven tools of quality have been developed. These tools are *flow charts, cause-and-effect diagrams* (also called fish-bone or Ishikawa diagrams), *check sheets, histograms, scatter diagrams, Pareto charts,* and *control charts.* These tools have had widespread success because they enable quality control engineers to "see through" their data, understand the reasons for quality problems, and come up with solutions for eliminating them.

Figure 11.3 shows a functional classification of the seven quality control tools. In order to control quality one must understand the underlying process, collect relevant data that describes the process, analyze important relationships within the process, identify the most critical problems to be addressed, and detect change (in the critical parameters). The seven most popular quality control tools and their role in overall quality control have been outlined above. Flow charts and cause-and-effect diagrams provide alternative ways of understanding the process, while data can be collected using check sheets and summarized using histograms. In practice, data may also be collected using automated data-logging equipment, and data may be summarized and presented using a wide range of statistical and data presentation methods. Scattergrams can be used to analyze relationships with the data. These relationships can also be quantified using statistical correlation, and more complex methods can be used to analyze relationships within the data (regression analysis and a variety of multivariate statistical methods). Each of the seven basic tools of quality control is described below.

**11.3.3.1** *Flow Charts*  One of the tasks in quality control is to describe or represent the process of interest. A flow chart is a method of representing a process that is used not only in quality control, but also in computer programming and in time and motion study (e.g., Barnes 1980).

A flow chart is basically a set of boxes (or pictures) connected with arrows. Different types of flow chart can be constructed by using different types of box or arrow. For instance, in a computer flow chart, a distinction is made between data and decisions. So a diamond might indicate some kind of test condition with two outgoing arrows (one for a yes answer, the other for a no answer). Flow diagrams are also related to state-transition diagrams (used in engineering). However, for quality control, flow diagrams generally have well-defined start and end points and time is an important

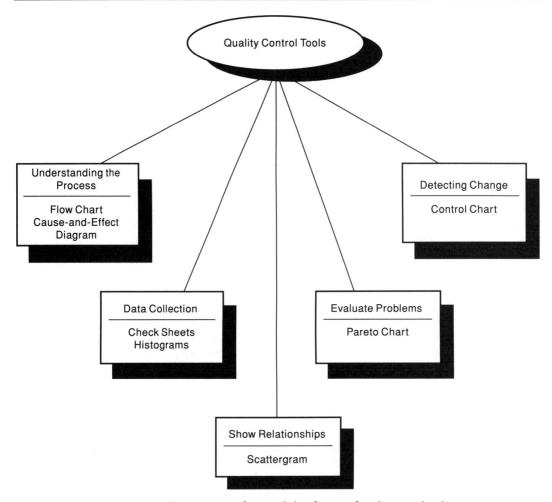

**Figure 11.3** A functional classification of quality control tools.

factor, so that the whole chart corresponds to the flow of products, people, or parts through some process over time. An example of a flow chart is shown in Figure 11.4.

Flow charts help answer questions (Burr 1990) such as "Where does the service or material come from? How does the service or material get to the process? Who makes the decisions that are needed? What happens for each outcome of each decision?"

Flow charts are particularly important in ensuring that the people who work in a process understand that process and see where they fit into it. Once workers understand a process they are in a better position to improve it.

***11.3.3.2 Cause-and-Effect Diagrams*** The flow chart is good at representing what is happening, but not why things are happening, or what factors are causing poor quality. In general, a cause-and-effect diagram represents the causal structure of a process (Figure 11.5 on page 472). In quality control, variants of such diagrams are often used where the

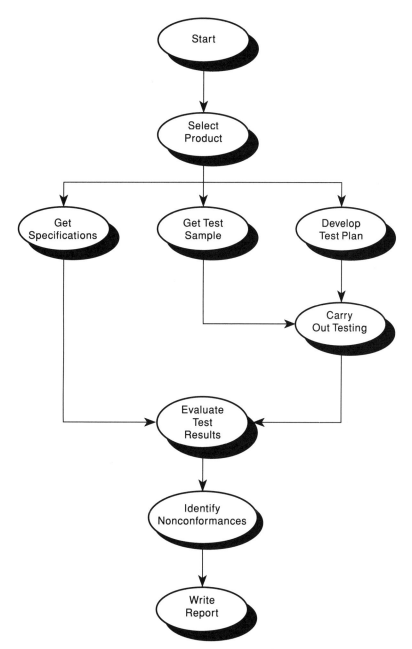

**Figure 11.4** A flow chart example.

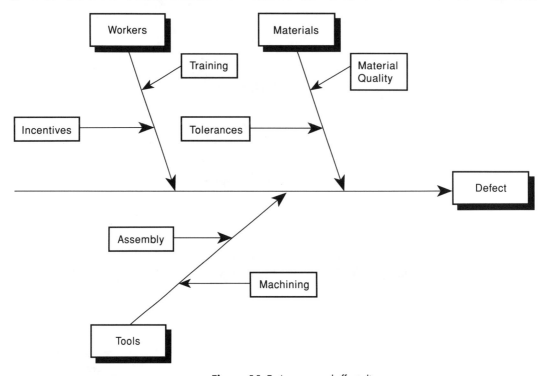

**Figure 11.5** A cause-and-effect diagrm.

effect of interest is a defect and the task is to identify the main causes of this defect. Cause-and-effect diagrams are particularly useful when used by teams in tracking the causes of defects.

Cause-and-effect diagrams provide an excellent means to facilitate a brainstorming session. Sarazen (1990) gives the example of an organization that is having problems with customer complaints. Several people with different functions meet to work on the problem and understand its causes. They begin by agreeing on the problem (i.e., customer dissatisfaction). One of the team (or a facilitator) then writes the problem down and draws a box around it, with an arrow running into it. The team now generates ideas about what is causing the effect of customer dissatisfaction (e.g., product quality, service, order processing, and so on). Each of these causes may then be treated as effects that have their own underlying causes. Upstream causes flow into effects which then become the causes of effects further downstream. This is illustrated in the cause-and-effect diagram shown in Figure 11.5. Diagrams such as this are sometimes referred to as fish-bone diagrams because of their appearance.

An important variation of the cause-and-effect diagram is the process-classification diagram. Here the key quality-related characteristics are listed for each of the steps in the process. Thus a process-classification diagram may be thought of as a kind of merger between a flow chart and a cause-and-effect diagram. A natural way to build the process-classification diagram is to build a flow process chart and then annotate that chart with all the causes or influences that may affect the quality of each step. As with the flow process chart, brainstorming with qualified people should make this a useful and valid representation of the process.

**11.3.3.3** *Check Sheets*     Quality control requires collection and summarization of data, in addition to description and representation of the underlying process. Check sheets are tools that simplify the data collection process. They are important because analysis of quality typically requires a lot of data. This data itself should be of high quality (i.e., valid and representative) so that conclusions drawn and modifications made do in fact improve the process. A check sheet serves as a template for recording data, thus ensuring the validity and integrity of the data.

Check sheets are forms or templates that guide operators in collecting data that is relevant to quality assessment. Check sheets are methods for "questioning" the process in a standard way. Considerable care should be taken in designing check sheets. The data collected should directly address the question being asked, and the form of the check sheet should encourage accurate tabulation of the data.

An example of a check sheet is shown in Figure 11.6. In this figure the value of a continuous variable (humidity) is plotted directly on a graph. Note here that in some situations this data might have been collected by a machine (e.g., a chart recorder of humidity in an art museum). Another type of check sheet simply counts (tabulates) the number of each type of error that is encountered. For instance, a photocopier repair man might tabulate all the problems encountered during service calls and this information could then improve the design or manufacture of future machines (note that in this example there is a long lag in the system, however, this lag may be acceptable with a stable product line).

Check sheets may also be merged with layout representations of the product to produce topographic models of quality variation. For instance, a location plot of chip rejects within an integrated circuit may be shown. Locations with extensive defects are marked on the chip's location plot. Armed with this information it may then be possible to find a cause in the manufacturing or handling process for this pattern of rejects.

**11.3.3.4** *Histograms*     Data collection is typically followed by data summarization and analysis. Histograms are one of the most popular ways of summarizing data. A histogram shows the distribution or variation in a set of data. Histograms allow people to detect patterns that they could never see in a table of numbers.

Each bar in a histogram represents a range of values. The height of each bar represents the frequency (count) of data points that were observed in that range. It is much easier to the overall pattern in the data when it is presented as a histogram, rather than as a table (Figure 11.7 on page 475).

Histograms are a way of representing the distribution of data. We can ask questions such as "Is there one value, or range of values, where a larger number of observations tend to occur, or are the observations distributed fairly evenly across the entire range?" Questions such as this can be answered by looking at the shape of the distribution. Figure 11.7 shows some different histogram shapes. Panel *a* shows a symmetrical single peaked distribution, while panel *b* shows a bimodal (two-peaked)

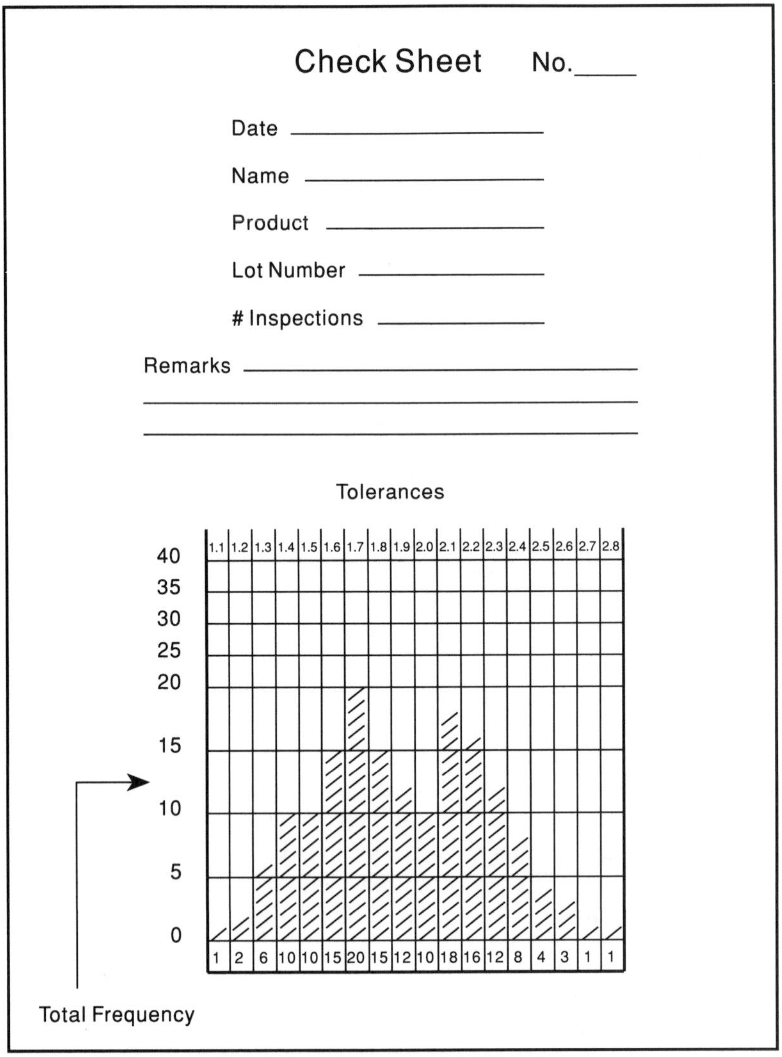

**Figure 11.6** A check sheet.

distribution. Panel *c* shows a skewed (asymmetrical) distribution where there are a lot of data points on one side of the range and then a "tail" spreading out over the other end of the range. Finally, panel *d* shows a flat (uniform) distribution.

There are in fact many different shapes that can be encountered in data, but for practical purposes the interest here is in the shape of a distribution because it can sometimes provide clues about the process which generated the data values. For instance, a skewed distribution may occur when a practical limit exists on one side of the range but not the other. A common example of this occurs with time (duration). A zero second duration imposes a practical limit on the left edge of any time

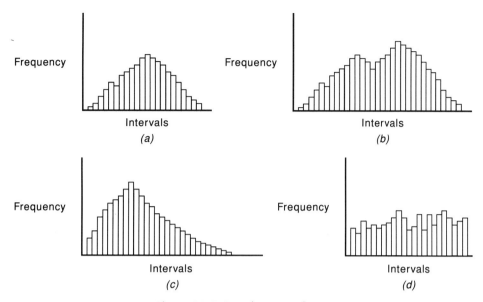

**Figure 11.7** Some histogram shapes.

distribution (one can't have negative time duration) so that quicker times are bunched up towards this practical limit while slower times can extend out over longer durations indefinitely.

***11.3.3.5  Scatter Diagrams***     Histograms summarize the distribution of a single variable or attribute. Basic scatter diagrams are a way of viewing the relations between two variables. 3D and N-D scattergrams may be used to plot the relationship between more than two variables. This type of "multidimensional" data plotting was discussed earlier in the context of data visualization (Chapter 5), but has not traditionally been used in quality control. The problem of plotting higher dimensional data for quality control applications will be returned to in a later section of this chapter.

Figure 11.8 shows some examples of scatter diagrams. Here one variable is plotted on the x-axis and the other variable is plotted on the y-axis. Each piece of data is then represented as a point corresponding to x and y coordinates. In scattergrams a positive relationship is indicated when the points fall roughly in line going from lower left to upper right (panel *a* of Figure 11.8), while a negative relationship is indicated by a similar line going from upper left to lower right of the diagram panel *b*. While the scattergram provides a visual representation, the relation can also be quantified as a number between −1 and 1 using a measure of statistical correlation. A correlation of −1 means that there is a perfect negative relation between the two variables (i.e., the value of one of the variables consistently decreases as the other increases), +1 means a perfect positive relation, and 0 means no relation at all (knowing the value of one variable does not help in any way in predicting the corresponding value of the other variable).

Relations between variables can be helpful in identifying problems. Consider a

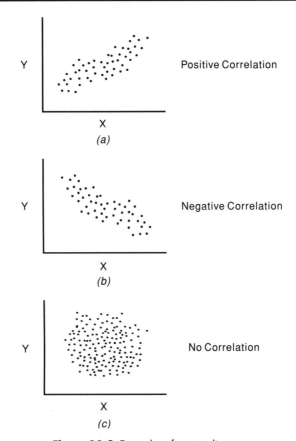

**Figure 11.8** Examples of scatter diagrams.

hypothetical situation where an inspection process is being monitored. Figure 11.9 shows the scattergram plotting the product flaws detected during 15-minute intervals across an eight hour working day. In this hypothetical data, there is a strong negative correlation between detection rate and time. One explanation for this is that there is a fatigue process and that quality of inspection may improve by scheduling more rest breaks or by improving the lighting. Figure 11.10 shows similar data plotted for each day in a five day week. The consistent pattern of negative correlation across the five days supports the idea that a fatigue process may be influencing inspection performance.

***11.3.3.6 Pareto Charts*** Histograms and scattergrams are "generic" charts that can be used for a wide variety of purposes. Pareto charts are more focused in their emphasis on presenting information of particular interest in quality control. A Pareto chart (e.g., Figure 11.11 on page 478) is a type of bar chart where the bars are generally ordered according to decreasing value. The purpose of a Pareto chart is to identify the most important issues or defects that need to be addressed.

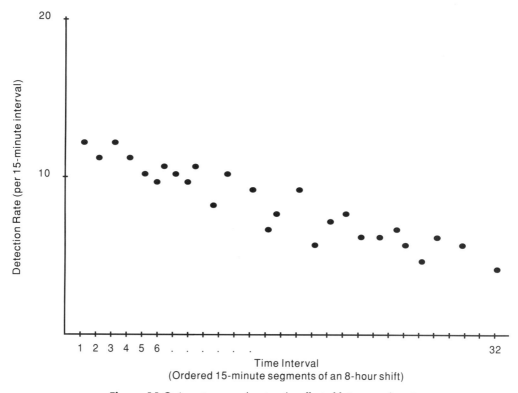

**Figure 11.9** A scattergram showing the effect of fatigue on detection rate.

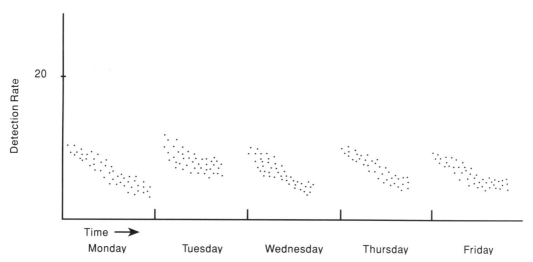

**Figure 11.10** Scattergrams showing daily fluctuations in detection rate during a 5-day working week.

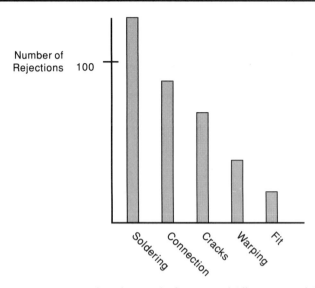

Number of
Rejections   100

Soldering   Connection   Cracks   Warping   Fit

**Figure 11.11** A Pareto chart showing the frequency of different types of defects.

The use of Pareto charts reflects the need to get "the biggest bang for the buck" since it is often necessary to balance costs and benefits in analyzing and controlling quality. There may be a limited budget for improving the production process, and one should maximize the impact on quality that is possible with the resources available. The Pareto chart indicates how the Pareto principle should be applied. The Pareto principle was named after an Italian economist of the nineteenth century who found that a large share of the wealth was owned by relatively few people. The Pareto principle has been generalized to cover a wide range of situations and is sometimes referred to as the 80/20 rule. For instance, 80% of the progress is made with 20% of the effort, or 80% of scrap or other quality-related costs come from 20% of the possible causes.

The Pareto principle implies that we should chase up the problems and causes that have the biggest impact on quality and cost. Pareto charts are methods for identifying these problems and causes from the data. Relevant data might include number of customer complaints, number of errors (e.g., rejected parts) or number of jobs that have to be redone. Once a measurement variable is chosen, the data is then plotted according to the categories or causes of interest. For instance, Figure 11.11 shows a Pareto chart for percentage of rejects versus reason for rejection. This chart is actually a bar chart, but the bars have been ordered in terms of decreasing size. If we assume in this case that the rejects are equally costly, regardless of the cause, then it can be seen that eliminating the most frequent cause of rejection is the best place to start.

A modified version (double) Pareto chart may then be used to make comparisons. Figure 11.12 shows hypothetical data for rejection rates before and after a quality improvement program. Here it can be seen immediately that the bars in the left-hand side of the figure (after the program) are generally lower than the bars in the right-hand side of the figure (before the program).

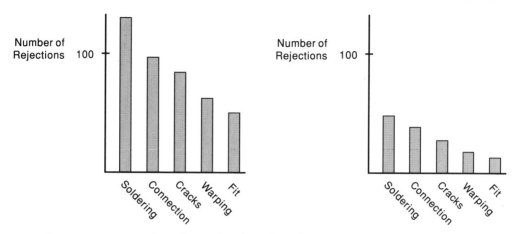

**Figure 11.12** Pareto charts showing hypothetical data for rejection rates before and after improvement.

***11.3.3.7 Control Charts*** Flow charts and cause-and-effect diagrams are good tools for understanding processes, and check sheets, histograms, scattergrams, and Pareto charts are good for summarizing and analyzing data, but they don't provide control information in relation to an ongoing process. In contrast, a control chart is specifically designed to detect when a process has changed (and consequently, when control inputs are needed).

Control charts are the main tool for statistical process control (SPC). The statistical approach recognizes that there will always be some random variation in any process, and seeks to detect change against this noise (background variation). Consider the distribution of data represented in Figure 11.13. This figure is called a frequency distribution and represents the number of times that each particular data value is encountered across the range of data values. Even with natural variation alone we can often expect this distribution to be fairly wide. Thus extreme events will sometimes happen (e.g., a person who stands over eight feet tall) without a specific cause (e.g., a diet of growth hormone during the formative years). However, extreme events are very unlikely and when they occur they may in fact indicate a systematic variation in the process being studied.

The essence of the statistical approach is to flag those events that are extremely unlikely to occur by chance alone. This is done by comparing the results obtained to a model distribution (typically a Gaussian or normal distribution). The normal distribution has well-known statistical properties and is generally applicable when the values being tested are actually averages contained from groups of data (samples). The approximate normality of such averages is supported by a theorem in mathematical statistics known as the central limit theorem. For control charts, the central limit theorem predicts three important properties of averaged data:

- If separate samples are taken from a distribution, and the items within each sample are averaged, then the distribution of the averages will approach a normal (Gaussian) shape as the subgroups become larger.

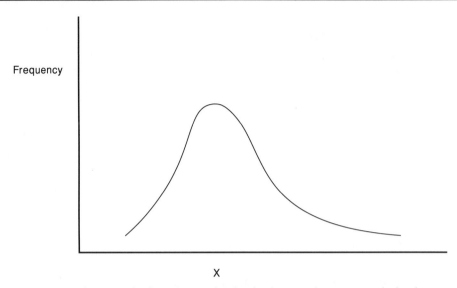

Frequency

X

**Figure 11.13** A frequency distribution. (Note that this distribution is drawn as an "idealized" curve representing the underlying population.)

- The distribution of averages will have the same mean as the distribution of individuals.
- The standard deviation ( an important statistical measure of variation) of the distribution of averages will be narrower than the corresponding standard deviation for the distribution of individuals.

The major contribution of the control chart technique has been to take the properties of the central limit theorem and fashion a workable technique for assessing change within a process based on sample data. Generally, the averages will be close enough to normally distribute if each sample contains at least four data points (regardless of the shape of the underlying distribution that produced those data points). The standard deviation can then be estimated from the average of the sample ranges (i.e., the difference between the highest and lowest values in the sample) as long as at least 25 subgroups are used.

Estimates of the mean and variance of the distribution may then be used to set control limits. Data points which lie outside the control limits are assumed to indicate that a systematic change in the underlying process has occurred. Control limits can be set on both the mean (location) and range (variation) of the data, since a change in either the location or the variation of the data points will be indicative of a change in the underlying process.

Figure 11.14 shows control charts averages. The upper and lower control limits for averages are usually set at three standard deviations above and below the mean respectively. Due to the properties of the normal distribution, only about one quarter of one percent of the points would be expected to be more than three standard deviations away from the mean. Thus points outside the upper and lower control limits

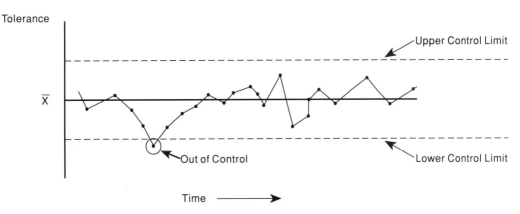

**Figure 11.14** A control chart for averages.

are very unlikely events and are typically taken as evidence that the process is "out of control" (i.e., that it has shifted in some way). When control charts are constructed automatically using a computer, the standard deviation can be calculated using the usual formula:

$$variance = \sum_{i=1}^{N} (X_i - \overline{X})^2/(N - 1)$$

$$s = (variance)^{.5}$$

The upper control limit is then defined as $\overline{X} + 3 * s$, while the lower control limit (for the mean) is $\overline{X} - 3 * s$, where $\overline{X}$ is the mean of all the sample averages and $s$ is the standard deviation.

In situations where the control limits are calculated manually (e.g., on the factory floor), methods of calculating the control limits have been developed that simplify the manual computation. In these situations, the upper control limit is defined as $\overline{X} + A * \overline{R}$, where $\overline{X}$ (sometimes referred to as *xbar*) is the mean of all the sample averages and *rbar* is the mean of all the sample ranges (a simpler measure of variability that is easier to calculate than the standard deviation).

In manual computation the lower control limit is defined as $\overline{X} - A * \overline{R}$. For the range (variability), the manual upper control limit is $D1 * \overline{R}$, and the lower control limit is $D2 * \overline{R}$, where $A, D1,$ and $D2$ are factors that depend on the subgroup size, $n$.

Once the control limits are known (e.g., by taking 25 samples of four data points each and calculating the control limits as described above) subgroups can be collected from time to time and plotted on the control chart. Averages that fall outside the control limits indicate that the distribution for that variable has changed or gotten wider. The process is then said to be "out of control." This acts as a red flag, and the reason for the change is then investigated. Control charts are used to flag changes in the process, but they do not by themselves assist in identifying the cause or eliminating it.

Control charts track the variation in various processes. Every quantity that can be measured is subject to certain variation, providing the measuring instrument is sensitive enough to detect the variation. Even things that we think of as constant can be shown to vary. Consider for instance the attribute of height. We think of height as a constant, a number that stays fixed on the driving license, year after year. Yet human stature is no more a constant than any other quantity. For young children, height increases relatively rapidly, which the constant need to find larger clothing serves to underscore for many parents. However, after we reach adulthood there tends to be a slow shrinkage in stature so that people are an inch or so shorter after retirement age than they were twenty or thirty years earlier (e.g., Konz 1990, Figure 11.5).

What may surprise some people though is that the height of an individual may vary significantly during a single day. Generally people are "taller" when they get out of the bed in the morning than they are when they go to sleep at night. This is because gravity acts as a compressive force during the day. Thus, if we measured the height of a person at different times of the day with a sensitive enough instrument we would find variations in stature.

Since attribute values are always subject to variation, there is the problem of determining what variation is natural or random and what variation is systematic and indicative of some change in an underlying process. The task of sorting out random from systematic variation is the task of statistics. Statisticians have developed a number of tools for assessing variation and detecting changes in variation, and control charts are a practical usage of these tools as applied to the problem of quality control. One basic idea in quality control and statistics is that the observations or measures

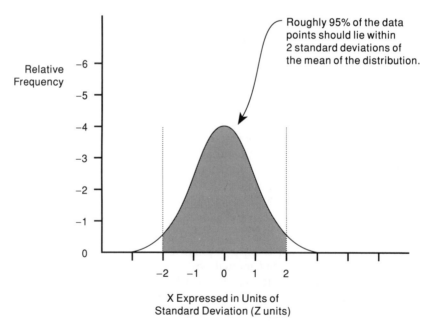

**Figure 11.15** The normal distribution.

that are made of processes and product features are in fact samples from an underlying population. Even if there is no change in the production process, these sampled values may change due to the background (random) variation that is always present during measurement.

Thus the task of the control chart is to set the limits of natural variation and to signal situations where the process appears to have changed. In general, the greater the distance of an observation point from the mean of a population distribution, the more likely that the new observation does not belong to the population. In statistics, a difference of two standard deviations is often taken as evidence that a new point comes from a different distribution (see Figure 11.15), while in quality control the corresponding figure is generally taken as three standard deviations. Practically, this means that if an observation is more than three standard deviations from the mean, then there are very good grounds to suppose that the process has changed in some way.

The effect of natural variation can be seen most clearly in small experiments, and such experiments are often used in the training of quality engineers. Imagine for instance that the distribution of some production value had shifted to the right (as shown in Figure 11.16. If we carried out a small experiment to simulate this change we could put a set of numbers in one bowl to simulate distribution A, and then put a different set of numbers into a second bowl to simulate distribution B. If distribution B were shifted to the right, the numbers on the chips in the second bowl would tend to be a little larger than those on the corresponding chips in the first bowl. However, there would still be some overlap between the two distributions, so that some chips in the first bowl would still be larger than some chips in the second bowl.

If we then sampled seven numbers at a time for distribution A and plotted the mean of each sample on the control chart we would get a chart that looked something like

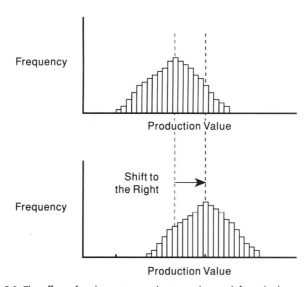

**Figure 11.16** The effect of a change in production value in shifting the histogram distribution.

the left panel of Figure 11.17. Here we see evidence of natural variation, but all the points fall within the control limits. If we now move to the next panel of the figures we see that the corresponding points for distribution B have been shifted upwards and that several of them fall outside the control limits. In this case the control chart is doing a good job of signaling that the distribution has changed. Distribution C represents a third situation where the mean is the same as for distribution A, but now the variation has increased. Looking at the right panel of Figure 11.17 we see that this results in more "jumping around" in the corresponding control chart, with one of the points exceeding the control limit.

The preceding example shows that a control chart can distinguish both changes in the mean and in the variation of a distribution. However, the effect of changes in the variation are shown more clearly in the R control chart shown in Figure 11.18. Here it can be seen that the variation did not change between distributions A and B, whereas the variation for distribution C is generally much higher and exceeds the control limits of variation in a number of places.

One can imagine frequency curves of many different shapes and many of the common types of frequency curve (distribution) that are encountered have been encapsulated in mathematical equations. The normal distribution is one of the most frequently encountered and used of these distributions. The central limit theorem (introduced above) guarantees that the means of successive samples of (four or more) data points will approximate a normal distribution.

Thus the bell-shaped symmetrical form of the normal distribution is generally assumed to underlie the sampling distribution of quality control data. Although most of the area under the normal distribution is within three standard deviations of the mean (as shown in Figure 11.15), the tails of the distribution actually spread much wider, but at vanishingly small probabilities. In normal distributions, about two-thirds of the data points fall within one standard deviation either side of the mean.

There is a great deal of statistical theory concerning the properties of the normal distribution, which is not surprising since it is the foundation of parametric statistics in general, and the widely used analysis of variance (ANOVA) method in particular. In the long run, the standard deviation of the frequency distribution of data values

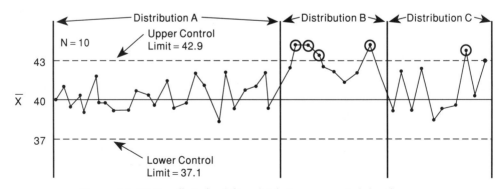

**Figure 11.17** The effect of a shifting distribution on a control chart for averages.

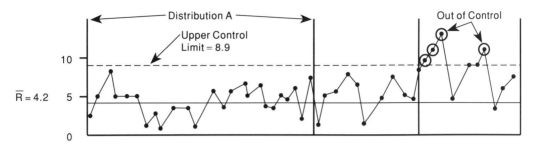

**Figure 11.18** The effect of a shifting distribution on an R control chart.

will be sd/(N).5, that is, the standard deviation divided by the square root of the sample size. Thus if samples of size 4 are drawn from a normal distribution, the standard deviation of the sample means will tend to be only half as great as the standard deviation of the underlying distribution. These, and other statistical principles based on normal distribution theory are then used to justify the method of control charting used in quality control.

### 11.3.4  Additional Quality Tools

Our analysis of existing quality control tools suggests that they are best suited for examining one or two variables that are closely related to process quality. Some of the features of the quality control tools described thus far are that they:

- Provide low dimensionality views of the data (examining one or at most two attributes at a time)
- Are designed for manual use and take little advantage of computer capabilities
- Are designed to use current or new data and do not consider the large amount of historical data that may be stored in databases
- Are based purely on the numerical properties of the data (they don't consider the qualitative effects of different attribute values)

In complex processes quality may be determined by complex interactions between a large number of variables. These interactions are hard to discover by plotting relations between two variables at a time. Existing quality control methods are also designed to handle a relatively small amount of data. But, as is becoming more and more the case, there are in fact huge amounts of information that are potentially relevant to quality control and we cannot simply identify one or two variables that critically determine quality. In such cases, information discovery and visualization can be used to make the process manageable. In addition, as this book emphasizes, there are a number of techniques for utilizing the data stored in large databases, and thus new tools are needed that can take advantage of existing quality data.

Before considering the use of hypermedia, information discovery, and data visualization in quality control, some other tools that aid in the understanding of tasks and processes will be looked at. The importance of understanding tasks and processes is reflected in the use of the cause-and-effect diagram as one of the basic tools of quality control.

The cause-and-effect diagram is fundamentally different from the other quality tools discussed so far in that it shows the aspects of the task that lead to quality problems. Consequently, it has a diagnostic purpose and aids in the understanding of tasks and processes. This section will describe a number of related tools that can also be used to enhance understanding of tasks and processes. This improved understanding can be invaluable in regulating activities and improving quality.

**11.3.4.1** *Affinity Diagrams*    The term "affinity diagram" has been used by Ozeki and Asaka (1990) to denote a type of qualitative modeling where concepts are grouped together. One way of generating an affinity diagram is to write relevant concepts and ideas on self-adhesive notes and stick them onto a large sheet of cardboard, arrange them in groups and then label the groups. The diagram may also be augmented to include arrows connecting between groups and arrows connecting the concepts within a group. These arrows may then be labeled to reflect relationships such as "part-of," "follows-from," "causes," and so on. In our experience, affinity diagrams are an easy and natural method of developing qualitative models of processes. For instance, Figure 11.19 shows an affinity diagram that was developed to understand how people used the manual for a complicated high-end facsimile (fax) machine.

**11.3.4.2** *Entity-Relationship Diagrams*    Entity-relationship diagrams can also be applied to quality control. This is a particularly interesting topic because it forms a natural bridge between tools for understanding tasks and systems on the one hand, and models of quality-relevant data on the other.

An entity relationship (E-R) diagram is a way of summarizing the different relationships that exist between data entities. An example of an E-R diagram was shown earlier in Figure 2.13 (page 51). In an E-R diagram such as the one shown in that figure, entities (entity sets) are represented as rectangles, while attributes of entities are represented as circles (attached to the corresponding rectangles/entities). Links are indicated by edges (lines). Relationships are represented as diamonds that connect the corresponding entities. For instance, we might have a relationship "manager" (Ullmann 1988) that connects the managers entity set to the employees entity set.

Entity-relationship diagrams provide a static representation of relationships between data objects. Since they tend to be declarative, rather than descriptive in nature (Winograd 1975), they complement the type of information that is provided in a flow chart.

**11.3.4.3** *Hierarchical Views*    Cause-and-effect diagrams are one method for developing a strategy for identifying and removing the causes of quality problems, while E-R diagrams describe the relationships that exist between data objects. Hierarchical views represent a related technique that may be easier to apply in some cases. The method for building hierarchies from sorting data was explained by Parsaye and Chignell (1988). In the context of quality control, the method normally begins with a goal such as "eliminate a problem that is affecting the quality of a product."

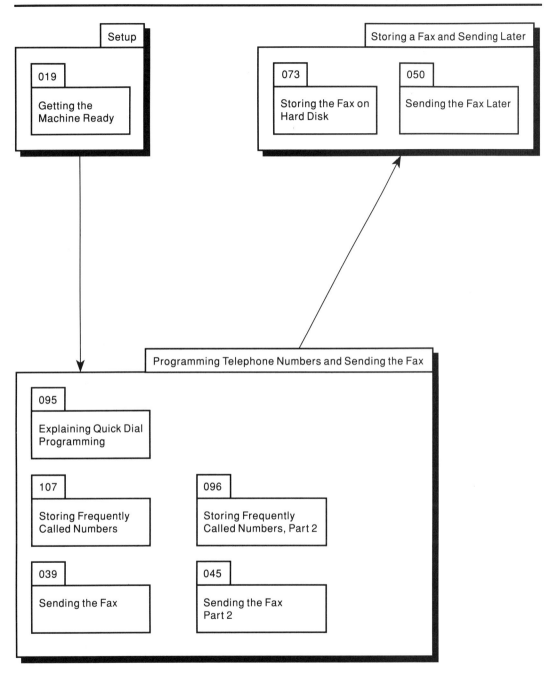

**Figure 11.19** An affinity diagram representing one person's understanding of a manual for a fax machine.

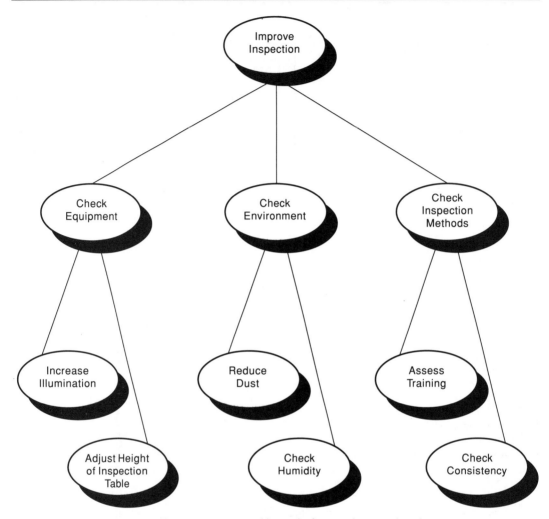

**Figure 11.20** A goal hierarchy for a quality control application.

The hierarchical representation of the solution to this problem may then be built in a top-down or bottom-up approach. In the top-down approach the quality engineer begins with the overall goal and then identifies the subgoals that are needed to achieve the goal. These subgoals then form the first level of the hierarchy. Each subgoal is then expanded into its own subgoals, creating new levels in the hierarchy. The process of expanding new levels of the hierarchy is completed at the lowest level when the subgoals are expressed as single actions that can be taken.

Building the hierarchy bottom-up begins with a listing of actions that should be taken. Actions are then grouped according to similarity, and groups of actions are then identified in terms of the shared subgoal that they represent. The subgoals thus formed are then grouped to form higher subgoals (levels) in the hierarchy. The process is concluded when a group of subgoals is combined to fulfill the main goal at the top of the hierarchy.

In many situations it may be useful to build both top-down and bottom-up versions of the goal hierarchy. Differences between the two versions of the hierarchy may indicate fuzzy thinking, uncertainty, or poorly defined subgoals and activities, and the process of merging the two versions into a single hierarchy can be very instructive. An example of a goal hierarchy for a quality control application is shown in Figure 11.20.

**11.3.4.4** *Matrix Diagrams and Process Charts*    There are a large number of matrix diagrams and process charts that have been developed by industrial engineers to describe the structure of work activity (Ozeki and Asaka 1990). Flow charts may be regarded as specialized versions of these diagrams. Typically these diagrams consist of rows and columns, often with different types of process or activity serving as rows in the diagram and different resources or action types filling the columns of the diagram. This basic type of chart can be specialized for quality control purposes by putting defects and causes in the columns as shown in Figure 11.21.

## ∎ 11.4 INTELLIGENT DATABASES FOR QUALITY CONTROL

The essence of quality control is to understand and improve processes using appropriate information. This information needs to satisfy two main requirements: (1) the information should be diagnostic, and (2) the information should be representative. Diagnostic information doesn't simply tell us that there is something wrong, it also gives us clues about what is wrong. Traditional quality control tools, in most cases, do not provide a great deal of diagnostic information. In fact, of the seven tools, only two provide any diagnostic information at all (i.e., cause-and-effect diagrams and Pareto charts). Cause-and-effect diagrams are useful, but they generally result from brainstorming and subjective evaluation rather than from ongoing data analysis. This restricts the usefulness of such diagrams, particularly at the shop floor level, or where there are hidden causes that cannot be uncovered by brainstorming. Pareto charts provide a method of ranking the importance of causes, but they do not identify them. The categories selected for plotting in a Pareto chart must already have been selected through some other process.

Thus the seven traditional quality control tools provide too little diagnostic information, particularly in terms of ongoing evaluation based on detailed analysis of data. The representativeness of information provided by quality control tools is also an issue. Flow charts and cause-and-effect diagrams rely on the skills of the workers to be able to represent the essential issues in the process. To some extent, the resulting diagrams will be biased by individual views on the process. Similarly, the way that check sheets are designed, or variables are chosen for plotting in histograms, scattergrams, Pareto charts and control charts, will also be heavily influenced by who is managing the quality control analysis.

A richer picture of the process would be the ideal, with multiple views of the information providing different insights into existing problems and how quality can

| | A | B | C | D | E |
|---|---|---|---|---|---|
| Defect A | + | | + | | ++ |
| Defect B | | + | + | | |
| Defect C | + | | | | + |
| Defect D | | + | | ++ | |
| Causes ⟶ | A | B | C | D | E |

| Process 1 | Element 11 | + | | | | + |
|---|---|---|---|---|---|---|
| | Element 12 | | + | | + | |
| | Element 13 | | + | + | | |
| Process 2 | Element 21 | | | + | + | ++ |
| | Element 22 | + | ++ | | | |
| | Element 23 | | + | + | + | |
| Process 3 | Element 31 | | | ++ | | + |
| | Element 32 | + | | | ++ | |
| | Element 33 | | + | | | |
| | Element 34 | | | + | | + |

+ = Relationship

++ = Strong Relationship

**Figure 11.21** An example of a matrix diagram used for quality control.

be improved. This is where the intelligent database approach can help by supplementing the traditional methods with new ways of focusing and presenting information.

The traditional tools for quality control were invented a number of years ago, when the computer industry was in its infancy. These tools have not kept up to date with new advances in computer technology. In addition, the statistical approaches underlying some of the tools do not provide the type of value-based information that is essential in troubleshooting quality problems. This section discusses three new tools for quality control, based on intelligent databases and data visualization, to complement the existing seven tools of quality. These tools are information discovery, data visualization, and hypermedia.

### 11.4.1 Quality and Executive Information Systems

Quality is an ideal application for an executive information system like Corporate Vision. Quality improvement generally requires information in the form of summarized data. The existing tools of quality represent this summarized information in the forms of charts and graphs.

An executive information system provides a convenient environment for exploring the information in these charts. Consider, for instance, the task of a manager who is managing a training program for a large company. Relevant quality data might include the proportions of different types of worker that have the skills required by their job, the cost and graduation rate of training programs, assessments of the effectiveness of training, and a tabulation of errors attributed to poor or inadequate training.

The quality data could be expressed as a variety of visual charts and then linked in a hyperdata environment. For instance, graphs showing training program costs would be linked to charts showing graduation rates. Examples of drill down in this case would be looking at more detailed cost breakdowns within a cost hierarchy, and drilling down to the employing history, training, and attributed errors for specific employees.

## 11.4.2 Quality Through Discovery

Quality Through Discovery™ (QTD) is a commercial system developed by IntelligenceWare as an extension to the Corporate Vision and IDIS systems. It provides measures of quality by extending the traditional seven tools for the analyst and by providing TQM reporting facilities for managers and executives.

The architecture of QTD is shown in Figure 11.22. The system has two distinct interfaces, one based on Corporate Vision, for managers and executives; the other, based on IDIS, for quality analysts and quality engineers. The executive can thus monitor quality immediately by using hyperinformation. The analyst can use the new technologies of discovery and 3D visualization to obtain diagnostic information about

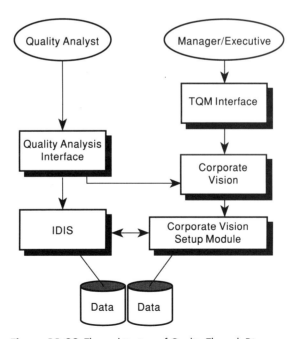

**Figure 11.22** The architecture of Quality Through Discovery.

quality. The key technologies QTD offers are as follows:

1. The use of automatic discovery and error detection as fundamental technologies that go beyond statistics.
2. New 3D hypervisualization techniques that extend the 2D diagramming techniques used in traditional quality tools.
3. Reliance on customizable hyperinformation frontends for providing total quality information to managers and executives.

For the analyst, the key improvement is based on the fact that existing quality control tools do not directly answer the question: "What set of conditions produces an error of this type?" For instance, we might want to know why some cars are made with faulty transmissions, or why certain models of television fail earlier than others. What we are looking for in such cases is diagnostic information that tells us what combinations of factors produce errors.

The representativeness of information provided by quality control tools is also an issue. When large amounts of data are available it makes sense to discover information from the data directly, searching for the reasons that underlie errors and failures. Statistics turn out to be a clumsy tool for getting this diagnostic kind of information. However, the relations between components of the process and resulting errors or quality levels can often be better expressed in the form of rules. For instance, we might have a rule that says that all the faulty transmissions for a particular model of car were manufactured in Cincinnati. This is useful information because it allows us to focus our analysis.

Expressing relationships as rules (e.g., if A and B then C) is quite intuitive and easy to understand. Logical rules can often pinpoint and characterize quality problems very quickly. Modern computer systems can automatically search a database and discover significant and important rules by themselves. The "hypotheses" for which rules will be generated automatically can either be input manually or calculated automatically. With manual input, quality control engineers can use their knowledge to focus the analysis. However, automatic hypothesis generation often leads to the discovery of unexpected information, uncovering hidden causes for quality control problems.

For example, rules of the form

```
% Rule 58
CF = 97%
"PROBLEM" = "Transmission"
If
    "MODEL" = "Rhombus"
And
    "86" <= "YEAR" <= "87"
And
    "12-30-1986" <= "SALES_DATE" <= "12-24-1987"
```

identify a relationship between Transmission problems existing with the model

Rhombus sold at specific dates. This type of information is hard to obtain from traditional tools. As another example, consider the problem discussed in section 11.4.2.2 based on IDIS found rules of the form

```
% Rule 2
CF = 100
"77.83" <= "PRODUCT HARDNESS" <= "78.04"
If
    "66.46" <= "MATTER HARDNESS" <= "66.78"
And
    "780.5" <= "TREATMENT TEMP" <= "810.2"
And
    "1" <= "3-MACHINES" <= "2"
```

that relate specific temperatures and manufacturing conditions to product quality. One could not even begin to pose these problems with traditional quality control tools because those tools are statistical, not rule-based.

Rule discovery is an important new quality control tool that provides diagnostic information missing in the existing tools. Anomaly detection is a related part of information discovery that is in essence the reverse of rule discovery. Instead of looking for consistent patterns which can be expressed as rules, anomaly detection identifies those items that are unusual (i.e., which contradict the patterns or implied rules that otherwise exist in the data). This helps identify what may have gone wrong in the production process. Anomaly detection may be thought of as the rule-based analog of control charts. In both cases the goal is to detect changes in the production process.

In the statistical approach, anomalies are detected as outliers (i.e., points that are more than three standard deviations away from the mean). However, statistical anomalies can only be detected if one has drawn up the appropriate control chart. Control charts normally work with a single variable at a time. What happens if an anomaly is defined by a combination of two or more variables? For instance, weighing 90 pounds does not constitute an anomaly (the person might be short), but being six foot tall and weighing 90 pounds would certainly be considered an anomaly by most people. Once anomalies are defined as specific combinations of values on two or more variables it becomes more difficult to characterize them as outliers in the statistical sense.

For complex combinations of variables it makes sense to define anomalies as exceptions to a rule. In this view, anomaly detection is a by-product of automatic rule discovery.

The distinction between rules and exceptions (anomalies) is in some senses rather arbitrary. If we think back to how control charts work, an out-of-control data point is defined in terms of the control limits set on the basis of the distribution of previous values. In similar fashion, an anomaly is defined as a data point that doesn't fit into the existing patterns of rules. Over time, a collection of anomalous data may eventually lead to updating of rules (the exception that becomes the rule). Thus methods of information discovery and anomaly detection have to be adapted to the quality control task so that rules can be updated over time, in the same way that control limits are sometimes adjusted as the distribution of the controlled variable changes.

One of the useful by-products of the machine-learning approach to quality control (i.e., information discovery and anomaly detection) is that it produces a knowledge base of rules and database facts that serves as a "theory" of how errors are produced. This knowledge base can then be used to derive causal explanations of error and to develop strategies for improving the process and enhancing quality.

The following sections will illustrate the use of intelligent quality control with three different examples.

**11.4.2.1** *Disk Drive Fault Analysis*    Consider a company called SuperDrive, Inc. which is in the business of manufacturing disk drives. This is a real company whose name has been changed here, for obvious reasons. The company manufactures dozens of types of disk drive. Tens of thousands of disk drives are manufactured and tested each month and test results are kept in a database for future reference. This following example illustrates how SuperDrive, Inc. can take advantage of automatic rule discovery, anomaly detection, and 3D visualization to analyze the database and find the causes of their manufacturing problems.

The disk drives had sporadic defect problems whose cause could not be identified. A sample from the database (3354 records) is shown in Table 11.1. This database is too large for visual analysis, although descriptive information (provided by IDIS) would be a good start. In this case, information discovery revealed that one particular operator was causing most of the problems in one particular manufacturing step. One of the rules that IDIS produced very quickly to identify the source of the problem looked like this:

```
% Rule 10
CF = 82
 "FAILURE MODE" = "932"
If
 "OPER" = "213272"
And
 "STEP" = "FSI"

% Margin of Error: 4.7 %
% Applicable percentage of sample: 11.3 %
% Applicable number of records: 379
```

This means that when operator 213272 performs the manufacturing step FSI, 82% of the time he will make error 932. As it turned out, some operators were not properly trained and quality was improved by providing the necessary additional training.

Here are some other rules discovered in the disk drive example:

```
% Rule 1
CF = 99
 "ERROR_CODE" = "931"
If
 "STEP" = "MA1"
```

```
% Rule 5
CF = 79
"ERROR_CODE" = "931"
If
"PRODUCT" = "5418172"
```

These rules indicate possible problems with process step MA1 and with product number 5418172.

The SuperDrive database was then subjected to anomaly detection analysis (another form of information discovery). The field ERROR_CODE was selected as the target of the analysis, and consequently suspicious ERROR_CODE results were found and reported. For instance, one of the anomalies detected in the SuperDrive data was

```
Record Number: 5
    Field: STEP, Value: CAM
    Field: PRODUCT, Value: 5418172
    Field: LOT_NO, Value: 44
    FieldRecord : OPERATOR, Value: 67890
  * Field: ERROR_CODE, Value: 931, Reason: Very frequent value
```

The anomaly reports also showed that the error codes 931 and 932 for the products XMI14 and 5418172 are very frequent when two particular operators were on duty.

We can also get alternative views on the data using data visualization. For instance, 3D bar charts can show visually the patterns in the data that led to the discovery of different rules.

**11.4.2.2** *Materials Manufacturing*    This example demonstrates effectiveness of rule discovery in the quality control of manufactured materials. If a manufacturing process is tested at a variety of settings, rule discovery can potentially determine which combination of settings will result in the optimal product, in terms of any qualitative criteria. In this example, a metal product is developed from raw materials of varying hardness, and processed at a variety of temperatures using several different machines and chemical additives. The criterion for quality control is product hardness.

**Table 11.1  Sample Records for a Disk Drive Fault Database**

| STEP | PRODUCT | LOT_NO | OPERATOR | ERROR_CODE |
|------|---------|--------|----------|------------|
| FSI | XMI14 | 24 | 213272 | 931 |
| FSI | XMI14 | 24 | 213272 | 931 |
| CB2 | 5418172 | 37 | 67890 | 932 |
| CAM | 5418172 | 44 | 67890 | 931 |
| FSI | 5418172 | 37 | 51512 | 932 |
| FSI | 5418172 | 43 | 213272 | 932 |
| MA1 | XMI14 | 24 | 38978 | 931 |
| MB1 | XMI14 | 25 | 38978 | 932 |
| MA1 | 5418172 | unknown | 115118 | 931 |
| CB4 | XMI14 | 25 | 51512 | 932 |

**Table 11.2 Sample Records for a Metallurgy Database**

| No. | Prod-hd | Mat-hd | Time | Temp | Med | Mach | Add | Test |
|---|---|---|---|---|---|---|---|---|
| 1 | 77.83 | 66.090 | 10.43 | 801 | 36.1 | 1.0 | 2.0 | 1.0 |
| 2 | 78.16 | 66.36 | 7.51 | 825.4 | 36.58 | 2.0 | 1.0 | 1.0 |
| 3 | 78.15 | 66.77 | 5.64 | 819.8 | 35.92 | 2.0 | 2.0 | 1.0 |
| ... | ...... | ...... | .... | ...... | ...... | ... | ... | ... |
| 99 | 78.20 | 66.85 | 6.84 | 820.5 | 36.23 | 3.0 | 2.0 | 1.0 |
| 100 | 78.00 | 67.16 | 8.29 | 820.6 | 36.35 | 2.0 | 2.0 | 1.0 |

The data was obtained from a demonstration disk provided by JUSE/QCASE, which is a very effective implementation of the traditional quality control systems—in fact, one of the best such tools on the market, and the best selling in Japan. Many of the system's features are very impressive, but automatic discovery could improve upon its results.

The description of this metallurgical database is "Special treatment of steel materials." The database consisted of 100 different combinations of processing machine, raw material hardness, alloy content, processing time and temperature, chemical additive, and testing machine. Sample records are shown in Table 11.2.

Information discovery was carried out in this case. The goal of rule discovery was to identify the optimal combination of raw materials and processing conditions for maximizing the quality of the product. Some of the rules found by IDIS are shown below.

```
% Rule 2
CF = 100
    "77.83" <= "PRODUCT HARDNESS" <= "78.04"
If
    "66.46" <= "MATTER HARDNESS" <= "66.78"
And
    "780.5" <= "TREATMENT TEMP" <= "810.2"
And
    "1" <= "3-MACHINES" <= "2"

% Margin of Error: 8.3 %
% Applicable percentage of sample: 6.0 %

% Rule 9
CF = 100
    "77.83" <= "PRODUCT HARDNESS" <= "78.08"
If
    "7.19" <= "TREATMENT TIME" <= "8.21"
And
    "780.5" <= "TREATMENT TEMP" <= "807.8"
And
    "1" <= "3-MACHINES" <= "2"

% Margin of Error: 10.0 %
% Applicable percentage of sample: 5.0 %
```

```
% Rule 21
CF = 100
     "78.2" <= "PRODUCT HARDNESS" <= "78.64"
If
     "67.03" <= "MATTER HARDNESS" <= "68.07"
And
     "800.4" <= "TREATMENT TEMP" <= "818.3"
And
     "2" <= "3-MACHINES" <= "3"

% Margin of Error: 8.3 %
% Applicable percentage of sample: 6.0 %
```

According to Rule 9, we can say with 100% certainty (allowing for a 10% margin or error) that Product Hardness will be within the range of 77.83 and 78.08 if the treatment time is between 7.12 and 8.21 minutes, the treatment temperature is between 780.5 and 807.8 degrees centigrade, and either Machine 1 or 2 is used for processing. Of the total sample, 36% had a Product Hardness measured within the range of 77.83 and 78.08. However, of the 36 observations specified by the rule's conclusion, only five (5% of the sample) fulfilled all of the premises of the rule.

With this type of information, it is then possible for a manufacturer to determine which equipment or processing method will most effectively fulfill the production quality goals. By specifying the criteria which should be measured for quality control as the goals for rule generation, a quality assurance professional can ascertain the optimal combination of time, labor, machinery, environmental conditions, and other criteria for quality maximization.

The key issue here is that IDIS can automatically discover specific ranges involving several values that give rise to a specific condition. With statistics alone this is practically impossible. Moreover, imagine what would happen if the database is really large. In such cases the advantages of discovery are further multiplied.

**11.4.2.3** *Automobile Manufacturing*    This section deals with World Motors Corporation, a real company whose name, plant locations, and models have been changed. World Motors has large databases which include information about cars, their manufacture, sales, and maintenance. Our task is to find out why World Motors is having too many returned cars. The following sources of information are relevant to the problem:

- *Sales* — This file contains information about the sale of the vehicle: the date the car was sold, the dealer, the year, and the model of the car.
- *Problems* — This file reflects the part causing the problem (Faulty Part), the date of the problem, and the mileage of the car at the time of the problem.
- *Shipping* — This file includes information about where the car was picked up (thus identifying the plant of final assembly), and the dates for pickup and delivery to the dealer.
- *Inspect* — This file gives an INSPECT_DATE, LOT_NO, as well as a PART_NO for the part responsible for the fault. The LOT_NOs are used to identify dates and plants of manufacturing.

- *Parts* — This file includes information about parts, lots, and manufacturers. Given a PART_NO and a LOT_NO, this file is used to identify the manufacturer and the date on which the part was manufactured.

These files were then joined into a large constructed file (called Total Info), with the following fields:

| | |
|---|---|
| SERIAL_NO | TRUCKER |
| MODEL | PICKUP |
| YEAR | DELIVERY |
| DEALER | INSPECT_DATE |
| SALE_DATE | PART_NO |
| PROBLEM | LOT_NO |
| PROBLEM_DATE | MANUFACTURER |
| MILEAGE | MANUFACT_DATE |
| PLANT | |

This file contains a great deal of information. Information discovery was then carried out using different problem conditions as goals. For instance, one analysis used the value Transmission for the field PROBLEM. In this case, rules for faulty transmissions were discovered. The following rules reflect the discovery with faulty transmission.

```
% Rule 58
CF = 100
"PROBLEM" = "Transmission"
If
    "MODEL" = "Rhombus"
And
    "86" <= "YEAR" <= "87"
And
    "12-30-1986" <= "SALES_DATE" <= "12-24-1987"

% Margin of Error: 8.3 %
% Applicable percentage of sample: 6.0 %


% Rule 85
CF = 100
"PROBLEM" = "Transmission"
If
    "MODEL" = "Rhombus"
And
    "12-30-1986" <= "PROB_DATE" <= "12-30-1987"
And
    "6-19-1986" <= "MANUFACT_DATE" <= "6-15-1987"

% Margin of Error: 10.0 %
% Applicable percentage of sample: 5.0 %
```

*% Rule 115*
*CF = 100*
*"PROBLEM" = "Transmission"*
*If*
   *"MODEL" = "Rhombus"*
*And*
   *"81058" <= "LOT_NO" <= "94138"*
*And*
   *"MANUFACTURER" = "Cincinnati"*

*% Margin of Error: 6.3 %*
*% Applicable percentage of sample: 8.0 %*

*% Rule 121*
*CF = 91*
*"PROBLEM" = "Transmission"*
*If*
   *"MODEL" = "Rhombus"*
*And*
   *"MANUFACTURER" = "Cincinnati"*
*And*
   *"PLANT" = "Detroit"*

*% Margin of Error: 14.3 %*
*% Applicable percentage of sample: 22.0 %*

According to Rule 58, 100% of transmission problems existed with the model Rhombus of the year 1986-87 which were sold between December 30, 1986 and December 24, 1987.

Anomaly detection was also carried out and some results were as follows:

*\*\*\**
   *Field: SERIAL_NO, Value: 2869*
   *Field: MODEL, Value: Rhombus*
   *Field: YEAR, Value: 86*
   *Field: DEALER, Value: 1668*
   *Field: SALE_DATE, Value: 19861230*
  *\* Field: PROBLEM, Value: Transmission, Reason: Very frequent value*
   *Field: PROB_DATE, Value: 19861230*
   *Field: MILEAGE, Value: 4536*
   *Field: INSPT_DATE, Value: 19861230*
   *Field: PART_NO, Value: 3900*
   *Field: LOT_NO, Value: 38189*
   *Field: MANUFACTURER, Value: Cincinnati*
   *Field: MANUFACT_DATE, Value: 19861023*
   *Field: PLANT, Value: Detroit*
   *Field: TRUCKER, Value: Zeno*
   *Field: PICKUP, Value: 19861128*
   *Field: DELIVERY, Value: 19861130*
   *Field: Class, Value: Full Size*

These anomaly reports show that the problem "Transmission" is a very frequent value in the database. This problem occurs mostly with the car model "Rhombus" and the parts were manufactured in Cincinnati. In this case, anomaly detection confirmed the results of information discovery. Moreover, some unusual problems at other plants were also detected.

### 11.4.3  Data Visualization

Most diagramming techniques used within the seven existing tools of quality control are two-dimensional, not reflecting state of the art developments in computer technology. However, graphic visualization of large databases can represent up to six-dimensions (three Euclidean dimensions, plus box size, color, shading) of information without difficulty. This allows a quality control engineer to readily see the real reasons for quality problems.

Data visualization is essential for understanding data and interpreting information. People are highly visual creatures and see patterns in a well-presented figure that they would not be able to see in the corresponding tables of numbers. Some data visualization capabilities particularly useful in quality control will now be described.

**11.4.3.1**  *The 2D Box Plot*    The box plot enables one to view the range of values on one variable that are associated with a specific range of values on another variable. Furthermore, the size of each box is proportional to the number of observations which fall into the specified ranges of the two variables. The box plot is useful when you want two-dimensional, bivariate (i.e., two-field) map values, and you want to be able to quickly assess which combinations of values are most prevalent in terms of the relative sizes of the mapped boxes. A box plot is like combining a scattergram with a Pareto chart.

Figure 11.23 shows a 2D box plot in the upper left panel. It can be seen that the boxes for two of the variable combinations are much larger than the rest and following the Pareto principle they would be the places to start looking for improvements. The larger boxes in box plots suggest the most fruitful starting points for eliminating errors and improving quality.

**11.4.3.2**  *The 3D Bar Chart*    The 3D bar chart displays the relative frequencies (scaled along the z-axis) of groups identified as falling within specific ranges on two variables (plotted along the x- and y-axes). The 3D bar chart provides a three-dimensional representation of the data, and represents the relative frequencies of bivariate (i.e., two-field) range combinations in terms of the heights of bars as opposed to the size of boxes. The upper left panel of Figure 11.24 on page 502 shows a bar chart indicating the sources of problems in a disk drive database.

**11.4.3.3**  *The 3D Box Diagram*    The 3D box diagram is similar in concept to the two-dimensional box plot. Each box is centered at a point which represents its mean value within a combination of ranges along the x-, y-, and z-axes. Whereas the area of each box in a box plot indicates the relative frequency of its combination of field values, it is the volume of each box in a 3D box diagram which expresses the relative frequency of its combination of field values.

The interpretation of the 3D box diagram is similar to that of the box plot, with one additional dimension. Like the 2D box diagram the 3D box diagram can function as

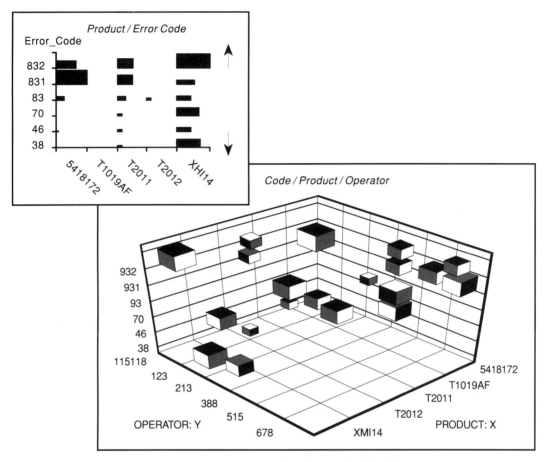

**Figure 11.23** Examples of 2D and 3D box diagrams.

a type of Pareto chart, but with the advantage of being able to describe an extra (third) dimension. In quality control applications where one of the dimensions is some type of error or problem, one is typically most interested in the largest boxes. The location of the large boxes indicates which combinations of machine, operator, or whatever should be focused on first in trying to improve quality. Figures 11.23 and 11.24 show examples of 3D box diagrams in their lower right panels.

**11.4.3.4** *Hyperinformation*    Having a richer picture of production processes, with multiple views of the information that can provide different insights into existing problems and how quality can be improved would be the ideal. The interrelation of the various quality control tools means that an application interface that links these tools together and allows users to smoothly move between the tools would be very useful. This suggests that hypermedia will be a useful strategy for integrating quality control tools.

Hypermedia is a way of linking all the tools of quality control together. For

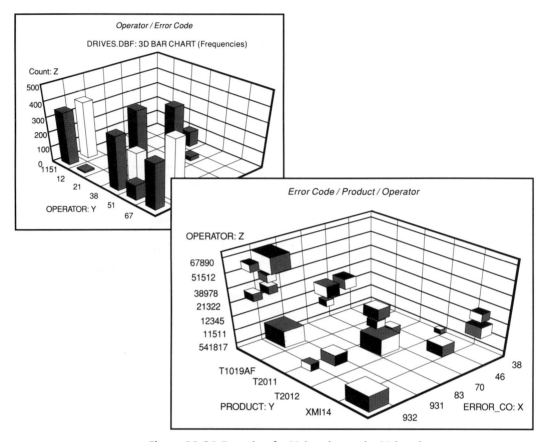

**Figure 11.24** Examples of a 3D bar chart and a 3D box diagram.

instance, all the tools involve visualization of one form or another. Even information discovery, which generates textual output (rules) can be expressed in terms of charts and figures. Simple rules and anomalies (with two or less preconditions) can be "seen" in 3D visualizations. For instance, rules will show up in 3D box plots as large boxes (in rows and columns that are otherwise fairly empty), while anomalies will show up as single points or clusters of points that share one or two, but not all of the values of the rule.

Different types of diagram may be displayed in a hypermedia interface. Regions of each chart or diagram may then be defined as hot spots. For instance, clicking on one of the segments of the pie chart might allow the user to see a hypertext description of that category or a more detailed breakdown of the data.

Information discovery and data visualization are complementary ways of reporting patterns in the same data. This analysis can be extended to include the earlier tools of quality control. A flow chart or cause-and-effect diagram is a way of explicitly relating the variables that are plotted or used for information discovery. Using a hypermedia interface, the analyst may choose to call up the cause-and-effect diagram where the current variable is the cause (or various pie charts, bar charts and scatter diagrams). The analyst may also choose a "Pareto view" of a 3D box chart. In this case, the levels of a chosen variable (e.g., errors) are reordered according to frequency of occurrence.

Control charts provide an alternative way of tracking anomalies over time based on a single control variable. Control regions may also be superimposed on the 3D charts, and out of control data points may be highlighted (e.g., in red). In advanced hypermedia interfaces, animated displays may be created where the data is plotted by time segments and then the frames corresponding to time segments are run in sequence. For a 3D box chart one would then see individual boxes expanding and shrinking over time, and turning red when they became out of tolerance. It is hard to overestimate how compelling and useful this type of animated, three-dimensional, color display is in helping people to interpret patterns in large amounts of complex data.

Animation allows people to synthesize patterns over time, while hierarchical structuring of data allows people to synthesize data over different levels of detail or abstraction. When a quality control engineer is viewing a graph or diagram, it is essential for him to be able to zoom into or zoom out of a portion of the screen, or get feedback and hypertextual information about items. Figure 11.25 shows an example where the quality assurance specialist has called up the image of a disk drive from within an analysis of the disk drive data.

Thus the engineer can see pictures of defective items and other information by clicking on a graph,or can view the original check sheets to ensure that the way in which the data was collected meets his expectations.

### 11.4.4 Hyperinformation and Intelligent Quality Control

The discussion above treats the three tools (automatic rule discovery, anomaly detection, and data visualization) as if they were completely distinct. In fact they are closely related. Anomalies are defined as exceptions to the rules, and simple rules or anomalies (with two or less preconditions) can be "seen" in 3D visualizations. For instance, rules will show up in 3D Box plots as large boxes (in rows and columns that are otherwise fairly empty), while anomalies will show up as single points or clusters of points that share one or two, but not all of the values of the rule.

Thus in some senses, rule discovery, anomaly detection, and data visualization, are different ways of thinking about and viewing the same data. This analysis can be extended to include the other seven quality control tools. A flow chart or cause-and-effect diagram is a way of explicitly relating the variables that are plotted or used for information discovery. Histograms, scattergrams, and Pareto charts are also alternative ways of plotting the data. Control charts provide an alternative way of tracking anomalies over time based on a single control variable. Finally, check sheets are a way of prescribing manual entry of data (as an alternative to automatic logging of data or downloading of data from an existing database).

The interrelation of the various quality control tools means that an application interface that links these tools together and allows users to smoothly move between the tools would be very useful. This suggests that hypermedia will be a useful strategy for integrating quality control tools.

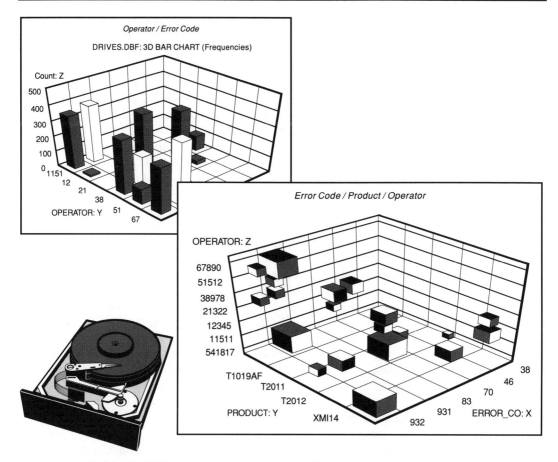

**Figure 11.25** Viewing a scanned image of a disk drive from within an analysis of disk drive data.

When a quality control engineer is viewing a graph or diagram, it is essential for him to be able to zoom into or zoom out of a portion of the screen, or get feedback and hypertextual information about items. In addition, the engineer can, for instance, see pictures of defective items by clicking on a graph or can view the original check sheets to ensure that the way in which the data was collected meets his expectations.

## ■ 11.5 METHODOLOGIES FOR QUALITY CONTROL

Earlier sections of this chapter outlined a number of tools for assisting in quality control, including a variety of charts (data visualizations) as well as information discovery and hypermedia. This section will look at the integrating methodologies that are used to put these tools into practice. In particular, the need for positive use of quality (i.e., designing out defectives rather than inspecting them out) will be discussed as will methods for managing quality and for achieving total quality management (TQM).

### 11.5.1 Management of Quality

Quality tools are useful, but they have to be used effectively within a quality assurance process. Understanding when quality problems have occurred and how they should be changed has to be followed up by managerial policies that implement the necessary changes and ensure that new standards and procedures are adhered to. For instance, one interpretation of the Challenger disaster is that it resulted at least in part from a failure of management to follow up on the known problems with the O-rings. The problems with the Hubble space telescope is another example where management practice may have failed, with costly results. The curvature of the lens in the telescope had to be machined to very fine tolerances. Initial test data indicated a possible problem, but this problem was not thoroughly investigated and the result was a telescope that was launched at great expense but which could not fulfill its assigned mission.

Effective quality management requires an on-going process of quality assessment and active striving for improved quality. This requires not only the use of quality tools, but also the appropriate motivation of all the workers whose actions affect quality. Ultimately, this requires a quality motivation not only in the workers within one's own organization but also in organizations that act as suppliers.

Controlling and enhancing quality requires attention to all aspects of the production process. Defects generally propagate, so that defects in parts provided by suppliers will later show up as defects in the products that are shipped. Thus a large company may be forced to serve as a type of quality control department for its upstream suppliers by warning them of defects or encouraging them to ship better quality parts, while its downstream customers will in turn provide useful quality information about the products that it in turn ships (Figure 11.26).

The way that a complex product is produced by a network of companies is a bit like the way that nutrients are used and transformed within a food chain. Consider the analogy of the production of a chicken. The chickens are fed on corn which in turn is

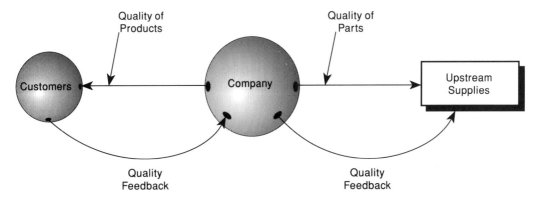

**Figure 11.26** Propagation of quality in the chain of suppliers and customers.

produced by the corn (maize) plant with the assistance of sun, soil, and water. The production of the corn will be adversely affected by poor weather or plant disease. Even if good corn is produced, it may spoil during shipment or storage. Thus the production of a healthy chicken depends on good feed (among other things) and the quality of the "suppliers" (e.g., sun, soil, water, storage silos, truckers) will critically affect the quality of the feed. The food chain of corn to chicken is short. Complex production processes, or the food chain from savannah grass to major predator, can be much longer and more complex.

One method for motivating and evaluating the quality of performance both within and between organizations or companies is to use quality audits and reviews. Such reviews may be useful, not only in maintaining quality performance within a company but also in ensuring that suppliers deliver quality parts. For example, a customer may audit a supplier to examine how closely contract conditions are being met, or it may lead to better understanding by the supplier of the user's needs, resulting in a better relationship between supplier and purchaser (user).

Quality management requires the establishment and maintenance of a suitable quality process. In some companies, responsibility for quality is delegated to a quality assurance department. However, considerable success (particularly in Japan) has been achieved by making quality the official responsibility of all workers. The task of management in this later case is to create a culture and process where workers can be directly involved in the quality process (e.g., the use of quality circles).

Managing for quality (Feigenbaum 1990) is a complex topic that lies outside the scope of this discussion which is mainly concerned with the presentation of information that can assist in making decisions that will maintain or enhance quality. Armed with the appropriate information, managers can then:

- Identify avoidable mistakes, problems, and nonconformance
- Assess the magnitude and relevance of external complaints, warranty recalls, and replacements
- Identify problems that are significantly increasing or decreasing
- Take corrective action based on relevant data

### 11.5.2  Detection is the Worst Form of Quality Control

As Deming has pointed out, detection often comes too late. Faults need to be prevented before they occur. How is preventive quality to be attained? One approach, which has been all too common, is to retain a "pre-quality" production process while weeding out defectives through an inspection process. Detection and removal of defectives can certainly improve the quality of products that are shipped to the customer, but it is an expensive form of achieving quality.

Other examples of detection may seem more mundane, but they underline the need to establish quality as a process as well as an end result. When people think of quality, they tend to think of widgets on an assembly line and gages being used to measure tolerances of various part geometries. Yet quality is in fact a process that can be applied to almost any activity, not just production. Furthermore, the relationship between producer and customer can appear in many different contexts. In one case the producer may be a manufacturer and the customer a consumer, but in another case the producer may be a database vendor and the customer may be the MIS department of a different company.

Consider a customer service situation where representatives answer a large number of calls each day and handle a variety of inquiries and complaints that relate to a product line. They are provided with a computer system that helps them enter orders, retrieve customer information, and the like. In a complex situation such as this, there may be a number of different quality goals that are relevant. First there is the obvious quality goal of handling customer calls professionally, efficiently, and effectively. However, this main goal can be propagated backwards, leading to other quality goals such as developing an information system that can facilitate the performance and productivity of the representatives, and development of selection and training programs that can get highly motivated and qualified people answering the phones.

In the customer service situation the detection method might be used to maintain quality. In practice this would mean monitoring the performance of the representatives. Defective performance might be indicated by customer complaints or excessively long phone calls. The consequences of defective performance (e.g., providing wrong information about company policy) angers customers and creates stressful situations for the representatives, leading to high turnover among representatives. In this case, the replacement of representatives who leave because they cannot handle the task involves the cost of hiring a replacement (e.g., advertising, interviewing, etc.) and the cost of training the replacement. In addition, the new representatives will continue to need additional support from experienced representatives while they learn the task. Thus new representatives will not only be relatively inefficient, but they will also be lowering the productivity of the experienced representatives while they learn. Thus the quality goal in this situation is one of maintaining a staff of highly qualified and motivated customer service personnel. Fulfillment of this goal will then result in quality service to the customer. Whereas, detection of problems after they occur will be costly, both in terms of poorer relations with customers and in terms of the tens of thousands of dollars it takes to recruit and train replacement personnel.

### 11.5.3 Total Quality Management

A commitment to quality is a commitment to the customer. This is wise, since it is the customer that keeps the company in business. No business can survive for long if it alienates its customers. Quality is the confidence a customer has that a product will work as advertised.

The movement towards total quality has evolved in stages. The first involved the use of inspection to eliminate defects before they reached the customer. The second involved controlling the processes that produced parts and goods so that defects could be avoided.

However, even when a process is rigidly controlled, there are aspects of quality that may not be addressed. The product may not be completely usable for certain types of customers. For instance, it may be difficult to load heavy items into the trunk of a car, or a stapler might require excessive force to operate.

Total quality is the third stage of quality. It looks at every aspect of a product. Other problems may arise because of defects in materials and parts provided by suppliers. Thus a commitment to total quality has to ensure not only that one's own processes and operations meet the highest standards, but also that the materials and parts supplied are of equally high quality.

One of the most critical areas for enhancing quality is in new product development. Much of the quality in products is designed into them. Quality products meet the needs of customers, are durable and reliable, and can be produced reliably and in the quantities needed.

Total quality management (TQM) is a group activity that requires teamwork and a shared commitment to quality. The concept of total quality management grew out of the earlier idea of total quality control originated by Armand Feigenbaum. According to him it is "an effective system for integrating the quality development, quality maintenance, and quality improvement efforts of the various groups in an organization so as to enable production and service at the most economical levels which allow for full customer satisfaction."

Parameters that are addressed in total quality management include cost control, management of inventory and work in progress (WIP), and control of delivery date. Total quality management requires a very strong commitment to quality and the structural change necessary to produce it (Ishikawa 1985). Increasingly total quality management is seen as a means of achieving the broad goals of a company, which include maintaining corporate health and character, motivating employees and using them to their potential, obtaining the confidence of customers, achieving world class quality and recognition, creating a responsive company that can adapt to rapid changes in the economy and marketplace, nurturing human resources, and integrating a full range of quality methods into the normal operation of the company.

TQM requires participation throughout the company, including the divisions of marketing, design, manufacturing, inspection, and shipping. Each of these participants should be committed to improvement. While sudden or large improvements should be encouraged and rewarded, more gradual incremental improvement as in the Kaizen approach should also be the goal of management. In many situations, rapid or large improvements may be hard to achieve, but gradual and steady improvement is almost always possible.

TQM should be buttressed and serviced by specialists in the area of quality control. Total quality management requires that everyone in the company must study, practice, and participate in quality improvement. This means that every worker must be educated about quality and motivated to improve quality wherever possible. Quality should never be considered separately from its cousins, cost control and control of the delivery date. All of these functions can be assisted by the appropriate use of an intelligent database to support quality improvement and management.

An idea that is closely related to total quality is that of the world-class company. Companies have to compete in an increasingly global marketplace. Often, their competitors may have intrinsic advantages such as access to cheaper labor or lower transportation or resource costs. In competitive industries, companies have to be world class in order to survive, and commitment to total quality is part of the recipe for creating a world class company.

Thus the goal of quality improvement has shifted from "satisfying," where it is enough just to meet the minimum needs of the customer to "world-class quality," where it is recognized that in a global marketplace with discerning customers one has to be the best in the world to dominate the market. In pursuing world-class quality, companies must also pursue high-quality information about quality that they can make available to their managers and workers in a highly interpretable way.

## ■ 11.6  CONCLUSIONS

This chapter reviewed methods of quality control and improvement and discussed the role of new technologies in assisting the quality improvement process. A distinction was made between the different methods and approaches to quality, beginning with a review of the seven traditional tools of quality. These were then extended using an intelligent database approach. It was also seen how quality tools were alternative ways of looking at information relevant to quality, and how the various tools could be merged within hyperinformation and used as part of an executive information system for quality.

The material in this chapter has also emphasized the importance of two further principles in intelligent database applications: Information should be diagnostic and it should be representative.

In pursuing the goal of quality it is necessary to exploit all relevant information. Now that computer databases are the rule rather than the exception, the necessary information for determining quality is already available and it becomes a matter of putting that information to appropriate use. In the intelligent database applications studied in earlier chapters of this book, there was a tendency for each application to emphasize either control or exploitation. For instance, project visualization was an example of a "control" situation, while point-of-sale marketing analysis is an example of an "exploit" situation (recognizing that no pejorative meaning is intended for "control" or "exploit"). In quality control, the need to control a process is paramount.

While the existing tools of quality control have proved useful over the years, they have not been updated along with new advances in computer technology. This chapter presented three new tools for quality control based on intelligent databases and visual data analysis: automatic discovery, 3D visualization, and hyperinformation.

These new tools complement the existing array of quality tools. The new tools are characterized by their ability to automatically generate hypotheses, discover unexpected information, visualize multidimensional data, and link all of the quality tools, along with additional information, within a hypermedia interface.

Information discovery adds value to data by extracting rules and anomalies that cannot be uncovered using statistical analysis. Hypermedia provides an intuitive interface within which the various quality tools are integrated. This encourages a "big picture" view of the data and allows the analyst to see the link between quality data and related production parameters (e.g., characteristics of operators and machines).

Examples were used in this chapter to illustrate how these new tools can assist the quality control process. It was also shown how these tools were alternative ways of looking at information relevant to quality. One of the useful by-products of the machine-learning approach to quality control (i.e., information discovery and anomaly detection) is that it produces a knowledge base of rules and database facts that serves as a "theory" of how errors are produced. This knowledge base can then be used to derive causal explanations of error and to develop strategies for improving the process and enhancing quality. Similarly, data visualizations provide highly interpretable charts and graphs that can be used in reports and presentations to management.

The new eighth, ninth, and tenth tools of quality control provide quality information to a wider audience and should form the backbone of quality information systems of the future.

# 12

# CONCLUSIONS

*Because it reduces the need for raw materials, labor, time, space and capital, knowledge becomes the central resource of the advanced economy. And as this happens, its value soars. For this reason, "info-wars" are breaking out everywhere.*

— Alvin Toffler*

*Corollary*: Information has become such a key asset that it deserves its own form of currency; its value can no longer be adequately measured in money alone.

## ■ 12.1 INTRODUCTION

Modern society is being challenged by the competitive requirements of global connectivity. Yet some challenges are much more visible than others. When David challenged Goliath the challenge was obvious. In contrast, the information challenge is less clear and therefore easier to overlook. The information challenge is not being posed by any individual, organization, or nation. It is more akin to pollution, a side effect of human activity that threatens to overwhelm us.

If we don't master information, then it will master us. This is already happening in many segments of society as people reach a stage of profound information dependence. In the face of routine storage of massive amounts of information, we are dependent on any number of databases. In a world that is overflowing with data, the people who can extract information from data effectively have an immense competitive advantage. If we are to successfully respond to the information challenge, we must develop means for adding value to data, interpreting it, and understanding it, so that the mass of data is focused and becomes usable information. Intelligent database applications are the tools for this purpose.

Intelligent database applications are tools that promote the development of understanding. They are particularly important in dealing with large amounts of data in

---

* *PowerShift*, Bantam, 1990. Alvin Toffler was born in 1928 in New York City and graduated from Washington Square College. He worked as a factory worker for five years, until his books afforded him the reputation of being an eminent futurist. His books are read throughout the world.

complex tasks. Understanding requires placing things in context. Disconnected details are relatively meaningless. With complex systems one needs to step back and look at the big picture from time to time or else one is blinded by detail. Thus the intelligent database approach emphasizes the summarization and visualization of data.

While most people are now besieged by data, in earlier times, data was often collected on an as-needed basis. There were no software tools for massaging and filtering information, so executives and commanders had to muster their information resources carefully, whether they were spies or auditors. In many cases, not knowing the right question to ask was the undoing of a commander or executive. The battle of Waterloo is now known as the battle where the Duke of Wellington and his Prussian allies disproved the myth of Napoleonic invincibility. Yet Waterloo was preceded by a Napoleonic victory over the allies, achieved in large part by the element of surprise. The "Iron Duke" and his allies had no idea where Napoleon's army was until it was almost upon them, assuming that Napoleon was still somewhere in France. Apparently, no one thought to ask, "Is Napoleon already here in Belgium, and if so, where?"

The questions that motivate the use of intelligent databases are age-old, whether they relate to war or competition in the modern marketplace. Economics, ecology, demographics, politics, science, and technology are the driving forces that have motivated the search for information and understanding since prehistoric times. In the modern information society, there are many information structures that range, from well-defined hierarchies to complex and messy networks, and many questions that may be asked of information.

A genuinely global perspective on data provides focused and interpretable information to a wide range of users. The same set of underlying data can then provide different types of information for different users. Intelligent database applications integrate diverse sources of information, create suitable visualizations, and provide access to them within a navigable interface. We need a global perspective to avoid making narrow and shortsighted decisions. Without it decisions are made in a narrow context and as a result people fail to see the full consequences of their actions.

Data, and the information it contains, is the resource that we have only begun to appreciate. Like a sudden downpour in a desert, we are flooded with data, yet much of it goes wasted, unanalyzed, and we are soon left thirsting for more information. The true cost of this wastefulness is hidden from us, because we have no knowledge of all the opportunities that are missed. It is hard to price our mistakes when we don't know what the alternatives were.

Information is the "lifeblood" of our increasingly complex world. It will be the key resource of the twenty-first century. Both in dollar volume and criticality, information greatly dominates society in increasingly larger segments to the near exclusion of physical elements.

Intelligent database applications have a tremendous impact on modern society because they directly affect our ability to deal with its most important and crucial resource—information. They help us to create information anew through discovery, maintain its quality through anomaly detection, and provide larger numbers of people easy and immediate access to it.

We can no longer deal with information without intelligent database applications. We have passed the point of no return.

# REFERENCES

Aaker, D. A. and Day, G. S. (1990). *Marketing Research.* New York: John Wiley & Sons.

Ackoff, R. and Emshoff, J. (1975). Advertising research at Anheuser-Busch (1968–1974). *Sloan Management Review,* 16, Spring, 1–15.

Akscyn, R., McCracken, D., and Yoder, E. (1988). KMS: A distributed hypermedia system for managing knowledge in organizations. *Communications of the ACM,* 31(7), 820–835.

Alderson, W. and Cox, R. Towards a theory of marketing. *Journal of Marketing,* 13(4), 139.

Anderson, J. R. (1982). *Cognitive Psychology and its Implications.* San Francisco: W. H. Freeman and Company.

Anderson, J. R. (1987). *Cognitive Psychology and its Implications,* (2nd ed.). San Francisco: W. H. Freeman and Company.

Applegate, L. M., Konsynski, B. R., and Nunamaker, J. F. (1986). A group decision support system for idea generation and issue analysis in organization planning. In *Proceedings of the First Conference on Computer-supported Cooperative Work,* (Austin, Texas). New York: ACM Press.

Asaka, T. and Ozeki, K. (1988). *Handbook of Quality Tools: The Japanese Approach.* Cambridge, MA: Productivity Press.

Assael, H. and Roscoe Jr., A. M. (1976). Approaches to market segmentation analysis, *Journal of Marketing,* 40, 67–76.

Astrahan, M. M., Chamberlin, D., Blasgen, M. W., *et al.* (1976). System R: Relational approach to database management. *ACM Transactions on Database Systems*, 1, 97–137.

Attneave, F. (1957). *Applications of Information Theory to Psychology: A Summary of Basic Concepts, Methods, and Results.* New York: Holt, Rinehart & Winston.

Auerbach, R. (1974). *Auerbach on Point of Sale Systems.* New York: Auerbach Publishers.

Barnard, P. and Marcel, A. (1984). Representation and understanding in the use of symbols and pictograms. In R. Easterby and H. Zwaga (eds.), *Information Design.* New York: John Wiley & Sons.

Barnes, R. M. (1980). *Motion and Time Study: Design and Measurement of Work* (7th ed.). New York: John Wiley & Sons.

Barney, J. (1991). Survey of marketing practices. *Direct: The Magazine of Direct Marketing,* January.

Barron, D. W. (1989). Why use SGML? *Electronic Publishing — Origination, Dissemination and Design,* 2(1), 3–24.

Barron, J. J. (1991). Prioritizing Information. *Byte Magazine,* May, 169–174.

Bartels, R. (1965). Development of marketing thought: A brief history. In G. Schwartz (ed.), *Science in Marketing.* New York: John Wiley & Sons.

Bayliss, J. S. (1985). *Marketing for Engineers.* London: Peter Peregrinus.

Bearden, W. O., Teel, J. E., and Durand, R. M. (1978). Media usage, psychographic, and demographic dimensions of retail shoppers. *Journal of Retailing,* Spring, 54, 65–74.

Benest, I. D. and Dukic, D. (1990). Some design issues in the automated office metaphor. *Proceedings of the European X User Group Conference,* (Guildford, England), 56–69.

Bernstein, R. (1991). Videoconferencing: Seeing is believing. *Insurance & Technology,* December/January, 18–20.

Blattberg, R. C. and Sen, S. K. (1974). Market segmentation using models of multidimensional purchasing behavior. *Journal of Marketing,* 38, 17–28.

Blum, R. (1982). Dicovery, confirmation and incorporation of causal relationships from a large time oriented clinical database: The RX project. *Computers and Biomedical Research.*

Blum, R. (1986). Computer-assisted design of studies using routine clinical data: Analyzing the association of prednisone and serum cholestorol. *Annals of Internal Medicine.*

Borgman, C. L. (1986). Why are online catalogs so hard to use? Lessons learned from information-retrieval studies. *Journal of the American Society for Information Science,* 37, 387–400.

Box, G. E. P. and Cox, D. R. (1964). An analysis of transformations. *Journal of the Royal Statistical Society, Series B,* 26, 211.

Box, G. E. P., Hunter, W. G., and Hunter, J. S. (1978). *Statistics for Experimenters: An Introduction to Design, Data Analysis, and Model Building.* New York: John Wiley & Sons.

Broadbent, D. E. (1958). *Perception and Communication.* London: Pergamon Press.

Burr, J. T. (1990). The Tools of Quality Part VI: Pareto Charts. *Quality Progress,* 23 (November), 59–61.

Bush, V. (1945). As we may think. *Atlantic Monthly,* 176, 101–108.

Campagnoni, F. R., and Ehrlich, K. (1989). Information retrieval using a hypertext-based help system. *ACM Transactions on Office Information Systems.*

Card, S. K., English, W. K., and Burr, B. J. (1978). Evaluation of mouse, rate-controlled isometric joystick, step keys and text keys for text selection on a CRT. *Ergonomics,* 21, 601–613.

Card, S. K., Robertson, G. G., and Mackinlay, J. D. (1991). The information visualizer, an information workspace. *CHI '91 Conference Proceedings,* (New Orleans, LA), 181–188. New York: ACM Press.

Cattell, R. B. (1943). The measurement of adult intelligence. *Psychological Bulletin,* 40, 153–193.

Chaffin, R. and Herrmann, D. J. (1988). The Nature of Semantic Relations: a comparison of two Approaches. In M. W. Evens (ed.), *Relational Models of the Lexicon: Representing Knowledge in Semantic Networks.* Cambridge, MA: Press Syndicate of The University of Cambridge.

Chamberlin, D. D., Astrahan, M. M., Eswaran, K. P., Griffiths, P. P., Lorie, R. A., Mehl, J. W., Reisner, T., and Wade, B. W. (1976). SEQUEL 2: A unified approach to data definition, manipulation, and control. *IBM Journal of Research and Development,* 20, 560–575.

Chambers, J. M., Cleveland, W. S., Kleiner, B., and Tukey, P. A. (1983). *Graphical Methods for Data Analysis*. Boston: Duxbury Press.

Chen, P. P. S. (1976). The entity-relationship model: Towards a unified view of data. *ACM Transactions on Database Systems*, 1(9), 9–36.

Cherington, P. T. (1913). *Advertising as a Business Force*. Garden City, NY: Doubleday.

Cherington, P. T. (1920). *The Elements of Marketing*. New York: Macmillan.

Chignell, M. H. and Lacy, R. M. (1991). Instructional Resources for Research and Writing: The Jefferson Notebook. *Journal of Computing in Higher Education*, 2(2), 18–43.

Chignell, M. H., and Parsaye, K. (1991). Principles of intelligent database application. *AI Expert*, 6(10), 34–41.

Cleveland, W. S. (1988). *The Elements of Graphing Data*. Monterey, CA: Wadsworth Advanced Books and Software.

Clocksin, W. F. and Mellish, C. S. (1984). *Programming in Prolog* (2nd ed.). Berlin: Springer-Verlag.

Codd, E. F. (1970). A relational model for large shared data banks. *Communications of the ACM*, 13, 377–387.

Conklin, J. (1987). Hypertext: A survey and introduction. *IEEE Computer*, 20(9), 17–41.

Conklin, J. and Begeman, M. L. (1988). gIBIS: A hypertext tool for exploratory policy discussion. *MCC Technical Report Number STP-082-88*. Austin, TX.

Cowles, M. (1989). *Statistics in Psychology: An Historical Perspective*. Hillsdale, NJ: Erlbaum.

Darden, W. R. and Ashton, D. (1975). Psychographic profiles of patronage preference groups. *Journal of Retailing*, 50, 99–112.

Davis, L. (ed.) (1991). *Handbook of Genetic Algorithms*. New York: Van Nostrand Reinhold.

de Baar, D. J. M. J., Foley, J. D., and Mullet, K. E. (1992). Coupling application design and user interface design. *CHI '92 Conference Proceedings*, (Monterey, CA), 259–266. New York: ACM Press.

Deerweister, S., Dumais, S. T., Furnas, G. W., Landauer, T. K., and Harshman, R. (1990). Indexing by latent semantic analysis. *Journal of the American Society for Information Science*, 41(6), 391–407.

Dichter, E. (1947). Psychology in Market Research. *Harvard Business Review*, Summer, 25.

Dillon, A. and McKnight, C. (1990). Towards a classification of text types: A repertory grid approach. *International Journal of Man-Machine Studies*, 33.

Dillon, A., Richardson, J., and McKnight, C. (1988). Towards the design of a full-text, searchable database: implications from a study of journal usage. *British Journal of Academic Librarianship*, 3, 37–48.

Dolich, I. J. (1969). A study of congurence relationships between self-images and product brands. *Journal of Marketing Research*, 6, 81–84.

Duda, R. O. and Hart, P. E. (1973). *Pattern Classification and Scene Analysis*. New York: John Wiley & Sons, Inc.

Dutka, S., Frankel, L. R., and Roshwalb, I. (1981). *A Marketer's guide to effective use of 1980 Census data*. New York: Audits and Surveys, Inc.

Egan, D. E., Remde, J. R., Gomez, L. M., Landauer, T. K., Eberhardt, J., and Lochbaum, C. C. (1989). Formative design evaluation of SuperBook. *ACM Transactions on Information Systems*, 7(1), 30–57.

Ellis, C. A., Gibbs, S. J., and Rein, G. L. (1991). Groupware: Some issues and experiences. *Communications of the ACM,* 34(1), 38–58.

Elrod, S., Bruce, R., Gold, R., Goldberg, D., Halasz, F., Janssen, W., Lee, D., McCall, K., Pedersen, E., Pier, K., Tang, J., and Welch, B. (1992). *Liveboard: A large interactive display supporting group meetings, presentations and remote collaboration. Proceedings of CHI '92,* (Monterey, CA). New York: ACM Press.

Engelbart, D. C. and English, W. K. (1968). A research center for augmenting human intellect. *AFIPS Proceedings, Fall Joint Computer Conference.*

Exter, T. (1991). Tiger shows its teeth. *American Demographics,* June, 23.

Fairchild, K., Poltrock, S. E., and Furnas, G. W. (1988). SemNet: three dimensional graphics representations of large knowledge bases. In R. Guindon (ed.), *Cognitive Science and its Applications for Human-Computer interaction.* Hillsdale, NJ: Erlbaum.

Farquhar, C. R. (1986). Taking aim at target markets. *Canadian Business Review,* 13(2), 32–36.

Feigenbaum, A. V. (1961). *Total Quality Control.* New York: McGraw-Hill.

Feigenbaum, A. V. (1991). *Total Quality Control* (3rd ed.). New York: McGraw-Hill.

Feldman, M. S. (1986). Constraints on communication and electronic mail. *Proceedings, MCC Conference on Computer-Supported Cooperative Work,* (Austin, TX), 73–90.

Fisher, R. A. (1951). *The Design of Experiments* (6th ed.). New York: Hafner Publishing Co.

Furnas, G. W. (1986). Generalized fisheye views. *CHI '86 Conference Proceedings,* 16–23. New York: ACM Press.

Furuta, R. (1987). Concepts and models for structured documents. In J. André, R. Furuta, and V. Quint (eds.), *Structured Documents.* Cambridge: Cambridge University Press.

Furuta, R., Plaisant, C., and Shneiderman, B. (1989). Automatically transforming regularly structured linear documents into hypertext. *Electronic Publishing,* 2(4), 211–229.

Gabor, A. (1990). *The Man Who Discovered Quality.* New York: Times Books/Random House.

Gaines, B. and Shaw, M. (1986). Induction of inference rules for expert systems. *Journal of Fuzzy Sets and Systems.*

Gibson, J. J. (1979). *The Ecological Approach to Visual Perception.* Boston: Houghton Mifflin.

Glenn, B. G. and Chignell, M. H. (1992). Hypermedia: design for browsing. In R. Hartson and D. Hix (eds.), *Advances in Human-Computer Interaction, Vol. 3,* 143–183. Norwood, NJ: Ablex.

Glushko, R. J. (1989). Transforming text into hypertext for a compact disc encyclopedia. *CHI '89 Proceedings,* 293–298. New York: ACM Press.

Goldberg, D. E. (1989). *Genetic Algorithms in Search, Optimization, and Machine Learning.* Reading, MA: Addison-Wesley.

Goldberg, A. and Robson, D. (1983). *SmallTalk-80: The Language and its Implementation.* Reading, MA: Addison-Wesley.

Golovchinsky, G. and Chignell, M. H. (1992). Making queries look like links: An interaction style for information exploration. *Computer Systems Technical Group Newsletter,* 19(1), 20–22.

Gordon, S., Gustavel, J., Moore, J., and Hankey, J. (1988). The effects of hypertext on reader knowledge representation. *Proceedings of the Human Factors Society 32nd Annual Meeting,* 296–300.

Gould, J. D. and Lewis, C. (1985). Designing for usability: Key principles and what designers think. *Communications of the ACM,* 28(3), 300–311.

Grant, E. L. and Leavenworth, R. S. (1988). *Statistical Quality Control,* (6th ed.). New York: McGraw-Hill.

Grudin, J. (1989). The case against user interface consistency. *Communications of the ACM*, 32, 1164–1173.

Guilford, J. P. (1954). *Psychometric Methods* (2nd ed.). New York: McGraw-Hill.

Halasz, F. G. & Schwartz, M. (1990). The Dexter Hypertext Reference Model. *Proceedings of the Hypertext Standardization Workshop, National Institute of Standards and Technology.* (Gaithersburg, MD), 95–133. (Available as NIST Special Publication 500-178, March 1990.)

Halasz, F. G., (1988). Reflections on NoteCards: Seven Issues for the Next Generation of Hypermedia Systems. *CACM* 31, 7, 836–852.

Harrison, B. L. (1991). Video annotation and multimedia interfaces: From theory to practice. *Proceedings of the Human Factors Society 35th Annual Meeting,* 319–323.

Harrison, D. (1990) Quality organization and programmes. In Lock, D. and Smith, D. J. (eds.), *Gower Handbook of Quality Management.* Aldershot, England: Gower Publishing Company.

Hebb, D. O. (1949). *The Organization of Behavior.* New York: John Wiley & Sons.

Hemm, R. (1991). Hitting Demographics Where They Live—In the Suburbs. *Direct: The Magazine of Direct Marketing,* January, 39.

Henderson, D. A. and Card, S. K. (1986). Rooms: The use of multiple virtual workspaces to reduce space contention in a window-based graphical user interface. *ACM Transactions on Graphics,* 5(3), 211–243.

Hewlett-Packard Company (1990). *HP Interface Architect Developer's Guide.* Corvallis, OR: Hewlett-Packard Company.

Hillier, F. S., and Lieberman, G. J. (1980). Introduction to Operations Research, (3rd ed.). San Francisco: Holden-Day.

Hinton, G. E., Sejnowski, T. J., and Ackley, D. H. (1984). Boltzmann Machines: Constraint Satisfaction Networks that Learn. *Technical Report CMU-CS-84-119.* Pittsburgh, PA.: Carnegie-Mellon University, Department of Computer Science.

Hisrich, R. D. and Peters, M. P. (1991). *Marketing Decisions for New and Mature Products.* New York: Macmillan.

Holland, J. H. (1975). *Adaptation in Natural and Artificial Systems.* Ann Arbor: University of Michigan Press.

Holland, J., Holyoak, K. J., Nisbett, R. E., and Tagard, P. R. (1986). *Induction: Processes of Inference, Learning, and Discovery.* Cambridge, MA: MIT Press.

Horton, W. (1991). *Illustrating Computer Documentation: The Art of Presenting Information Graphically on Paper and Online.* New York: John Wiley & Sons.

Hughes, J. W. (1991). Homeowners: Winners and Losers. *American Demographics,* June, 38.

Hunt, E. B., Marin, J., and Stone, P. J. (1966). *Experiments in Induction.* New York: Academic Press.

Huang, K. T. (1990). Visual interface design systems. In S. K. Chang (ed.), *Principles of Visual Programming Systems.* Englewood Cliffs, NJ: Prentice-Hall.

Hull, R. and King, R. (1988). Semantic database modeling: Survey, applications, and research issues. *ACM Computing Surveys,* 19(3), 201–260.

Imai, M. (1986). *Kaizen: The Key to Japan's Competitive Success.* New York: Random House.

IntelligenceWare (1987). *IXL User's Manual.* Los Angeles: IntelligenceWare.

IntelligenceWare (1989). *Database/Supervisor Manual.* Los Angeles: IntelligenceWare.

IntelligenceWare (1992). *IDIS: The Information Discovery System.*Los Angeles: IntelligenceWare.

Irler, R. and Colazzo, J. (1990). In E. Berk & J. Devlin (eds.), *Hypertext/Hypermedia Handbook.* New York: Intertext Publications, McGraw-Hill Publishing Company, Inc.

Ishii, H. and Miyake, N. (1991). Toward an open shared workspace: Computer and video fusion approach of TeamWorkstation. *Communications of the ACM,* 34(12), 37–50.

Ishikawa, K. (1976). *Guide to Quality Control.* Tokyo: Asian Productivity Association.

Ishikawa, K. (1985). *What is Total Quality Control? The Japanese Way.* Englewood Cliffs, NJ: Prentice-Hall.

J. Walter Thompson Advertising Agency (1988). *Marketing Information in transition: Scanner Services and Single-Source Systems,* New York.

Johnson, J., Roberts, T. L., and Verplank, W. (1989). The Xerox Star: A Retropspective. *IEEE Computer,* 22(9), 11–26.

Joloboff, V. (1987). Document Representation: Concepts and standards. In J. André, R. Furuta and V. Quint (eds.), *Structured Documents.* Cambridge: Cambridge University Press.

Jorna, G. C. and Snyder, H. L. (1991). Image quality determines differences in reading performance and perceived quality with CRT and hard-copy displays. *Human Factors, 33,* 459–470.

Jung, C. G. (ed.) (1964). *Man and His Symbols.* London: Aldus Books.

Kahneman, D. E. (1973). *Attention and Effort.* Englewood Cliffs, NJ: Prentice-Hall.

Kedsierski, B. I. (1982). Communication and management support in system development environments, *Proceedings of the Conference on Human Factors in Computer Systems,* (Gaithersburg, MD).

Kling, R. (1991). Cooperation, coordination, and control in computer-supported cooperative work. *Communications of the ACM,* 34(12), 83–88.

Konz, S. (1990). *Work Design: Industrial Ergonomics,* (3rd ed.). Worthington, Ohio: Publishing Horizons.

Kuhn, T. S. (1971). *The Structure of Scientific Revolutions,* (2nd ed.). Chicago: University of Chicago Press.

Lai, E. P. and Chua, T. S. (1991). Supporting composition in a hypertext environment. *Hypermedia,* 3(3), 207–238.

Langley, P. W., Zytkow, J., Simon, H. A., and Bradshaw, G. L. (1986). The search for regularity: Four aspects of scientific discovery. In R. S. Michalski, J. G. Carbonell, and T. M. Mitchell (eds.), *Machine Learning: An Artificial Intelligence Approach.* Los Altos, CA: Morgan Kaufmann.

Leech, G. N. (1974). *Semantics.* Harmondsworth: Penguin.

Lindsay, P. and Norman, D. A. (1977). *Human Information Processing: An Introduction to Psychology,* (2nd ed.). New York: Academic Press.

Lock, D. and Smith, D. J. (eds.) (1990). *Gower Handbook of Quality Management.* Aldershot, England: Gower Publishing Company.

Lynch, K. (1959). *The Image of the City.* Cambridge, MA: MIT Press.

Mackinlay, J. D., Card, S. K., and Robertson, G. G. (1990). Rapid controlled movement through a virtual 3D workspace. *Computer Graphics,* 24(4), 171–176.

Mackinlay, J. D., Robertson, G. G., and Card, S. K. (1991). The perspective wall: Detail and context smoothly integrated. *Proceedings of CHI '91,* 173–179. New York: ACM Press.

Mahnke, J. (1988). IXL Tool Discovers Database Patterns. *MIS Week.*

Malone, T. W., Grant, K. R., Turbak, F. A., Brobst, S. A., and Cohen, M. D. Intelligent information sharing systems. *Communications of the ACM,* 30(5), 390–402.

Malone, T. W. and Rockart, J. F. (1991). Computers, Networks and the Corporation. *Scientific American,* September, 92–99.

Mander, R., Salomon, G., and Wong, Y. Y. (1992). A "pile" metaphor for supporting casual organization of information. *Proceedings of CHI, '92,* 627–634. New York: ACM Press.

Mantei, M., Baecker, R., Sellen, A., Buxton, W., and Milligan, T. (1991). Experiences in the use of a media space. *CHI '91 Proceedings,* (New Orleans, LA), 203–208.

Mantei, M. M. and Teorey, T. J. (1988). Cost/Benefit analysis for incorporating human factors in the software lifecycle. *Communications of the ACM,* 31(4), 428–439.

Martino, R. L. (1964). *Project Management and Control, Volume 1, Finding the Critical Path.* New York: American Management Association.

Maslow, A. (1970). *Motivation and Personality.* New York: Harper and Row.

Maslow, A. (1971). *The Farther Reaches of Human Nature.* New York: Viking Press.

McKenzie, I. S., Sellen, A., and Buxton, W. (1991). A comparison of input devices in elemental pointing and dragging tasks. *CHI '92 Conference Proceedings,* (Monterey, CA), 161–166. New York: ACM Press.

McKnight, C., Dillon, A., and Richardson, J. (1991). *Hypertext in Context.* Cambridge: Cambridge University Press.

Meredith, J. R. and Mantel, S. J. (1989). *Project Management: A Managerial Approach,* (2nd ed.). New York: John Wiley & Sons.

Michalski, R. S., Carbonell, J. G., and Mitchell, T. M. (eds.) (1983). *Machine Learning: An Artificial Intellligence Approach.* Palo Alto, CA: Tioga Press.

Michie, D. (1984). Automating the synthesis of expert knowledge. *ASLIB Proceedings,* (London), 337–343.

Microsoft (1990). *PowerPoint Reference Guide.* Bellevue, WA: Microsoft Corporation.

Miller, D. W. and Starr, M. K. (1969). *Executive Decisions and Operations Research.* Englewood Cliffs, NJ: Prentice-Hall.

Minoura, T. and Parsaye, K. (1984). Version Based Concurrency Control of a Database System, *Proceedings of the 1984 ACM/IEEE Conference on Data Engineering,* (Los Angeles, CA).

Mintzberg, H. (1973). *The Nature of Managerial Work.* Englewood Cliffs, NJ: Prentice-Hall.

Mitchell, A. (1983). *The Nine American Lifestyles.* New York: Macmillan.

Monmonier, M. (1991). *How to Lie with Maps.* Chicago: The University of Chicago Press.

Monk, A. F, Walsh, P., and Dix, A. J. (1988). A comparison of hypertext, scrolling and folding mechanisms for program browsing. In D. M. Jones and R. Winder (eds.), *People and Computers IV.* Cambridge: Cambridge University Press.

Myers, B. (1990). Creating user interfaces using programming by example, visual programming, and constraints. *ACM Transactions on Programming Languages and Systems,* 12(2), 143–177.

Myers, B. and Rosson, M. B. (1992). Survey on user interface programming. *CHI '92 Conference Proceedings,* (Monterey, CA), 195–202, New York: ACM Press.

Mylopoulos, J., Bernstein, P. A., and Wong, H. K. T. (1980). A language facility for designing interactive data-intensive systems. *ACM Transactions on Database Systems,* 5(2), 185–207.

Neisser, U. (1967). *Cognitive Psychology.* New York: Appleton Century Crofts.

Nelson, M. M. and Illingworth, W. T. (1991). *A Practical Guide to Neural Nets.* Reading, MA: Addison-Wesley.

NeXT Computer Inc. (1990). *NeXTstep Concepts.* Redwood City, CA: NeXT Computer, Inc.

Nielsen, J. (1990). *HYPERText and HYPERMedia.* New York: Academic Press.

Norman, D. A. (1981). The trouble with UNIX. *Datamation.* November, 139–150.

Ooi, B. C. (1990). Efficient query processing in Geographic Information Systems. No. 471, *Lecture Notes in Computer Science.* Berlin: Springer-Verlag.

Ouchi, W. (1984). *The M-Form Society: How American Teamwork Can Recapture the Competitive Edge.* Reading, MA: Addison-Wesley.

Packard, V. (1957). *The Hidden Persuaders.* New York: David McKay.

Parsaye, K. (1983). Database management, knowledge base management and expert system development in Prolog. *Proceedings of the ACM SIGMOD Database Week Conference,* (San Jose, CA).

Parsaye, K. (1983). Prolog, A Programming Language with a Built-in Relational Database, *Computer-World,* October.

Parsaye, K. (1983). Logic programming and relational databases. *IEEE Transactions on Database Engineering,* December.

Parsaye, K (1985). The next 700 expert system languages. *Proceedings of the IEEE COMPCON Conference,* (San Francisco, CA).

Parsaye, K (1985). The evolutionary road to expert systems. *Proceedings of the Expert Systems in Government Conference,* (Washington DC).

Parsaye, K. (1986). Knowledge Compilation, *Proceedings of the 21st Annual meeting of the Association for the Advancement of Medical Instrumentation,* (Chicago, IL).

Parsaye, K. (1987). Machine learning: The next step. *Computer World.*

Parsaye, K. and Chignell, M. H. (1988). *Expert Systems for Experts.* New York: John Wiley & Sons.

Parsaye, K. and Chignell, M. H. (1992). Information made visual using HyperData. *AI Expert,* 7(9), 22–29.

Parsaye, K., Chignell, M. H., Khoshafian, S., and Wong, H. K. T. (1989). *Intelligent Databases: Object-Oriented, Deductive Hypermedia Technologies.* New York: John Wiley & Sons.

Parsaye, K. and Lin, K. (1987). An Expert System Approach to Automatic Fault Tree Generation for Emergency Feedwater Systems for Nuclear Power Plants, *Proceedings of the 2nd Annual IEEE Westex Conference,* (Anaheim, CA).

Perez, E. (1991). Tools for Authoring Hypertexts. In E. Berk and J. Devlin (eds.), *Hypertext/Hypermedia Handbook.* New York: Intertext Publications, McGraw-Hill Publishing Company, Inc.

Perin, C. (1991). Electronic social fields in bureaucracies. *Communications of the ACM,* 34(12), 64–73.

Perlman, G. (1989). Asynchronous design/evaluation methods for hypertext technology development. *Proceedings of Hypertext '89,* 61–81. New York: ACM Press.

Piirto, R. (1991). *Beyond mind games.* New York: American Demographics Books.

Porter, B. W. and Mooney, R. J. (eds.) (1990). *Machine Learning: Proceedings of the Seventh International Conference on Machine Learning.* San Mateo, CA: Morgan Kaufmann.

POS News, POS terminal leasing: When ownership isn't the answer. *POS News,* 7(8), December 1990, pp 1–2.

Quinlan, J. R. (1979). Discovering rules from large collections of examples: A case study. In D. Michie (ed.), *Expert Systems in the Micro Electronic Age.* Edinburgh: Edinburgh University Press.

Quinlan, R. J. (1983). Learning efficient classification procedures and their application to chess end-games. In R. S. Michalski, J. G. Carbonell, and T. M. Mitchell (eds.), *Machine Learning: An Artificial Intelligence Approach.* Palo Alto, CA: Tioga Press.

Rada, R. (1991). *Hypertext: From text to expertext.* London: McGraw Hill (UK).

Rechtin, E. (1990). *Systems Architecting.* Englewood Cliffs, NJ: Prentice-Hall.

Remde, J. R., Gomez, L. M., and Landauer, T. K. (1987). SuperBook: an automatic tool for information exploration — hypertext? In *Proceedings of Hypertext '87,* (Chapel Hill, NC), 175–188.

Robertson, G. G., Card, S. K., and Mackinlay, J. D. (1989). The cognitive co-processor architecture for interactive user interfaces. *ACM SIGGRAPH Conference on User Interface Software Technology.* New York: ACM Press.

Robertson, G. G., Mackinlay, J. D., and Card, S. K. (1991). Cone trees animated 3D visualizations of hierarchical information. *CHI '91 Conference Proceedings,* (New Orleans, LA), 189–194, New York: ACM Press.

Root, R. W. (1988). Design of a multi-media vehicle for social browsing. In *Proceedings of the Second Conference on Computer-Supported Cooperative Work,* (Portland, OR). New York: ACM Press.

Rosenblatt, F. (1959). Two theorems of statistical separability in the perceptron. In *Mechanization of Thought Processes: Proceedings of a symposium held at the National Physical Laboratory,* Vol. 1, 421–456. London: HM Stationery Office.

Saint-Martin, F. (1990). *Semiotics of Visual Language.* Bloomington, IN: Indiana University Press.

Salomon, G., Oren, T., and Kreitman, K. (1989). Using guides to explore multimedia databases. *Proceedings of the 22nd Hawaii International Conference on System Sciences,* (Kailua-Kona, HI) 3–12.

Salton, G. and McGill. M. (1983). *Modern Information Retrieval.* New York: McGraw-Hill.

Samuel, A. (1963). Some studies in machine learning using the game of checkers. In A. Feigenbaum (ed.), *Computers and Thought.* New York: McGraw-Hill.

Samuelson, P. and Glushko, R. J. (1990). Survey on the look and feel of lawsuits. *Communications of the ACM,* 33(5), 483–487.

Sarazen, J. S. (1990). The tools of quality: Cause-and-effect diagrams. *Quality Progress,* 23 (July), 59–62.

SAS (1988). *SAS System Guide.* Cary, NC: SAS Institute, Inc.

Schank, R. (1975). *Conceptual Information Processing.* Amsterdam: North-Holland.

Searle, J. R. (1979). *Expression and Meaning Studies in the Theory of Speech Acts.* Cambridge: Cambridge University Press, 1979.

Selfridge, O. G. (1959). Pandemonium: A paradigm for learning. In *Mechanization of Thought Processes: Proceedings of a symposium held at the National Physical Laboratory,* Vol. 1, 421–456. London: HM Stationery Office.

Shackel, B. (1991). Usability—Context, framework, definition, design and evaluation. In B. Shackel and S. J. Richardson (eds.), *Human Factors for Informatics Usability.* Cambridge: Cambridge University Press, 21–37.

Shannon, C. E. and Weaver, W. (1949). *The Mathematical Theory of Communication.* Urbana, IL: University of Illinois Press.

Shepard, R. N. (1974). Representation of structure in similarity data: Problems and prospects. *Psychometrika,* 39, 373–421.

Shneiderman, B. (1989). Evaluating three museum installations of a hypertext system. *Journal of the American Society for Information Science,* 40, 172–182.

Shneiderman, B. and Kearsley, G. (1989). *Hypertext Hands-on! An Introduction to a New Way of Organizing and Accessing Information.* Reading, MA: Addison-Wesley.

Singh, G. and Chignell, M. H. (1990). Components of the visual computer: A review of relevant technologies. *Technical Report TR90-46-0.* Singapore: Institute of Systems Science, National University of Singapore.

Smith, S. B. (1983). *The Great Mental Calculators: The Psychology, Methods, and Lives of Calculating Prodigies, Past and Present.* New York: Columbia University Press.

Smith, D. K. and Alexander, R. C. (1988). *Fumbling the Future: How Xerox Invented, then Ignored, the First Personal Computer.* New York: W. Morrow.

Smith, D. C., Irby, C., Kimball, R., Verplank, W., and Harslem, E. (1982). Designing the Star user interface. *BYTE,* 7(4), 242–282.

Smith, D. J. and Edge, J. (1990). Essential Quality Procedures. In D. Lock and D. J. Smith (eds.), *Gower Handbook of Quality Management.* Aldershot, England: Gower Publishing Company.

Sokal, R. R. and Sneath, P. H. A. (1963). *Principles of Numerical Taxonomy.* San Francisco: Miller Freeman Publications, Inc.

Sonquist, J. A. and Morgan, J. (1969). The Detection of Interaction Effects—A Report on a computer Program for the Selection of Optimal Combinations of Explanatory Variables. *Monograph No. 35.* Ann Arbor: University of Michigan, Institute for Social Research.

Spearman, C. (1927). *The Abilities of Man.* New York: Macmillan.

Spencer, R. H. (1990). Managing Non-conformances. In D. Lock and D. J. Smith (eds.), *Gower Handbook of Quality Management.* Aldershot, England: Gower Publishing Company.

Staple, G. (1990). Quality Audits and Reviews. In D. Lock and D. J. Smith (eds.), *Gower Handbook of Quality Management.* Aldershot, England: Gower Publishing Company.

Stigler, S. M. (1986). *The History of Statistics: The Measurement of Uncertainty Before 1900.* Cambridge, MA: Harvard University Press.

Stonebraker, M., Wong, E., Kreps, P., and Held, G. (1977). The design and implementation of INGRES. *ACM Transactions on Database Systems,* 1, 189–222.

Strasser, S. (1989). *Satisfaction Guaranteed: The Making of the American Mass Market.* New York: Pantheon Books.

Streitz, N. A., Hannemann, J., and Thuring, M. (1989). From Ideas and Arguments to Hyperdocuments: Travelling through Activity Spaces. In *Proceedings of the 2nd ACM Conference on Hypertext (Hypertext'89),* (Pittsburgh, PA), 343–364.

Sun Microsystems, Inc. (1990). *Open Windows Developer's Guide 1.1, Reference Manual. Part No. 800-5380-10.*

Sutton, J. A., and Sprague, R. H. (1978). A study of display generation and management in interactive business applications. *Tech. Rept. RJ2392, IBM Research Report,* November.

Tang, J. C. and Minneman, S. L. (1991). VideoWhiteboard: Video shadows to support remote collaboration. *CHI '91 Proceedings,* (New Orleans, LA), 315–322.

Tatsuoka, M. (1971). *Multivariate Analysis.* New York: John Wiley & Sons.

Taylor, M. M. (1988). Layered protocols for comuter-human dialogue. I: Principles. *International Journal of Man-Machine Studies*, 28, 175–218.

Torgerson, W. S. (1958). *Theory and Methods of Scaling.* New York: John Wiley & Sons.

Trigg, R. H. (1983). A network-based approach to text handling for the online scientific community (PhD Thesis). Department of Computer Science, University of Maryland.

Trimble, J. H. and Chappell, D. (1990). *A Visual Introduction to SQL.* New York: John Wiley & Sons.

Tufte, W. (1983). *The Visual Display of Quantitative Information.* Cheshire, CT: Graphics Press.

Tukey, J. W. (1988). *The Collected Works of John W. Tukey: Vol. V Graphics 1965–1985,* (edited by W. S. Cleveland). Pacific Grove, CA: Wadsworth and Brooks/Cole Advanced Books and Software.

Tull, D. S. and Hawkins, D. I. (1987). *Marketing Research: Measurement and Method,* (4th ed.). New York: Macmillan.

Ullmann, J. D. (1988). *Principles of Database and Knowledge-Base Systems, Volume 1.* Rockville, MD: Computer Science Press.

U. S. Navy. (1960). *PERT Instruction Manual and system and Procedures for the Program Evaluation System.* Washington, D.C.: Special Projects Office, Bureau of Naval Weapons, Department of the Navy, U. S. Government Printing Office.

Valdez, J. F. (1992). Navigational Strategies in Using Documentation (Unpublished Ph.D Dissertation). Department of Industrial and Systems Engineering, University of Southern California.

Valdez, J. F., Chignell, M. H., and Glenn, B. (1988). Browsing models for hypermedia databases. *Proceedings of the Annual Meeting of the Human Factors Society.*

Wainer, H. (1979). Making newspaper graphs fit to print. In P. A. Kolers, M. E. Wrolstad, and H. Bouma (eds.), *Processing of Visible Language.* New York: Plenum Press.

Walker, J. H. (1987). Document Examiner: Delivery interface for hypertext documents. *Proceedings of Hypertext '87*, 307–323.

Walker, J. H., Young, E., and Mannes, S. (1990). A case study of using a manual online. *Machine Mediated Learning*, February.

Wareham, J. (1991). *The Anatomy of a Great Executive.* New York: Harper and Collins.

Waterworth, J. A. and Chignell, M. H. (1989). A manifesto for hypermedia usability research. *Hypermedia*, 1(3), 205–234.

Waterworth, J. A. and Chignell, M. H. (1991). A Model of Information Exploration. *Hypermedia,* 3(1), 35–58.

Weiss, M. J. (1988). *The Clustering of America.* New York: Harper and Row.

Wickens, C. D. (1984). *Engineering Psychology and Human Performance.* Columbus, OH: Charles E. Merril.

Wickens, C. D. (1992). *Engineering Psychology and Human Performance,* (2nd ed.). New York: Brooks Cole.

Winograd, T. ( 1975). Frame representations and the declarative/procedural controversy. In D. G. Bobrow and A. Collins (eds.), *Representation and Understanding: Studies in Cognitive Science.* New York: Academic Press.

Winograd, T. and Flores, F. (1986). *Understanding Computers and Cognition.* Norwood, NJ: Ablex.

Wright, P. (1991). Cognitive overheads and prostheses: Some issues in evaluating hypertexts. *Hypertext '91 Proceedings,* 1–12.

Yankelovitch, D. (1981). *New Rules*. New York: Random House.

Yankelovitch, D. (1964). New criteria for market segmentation. *Harvard Business Review,* March, 42.

Yankelovitch, D. (1958). A marketing concept should be the sum of psychoanalysis and nose-counting. *Printer's Ink,* April.

Yankelovich, N., Haan, B., and Meyrowitz, N. (1988). Intermedia: The concept and the construction of a seamless information environment, *IEEE Computer 21,* 81–96.

Young, S., Ott, L., and Feigin, B. (1978). Some practical considerations in market segmentation. *Journal of Marketing Research,* 15, 405–412.

Zadeh, L. A. (1965). Fuzzy sets. *Information and Control,* 8, 338–353.

Zloof, M. (1975). Query by example. Proc. National Computer Conference, AFIPS Press, 431–437.

Zloof, M. M. (1977). Query-by-example: A database language. *IBM Systems Journal*, 16, 324–343.

Zuboff, S. (1988). *In the Age of the Smart Machine. The Future of Work and Power*. New York: Basic Books.

# INDEX

# ■ ABOUT THE AUTHORS

Kamran Parsaye is CEO of IntelligenceWare, Inc. He received his B.S. and M.S. degrees in Mathematics from King's College London and his Ph.D. in Computer Science from UCLA. He has a wide range of both research and industrial management experience, and has initiated a number of new directions both in computer science and the computer industry; including automatic discovery from large databases, interactive knowledge acquisition, automatic data quality management, higher-order data types, dynamic logic data access, object-based language semantics, iconic hypertext data access, project visualization, and hyperinformation, as well as a number of other domain specific patents and inventions. He has also provided guidance to top level management of key industrial and government organizations for the use of information technology for competitive advantage.

Mark Chignell has been an Associate Professor of Industrial Engineering at the University of Toronto since 1990. He received his B.S. and Ph.D. degrees in Psychology from the University of Canterbury in New Zealand, and he has an M.S. degree in Industrial and Systems Engineering from Ohio State. Previously, he was an Assistant Professor of Industrial and Systems Engineering at the University of Southern California. He has done extensive research in the areas of user interfaces, hypertext, on-line textual databases and hyperinformation. His current research involves the use of multimedia in user interface design and information management. He is particularly interested in portable computing and the development of electronic books.

# ■ ABOUT INTELLIGENCEWARE

IntelligenceWare was formed in December 1984 as a private corporation to improve productivity in business through innovative software solutions. The first software package for personal computers was released in July 1985 and a number of leading and popular products on several computer platforms have since followed. These products are in use within diverse institutions — from manufacturing, to design, to market research, to the Coast Guard, to Wall Street, among others, and have already made an impact in many branches of science, business, and industry.

IntelligenceWare has created the Intelligent Database Industry with products that are positioned to fit on top of existing database engines, adding functionality and intelligence to data. The company also has cultivated significant industrial ties by applying technologies to diverse industrial segments through its Consulting and Professional Services Division, delivering complete and customized business solutions with intelligent databases.